SHATTERZONE
OF
EMPIRES

SHATTERZONE OF EMPIRES

COEXISTENCE AND VIOLENCE IN THE GERMAN, HABSBURG, RUSSIAN, AND OTTOMAN BORDERLANDS

Edited by
Omer Bartov and Eric D. Weitz

INDIANA UNIVERSITY PRESS
Bloomington and Indianapolis

Publication of this volume was supported by the Watson Institute for
International Studies at Brown University and the Arsham and Charlotte
Ohanessian Chair in the College of Liberal Arts at the University of Minnesota.

This book is a publication of

Indiana University Press
601 North Morton Street
Bloomington, Indiana 47404-3797 USA

iupress.indiana.edu

Telephone orders   800-842-6796
Fax orders   812-855-7931

Library of Congress Cataloging-in-Publication Data

Shatterzone of empires : coexistence and violence in the German, Habsburg, Russian, and Ottoman borderlands / edited by Omer Bartov and Eric D. Weitz.
    p. cm.
  Includes bibliographical references and index.
   ISBN 978-0-253-00631-8 (cloth : alk. paper) — ISBN 978-0-253-00635-6 (pbk. :
alk. paper) — ISBN 978-0-253-00639-4 (e-book) 1. Ethnic conflict—Europe, Eastern—History—19th century. 2. Ethnic conflict—Europe, Eastern—History—20th
century. 3. Europe, Eastern—Ethnic relations—History—19th century. 4. Europe,
Eastern—Ethnic relations—History—20th century. 5. Borderlands—Europe, Eastern. 6. Europe, Eastern—Boundaries. I. Bartov, Omer. II. Weitz, Eric D.
  DJK26.S53 2013
  305.800947'09041—dc23
                                    2012025509
1 2 3 4 5 18 17 16 15 14 13

CONTENTS

ACKNOWLEDGMENTS

The present volume is the result of a multiyear project that involved workshops, conferences, symposia, and lecture series at Brown University, the University of Minnesota, and the Herder Institute in Marburg, Germany. More than one hundred scholars participated in one or more of the events that we held. We could not include every person in a volume that is already quite large, but we gratefully acknowledge everyone's participation in our various events. All of the various scholars gave us new insights into the problems of ethnic and national identity in the borderlands and helped us sharpen our understandings.

We would not have been able to organize the project without the generous support of numerous institutions, programs, and centers. We thank each and every one of them. At Brown University, the Watson Institute for International Studies provided an institutional home for the Borderlands Project and generous financial support. At the University of Minnesota, the Institute for Global Studies and many of its constituent centers—the Center for Austrian Studies, the European Studies Consortium, the Center for German and European Studies, Modern Greek Studies, and the Center for Holocaust and Genocide Studies—also provided generous financial support and major intellectual resources. In addition, the College of Liberal Arts, the History Department, and the Arsham and Charlotte Ohanessian Chair in the College of Liberal Arts provided much-needed resources. Two University of Minnesota research assistants, Melissa Kelley and Eric Roubinek, provided excellent technical help. Our final conference was graciously and generously hosted by the Herder Institute in Marburg, Germany. We thank two of its directors, Professor Eduard Mühle and Professor Peter Haslinger, for their enthusiastic support.

Two anonymous reviewers for Indiana University Press provided insightful comments on the manuscript. We thank them immensely for their very helpful criticism. Dimitri Karetnikov was our excellent mapwriter for maps 1–7. We also would like to thank Paul Robert Magosci for providing two additional maps on the Carpathian Rus' (chapter 24). We are very grateful to our editor, Janet Rabinowitch, for her enthusiasm for the project and the skill and efficiency with which she guided it through the review and production process.

Finally, we thank our contributors, whose abiding commitment to scholarship and intellectual engagement made the project so stimulating and fulfilling, and even—despite the grimness of the topic at times—eminently enjoyable.

Omer Bartov	Eric D. Weitz
Providence, Rhode Island	New York City

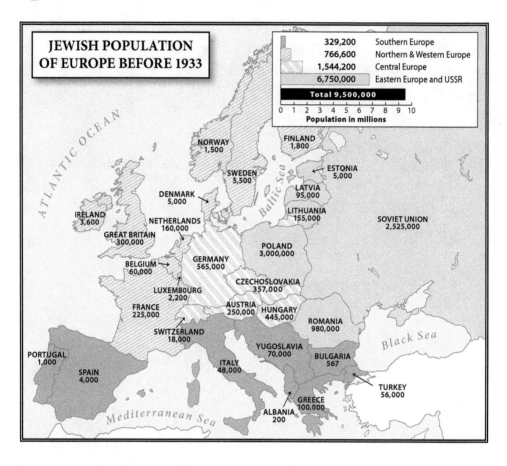

JEWISH POPULATION OF EUROPE BEFORE 1933

Population	Region
329,200	Southern Europe
766,600	Northern & Western Europe
1,544,200	Central Europe
6,750,000	Eastern Europe and USSR
Total 9,500,000	

Population in millions

NORWAY 1,500
FINLAND 1,800
SWEDEN 5,500
ESTONIA 5,000
DENMARK 5,000
LATVIA 95,000
LITHUANIA 155,000
SOVIET UNION 2,525,000
IRELAND 3,600
NETHERLANDS 160,000
GREAT BRITAIN 300,000
POLAND 3,000,000
BELGIUM 60,000
GERMANY 565,000
LUXEMBOURG 2,200
CZECHOSLOVAKIA 357,000
FRANCE 225,000
AUSTRIA 250,000
HUNGARY 445,000
ROMANIA 980,000
SWITZERLAND 18,000
YUGOSLAVIA 70,000
BULGARIA 567
PORTUGAL 1,000
ITALY 48,000
TURKEY 56,000
SPAIN 4,000
GREECE 100,000
ALBANIA 200

Atlantic Ocean
Baltic Sea
Black Sea
Mediterranean Sea

GERMAN AND SOVIET OCCUPATION OF POLAND AND THE BALTIC STATES, 1939-41

SWEDEN

Stockholm

Baltic Sea

FINLAND

Gulf of Finland

Leningrad

ESTHONIA

LATVIA

LITVANIA

East Prussia

SOVIET UNION

Moscow

Smolensk

Minsk

German advance December 1941

German advance August 1941

Poznan

Warsaw

GERMANY

GENERALGOUVERNEMENT

Galicia

Kiev

Vienna

Soviet occupation 1939–June 21, 1941

German occupation 1939–June 21, 1941

German occupation June 22 – December, 1941

Poland's borders 1919-39

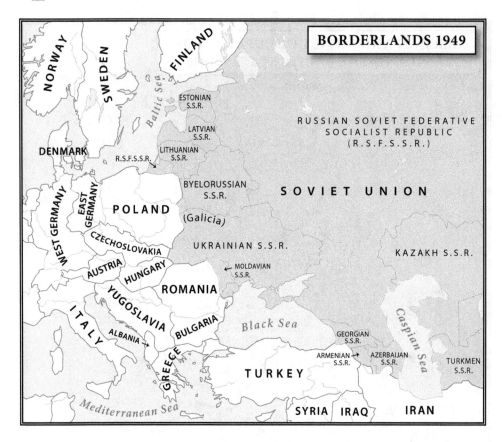

SHATTERZONE
OF
EMPIRES

INTRODUCTION

COEXISTENCE AND VIOLENCE IN THE GERMAN, HABSBURG, RUSSIAN, AND OTTOMAN BORDERLANDS

Omer Bartov and Eric D. Weitz

Borderlands are places of interaction. They are regions intersected by frontiers that separate states, where crossing from one side to the other means switching the sovereign political authority under which one lives. But borderlands are frontiers in another sense as well. They are spaces-in-between, where identities are often malleable and control of the territory and the population is subject to dispute. Most often, borderlands are geographically or culturally distant from the seat of power, and states expend great energy trying to subsume and integrate them. Borderlands are therefore also constructs of the political imaginary and products of ideological fantasies. As such they become sites for all sorts of political, military, and economic projects, as well as scholarly pursuits and literary representations. The main protagonists constitute a diverse lot: states and social movements, political parties and nationalist activists, entrepreneurs and colonizers, intellectuals and ideologues, locals and newcomers. In the borderlands, diverse populations may coexist for long stretches of time, only to have the harmony ruptured by episodes of violence. Living side-by-side, diverse populations learn how to live with one another, but they may also come to perceive the other as essentially different and naturally hostile. In the borderlands, groups become both objects and generators of intense violence.

The borderlands with which we are concerned was a vast swath of territory running from the Baltic to the Black Sea, Lithuania to Anatolia, where four great powers encountered each other in the nineteenth and twentieth centuries along a variety of often changing and contested borders. Prussia (later transformed into the German Empire), along with the Habsburg, Russian, and Ottoman Empires, did not all share borders, nor were all of these borders disputed. Each of the empires had, of course, its distinctive characteristics. But a number of essential factors unified the region, making it a compelling object of study in its entirety. First, the Borderlands was a region of great ethnic and religious diversity. Each of the empires presided over a multitude of populations. Second, in the modern period, each of the empires had to grapple with national and racial movements that, in place of diversity, sought to establish sovereign states that represented one particular nationality. Third, the four empires competed for power and influence in this large region. At particular junctures, each of the empires and many of their successor states sought to revise existing borders and expand their territorial writ. As a result (and fourth), the Borderlands became the major site of the European wars of the twentieth century. A floodtide of ethnic and national violence ensued, some of it stimulated by war between states, some by internal conflicts among varying nationalities. In wartime, states and political movements sought to reshape dramatically the demographic landscape of the Borderlands.[1]

By examining this large, highly diverse region in its entirety and at multiple levels—local, national, imperial, interstate; social, cultural, political, and economic—we gain a much greater understanding of how the many populations of this borderland managed to coexist, and how they eventually descended into and became, in many instances, the perpetrators and objects of the worst violence imaginable. That, in brief, is our argument for researching the Borderlands; that is the ambition of this volume.

Nations and Empires

Article 3 of the Declaration of the Rights of Man and Citizen, pronounced on 26 August 1789, declares: "The principle of all sovereignty resides essentially in the nation." The French Revolution's assertion of popular sovereignty and the principle of national self-determination thus became the rallying cry of all emergent national movements. At that historical moment, the concept of the nation state was born and it would then become the preeminent political force in the modern world. The idea, though hardly the reality, that the state should be the representative of one particular people, spread like the proverbial prairie fire throughout nineteenth-century Europe and, especially after World War I, across the rest of the world.

Yet the borderlands region that is our concern was the world of empires, the zone where four powers challenged one another for political and military predominance. There, every empire presided over highly diverse populations, many of which had religious or ethnic counterparts and kin across one or several imperial borders and under the rule of a different imperial house. These empires, emblematic of the preeminent form of political organization over more than two millennia, were by definition multiethnic and multiconfessional.[2] No Ottoman sultan, Russian czar, or Habsburg emperor ever for a moment thought that all his subjects should or could share one religious belief or one ethnic identity. Yet in all four empires, particularly toward their demise, millions of people were moving, or being moved, across the borders. They sought opportunities or fled wars and pogroms. Sometimes, they were expelled or killed in the name of national or racial purity.

In our period, the four empires were anything but static entities. Unlike the other three, Imperial Germany was only formed in 1871, though in many ways it inherited Prussia's imperial ambitions in the Polish lands, as well as its overall suspicion of Catholicism. The Habsburg, Russian, and Ottoman empires followed distinctive reform courses, including liberal constitutionalism, limited political representation, or, conversely, the reassertion of authoritarian rule, all with varying degrees of success. In the second half of the nineteenth and into the twentieth century, the empires were tested, reformed, destroyed, or reconstructed—or all of the above, sometimes at one and the same time. Primarily, the challenge to them came from the combination of nationalist, sometimes racist, movements and great power rivalries. Unlike empires, which are distinguished by the diversity of their populations, nation states are most typically promoters of one language, one national identity, and one religion, even if the state consists of more than one nation or agrees to tolerate some aspects of minority nations within its borders.

The national movements and the nation states that emerged in the borderlands region did not simply replace empires. In the borderlands, two of the great landed empires, the Ottoman and Habsburg, collapsed as part of the wreckage of World War I, but twentieth-century communists created a vast Soviet empire and the Nazis erected a short-lived but virulent racial empire whose impact on the twentieth century is incalculable. In the long nineteenth century that began in 1789 and ended with World War I, the empires of the borderlands indeed faced great challenges from the reality and the lure of the nation. Poles in the Russian and German Empires, Bulgarians and Armenians in the Ottoman Empire, Croatians under the Habsburgs and the Hungarians, and many others developed national movements that sought the creation of their own nation states. In response, the empires made concerted efforts to absorb some of the characteristics of the nation state by asserting the importance of one ethnic or national group. Russians in the Romanov Empire, Turks (and not just Muslims) in the last decades of Sultan Abdul Hamid II's rule over the Ottoman Empire, Germans in the Habsburg Empire, and Protestant Germans under Bismarck all became the intended beneficiaries of imperial policies. For the new breed of twentieth-century activists, such as the Young Turks in the Ottoman Empire, or the German nationalists in the Habsburg and the German Empires, the idea of transforming their troubled empires and reconstructing them along particular ethnic and national lines seemed a most appealing solution, a way to revive imperial power, establish national greatness, and secure internal stability. In this view, the multinational character of the old empires was precisely the problem. They suppressed the dominant nationality and prevented it from achieving its historical destiny, while incessant ethnic conflict destabilized the political and social order and provided opportunities for foreign meddling. Despite their vastly different backgrounds, self-perceptions, and articulations of goals, Soviet party militants were involved for decades in a large-scale effort to maintain and expand their empire, promoting "friendly" nationalities, violently purging the perceived enemies of the Soviet "homeland," and asserting the dominance of (Great) Russians. Most radically, the Third Reich was planned to be a vast improvement over the previous two German Empires by being built on the principle of a Master Race (which included activist ethnic Germans from the Baltic and former Habsburg lands) lording it over a hodgepodge of enslaved and debilitated groups and eradicating those deemed to be unworthy of life or obstacles to Aryan supremacy.

Mutual Interactions, Peaceful and Violent

Many of the chapters that follow deal with the extraordinary violence that marred the Borderlands region, especially between the latter part of the nineteenth century and the aftermath of World War II. But violence was never natural or inevitable, as so many commentators presumed when they watched the former Yugoslavia descend into ethnic cleansing and genocide in the 1990s.[3] For centuries, in some areas for over two millennia, diverse populations had lived side-by-side and sometimes interacted quite peaceably. To be sure, they were divided by religion, language, ethnicity, and social class; marriage across certain religious and ethnic lines may have been limited in some cases, invisible in others. Yet the economic and social relations among diverse communities could only be sustained on a foundation of peaceable interactions. In the era of empires, more often than not the rulers sought to maintain social tranquility because they prized order and knew that violence, once unleashed, was very difficult to control. There were exceptions, of course, perhaps most notoriously the massacres of Armenians in the Ottoman Empire in the 1890s and 1909, and the anti-Jewish pogroms in the Russian Empire in 1881–1884 and 1903–1906. But by and large, pogroms were generally not the work of the state but of mobs that the state sought to bring under control. The state even prosecuted people who committed crimes against those deemed minorities. Local populations as well as state officials had a direct interest in maintaining conditions that permitted the proverbial Jewish cattle dealer to offer his services to the local peasants, the Armenian and Greek merchants to act as intermediaries between international markets and more local-oriented Muslim shopkeepers, and German-speaking and Slovenian-speaking peasants to live side-by-side and, in fact, to switch languages as need arose without any sense that they had to make a fixed choice between them.

Certainly, our intent is not to idealize the long epoch of empires, nor should premodern interethnic relations be confused with modern notions of multiculturalism and social harmony. Jews had been expelled from England, France, and Spain from the twelfth to the fifteenth centuries by kingdoms that defined themselves in religious terms. Pogroms devastated the Jews of the Rhineland and elsewhere during the Crusades. The Thirty Years War became so violent because of the mix of religious, political, and social conflict, and the devastation of the war affected primarily civilians. The Khmelnitsky Cossack and peasant uprising of 1648 not only devastated large parts of Eastern Europe, but also had far reaching economic, political, and demographic ramifications. The uprising targeted Poles and Jews who had colonized, urbanized, and brought new modes of commerce to the newly acquired lands of the Polish-Lithuanian Commonwealth. They thus came to be seen as the oppressors and exploiters of peasants subsequently described as Ukrainians and of freebooting Cossacks who either wanted to maintain their autonomy or to enter the ranks of the Polish *szlachta* (gentry). Tens of thousands of Armenians were killed in large-scale pogroms that resulted from a combination of long-standing religious prejudices and social resentments against Christians who were often wealthier, better educated, and more worldly than their Muslim neighbors.

Still, there were fundamental differences between such premodern eruptions, driven by a combination of religious strife, socioeconomic resentment, and political ambition, and modern instances of interethnic conflict, motivated by a new sense of national identity, even if the new nationalists liked to retell the story of earlier conflicts as harbingers of contemporary national struggles. At the same time, the division of populations into religiously defined groups and the episodes of violence did leave historical traces still evident in the modern era. A repertoire of repressive acts could easily be mobilized and reenacted, even with the same tools of violence—pitchforks, clubs, swords, and worse.[4] But both state-directed violence and communal interethnic conflict became more sustained and more brutal in the latter part of the nineteenth century, largely for political, ideological, and technological-logistical reasons. The sea change in the nineteenth and twentieth centuries, the great distinction between the modern era and everything that came before, was the connection drawn between populations conceived in national and racial terms and sovereignty. To this must be added the rapid expansion in the state's ability to mobilize its new industrial, logistical, and administrative resources in order to propagate ideas and enact policies on a scale and at a pace entirely unthinkable in the premodern world. This profound transformation has led in the modern era to the great intensification of population separation via migrations, forced deportations, and genocides, as it has, of course, transformed the nature of war.[5] The claim that people were essentially constituted as nations and that their destiny would be fulfilled when they acquired their own state proved vibrant, powerful, and alluring; in its racial form, as under the Nazis, it could become limitless in its violence and in its conception of the territory appropriate to the dominant race.

Nationalism was not just a sentiment of belonging related to religion, language, and locality. Nationalism was expansive, indeed revolutionary, in its claim that the conformity of territorial and ethnic borders was the natural state of being. Whether espoused by Muslim Turks, Baltic Germans, *shtetl* Jews, or Hungarian landlords, nationalism directly challenged the multiethnic and multiconfessional empires with their far more extensive borders. Often, nationalism created its own fantasies of great territories. Many nationalists could not rest content in a small state and loudly proclaimed their irredentist dreams, whether of a revived Hellenic Mediterranean empire, a Pan-Turkish realm that stretched into Central Asia, or a Poland whose borders reached from the Baltic to the Black Sea. But there were many other nuances: Zionists preferred a small Jewish state to Jewish minority status throughout many countries (though the process of creating that state indeed triggered irredentist fantasies); nationalists in countries with large minorities, such as interwar Poland, had to decide whether to maintain their extended borders and assimilate or tolerate their minorities, as advocated by Józef Piłsudski, or to limit the state to the frontiers of its core ethnicity, as argued by Roman Dmowski.[6] Nazi irredentism was transformed into racial domination; communist internationalism was turned into Soviet-Russian hegemony. Conversely, some minorities, such as non-Zionist Jews or Muslim Arabs and Turks in Europe, have had to negotiate between their own sense of ethnic, religious, and national identity, their relationship to their so-called host countries, and their ties to Israel, the Arab world, or Turkey.

Nationalism created minorities and majorities. Those terms, as we understand them today, are essentially modern and date only from the late nineteenth century.[7] They constitute the language of nationalism and the nation state. The empires had various subjects under their domain who differed from the predominant ethnicity and religion of the ruling house. Jews and Christians in the Ottoman Empire; Czechs and Slovaks, Poles and Ruthenians, Romanians and Magyars, Croatians and Italians, Roma, Jews, and others in the Habsburg Empire; literally hundreds of groups that were Muslim, Jewish, Catholic, or something else entirely in the Russian Empire; Poles, other Catholics, and Jews in the German Empire— from imperial subjects they became minorities who, by their very existence, challenged the claims of the nationalists that their own population was, or would become, homogeneous or dominant under the state. If Poland was to be the country of Poles, Bulgaria of Bulgarian Christians, Turkey of the Turks, then everyone else was now consigned to minority status. And that meant a wide range of policies. Minorities could be assimilated into the dominant group or even protected, as was the goal of the post-World War I treaties and the League of Nations' Permanent Minorities Commission. Or they could be driven out or killed. Only one thing was certain: minorities could never be ignored.

Ultimately, then, the more virulent and sustained character of the violence of the borderlands in the past two centuries was a result of the emergence of national claims in a world of empires. As we noted, this violence was distinguished from numerous earlier examples of brutalities by being far more extensive and reaching more consistently into civilian populations. The Balkan Wars of 1912–1913 provide a good example. Many observers remarked on the particularly brutal character of the warfare.[8] Armies did not just crisscross the lands and defeat one another in battle. They tortured the living and mutilated the dead, raped women and butchered children en masse. Irregular forces and civilians joined in the activities and seized the properties and possessions of minorities that were driven out. Since nation building was the goal, civilians who were not of the same nation had to be removed and violence was the best method to accomplish this end. War of any kind unleashes all sorts of passions and some people are attracted by the appeal of total domination that war makes possible. But when those passions are played out in a framework of national conflicts, soldiers and civilians may be given license to enact even greater brutalities.

Great Power rivalries often stimulated local violence. In the Borderlands the four empires vied for territorial expansion and greater influence. But that was not all. The system of alliances drew in the other European powers, France and Britain most notably, but also Italy after 1871. The fabled "Eastern Question"—the Great Power concentration on the fate of the Ottoman Empire—reverberated from the Eastern Mediterranean to deep into Eastern Europe.[9] Russian–Ottoman wars were often the fulcrum whose reverberations extended outward to set off local episodes of violence within the larger context of imperial wars. It is no accident that waves of ethnic, national, and racial violence continued well after the armistices or peace treaties that ended the Russo-Turkish War of 1877–1878, the Balkan Wars of 1912–1913, and both world wars. In all these settings, modern technology and the modern public sphere enabled the speeding up and intensification of violence. Armies and mobs could travel quickly by rail from one destination to another. Ideas could be disseminated in mass-circulation and fast-printed newspapers, orders communicated via telegraph and telephone.

Often the violence became so extensive because national or racial claims were increasingly enmeshed with deep-seated political and social conflicts. At acute moments like the immediate post-World War I period, it is almost impossible to disentangle the various strains of the huge conflagrations that devastated the borderlands. Peasant uprisings, worker strikes, white terrors, red terrors, pogroms, genocidal assaults on minorities, national armies, imperial armies—all deeply scarred the entire region from the Baltic to the Black Sea and beyond from 1917 to 1923. Time and again, these social and economic conflicts were "nationalized." Armenian and Greek merchants, Polish landowners, Jewish traders—all became targets, especially if they were more prosperous than their neighbors. When outright violence was contained, discrimination became more pronounced as new national states from Republican Turkey to interwar Poland sought to develop their own national bourgeoisies. Even without the still more virulent violence of the Nazi era, the overall situation looked bleak for minorities as nation states came to dominate the region.[10]

Political Imaginary

Borders exist in the geopolitical reality of cartography and international treaties, fences and watchtowers, customs posts and army patrols. On either side of the line is another country, characterized by a different regime, and often a different language, different customs, even a different history. Of course, the geopolitical reality of cartography and international treaties can and often does also make for borders that cut across shared languages, customs, and histories, so that, at least for a while, the only difference between one side of the line and the other is the line itself and the regimes that sketch it on the map and enforce it on the ground. Drawing this line can be an attempt to create a new, separate reality rather than a reflection of existing differences, as was the case of divided Germany after World War II. States and their rulers, social elites, and bureaucracies often try to fix borders even as they may also wish to expand them. Others constantly try to undo them, whether for economic or ideological reasons, in order to reunite families, or to bring together dispersed ethnic groups. Historically, what at one point appeared as unchangeable frontiers separating one political entity from another often turn out to have been neither permanent nor impregnable. Where the Berlin Wall solidly separated the city into two parts two decades ago, now only a few quaint remnants stand; where the Iron Curtain divided Europe into irreconcilable blocks, traffic streams in both directions with little attention to the rotting leftovers of elaborate systems erected to keep some in and others out.

While borders separate and block, they also often serve as sites of contact and transition. Moving past the stern officials at the border crossing points is a constant flow of humanity and its products. The firm yet transitory nature of such lines drawn on the ground, and their predilection to both block and channel through, indicates a certain ambiguity that is all the more visible in borderland regions. For it is there that one becomes aware of the possible affinity between those residing on either side of the border, on the one hand, and the differences between the border-dwellers and their respective compatriots living closer to the political centers of their separate states, on the other hand. We might suggest that the nature of the association between frontier nationalities and the nationality of the metropole indicates the fluidity or opaqueness of that state's borderlands. Where the periphery adheres more strongly to the national idea of the center, the border may be less porous at least in that it truly divides between two (or more) nationalities; but where the frontier nationality expresses or displays a closer affinity with a national group across the border or even with the core national idea of another state, then we can speak of these borderlands as regions of transition and overlap rather than clearly demarcated separations, despite the line that bisects them.

The transition from one set of customs, languages, traditions, or even physical appearance to another was often not abrupt but gradual, especially in prenational circumstances. Hence the notion of borderlands peoples who appeared to display mixed characteristics that included features of the two peoples on either side of the borderland region. For that reason borderlands peoples or frontier nationalities were often a disturbing, if also an alluring, phenomenon to integral nationalists. Minorities in one state who have national affinities with another nation state across the border may be living side-by-side with a national group for which the border is indeed a line of national demarcation. Hungarians in Romania provide a good example.[11] The Hungarian minority has clear affinities with people living across the border, yet the Romanian majority perceives that same border as a firm and necessary separation both because it indicates the difference between the majority in one state and another, and because it defines the minority as just that, as, in a sense, a group that is on the "wrong" side of the border. This is very different from the case of minorities that cannot be identified with any existing nation state, as were the Jews in Europe before the creation of the State of Israel. Especially in a world of nation states, such groups may evolve a general sense of themselves as an intrinsic minority, a marginal or guest people, an inherently foreign entity wherever they reside, as borderlands people irrespective of their location vis-à-vis the border. This is to some extent still the condition of the Roma in Europe today. In other words, borderland identities may lead to a greater insistence on adherence to a national, ethnic, or religious collective; or, they may make for more ambiguity and uncertainty regarding affiliations to a larger whole. But in either case, they are rooted in an awareness of living on the margins where one state ends and another begins.[12]

Here is the paradox of the borderlands' political imaginary: while reality consists of arbitrary separation, the imaginary takes one across the line to peoples, cultures, and landscapes cut off by political and military fiat; yet long-term cultural and kinship associations across the line constitute a powerful reality that pits itself against the fantasy of political leaders striving to tear peoples and families apart for perceived reasons of state and power. Borders are drawn to separate those who allegedly cannot or should not be mixed, and in order to create zones of homogeneous nations. Yet borderlands by their very nature often defy this goal by remaining regions of ethnically, culturally, and religiously mixed populations.

In some sense, borderlands are imagined most in their absence, only after they have disappeared into a simplified system of ethnic and political division. During their lifetimes, perhaps precisely because of their geographical marginality, borderlands are often the prime sites where contesting national myths, narratives, and identities are created.[13] Hence also the predilection of borderlands to be both zones of coexistence and multiethnicity, and of violence and devastation. Such violence is generated from without by the states that claim the borderlands for themselves and try to transform them into more clearly identifiable national regions. But it is also generated from within by the inhabitants of the borderlands, who are either taken in by the new rhetoric of separation and exclusion, or in fact become its main carriers and leaders.

Protean Borderlands

Whether a place or a region is or ever was in the borderlands may itself be a contested assertion. For the notion of borderlands can have various uses, ranging from a license for conquest and annexation to a preoccupation with nostalgia and marginality. The scope, definition, and meaning of borderlands are, therefore, fluid and unstable: just as their typical mix of populations suggests their hybridity, so too their ever-changing contours reveal their protean nature.

This was the case, to offer just one telling example, of a southeastern territory of Poland annexed by the Habsburg Empire in 1772 and given the name Galicia in an attempt to legitimize a bare-knuckled land grab by appealing to the region's obscure medieval genealogy. By the time the province reverted to the resurrected Polish state in the wake of World War I, it had evolved a unique sense of identity, not least thanks to its status as the Habsburg Empire's eastern borderland.[14] And yet, what became Eastern Little Poland in the interwar period also experienced a growing interethnic conflict between Poles and Ukrainians.[15] With the outbreak of World War II, the former Eastern Galicia was taken over by the Soviet Union and joined to Soviet Ukraine. The Soviets perceived this western borderland as more prosperous and diverse than their own lands, and they quickly set out to transform it along Soviet lines. In fact, they reduced it to even greater economic deprivation, cultural paralysis, and political chaos, to say nothing of the widespread police brutality, arrests, and deportations that characterized their rule.[16] Two years later it was occupied by the Germans, renamed Ostgalizien (Eastern Galicia), and treated as part of the vast, savage, and dangerous eastern frontier that had to be occupied, subjugated, racially cleansed, and Germanized.[17]

By the time the Soviets and Germans were done with their respective political, social, and demographic restructuring of the region, accompanied by the actions of Ukrainian nationalists, the former Galician province was transformed into a relatively homogeneous Ukrainian land whose Polish population had been expelled, Jewish inhabitants murdered, and remaining or newly arrived residents professed little knowledge or memory of its previous multiethnic identity.[18] Since Ukrainian independence in 1991 the region constitutes part of that state's western provinces. Although officially it has not been called Galicia since World War II, many Poles, Ukrainians, and Jews (as well as some Germans and Austrians) still refer to it by this name even today.[19]

The nature and characteristics of this borderland were molded and transformed over several centuries. For the Polish nobility, which lined it with fortified towns and castles in the early modern period, this frontier served to fend off invading Ottomans, Tartars, and Cossacks. Meanwhile its demographic pattern was established along lines eventually to be ethnicized and nationalized, made up of majority Greek Catholic Ruthenian (later Ukrainian) peasants; a powerful Roman Catholic Polish nobility and urban class; and a significant population of Jewish city dwellers, artisans, estate managers, leasers of noble properties, and merchants.[20] Hardly prosperous under Polish rule, following its annexation by the Habsburg Empire, the newly named Galicia came to be known as the Empire's poorest and most backward province.[21] Yet the unhappy state of many of its inhabitants did not prevent Galicia from becoming, especially in retrospect, a site of fascination and fantasy.

Long after its loss, Galicia featured in much Austrian literature as an essential component of the empire's unique blend of cultures and languages, bureaucratic centralism and chaotic periphery.[22] Similarly, despite its years of political strife and economic underdevelopment under Polish rule, and even as Poland's borders were shifted away from it after World War II, in the Polish imaginary Galicia remained a crucial part of the lost *Kresy*, the borderlands in which much of the nation's identity and lore was forged as it carried its self-proclaimed, centuries-long "civilizing mission" to the "wild east."[23] And, not least, Galicia remained on the borderlands of Jewish identity, a place of mystical rabbis and practical merchants, of Hasidim and *Maskilim* (Enlightenment-influenced Jews), socialists and Zionists, humor and tragedy. Increasingly a site of departure to lands of greater opportunity and fewer dangers, Jewish Galicia featured also as a borderland of transition and a launching pad for self-transformation. The "Galitzianer" embodied all the qualities of the *Ostjude* on the threshold of modernity, the borderland Jew par excellence, with one foot in the ghetto and another in the modern world.[24] By definition, this was a transitional figure; he too remains only as a literary trope and a cultural icon for those long-vanished Jewish borderlands, where these days Polish, Jewish, and occasional Austrian and German tourists can be seen seeking their respective imagined roots.[25]

Local Violence

A deeper understanding of the borderlands paradigm also calls for a focus on the local, on those multiethnic towns and cities that dotted the landscapes of Europe's eastern frontier regions. These sites on the map may enter and exit the borderlands without ever changing location. They may also maintain a borderland identity long after their actual position has fundamentally changed. The borderlands of reality and imagination are part and parcel of the mundane fabric of local community life.

In many towns located in the former Eastern Galicia, for example, we find that as early as the seventeenth century relations between the Polish, Jewish, and Ruthenian inhabitants had settled into a division of roles that changed very little for the next three centuries, despite several political transformations. This ethno-religious balance depended on a premodern view of society that was eventually undermined by the idea of nationalism combined with slow economic development in the nineteenth century. To be sure, long before the modern era this socioeconomic reality could become a source of violence. Yet for much of the time widespread communal violence was uncommon, and the rhetoric of exclusion and excision was rarely heard.[26] But in the latter part of the nineteenth century, Poles, Ukrainians, and Jews began organizing themselves separately from and in some ways against each other, a phenomenon that emerged all over the borderlands. While violence was still rare, the implicit message of integral nationalism was that eventually the region would have to belong to either Poles or Ukrainians, and that Jews would remain either a tolerated minority or not at all, since they had no "natural" place in the towns or the land.[27] For their part, some Jews began to envisage their own national solution, one that would be located in Palestine, far from the existing borderlands.

A similar pattern can be identified in the city of Vilnius (Wilno, Vilna), located in the northern part of the borderlands. As outlined by Theodore Weeks in his contribution to this volume, the city had a particularly wide range of ethnic groups and religions, including Roman Catholic or Eastern Orthodox Poles, Lithuanians, Belorussians, and Russians, as well as Jews. Yet while these different groups lived side by side without any major outbreaks of violence prior to 1914, they often entirely ignored each other's existence, speaking and writing about the city as if it belonged only to their own group. The emergence of electoral politics in the early twentieth century only accentuated the tendency of local national groups to identify by and large only with their own members. Ironically, but according to a pattern seen elsewhere as well, hostility to Jews increased in direct correlation to the growing involvement of Jews in the larger society. The advent of nationalism, which in some ways replaced religion as a focus of identification, only deepened the rift between ethnic groups and was especially detrimental to the Jews of Vilnius, as to those of the borderlands as a whole.

In the Ottoman realm, an empire setting far removed from modern notions of legal equality among all the citizens or subjects of the state, Jews and Christians occupied a subordinate legal status. At the same time, their communities exercised a great deal of autonomy. Jewish life in particular fared much better in comparison with Europe in the premodern era. Despite Muslim prejudices against Christians, Armenians also lived in fairly secure status despite their legally subordinate position, and were even known as the "most loyal millet." But over the course of the nineteenth century, conditions deteriorated for Armenians precisely as some Armenians prospered economically and became more tied to Western Europe—in short, became more modern—and as the European powers threatened the integrity of the Empire and Ottoman sultans hesitantly and intermittently pursued policies that would have made all the Empire's subjects at least formally equal. Such policies aroused the intense ire of traditionally minded Muslims. At the local level, Armenians became more subject to arbitrary land seizures, oppressive taxation, and extensive violence. Armenian activists, beginning in the late nineteenth century, organized their own political parties, while the initial multiethnic and multiconfessional character of the Committee of Union and Progress, the Young Turk party, proved very short-lived. Under these conditions, the fabric of communal coexistence that had characterized so much of Ottoman history became badly frayed.[28]

Three main events transformed the implicit logic of nationalist rhetoric into a brutal national and local reality with lasting and permanent consequences. The first was World War I, whose sheer violence as well as policies and ideologies left deep scars all over the borderlands. In the town of Buczacz (Buchach), Eastern Galicia, for instance, more than half of the houses were destroyed. Thousands of Jews fled from widespread pogroms by the Russian army. The delicate political balance between the ethnic groups was finally shattered through subsequent wars between Poles, Ukrainians, and Bolsheviks.[29] Poland's interwar rule became increasingly xenophobic and antisemitic. Growing impoverishment, police suppression of nationalists and communists, the organization of underground insurgent groups, and the exclusion of suspected minorities from higher education and political posts all created an atmosphere of impending eruption.[30] Finally, the Soviet occupation of 1939–1941 undid whatever potential had remained for interethnic cooperation, pitting one group against the other and favoring formerly underprivileged groups such as Jews and Ukrainians over the previously dominant Poles.[31] The Nazis, of course, then exercised the most extensive violence with a deliberate program of the annihilation of Jews and the brutal and lethal subordination of Poles and other Slavs.

Vilnius presents a similar case of this eventually deadly process. Here too, World War I was a disaster for all inhabitants of the city. A combination of anti-Jewish Russian policies and economic measures by both the Russian and German occupiers had an especially deleterious impact on the Jewish community. Polish rule of the city began with a pogrom in April 1919. Over the next two decades, Jews came to be identified both by Poles and subsequently also by Lithuanians with the communists. As was also the case in many Galician towns, Vilnius was both economically depressed and culturally vibrant, and Jews played a prominent part in cultural, educational, and political activities. Yet here as elsewhere, government policies discriminated against Jewish businesses in favor of ethnic Polish economic growth, while the expanding influence of the antisemitic National Democrats, especially among university students, restrictions on Jewish kosher food, and widespread popular expressions of anti-Jewish sentiments meant that by the late 1930s life in Vilnius had become increasingly difficult for its Jewish residents, estimated at about a quarter of the total population of the city. Finally, in October 1939 Vilnius was handed over to Lithuania by the Soviet regime, setting off a process of Lithuanization directed especially against Polish institutions and civil servants.[32] Once the Soviets occupied Lithuania in June 1940, their own policies of arrests and deportations had a similar effect to those implemented in Galicia, destroying the local elites and further exacerbating interethnic hostility. Here too, then, the scene was set for an outburst of even greater violence once Germany attacked the Soviet Union the following year.

World War I was the decisive event also for the fate of Ottoman Christians. By 1914 the Young Turks dominated the regime. The catastrophe of the Balkan Wars had made the Young Turks hyper-alert to any possible further dismemberment of the Empire. So when Germany, on the very eve of World War I and on an explicit directive from Kaiser Wilhelm II, offered an alliance, they accepted.[33] Germany promised their party, the Committee of Union and Progress, that it would fight the war until the Ottoman Empire had recovered much of the territory it had lost in the preceding decades. But the war went badly for the Ottomans. The specter of defeat and total war offered the Young Turks the opportunity to radically revamp the demography of the Empire, making its core regions more decisively Muslim and Turkic and asserting the political domination of Turks in the polity and society against the leading positions that Armenians and Greeks had held in the economy. This was the setting in which the deportations and killings of Armenians and Assyrians unfolded, beginning in February 1915 and accelerating through the spring and summer and into 1916 in its most concentrated phase. The Pontic and Aegean Greeks were meanwhile subject to on-again, off-again deportations to Greece.[34] While the violence was initiated by the state, it played out at the local level. If some Muslims tried to protect their Christian neighbors, others turned on them through the direct exercise of violence or by seizing the lands, homes, and furniture of those sent off on deportation columns. Along the way, many Armenians faced further depredations by Kurdish bands that operated with the full knowledge of the state.

Local violence tends to be particularly gruesome and gratuitous, perhaps precisely because it is visited upon neighbors and acquaintances, not foreigners and outsiders. This was evidenced in the borderlands and seen most recently is such cases as the Rwandan genocide and the war in Bosnia, as well as in many other cases of genocide, mass murder, ethnic cleansing, and communal massacres.[35] Proximity and familiarity appear to call for the kind of ruthless brutality that will transform friends and colleagues into faceless outsiders. Where there has been no social reality of separation, local violence is intended not only to evict or to kill members of other ethnic and religious groups but also to erase a past whose memory would deny the legitimacy of the perpetrators. Thus this is violence generated by historical myths even as it strives to realize them in the present by eradicating the traces of its victims.

In all of these cases, external violence was further incited and abetted by internal strife, greed, and pent-up aggression.[36] On the local level, such terms as "perpetrators" and "victims" often become blurred, while the supposedly common phenomenon of the "bystander" loses almost all meaning and relevance. Finally, especially in the borderlands, in order to understand the full implications of state-organized genocide we need to study local massacres and their long-term ramifications. This, in turn, leads us to make greater use of evidence provided by local protagonists, in the form of diaries, letters, eyewitness accounts, testimonies, interviews, and memoirs. Only in this manner, the combination of standard state documentation with locally-generated sources, can historians reconstruct local events in all their complexity and thereby gain more insight into the socio-psychological make up of interethnic violence, its motivations, rationalizations, dynamics of perpetration, and subsequent narratives.[37]

Contested Memories

When the sociopolitical reality of borderlands ceases to exist, their memory still lingers in the mind, in photographs and writing, but also in the shape of tangible remnants on the ground—empty shells, collapsing ruins, converted buildings—echoes of civilizations whose living representatives are gone forever. Memory is not merely fading, it is also contested, not least through the erection of memorials, which try to recall and eternalize one narrative of the past while forgetting and erasing another. In numerous towns throughout the borderlands, the memory of the slaughtered and expelled has been wiped clean; the mass graves are unmarked; little, if any, information is provided about the fullness of prewar life and its wartime destruction. The few remaining edifices that still assert a forgotten past are rapidly collapsing or being demolished.

The memory and commemoration business is thriving in the Borderlands, but often the industry is focused on self-glorification, ritualized mourning for the victims of Soviet-

Communist rule, and the creation of a history cleansed both of the murdered or expelled minority populations and of the local collaborators who facilitated the crime. This is especially blatant in such regions of the borderlands as the former Galicia, where Ukrainian liberation fighters are lauded for their struggle against the Soviets, while their participation in war crimes against Jews and Poles is unremembered. And, what is perhaps the saddest of all, the memory of the few heroic rescuers of the victims is invoked only as a rhetorical tool to fend off accusations of collaboration in genocide.[38] But obviously the complex history of a multiethnic past that was violently "unmixed" not merely by external forces but also by local protagonists has had repercussions throughout the borderlands. Outright denial by the direct perpetrators is rare, although the official policy of the Turkish government on denying the genocide of the Armenians is a major exception. But a twisting of narratives, obfuscation, insistence on one's own victimization, and attempts to blame one's victims for their own fate are much more common.[39]

Thus, for instance, L'viv recently saw the opening of the National Memorial Museum "Lonsky Street Prison," dedicated to Ukrainian victims of the Soviets, which fails to make any mention of the thousands of Jews who were murdered in the city by the Germans and numerous local collaborators in alleged reprisal to the murder of Ukrainian nationalists by the Soviets; Vilnius has a "Museum of Genocide Victims," which makes no mention of Lithuanian units that participated in mass killings of Jews throughout Eastern Europe or, indeed, anything about the Holocaust at all; Budapest features the very successful "House of Terror" museum, which devotes a minute portion of its exhibit to Hungarian collaboration in the murder and deportation of Jews and the rest of its ample space to the following decades of Soviet rule and oppression. In contemporary Germany debates rage about the memorialization of the approximately 13 million ethnic Germans deported from Central and Eastern Europe right after World War II. Meanwhile, the Republic of Turkey expends great efforts to deny the Armenian genocide.[40]

There are, of course, various gradations of this politics of memory, ranging from Belarus, with its almost total absence of Jewish and Holocaust memory, to Poland, where the vast "Museum of the History of Polish Jews" is about to be completed on the site of the Jewish Warsaw Ghetto. Memoirs and autobiographies often tell a different story, a search for a lost world of interactions across ethnic and national lines, even within families. Fethiye Çetin's memoir, *My Grandmother*, caused a sensation when it was published in Istanbul in 2004. Her grandmother had been one of the many Armenian children who were taken, sometimes forcibly, into Muslim households and raised as Turks. But in her old age, she would sometimes slip into Armenian when conversing with Kurdish neighbors.[41] Sometimes, family realities defy the logic and claims of nationalists.

Indeed, even in Ukraine this is not only a tale of destruction and erasure. In L'viv attempts are being made to remind the current inhabitants of their city's rich, diverse, and multiethnic past.[42] Moreover, nowadays there is in fact a certain cachet in the very borderland status of these regions, seen perhaps as linking parts of the world that had been separated from each other by totalitarian regimes, integral nationalists, exclusive memories, and narratives of violence and excision. Now borderlands can be presented in a positive light as vehicles of globalization and pluralism. But of course they have become merely borderlands of memory and imagination.[43] We must shift our gaze to other parts of the world to find living multiethnic borderlands, and in those sites, the reigning sentiment is not nostalgia, but often fear of communal strife and violence.

The Chapters

The individual contributions to this volume reflect the range of approaches discussed above. They focus on states, national and imperial; violence, local and global; coexistence; rituals; and cultural imaginings. They span the entire region of the borderlands, from the Baltic to the Black Sea, from the Urals to the Rhine.

The first section, "Imagining the Borderlands," opens with Larry Wolff's rumination on travel between west and east and the invention of Central Europe as a multiethnic transitional borderland linking the German and Slavic worlds. The term Central Europe—not coined until 1915 but already epitomized by the Habsburg Empire—reemerged with the Soviet Union's demise. Wolff sees Central Europe as both an unstable geographical entity and a literary and political fantasy, which for Czech writer Milan Kundera was embodied in the longing "to be a condensed version of Europe itself in all its cultural variety." Yet in the twentieth century massive ethnic cleansing and genocide deprived this in-between region of precisely that quality of having "the greatest variety within the smallest space." This eruption of violence, argues Gregor Thum in his chapter, can be traced back to the formation and representation of the eastern borderlands in nineteenth-century Germany and the meaning these lands acquired within German national culture. It was, he contends, the creation of myths about these borderlands that prepared the ground for Germany's ethnic war against its eastern Slavic neighbors.

Dan Diner takes us to the Jewish experience of transition from a premodern multiethnic Europe to the modern world of nation states that emerged in the Eastern borderlands after World War I. He argues that integrating the transnational, diasporic Jewish experience into the mainstream of European history can productively undermine the conventional nation state paradigm that guides much of continental historiography. For Diner, the Jews as a people were not agents of modernity, as is often argued, but rather remained as residues of the premodern *nationes* well into the modern era. These Jewish hybrid cultures were left behind as fragments of former corporate estates and remnants of the shattered multiethnic empires—only to be eventually swept away in the Holocaust. Theodore Weeks then turns to the specific relationship between Jews and others in the city of Vilnius, and demonstrates how different national groups employed selective examples and strategic rhetoric to claim the city as belonging primarily to their own ethnic-cultural group. The growing tendency toward cultural uniformity in the first half of the twentieth century resulted in a process of repressing, exiling, or murdering neighbors of other ethnicities. The predilection of political ideologies and groupings to "play the ethnic card" reduced toleration and exacerbated conflict—ultimately taken by the Nazis to its most murderous conclusion.

Gary Cohen provides a different kind of analysis in the chapter that leads off the section "Imperial Borderlands." Cohen shows that the Habsburg Empire, far from being another "sick man" of Europe wrenched apart by conflict among the nationalities, in fact commanded a great deal of loyalty from its subjects and citizens. The chapter demonstrates how various parties and movements used the laws and institutions of the Empire effectively for their own interests. Until the devastating end of World War I, even nationalists sought primarily reform, not dissolution. From the local vantage point, Pieter Judson argues similarly: so many of the subjects of Emperor Franz Joseph were, quite simply, not nationalists. In fact, they moved easily among different languages, to the frustration of nationalist activists and census takers. Nationalists engaged in an ideological and political struggle in which they depicted these internal borderlands as wild, untamed areas with populations desperately in need of the civilizing influence of nationalism. The very intensity of the struggle, Judson shows, undermines the claims of nationalists that they represented some kind of natural force and the inevitable logic of history.

Nationalism was modern, and so was the railroad. Frithjof Benjamin Schenk shows how railroads became a kind of mobile borderland, one in which the various ethnicities of the Russian Empire encountered one another, often for the first time. The shock of the new, however, did not necessarily breed tolerance. Quite the contrary: it often led to the assertion of ugly stereotypes, and railroads became the means by which pogroms spread rapidly.

The last two chapters in this section address the borderlands of the Ottoman Empire. Eric Weitz shows how international and domestic concerns became inextricably entwined as Germany sought to exercise predominant influence in the Ottoman Empire. Imperial competition and national conflicts within the Empire developed in tandem, leading Germany, ultimately, to become complicit in the genocide of Armenians and Assyrians. Elke Hartmann shifts the focus to Eastern Anatolia and demonstrates how, paradoxically, the Ottoman Empire's efforts to assert greater central control actually led to the fragmentation of power and intensified ethnic violence. As part of its overall reform efforts, the Empire sought to secure more firmly its eastern borders and eliminate the powers of semi-independent tribes. But it ended up arming some Kurdish groups, who then taxed and seized Armenian land and perpetrated violence against Armenian villagers.

The chapters in part 3, "Nationalizing the Borderlands," also range across Central and Eastern Europe and Anatolia. Patrice Dabrowksi investigates one of the quintessential borderlands, the Carpathian Mountains. In particular, she demonstrates how nationalist Poles from the lowlands entered the mountain regions and expended great efforts to nationalize the Tatra highlanders, and how Ukrainian nationalists sought to do the same with the Hutsul mountain people. The Carpathians became a site of conflict among competing nationalisms, even as the actual borders kept shifting among the various empires and successor states in the region. Robert Nemes also uses a local case—the Bihar/Bihor County on the Hungarian–Romanian borderland—to demonstrate how nationalisms were made around the turn of the twentieth century. Nemes shows that nationalists sought to draw a fixed border across what had long been an area of cross-cultural interaction. Ultimately, the Great Powers drew the line at the end of World War I, making a very real border.

Yaroslav Hrytsak focuses on the Ukrainian writer Ivan Franko. Hrytsak situates Franko in the great ethnic diversity and emerging modernization of Habsburg Galicia in the late nineteenth century. Galicia had a very substantial Jewish population, and Franko's writings conveyed the Judeophobia common among other groups. Yet Franko was repelled by the pogroms he witnessed and also expressed philosemitic sentiments. Hrytsak's chapter captures the complexity of attitudes toward Jews in the borderlands.

Tomas Balkelis turns to another compact yet highly complex region, Lithuania in the first months of the Second World War. Crisscrossing national, political, and territorial claims among Poles and Lithuanians only worsened under German and Soviet occupation (during the period of the Nazi–Soviet Non-Aggression Pact), and a spiraling refugee crisis added to the difficulties. Vilnius was the focal point of the territorial dispute, and its fate would ultimately be decided by Soviet power, but it was the "umixing" of populations, including the genocide of the Jews, that had the most fateful, long-term consequences for the region. Taner Akçam explores another form of population displacement—Young Turk plans for the ethnic homogenization of Anatolia before and during World War I. Drawing on intensive research in the Ottoman archives, Akçam shows the very deliberate character of the policies of the Committee of Union and Progress (CUP) toward Greeks and Armenians from 1913 to 1916. As a guiding principle, the Young Turks secretly decreed that in each Ottoman province, non-Muslims (and sometimes that meant non-Turks) should comprise no more than five to ten percent of the overall population. Forced deportations and genocide were the consequence.

The first three chapters of part 4, "Violence on the Borderlands," also address the history of the area of the Ottoman Empire. Complementing Akçam's contribution, Eyal Ginio explores CUP policies toward Bulgarians during and after the Balkan Wars of 1912–1913. Ginio shows that although the Ottoman government did not pursue a systematic policy of deportations, Ministry of Interior officials exerted great pressure on Bulgarians to leave, actions that were then legitimated by the bilateral Ottoman–Bulgarian treaty. These actions, Ginio argues, were far different from traditional Ottoman policies and marked a new stage in population politics. Keith Brown explores the narratives of Greek atrocities against Bulgarians during the Balkan Wars. Brown bases his chapter on letters written by Greek soldiers and incorporated into the Carnegie Endowment's widely circulated report on the war. He is less concerned with demonstrating the "truth" of the accounts than with showing how these reports became a critical feature in the public and historical debate about the nature of the Balkan conflicts, and how Greek and Bulgarian identities were made through these narratives. Finally, David Gaunt writes about the little-known Assyrian communities of the Ottoman Empire during World War I. Too small in number and too divided to be of critical political significance to the Ottoman government, the Assyrians were nonetheless caught up in the maelstrom of Ottoman population politics and underwent genocide. After the war, their internal divisions and political inexperience prevented the Assyrians from effectively articulating their sufferings before the Allied Powers at the Paris Peace Conference.

Peter Holquist also addresses territories of the Ottoman Empire, but this time from the perspective of Russian occupation policies in the borderland region of the Caucasus and northern Anatolia during World War I. He argues that the conduct of the Russian Army was a major contributing factor to the spiral of violence which culminated in the massacre of the Armenian population but also found expression in massacres and expulsions of Muslims and especially Kurds. Holquist notes the transformation of Russia's militarized violence, which initially operated within certain bounds, into a much more destructive form of revolutionary violence, caused in large part by the breakdown of military discipline and order, and spilling over into Russia proper in 1917–1921.

The last three chapters in this section take us to the Polish–Ukrainian borderlands. Alexander Prusin explores the dynamics and mechanisms of anti-Jewish violence in Eastern Galicia during the Russian occupation of 1914–1915 and the German invasion of 1941. He argues that dormant interethnic hostility was activated by invading armies whose occupation policies were predicated upon the elimination of Jews as not capable of fitting into the new state order. Thus state-driven violence was sustained and exacerbated by the active participation of Polish and Ukrainian "neighbors" who strove to gain access to power and economic resources at the expense of the Jews. John-Paul Himka, in his chapter, examines how an important nationalist Ukrainian newspaper published under the German occupation reported on two cases of mass violence by the Soviets in 1941 and 1943. Himka shows that the daily *Krakivs'ki visti,* published in Kraków, ethnicized both perpetrators and victims, ascribing primarily Jewish identity to the former and depicting the latter as almost exclusively Ukrainian. Thus, he argues, this Ukrainian organ used Soviet violence to justify German genocide and to advance the nationalist goal of "Ukraine for the Ukrainians."

Finally, Omer Bartov's chapter analyzes interethnic relations in the Eastern Galician town of Buczacz during World War II as reflected in personal accounts. He argues that testimonies contain crucial insights into the dynamic of denunciation and collaboration, as well as rescue and resistance, and undermine the conventional categories of perpetrators, victims, and bystanders. Bartov notes that such accounts "save" from oblivion events missing from official documentation. He further claims that local studies of Europe's eastern borderlands transform our overall picture of the Holocaust by demonstrating that much of it occurred as communal massacres and mass shootings and included large-scale local transfers of property.

The last section of the book, "Ritual, Symbolism, and Identity," opens with Pamela Ballinger's discussion of the Adriatic as a "watery borderland." This sea has separated such powers as Venice and the Ottomans; it has also provided for distinctions between those who lived along its eastern coast ("Italians") and those who dwelled in the interior ("Slavs"). A facilitator of transborder contact, the Adriatic has been and remains also a space of contestation over rights and identities, most recently between coastal Slovenes and Croats. More terrestrial contacts are examined by Myroslav Shkandrij, who reconstructs Ukrainian and Jewish attempts to establish a cultural and political identity in the early twentieth century by combining a modernist style with elements of their national traditions. In the wake of the 1917 revolution, a Ukrainian "cultural renaissance" was accompanied by a Jewish "cultural revival," embodied in the Kyiv-based Kultur-Lige. Shkandrij argues that the two movements were linked both as products of the Ukrainian revolution and in their mutual creation of "national modernism" as an important element of post-revolutionary culture.

Paul Robert Magocsi takes us to another instance of peaceful interethnic coexistence, this time in Carpathian Rus'. Constituting a religious, ethnolinguistic, and climatic-cultural borderland, the region has experienced its share of state-inspired violence. Yet, argues Magocsi, it has been remarkably free of ethnic, religious, and social violence, largely because this poor land witnessed little ethnically defined socioeconomic differentiation and because ethnic groups feared the state much more than each other. As Kai Struve's chapter demonstrates, things were very different in Eastern Galicia in 1941, when a wave of pogroms by local Christians and mass executions by German mobile killing units combined to wreak havoc on the Jewish population. This violence, argues Struve, acted as a ritual of blaming the Jews for the crimes of the Soviets. And while the Nazis encouraged local pogroms, Ukrainian anti-Jewish riots in summer 1941 were directly motivated by resentment against Jews whose social status had improved under Soviet rule, as well as by nationalist rhetoric against Jews as obstacles to national renewal.

Closing this section and the book as a whole is Philipp Ther's chapter on border regions. Particularly in Central Europe, such "lands in-between"—shaped by distinct mixtures of cultures and languages—became sites of struggles between national movements and nation states, which both wanted ownership over these areas and perceived regional movements as a threat to their administrative and ideological domination. Ambiguous or hybrid identities were anathema to nation states that demanded distinct and unequivocal belonging. Yet, as the example of Upper Silesia demonstrates, while the region has changed dramatically in the last century, regional loyalties have persisted and national identities remain unstable, as is arguably the cases with many other European regions. Under the impact of the enlarged

European Union, the question is, will the "Europe of nations" of the past two centuries develop into a "Europe of regions"?

However things may turn out, what we have learned from this book is that, as Ther notes, the study of borderlands helps historians overcome the dominant national paradigm, introduces contingency into the process of nation building and nation state formation, and demonstrates that territorial and group identifications, be they national, regional or local, are always fluid and transitory. But however contingent, the violent events of the twentieth century transformed the borderlands in ways that would have been unimaginable to a traveler in the early or mid-nineteenth century. Every village, town, and city, every society, is far more homogeneous than it was at any previous time in its history. The wars, genocides, and intercommunal violence that so marked the first half of the twentieth century have left their traces. And they have left us to ponder their origins and contemplate their meanings, for history and for the present.

NOTES

1. Unlike Timothy Snyder's *Bloodlands: Europe between Hitler and Stalin* (New York: Basic Books, 2010), our volume argues that the regions of bloody conflict were far larger than those delineated by the "bloodlands," not least because of the crucial Ottoman case. *Shatterzone of Empires* also amply documents that, contrary to Snyder's view, violence could hardly be ascribed only to the conflict between the Soviet Union and Nazi Germany, both because violence predated these regimes and because much of it was generated from within the borderlands rather than strictly imposed from without.

2. See Jane Burbank and Frederick Cooper, *Empires in World History: Power and the Politics of Difference* (Princeton: Princeton University Press, 2010).

3. Notorious in this regard is Robert Kaplan, *Balkan Ghosts: A Journey through History* (New York: St. Martin's, 1993).

4. Norman Naimark, "Three Hundred Years of Mass Killing in the Borderlands of Russia, Ukraine, and Poland, 1648–1848," presented at Princeton University Colloquium on Human Rights and Crimes against Humanity, December 2008, cited by permission.

5. See Eric D. Weitz, *A Century of Genocide: Utopias of Race and Nation* (Princeton: Princeton University Press, 2003).

6. Timothy Snyder, *Sketches from a Secret War: A Polish Artist's Mission to Liberate Soviet Ukraine* (New Haven: Yale University Press, 2005).

7. See Eric D. Weitz, "From the Vienna to the Paris System: International Politics and the Entangled Histories of Human Rights, Forced Deportations, and Civilizing Missions," *American Historical Review* 113: 5 (2008): 1313–43.

8. See, for example, International Commission to Inquire into the Causes and Conduct of the Balkan Wars, *The Other Balkan Wars: A Carnegie Endowment Inquiry in Retrospect* (Washington, D.C.: Carnegie Endowment for International Peace, 1993 [1913]).

9. Still important is M. S. Anderson, *The Eastern Question, 1774–1923: A Study in International Relations* (London: Macmillan, 1966).

10. William W. Hagen, "Before the 'Final Solution': Toward a Comparative Analysis of Political Anti-Semitism in Interwar Germany and Poland," *Journal of Modern History* 68: 2 (1966): 351–81; Çağlar Keyder, *State and Class in Turkey: A Study in Capitalist Development* (London: Verso, 1987); idem, "Class and State in the Transformation of Modern Turkey," in *State and Ideology in the Middle East and Pakistan,* ed. Fred Halliday and Hamza Alavi (Houndmills, Basingstoke, U.K.: Macmillan Education, 1988), 191–221; and Ayhan Aktar, "Economic Nationalism in Turkey: The Formative Years, 1912–1925," *Boğazici Journal: Review of Social, Economic, and Administrative Studies* 10: 1–2 (1996): 263–90.

11. Rogers Brubaker et al., *Nationalist Politics and Everyday Ethnicity in a Transylvanian Town* (Princeton: Princeton University Press, 2006).

12. Larry Wolff, *Inventing Eastern Europe: The Map of Civilization on the Mind of the Enlightenment* (Stanford University Press: Stanford, 1994); Walter Kolarz, *Myths and Realities in Eastern Europe* (Port Washington, N.Y.: Kennikat Press, 1972).

13. Timothy Snyder, *The Reconstruction of Nations: Poland, Ukraine, Lithuania, Belarus, 1569-1999* (New Haven: Yale University Press, 2003).

14. Larry Wolff, *The Idea of Galicia: History and Fantasy in Habsburg Political Culture* (Stanford, Calif.: Stanford University Press, 2010).

15. Economics also played a role. See Alison Fleig Frank, *Oil Empire: Visions of Prosperity in Austrian Galicia* (Cambridge, Mass.: Harvard University Press, 2005), 205-36.

16. Jan T. Gross, *Revolution from Abroad: The Soviet Conquest of Poland's Western Ukraine and Western Belorussia*, 2nd ed. (Princeton, N.J.: Princeton University Press, 2002).

17. Dieter Pohl, *Nationalsozialistische Judenverfolgung in Ostgalizien 1941-1944: Organisation und Durchführung eines staatlichen Massenverbrechens* (Munich: Oldenbourg, 1996).

18. Roman Szporluk, *Russia, Ukraine, and the Breakup of the Soviet Union* (Stanford: Hoover Institution Press, 2000), 109-60.

19. See, e.g., Christopher Hann and Paul Robert Magocsi, eds., *Galicia: A Multicultured Land* (Toronto: University of Toronto Press, 2005).

20. A. J. Brawer, *Galizien, wie es an Österreich kam: Eine historisch-statistische Studie über die innere Verhältnisse des Landes im Jahre 1772* (Vienna: G. Freytag: Leipzig and F. Tempsky, 1910).

21. Paul Robert Magocsi, *A History of Ukraine* (Seattle: University of Washington Press, 1996), 170-216, 290-302, 385-96.

22. See, e.g., Joseph Roth, *The Radetzky March,* trans. Michael Hofmann (London: Granta, 2002 [1932]).

23. See, e.g., Henryk Sienkiewicz, *With Fire and Sword,* trans. W. S. Kuniczak (New York: Collier Books, 1991 [1884]).

24. See, e.g., Shmuel Yosef Agnon, *A Guest for the Night: A Novel,* trans. Misha Louvish (Madison, Wis.: The University of Wisconsin Press, 2004 [1938]).

25. See, e.g., Grzegorz Rąkowski, *Podole: Przewodnik krajoznawczo-historyczny po Ukrainie Zachodniej* (Białstok: Pruszków, 2006).

26. Joel Raba, *Between Remembrance and Denial: The Fate of the Jews in the Wars of the Polish Commonwealth During the Mid-Seventeenth Century as Shown in Contemporary Writings and Historical Research* (New York: Columbia University Press, 1995).

27. Brian Porter, *When Nationalism Began to Hate: Imagining Modern Politics in Nineteenth-Century Poland* (New York: Oxford University Press, 2000); Paul Robert Magocsi, *The Roots of Ukrainian Nationalism: Galicia as Ukraine's Piedmont* (Toronto: University of Toronto Press, 2002).

28. Ronald Grigor Suny, Fatma Müge Göcek, and Norman Naimark, eds., *A Question of Genocide: Armenians and Turks at the End of the Ottoman Empire* (New York: Oxford University Press, 2011). See also chapter 9 in this volume, by Elke Hartmann.

29. Wykaz: Budynków miejskich zupełnie zniszczonych, June 1918, Tsentralnyi derzhavnyi istorychnyi arkhiv Ukrainy, Lviv (TsDIAL), fond 146, op. 48, spr. 31; Alexander Victor Prusin, *Nationalizing a Borderland: War, Ethnicity, and Anti-Jewish Violence in East Galicia, 1914-1920* (Tuscaloosa: The University of Alabama Press, 2005).

30. Yisrael Gutman et al., eds., *The Jews of Poland Between Two World Wars* (Hanover, N.H.: University Press of New England, 1989).

31. Ben-Cion Pinchuk, *Shtetl Jews under Soviet Rule: Eastern Poland on the Eve of the Holocaust* (Cambridge, Mass.: Basil Blackwell, 1990); Bogdan Musial, *"Konterrevolutionäre Elemente sind zu erschiessen": Die Brutalisierung des deutsch-sowjetischen Krieges im Sommer 1941* (Berlin: Propyläen, 2000).

32. See further in Tomas Balkelis's contribution to this volume, chapter 13.

33. See Michael A. Reynolds, *Shattering Empires: The Clash and Collapse of the Ottoman and Russian Empires, 1908-1918* (Cambridge: Cambridge University Press, 2010), and Mustafa Aksakal, *The Ottoman Road to War in 1914: The Ottoman Empire and the First World War* (Cambridge: Cambridge University Press, 2008). Aksakal effectively challenges the older, standard view that Enver,

Talaat, and Djemal dragged a reluctant Ottoman society into war on the side of the Central Powers. See also M. Şükrü Hanioğlu, *A Brief History of the Late Ottoman Empire* (Princeton: Princeton University Press, 2008), 174–75.

34. Taner Akçam, *The Young Turks' Crime against Humanity: The Armenian Genocide and Ethnic Cleansing in the Ottoman Empire* (Princeton: Princeton University Press, 2012); idem, chapter 14 in this volume.

35. Philip Gourevitch, *We Wish to Inform You that Tomorrow We Will be Killed with Our Families: Stories from Rwanda* (New York: Picador, 1999); Eric Stover and Harvey M. Weinstein, eds., *My Neighbor, My Enemy: Justice and Community in the Aftermath of Mass Atrocity* (New York: Cambridge University Press, 2004); Donald L. Horowitz, *The Deadly Ethnic Riot* (Berkeley: University of California Press, 2001).

36. Omer Bartov, "Eastern Europe as the Site of Genocide," *The Journal of Modern History* 80: 3 (September 2008): 557–93. See also Kai Struve, chapter 25 in this volume.

37. See chapter 21 by Omer Bartov this volume. See also Elizabeth Neuffer, *The Key to My Neighbor's House: Seeking Justice in Bosnia and Rwanda* (New York: Picador, 2002).

38. Omer Bartov, *Erased: Vanishing Traces of Jewish Galicia in Present-Day Ukraine* (Princeton: Princeton University Press, 2007).

39. For a comprehensive survey of Eastern Europe's politics of Holocaust memory, see John-Paul Himka and Joanna B. Michlic, eds., *Bringing the Dark Past to Light: The Reception of the Holocaust in Postcommunist Europe* (Nebraska University Press, forthcoming spring 2013).

40. See the official website of the Ministry of Foreign Affairs: http: //www.mfa.gov.tr/the-armenian-allegation-of-genocide-the-issue-and-the-facts.en.mfa. For one critique, see Ronald Grigor Suny, "Truth in Telling: Reconciling Realities in the Genocide of the Ottoman Armenians," *American Historical Review* 114: 4 (2009): 930–46. See also, Göcek, Suny, and Naimark, *A Question of Genocide.*

41. Fethiye Çetin, *My Grandmother: A Memoir,* trans. Maureen Freely (London: Verso, 2008).

42. Hermann Simon, et al., eds., *Lemberg: Eine Reise nach Europa* (Berlin: Links Verlag, 2007), companion volume to the exhibition: "Wo ist Lemberg," shown in L'viv in 2008; "Forum: The Jewish Heritage in Ukraine and Representation of the Holocaust: A Discussion of Omer Bartov's *Erased,*" *Ukraina Moderna* 15: 4 (2009): 273–348 (in Ukrainian).

43. As Weeks notes in his contribution to this volume, chapter 4, unlike many other borderlands sites, Vilnius once more became a multiethnic city by the late 1940s, but one almost entirely inhabited by newcomers, defined officially as Lithuanian and Soviet, and focused on celebrating its Lithuanian character while paying little heed to its Jewish and Polish pasts. The Jewish Museum of Vilnius was resurrected in 1989 as a state-sponsored institution, which also now contains a Holocaust exhibition.

PART ONE

Imagining the Borderlands

1

THE TRAVELER'S VIEW OF CENTRAL EUROPE

GRADUAL TRANSITIONS AND DEGREES OF DIFFERENCE IN EUROPEAN BORDERLANDS

LARRY WOLFF

Introduction: "Traveling in the Central of Europe to Get Educated"

In 1925 the American writer Anita Loos published a celebrated comic novel under a title that was to become one of the most famous mottoes of American popular culture: *Gentlemen Prefer Blondes*. The novel followed the fictional European travels of the irresistibly preferable blonde heroine, Lorelei Lee, a spectacularly uneducated and uncultivated young American woman from Arkansas. Lorelei Lee appeared as the comic caricature of the American gold-digger as she sought to exercise her blonde American charms upon men with money in the great metropolises of Europe. She dismissed England with the chapter title "London is Really Nothing," and celebrated France illiterately with the title "Paris is Devine," but when she turned eastward toward Germany, the native land of the mythological Lorelei, the American heroine summed up her experiences under the chapter title, "The Central of Europe." With this goofy malapropism, Anita Loos seemed to suggest that her heroine was quite unable to understand the meaning of "Central Europe," an epithet that was already broadly current in the 1920s. The German politician Friedrich Naumann had published his landmark book *Mitteleuropa* in Berlin in 1915, and it was translated into English as *Central Europe* and published in London in 1916 and New York in 1917.

The idea of Central Europe was pervasive in the 1920s and 1930s, as prominent as it would ever be until, perhaps, its rediscovery in the 1980s and 1990s. Yet, then as now, "Central Europe" could be a frustratingly vague and elusive notion, and this was perhaps part of what Loos meant to suggest when she permitted her completely unintellectual heroine to become cheerfully confused about its meaning. Indeed there was room, then as now, for legitimate uncertainty about whether Central Europe represented a concretely specifiable geographical region, or whether it was actually more of a slippery cultural concept. Accordingly, Lorelei Lee, traveling around Europe, jumped to the preposterous conclusion that Central Europe was some sort of telephone exchange, or perhaps a train station, the Grand Central of Europe. While Anita Loos was certainly ridiculing her heroine, the author was perhaps also satirizing the puzzlingly problematic concept of Central Europe.

"So now we have a telegram," remarks Lorelei Lee, "and Mr. Eisman says in the telegram for Dorothy and I to take an oriental express because we really ought to see the central of Europe because we American girls have quite a lot to learn in the central of Europe." Central Europe, after all, must be "central," poised between east and west, and so the traveler can only arrive in Central Europe by following either an easterly or westerly vector, like an "oriental express," that is, the Orient Express. What could American girls "learn" in the Central of Europe, especially American girls who had already mastered the universally valid lessons of sex and money?

> And I really think it is quite unusual for two American girls like I and Dorothy to take an oriental express all alone, because it seems that in the Central of Europe they talk some other kinds of landguages [sic] which we do not understand besides French. But I always think that there is nearly always some gentleman who will protect two American girls like I and Dorothy who are all alone and who are traveling in the Central of Europe to get educated.[1]

In her ungrammatical and illiterate musings Lorelei Lee unerringly identified a characteristic experience of the western traveler making an oriental voyage into Central Europe: hearing "some other kinds of landguages which we do not understand besides French." Linguistic commingling and complication has always been fundamental to the traveler's experience of Central Europe. Lorelei Lee surely had no intention of actually learning any of the languages of Central Europe, or even French, but the discovery of the diversity and heterogeneity of languages was in itself an educational experience. If it provoked any anxiety, or even foreboding of danger, the certainty of finding some gentleman to provide protection, or perhaps translation, was sufficient reassurance.

The experience of travel may permit the observation of difference among the regions of Europe, but at the same time, more subtly, the traveler may actually produce that difference as a consequence of subjective impressions on the road or in the train. In the eighteenth century, the subjective experience of travelers helped to produce the most important modern orientation and division of Europe, that is, the conviction that Europe was fundamentally divided between east and west, Eastern Europe and Western Europe.[2] In the 1780s the Count Louis-Philippe de Ségur traveled from Paris to St. Petersburg, to take up his position as French minister to the court of Catherine the Great. On the way, as he traveled from Berlin to Warsaw, he crossed from Prussia into Poland, and he experienced that crossing as the boundary between realms of tremendous difference.

> When one enters Poland, one believes one has left Europe entirely, and the gaze is struck by a new spectacle: an immense country almost totally covered with fir trees always green, but always sad, interrupted at long intervals by some cultivated plains, like islands scattered on the ocean; a poor population, enslaved; dirty villages; cottages little different from savage huts; everything makes one think one has been moved back ten centuries, and that one finds oneself amid hordes of Huns, Scythians, Veneti, Slavs, and Sarmatians.[3]

This powerful subjective sense of difference between Poland and the lands further west marked the boundary between the modern domains of Eastern Europe and Western Europe. The traveler believed that he was leaving Europe entirely, despite remaining unequivocally in Europe according to every atlas. The notion of traveling backward in time through ten centuries was even more extravagantly subjective.

The conception of Europe as divided so abruptly between Western Europe and Eastern Europe almost ruled out the possibility of Central Europe, since there seemed to be no geographical space in between the sharply separated spheres of east and west. In fact, the idea of Central Europe was never discussed in the eighteenth century; it began to emerge in nineteenth-century discussions concerning the integration of the multinational and multilinguistic Habsburg Empire. Yet, the travel accounts of the eighteenth century offer intimations of the idea of Central Europe, discernible in a kind of traveler's experience that stood in clear contrast to Ségur's sense of radical continental demarcation. If the idea of Eastern Europe depended upon the subjective experience of abrupt discontinuity, the idea of Central Europe emerged from a different subjective experience of gradual transition, moving from west to east or from east to west. The idea of Central Europe, to the extent that it was implicitly present in eighteenth-century travel accounts, was dependent upon the distinction between east and west, and especially the philosophical emphasis on the supposed "civilization" of Western Europe in contrast to the alleged backwardness of Eastern Europe. However, instead of affirming an absolute contrast and dichotomy between west and east, the idea of Central Europe suggested gradual transition in a domain of variation and heterogeneity. In this regard, the idea of Central Europe was also important for representing the character of European borderlands.

The eighteenth-century diary of the philosopher Johann Gottlieb Fichte, who traveled as a young man in 1791 from Saxony through Silesia into Poland, offers an instance of such a gradualist experience of travel from west to east; it was very different from Ségur's sense of a sudden continental divide, but conditioned by the same philosophical principles of the Enlightenment. The roughly contemporary travels of the Polish writer Julian Niemcewicz indicate how such a voyage into Central Europe might have seemed from the other direction, from east to west. Finally, several twentieth-century travel narratives, including those of Alfred Döblin, Rebecca West, Czesław Miłosz, and Patrick Leigh Fermor, suggest how the subjective experience of travel was relevant to the idea of Central Europe after its explicit formulation.

Above all, it must be emphasized that the traveler's experience of Central Europe was not so much determined by the particular terrain of travel, but rather by the mode of perceiving and reporting. Indeed, it was not only the terrain that produced the idea of Central Europe in the traveler, but also the traveler who imposed the idea of Central Europe on the terrain. This perspective may offer some insight into the political plasticity of the idea of Central Europe in the twentieth century, successively invoked to serve a variety of political purposes, from Naumann's concern with German economic regional power during World War I, to Milan Kundera's affirmation of anticommunist regional solidarity in the 1980s.

Fichte: "The Virtues of the Saxon and the Pole"

Fichte, traveling in 1791, was not yet 30. Far from being the famous philosopher he would one day become, he was actually traveling to Warsaw to take up a rather humble position working as a private tutor for a noble Polish family. He set out from his native Saxony, from

Dresden, traveled through Silesia in Prussia, and then into Poland. Especially in his passage through Silesia he was extremely sensitive to transitions between the German world and the domain of Eastern Europe, and since he actually walked for much of the journey he was able to make observations of the most gradual nature. "I went a large part of the way on foot," he noted, and it took him a full month, from 8 May until 7 June, to travel from Dresden to Warsaw.[4] This left him all the more capable of observing and registering in his diary from day to day the subtle and gradual transitions, continuities, and differences along the itinerary from west to east. Fichte would not have characterized the territory as Central Europe, for no such notion explicitly existed yet in the eighteenth century. However, the province of Silesia would belong to almost anyone's modern conception of Central Europe, and Fichte's sensibilities and observations were notably modern in their recognition of some of the categories and considerations that would eventually lead to the construction of Central Europe.

A native subject of the elector of Saxony, Fichte would have been well aware of the political relation between Saxony and Poland, inasmuch as they had been ruled jointly by the Wettin dynasty through the first six decades of the eighteenth century; Augustus II and Augustus III, kings of Poland, were also electors of Saxony. The latter Augustus died in 1763, the year after Fichte's birth in 1762. The Wettins, however, were declared the hereditary dynasty of Poland according to the constitution of 3 May 1791, adopted in Warsaw only days before Fichte set out from Dresden. In the context of these political connections between Saxony and Poland, Fichte was sensitive to distinctions of civilization and backwardness according to the eighteenth-century philosophical sorting of west and east. At the same time, the future philosopher of German nationalism was already in 1791 attentive to ethnographic differences as he traveled from Germany to Poland.

The entrance into Silesia was also the political boundary between Saxony and Prussia, and up until that point Fichte observed the landscape with distinctly western resemblances in mind. He noted, for instance, in the mountains along the Saxon–Bohemian border "an exceptionally pretty village, that lies in bushes, boulders, and waters, whose mountains are like Switzerland (*ganz Schweitzerisch*)." Yet everything began to seem a little less Swiss when Fichte crossed the Saxon border into Prussian Silesia, arriving in the town of Naumburg on 17 May. There he admired a monastery tower, "altogether Catholic," and an urban landscape notable for "the baroque aspect (*der baroke Anblick*)."[5] Prussian Silesia had been Habsburg Silesia up until Frederick the Great seized the province from Maria Theresa in the 1740s. Fichte's usage of the term "baroque" must be understood as a negative comment implying irregularity and roughness. Yet, any modern attempt to recognize Central Europe in terms of architectural impressions would inevitably consider the presence of baroque architecture as one of the stylistic hallmarks of the region, the style that was sponsored by the Habsburgs in the age of the Counter-Reformation. In fact, as the historian R. J. W. Evans has noted, under Habsburg rule baroque style influenced the joint artistic development of both Catholic and Protestant culture in Silesia, while the art historian Thomas DaCosta Kaufmann has further emphasized the importance of baroque style for the art and culture of Central Europe.[6]

Though Fichte initially commented on "the good Silesian honesty" (*die gute Schlesische Ehrlichkeit*), he noted increasingly mixed impressions of Silesia as he traveled further, passing material judgment on the Silesian economy and moral judgment on the Silesian character.

> Through woods for the most part, and worse villages than the Saxon ones, villages that already appear very Polish [*schon sehr polnisch aussehen*], to Bunzlau. . . . A pretty female, in the

becoming Silesian costume. . . . The town itself is built quite regularly. The houses maybe less solid than in the beautiful Saxon towns, but a more beautiful appearance. . . . The daughter of the innkeeper—very pretty, good-hearted, though not notably polite, less delicatesse, the whole Silesian character, as I see it. But she was embarrassed, because there were sour pickles that they didn't want to give me. The lack of foodstuffs, business, trade, and so on. The Jews—especially one whom I took for a good man. The dispositions of the housemaid against the Jews, against me. . . . Everything not as it would have been in Saxony. [*Alles nicht, wie es in Sachsen gewesen sein würde.*] The bill cheap. Here Silesian accounting begins.[7]

The passage from Saxony through Silesia into Poland constituted the intermediary or central leg of a journey from west to east, and the centrality of Silesia was defined by Polishness and Saxonism as eastern and western points of reference. Villages began to appear "very Polish" in Silesia, on the way to becoming completely Polish in Poland itself, though Fichte never defined what it meant for a village to be "very Polish." Presumably this was related to the scale of greater and lesser solidity that he applied to the comparison of Saxon and Silesian towns.

The Silesian character, as Fichte saw it, was a matter of good-heartedness and the relative absence of politeness; he thus measured civilization according to the refinement of manners, matching the historical model that has been proposed by Norbert Elias in *The History of Manners*. At the same time, the lack of politeness corresponded to the lack of foodstuffs and business, so that economic indicators were correlated with the evidence of civility. The same criteria of backwardness and civilization that defined the difference between Eastern Europe and Western Europe in the age of Enlightenment became the polar coordinates of a perceptibly gradual transition in Central Europe.

Fichte's cryptic notation of the Jewish presence in Silesia ("the Jews—especially one whom I took for a good man") was fully consistent with modern attempts to define Central Europe in terms of its Jewish cultural elements. "In their destiny," wrote Kundera about the Jews, "the fate of Central Europe seems to be concentrated, reflected, and to have found its symbolic image."[8] Fichte's account of Silesia alluded to antisemitism as well as to Jews: "the dispositions of the housemaid against the Jews." Fichte himself seemed to have some strong feeling about the one Jew whom he "took for a good man"—but the comment almost seems to imply that he had found a reason to change his mind about this particular Jew.

19 May was Fichte's 29th birthday, and the next day, passing through the town of Neumarkt, he was celebrating with Silesian beer and schnapps.

> A Silesian roundhead of an innkeeper says to me, that I should move my mouth over his beer: oh it tastes good, it is so sweet and sour at the same time. Another says to me when I ask for good schnapps, he wants to give me a glass, like none other I've ever drunk in my life, and that sort of thing. The whole character free, without being coarse [*frei, ohne grob*], confiding, joking, without insult. In the village the inns are as good as the Saxon ones . . . but the real Silesian character is here. One might think here of a Polish German [*an einen Polnisch Deutschen*]. God what a difference! [*Gott welcher Abstand!*] Does the Silesian have the virtues of the Saxon and the Pole, between whom he lies [*zwischen denen er liegt*], without their faults?[9]

There could hardly have been any clearer expression of the idea of Central Europe negotiating the cultural difference ("God what a difference!") between east and west. The Silesian was a sort of ethnographic hybrid, a paradoxical "Polish German"—which, for the moment, after beer and schnapps, appeared to Fichte as a desirable amalgam.

Though he did not explicitly explain what were the divergent poles of Polish and German character that combined in the Silesian, the formula "free, without being coarse" (*frei, ohne grob*) seemed to suggested that the Polish character was too coarse and the German character insufficiently free. The issue of coarseness was entirely consistent with the values of civilization that made manners, politeness, and refinement into crucial points of reference for evaluating the difference between east and west. Proceeding on foot, Fichte continued to measure by his observations the distance he had come from Saxony and the proximity of Poland as he approached the border. The centrality of Silesia was emphasized as a geographical as well as an ethnographic fact; the Silesian was the central term between the Saxon and the Pole, "between whom he lies."

One week later, on 26 May Fichte observed changes in both the topographical landscape and the linguistic environment:

> Beyond Breslau the region changes. Small mountains surround the horizon, behind which bigger ones tower like an amphitheater. The ground becomes limier and firmer, but is just as little built up. The people more Slavic, their language rougher [*das Volk sclavischer, seine Sprache rauher*]: *Bausch* instead of *Busch*, *Hauf* instead of *Hof*, and the like.[10]

Taking the city of Breslau (today Wrocław) as the geographical hinge of the province, Fichte represented Silesia as a region of multiple transitions. He described in detail the changing landscape and gave specific examples of the varying pronunciation of German words, which became "rougher" as he walked eastward. This "roughness" of speech was clearly aligned with the "coarseness" of manners that he also perceived as the Polish end of the Silesian spectrum.

Fichte, however, left unspecified and undetailed the most striking note of his observations: that the people became "more Slavic" as he proceeded. Though this was associated with the increasing roughness of speech, it was not fundamentally a linguistic observation since the "rough" pronunciations cited were of German words, not Slavic words—that is, not Polish. Rather, Fichte's observation—*das Volk sclavischer*—must be interpreted as an anthropological judgment concerning character and customs, and perhaps also a racial judgment concerning the physical appearance of the people. Fichte did not add details of custom or appearance to clarify his comment here, but elsewhere in the diary he showed himself interested in trying to discern the Silesian character through the regional customs. In fact, 1791, the year of Fichte's journey, was also the year that Johann Gottfried Herder published the fourth volume of his *Ideas for the Philosophy of the History of Mankind*, introducing the anthropological category of "Slavic Peoples" (*Slavische Völker*). This effort to generalize anthropologically and ethnographically over all of Eastern Europe was something new in the intellectual history of the Enlightenment.[11] Fichte, making his observations on only the limited terrain of Silesia, was evidently attuned to Herder's anthropological sensibility. However, while Herder's category of "Slavic Peoples" was fundamental for defining "Eastern Europe" in terms of Slavic ethnography, Fichte's travel experience could be considered more relevant for defining "Central Europe," inasmuch as he made "Slavic" into a comparative adjective: *sclavischer*, more Slavic. For Fichte, in Silesia, "Slavic" was not a designation of absolute difference, but a matter of degree, of more or less, as he described the gradual transitions that he experienced on the way from west to east in Central Europe.

The next day, on 27 May Fichte registered further transitions: "There lie true Polish villages [*ächtpolnische Dörfer*] that even have Polish names. . . . Here the country people are for the most part Catholic."[12] It was characteristic of Fichte's sensibility that Polishness appeared as a true and essential character which could also influence the phenomena of Silesia in varying degrees and amalgams. A "Polish German" might seem to be an odd amalgam, the quality of Polishness qualifying the German subject. Beyond this possibility of hybridization, however, it was also possible to identify phenomena that were not just Polish (*polnisch*) but true Polish (*echtpolnisch*). As with Slavic character, "Polish" could be a matter of degree in Central Europe.

One day later, on 28 May, Fichte was already crossing the state border, leaving Prussian Silesia to enter the Polish-Lithuanian Commonwealth. Yet, he clearly felt that he had left "Germany" behind him long before, and that all of the Silesian stretch of travel was a transitional approach to Poland.

> Through a region pretty at first, in villages that already have real Polish names [*lauter polnische Namen*]. . . . The German here is no longer to be understood [*gar nicht mehr zu verstehen*]. The region is desolate, sad, and joyless [*wüste, traurig, freudenleer*]. At noon I crossed over the border. The first village is Ponnichowo, German, but a shudder came over me, especially at the sight of the big dogs, running freely around. . . . The costume of the peasants has already here in the first village something wild, and abandoned [*etwas wildes, und vernachlässigtes*].[13]

The border did not represent a definitive or abrupt boundary for Fichte's observations. Even before entering Poland the villages had "real Polish names," and even after entering Poland the first village could still be described as German.

Compared to Ségur, who felt that upon entering Poland he was leaving Europe entirely and stepping backward ten centuries in time, Fichte's travel experience was very different; his orientation of west versus east was qualified by the transitional approach to Poland through the "central" region of Silesia. Ségur subjectively found the Polish landscape to be "always sad," projecting his own inner mood onto the country around him, while Fichte found the border region "desolate, sad, and joyless"—before he actually crossed the border. Indeed, Fichte seemed much more self-conscious than Ségur about his own susceptibility to projecting personal emotions onto the landscape. He seemed to recognize that there was something subjectively emotional at work in the shudder that came over him when he saw the dogs on the Polish side of the border, even though the village was German. Indeed the seeming wildness of the dogs was somehow projected onto the costumes of the peasants—"something wild and abandoned." Clearly, Fichte knew that crossing the border into Poland was not actually any sort of sudden descent into anthropological savagery, and he knew it all the more surely for the fact that he himself had been recording a journey through increasingly perceptible coarseness and roughness over the previous ten days in Silesia.

Though Fichte traveled long before the idea of Central Europe was formulated, and just as the conceptions of Western Europe and Eastern Europe were emerging in the age of Enlightenment, his sensibility as a traveler sensitive to gradual transitions makes it possible to consider him as an early observer of Central Europe. Indeed, the modern ingredients of Central Europe—the ethnography of Germans, Slavs, and Jews, the material culture of beer, schnapps, and baroque architecture—were notably present in Fichte's diary. Above all, his travel account conveyed the ethnographic and linguistic heterogeneity of Silesia, which would eventually be recognized as the hallmark of Central Europe. Fichte found a commingling of qualities in a gradual and transitional travel experience, reflected in everything that he observed, from manners to mountains. Indeed his final shudder, on crossing the Polish border, was the culmination of a persistent anxiety throughout his trip, as he confronted uncertainty, ambiguity, and miscellany. By 1807 and 1808 Fichte would offer his "Addresses to the German Nation" as the philosophical founding of modern German nationalism, without regard to the ambiguities of Central Europe. In this regard it may be noted that in modern European history Central Europe has often been the crucible for the forming of modern nationalist passions, precisely in reaction to the heterogeneous ethnographic mélange of the region.

Fichte did not last long in Warsaw, but ended up moving on, further east, to Königsberg, where he would study philosophy with Immanuel Kant and embark upon a philosophical career. His problem as a tutor in Warsaw was that he failed to satisfy his employers, because his French was considered inadequate to give instruction. In Central Europe, after all, "they talk some other kinds of landguages which we do not understand besides French"— and a mastery of French would therefore have been an important skill for an itinerant tutor to offer. Fichte himself discovered during his journey through Silesia the tremendous variation and complication of language in the intermediary region that would later be called Central Europe.

Niemcewicz: "The Sound of Our Language"

The consciousness of linguistic complication was equally evident in the travel writing of Fichte's contemporary, the Polish writer Julian Niemcewicz, who traveled from east to west at roughly the same time. For illustrative purposes he may thus serve as Fichte's counterpart, pursuing reciprocal voyages in the reverse direction through intermediary regions that would later be characterized as Central Europe. Niemcewicz even traveled outside of Europe to America, and left a full account of New Jersey in the late eighteenth century, so his traveler's perspective was conditioned by worldwide experience. While Fichte recorded his impressions immediately in a diary, Niemcewicz remembered his eighteenth-century travels in his nineteenth-century memoirs, writing with the full benefit of retrospective experience.

In 1784 Niemcewicz was traveling from Vienna to Venice, and passing through the provinces of Styria and Carinthia, at the intersection of Austrian and Slovenian lands, of German and Slavic languages, in the borderlands of Central Europe.

> We set out on the 16th of March 1784, taking the road for Styria and Carinthia. It was agreeable for me to hear in these provinces the ordinary people speaking Slavic, fraternally related to my own paternal language. Thus it is that in spite of all invasions, conquests, and usurpations, in you alone, peasant people, is preserved the memory of original generations and the native inhabitants of the land.[14]

Like Fichte, Niemcewicz was sensitive to the languages being spoken around him as he traveled, and used his own native language, Polish, as the standard for recognizing and evaluating the languages that he heard on the way. The lands of the Habsburg monarchy were crucial terrain for exercising the sensibility attuned to the multifariousness of Central Europe.

Niemcewicz paused in Trieste, and then moved on to Dalmatia: "Before going to Venice we resolved to visit the fraternal Illyrian land." Making his way among various lands, languages, and nationalities, he guided himself by a sense of his own fraternal relation to other Slavic peoples, well aware that in Central Europe they were intermingled among other populations. Fraternity was the key to exploring diversity. In Split, along the Adriatic esplanade, he fell asleep: "What a surprise! When I opened my eyes, drowsy with sleep, I saw the port by the rising sun, and the walls of the town, and I heard people standing by the shore, conversing in Polish. Unfortunately, where the Slavic language did not spread . . . we lost both land and rule."[15] What he actually heard, of course, was not Polish, but the language that is today called Croatian. His sense of a unified Slavic linguistic domain was rooted in the Herderian moment at which Niemcewicz and Fichte both traveled, and their reciprocal perspectives of Central Europe involved the jostling and commingling of Slavic speech with German or Italian. For Niemcewicz, whose perspective on Central Europe was complicated by nineteenth-century retrospective vision, linguistic heterogeneity already assumed the air of national competition.

Fichte reached Warsaw a month after the adoption of the Polish Constitution of 3 May 1791, a revolutionary political moment in which Poland's political condition was transformed, and the country declared its independence from Russia. For all Fichte's traveling interest in what was Polish and what was "true Polish," there was not the slightest reference in his diary to the extraordinary Polish political circumstances. Niemcewicz, however, was a deputy to the Warsaw assembly, the Four-Year Sejm, which adopted the constitution, and had even contributed directly to the constitutional movement with his drama *The Return of the Deputy* (*Powrót Posła*) of 1790. The Constitution of 1791 was overturned by a Russian invasion of Poland in 1792, and in 1793 Niemcewicz went abroad. In fact, he traveled from Poland to Saxony, exactly the reverse of Fichte's journey two years before:

> So we set out together for Dresden. Not without sad emotion I looked upon the virtuous Saxon elector and his daughter, chosen by us as our lords in the short moments of our independence. From Dresden, on the road to Berlin, we visited Dessau and Wörlitz. We stayed in a guest house, as orderly and pretty [*tak porządnym i pięknym*] as any I ever happened to find anywhere except England.[16]

Though his sad emotions lingered over the fate of Poland, the orderliness of the inn put Niemcewicz on a western train of thought, an occidental express, and his traveler's imagination was already looking beyond Central Europe to England.

Yet, in the cities of Central Europe, Niemcewicz remained attuned to the mingled sounds of different languages:

> Going through Prague we stayed in Vienna in October. With regret I saw how the Czechs, our brothers, are transformed more and more into Germans [*oraz bardziej przemieniają się w Niemców*] by the efforts of the government. The nobility already does not know our paternal language. Unfortunately, I thought to myself, it will be thus with our unfortunate Poland: the sound of our language will remain only among the good farmers.[17]

Fichte's astonishment at the thought of a Polish German was echoed in a spirit of national regret by Niemcewicz, who also believed that Central Europe, with its intermingled languages and ethnicities, was the domain of a national metamorphosis in which Slavs might become transformed into Germans.

Such were the reflections of Niemcewicz as he traveled from Prague to Vienna. Another traveler, just a few years before, went from Vienna to Prague and was inspired in a very different spirit by the linguistic circumstances of Central Europe. Wolfgang Amadeus Mozart was on the way to Prague in January 1787 for the first Prague production of *Le Nozze di Figaro*. Far more than either Fichte or Niemcewicz, Mozart was a man of aural sensibility, guided by his ear, and therefore naturally attuned to linguistic complications. Mozart, whose native language was German, was also perfectly comfortable in French and Italian, but on the way to Prague he inevitably encountered in Central Europe a language that he did not understand, namely Czech. From Prague he wrote to his friend Gottfried von Jacquin, back in Vienna, describing the musical success of Figaro, and concluding with an outburst of characteristically Mozartean nonsense.

> Now farewell dearest friend, dearest Hikkiti Horky! That is your name, so you will know it; we have all of us on our trip invented names; they follow here. I am Punkititi.—My wife is Schabla Pumfa. Hofer is Rozka Pumpa. Stadler is Notschibikitschibi. Joseph my servant is Sagadarata. Goukerl my dog is Schomanntzky—Madame Quallenberg is Runzifunzi.[18]

Mozart spoke German in Vienna and also in Prague, but on the way to Prague, traveling through the province of Bohemia, he must have heard Czech being spoken, an incomprehensible concoction of alien sounds to his Austrian ear, and he responded with gibbering linguistic delight.

While Niemcewicz lamented the transformation of Czechs into Germans, Mozart enthusiastically transformed himself and his friends into pseudo-Oriental (*Schabla Pumfa*), pseudo-Slavic (*Schomanntzky*), supremely nonsensical aliens. Fichte had also noted the strange sounds of German pronunciation in Silesia (*Bausch* instead of *Busch*), up to the point where it was no longer intelligible to him (*gar nicht mehr zu verstehen*). Mozart responded to linguistic incomprehensibility by playfully inventing silly names and identities for himself and his friends. He became Punkititi. Indeed the serious lesson of his nonsensical game might be, perhaps, the uncertainty, ambiguity, and malleability of identity in Central Europe.

Twentieth Century: "The Unfamiliar Hubbub"

The eighteenth-century traveler, when he perceived, assimilated, integrated, and responded to the transitions and complications of the passage between east and west, anticipated the twentieth-century idea of Central Europe. In this sense, Central Europe may be understood as a cognitive mode of apprehension, registering the complexity of gradual transition rather than emphasizing the dichotomy of abrupt separation. Central Europe's geographical domain was necessarily undetermined, a matter of subjective construction, but the most plausible locus for observing the variety of detail and attempting the integration of diversity was the Habsburg monarchy. This was precisely because the Habsburg monarchy had every motivation for pursuing the political integration of ethnically and linguistically diverse lands, and the details of diversity could not be denied.

In the eighteenth century Habsburg integration might take the cultural form of baroque architecture, the political form of administrative centralization, or the economic form of state cameralism, but in the nineteenth century the crystallization of the "nationalities problem"—in politics, education, language, culture, and administration—made the heterogeneity of Central Europe into the ongoing agenda of Habsburg policy. After the demise of the Habsburg monarchy in 1918, the idea of Central Europe in some sense displaced the monarchy, providing a new name for the lands that were no longer politically linked. Indeed, to the extent that Central Europe might be said to possess historical reality as something more concrete than a cultural construction, it may be regarded as the legacy of the Habsburg monarchy, the intersecting factors—languages, customs, cultures—that remained after the passing of the dynasty. Paradoxically, that common legacy of the former Habsburg lands was premised on the shared experience of extreme and complex diversity.

While the idea of *Mitteleuropa* first emerged in relation to the Habsburg monarchy, in the later nineteenth century industrialists in Imperial Germany became very interested in the possibility of a Central European customs union, and their interest was reflected in the program of the *Mitteleuropäische Wirtschaftsverein,* established in 1904. Historian Fritz Fischer has shown that such economic concerns were related to German war aims at the outbreak of World War I. Chancellor Theobald von Bethmann Hollweg noted in September 1914: "We must create a central European economic association through joint tariff agreements. . . . This association . . . will in fact be under German leadership and must stabilize Germany's economic domination of Mitteleuropa."[19] Such was the German government's interest in Central Europe at the time of the publication of Naumann's *Mitteleuropa* during the war. Naumann's vision also involved the advancement of German economic power in the region as an integrating force, and this drive toward German influence in some sense reached its evil apogee in the Nazi policy of conquest during World War II. After World War II the historian Felix Gilbert analyzed Nazi policy under the title "Mitteleuropa—The Final Stage."[20] The Nazis were well aware of the complex diversity of Central Europe, especially what they saw as racial diversity, and they addressed it radically through policies of enslavement, deportation, and extermination. After World War II the conception of Mitteleuropa organized under German hegemony was thoroughly discredited.

Between the wars, however, the idea of Central Europe received considerable attention, sufficient to invite parody as "The Central of Europe" in *Gentlemen Prefer Blondes* in 1925. A sampling of authentic travelers from the 1920s and 1930s reveals some continuities of perception dating back to the eighteenth century, complicated by the modern political tension that followed from Woodrow Wilson's principles of national self-determination, as put into practice at the peace of Versailles. The linguistic and ethnographic commingling noted by eighteenth-century travelers like Fichte and Niemcewicz seemed all the more unstable and unsettling in the modern context of a continent whose borders had been recently redrawn to accommodate such distinctions. Alfred Döblin, Rebecca West, Czesław Miłosz, and Patrick Leigh Fermor all traveled between east and west, or west and east, in the 1920s and 1930s, and showed themselves deeply attentive to the subtleties of transition in Central Europe.

The German writer Alfred Döblin traveled by train from Berlin to Warsaw in 1924, departing from the Schlesischer Bahnhof, and his voyage may be read in counterpoint to Fichte's Silesian passage from Germany to Poland in 1791. Döblin, on the train, had a strong sense of direction: "The train, the reverberating edifice, is taking me east. This is still Germany, I am still almost at home, here comes Frankfurt on the Oder: I can't believe it, I don't recognize the countryside." The landscape already appeared alien to Döblin, though he was still in Germany. "Anxiously, I think of Poland," Döblin noted, without feeling the need to explain his anxiety. "I think of my plans. But they are not my plans now, I do not recognize them."[21] Though the train was still in Germany, the traveler's thoughts had leaped ahead to Poland, so that the passage through Central Europe permitted him to be in both places, east and west, simultaneously. Unable to recognize his own plans, Döblin's very identity was rendered unstable by the reverberations of the eastbound train through Central Europe.

Published in Berlin in 1925, Döblin's *Reise in Polen* (*Journey to Poland*) was exactly contemporary with *Gentlemen Prefer Blondes,* and he too, like Lorelei Lee, was traveling for an education. Döblin was of Jewish origin, and he wanted to know more about Jews. As he approached the Polish border, the Jewish intimations of Central Europe reached his ear:

Night. The train surges about us. The border is coming, three hours east of Berlin. The three elegant gentlemen occasionally speak a different language than before. I notice eyes moving, hunting peculiarly, shoulders shrugging in a certain way: the voices coo and carol Yiddish. They stick their heads together with their British caps. Then the train stops.[22]

As with so many other travelers in Central Europe Döblin's ear was attuned to the intonations of a different language, in this case foreign but not altogether alien to him. He was further prepared to interpret the language of eyes and shoulders, peculiarly expressive of the inner nature of these elegant gentlemen. They seemed to metamorphose before Döblin's eyes and around his ears, betraying a different identity by the shifting of language and the shrugging of shoulders.

The stopping of the train meant that they had finally reached the German–Polish border: "The signs on the staircase walls contain words, syllables, whose meaning I can't surmise. They are probably just saying: Such and such a train departs from the platform. But in the foreign language, these words excite me, arouse my expectations."[23] His thoughts had already crossed the border into Poland ahead of the train, but the station signs in an incomprehensible language gave the border its emotional impact. In fact, Döblin knew that the meaning of the signs was predictable and banal, and that the border was important for entirely subjective reasons. Like Fichte projecting his sense of Polish wildness onto women's costumes, Döblin found himself aroused by the emotional aphrodisiac of incomprehensible syllables. The Polish poet Czesław Miłosz made a "Journey to the West" in 1931, when he was 20, and, passing from Czechoslovakia into Germany by train, noted his own disorientation as the sound of German surrounded him: "Then the train again, and a feeling of strangeness (*nieswojość*) as I passed over the German frontier—all around me people were speaking a language I did not understand. Furious with myself, I made an act of will and entered, for the first time in my life, the dining car."[24] The word *nieswojość* actually suggested something more than external strangeness, something more like internal dislocation and uneasiness. Like Döblin, moving in the other direction, Miłosz found himself psychologically challenged by the linguistic alternations of Central Europe, and the young poet furiously determined to collect himself and reestablish his sense of identity.

Döblin's train moved on from the border, and he continued to find himself inexplicably excited by the most banal and familiar sights outside his window: "What's this? Herds of cattle. New farmland. Many white geese. This is Poland." Yet he had to try to grasp the difference between Germany and Poland, and like Fichte, who found the people becoming "more Slavic" as he proceeded, Döblin practiced a sort of racial physiognomy from the window of the moving train. "The faces of the Polish women," he observed. "Broad foreheads, not high; full faces. The root of the nose starting low, sometimes with an almost saddle-shaped recess. The nose sloping flat toward the cheeks; very strong nostrils; the dark openings turned up."[25] Ironically, it would be Nazi anthropologists who ultimately made use of such physiognomic criteria as they sorted through the population of Central Europe, distinguishing between desirable and undesirable racial subjects. Yet, dating back to the eighteenth century, this had been a domain of heterogeneous ethnography, challenging the traveler to sort out his impressions into the familiar and the unfamiliar.

The English writer Rebecca West traveled to Yugoslavia in 1937, and ended by writing an epic portrait of that country, published as *Black Lamb and Grey Falcon* in 1941. She experienced profound spiritual epiphanies in the deep southeastern domains of Macedonia and Kosovo, exploring the Byzantine legacy of Europe, but she initially passed from west to east, through Central Europe, on the train from Salzburg to Zagreb, from Austria to Croatia. This was the inner, intermediary leg of the spiritually and geographically longer journey that West was undertaking to the Balkans and Byzantium. Like Döblin she was attuned to details of Slavic physiognomy: "It was dark when we crossed the Yugoslavian frontier. Handsome young soldiers in olive uniforms with faces sealed by the flatness of cheekbones asked us questions softly, insistently, without interest." She was sharing the train compartment with a party of Germans on their way from Nazi Germany for a vacation on the Yugoslav Dalmatian coast. They were, in fact, traveling to Split, where Niemcewicz had enjoyed a sense of Slavic fraternity in the 1780s, but the German tourists of the 1930s were apprehensive of the Slavic world. As soon as they crossed the border they began to complain about the bad food that they would have to eat in Yugoslavia: "They all sat, nodding and rocking, entranced by a vision of the warm goodness of German life, the warm goodness of German food, and of German superiority to all non-German barbarity." West asked them, "But why are you going to Yugoslavia if you think it is all so terrible?" They replied, "We are going to the Adriatic coast where there are many German tourists and for that reason the hotels are good."[26] The idea of Central Europe, in the generation after Naumann's *Mitteleuropa,* was deeply imbued with a sense of German precedence and presumption; economic domination was accompanied by total cultural condescension. In 1941, the year that West published *Black Lamb and Grey Falcon,* the Nazis would invade and destroy the state of Yugoslavia.

In the marketplace of Zagreb in 1937 Rebecca West observed the Croatians, and self-consciously reflected upon whether she was actually in Central Europe.

> They all spoke some German, so we were able to ask the prices of what they sold; and we could have bought a sackful of fruit and vegetables, all of the finest, for the equivalent of two shillings: a fifth of what it would have fetched in a Western city. This meant desperate, pinching poverty, for the manufactured goods in the shops are marked at nearly Western prices. But they looked gallant, and nobody spoke of poverty, nobody begged. It was a sign that we were out of Central Europe, for in a German and Austrian town where the people were twice as well off as these they would have perpetually complained. But there were signs that we were near Central Europe. There were stalls covered with fine embroidered handkerchiefs and table linen, which was all of it superbly executed, for Slav women have a captive devil in their flying fingers to work wonders for them. But the design was horrible. It was not like the designs I had seen in other parts of Yugoslavia, in Serbia and Macedonia; it was not even as good as the designs on the dresses of the peasant women who were standing by the stalls, inferior though they were. It was severely naturalistic, and attempted to represent fruit and flowers, and it followed the tradition of Victorian Berlin woolwork. In other words, it showed German influence.[27]

Zagreb had been a Habsburg city up until 1918, and the presence of German language in the Croatian marketplace followed naturally from that recent history, while the commingling of languages preserved some sense of Central Europe. For Rebecca West the idea of Central Europe was interpreted as a matter of German influence. West herself considered German influence to be an entirely pernicious force—producing beggars and bad embroidery—and she therefore regarded Central Europe as a negative domain; she would find her preferred embroideries and personal epiphanies further to the east.

In Zagreb West could not quite decide whether or not she was in Central Europe, for, of course, Central Europe was an idea, a set of impressions, an imaginary space, not a precisely designated geographical agglomeration of territories, and all the more uncertain with the abolition of the Habsburg monarchy. West looked for signs of whether she was "out of Central Europe" or "near Central Europe," and the crucial factor was German influence. "Yes, the German influence was like a shadow on the Croat World," she exclaimed, regretfully.[28] Central Europe was always a shadowy domain, with its imprecise landmarks and permeable borders, but in the late 1930s the shadow of Germany added new anxieties to a region of unstable identity.

In 1933 Patrick Leigh Fermor, at the age of 18, set out to walk all the way across Europe, from Rotterdam to Constantinople. The intermediary passage through Central Europe followed the Danube, from Vienna to Bratislava, and Fermor summed it up in a chapter entitled "The Edge of the Slav World." Like Fichte in 1791, Fermor, by traveling on foot, was especially sensitive to transitions and the overlapping of cultural spheres. His ear told him that he was in Central Europe as he picked up the incomprehensible syllables of unknown languages along the Danube. "Listening to the unfamiliar hubbub of Slovak and Magyar," he wrote, in the memoir that he published almost half a century later, "I realized I was at last in a country where the indigenous sounds meant nothing at all; it was a relief to hear some German as well."[29] Like Mozart on the way to Prague in 1787, so Fermor too, 150 years later, discovered that the linguistic heterogeneity of Central Europe was perfectly evident to the sensitive ear.

Fermor detoured from the Danube to visit Prague, and declared that it was "the place which the word Mitteleuropa, and all that it implies, fitted most aptly." He had been born in 1915, the year of Naumann's *Mitteleuropa,* and in 1933 Fermor's own somewhat confused teenage erudition and imagination supplied the fitting "implications" of Central Europe.

> Ever since their names were first recorded, Prague and Bohemia had been the westernmost point of interlock and conflict for the two greatest masses of population in Europe: the dim and mutually ill-disposed volumes of Slavs and Teutons; nations of which I knew nothing. Haunted by these enormous shadows, the very familiarity of much of the architecture made Prague seem more remote. Yet the town was as indisputably a part of the western world, and of the traditions of which the West is most justly vain, as Cologne, or Urbino, or Toulouse or Salamanca.[30]

Fermor's vague historical sense of ethnographic "interlock and conflict" echoed the jumbling of languages that he himself experienced as he traveled in Central Europe. His apprehension of haunting shadows in Bohemia in the 1930s corresponded to Rebecca West's impression of Croatia. Finally, he was himself personally disoriented by the interplay of what was familiar (the architecture!) and what was unfamiliar (the hubbub!)—so that even as he dubbed Prague the quintessential locus of Central Europe he recognized its indisputable relation to Western Europe.

When Czesław Miłosz came to Prague on his "Journey to the West" in 1931, he identified it as "the first Western European capital I saw."[31] If Prague was indeed the perfect expression of Central Europe, with all that implied, then one of the implications was the paradoxical uncertainty in Central Europe of determining whether or not some particular place was actually in Central Europe at all. Like Rebecca West puzzling over Croatia's status, Fermor was by no means absolutely certain about Bohemia. By the time he published his book in 1977, long after World War II, Prague was widely considered to be a capital of Eastern Europe, a communist capital behind the Iron Curtain. "I thought about Prague often later on," remarked Fermor, "and when evil times came, sympathy, anger and the guilt which the fate of Eastern Europe has justly implanted in the West, coloured my cogitations."[32] Prague could thus be classified as belonging to Western Europe, Central Europe, or Eastern Europe, depending upon the coloring of the traveler's cogitations. The paradoxical character of Central Europe was partly expressed in the uncertainty and instability that it inspired in the impressionable traveler.

Conclusion: "The Train of Time"

The Czech perspective was, in fact, fundamental for the relaunching of the idea of Central Europe in the 1980s, dating from Milan Kundera's publication in *Le Debat* in 1983, and *The New York Review of Books* in 1984, of his essay on "The Tragedy of Central Europe." He passionately argued that the Central Europe of Poles, Czechs, Slovaks, and Hungarians had been "kidnapped" from the West by Soviet communism, and further affirmed that Russia and Central Europe were absolutely antithetical in their cultural values. Kundera asked, "Does Central Europe constitute a true cultural configuration with its own history?" and he answered that "its borders are imaginary and must be drawn and redrawn with each new historical situation." Thus, in the historical situation of the late Cold War, Kundera sought to redraw the borders of Central Europe in such a way as to deny the validity of Soviet domination and challenge the lethargy of Western indifference. Kundera was well aware of himself as a writer from Central Europe: "But if to live means to exist in the eyes of those we love, then Central Europe no longer exists. More precisely, in the eyes of its beloved Europe, Central Europe is just a part of the Soviet empire and nothing more, nothing more."[33] Kundera's Central Europe, varying according to the "historical situation," had a very different geopolitical orientation from that of Naumann's Central Europe. Naumann's idea of Mitteleuropa had revolved around the circumstances of German power in the region, but Kundera's idea of Central Europe was formulated in reaction to the imperial presence of Soviet power.

Through the 1980s the idea of Central Europe functioned as an intellectual point of reference for anticommunist dissidents, especially in Czechoslovakia, Poland, and Hungary. "Central Europe is back," declared the British journalist and historian Timothy Garton Ash in 1986. "For three decades after 1945 nobody spoke of Central Europe in the present tense: The thing was one with Nineveh and Tyre. In German-speaking lands, the very word Mitteleuropa seemed to have died with Adolf Hitler."[34] Ever since Yalta, argued Garton Ash, Europe recognized only the Cold War dichotomy between Western Europe and Eastern Europe. Now, in the 1980s, the idea of Central Europe became a kind of ideological wedge to unsettle and overturn the Cold War conventions about east and west. After the collapse of communism in Eastern Europe in 1989, the slogan of Central Europe was deployed as an argument for the priority of Czechoslovakia, Poland, and Hungary among the post-communist countries seeking affiliation with the European Union. The historian Maria Todorova and the political scientist Iver Neumann have both critically analyzed the ways in which the idea of Central Europe became a formula of exclusion for denigrating the supposedly less "central" (and therefore more "eastern") post-communist states.[35]

When Kundera celebrated Central Europe he emphasized "variety" as crucial to the identity of the region: "Central Europe longed to be a condensed version of Europe itself in all its cultural variety, a small arch-European Europe, a reduced model of Europe made up of nations conceived according to one rule: the greatest variety within the smallest space."[36] This was precisely the regional character that an eighteenth-century traveler like Fichte considered most remarkable as he walked from west to east and noted the transitions, alterna-tions, and combinations of languages and customs in Silesia in 1791. Yet, this variety, sup-posedly the hallmark of Central Europe, had been rendered far more uniform by the time Kundera was writing two centuries later. The Jews of Central Europe were murdered during World War II, and the Germans largely deported after the war; Silesia itself had become a predominantly Polish province of postwar Poland after being subject to massive transfers of population. The linguistic and ethnographic heterogeneity of Central Europe experienced by eighteenth-century travelers had been radically reduced by the time the idea of Cen-tral Europe reemerged in the 1980s. Czechoslovakia, Poland, and Hungary, the bastions of Kundera's Central Europe, were largely consistent national states, and Czechoslovakia sur-rendered even its dual national status in the 1990s when it separated itself into the Czech Republic and Slovakia. In spite of Kundera's eloquent devotion to variety, the definition of Central Europe according to the perception of heterogeneity was already losing its validity.

"I am in a country located right in the middle of Europe," wrote Voltaire to Madame du Deffand in 1764 ("*Je me trouve dans un pays situé tout juste au milieu de l'Europe*").[37] He was writing from his villa, Les Délices, just outside Geneva. There he obviously considered himself to be living in "central" Europe—right in the middle—although the modern idea of Central Europe would certainly bear no relation to his Swiss geographical coordinates. In fact, Voltaire described himself as being in the middle of Europe, because he was envision-ing Europe according to an older convention: Europe divided between north and south, divided by the Alps. In this sense, Voltaire's Swiss home could be considered to be right in the middle of Europe. Voltaire did sometimes articulate a conception of Eastern Europe, as in the *Essai sur les Moeurs* in the 1750s, when he wrote, with reference to the Cossacks of Ukraine, that "to the north and the east of Europe [*à l'orient de l'Europe*], all that part of the world is still rustic [*agreste*]."[38] This sense of the backwardness of the east of Europe would be implicit in the observations of a traveler like Fichte as he negotiated the intermediary passage between east and west. Though Fichte never named "Central Europe," his reflections on variety, transition, and heterogeneity closely corresponded to the concept as it would be eventually articulated.

"And in the good old days when the Austrian Empire still existed, one could in such a case get off the train of time [*den Zug der Zeit verlassen*], get on an ordinary train of an or-dinary railroad, and travel back to one's home," remarked Robert Musil in his epic novel *Der Mann ohne Eigenschaften* (*The Man without Qualities*). The first volume appeared in 1930, but the scenario referred back to the Habsburg monarchy before World War I, the state that Musil dubbed "Kakania" as he explored its contradictory combinations of modernity and tradition. Where was Kakania? Musil specified its coordinates thus: "Here at the very center of Europe (*im Mittelpunkt Europas*), where the world's old axes crossed."[39] Musil's sense of the middle of Europe was clearly more modern than Voltaire's, and the association of Cen-tral Europe with the former Habsburg monarchy ("when the Austrian Empire still existed") was historically apt. In fact, the Habsburg monarchy, with its problematic heterogeneity, was precisely the locus of Central Europe, and it was exactly at the time of the demise of the monarchy, during World War I, that the name "Central Europe" or "Mitteleuropa" became explicitly prominent.

The borders of Central Europe have always been, as Kundera conceded, largely imag-inary, and the region acquired its character according to particular modes of perception, which were sometimes evident in travelers' accounts. Yet, if there is any concrete historical character to Central Europe it would have to be defined as the legacy of the Habsburg monarchy, the common character and mutual relations that survived from the experience of commingled social and cultural existence within the multinational empire. That legacy may have been quite vivid in the period immediately after the empire's abolition in 1918, but has certainly become less potent over the course of almost a century since then. Today it is historical memory which seeks to preserve the importance of historical legacy: when a portrait of Emperor Franz Joseph hangs in a café in L'viv, in post-communist Ukraine, in the former Galicia, it serves as a reminder that this city was once a part of the Habsburg monarchy, when the monarchy still existed.[40]

Musil invoked the metaphor of the train for describing Kakania's oblique relation to "the train of time." It was a fitting image for representing Central Europe, which was so often observed from the window of a train in the early twentieth century, as in the cases of Alfred Döblin and Anita Loos's fictional Lorelei Lee. When Lorelei Lee looked out the window of her train, and observed the landscape of Central Europe, she did not always like what she saw:

> So now we are on an oriental express and everything seems to be quite unusual. I mean Dorothy and I got up this morning and we looked out of the window of our compartment and it was really quite unusual. Because it was farms, and we saw quite a lot of girls who seemed to be putting small size hay stacks onto large size hay stacks while their husbands seemed to sit at a table under quite a shady tree and drink beer . . . and Dorothy said, "I think we girls have gone one step too far away from New York, because it begins to look to me as if the Central of Europe is no country for we girls."[41]

In this comic fictional travelogue Anita Loos actually captured some of the truth about travel in Central Europe, that is, the ways in which unfamiliar circumstances might become unsettling to travelers moving from west to east. Central Europe, however, always represented a balance between the familiar and the unfamiliar, so that Lorelei Lee was reassured to learn that she would find a familiar Ritz hotel, even in Budapest: "So we will soon be at a Ritz hotel again and I must say it will be delightful to find a Ritz hotel right in the Central of Europe."[42] Thus it was clear that Central Europe was Europe after all.

NOTES

An earlier version of this work was published as "The Traveler's View of Central Europe: Gradual Transitions, Degrees of Difference, and the Shadows of Influence," *Comparare: Comparative European History Review* 2003: 18–35.

1. Anita Loos, *Gentlemen Prefer Blondes* (New York: Curtis Books, 1963 [1925]), 104.

2. Larry Wolff, *Inventing Eastern Europe: The Map of Civilization on the Mind of the Enlightenment* (Stanford: Stanford University Press, 1994).

3. Louis-Philippe de Ségur, *Mémoires, souvenirs, et anecdotes, par le comte de Ségur*, Volume I, in *Bibliothèque des mémoires: relatif a l'histoire de France: pendant le 18e siècle*, Volume XIX, ed. M. Fs. Barrière (Paris: Firmin Didot Frères, 1859), 300.

4. Johann Gottlieb Fichte, "Tagebuch meiner Oster Abreise aus Sachsen nach Pohlen u. Preussen. Im Jahr. 1791," in *Nachgelassene Schriften 1780–1791*, ed. Reinhard Lauth, Hans Jacob, & Manfred Zahn (Stuttgart-Bad Cannstatt, Germany: Friedrich Frommann Verlag, 1962), 386; see also Wolff, *Inventing Eastern Europe*, 332–35.

5. Fichte, "Tagebuch meiner Oster," 389, 391.

6. R. J. W. Evans, *The Making of the Habsburg Monarchy, 1550–1700*, (Oxford: The Clarendon Press, 1984 [1979]), 298–304; Thomas DaCosta Kaufmann, *Court, Cloister, and City: The Art and Culture of Central Europe, 1450–1800*, (Chicago: University of Chicago Press, 1995).

7. Fichte, "Tagebuch meiner Oster," 391.

8. Milan Kundera, "The Tragedy of Central Europe" (1983/1984) in *From Stalinism to Pluralism: A Documentary History of Eastern Europe since 1945*, ed. Gale Stokes (New York: Oxford University Press, 1991), 221.

9. Fichte, "Tagebuch meiner Oster," 393.

10. Fichte, "Tagebuch meiner Oster," 395.

11. Wolff, *Inventing Eastern Europe*, 310–15; see also Larry Wolff, *Venice and the Slavs: The Discovery of Dalmatia in the Age of Enlightenment*, 173–227.

12. Fichte, "Tagebuch meiner Oster," 395.

13. Fichte, "Tagebuch meiner Oster," 395–96.

14. Julian Ursyn Niemcewicz, *Pamiętniki czasów moich*, ed. Jan Dihm, (Warsaw: Pańtswowy Instytut Wydawniczy, 1957), vol. 1, 169.

15. Niemcewicz, *Pamiętniki czasów moich*, vol. 1, 171.

16. Niemcewicz, *Pamiętniki czasów moich*, vol. 2, 59.

17. Niemcewicz, *Pamiętniki czasów moich*, vol. 2, 61.

18. Wolfgang Amadeus Mozart, *Briefe*, ed. Horst Wandrey, (Zürich: Diogenes, 1982), 370–71; Larry Wolff, *Inventing Eastern Europe*, 106–107.

19. Fritz Fischer, *War of Illusions: German Policies from 1911 to 1914*, trans. Marian Jackson, (New York: W. W. Norton, 1975 [1969]), 8–12, 38–39, 536–39.

20. Felix Gilbert, "Mitteleuropa—The Final Stage?" *Journal of Central European Affairs* 7: 1 (April 1947): 58–67; Paul Sweet, "Recent German Literature on Mitteleuropa," *Journal of Central European Affairs* 3: 1 (April 1943): 1–24; Stephan Verosta, "The German Concept of Mitteleuropa, 1916–1918 and its Contemporary Critics, " in *The Habsburg Empire in World War I: Essays on the Intellectual, Military, Political and Economic Aspects of the Habsburg War Effort*, ed. Robert Kann, Bela Kiraly, Paula Fichtner (Boulder, Colo.: Eastern European Quarterly, 1977), 203–220; Peter Stirk, "The Idea of Mitteleuropa," in *Mitteleuropa: History and Prospects*, ed. Peter Stirk, (Edinburgh: Edinburgh University Press, 1994), 1–35; Henry Cord Meyer, *Mitteleuropa in German Thought and Action 1815–1945*, (The Hague: Martinus Nijhoff, 1955); Catherine Horel, *Cette Europe qu'on dit centrale: des Habsbourg à l'intégration européenne* (Paris: Beauchesne, 2009).

21. Alfred Döblin, *Journey to Poland*, trans. Joachim Neugroschel, ed. Heinz Graber, (London: I. B. Tauris, 1991), 2; see also Larry Wolff, *The Idea of Galicia: History and Fantasy in Habsburg Political Culture*, (Stanford: Stanford University Press, 2010), 385–89.

22. Döblin, *Journey to Poland*, 2.

23. Ibid., 3.

24. Czesław Miłosz, *Native Realm: A Search for Self-Definition*, (Berkeley: University of California Press, 1981), 151; idem, *Rodzinna Europa*, (Paris: Instytut Literacki, 1989), 130.

25. Döblin, *Journey to Poland*, 3.

26. Rebecca West, *Black Lamb and Grey Falcon: A Journey through Yugoslavia* (New York: Penguin Books, 1982), 33–35.

27. West, *Black Lamb and Grey Falcon*, 48.

28. West, *Black Lamb and Grey Falcon*, 68.

29. Patrick Leigh Fermor, *A Time of Gifts* (1977; New York: Penguin Books, 1979), 224.

30. Ibid., 250.

31. Miłosz, *Native Realm*, 150.

32. Fermor, *A Time of Gifts*, 251.

33. Kundera, "The Tragedy of Central Europe," 220–23.

34. Timothy Garton Ash, "Does Central Europe Exist?" (1986) in *The Uses of Adversity: Essays on the Fate of Central Europe* (New York: Vintage Books, 1990), 179; see also Robin Okey, "Central Europe/Eastern Europe: Behind the Definitions," *Past and Present* no.137 (November 1992): 102–33; Rudolf Jaworski, "Die aktuelle Mitteleuropadiskussion in historischer Perspektive," *Historische Zeitschrift* 247: 3 (December 1988): 529–50; H. Burmeister, F. Boldt, Gy. Meszaros, eds. *Mitteleuropa: Traum oder Trauma?* (Bremen: Edition Temmen, 1988).

35. Maria Todorova, "Between Classification and Politics: The Balkans and the Myth of Central Europe," in *Imagining the Balkans,* (New York: Oxford University Press, 1997), 140–60; Iver Neumann, "Making Regions: Central Europe," in *Uses of the Other: "The East" in European Identity Formation* (Minneapolis: University of Minnesota Press, 1999), 143–60.

36. Kundera, "The Tragedy of Central Europe," 218.

37. Voltaire to Mme. du Deffand, 4 June 1764, in Voltaire, *Correspondence and Related Documents,* Definitive Edition, ed. Theodore Besterman, Volume 27, Letter D11904, 403; in *The Complete Works of Voltaire* III (Oxford: The Voltaire Foundation, 1973).

38. Voltaire, *Essai sur les mœurs et l'esprit des nations,* ed. René Pomeau, (Paris: Garnier Frères, 1963), vol. 2, 741.

39. Robert Musil, *The Man without Qualities,* trans. Sophie Wilkins, ed. Burton Pike, (New York: Vintage International, 1996), 28–29; idem, *Der Mann ohne Eigenschaften,* (Hamburg: Rohwolt Verlag, 1965), 32–33.

40. Wolff, *The Idea of Galicia,* 411–19.

41. Loos, *Gentlemen Prefer Blondes,* 104–105.

42. Loos, *Gentlemen Prefer Blondes,* 128.

2

MEGALOMANIA AND ANGST

THE NINETEENTH-CENTURY MYTHICIZATION
OF GERMANY'S EASTERN BORDERLANDS

GREGOR THUM

The last German Emperor, Wilhelm II, was notorious for his offensive speeches. On 5 June 1902, Wilhelm delivered an address in the Marienburg Castle, the former seat of the Teutonic Order in the German-Polish borderlands of the Prussian east. In front of dignitaries of the Prussian-German state, the Austrian-based Teutonic Order, and the Order of St. John seated in Berlin, who had all convened to celebrate the historical reconstruction of the Marienburg, the German monarch declared:

> In this castle, at this very place, I once took the opportunity to highlight how the old Marienburg, this former bulwark in the east, the starting point for the culture of the countries east of the river Vistula, should forever remain a symbol of the German tasks. Now it is time again. Polish presumption wants to challenge Germandom, and I am obliged to call on My people to preserve its national goods.

Wilhelm II closed his address with an appeal to Pan-German cooperation in order "to protect all that is German here and beyond the border."[1] According to the Imperial Chancellor Bernhard von Bülow, who claimed to have toned down the speech prior to its publication, the emperor's actual address was far more aggressive. Wilhelm summoned the convened knights "to charge the Sarmatians with the Teutonic Order's sword in the strong fist, to punish their impudence, to exterminate them."[2]

Most striking, however, is not the aggressive anti-Slavic rhetoric, but the speech's contradictory message. On the one hand, the emperor claimed that the regions east of Germany owed their cultural development to the Germans and that this legacy should continue to define "German tasks" in the east. On the other, he apparently considered a united German front necessary in order to defend the "national goods" against a Slavic menace. In the context of German perceptions of Eastern Europe, this oscillation between megalomania and angst was anything but unusual. In fact, it was the very essence of the myth of Germany' eastern borderlands. From the myth's emergence in the early nineteenth century to its disappearance well after the Second World War, large parts of German society believed it was Germany's calling to play a dominant political role in the European East; at the same time, however, they feared being overrun by a Slavic wave from the east.[3]

The Marienburg Castle was the ideal embodiment of these conflicting visions. A fortress is as much a bridgehead for offensive operations as a defensive structure in a moment of danger. The Marienburg, in particular, stood for both the eastward expansion of the Teutonic Order in the Middle Ages and a German position in the east that had become fragile in the age of nationalism. In the German-Slavic borderlands, the territorial claims of the German national movement clashed with those of their East European counterparts, in particular with the national movements of Poles and Czechs. When Wilhelm II gave his speech at the Marienburg, the medieval fortress of the Teutonic Order had become the symbol of these clashes and the most prominent emblem of Germany's eastern borderlands.

The purpose of this chapter is to shed light on the representation of the eastern borderlands in German political discourse of the nineteenth century. This will not only allow for a better understanding of the place of these borderlands in the emerging German national culture, but also explain why the borderlands' mythicization in the nineteenth century laid the ground for the particularly violent clashes of the twentieth century. A century before Nazi Germany embarked on a policy of "ethnic cleansing" in the east, a political discourse driven by both megalomania and angst began to shape German perceptions of the eastern borderlands. Even the term "extermination" entered German political discourse—long before a policy of extermination was conceivable in the context of Central European politics. Language precedes action.

This chapter, however, will not argue in favor of simple continuities. After all, right-wing radicalism was never more than a minority position in German politics until 1914.[4] But in order to understand the culmination of ethnic conflict in East Central Europe between 1918 and 1948, by the end of which time tens of millions of people were expelled and massacred for the sake of ethnically-cleansed borderlands, we have to look more closely at the discourses of the long nineteenth century. These discourses established perceptions that preconfigured political actions in the twentieth century. As for the German discourse over the eastern borderlands, elites of the German national movement established an image of the borderlands as a zone of conflict, in which Germans had to prevail over their (mostly) Slavic neighbors so that the German nation could assume its deserved place among the leading powers of the time. The borderlands were portrayed as a German frontier, the place where the German nation pursued its own civilizing mission, be it in spreading European civilization to the east, or defending it against assaults from there. In this way, local conflicts were charged with meaning, which made it increasingly difficult to find pragmatic political solutions.

To be sure, the borderlands and the nationality conflicts in the east hardly played a dominant role in German political discourses before 1914. German society had many things to worry about: the social question, the national question, the constitutional question, and the conflicts between executive and legislative, between state and church, and between Protestants and Catholics; these concerned German society as a whole and shaped many aspects of daily life. When it came to the popular appeal of imperial politics, colonialism and navalism were far more fascinating for people than the backwater provinces in the east. Yet it was exactly the borderlands' marginal position in German political discourse in the second half of the nineteenth century that allowed the political right to establish an image of the eastern borderlands that wasn't seriously challenged by alternative interpretations. The idea of a German frontier in the east, which had emerged out of the megalomaniac dreams and inflated fears of the nineteenth century, was the only concept available to a German society eager to make sense of the dramatic developments along the eastern borders during World War I: the Russian invasion of East Prussia in 1914, followed by unexpectedly large conquests of Russian territory after 1915, and the loss of German territory in 1919, when Poland reemerged as an independent nation.

The Rediscovery of the Marienburg and Prussia's Imagined Frontier

At the end of the eighteenth century, the Marienburg was a forgotten ruin at the periphery of the Prussian monarchy. After having been used for more than two centuries as barracks, an arsenal, a grain depot, and a stone pit, the large brick fortress revealed little of its former splendor. In 1794, the Prussian government sent the architect David Gilly to examine the dilapidated ruin and to make suggestions about its further use. While the government had considered razing the remains of the castle to the ground, the young Friedrich Gilly, who accompanied his father on his trip to the Marienburg, was so fascinated by the medieval ensemble that he produced a number of drawings.[5] After the Berlin artist Friedrich Frick had turned them into a fine collection of engravings, the Prussian public suddenly took an interest in the medieval fortress. Protests against the neglect of a unique piece of ancient architecture in Prussia led King Friedrich Wilhelm III to issue a royal order in 1804 that mandated safeguarding the castle from further dilapidation. A decade later, after the Napoleonic Wars had come to an end, the Prussian government was ready to sponsor the reconstruction of the Marienburg. The castle's ascendancy to status as one of the most prominent German historical landmarks began.[6]

Initially, the interest in the Marienburg was driven by a romanticist fascination for medieval architecture. In the course of the nineteenth century, however, the castle assumed political meaning. The rise of the national movements put pressure on the dynastical states to legitimize their territorial possessions and to dismiss allegations that the lands under their scepter had been brought together solely by the arbitrariness of dynastical politics. Ever since the partition of the Polish-Lithuanian Commonwealth in the late eighteenth century, the partitioning powers—Russia, Austria, and Prussia—had to defend their territorial acquisitions against demands for the reestablishment of an independent Poland. As far as Prussia was concerned, Frederick the Great liked to point to the alleged political squalidness of the Polish nobility, blaming them for gambling away Poland's right to existence. In the nineteenth century, however, a more elaborate justification was required. After the Polish national movement had demonstrated its vitality in the Napoleonic Wars, the Congress of Vienna officially recognized the existence of a Polish nation in 1815 and forced the partitioning powers to concede Polish representations and national institutions in their respective Polish provinces.

The Prussian government established the Grand Duchy of Posen in 1815 and provided the province with a considerable degree of political autonomy. No such status was given to West Prussia, although the province had also been part of Poland and continued to be inhabited by a substantial Polish-speaking population. West Prussia, however, provided the strategically important land bridge between the older Prussian provinces of Pomerania and East Prussia, and was home to the city of Danzig, one of the Baltic Sea's largest port cities. Without the possession of West Prussia, the province of East Prussia would have been separated from the rest of the Hohenzollern territories. Given the political importance of Prussia's northeastern provinces, on which the monarchy's kingship formally rested and from where the state name "Prussia" derived, the government in Berlin insisted on their indissoluble connection to the Hohenzollern monarchy. In order to establish a stronger historical link between the monarchy's political center in Brandenburg and the provinces in the northeast, Prussian elites began to appropriate the tradition of the Teutonic Order in the early nineteenth century.

The Teutonic Order was the creator of the Monastic State, which was established on the southeastern shores of the Baltic Sea after the subjugation of the Old Prussians in the thirteenth century. Through this act of state building, the Teutonic Knights shaped the early political, economic, and cultural development of the later provinces of West and East Prussia, which the Hohenzollern monarchy took over from the Polish crown in the seventeenth and eighteenth centuries. Until the early nineteenth century, however, the Teutonic Order enjoyed a less than favorable reputation in Berlin. Particularly during the Enlightenment, the Teutonic Knights, who never accepted the loss of the Monastic State, were primarily associated with the violent Christianization of the Old Prussians, cruel suppression of their subjects, and an aggressive foreign policy that resulted in constant conflicts with their neighbors.

Yet at the end of the eighteenth century, this image changed dramatically. Prussian-German historians began to portray the Teutonic Knights as the bearers of a German civilizing mission in Europe's northeast. It was this perception that paved the way for positive references to the Teutonic Order in Prussia and eventually allowed for the integration of its state-building tradition into the Prussian state ideology.[7] The glorification of the Teutonic Order in nineteenth-century Prussia provided the Hohenzollern monarchy with an ancient history, and it offered new arguments for the defense of Prussia's eastern border against the demands of the Polish national movement. By placing the Hohenzollern state in the tradition of the Teutonic Order, its eastern borders no longer appeared as the product of dynastical politics, but as the result of the Order's alleged civilizing mission in the east. In other words: Prussia's eastern borders constituted a cultural frontier.

Frontiers were a political phenomenon familiar to the societies of nineteenth century Europe.[8] Newspapers, travelogues, and novels, along with private letters and oral reports spread the knowledge of the dynamic borders in the colonies and at the peripheries of the European empires. In order to undermine the claims of the Polish national movement, Prussian elites tried to present the eastern border of the monarchy as such a frontier, which had to be defended against indigenous populations hostile to European civilization. This required them, however, to depict the indigenous populations as culturally inferior and incapable of making full use of the land; their resistance against Prussian rule was portrayed as an unwillingness to embrace European civilization.[9] The propaganda battle accompanying the evolving German-Polish conflict over territory in the Prussian east can be reduced to the promotion—or the deconstruction—of this Prussian-German frontier myth.

The reconstruction of the Marienburg Castle in the first half of the nineteenth century, accompanied by the portrayal of the Teutonic Knights as the forebears of the modern Prussians, offered ample opportunities to promote and visualize the frontier myth and to provide it with an emblematic historical landmark. The myth found a particularly vivid expression in the stained glass windows created for the Summer Refectory of Marienburg's Grandmaster

Palace in the 1820s.[10] By depicting scenes from the history of the Teutonic Order, the ten windows present the Teutonic Knights as the venerable bearers of a Christian civilizing and state-building mission in the Baltic region.

Two of the windows, produced by Karl Wilhelm Kolbe, a Berlin artist and member of the Prussian Academy of Arts, explicitly promoted the frontier myth. The first, titled "Bishop Christian asks the Teutonic Order for help," dealt with the arrival of the Teutonic Order at the Baltic Coast in the early thirteenth century.[11] The window juxtaposed two scenes in sharp contrast: whereas in the image's dark-colored background the Old Prussians are portrayed as pillaging barbarians who slaughter civilians and burn down churches, the Teutonic Knights appear in the image's bright-colored foreground in an idealized fashion as noble warriors who have come to rescue hard-pressed Christians from their destruction.

The window "The Defense of Marienburg Castle" offered a similar interpretation of the Order's mission.[12] In this case, Kolbe created a dramatic battle scene in which the Teutonic Knights defended the Marienburg's walls against a Polish-Lithuanian attack—a historical event of the year 1410. Again, this image generated a dichotomy between barbarians and the defenders of European civilization. While the representatives of the Teutonic Order appear as dignified knights in flowing white cloaks, their enemies are portrayed as a wild horde, with facial features, hairstyles, dresses, and arms that suggest the troops of the Polish King Władysław II Jagiełło had consisted mainly of Tatars. This orientalization of the Polish-Lithuanian army associated the Order's enemies with the Asian invaders that European societies had been terrified of since the Middle Ages. The painting's light effects and the arrangement of the figures enhanced this dichotomy. The Teutonic Knights were placed in the upper half of the image and surrounded by bright light, whereas the offenders rose from the image's dark bottom—a composition that recalled depictions of heaven and hell in Christian art.

The Prussian–Polish conflict, which was one between a dynastic state and a rising national movement, both of which were rooted in the European tradition, was presented through the iconological program of the restored Marienburg Castle as one between civilization and barbarism. The idea of Poland as the eastern bulwark of Western Christendom was rejected. Instead, the windows ascribed this role to the Teutonic Knights and their Prussian heirs. True to this historical interpretation, which incorporated Western stereotypes about Eastern Europe prevalent since the Age of Enlightenment, the Prussian king Friedrich Wilhelm IV called his monarchy's northeastern province in a letter from 1842 a land "the Lord has pushed forward as a bulwark of German character into the Slavic-Sarmatian chaos [*Wirrleben*]."[13]

The creation and promotion of the Prussian frontier myth speaks to how strongly Prussian elites believed in the need to defend the monarchy's territorial integrity against the claims of the Polish national movement. Had the liquidation of the Polish state been followed by the gradual assimilation of Prussia's Polish citizens, the frontier myth would hardly have emerged. But the Polish national movement was on the rise in the nineteenth century, and the processes of assimilation and migration pointed to the strengthening of the Polish element in Prussia's east rather than its weakening. This explains the growing importance of the frontier myth in Prussian political discourse after 1815 and the Marienburg's central place in Prussian state propaganda.

Theodor von Schön, the provincial governor of West and East Prussia and the guiding spirit of the Marienburg's first reconstruction between 1817 and 1856, hoped to turn the medieval castle into a Prussian national monument comparable to England's Westminster.[14]

Although the Marienburg never gained such significance, the castle became a celebrated national monument and the eastern borderlands' most prominent symbol. In the mid-nineteenth century, the Prussian government built the main railroad connection between Berlin and Königsberg in such a way that travelers, soon after passing the monumental bridge over the Vistula that was built in an architectural style referring to the Marienburg, were granted a spectacular view of the medieval structure. When the German national movement superseded the modest attempts of Prussian nation building and absorbed its symbols, the frontier myth and the Marienburg became part of the German national cult.

1848 and the Expansion of the Frontier from the Baltic to the Balkans

When a German National Assembly convened in Frankfurt in the wake of the 1848 Revolution to bring a unified German nation state into being, the question of its future boundaries figured prominently in the ensuing debates. The borders of the German Confederation, established at the Congress of Vienna in 1815, served as a general orientation. But in the east especially, they were not congruent with the borders of German settlement. The German Confederation included regions with a partly Slavic character like Bohemia and Carniola, while excluding the German-speaking populations of Prussia's and Austria's eastern provinces.

The difficulty of drawing national borders in a region of ethnically mixed settlement was exacerbated by the fact that national movements strove not only to for unified nation states but also to provide them with the largest possible territories. In his excellent study of the imperialist visions of the Frankfurt Assembly, Günter Wollstein demonstrated that most delegates aimed for more than just the creation of a unified Germany. They believed in their nation's right and destiny to advance to the position of a "world power" on par with France, England, Russia, and the rising United States of America.[15] These imperial dreams generated far-reaching territorial demands. Without the retention of Austria's and Prussia's non-German provinces, argued imperial proponents, Germany would be deprived of strategic positions that were mandatory for the envisioned "world power" status. As was the case with most national movements, liberal and imperial dreams went hand-in-hand in Germany.[16]

Heinrich von Gagern, a prominent liberal from Hessen-Darmstadt and the first president of the German National Assembly, advocated a Germany that included all of Austria, despite the predominantly non-German character of its eastern provinces. Von Gagern stated that he had always thought of "the German people's calling as a great one, as one of a world ruler (*weltgebietend*)," and that he would lose his pride in belonging to this people if he had to give up his belief in this "higher destiny."[17] Therefore, the purpose of German unity was to "live up to our destiny towards the Orient, to include those peoples of the Danube Basin who have neither the calling for nor the claim to independence like satellites in our planetary system." He urged the German nation to take over

> . . . Austria's mission to spread the German culture, language and way of life following the Danube to the Black Sea, into those lands sparsely populated by various peoples, but lands full of hope, the entire civilization of which is used to leaning on the German one, which is longing for Austrian-German protection and increased influence, and which would open a rich market to German industriousness.[18]

The call for a large Central European state, stretching from the western rim of German settlement to the borders of Russia and the Ottoman Empire, mirrored ideas already developed in the 1830s and 1840s.[19] Among others, the influential German-American political economist Friedrich List believed that the future would belong to large national economies, and that Central Europe, if united under German leadership, would rise, alongside the United States of America, to become a truly global power. List therefore promoted a German-led economic space that stretched beyond the sum of ethnically undisputable German territories. The territories east of the German Confederation in particular, already characterized by a privileged position of German culture and language and an economic orientation toward Germany, seemed to be destined for inclusion in a larger German empire.

Those among the National Assembly's delegates who subscribed to the imperial dream of German greatness believed in the necessity of strengthening German culture in the east in order to advance Central Europe's political integration under German leadership. Von Gagern and others, therefore, did not want to rely exclusively on Germanization through the assimilation of the borderlands' non-German populations. They hoped to open Austria's eastern provinces to a wave of German settlement.[20] Accordingly, Friedrich Schulz, a teacher from Hesse, declared: "If the Austrian government is not entirely incompetent, it cannot completely fail to appreciate the obligation of our Eastern March; as a start, it will try to win through favorable conditions millions of poor settlers for the empty stretches of land along the Danube. There, at our borders, is our Texas, is our Mexico."[21] Regardless of how unrealistic these ideas were and how little the American West had in common with Austria's east, many nineteenth-century German nationalists saw Germany and the United States as nations on the same path to world power through the creation of economically advanced continental empires. As a consequence of this perception, the American frontier became an important inspiration for the conceptualization of Germany's eastern borderlands. What the West was for the United States, the East should become for Germany. Tellingly, the youngest member of the National Assembly, Julius Ostendorff, claimed for the Germans during the debate on the Polish question in July 1848 the "right of conquest through the plow, the same right the free North American is exercising with respect to the indigenous Indian."[22] While the focus on the Teutonic Knights betrayed the aristocratic orientation of the frontier myth promoted by the Prussian state, the national revolution of 1848 generated a decisively bourgeois, "Americanized" version of the frontier.[23] The parallelization of Poles and American Indians was one of the narrative strategies used to assimilate Prussia's eastern borderlands to the American West. In a travel report published in 1848, the writer Gustav Freytag, alias William Rogers, compared a group of Polish aristocrats in the province of Posen with "a gang of coarse Indians, a horde of Pawnee Loups in the plains of Missouri, well-suited for frontier wars, for novels and tragic dramas, but useless for life."[24] "Asianizing" or "Blackening" Poles were alternative ways of "othering" the borderland's non-German population and emphasizing the region's frontier character.[25]

Against the backdrop of these early attempts to racialize the territorial conflicts in the east, it is important to note, however, that most of the Frankfurt parliamentarians in 1848 understood the "Germandom" (*Deutschtum*) to be spread in the eastern borderlands as a cultural concept open to all ethnic groups. To become German was primarily a commitment to German language and culture.[26] Since the delegates of the German National Assembly were convinced that they represented a superior culture, they had a hard time understanding why their eastern neighbors would not embrace a German-led Central Europe and accept their Germanization as a ticket to civilizational advancement.

There was nothing peculiar about these views. The elites of the Polish national move-ment dreamed of a Polish empire that would stretch from the Baltic to the Black Sea, and would assimilate the Lithuanian-, Belorussian- and Ukrainian-speaking people of its eastern borderlands into Polish culture.[27] Czech nationalists promoted a nation state that not only covered all of Bohemia, including its German-speaking regions, but also wide stretches of land of Slovak and Hungarian character. Hungarian, Romanian, Croatian, and Serbian na-tionalists harbored similar imperial dreams. Modern Central Europe was a region with a particularly high density of imperial projects, criss-crossed by various imagined frontiers and civilizing missions. Clashes between these mutually exclusive projects were inevitable.

In the German case, the anticipation of conflict found its expression in the reintro-duction of the medieval term "march" into German political discourse. In the Carolingian Empire, the marches were border provinces that were granted a privileged political status in order to fulfill their special duties in defending and expanding the Empire's boundar-ies. Whereas the term "march," which is the German equivalent of "frontier," appeared only sporadically in the first half of the nineteenth century to denote the eastern borderlands, the Eastern March (*Ostmark*)—sometimes known also as Eastern Marches—became a catch-phrase after 1848.[28]

A precursor of looming ethnic conflict over territory in the German-Slavic border-lands was František Palacký's famous letter sent to Frankfurt in April 1848. The highly es-teemed Prague historian declined the offer to join the prestigious Pre-Parliament of the Fifty on the simple grounds that he was Czech, not German. Palacký sent his best wishes to the Frankfurt parliamentarians, but made it clear that his Bohemian homeland could not pos-sibly be part of a German nation state. Two months later, in early June, a Slav Congress convened in Prague under Palacký's presidency. The congress' purpose was not entirely clear, since even the political unification of the Austrian Slavs was hardly feasible given their lin-guistic and cultural diversity. But Prague's message to Frankfurt was unmistakable: German national claims to territory predominantly inhabited by the speakers of Slavic languages would trigger fierce resistance.[29]

Similar signs came from Posen. Leaders of the Polish national movement in Prus-sia's most Polish province, who in March of 1848 had formed a Polish National Committee, protested against the presence of delegates from the Grand Duchy of Posen in the German National Assembly. Regardless of the fact that about a third of the province's population con-sidered themselves Germans, Polish national leaders accused the assembly of undermining the hitherto existing solidarity of the national movements by disrespecting the province's autonomy and historically Polish character. The conflict could not be resolved. During the assembly's notorious debate on the Polish question in July of 1848, many parliamentarians took an openly anti-Polish stance, while only few showed respect for the Poles' national sen-sitivities and historical rights to territory. In the end, the assembly voted overwhelmingly for the inclusion of large parts of the province of Posen into the future German nation state. The national movements of Poles and Germans had turned onto a collision course. Prussia's eastern borderlands became a zone of conflict between two competing nationalisms.[30]

In the summer of 1848, the Committee for Austrian-Slavic issues warned of a "blood bath" and a "national war of extermination to which the Slavic fanaticism in Bohemia might lead."[31] Ignaz Kuranda, an influential Jewish-German liberal from Prague, urged the Assem-bly to defend Bohemia's Germans against the "tyrannical desires of the Slavs."[32] Adolph Go-eden, a delegate from Posen, argued that hatred against the Germans was "the Pole's gospel," and that Poles had already decided upon the "extermination" (*Vertilgung*) of the Germans during the insurgence in Posen in 1846.[33] His fellow delegate Samuel Gottfried concurred: the Poles were conducting "the most terrible war of extermination against the Germans"; if the latter failed to act, "it might easily be that the great German people will become homeless, the laughing stock of all peoples on earth."[34]

As Brian Vick has pointed out, in the context of 1848, Germans perceived themselves as the possible victims, but never as the agents of a policy of extermination.[35] To be sure, their extermination by their fellow Slavic citizens, who neither controlled the government nor had an army at their disposal was not exactly a likely scenario. But where self-image rested on dreams of empire, the difficulties in controlling the national aspirations of Czechs and Poles might explain the inflated fears of some members of the German National Assembly. It was not so much the life of Germans that they saw at stake as the feasibility of a German-led Central Europe. After all, the control of the eastern borderlands and the eventual absorption of the region's non-Germans into the German national sphere was the prerequisite of the envisioned empire. It was a question of both strategic considerations and national prestige.

Inventing the Wild East

Despite the failure of the national revolution in 1849, and despite the assembly's eventually pragmatic decision in favor of the "lesser German" solution that excluded the Habsburg Monarchy from the German nation state for the time being, the idea of the German frontier lived on. However, where the scope for political action is limited, literary imaginations gain in importance. In the second half of the nineteenth century, the new genre later known as *Ostmarkenroman*—Eastern March novel—emerged.[36] These novels popularized the idea that a battle over territory was taking place in the eastern borderlands between the representatives of a superior German civilization and their Slavic enemies. One of its first and most successful products was Gustav Freytag's *Debit and Credit* (*Soll und Haben*). Published in 1855, it became one of the bestselling German novels of the nineteenth and early twentieth centuries.[37] *Debit and Credit* tells the story of the young German middle-class hero Anton Wohlfart, who has to stand his ground in a conflict with Polish insurgents in Prussia's eastern borderlands. The novel reads in large part like a literary adaptation of the National Assembly's imperial visions and its most radical anti-Polish statements. In one of its key scenes, Wohlfart tells his friend Karl Stumpf, who has left the city to become a farmer at the German frontier: "You got used to living among foreign people, you fulfill all the requirements of being a colonist on newly gained soil. [. . .] With the plow in your hand, you will be a German soldier who will push the boundary stone of our language and customs further against our enemies."[38] As Kristin Kopp and Izabela Surynt have demonstrated, *Debit and Credit* likened Germany's eastern borderlands to a colonial setting, with the Germans appearing as the bearers of a culture on a civilizing mission against both an untamed nature and the resistance of the indigenous Polish population.[39] In the novel, the borderlands' Poles threaten the cultural advance and life of the German settlers, whose fragile position is symbolized through the exposed land estate of the von Rothsattel family. The position can only be held after the manor house is temporarily turned into a fortress, manned by German settlers who are ready to sacrifice their life for the defense of the frontier. With the Polish onslaught fought off, the manor house becomes a bridgehead of expansion once again: ". . . and a flock of strong boys will jump out of the Slavic castle, and a new German generation, peasant-like in body and soul, will spread over the land, a generation of colonists and conquerors."[40]

Debit and Credit is arguably the first text that introduced a large German readership to the idea of a frontier situation in the east. Also, the novel's Prussian orientation testified to a shift of attention from the Austrian to the Prussian borderlands after 1848. With the fusion of Prussian state patriotism and German nationalism, followed by the foundation of a German nation state under Prussian leadership in 1871, the strong presence of Polish speakers in Prussia's eastern provinces and calls for the provinces' Germanization took center stage in German national discourses. The Austrian government, on the other hand, was forced onto a course of institutionalized compromise with the monarchy's various nationalities in the second half of the nineteenth century. A state-sponsored Germanization policy ceased to be an option.

From its early days on, the German Empire strongly promoted the use of German by all its citizens and suppressed the public use of Polish as the native language of its largest national minority.[41] Although the "Kulturkampf" of the 1870s was directed against the influence of the Catholic Church in Germany in general, it had an important anti-Polish aspect.[42] The most remarkable component of the Germanization policy, however, was the establishment of the "Royal Settlement Commission for the Provinces of West Prussia and Posen" in 1886. The purpose of this state-funded institution was to substantially increase the number of German inhabitants in Prussia's eastern borderlands by purchasing large land estates and reselling them after their parcellation to German farmers.[43] Bismarck defended the settlement policy in the Prussian House of Representatives as a defensive measure to counteract the exodus of ethnic Germans from Prussia's eastern provinces and to stop the provinces' creeping Polonization: "We do not want to exterminate Polish culture but we want to protect Germandom from extermination."[44] With the establishment of the Settlement Commission, the policy of ethnic homogenization of the borderlands acquired a new quality. The very idea of changing the ethnic composition of the borderlands through a state-sponsored, large-scale population movement foreshadowed the far more radical resettlement politics of the twentieth century. It is important to note, however, that the Prussian settlement policy not only had to operate within the narrow confines set by the rule of law, but it also met with fierce opposition in the parliaments, mostly from socialist and Catholic politicians who defended the equality of all citizens, regardless of their ethnic or religious background.

Political action requires symbolization in order to generate popular support. With the shift toward a comprehensive Germanization policy in Prussia's east and the opposition this caused, the frontier myth gained new relevance. In 1882, a second and much more comprehensive reconstruction of the Marienburg began. Reflecting the professionalization of historic preservation in the late nineteenth century, its leading architect, Conrad Steinbrecht, strove for the reconstruction of the fortress' authentic appearance during its heyday around 1400.[45] The funds flowing into the project were substantial, and the Hohenzollern family took renewed interest in the construction works. Wilhelm II, in particular, became a frequent visitor to the Marienburg and used the medieval castle as a stage for political ceremonies.

Despite Steinbrecht's pursuit of historical authenticity, the Marienburg assumed the quite ahistorical meaning of an eastern bulwark of Germandom. When German citizens called a fundraising organization into being in 1884 in order to support the second reconstruction, their public announcement began with the following statement: "The Marienburg, the most magnificent landmark of medieval architecture in our country, has to be adored by every German as the site from where the [Teutonic] Order's powerful and organizing hand won a large territory for the German Empire and for German culture."[46] Statements like these mirrored Heinrich von Treitschke's interpretation of the Monastic State, which he had begun to promote in the 1860s. The influential German historian, notorious for his chauvinistic nationalism, praised the Baltic conquests of the Teutonic Knights through which "our people already developed on a small territory the main directions of colonial politics—the same ones that the Spaniards and English later carried out with similar success in the enormous spaces of the Americas."[47]

Treitschke offers evidence for German perceptions of the eastern borderlands as a quasi-colonial space—a view that emerged during the nineteenth century[48] but became prevalent in the mid-twentieth, when Nazi Germany tried to establish a colonial empire in Eastern Europe. Recent studies inspired by postcolonialism have to be credited for shedding light on the connection between overseas colonialism and German perceptions of the European east.[49] It is important, however, not to overlook the principal differences between Germany's borderlands and colonies. Unlike the indigenous populations in Europe's overseas colonies, Prussia's Poles were full-fledged citizens. They were able to defend themselves in the courts, to mobilize national and international public support against their discrimination, and to undermine the government's Germanization and settlement policy through the use of highly effective economic countermeasures. What caused the intensity of the conflict in Germany's eastern borderlands was the very fact that the alleged colonial "subjects" did not behave like colonial subjects were supposed to. The power relation between the would-be colonizers and intended colonized lacked the extreme asymmetry of a classical colonial situation. Therefore, depicting the German-Polish borderlands as a quasi-colonial space, for which Kristin Kopp suggested the useful term "colonialization,"[50] was both a strategy of legitimizing radical political measures, and wishful thinking on the part of those who did not want to recognize the political strengths of the Polish national movement.

At the turn of the century, most of the German literature on the Eastern Marches reflected fears that the entire Germanization project might fail and that the eastern borderlands might fall victim to a process of reverse colonization. In his book on *The Battle over the Eastern March,* Carl Fink described the pockets of Polish settlements in eastern Germany as the "foamy splashes of an approaching large Slavic wave." He called for the erection of a "firm bulwark where the waves can break."[51] Similarly, Christian Petzet's book on *Prussia's Eastern Marches* is dominated by concerns about the Polish advance in the east.[52] In Petzet's view, "the preservation and strengthening of Germandom against imminent Polonization" was the Eastern Marches' "vital question."[53] As he outlines in a chapter on "the borderland," Prussia's already disadvantageous boundary in the east does not allow for any westward shift without substantially weakening the German position.[54] Petzet registered with concern that the economic gap between Germans and Poles was closing. Polish farmers achieved productivity levels on par with their German counterparts. Unlike in the colonies, it was a strong economic competitor with full access to the arena of parliamentary politics in Germany, rather than a violent insurgency, that challenged the position of the Germans in the eastern borderlands.[55]

Failure and Radicalization: The Path toward "Ethnic Cleansing"

In 1904, Clara Viebig published her bestselling novel *The Sleeping Army.*[56] The book describes the effects of the Prussian settlement policy through the lens of a German village created in the solidly Polish environment of the eastern provinces. Far from advancing the Germanization of the east in any significant way, the German settlement antagonized the region's Polish inhabitants without binding the new settlers to the land. If we are willing to treat *The Sleeping Army* as evidence of the views of those who supported the Germanization policy, the novel's apocalyptic visions suggest a significant change of mood around 1900. Freytag's self-confidence has given way to Viebig's anticipation of possible defeat. In many ways, Viebig provided an accurate description of the problems the Settlement Commission policy faced. Despite enormous investments, the overall results of the settlement policy fell short of the expectations. The number of German families settled in the predominantly Polish counties of the eastern provinces was too low to challenge the Polish majority. By irony of history, the share of Poles, which had been on the decline over the course of the nineteenth century, began to rise again after the Prussian Settlement Commission was created.[57] Instead of weakening the Polish element, the government's anti-Polish policy strengthened the national consciousness among its Polish-speaking citizens. Even the Commission's effect on landownership was not convincing. Thanks to Polish countermeasures, such as the establishment of Polish credit unions for the support of Polish farmers in financial trouble, or the exertion of intense social pressure on Poles to sell their land only within the Polish community, Polish landownership did not decrease but instead increased after 1886.

The aggressive rhetoric of the "Eastern Marches Society" (*Ostmarkenverein*), a private German organization founded in 1894 to pressure the government to pursue an uncompromising Germanization policy,[58] or Chancellor von Bülow's condescending remarks regarding the Poles' "rabbit-like fertility," were signs of growing desperation at the turn of the century.[59] The Polish national movement had proven its ability to successfully counteract the Prussian settlement policy and to mobilize Prussia's Polish citizens against the government's discriminatory language policy. The school strike in the town of Wreschen in the province of Posen in 1901 demonstrated the popular appeal of Polish nationalism and the government's helplessness in breaking the Polish resistance to the Germanization policy.[60] Against this backdrop, German right-wing nationalists demanded a radicalization of means. In particular, they promoted a Germanization policy no longer bound to the rule of law.[61] During the convention of the Pan-German League in the spring of 1902, the editor of the *Alldeutsche Blätter,* Paul Samassa, echoed a rapidly spreading conviction: "The sharpest weapon the Poles can use against Germandom is the Prussian constitution."[62]

This is the political context in which we have to place Viebig's *The Sleeping Army.* The novel created a scenario of imminent danger: while the German settlers in the eastern borderlands lack the numbers, the determination, and the political wisdom to defend the German frontier, Polish peasants are depicted as an anarchic force that might at any time roll over the islands of German settlement with a pogrom-like temper. Telling are the dark prophecies of the novel's most mysterious figure, the old Polish shepherd Dudek, whose predictions regarding the rise of a mythical Polish army gave the novel its title. In one of the key scenes, Dudek tries to instigate the Polish peasants by reminding them of their ancestors' willingness to fight against the Germans:

> Your fathers did not sleep. They ground their scythes until they became sharper than swords, and then they mowed the German dogs at Koschmin and Tschemieschno, at Minoslaw and Sokolowo. At Stenschewo the bullets flew around like hailstones, but the Holy Mother caught them in her pinafore. And the Polish mothers did not sleep either. Listen!

As the German militia was stationed in Buk, in every house two or three of them, Virgin Mother strengthened the women's hearts so that the pigeons turned into eagles. And they gave the Germans to drink—a lot—until all of them were drunk. And when they slept in the cots and barns, on the barn floors and haylofts, the Polish mothers sneaked up to them with their knives, and they cut off the devils' beards, the noses and ears, the fingers and toes, and made the blood of Poland's enemies flow like water.[63]

Scenarios of threat provide the strongest arguments for radical "defensive" measures. With her gruesome prophecies, Clara Viebig warned of the dire consequences of a failing Germanization policy. It was the same perception of danger that drove Wilhelm II's call to close the ranks in defense of the Eastern Marches in his aforementioned address, and the announcement of his chancellor von Bülow in 1902 that a harsher course of action against the activities of Polish nationalists would be required.[64]

The beginning of the new century was a watershed moment for the proponents of German imperialism. They began to believe in a chain of defeats that the German Empire had allegedly been suffering on the eastern frontier, in its colonies, and in its competition with imperial rivals.[65] The aggressive political rhetoric of Wilhelm II and his last prewar administration, the alarmism of the nationalistic organizations such as the Pan-German League and the Eastern Marches Society, and the excessively brutal suppression of the Herero, Nama, and Maji Maji uprisings in Germany's African colonies between 1904 and 1907 were not signs of self-confidence. They testified, rather, to German fears that the nation was perhaps incapable of reaching the self-set imperial goals.

Driven by right-wing political forces, the government was increasingly ready to violate generally accepted legal norms in order to increase the effectiveness of the Germanization policy.[66] In 1904, the Prussian parliament passed a law that gave the authorities the right to deny building permits in cases where the construction contradicted the aims of the Prussian settlement policy. This was the case with any farmhouse in the east built or modernized by Polish citizens.[67] 1908 saw a new national Association Law, which forced Polish-speaking citizens to conduct public meetings exclusively in German.[68] In the same year, the Prussian Diet passed the "Law for the Strengthening of Germandom in the provinces of Posen and West Prussia." Since the Settlement Commission had run out of land estates to purchase as a result of Polish organized resistance against the settlement policy, the new law allowed for the expropriation of (Polish) farmland.[69] With the Expropriation Law of 1908, Prussia crossed the Rubicon. Basic legal principles, such as the equality of all citizens before the law and the protection of private property, were sacrificed for the sake of the Germanization policy. If the twentieth century was the century of expulsions, the Expropriation Law was Germany's step into that century, during which Germans figured prominently both as perpetrators and as victims of large-scale forced migration.

To be sure, the law of 1908 faced massive political resistance before it was passed. In fact, both the domestic opposition to the discrimination against Prussia's Polish citizens and the international protests were so strong that the Prussian administration hesitated to enforce the law. In the end, the law didn't amount to any more than the expropriations—against compensation according to market prices—of four land estates in 1912. Therefore, the history of the Prussian expropriation law testifies to both the political radicalization of the German borderland policy before 1914, and the stability of the political and constitutional dams against large-scale expropriations for the sake of the Germanization policy. By irony of history, it was the government of the Polish state—reestablished after the First World War—that made systematic use of a similar law in order to advance the Polonization of the same region, after it had become the western borderland of Poland in 1919.[70]

We still lack a sufficient amount of comparative research on this issue. But it is likely that Prussia's settlement policy became a model—in the Polish case also the justification—for the borderland policies pursued by the new East Central European nation states established after the war. The governments of Poland and Czechoslovakia pursued a similar policy in their respective borderlands by combining socially and economically motivated land reforms with the goal of weakening the position of minority populations.[71] Throughout interwar East Central Europe, fears of "internal enemies" and "fifth colonies," fears of losing control over the fringes of the state territory, and fears of proving unable to unify the national society led to the policy of forced ethnic homogenization. Yet it took the experience of another world war, and of the brutality of Germany's war of extermination in the east, before large-scale forced resettlements became a widely accepted means of clearing East Central Europe's borderlands of minority populations and creating ethnically homogeneous nation states.

Returning to the German discourse on the eastern borderlands and the legacy of the nineteenth century, there is no question that the experience of World War I—which ended for Germany with defeat and the loss of large parts of the former borderlands to Poland—contributed to a further radicalization. Although Germany entered the war with the experience that the Germanization policy in Prussia's Polish provinces did not produce the expected results, political and military leaders considered implementing a similar Germanization policy in Russia's Baltic provinces occupied by German troops in 1915.[72] In the case of the envisioned annexation of a Polish border strip, however, the continuation of the traditional Germanization policy was no longer considered. The government officials, military leaders, and scholarly experts involved agreed that the annexation of additional Polish land would require the removal of the Polish population. No longer did anyone harbor hopes that Poles—or any other ethnic group with a comparably strong sense of nationality—could be Germanized.[73] Wherever land was inhabited by people who were likely to resist assimilation, annexation was perceived as an attractive option only if the land could be emptied of its foreign inhabitants.

In December 1914, only a few months after the outbreak of the war, Adolf von Batocki, Governor of East Prussia, proposed in a memorandum to the German government that the acquisition of new land in the east be followed by a "comprehensive resettlement." Von Batocki stressed the modernity of such a policy and believed that the Prussian state would be capable of organizing large-scale resettlements with minimal collateral damage. In March 1915, Friedrich von Schwerin, then head of the provincial administration in Frankfurt/Oder and chairman of the Society for Inner Colonization, seconded such views with another memorandum: "The German people, the greatest colonizing people on earth, have again been given a great colonizing task. . . . The current world war provides the opportunity—maybe for the last time in world history—for Germany to resume in a resolute way its colonizing mission in the east."[74] Von Schwerin left no doubts that this mission would entail massive population movements. "Since almost the entire earth is settled, new land can usually only be won at the expense of those who own the land," he declared, and thus, one has to get used to the "idea of the 'resettlement' of large masses of people."[75]

We should not overestimate the radicalizing effect of the war, though. The views expressed by people like von Schwerin and von Batocki were not so much the product of the war as they were the result of the prewar experiences. In fact, none of the large-scale Germanization and resettlement fantasies materialized during the war. The factual constraints of a war of attrition fought with limited resources, the sheer need to avoid unrest in the occupied territories and to secure the cooperation of their non-German inhabitants, forced the German policy in the east onto a path of moderation rather than radicalization. Pragmatism tended to prevail over the utopian ideas from the early days of the war. Signs of this pragmatism can be found Friedrich Naumann's bestselling book *Mitteleuropa,* published in 1915.[76] Although Naumann called for the unification of Central Europe under German leadership, the book's most remarkable message was the rejection of the former Germanization policy, and the promotion of tolerance for the languages and cultures of East Central Europe:

> In former times, they [the Teutons] transformed many Slavs and other alien people into Germans (Brandenburg, Lusatia, Silesia, Pomerania, Prussia). Suddenly, however, they stood still as though in front of a wall. Today, they are still standing in front of the same wall. How great would it be for us if Czechs could be turned into Germans! But this is simply impossible. Those days are gone; both sides are too old for this. . . . It is the tragic guilt of the current Pan-German Germanizers that they fail to recognize the turn of the tide.[77]

It took the experience of Germany's military defeat in 1918 to bring the radical forces to the fore again. The worst German anxieties of the prewar years seemed to be confirmed by the territorial losses in the east, the dissolution of the Habsburg Monarchy, the emergence of new nation states in East Central Europe, where German-speaking citizens found themselves as national minorities deprived of their formerly privileged status, followed by the exodus of hundreds of thousands of Germans from East Central Europe.

Whereas the demands of right-wing radicals regarding the borderland policy met with considerable opposition within German society before 1914, Germany's postwar governments could count on overwhelming support for the defense of the Eastern Marches and the reclamation of lost territories. These sentiments would soon find their most comprehensive expression in the imperial utopias of the Nazi party and the quest for *lebensraum* in the east. Little was new about these fantasies. The Nazis only had to adopt the radical ideas developed before 1914, when the Germanization policy in Prussia's Polish provinces did not produce the expected results. One of the most important elements of these prewar ideas was the belief that the value of the borderlands (and later of the conquered territories in the east) would increase with the removal of its alien inhabitants. It had made its inroads far into the bourgeois camp and the government circles before 1914. After 1918, it became a widely held view not only in Germany, but also among the elites of Central and Eastern Europe's new nation states. The stage was set for a century of "ethnic cleansing." At the end of this century, little was left of the ethnic heterogeneity that once characterized Central Europe's borderlands.

NOTES

1. Johannes Penzler, ed., *Die Reden Kaiser Wilhelms II* (Leipzig: Reclam, [1907]), vol. 3, 84–89; on the celebrations, see Hartmut Boockmann. *Die Marienburg im 19. Jahrhundert* (Frankfurt am Main: Propyläen, 1982), 38–39.

2. Quoted in Jürgen Vietig, "Die polnischen Grunwaldfeiern im Jahre 1902 und 1910," *Germanica Slavica* 2 (1981): 237–62, esp. 244.

3. Gregor Thum, "Mythische Landschaften. Das Bild vom 'deutschen Osten' und die Zäsuren des 20. Jahrhunderts," in *Traumland Osten. Deutsche Bilder vom östlichen Europa im 20. Jahrhundert*

(Göttingen: Vandenhoeck & Ruprecht, 2006), 181–211; see also Vejas G. Liulevicius, *The German Myth of the East: 1800 to the Present* (Oxford: Oxford University Press, 2009).

4. See the excellent survey: Peter Walkenhorst, *Nation—Volk—Rasse. Radikaler Nationalismus im deutschen Kaiserreich 1890–1914* (Göttingen: Vandenhoeck & Ruprecht, 2007).

5. Friedrich Gilly, "Über die vom Herrn Oberhof-Bauamts-Kondukteur Gilly im Jahr 1794 aufgenommenen Ansichten des Schlosses der deutschen Ritter zu Marienburg in Westpreussen," in *Essays zur Architektur, 1796–1799,* ed. Fritz Neumeyer (Berlin: Ernst & Sohn, 1994), 117–24.

6. See the excellent studies of the Prussian/German reconstructions of the Marienburg Castle: Hartmut Boockmann, "Das ehemalige Deutschordensschloß Marienburg 1772–1945. Die Geschichte eines politischen Denkmals," in *Geschichtswissenschaft und Vereinswesen im 19. Jahrhundert. Beiträge zur Geschichte historischer Forschung in Deutschland,* ed. Hartmut Boockmann and Arnold Esch (Göttingen: Vandenhoeck & Ruprecht, 1972), 99–162; Sven Ekdahl, "Denkmal und Geschichtsideologie im polnisch-preussischen Spannungsfeld," *Jahrbuch für die Geschichte Mittel- und Ostdeutschlands* 35 (1986): 127–218; see also: Boockmann. *Die Marienburg im 19;* Knapp, Heinrich, *Das Schloss Marienburg in Preussen. Quelle und Materialien zur Baugeschichte nach 1456* (Lüneburg: Nordostdeutsches Kulturwerk, 1990); Maria Lubocka-Hoffmann, *Die Marienburg. Das Schloss des Deutschen Ordens. Geschichte, Architektur, Denkmalschutz* (Bydgoszcz: Excalibur, 2002).

7. Jörg Hackmann, *Ostpreußen und Westpreußen in deutscher und polnischer Sicht. Landesgeschichte als beziehungsgeschichtliches Problem* (Wiesbaden: Harrassowitz, 1996), 57–85; Wolfgang Wippermann, *Der Ordensstaat als Ideologie. Das Bild des Deutschen Ordens in der Geschichtsschreibung und Publizistik* (Berlin: Colloquium Verlag, 1979), chs. 3–4.

8. Jürgen Osterhammel, "Frontiers: Unterwerfung des Raumes und Angriff auf nomadisches Leben," in *Die Verwandlung der Welt. Eine Geschichte des 19. Jahrhunderts* (Munich: C. H. Beck, 2009), 464–564.

9. On the German stereotype of *Polnische Wirtschaft* (Polish economy), see the excellent study of Hubert Orłowski, *"Polnische Wirtschaft." Zum deutschen Polendiskurs der Neuzeit* (Wiesbaden: Harrassowitz, 1996); for the broader West European context see: Larry Wolff, *Inventing Eastern Europe: The Map of Civilization on the Mind of the Enlightenment* (Stanford: Stanford University Press, 1994).

10. Hartmut Boockmann, "Die Entwürfe von Karl-Wilhelm Kolbe und Karl-Wilhelm Wach für die Glasmalereien des Marienburger Sommerremters. Beiträge zu einer Ikonographie des Deutschen Ordens," in *Preußen und Berlin. Beziehungen zwischen Provinz und Hauptstadt,* ed. Udo Arnold (Lüneburg: Nordostdeutsches Kulturwerk, 1981), 9–39. The windows were destroyed during the siege of the Marienburg in 1945, but records of their imagery survived: Boockmann. *Die Marienburg im 19,* 27.

11. See Boockmann, *Die Marienburg im 19,* image 35.

12. See Boockmann, *Die Marienburg im 19,* image 40.

13. Letter to Theodor von Schön, quoted in Wippermann, *Der Ordensstaat als Ideologie,* 137.

14. Ekdahl, "Denkmal und Geschichtsideologie," 142; Wipperman, *Der Ordensstaat als Ideologie,* 149; Boockmann, *Die Marienburg im 19,* 115.

15. Günter Wollstein, *Das "Grossdeutschland" der Paulskirche. Nationale Ziele in der bürgerlichen Revolution von 1848/1849* (Düsseldorf: Droste, 1977).

16. Hans Fenske, "Ungeduldige Zuschauer. Die Deutschen und die europäische Expansion 1815–1880," in *Imperialistische Kontinuität und nationale Ungeduld im 19. Jahrhundert,* ed. Wolfgang Reinhard (Frankfurt am Main, 1991), 87–123; Matthew Fitzpatrick, *Liberal Imperialism in Germany: Expansionism and Nationalism 1848–1884* (New York: Berghahn Books, 2008); Frank L. Müller, "Imperialist Ambitions in Vormärz and Revolutionary Germany: the Agitation for German Settlement Colonies Overseas, 1840–1949," *German History* 17: 3 (1999): 346–68.

17. Franz Wigard, ed., *Stenographischer Bericht über die Verhandlungen der Deutschen constituirenden Nationalversammlung zu Frankfurt am Main,* (Frankfurt am Main: Sauerländer, 1848–1849), vol. 4, 2898 (parliament session of 26 October 1848).

18. Ibid., 2898–99 (26 October 1848)].

19. Sönke Neitzel, *Weltmacht oder Untergang. Die Weltreichslehre im Zeitalter des Imperialismus* (Paderborn: Schönigh, 2000), 31–55; Henry C. Meyer, *Mitteleuropa in German Thought and Action 1815–1945* (The Hague: Martinus Nijhoff, 1955).

20. Wigard, *Stenographischer Bericht,* vol. 4, 2899 (26 October 1848).

21. Wigard, *Stenographischer Bericht,* vol. 8, 5721 (16 March 1849).

22. Wigard, *Stenographischer Bericht,* vol. 2, 1175 (25 July 1848). Recent studies have pointed to the significance of the American Frontier as a model for Germany's eastern borderlands, particularly in the late nineteenth and twentieth centuries, e.g.: Alan E. Steinweis, "Eastern Europe and the Notion of the 'Frontier' in Germany to 1945," in *Yearbook of European Studies* 13: *Germany and Eastern Europe: Cultural Identities and Cultural Differences,* ed. Keith Bullivant, Geoffrey Giles, and Walter Pape (Amsterdam: European Cultural Foundation, 1999); David Blackbourn, *The Conquest of Nature: Water, Landscape, and the Making of Modern Germany* (New York, London: W. W. Norton, 2006), 293–309. This nexus was not yet systematically researched for the first half of the nineteenth century.

23. Gregor Thum, "Eine deutsche Frontier? Die deutsch-polnische Grenze und die Ideen von 1848." In *Granica: Die deutsch-polnische Grenze vom 19. bis zum 20. Jahrhundert,* ed. Karoline Gil and Christian Pletzing (Munich: Meidenbauer, 2010), 19–38.

24. William Rogers, "Beobachtungen auf einer Geschäftsreise in das Großherzogtum Posen," *Die Grenzboten* 3, no. 27 (1848): 35–43, 39; on the parallelization of Poles and Indians, see Eva and Hans Hennig Hahn, "Nationale Stereotypen. Plädoyer für eine historische Stereotypenforschung," in *Stereotyp, Identität und Geschichte: Die Funktion von Stereotypen in gesellschaftlichen Diskursen,* ed. Hans Hennig Hahn (Frankfurt am Main: Peter Lang), 2002, 17–56, in particular, 29–31.

25. Kristin Kopp, "Constructing Racial Difference in Colonial Poland," in *Germany's Colonial Past,* ed. Eric Ames, Marcia Klotz, and Lora Wildenthal (Lincoln: University of Nebraska Press, 2005), 76–96; Izabela Surynt, "Polen als Raum des 'Anderen' am Beispiel der deutschsprachigen Literatur der 1820er und 1830er Jahre," in *Romantik und Geschichte. Polnisches Paradigma, europäischer Kontext, deutsch-polnische Perspektive,* ed. Alfred Gall et al. (Wiesbaden: Harrassowitz, 2007), 295–310; for the later period, see David Blackbourn, "The Conquest of Nature and the Mystique of the Eastern Frontier in Nazi Germany," in *Germans, Poland, and Colonial Expansion to the East: 1850 Through the Present,* ed. Robert L. Nelson (New York: Palgrave Macmillan, 2009), 141–70.

26. Brian E. Vick, *Defining Germany: The 1848 Frankfurt Parliamentarians and the National Identity* (Cambridge, Mass.: Harvard University Press, 2002), 110–38; Pieter Judson, "Changing Meanings of German Habsburg East Central Europe," in *The Germans and the East,* ed. Charles Ingrao and Franz A. J. Szabo (West Lafayette, Ind.: Purdue University Press, 2008), 109–28.

27. Stefan Troebst, "'Intermarium' and 'Wedding to the Sea': Politics of History and Mental Mapping in East Central Europe," *European Review of History* 10: 2 (2003): 293–321.

28. On the terminology, see Lucien Febvre, "Frontière: The Word and the Concept," in *A New Kind of History: From the Writings of Lucien Febvre,* ed. Peter Burke (New York: Harper Torchbooks, 1928), 208–18.

29. Josef Kolejka, "De Slawenkongreß in Prag im Juni 1848," in *1848/1849. Revolutionen in Ostmitteleuropa,* ed. Rudolf Jaworski and Robert Luft (Munich: Oldenbourg, 1996), 129–47; Andreas Moritsch, ed., *Der Prager Slavenkongreß* (Wien: Böhlau, 2000); Lawrence D. Orton, *The Prague Slav Congress of 1848* (New York: Columbia University Press, 1978).

30. Józef Feldman, *Sprawa polska w roku 1848* (Kraków: Nakład Polskiej Akademii Umiejętności, 1933); Krzysztof Makowski, "Das Großherzogtum Posen im Revolutionsjahr 1848," in *1848/1849. Revolutionen in Ostmitteleuropa,* ed. Rudolf Jaworski and Robert Luft (Munich: Oldenbourg, 1996), 149–72; Michael G. Müller and Bernd Schönemann, *Die "Polen-Debatte" in der Frankfurter Paulskirche* (Frankfurt am Main: Diesterweg, 1991).

31. Report of Hermann von Beisler from Munich, quoted in Wigard, vol. 1, 662 (1 July 1848).

32. Wigard, *Stenographischer Bericht,* vol. 1, 665.

33. Wigard, *Stenographischer Bericht,* vol. 2, 1137–38 (24 July 1848).

34. Wigard, *Stenographischer Bericht,* 1169–70 (25 July 1848); on the bellicose language of the German National Assembly, see also Vick 2002, 191.

35. Brian E. Vick, "Imperialism, Race, and Genocide at the Paulskirche. Origins, Meanings, Trajectories," in *German Colonialism and National Identity,* ed. Michael Perraudin, Jürgen Zimmerer, and Katy Heady (New York: Routledge, 2011), 9–20, 16

36. Maria Wojtczak, "Hinter den Kulissen des Ostmarkenvereins. Zur Entstehungsgeschichte der 'Ostmarkenromane,'" *Studia Germanica Posnaniensia* 22 (1995): 65–76.

37. Hartmut Steinecke, "Gustav Freytags Soll und Haben (1855). Weltbild und Wirkung eines deutschen Bestsellers," in *Romane und Erzählungen des bürgerlichen Realismus,* ed. Horst Denkler (Stuttgart: Reclam, 1980), 138–52.

38. Gustav Freytag, *Soll und Haben* (Leipzig: Fikentscher, [ca. 1930]), 757.

39. Kristin Kopp, "Reinventing Poland as German Colonial Territory in the Nineteenth Century: Gustav Freytag's *Soll und Haben* as Colonial Novel," in *Germans, Poland, and Colonial Expansion to the East: 1850 Through the Present,* ed. Robert L. Nelson (New York: Palgrave Macmillan, 2009), 11–37; Izabela Surynt, *Das 'ferne', 'unheimlich' Land. Gustav Freytags Polen* (Dresden: Thelem bei w.e.b., 2004).

40. Freytag, *Soll und Haben,* 840.

41. Eva Rimmele, *Sprachenpolitik im Deutschen Kaiserreich. Regierungspolitik und veröffentlichte Meinung in Elsaß-Lothringen und in den östlichen Provinzen Preußens* (Frankfurt am Main: Lang, 1996).

42. Lech Trzeciakowski, *The Kulturkampf in Prussian Poland,* trans. Katarzyna Kretowska (New York: Columbia University Press, 1990).

43. Witold Jakóbczyk, *Pruska Komisja Osadnicza 1886–1891* (Poznań: Wyd. Poznanskie, 1976); Scott M. Eddie, "Ethno-nationality, Property Rights in Land, and Territorial Sovereignty in Prussian Poland, 1886–1918: Buying the Land from under the Poles' Feet?" in *Land Rights, Ethno-Nationalism, and Sovereignty in History,* ed. Stanley Engerman and Jacob Metzer (London: Routledge, 2004), 55–86.

44. "Speech of Bismarck in the Prussian House of Representatives on 15 April 1886," *Reden des Fürsten von Bismarck,* vol. 6, ed. Otto de Grahl (Cöthen: Paul Schettler's Erben, 1888), 217–18.

45. Rudy Koshar, *Germany's Transient Pasts. Preservation and National Memory in the Twentieth Century* (Chapel Hill: University of North Carolina Press, 1998); Boockmann 1972, 139.

46. Ekdahl, "Denkmal und Geschichtsideologie," 205–207.

47. Heinrich von Treitschke, "Das Deutsche Ordensland Preußen, " *Preußische Jahrbücher* 10 (1862), 110.

48. Izabela Surynt, "O misjonarstwie cywilizacyjnym. Zakon krzyżacki i kolonizacja 'Wschodu' w niemieckim piśmiennictwie drugiej połowy XIX wieku," in *Opowiedziany naród. Literatura polska i niemiecka wobec nacjonalizmów XIX wieku,* ed. Izabela Surynt (Wrocław: Wyd. Uniwerstytetu Wrocławskiego, 2006), 185–208. See also: Tomasz Torbus, "Deutschordensideologie in der polnischen und deutschen Kunst des 19. und 20. Jahrhunderts," in *Preussen in Ostmitteleuropa. Geschehensgeschichte und Verstehensgeschichte,* ed. Matthias Weber (Munich: Oldenbourg, 2003), 209–257.

49. David Furber, "Near as Far in the Colonies: The Nazi Occupation of Poland," *International Historical Review* 26, no. 3 (2004): 541–79; Pascal Grosse, "What Does German Colonialism Have to Do with National Socialism?" in *Germany's Colonial Past,* ed. Eric Ames, Marcia Klotz, and Lora Wildenthal (Lincoln, Neb.: University of Nebraska Press, 2005), 115–34; Kristin Kopp, "Gray Zones: On the Inclusion of 'Poland' in the Study of German Colonialism," in *German Colonialism and National Identity,* ed. Michael Perraudin, Jürgen Zimmerer, and Katy Heady (New York: Routledge, 2011), 33–42; Mark Mazower, *Hitler's Empire: How the Nazis Ruled the World* (New York: Penguin, 2008); Jürgen Zimmerer, "The Birth of the *Ostland* out of the Spirit of Colonialism: A Postcolonial Perspective on the Nazi Policy of Conquest and Extermination," *Patterns of Prejudice* 39, no. 2 (2005): 197–219. For colonialism's impact on German perceptions of the east in the nineteenth century: Kristin Kopp, *Germany's Wild East: Constructing Poland as Colonial Space* (Ann Arbor: University of Michigan Press, forthcoming); Philipp Ther, "Imperial Instead of National History: Positioning Modern German History on the Map of European Empires," in *Imperial Rule,* ed. Alexey Miller and Alfred J. Rieber (Budapest: CEU Press, 2004), 47–66; Izabela Surynt, *Postęp, kultura i kolonializm: Polska a niemiecki projekt europejskiego Wschodu w dyskursach publicznych XIX wieku* (Wrocław: Atut, 2006).

50. Kristin Kopp, "Positioning Eastern Europe in Fin-de-Siècle Colonialist Cartography," paper given at the Annual Meeting of the American Historical Association, New York, 2009.

51. Carl Fink, *Der Kampf um die Ostmark. Ein Beitrag zur Beurtheilung der Polenfrage* (Berlin: Walther, 1897), 5.

52. Christian Petzet, *Die preussischen Ostmarken. Mit einer Sprachenkarte* (Munich: Lehmann, 1898).

53. Petzet, *Die preussischen Ostmarken*, 1.

54. Petzet, *Die preussischen Ostmarken*, 3–5.

55. Petzet, *Die preussischen Ostmarken*, 49.

56. Clara Viebig, *Das schlafende Heer* (Berlin: Egon Fleischel & Co., 1904).

57. Leszek Belzyt, *Sprachliche Minderheiten im preußischen Staat. Die preußische Sprachenstatistik in Bearbeitung und Kommentar* (Marburg: Herder-Institut, 1998), 17–24.

58. Jens Oldenburg, *Der deutsche Ostmarkenverein, 1894–1934* (Berlin: Logos 2002).

59. William Hagen, *Germans, Poles, Jews: The Nationality Conflict in the Prussian East, 1772–1914* (Chicago: University of Chicago Press, 1980), 181.

60. John J. Kulczycki, *School Strikes in Prussian Poland, 1901–1907* (New York: Columbia University Press, 1981).

61. Hagen, *Germans, Poles, Jews*, 159–207; Walkenhorst, *Nation—Volk—Rasse*, 252–282.

62. Report of Paul Samassa regarding "The Slavic Peril," (May 1902), in *Zwanzig Jahre alldeutscher Arbeit und Kämpfe*, ed. Alldeutscher Verband (Leipzig: Dieterichsche Verlagsbuchhandlung, 1910), 135.

63. Viebig, *Das schlafende Heer*, 228–29.

64. Sabine Grabowski, *Deutscher und polnischer Nationalismus: Der deutsche Ostmarken-Verein und die polnische Straż 1894–1914* (Marburg: Herder-Institut, 1998), 168–69.

65. Helmut Bley, "Der Traum vom Reich? Rechtsradikalismus als Antwort auf gescheiterte Illusionen im Deutschen Kaiserreich 1900–1918," in *"Phantasiereiche." Zur Kulturgeschichte des deutschen Kolonialismus*, ed. Birthe Kundrus (Frankfurt: Campus, 2003), 56–70; see also Walkenhorst, *Nation—Volk—Rasse*.

66. Hagen, *Germans, Poles, Jews*, 180–94; Grabowski, *Deutscher und polnischer Nationalismus*, 187–89.

67. Eddie, "Buying the Land," 76.

68. Hagen, *Germans, Poles, Jews*, 191; Rimmele, *Sprachenpolitik*, 147–60.

69. Hagen, *Germans, Poles, Jews*, 183–90; Grabowski, *Deutscher und polnischer Nationalismus*, 192–96; Michał Pirko, *Niemiecka polityka wywłaszczeniowa na ziemiach polskich w latach 1907–1908* (Warszawa: Wyd. Ministerstwa Obrony Narodowej, 1963); Walkenhorst, *Nation—Volk—Rasse*, 272–73.

70. Richard Blanke, *Orphans of Versailles: The Germans in Western Poland, 1918–1939* (Lexington, Ky.: University of Kentucky Press, 1993), 111–15.

71. Mark Cornwall, "National Reparation? The Czech Land Reform and the Sudeten Germans 1918–1938," *Slavonic and East European Review* 75: 2 (1997): 259–80; Joachim von Puttkamer, "Die tschechoslowakische Bodenreform von 1919," *Bohemia* 46, no. 2 (2005): 313–42; Wilfried Schlau, "Die Agrarreformen und ihre Auswirkungen," in *Ostmitteleuropa zwischen den beiden Weltkriegen 1918–1939: Stärke und Schwäche der neuen Staaten, nationale Minderheiten*, ed. Hans Lemberg, 145–59 (Marburg: Herder-Institut, 1997); for a comparative study in a global perspective, see Stanley L. Engerman and Jacob Metzer, ed. *Land Rights, Ethno-Nationality, and Sovereignty in History* (London and New York: Routledge, 2004).

72. Vejas G. Liulevicius, *War Land on the Eastern Front: Culture, National Identity, and German Occupation in World War I* (Cambridge: Cambridge University Press, 2000).

73. Imanuel Geiss, *Der polnische Grenzstreifen 1914–1918. Ein Beitrag zur deutschen Kriegszielpolitik im Ersten Weltkrieg* (Lübeck: Matthiesen, 1960); Liulevicius *War Land on the Eastern Front*, 94–96.

74. "Die Notwendigkeit und Möglichkeit, als Ziel des Krieges neues Siedlungsland im Anschluß an die Grenzen Deutschlands zu schaffen," quoted in: Geiss, *Grenzstreifen*, 81–86, here 82–83.

75. Geiss, *Der polnische Grenzstreifen*, 82, 84.

76. Friedrich Naumann, *Mitteleuropa* (Berlin: Reimer, 1915).

77. Ibid., 84.

3

BETWEEN EMPIRE AND NATION STATE

OUTLINE FOR A EUROPEAN CONTEMPORARY HISTORY OF THE JEWS, 1750–1950

DAN DINER

This chapter explores the epistemic and conceptual advantages of integrating the transnational or diasporic Jewish experience into European History in order to overcome the nation state paradigm that is so inherent to continental historical thought. The experience of the Jews as a physically dispersed population united nevertheless by religion and liturgy, as well as by semi-religious memorial and ethnic bonds, makes for a unique store of preconceptual knowledge that can be cognitively transformed into actual notions of historical understanding. This understanding focuses first and foremost on the institutional, political, and cultural fabric of substantial changes in the age of transition from premodern patterns of life and modes of social intercourse into modernity.

Seen through this lens, the Jewish experience serves as a seismograph of knowledge and understanding in an age of profound changes—not least the conflict-ridden transformation that accompanied the shift from the variety of imperial integration into the homogeneity of emergent nation states—that extends well into the web of the first half of the twentieth century, but removing the Holocaust from the core to the margin. Removing the core event of the century from the center to the margin seems to become justified by methodological and ethical reasons that need not be elaborated here. Just one reason should be mentioned: by avoiding the Holocaust, the narration of modern Jewish history proposed in this chapter permits a closer look at the events *up to* the Holocaust. Such an approach highlights the role and nature of *contingency* in historical understanding, the recognition of which is urgently needed in the case of the Holocaust, especially in view of narratives that tend to assert alleged and/or largely overstated modes of a supposed continuity. This approach allows the actual contemporary human experience a more appropriate share in the reconstruction of the past, and avoids—to the extent that it is possible—being overwhelmed by the impact of teleology.

This methodological preference is valid despite our awareness of the evident and unavoidable truth that catastrophic intrusions draw events that occurred before and after them into their vortex.

Embarking from a perspective located in a period *up to* the Holocaust and not of the Holocaust itself, I attempt here to sketch the contours of a European narrative focusing on the experiences of the Jews as an exceptional population whose religious, institutional and cultural fabric in the continent was traditionally situated beyond, beside, and above that of the body politic generally considered to be the nation state. Indeed, the Jews as a diasporic population fit rather well into the framework of multinational empires and apparently less well into homogeneous and therefore assimilatory nation states, no matter how liberal they may have been.[1] The Jews and their respective institutions, forms of social intercourse, habits, and languages as well as their hybrid cultures more generally—had an exceptionally premodern proclivity. In modernity—and that is the core of the thesis presented here—the Jews represented residues of premodern *nationes,* remaining as fragments of former corporate estates in modernity, remnants of Empire, so to speak.[2]

This sounds like a forthright repeal of everything generally accepted, namely the largely undisputed assumption that the Jews were—as Horkheimer and Adorno put it in their *Dialectic of Enlightenment*—pioneers *of* modernity. Conversely, here they are portrayed as distinctive agents of lingering premodern patterns *within* modernity. True, as individuals the Jews were quite evidently pioneers of modern time. The whole history of innovations in the nineteenth and twentieth centuries is packed with Jews.[3] But is this assumption really true for the Jews as a collective? At the level of collectivity, premodern patterns stubbornly prevailed. The history of Jewish integration into modernity was accompanied by ambiguity and conflict. This applies first and foremost to questions of belonging—to citizenship, equality, and nationality,[4] and this quite apart from the problematic record of secularized Christianity's attitude toward the Jews. By and large, modernity, in the guise of the territorial nation state and its striving for homogeneity and loyalty, confronted different Jewries with constant demands for accommodation. And these demands were accompanied by inner upheavals and conflicts regarding never-ending question of belonging—evoking the fundamental internal and external query as to who, after all, are the Jews?[5] Emancipation and modernity brought about the right of citizenship on the one hand, and its contractions and warping on the other. This phenomenon of continuous and unresolved tension, so distinctive to Jewish existence in modernity, can be read or re-read through the proposed perspective, namely, the very prism of perceiving Jewish existence as impregnated with prevailing residues of premodernity in modernity. This perspective—focusing on the transformation of premodern modes of social intercourse and their institutional patterns into those of modernity, all in the wake of an overall transformation from (premodern) empires into (modern) nation states, has to be chosen as our perspective on the Jewish catastrophe *up to* the Holocaust.[6] And this as a pivot and as an epistemic angle for our general agenda: an integrated European historical narrative of understanding beyond the nation state—following the experience of different Jewries as a collective as well as Jews as individuals against the backdrop of the upheavals of modernity.

Sorting out our subject from the early modern period to the heyday of the nation state requires that we begin with Jewish institutional autonomy—and do so largely from an East European perspective.[7]

In the beginning was the *Va'ad Arba Aratsot*—the Jewish Council of the Four Lands, the synod of Jewry in the realm of the Polish-Lithuanian Commonwealth, a corporate social order in a premodern imperial context.[8] The synod embodied a degree of autonomy and self-administration that was obviously unattainable for Jews elsewhere in their diasporic existence. Its origin can be traced back to a royal charter, a privilege obtained in 1551 from Sigismund II Augustus. This privilege was derived from the poll tax the Jews had to pay collectively. And this collectively demanded requirement and liability gave rise to a whole network of self-administering Jewish institutions, in particular for legal regulation in almost all social, religious, and personal affairs—including the election of rabbis and judges.[9] It was no accident that Simon Dubnow, the renowned Russian-Jewish historian of the late nineteenth and early twentieth centuries—and the foremost protagonist of a modern, transterritorial autonomy of the Jews in the realm of the Russian empire and beyond—would come to celebrate the royal charter of 1551 as the very "Magna Carta" of Jewish independence.[10]

This dense and complex network of self-administering institutions drew upon the administrative body of the *kahal*, the communal council, which, according to Dubnow, was the "nucleus" of the cultural autonomy that he would seek grow for the Jews.[11] The communal institution of the *kahal*, formally abolished in Russia in 1844, led to all manner of speculations about and hostility toward Jewish autonomy, disparagingly called "a state within the state" during the fairly lengthy period in which absolutist rulers were engaged in increasing integration, unification, rationalization, and homogenization of their realms.[12] The Habsburg Emperor Joseph II, for instance, decreed in 1782 that business documents written in Hebrew or Yiddish would not be admissible as evidence in the courts.[13] Moreover, he abolished group responsibility for toleration taxes and subjected the Jews to all the political, civil, and juridical processes of the land. The Austrian emperor was resolved to grant the Jews equal rights, but on condition of putting an end to their political separation, in such a fashion that their religion would remain the only distinction between them and their compatriots. Finally the French Revolution challenged corporate Jewish autonomy thanks to its transformation of the previous vertical social order into an individualization of the person as citizen on the basis of a horizontal geometry of legal equality.[14] The anti-corporate agenda of the Revolution abhorred any institutional difference in the body of the nation. As individual citizens, the Jews were to be granted everything, but as a *natio*, a corporate body and vessel of premodern, residual emblems of collective belonging, as a *corps de nation*—they were to be granted nothing whatsoever. As Clermont-Tonnerre declared: "They should not be allowed to form in the state either a political body or an order."[15] Taking the civic oath entailed renunciation of all privileges and exceptions. Autonomy had come to an end.

By stripping the Jewish communities of their corporate formation and self-administration, a transformation of the emblems of Jewish belonging was engendered. While in the West religion could become internalized as simple personal faith and thus made to some extent invisible, in the East a traditional social order hampered the differentiation of religious belief, ethnic belonging, and social stratification.[16] In such an environment, changes toward modern forms of social intercourse and their proper institutional settings were evidently delayed. Collective Jewish self-awareness as well as Jewish visibility was largely preserved. Under the conditions of modernization and secularization, this tendency may be termed a process of ethnification—the transformation of the emblems of Judaism (and the sacred elements enshrined in it) into those of Jewishness (as a result of profanation). This ongoing process of secularization was accompanied by alteration of the realm of text on which the diasporic Jewish existence of Jews was "eternally" founded—the rule of divine law and its continuous interpretation by rabbinical authorities—into the profane modes of textual storytelling as history. This transformation was first triggered by the Jewish Enlightenment, the *Haskalah,* and disseminated by the different types of *maskilim.*[17] The transition from (divine) Law into (profane) History is one of the most substantive transformations of the age of Jewish Enlightenment.[18] It was part and parcel of a process that should be entitled the "secondary conversion"[19]—a Jewish conversion of the framework of Judaism and its transformation, so to speak, into Jewries. Among other phenomena of the "secondary conversion," such as in the domain of religious practices or especially in the establishment of profane hermeneutics in interpreting Jewish texts (as introduced by the *Wissenschaft des Judentums*),[20] the very meaning of the "Jew" as a collective underwent fundamental change, when the largely liturgical meaning of the People of Israel (*Am Yisrael*) was converted into a successively national and ethnic understanding of the Jewish People *(ha-am ha-yehudi).*[21]

This ongoing transformation from sacred text into historical thought brought about the emergence of a nationally oriented and more "sociologically" inclined Jewish historiography in the later nineteenth century, as proposed by Simon Dubnow.[22] Here a new concept of the *kahal* moved continuously to the forefront of collective self-perception. Unlike the original *kahal* that formed the basic institution of Jewish autonomy and was abolished by absolutist rule and the later French-inspired Civil Code, or similar undertakings of more hesitant reform further east, the newly conceptualized *kahal* constituted a historical paradigm and a subject of intellectual quest grounded in notions of a nonterritorial Jewish autonomy.[23] The vanishing religiously impregnated corporate political form was thus converted into the narration of a collective consciousness of national self-awareness, though situated beyond the notions and concepts of state, territoriality, and ethnic homogeneity, otherwise so distinctive of the general historiography of the nations in whose midst the Jews were dwelling. According to this transnational, diasporic understanding of Jewish history, the *pinkasim,* the protocols of the organs of Jewish self-administration, were moved to the forefront in order to become the main source for a modern Jewish historiography centering on the Jews as a collective and as a nation beyond the previous liturgical meaning of *Am Yisrael.*[24]

The ubiquitous process of further differentiation of the Jews on the basis of distinctive national citizenships and their associated loyalties to the various nation states in which they were living ran counter to the transterritorial and transnational strands which infused Jewish diasporic existence,[25] as is amply demonstrated by forms of Jewish diplomacy at the time.[26] This began happening when the balance of power and its regulations, as restored in the wake of the Congress of Vienna in 1815, started to disintegrate in the 1880s. The logic of this balance, which encompassed a system of continuous negotiations and clarifications of interests and conflicts among the powers, allowed the Jews throughout the nineteenth century to coordinate their interest "internationally." Jewish political intervention, using the diplomatic stage offered by a system of regulations based on a principle of balance, originated in the traditional organ of Jewish intercession as conducted within the framework of premodern and corporate Jewish autonomy. While traditional intercession, *shtadlanuth,* was carried out by the agents of the corporate order, the later stage of Jewish diplomacy—under conditions of full emancipation on the basis of citizenship or of a incomplete citizenship—was largely carried out by notables with access to courts and chancelleries.[27] The historian Salo W. Baron dealt in his doctoral dissertation with the Jewish intercessions and interventions at the Congress of Vienna in 1814–1815.[28] The further presence of Jewish individuals and organizations at future peace conferences, especially at the Berlin Congress, was rightfully characterized by

Fritz Stern as the "European Concert of Jewries." The goal of this common action was by and large to obtain legal equality for Jews, including civil rights.[29]

The first indication of such an evolution from premodern intercession to a more modern form of diplomatic action was seen at the Congress of Vienna. It was there that Jews from Frankfurt am Main, Lübeck, Hamburg, and Bremen demanded that safeguards be instituted for the rights they had obtained by Napoleonic reforms, especially property rights concerning real estate. The Jewish demands were supported by chief negotiators Hardenberg for Prussia and Metternich for Austria.

Another climactic event in Jewish diplomatic intervention at the threshold of modern forms of intercession occurred in the wake of the notorious Damascus Affair of 1840, a ritual murder or so called blood-libel charge. This event should be recognized as a kind of prototype of Jewish diplomatic intervention in favor of Jews under foreign rule. The Damascus Affair was widely discussed in the newly evolving European public sphere, communicated by an emerging culture of a widely circulating press. It erupted in the midst of the already heated discourse on the emancipation of the Jews, the so-called *Judenfrage,* the Jewish Question, as it emerged in the wake of emancipation and the demand for equal rights and citizenship.[30] In this debate, figures of prominence became involved, among them Heinrich Heine and Karl Marx. The Damascus Affair as a foundational event of modern Jewish politics generated via discourse a common Jewish realm of political awareness and solidarity, something like a common Jewish "public sphere," transgressing the different Jewries while encompassing the Jews of the West, the Jews in East, and the Jews of the Orient.[31] Subsequent to this seminal event in Jewish consciousness at the temporal watershed from the premodern to the modern, the kidnapping and compulsory baptism of a Jewish child in Rome in 1858, the notorious Mortara case, then brought the Paris-based *Alliance Israélite Universelle* into being in 1860.[32] Besides its intervention in behalf of persecuted Jews, this internationally active Jewish organization was involved in disseminating French language and culture as heralds of the emancipation of humankind. This engagement fit well with the policy of Napoleon III, who sought to disseminate the ideas of nationality inside the domains of multinational empires. In 1878, Jewish individuals and Jewish organizations, including the *Alliance,* were considerably involved at the Congress of Berlin—convened by Bismarck following the eighth Ottoman–Russian war—in order to attain equal rights for the Jews of Romania.[33] How deeply this politics of a more modern Jewish intercession on the stage of an international congress based on the principles of the balance of power was interwoven with traditional Jewish intercession was shown convincingly in Fritz Stern's *Gold and Iron.*[34]

The Congress of Berlin was by and large the last international conference of importance orchestrated by the Great Powers. From now on the common European imperial space of international order, based on the principle of balance of power, drifted apart. That also meant the end of the "European Concert of Jewry."

The so-called "revolution of alliances" of the European state-system acted to substantially narrow the scope and latitude for Jewish diplomacy, which was in any case marginal and ineffective. Emerging in the 1870s, the alliance system became increasingly destructive in the 1880s, culminating in the establishment of two opposing blocks based on rivalry and enmity—a tendency of dualistic opposition which brought about the "seminal catastrophe" of World War I. In any event, the structural prerequisites for a shared Jewish political commonality and common diplomatic action were continuously undermined. After the loss of internationalism, inherent in the previous balance-of-power system, the Jews were even more obliged to accommodate themselves to the growing demands for different national loyalties. The predicament of British Jewry on the eve of World War I and especially during the war is notorious.[35]

In 1907 the conflict between liberal England and autocratic Russia in the regions of the so-called Eastern Question and the Great Game was resolved, resulting in a functional division of Persia and paving the way for another alliance.[36] The association with Russia not only contradicted Britain's own parliamentary tradition, but was evidently opposed to its fundamental political orientation throughout the long nineteenth century. This unholy alliance required of British Jewry to remain silent regarding the restrictive policies pursued by the Tsar toward the Jews on the grounds of *raison d'état* and in contrast to their long-held tradition of criticism vis-à-vis imperial Russia. This was the moment of American Jewry, which, by establishing the American Jewish Committee in 1906 in reaction to the Kishinev pogrom, succeeded in bringing about the abrogation of the Russo-American commercial treaty of 1832.[37] This tendency accelerated after the irreversible downfall of continental empires in the wake of Word War I and the formation of a veritable myriad of nation states. All this served to augment expectations of loyalty, further impinging on the maneuverability of Jewish diplomatic action and initiatives—a quandary which would impose its dramatic consequences on Jews in the interwar period, especially those in East-Central Europe.

Conversely, the increasing tendency toward the nationalization of empire in the nineteenth century, as well as the centrifugal shifts this process generated, led to conceptual provisions of extraterritoriality, in an attempt to preserve the multinational fabric of empire and to safeguard imperial integrity. In order to neutralize the dismembering effects brought about by the combination of democratic representation on the one hand and the politicization of language and culture on the other, obviously resulting in a breakup of the imperial domain and its metastasizing into territorial entities, a quasi-corporate concept beyond the democratically obligatory majority-rule was required. Among these quasi-corporate institutions beyond and above majority and minority relations was the Austro-Marxist principle of national-personal autonomy, put forward at the dawn of the nineteenth century by Karl Renner und Otto Bauer.[38] Its aim was the preservation of the multinational composition of the empire. In hindsight it seems probably more than mere irony that Austrian Social Democracy—by objecting to secession from the Empire on the basis of nationality—had no other option but to preserve the imperial fabric, and by implication the monarchy.

Social Democracy attempted to combine the principle of majority rule, anchored in arguments of democracy and demography and based on horizontally buttressed equality, with a cultural and linguistic autonomy that bore corporate traits and was indifferent to the respective numerical relations of majority and minority. Such a vision seemed to mesh well with Jewish intentions to reconcile liberalism grounded in formal equality and citizenship, while at the same time recognizing diversity. In the specific Austrian case, however, Social Democracy neither recognized the one and a quarter million Jews as a distinctive nationality, nor Yiddish as a collective Jewish language.[39] With some instructive exaggeration, one can conclude that the most convenient preserver of the Jews as a nonterritorial and dispersed population happened to be the Emperor, delaying modernity while safeguarding the remnants of premodern life-worlds, of corporate multinationality so to speak—enshrined in the framework of monarchy.

The principle of nationality accomplished in 1918–1919 happened to be a dubious victory over that of empire in Central and East-Central Europe. It became increasingly obvious that the new and expanded nation states established on the ruins of the old empires were no less multiethnic than the empires they had so gladly conveyed to the graveyard of history. In order to paper over the evident gap between the newly established nations and their various minorities, the Paris Peace Conference stipulated a conception of minority protection for those new and enlarged nation states, while limiting their sovereignty. The protection of minorities, entrenched in the peace treaties and enshrined in the constitutions of the different new or enlarged states in Central, East-Central, and southeastern Europe, was attributed primarily to the efforts of Jewish organizations, individuals, and institutions at the peace conference, especially the *Committée des Delégations Juives,* headed mostly by individuals of Eastern and East-Central European imperial origin.[40] The Jewish diplomatic impact was, however, highly exaggerated in public opinion as well as in historiography. The regulations of minority protection were meant primarily for the safeguard of ethnic Germans.[41] The German Reich had suffered considerable losses in territory and population, especially in the East, and Germans—ethnic Germans as well as former citizens of the Reich—found themselves in the unusual condition of a national minority.

Nevertheless, a significant distinction has to be introduced: an ethnic minority is not just that. One can observe a noteworthy difference between those populations turned into ethnic minorities as a result of the secession of territories (newly established minorities, so to speak) carved out of a formerly majority population by dint of political readjustments, that is, minorities created by political circumstances, and to that extent obviously situational by character—and the minorities whose very formation was historical, formerly based on group privileges, so to speak. The latter never experienced any other condition than that of territorial dispersion, namely, living within a surrounding majority and without any proper chance for territorial aspirations. These latter minorities were imperial nationalities to the extent that they had emerged from premodern and multinational empires without any aspirations to achieve control and sovereignty over national territory—they included Jews, Baltic Germans, Armenians, and Greeks, in the Russian Empire. And just for the sake of the argument: the noble estate as well.[42]

The historian Dubnow, who was highly attentive to the deliberations at the Paris Peace Conference on the question of minority rights in 1919, assumed that the notions and concepts of minority protection contained basic outlines of the *kahal,* the premodern form of Jewish communal self.[43] After all, the institution of minority protection seemed to have been designed especially for such populations formerly living in imperial frameworks and endangered by probable politics of ethnic homogenization as pursued by newly established, restituted, or enlarged nation states—especially Poland and Romania. The minorities, historical and situational together, all in all 35–40 million people, established in 1925 a joint institution, the Congress of European Nationalities in Geneva, in order to safeguard their semi-corporate rights enshrined in the respective treaties.[44] This forum was led by individuals who had experienced the ethnic diversity of formerly existing empires—especially the Jewish international politician Leo Motzkin and the Baltic Germans Ewald Ammende and Paul Schiemann—and this continued down to the day when Nazi policy on the Jews in Germany brought that cooperation to an end.[45] The minorities were divided and driven apart by revisionist territorial schemes and anti-Jewish sentiments. Situational minorities—such as Germans and Magyars—living near redrawn borders in compact settlements, sought salvation through irredentism, while minorities of a more imperial type, being mostly scattered or of a peculiar urban character, could not aspire to effective attachments between ethnos and territory—Germans from the Baltic or the Banat for instance, and most especially, Jews.

At first, minority protection had become an issue in the wake of the anti-Jewish pogroms in Eastern Poland in 1918, especially the pogroms of Lemberg, or L'viv, or Lwów—the city's name depending on one's ethnic affiliation—and the pogrom of Pinsk.[46] This ethnic violence, committed in first place by Poles against Jews, was instigated by the rumors that the Jews were siding with the archenemies of Poland resurrected—either Bolsheviks or Ukrainians. These highly violent events at the traditionally conflict-ridden space of the *Kresy*, the historical borderlands of the East and the former Jewish Pale of Settlement, brought about the formation of an important American-Jewish organization: the American Jewish Congress, demanding a "Bill of Rights" for the Jews of Eastern Europe.[47] Such a Bill of Rights incorporated not only civil and religious rights for individual Jews in the newly established nation states in East and East-Central Europe, but collective "group rights" as well. This demand had a dual cause. First, it embodied an immediate and contingent reaction to the recent pogroms; second, it reflected a much more profound layer of Jewish traditional awareness of collectivity and its autonomous regulations embedded in the formerly abrogated concept of the *kahal*, amplified by a deep-seated Jewish mistrust with regard to the rising political ambitions of newly established nations based on principles of ethnicity rather than on citizenship—a constellation that was relatively muted by the previous, now defunct fabric of multinational and multiconfessional empires.

The complicated Polish–Jewish relationship was increasingly damaged even earlier—peaking in the wake of the Fourth Duma elections of 1912.[48] The Jews were watched ever more carefully by Polish nationalists who considered them to be a segment of the population that viewed the very idea of a Polish nation state with agnostic reserve.[49] This dangerously hostile perception had been exacerbated by the consequences of the Russian Revolution, although its roots were of a more profound nature. After the quelling of the Polish January uprising of 1863 and the subsequent Tsarist policy of enforced Russification in Congress Poland, ever more Jews emigrated from the Russian areas proper into that realm. This Jewish population was of a specific character. The so-called Litvaks or Litvaki had been culturally shaped by the Jewish-Russian Enlightenment and Russian integration politics.[50] Ethnic, i.e., Catholic, Poles regarded them as the trustees and compliant heralds of Empire; and as such they apparently had little enthusiasm for the prospects of Polish independence. Furthermore, the Litvaks favored Russian as an imperial and cosmopolitan language, facilitating a far greater prospect and scope for education, science, social communication, and imperial trade.

The attraction Jews felt for an imperial fabric—Stefan Zweig's "World of Yesterday"—its traditions and institutions, aroused suspicion among those who regarded the supranational Empires exclusively as hothouses of repression. With the establishment or "restoration" of Poland after World War I, the former premodern expanse of the Polish-Lithuanian Commonwealth was claimed by a new Polish nation state as its proper territorial space.[51] That created a powerful tension between the newly introduced principle of an ethnically homogenous nation state, based on general suffrage, and the reality of a population composed of a multitude of minorities, which, by and large and with the exception of the Jews, were situational minorities, dwelling in newly drawn border areas. This constellation became Poland's predicament in the interwar period: minority problems were often transmuted into "external" border strife with the surrounding countries, and continuous frictions about borders became chronically transformed into "internal" minority problems.

The unresolved self-perception of Poland—ethnically homogeneous or a federal body politic including ethnically different populations extending far into the East—triggered the largely forgotten Polish–Soviet War of 1920.[52] This war on and about the historical border-lands, which later brought about the "Curzon Line," an ethnic demarcation line favoring by and large Polish claims, encompassed national, imperial, and also class components. As the Soviet forces under the command of Tukhachevsky advanced on Warsaw as a reaction to the Polish onslaught on Kiev, Jewish soldiers and officers of the Polish army as well as Jewish nurses in the hospitals were suspected of probable disloyalty. The Jewish military person-nel were removed and interned in different camps. The most notorious of them was Camp Jablonna, actually established for Soviet prisoners of war.[53]

The advance and acculturation of Jews in the nineteenth century ensued mainly by adopting imperial languages and the canons of knowledge related to them. By contrast, local vernaculars were held in far less esteem. They had little utility for education and the universal and cosmopolitan cultures of science and learning. German, most particularly the German language of the Habsburg monarchy, can thus be qualified as an imperial language. After all, and along with its importance as a major cultural and academic language—*the* academic language of the nineteenth century—it was likewise the linguistic medium of administra-tion, justice, and the military. Though Habsburg German did not differ either in grammar or syntax or in any other form from the German spoken and written in the German Reich—it evidently did so in its application. When, where, by whom, and with whom and under what circumstances and conditions was German spoken—at home, in public, in academia, for spe-cific functions? In a volume of his autobiography *The Tongue Set Free* (*Die gerettete Zunge*), a Bulgarian-born German-language author of Sephardic-Jewish origin, Elias Canetti, provides an insightful everyday glimpse into the multitude of languages and their different meaning in a still multicultural although already waning setting, inherited from the imperial fabric of the Ottoman Empire in dissolution. The intriguing dialectics of language and belonging were highlighted ironically and to that extent quite accurately by the Austrian-Jewish émigré Felix Pollack, a poet and translator of German classics into English—and later a librarian at the University of Wisconsin in Madison—who also coined the saying "*Es ist immer das gleiche. Die einen sind Deutsch und die anderen können es*"—a distinction between those of German origin and those who command the German language.[54]

Clearly the manner and extent of German language usage by Jews in Prague under-went significant changes in the late nineteenth and early twentieth centuries. And this not only in the wake of the literary legacy of Franz Kafka, whose biography and literary opus reflect the experience of transformation, the successive conversion of the employment of the German language by ethnic Germans on the one hand, and by German-speaking Jews on the other.[55] Because of the notorious and ongoing struggle between Czechs and Germans in Bohemia and Moravia, the German-speaking Jews wedged between them progressively diminished their use of German, an imperial, and thus a cosmopolitan language, in the pub-lic sphere, relegating it to the realm of the private and accepting Czech as a public means of communication. Kafka's close friend, the Jewish poet Oskar Baum, was permanently blinded as a child in a scuffle with Czech school children because of the German schoolbooks he naïvely showed them. According to Kafka, he lost his eyesight as a German, a collective be-longings he never had nor wished to have. Kafka, who spoke Czech fluently, was sent by his father—the father to whom his famous letter was addressed—on at least three occasions to negotiate with angry Czech employees at their homes. The father's Czech, an allegedly "foreign" language, was simply not good enough to deal with a conflict situation. Ernest Gellner, who was not born in Prague but was educated there, recollects an embarrassing, even menacing event as a child in primary school, when he dared to provoke his classmates by singing a Czech folksong in German.

The Jewish experience in Prague, in the ambit of an imperial culture falling apart as it transformed into an array of exclusive and antagonizing ethnic affiliations, seems to assume an epistemic meaning for a scholarly deciphering of the phenomenon of nationalism. The Czech lands—becoming after 1918–1919 the multinational Czechoslovak Republic, Czechoslovakia without or with a hyphen—however strongly Czech-leaning, became something of a cache of memory as well as of future knowledge for scholarly research on the phenomena of nationalism and ethnicity on neutral ground. This is true for Ernest Gellner in the fields of sociology and cultural anthropology, and also holds for Hans Kohn in the discipline of history, as well as for Karl W. Deutsch and his theory on "nationalism and social communication" in political science.[56] All three originated in Prague. Karl Deutsch's uncle, Julius Deutsch, was, incidentally, the commander of the socialist militia in Vienna, the *Schutzbund*, which rose against the regime of Engelbert Dollfus in February 1934, and was subsequently crushed in the former imperial capital.[57]

In the late fall of 1939, Raphael Lemkin, a young lawyer and former state prosecutor in Warsaw, escaped the burning Polish capital and arrived via Lithuania in Riga, where he waited for passage to Stockholm and ultimately to the United States. In the Latvian capital, he went right away to meet the renowned historian Simon Dubnow, who had meanwhile become an icon of Jewishness, at his home in the neighborhood of Kaiserwald. Thanks to his liberal and anti-Bolshevik political stand and his leanings toward the Mensheviks, Dubnow had moved from Petrograd to republican Berlin in 1922, where he hoped to continue his work on the subsequently highly esteemed, ten-volume "World History of the Jewish People." The Bolsheviks despised him as a so-called "white" political émigré.[58] In 1933, Dubnow fled the Nazis and settled in the capital of still-independent Latvia, Riga. During their evening talk, Lemkin mentioned that he intended to exert himself—as he expressed it—to "outlaw the destruction of peoples." Dubnow agreed by replying that "the most appalling part about this type of killing is that in the past it ceased to be a crime when large numbers were involved and when all of them happened to belong to the same nationality, or race, or religion."[59] Lemkin arrived in April 1941 in the United States and became noted for having coined the term "genocide," and pushed hard for the acceptance of a United Nations Convention on such crimes.[60] Dubnow fell victim to collective destruction in the Ghetto of Riga that very same year.

The dialogue between Simon Dubnow and Raphael Lemkin sounds—against the backdrop of future events—indeed *unheimlich*, or uncanny; and this because of its apparently prophetic insight into the looming disaster. But neither Dubnow nor Lemkin imagined the coming catastrophe proper. Especially Dubnow, an epistemic empiricist of the Russian tradition and politically a liberal optimist of the nineteenth century type, could and would not dare to imagine an event of such a magnitude, one which only later, in distant hindsight, would be termed *Holocaust*. Moreover, in 1940, in a narrow temporal window of awareness between war and genocide, Dubnow's most outstanding younger followers, who had previously embraced diasporic Jewish politics such as autonomism, liberalism, or socialism, retreated into a mentality of profound disillusionment and pessimism. This reaction was not yet in anticipation of the still inconceivable looming catastrophe of the European Jews, but in reaction to the earlier phases, wherein they experienced a general refutation of everything related to emancipation, civil equality, and human rights. Some of them even published the newly established and short-lived journal *Afn sheydweg* in Paris in 1939, and in response to their deep disappointment with the promises of the Enlightenment proclaimed a "return to the ghetto."[61] Such a deliberately considered return to the forms and norms of premodern Jewish existence was evidently out of reach. That former world was gone forever. And it was gone not only because fundamental changes in material life and in institutional settings had long ago transformed the now desired past, but because people's minds and their comprehension of the world had been enlightened. The anger of disappointment and the energy it produced was not limited to the impact of the non-Jewish surroundings, but was ultimately directed against the Jewish adoption of enlightened culture in the guise of *Haskala.* This conjecture of the mind had tempted the Jews to leave their tradition and its meaning behind and enter the outside world by investing limitless faith in universal pledges. And having adopted the *Haskala* and abandoned the sacred interpretation of their holy texts in favor of the hermeneutics of modernity, they were blocked from any possible return to the origins of orthodoxy.

The disillusionment with universalism and its pledges among Jews in the twilight zone between war and genocide, or even before, in the later 1930s, was ubiquitous. Western Jews, having historically related the promises of emancipation to legal equality and individual acceptance, quarreled with the concept of human rights. Eastern Jews added to such disappointment the ongoing abrogation of their collective rights, formerly enshrined in the peace treaties concluding World War I. A Jewish collective existence under diasporic conditions seemed obviously doomed.

Hannah Arendt's fundamental inquiry into the very concept of universal human rights is eminently part and parcel of such a deep Jewish disappointment with universalism at that time. In her seminal treatise on the cataclysms of the twentieth century, the iconic *Origins of Totalitarianism,* while reflecting her own fate as a stateless refugee in France in the 1930s, she challenges that universal pledge in a remarkably short, yet extraordinarily substantial chapter entitled "The Perplexities of the Rights of Man."[62] Her question is conceptual as well as political. And the question put forward is extremely radical in its scope and meaning. It goes along the following lines: is the validity of human rights exclusively related to the existing framework of the nation state, a body politic granting political and legal sanctuary only to those whose belonging to the community seems beyond question—or does it conceptually as well as politically give shelter to any human being? The answer was Jewish as well as universal in its negativity. Exclusion from the political community was the German-Jewish experience in the Nazi Reich, and pending exclusion—peaking in the later 1930s—was the chronically experienced fate of the Jews as a minority among other minorities in the interwar period and in the successor states of dissolved empires. Stripped of his or her former citizenship by de-nationalization or simply by the dissolution of empire, the stateless person was denied the protection of any statehood whatsoever. He or she was stranded in an obscured sphere of the political realm, in a nowhere region, beyond any possible legal refuge. This somber condition was threatening millions of people who suddenly emerged as ethnic minorities in newly established or enlarged nation states after World War I. In the convulsive interwar period, in the twilight of time and in a the troubled political space in-between—between Germany and Soviet Russia—the future of minorities, especially historical minorities without territorial inclinations, remnants and residues of empire, so to speak, were exposed to the menace of discrimination, denationalization, expulsion, and ethnic violence. Already in the late 1920s and the early 1930s, when Raphael Lemkin endeavored to become legally involved in establishing the still nameless concept of collective destruction, critical inquiry could ominously anticipate the looming dangers. This state of creeping danger was quite poetically expressed in the German press already in 1929 as it mourned the toothless stipulations of minority protection: "There is in the League's glass palace a dark room in which the light never enters and no sound emerges. This is the place where the protection of minorities is implemented."[63]

In her "Perplexities," Hannah Arendt laments the fact that without state protection, minorities and individuals belonging to an endangered collective may encounter a perilous fate. The political philosopher is still thinking about the awkward fate of refugees, not the future disaster of ultimate destruction. Concerning the Jews, her argument tends in the direction of a territorial sanctuary. This argument entails a strong proto-Zionist strand.[64]

In 1940–1941—in between war and genocide—Hannah Arendt encounters Simon Dubnow. Obviously she did not encounter him in real life, but evidently there was a meeting in the realm of historical imagination and political expectation, an encounter exclusively in the realm of the mind.[65] And in contradistinction to the previous encounter between Dubnow and Lemkin, that dialogue was indeed *Heimlich*—transpiring exclusively in the domain of the text. To a certain extent, while embarking from a completely different experience of Jewish emancipation and its refutation—the German-Jewish experience—Arendt continued the discourse on the trail of Dubnow's ideas of a Jewish collectivity and, to that extent, of a political Jewish existence. When his voice was silenced by the extermination of 1941, she started speaking up in America in the name of a Jewish nation, even in the name of the "Jewish People." Following Dubnow's ideas on a militant participation in the war by the Jewish people as a fully accepted ally of the Allies, Hannah Arendt proposed in her public statements in 1940–1941 the establishment of a Jewish Army. This construct emphasized Jewish national claims in order to attain Jewish collective rights (minority rights enshrined in international law and obligations, in the language Dubnow was still using) at a future peace conference in the postwar period along the lines of the experience after World War I. Indeed, the very nature of the disaster, unfolding its inconceivable dimension, was yet not evident.[66]

In those crucial years of disillusionment even *before* the ultimate arrival of catastrophe, Jewish legal scholars, social scientists, and political activists established in 1941 in New York the Institute for Jewish Affairs, the research institute of the World Jewish Congress. Most of them had been on guard in the interwar period protecting the remnants of empire with the disabled means of a collapsing minority regime. Some of them succeeded in escaping the hellfire of Europe and found refuge in the United States. The institute was directed by Jacob Robinson, an international lawyer, who, after having been released as a Russian prisoner of war from German captivity after World War I, became the chairman of the Jewish fraction and leader of the minority block in the Lithuanian parliament until its dissolution in 1926.[67] He represented Lithuania on several occasions at the Permanent Court of International Justice in The Hague and served as a Jewish representative at the pan-European Nationalities Congress in Geneva mentioned above. Later, in New York, he was involved among other research activities in the preparations for the UN Declaration of Human Rights and (with Raphael Lemkin) became consultant to the American chief prosecutor at Nuremberg, Robert H. Jackson. Jacob Robinson and his brother Nehemia Robinson laid the ground for pressing legal questions of indemnification, reparations, and restitution in the wake of an age of destruction.[68] While dealing with different questions of Jewish interest in time of war, among them the question of restitution, it became horrendously clear that the ultimate destruction of *all* Jews was under way *everywhere* within the reach of the Germans.[69] That was indeed something new, and entailed numerous consequences—especially in the domain of legal concepts and further considerations emanating from them. Among others, the property question suddenly emerged in a new light. Because of the ultimate character of collective extermination, the property left behind had to be appropriated by the targeted collective, that is, by the "Jewish people." That was not just an ideological claim, although it fit well into those concepts of Jewish self-awareness that presumed a national Jewish collective analogous to other nations. The far more pressing circumstances behind the legal construction of a Jewish people or Jewish nation in the wake of destruction happened to be the fact that genocide also entailed, over and beyond the moral and human price of total destruction, the phenomenon of heirless property. However, heirless property cannot remain heirless, for property, by definition, must have a proprietor. If the proprietor does not exist, he has to be invented.

Generally, heirless property falls into the hands of the state in which the property is located—especially when real estate is involved. In the case of the event known later as the Holocaust, the following pressing question arose: should those nations where the murdered Jews dwelled in the past legally appropriate and inherit the titles left heirless following the mass murders of their owners? This is especially striking when considering Germany and the German nation, namely, those who perpetrated that very disaster upon the Jews. But other European nations and their actions toward the Jews during the catastrophe were not so much different, taking into account indigenous anti-Jewish measures and collaboration. Should they be legally entitled to appropriate Jewish assets that became heirless on their territory?

Such an appropriation on the basis of a general law of inheritance could by no means be morally applied to Jewish property deliberately made heirless. And this especially thanks to the anthropological fact that property, or the desired object, does not merely reflect an objective value to be realized at the market, but is also if not more a fetish of belonging and of memory, and therefore highly subjective. This is especially true when the victims' existence is symbolized through the artifact of property—all the more in the case of collective destruction, of genocide. To that extent, property anthropologically involves the material side of memory. Concurrently, the procedures of memory and commemoration are claims for justice as well. And justice, if feasible at all, has its material side in the restitution of or compensation for property.[70]

The construction of a Jewish People after the Holocaust had its explanation in the ultimate collective death of absolute genocide. The practical realization traced its path through the collective Jewish claim to Jewish property made heirless by total destruction. The general acceptance of the collective definition of the Jews as a people wound its way through the common religious denominator accepted everywhere by all Jews: its liturgical meaning. This ubiquitous liturgical meaning of the Jewish people was transformed at that time into a legal as well as a political meaning of a Jewish collective represented by international Jewish organizations as well as by the State of Israel. Consequently, the international legitimacy of the State of Israel relies on the collective destruction of the Jews of Europe—or more precisely, on the memory of that destruction.

The Jewish Restitution Successor Organization (JRSO), established in 1948, was charged with implementing the collective Jewish claim to heirless Jewish property.[71] Its early activities were limited to occupied Germany—more precisely to the American Occupation Zone, where it established its main offices in Nuremberg. According to its origins and tradition, it pursued the tradition and continuity of Jewish politics in the interwar period, relating first and foremost to the implementation and the protection of minority rights. Now, in the wake of the mass murder, the collectivization of heirless Jewish property had to be regulated. At the Board of Directors of JRSO we identify—among many others—such illustrious individuals as Hannah Arendt, Salo W. Baron, Norman Bentwich, and Isaiah Berlin.

The institution which prepared, intellectually and organizationally, the postwar, postgenocidal existence of the Jews as a collective, the New York–based Institute for Jewish Affairs, assembled persons whose biographies as well as public and academic legacy represented the spectrum of European Jewries and their experiences in the face of the surging upheavals from the late nineteenth century to the onset of disaster. The prosopography of those involved in the Institute for Jewish Affairs' academic board conspicuously reflected the European past and its previous discrete realms, which had long since waned. It was composed mainly of individuals from the lost imperial eras and the in-between times. Max Laserson, for example, formerly Associate Professor of Constitutional Law and Legal Theory at the University of St. Petersburg, Deputy Director of the Department of National Minorities in the Provisional (Democratic) Government of Russia, in 1917; or Mark Vishniak, Professor for Constitutional Law, Moscow, Secretary-General of the Russian Constituent Assembly of 1918, later dissolved by the Bolsheviks. In the advisory council we come across the great legal scholar Hans Kelsen, a former Viennese and, although not a socialist, a close collaborator of Otto Bauer and Karl Renner. His *Pure Theory of Law* can be historically interpreted as a belated attempt to neutralize the multitude of ethnic differences in the late Habsburg Empire by the most formal normative abstractions possible. And at the head of the board of trustees was Horace Kallen, the father of the concept of pluralism in the United States.[72]

The history of the Institute for Jewish Affairs has still to be written. Such an endeavor promises deep insight into the manner in which historical experiences are transformed in order to be converted into the respective collections of knowledge and meaning—in this case, the patterns, forms, and phenomena of dissolving empires and threatened minorities. Not the history of the Holocaust as such, but the history just *short* of destruction and thereafter—in the years just before and immediately after the twentieth century's foundational event.

NOTES

1. Rogers Brubaker, "Aftermath of Empire and the Unmixing of Peoples: Historical and Comparative Perspectives," *Ethnic and Racial Studies* 18 (1995): 189–218; Robert A. Kann, *The Multinational Empire: Nationalism and National Reform in the Habsburg Monarchy, 1848–1918,* 2 vols. (New York: Columbia University Press, 1950); Andreas Kappeler, *Rußland als Vielvölkerreich: Entstehung, Geschichte, Zerfall* (Munich: C. H. Beck, 1992).

2. Dan Diner, "Geschichte der Juden. Paradigma einer europäischen Geschichtsschreibung," in Diner, *Gedächtniszeiten: Über jüdische und andere Geschichten Munich* (Munich: C. H. Beck, 2003), 246–62; Diner, "Ambiguous Semantics: Reflections on Jewish Political Concepts," *The Jewish Quarterly Review* 98: 1 (2008): 89–102.

3. Arkadius Kahan, *Essays in Jewish Social and Economic History* (Chicago: University of Chicago Press, 1986); Derek J. Penslar, *Shylock's Children: Economics and Jewish Identity in Modern Europe,* (Berkeley: University of Chicago Press, 2001); Jonathan Karp, "Economic History and Jewish Modernity: Ideological Versus Structural Change," *Jahrbuch des Simon-Dubnow-Instituts* [*JBDI*] 6 (2007): 249–68. On the concentration of Jews in the sciences and specific professions, see the early

reflections by Thorstein Veblen, "The Intellectual Preeminence of Jews in Modern Europe," *Political Science Quarterly* 39 (1939): 33–42; and David Hollinger, "Why are Jews Preeminent in Science and Scholarship? The Veblen Thesis Reconsidered," *Aleph: Historical Studies in Science and Judaism* 2 (2002): 145–63; Shulamit Volkov, "Jewish Scientists in Imperial Germany," Parts 1 and 2, *Aleph* 1 (2001): 215–81. See as well the *Schwerpunkt* "Wissenschaftsgeschichte," ed. Ulrich Capa and Ute Deichmann, *JBDI* 3 (2004): 149–314; Rabin Yakov and Ira Robinson, eds., *The Interaction of Scientific and Jewish Cultures in Modern Times,* (Lewinston: E. Mellen Press, 1995); Shulamit Volkov, "Juden als wissenschaftliche Mandarine," in Volkov, *Das jüdische Projekt der Moderne* (Munich: C. H. Beck, 2001), 138–63.

4. Pierre Birnbaum and Ira Katznelson, eds., *Paths of Emancipation: Jews, States, and Citizenship* (Princeton: Princeton University Press, 1995); for the later importance of distinctive paths to citizenship, see Yfaat Weiss, *Deutsche Juden und polnische Juden vor dem Holocaust. Jüdische Identität zwischen Staatsbürgerschaft und Ethnizität 1933–1940* (Munich: Oldenbourg, 2000); Frederic C. Jaher, *The Jews and the Nation: Revolution, Emancipation, State Formation, and the Liberal Paradigm in America and France* (Princeton: Princeton University Press, 2002).

5. For the early beginnings of such a process, especially in the German Lands, see the seminal work by Jacob Katz, *Out of the Ghetto: The Social Background of Jewish Emancipation 1770–1870* (Cambridge, Mass.: Harvard University Press, 1973).

6. Still most instructive for this period is Joseph Rothschild, *East Central Europe between the Two World Wars* (Seattle: University of Washington Press, 1974); Ezra Mendelsohn, *The Jews of East Central Europe between the Two World Wars* (Bloomington: Indiana University Press, 1987).

7. For an instructive overview see Israel Bartal, "From Corporation to Nation: Jewish Autonomy in Eastern Europe, 1772–1881," *JBDI* 5 (2006), 17–31; for the German-Jewish experience see Andreas Gotzmann, *Jüdische Autonomie in der Frühen Neuzeit, Recht und Gemeinschaft im deutschen Judentum* (Göttingen: Wallstein, 2008).

8. Jacob Goldberg, "The Jewish Sejm: Its Origins and Functions," in *The Jews in Old Poland, 1000–1795,* ed. Antony Polonsky, Jakub Basista, and Andrzej Link-Lenczowski (New York: Tauris et al., 1993), 147–65; Goldberg, *Jewish Privileges in the Polish Commonwealth: Charters of Rights Granted to Jewish Communities in Poland-Lithuania in the Sixteenth to Eighteenth Centuries* (Jerusalem: Israel Academy of Science and Humanities, 2001).

9. Anatol Leszczynski, "The Terminology of the Bodies of Jewish Self-Government," in Polonsky et al., *Jews in Old Poland,* 132–46.

10. Simon Dubnow, *Weltgeschichte des jüdischen Volkes. Von seinen Uranfängen bis zur Gegenwart,* 10 vols. (Berlin: Jüdischer Verlag, 1927), vol. 6: *Die Neuzeit,* 344.

11. Ibid., 347; Israel Bartal, "'A Substitute for a Government, for a State and for Cizizenship': Simon Dubnov's Image of Medieval Autonomy," in *A Missionary for History: Essays in Honor of Simon Dubnov,* ed. Avraham Greenbaum and Kristi Groberg (Minnesota: University of Minnesota, 1998), 11–18.

12. Isaac Levitats, *The Jewish Community in Russia, 1772–1844* (New York: University Press New York, 1943); Levitats, *The Jewish Community in Russia, 1844–1917* (Jerusalem: Posner, 1981); Michael Stanislawski, *Tsar Nicholas I and the Jews. The Transformation of Jewish Society in Russia, 1825–1855* (Philadelphia: Jewish Publication Society of America, 1983); John D. Klier, *Russia Gathers Her Jews: The Origins of the "Jewish Question" in Russia, 1772–1825* (DeKalb, Ill.: Northern Illinois University Press, 1986); Klier, "The *Kahal* in the Russian Empire: Life, Death and Afterlife of a Jewish Institution, 1772–1883," *JBDI* 5 (2006): 33–50; Eli Lederhendler, *The Road to Modern Jewish Politics: Political Tradition and Political Reconstruction in the Jewish Community of Tsarist Russia* (New York: Oxford University Press, 1989), 36–57.

13. Lois C. Dubin, "Between Toleration and 'Equalities': Jewish Status and Community in Pre-Revolutionary Europe," *JBDI* 1 (2002): 219–38; Paul B. Bernard, "Joseph II and the Jews: The Origins of the Toleration Patent of 1782," *Austrian History Yearbook* 4–5 (1968/69): 101–119; Nancy Sinkoff, *Out of the Shtetl: Making Jews Modern in the Polish Borderlands* (Providence, R.I.: Brown Judaic Studies, 2004), 208–224.

14. Zosa Szajkowski, *Jews and the French Revolutions of 1789, 1830, and 1848* (New York: Ktav Pub. House, 1970), 358–70; Michael Graetz, *The Jews in Nineteenth-Century France: From the French Revolution to the Alliance Israélite Universelle* (Stanford: Stanford University Press, 1996), 17–40;

Graetz, ed., *The French Revolution and the Jews: The Debates in the National Assembly, 1789–1791* (Jerusalem: Mosad Byalik, 1989, in Hebrew); Frederic Cople Jaher, *The Jews and the Nation: Revolution, Emancipation, State Formation, and the Liberal Paradigm in America and France* (Princeton: Princeton University Press, 2002).

15. Jaher, *Jews and the Nation*, 60. Concerning the later Napoleonic policy on the Jews, see Simon Schwarzfuchs, *Napoleon, the Jews, and the Sanhedrin* (London: Routledge & Kegan Paul, 1979); Bernard Blumenkranz and Albert Soboul, eds., *Le Grand Sanhedrin de Napoleon* (Toulouse, France: E. Privat, 1979).

16. Max Wiener, *Jüdische Religion im Zeitalter der Emanzipation* (Berlin: Philo Verlag, 1933); Caesar Seligmann, *Geschichte der jüdischen Reformbewegung* (Frankfurt am Main: J. Kauffmann, 1922); Andreas Gotzmann, "From Nationality to Religion: Samuel Holdheim's Path to the Extreme Side of Religious Reform," in *Redefining Judaism in an Age of Emancipation: Comparative Perspectives on Samuel Holdheim (1806–1860)*, ed. Christian Wiese (Leiden, Netherlands: Brill, 2006), 23–62; Michael A. Meyer, *Response to Modernity: A History of the Reform Movement in Judaism* (Oxford: Oxford University Press, 1988). For the Eastern form of nationalization of the Jews, see Peretz Smolenskin, *Articles* (Jerusalem: n.p., 1925, in Hebrew); Moshe Leib Lilienblum, *Autobiographical Writings*, ed. Shlomo Braiman (Jerusalem: Mosad Byalik, 1970, in Hebrew). About the importance of Lilienblum's biographical writing as a paradigm of ethnic Jewish modern belonging, see Benjamin Nathans, "A 'Hebrew Drama': Lilienblum, Dubnow, and the Idea of 'Crisis' in East European Jewish History," *JBDI* 5 (2006): 211–30; Steven J. Zipperstein, *Imagining Russian Jewry: Memory, History, Identity* (Seattle: University of Washington Press, 1999).

17. Shmuel Feiner, *The Jewish Enlightenment* (Philadelphia: University of Pennsylvania Press, 2004); Shmuel Feiner and David Sorkin, eds., *New Perspectives on the Haskalah* (Portland, Ore.: Littman Library of Jewish Civilization, 2001); Shmuel Feiner and Israel Bartal, eds., *Varieties of Haskalah: New Studies in the History of Haskalah and its Literature* (Jerusalem: Magnes Press, 2005, in Hebrew).

18. Shmuel Feiner, *Haskalah and History: The Emergence of a Modern Jewish Consciousness* (Oxford: The Littman Library of Jewish Civilization, 2001).

19. Dan Diner, "Editorial," *JBDI* 3 (2004): 9–13.

20. Michael Brenner and Stefan Rohrbacher, eds., *Wissenschaft vom Judentum: Annäherungen nach dem Holocaust* (Göttingen: Vandenhoeck & Ruprecht, 2000).

21. Dan Diner, "Historische Anthropologie nationaler Geschichtsschreibung," in *Jüdische Geschichtsschreibung heute: Themen, Positionen Kontroversen: Ein Schloss Elmau-Symposion*, ed. Michael Brenner and David N. Myers (Munich: C. H. Beck, 2002), 207–16; Jeffrey Veidlinger, "The Historical and Ethnographical Construction of Russian Jewry," *Ab Imperio: Theory and History of Nationalism and Empire in the Post-Soviet Space* 4 (2003): 165–84.

22. Jeffrey Veidlinger, "Simon Dubnow Recontextualized: The Sociological Conception of Jewish History and the Russian Intellectual Legacy," *JBDI* 3 (2004): 411–27; Arye Tartakower, "Toward a Criticism of Dubnow's Sociological Approach," in *Sefer Shimon Dubnov*, ed. Shimon Ravidowicz (London: Ararat, 1954, in Hebrew), 77–88.

23. Simon Dubnow, "Das Problem der Gemeinde in der neuesten Geschichte des Judentums," *Bote der jüdischen Gemeinde* 1 (1913): 10ff.; Dubnow, *Nationalism and History: Essays on Old and New Judaism* (Cleveland, Ohio: Jewish Publication Society of America, 1958); Viktor E. Kleiner, "Nation der Gegenwart—Simon Dubnow über jüdische Politik und Geschichte," *JBDI* 2 (2003): 519–44, esp. 526.

24. For Simon Dubnow's historical agenda see his "Let Us Seek and Investigate: An appeal to the informed among us who are prepared to collect material for the construction of a history of the Jews in Poland and Russia," originally published in Odessa in 1892, translated from the Hebrew by Avner Greenberg, introduced by Laura Jockusch, in *JBDI* 7 (2008): 343–82.

25. Dan Diner, "Ubiquität in Zeit und Raum. Annotationen zum jüdischen Geschichtsbewusstsein," in *Synchrone Welten: Zeiträume jüdischer Geschichte*, ed. Dan Diner (Göttingen: Vandenhoeck & Ruprecht, 2005), 13–36.

26. Caron Fink, *Defending the Rights of Others: The Great Powers, the Jews, and International Minority Protection, 1878–1938* (Cambridge: Cambridge University Press, 2004).

27. François Guesnet, "Politik der Vormoderne—Shtadlanuth am Vorabend der polnischen Teilung," *JBDI* 1 (2002): 235–55.

28. Max J. Kohler, *Jewish Rights at the Congress of Vienna, 1814–1815, and Aix-La-Chapelle 1818* (New York: American Jewish Committee, 1918); Salo Baron, *Die Judenfrage auf dem Wiener Kongreß* (Vienna: Löwit, 1920).

29. Markus Kirchhoff, "Einfluss ohne macht. Jüdische Diplomatiegeschichte 1815–1878," in Diner, *Synchrone Welten*, 121–47.

30. Jacob Toury, "'The Jewish Question': A Semantic Approach," *Leo Baeck Institute Yearbook* 11 (1966): 85–106.

31. Jonathan Frankel, *The Damaskus Affair: "Ritual Murder," Politics, and the Jews in 1840* (Cambridge: Cambridge University Press, 1997).

32. David I. Kertzer, *The Kidnapping of Edgardo Mortara* (New York: Alfred Knopf, 1997); Graetz, *Jews in Nineteenth-Century France*, 249–88; Aron Rodrigue, *French Jews, Turkish Jews: The Alliance Israélite Universelle and the Politics of Jewish Schooling in Turkey, 1860–1925* (Bloomington: Indiana University Press, 1990).

33. Josef Meisl, *Die Durchführung des Artikels 44 des Berliner Vertrages in Rumänien und die europäische Diplomatie* (Berlin: Schwetschke, 1925); N. M. Gelber, "The Intervention of German Jews at the Berlin Congress 1878," *Leo Baeck Institute Yearbook* 5 (1960): 221–48; Immanuel Geiss, "Die jüdische Frage auf dem Berliner Kongress 1878," *Jahrbuch des Instituts für Deutsche Geschichte* 10 (Tel Aviv, 1981): 413–22; Lloyd Gartner, "Roumania, America, and World Jewry: Consul Peixatto in Bucharest, 1870–1876," *American Jewish Historical Quarterly* 58: 1 (September 1968): 25–117.

34. Fritz Stern, *Gold and Iron: Bismarck, Bleichröder, and the Building of the German Empire* (New York: Knopf, 1977).

35. David Ceserani, "An Embattled Minority: The Jews in Britain During the First World War," *Immigrants and Minorities* 8 (1989): 61–81; Werner Mosse, "Die Krise der europäischen Bourgeoisie und das Deutsche Judentum," in *Deutsches Judentum in Krieg und Revolution,* ed. Mosse (Tübingen: J. C. B. Mohr, 1971), 1–26; Philippe-E. Landau, *Les Juifs de France et la grande guerre: Un patriotisms républicain* (Paris: CNRS éd., DL, 1999); Egmond Zechlin, *Die deutsche Politik und die Juden im Ersten Weltkrieg* (Göttingen: Vandenhoeck u. Ruprecht, 1969).

36. "Max Beloff, Lucien Wolf, and the Anglo-Russian entente: 1907–1924," Lucien Wolf memorial lecture, London, 1951. Chimen Abramsky, "Lucien Wolf's Efforts for the Jewish Communities in Central and Eastern Europe," *Jewish Historical Studies: Transactions of the Jewish Historical Society of England* 29 (1982–86): 281–95; Mark Levene, *War, Jews, and the New Europe: The Diplomacy of Lucien Wolf, 1914–1919,* (Oxford: Oxford University Press, 1992). As a source into Wolf's views, see Lucien Wolf, *Notes on the Diplomatic History of the Jewish Question* (London: Spottiswoode, Ballantyne, 1919).

37. Nathan Schachner, *The Price of Liberty: A History of the American Jewish Committee* (New York: American Jewish Committee, 1948); Naomi W. Cohen, *Not Free To Desist: The American Jewish Committee, 1906–1966* (Philadelphia: Jewish Publication Society, 1972).

38. Roni Gechtman, "Conceptualizing National-Cultural Autonomy—From the Austro-Marxists to the Jewish Labor Bund," *JBDI* 4 (2005): 17–49.

39. Gerald Stourzh, "Recognizing Yiddish—Max Diamant and the Struggle for Jewish Rights in Imperial Austria," *JBDI* 1 (2002): 153–67; Tatjana Lichtenstein, "Making Jews at Home: Jewish Nationalism in the Bohemian Lands, 1918–1938" (Ph.D. Diss., University of Toronto, 2009); David E. Fishman, *The Rise of Modern Yiddish Culture* (Pittsburgh, Pa.: University of Pittsburgh Press, 2005).

40. "Arbeitsbericht des Comité des Délégations Juives für das Jahr 1920/1921," ed. Philipp Graf, *JBDI* 4 (20015): 175–208.

41. David Engel, "Being Lawful in a Lawless World: The Trial of Scholem Schwarzbard and the Defense of East European Jews," *JBDI* 5 (2006): 83–97, esp. 85–92.

42. Yuri Slezkine, *The Jewish Century* (Princeton: Princeton University Press, 2004); Dan Diner, "Editorial," *JBDI* 5 (2006): 9–13, and other introductions to volumes of the *JBDI*.

43. Simon Dubnow, "Das Problem der Gemeinde in der neuesten Geschichte des Judentums," *Bote der jüdischen Gemeinde* 1 (1913): 10ff.

44. Frank Nesemann, "Minderheitsdiplomatie—Leo Motzkin zwischen Imperien und Nationen," in Diner, *Synchrone Welten*, 147–71; Sabine Bamberger-Stemmann, *Der Europäische Nationalitätenkongress 1925 bis 1938: Nationale Minderheiten zwischen Lobbyistentum und Grossmachtinteressen* (Marburg: Herder-Institut, 2000); Fink, *Defending the Rights of Others*; Leon Chasanowitsch and Leo Motzkin, eds., *Die Judenfrage der Gegenwart: Dokumentensammlung* (Stockholm: Bokförlaget Judäa, 1919).

45. John Hiden, "Propagating the Anational State—Paul Schiemann's Concept of Minority Rights," *JBDI* 4 (2005): 99–109.

46. David Engel, "Lwów, 1918: The Transmutation of a Symbol and its Legacy in the Holocaust," in *Contested Memories: Poles and Jews During the Holocaust and Its Aftermath*, ed. Joshua D. Zimmerman (New Brunswick, N.J.: Rutgers University Press, 2003), 33–34; William W. Hagen, "The Moral Economy of Popular Violence: The Pogrom in Lwów, November 1918," in *Antisemitism and Its Opponents in Modern Poland*, ed. Robert Blobaum (Ithaca, N.Y.: Cornell University Press, 2005), 124–47; Henry Morgenthay, *All in a Life-Time* (Garden City: Doubleday, Page & Co, 1922), 348–84; Ana Filipa Vrdoljak, "Human Rights and Genocide: The Work of Lauterpacht and Lemkin in Modern International Law," *The European Journal of International Law* 20: 4 (2009): 1163–94; Caludia Kraft, "Völkermord als *delictum iuris gentium*—Raphael Lemkins Vorarbeiten für eine Genozidkonvention," *JBDI* 4 (2005): 79–98; Frank Golczewski, *Polnisch-jüdische Beziehungen, 1881–1922: Eine Studie zur Geschichte des Antisemitismus in Osteuropa* (Wiesbaden: Steiner, 1981).

47. Fink, *Defending the Rights of Others*, 126.

48. Golczewski, *Polnisch-jüdische Beziehungen*, 101–106; Mark Levene, "Resurrecting Poland—The Fulcrum of International Politics," *JBDI* 1 (2002): 29–40.

49. Marcos Silber, "Jews and Non-Jews in the Public Sphere in Poland (1848–1939): A Brief Prolegomenon," *JBDI* 7 (2008): 115–25.

50. Francois Guesnet, *Polnische Juden im 19. Jahrhundert: Lebensbedingungen, Rechtsnormen und Organisation im Wandel* (Cologne: Böhlau, 1998); Golczewski, *Polnisch-jüdische Beziehungen*, 96–101.

51. Dan Diner, *Cataclysms: A History of the Twentieth Century from Europe's Edge*, trans. William Templer and Joel Golb (Madison: University of Wisconsin Press, 2008).

52. Norman Davies, *White Eagle, Red Star: The Polish-Soviet War, 1919–20* (London: Macdonald and Co., 1972).

53. Celia Stopnicka Heller, *On the Edge of Destruction: Jews of Poland between the Two World Wars* (Detroit, Mich.: Wayne State University Press, 1994), 51.

54. Ron Wallace, "In Memoriam: Felix Pollak," *Wisconsin Academy Review* 34(2) (1988): 24–27.

55. Scott Spector, *Prague Territories: National Conflict and Cultural Innovation in Franz Kafka's fin de siècle* (Berkeley: University of California Press, 2000).

56. Ernest Gellner, *Words and Things: A Critical Account of Linguistic Philosophy and a Study in Ideology* (London: Gollancz, 1959); Gellner, *Nations and Nationalism*, 2nd ed. (Ithaca, N.Y.: Cornell University Press, 2008); Hans Kohn, *Nationalismus: Über die Bedeutung des Nationalismus im Judentum und in der Gegenwart* (Wien: R. Löwit, 1922); Kohn, *The Idea of Nationalism: A Study in Its Origins and Background* (New York: Macmillan, 1944); Karl W. Deutsch, *On Nationalism, World Regions, and the Nature of the West* (Berlin International Institute for Comparative Social Research, 1982).

57. Julius Deutsch, *Putsch oder Revolution? Randbemerkungen über Strategie und Taktik im Bürgerkrieg* (Karlsbad: Graphia, 1934).

58. Simon Dubnow, *Buch des Lebens: Erinnerungen und Gedanken. Materialien zur Geschichte meiner Zeit*, 3 vols., ed. Verena Dohrn (Göttingen: Vandenhoeck & Ruprecht, 2004), esp. vol. 2: *1903–1922*, trans. from the Russian by Barbara Conrad.

59. Anson Rabinbach, "The Challenge of the Unprecedented—Raphael Lemkin and the Concept of Genocide," *JBDI* 4 (2005): 419–20.

60. Raphael Lemkin, *Axis Rule in Occupied Europe: Laws of Occupation—Analysis of Government—Proposals for Redress* (Washington, D.C.: Carnegie Endowment for International Peace, Division of International Law, 1944); Dominik J. Schaller and Jürgen Zimmerer, eds., *The Origins of Genocide: Raphael Lemkin as a Historian of Mass Violence* (New York: Routledge, 2009); A. Dirk

Moses, "Introduction," in *Empire, Colony, Genocide: Conquest, Occupation, and Subaltern Resistance in World History,* ed. Moses (New York: Berghahn Books, 2008), 3–54; Dan Stone, ed., *The Historiography of Genocide* (Houndmills, U.K.: Palgrave MacMillan, 2008).

61. Joshua Karlip, "In the Days of Haman: Simon Dubnow and his Disciples at the Eve of WWII," *JBDI* 4 (2005): 531–64.

62. Hannah Arendt, *The Origins of Totalitarianism,* 2nd ed. (London: André Deutsch, 1986 [1951]), 290–302.

63. Lucien Wolf to Erik Andreas Colban, 30 January 1923, cited in Fink, *Defending the Rights of Others,* 267.

64. Dan Diner, "Marranische Einschreibungen. Erwägungen zu verborgenen Traditionen bei Hannah Arendt," *Babylon* 22 (February 2007), 62.

65. Hannah Arendt, *The Jewish Writings,* ed. Jerome Kohn and Ron H. Feldman (New York: Schocken Books, 2007), 46–133.

66. Karlip, "In the Days of Haman," 554–57. Arendt, *The Jewish Writings,* 134–85 (articles from *Aufbau*).

67. Jacob Robinson, *Uprooted Jews in the Immediate Postwar World* (New York: Institute of Jewish Affairs of the American Jewish Congress and World Jewish Congress, 1943).

68. Nehemiah Robinson, *Indemnification and Reparations: Jewish Aspects,* ed. Ephraim Fischoff (New York: Institute of Jewish Affairs of the American Jewish Congress and World Jewish Congress, 1944).

69. Ronald W. Zweig, *German Reparations and the Jewish World: A History of the Claims Conference,* 2nd ed. (London: Frank Cass, 2001), 12.

70. Dan Diner and Gotthart Wunberg, eds., *Restitution and Memory: Material Restoration in Europe* (New York: Berghahn Books, 2006); Martin Dean, Constantin Goschler, and Philipp Ther, eds., *Robbery and Restitution: The Conflict over Jewish Property in Europe* (New York: Berghahn Books, 2007); Inka Bertz und Michael Dorrmann, eds., *Raub und Restitution: Kulturgut aus jüdischem Besitz von 1933 bis heute* (Göttingen: Wallstein Verlag, 2008), esp. essays by Diner and Goschler.

71. Ayaka Takei, "The 'Gemeinde Problem': The Jewish Restitution Successor Organization and the Postwar Jewish Communities in Germany, 1947–1954," *Holocaust and Genocide Studies* 16(2) (Fall 2002): 266–88; Benjamin B. Ferencz, *A Visionary for World Peace: Stories of the Life and Times of Benjamin B. Ferencz, Nuremberg War Crimes Prosecutor and World Peace Advocate,* chapter 5: "Seeking Redress for Hitler's Victims (1948–1956)," Story 38: "Restitution for Confiscated Property," available at: www.benferencz.org.

72. See, e.g., Max M. Laserson, *The Status of the Jews after the War: A Proposal for Jewish Demands at the Forthcoming Peace Conference* (New York: Educational Committee Jewish National Workers' Alliance, 1940); Marc Vishniak, *The Legal Status of Stateless Persons* (New York: The American Jewish Committee, 1945); Hans Kelsen, *Pure Theory of Law,* 2nd rev. ed., trans. Max Knight (Berkeley: University of California Press, 1967); Horace M. Kallen, *Cultural Pluralism and the Critical Issues in Jewish Education* (New York: Farband-Labor Zionist Order, 1964).

4

JEWS AND OTHERS IN VILNA-WILNO-VILNIUS
INVISIBLE NEIGHBORS, 1831–1948

THEODORE R. WEEKS

The modern world loves precise, fixed borders. We consider it normal that where one country ends, another one starts. Conversely it would be peculiar, even outrageous for us to be simultaneously in two countries. But such a situation is both recent and rare. Even now borders retain a certain amount of fluidity, more so in the case of EU member states, far less so when one passes, say, from Israel to Egypt (or attempts to pass from Israel to Lebanon). But before World War II in East-Central Europe, borderlands were far more mixed and fluid than after the mid-twentieth century. The "unmixing of populations" that has taken place since 1914 and especially brutally in the 1940s, through assimilation, migration, forced exile, and mass murder, has radically changed the ethnic/national landscape of Europe east of the Oder River. However, living in close physical proximity in the past did not necessarily denote cultural mixing or even active toleration. Rather, I will argue, far more typical was simply a mutual ignoring of neighbors who followed a different pattern of everyday life, religion, and language.

Even today, the city known variously as Vilnius (the present-day capital of the Republic of Lithuania), Vilna (in Russian and for Jews), Vilnia (for Belorussians), and Wilno (for Poles), presents a case study of a borderland community.[1] One regularly hears Russian and Polish, as well as Lithuanian, spoken in the city's streets. The surrounding rural population, in particular to the east, is more likely to speak Belorussian or Polish as a native tongue than Lithuanian. While the majority of the population is Roman Catholic, the cityscape is marked by a number of Orthodox churches, a Karaite house of worship (*kenesa*), and one remaining—and magnificent—synagogue.

The ethnic and religious diversity of the city was, of course, considerably richer before the Holocaust and particularly before 1918, when Vilnius functioned as a major center for the Belorussian and Lithuanian national movements, traditional Jewish learning, and the

Jewish labor movement (the "Bund"), while also being claimed by Russian nationalists. Vilnius is located at the "borderline" between Catholicism and Orthodoxy, the last major city dominated by Catholics (it was not by chance that the Jesuits established their academy here in 1579). Until the twentieth century, these diverse religious and ethnic groups managed to live, if not in "harmony," then at least without major outbreaks of violence. The pogrom wave of 1881 that touched much of Ukraine (officially the "southwest provinces" of the Russian Empire) did not reach Vilnius, nor were there Jewish pogroms here during the 1905 Revolution. In short, until World War I this was an exemplary "borderland city" where no one religion, language, or ethnicity dominated and where religious and linguistic diversity was taken for granted.

Toleration of diversity is not, however, equivalent to mutual understanding and respect. The history of Vilnius demonstrates rather the ability of diverse ethno-cultural groups to live in close proximity almost without noticing each other. Not only in everyday life, but even more in writing about "their" city, each group tended to marginalize or simply leave out others. To be sure, as the twentieth century dawned and particularly after the Revolution of 1905 eased censorship and opened the way toward modern politics (by having elections to the Russian parliament, the Duma), it became increasingly difficult for, say, Poles to ignore their Jewish neighbors, if only because they had sometimes to seek allies in the other national group to support a Duma candidate.[2] Still, this mutual perception and cooperation remained rather superficial and tentative. Members of each nationality tended to identify with their own group and regard members of other nationalities with indifference or even hostility. Specifically for Jews, this blindness to the "national other" that in the twentieth century began to shift to suspicion and hostility meant ironically that as the impact of non-Jewish culture on Jewish life (politics, everyday life, language) grew, on the whole relations with non-Jewish neighbors became more and more strained. There is obviously no direct connection between frictions between Jews and Poles in Vilnius in the interwar period and the mass murder of the city's Jewish community in the years 1941–1944, but surely the fact that Poles generally defined their Jewish neighbors as "other" rather than "our own" made it less likely that Poles would risk their lives to assist Jews.

Throughout its history, this city has been inhabited by individuals of various faiths and ethnicities.[3] The still-Pagan Lithuanian ruler Gediminas founded the city in the early fourteenth century when, according to legend, an iron wolf instructed him to do so in a dream. Jews resided in the city at least from the later fifteenth century—their presence usually documented by attacks on them by their Christian neighbors or periodic expulsion orders by the rulers.[4] But from the late sixteenth century at least Jews formed a permanent presence in Vilnius.[5] The city's Great Synagogue was constructed at the end of the sixteenth century and survived to the mid-twentieth.[6] By the time of its construction, the language and culture of the surrounding Gentile population was mainly Polish and Catholic, a situation that would survive essentially as long as the synagogue itself: the building was heavily damaged in World War II and finally cleared away by the Soviet authorities in the mid-1950s; Vilnius's Polish population had been "repatriated" to Poland a few years earlier.[7]

This essay is mainly about identity and perceptions—of one's own and of the "other." Without falling into the trap of positivism, it would, I think, be of some use to look at the admittedly imperfect but not entirely fanciful statistical information we have on nationalities and religions inhabiting Vilnius during the century covered here. In the most detailed statistical work on Vilnius before 1897, the Polish historian Michał Baliński, using official statistics of the early 1830s, set the city's population at a minimum of 35,922 (and a maximum of 50,000). By "estate" (*stan*) Jews formed the majority—nearly two thirds—of the city's population. The second largest estate, remarkably, was not townspeople (*mieszczanie*, ca. 5,000) but nobles (*szlachta*), numbering nearly 6,600. Over 700 persons in Vilnius belonged to the clerical caste and around 300 serfs inhabited the city.[8] Even among the non-Jewish minority, Vilnius was a religiously and ethnically diverse city. To be sure, the majority (nearly two thirds) of the city's Christians were Roman Catholics, but almost 3,000 Orthodox believers also lived in Vilnius, along with Uniates, Lutherans (*Ewangelicko-Auszpurskiego*), Calvinists (*Reformanego*), and almost certainly a few Muslim Tatars and Karaites who do not, however, appear among Baliński's figures. Because "nationality" did not figure as a legal category in the Russian Empire, Baliński had to limit his statistics to religion. From all that we know about the city (memoir literature, official reports, etc.), it seems certain that the great majority of Catholics were Polish by language and culture, though of course among the Catholics one would have found some Belorussians and Lithuanians.

The first modern census in the Russian Empire was carried out in 1897. While nationality was still not used as a category, "native language" was. According to this census, the city boasted a population of 154,532 persons, 40 percent Jews (61,847 individuals), 31 percent Poles (47,795), 20 percent "Russians" (30,967; this figure would include Belorussians and Ukrainians), and 2.1 percent Lithuanians (3,238).[9] These figures must be regarded with some suspicion; in particular the number for "Russians" is probably too high, those for Poles and Jews a bit low. The city grew rapidly in the decades after 1897 and on the eve of the First World War probably had around 200,000 inhabitants.

World War I was devastating for the city. The population declined from over 200,000 at the beginning of the war to around 139,000 by September 1917. Of these, 110,000 were being fed (sparsely) in the 130 public soup kitchens set up by citizens' committees in the city.[10] By the time the city was officially incorporated into Poland (1922), its population was about half that of the prewar figure. Most of the Russian population (being administrators and soldiers) left when the Russian authorities pulled out in fall 1915, and the Jewish population also declined. During the interwar years, the Polish government's pro-Polish (and at times overtly anti-Lithuanian and anti-Jewish) policies encouraged the growth of the Polish ethnic element. By the late 1930s, the city's population had recovered to the pre-World War I figure of just over 200,000. According to the latest pre–World War II figures we have on nationalities in the city (1931), Poles made up 66 percent of the total city population, followed by Jews (28), Russians (nearly 4), and Lithuanians (under 1).[11] To be sure, the Polish authorities tended to exaggerate the percentage of Poles among this region's population, but these figures seem at least roughly correct. These official statistics almost certainly underestimated the number of Lithuanians in the city at 1,579, but their numbers were probably at most a few thousand.

Between 1939 and 1948, the population of Vilnius changed nearly totally. At war's end, the Jewish population of the city had been almost entirely murdered by the Nazis and thousands of Lithuanians had taken up residence there, but the city remained primarily Polish. According to NKVD figures, at the end of 1944 84,990 Poles and 7,958 Lithuanians lived in the city (which had a total population of 106,500—around half its population in 1939).[12] The Polish population of the city (though not of rural areas in the Lithuanian SSR) was almost entirely "repatriated" to Poland in the years 1944–1946, and thousands of Russians, Belorussians, Ukrainians, and Lithuanians moved into the city. In figures from 1951 we see the population of 195,000 divided fairly evenly between Russian, Lithuanians, and "others." Russians made up a third of the city's inhabitants (33.3 percent), followed closely by Lithuanians (30.8), and then Poles (21.2, mainly migrants from the rural areas around the city).[13] From 1951 onward, the Lithuanian percentage among the city's population would increase steadily.

Nationalizing Vilnius: Making the City "Our Own"

Having surveyed fluctuations in the city's population in a rather positivistic, statistical way, we may now turn to a more subjective (and, one hopes, more interesting) look at how individual national groups perceived the city as "their own." It is by now a banality in nationality studies that nations are not "born" but "created," essentially in the modern period under influences of European Romanticism (Johann Gottfried Herder), the French Revolution, and industrialization.[14] Without wanting to delve into the endless argument on the nature and timing of modern nationalism, using the example of Vilnius one can see clearly how individuals from each national group resident there used selective examples and strategic rhetoric to claim the city as theirs—if not theirs alone, then at least rightly belonging primarily to their ethnic-cultural group.

Poles had good reason to claim Wilno, as they called the city, for their own. During the nineteenth century, as far as we can tell from not-always-reliable statistics, their culture and language dominated in the city. As we have seen, Poles made up the largest Christian nationality in the city throughout the nineteenth century. In the first half of the nineteenth century, the appointed city government was made up mainly of Poles, and while over the decades Russian came to be used more and more in administration, before 1863 Polish was still quite prevalent.[15] High culture in the city, from schools to publishing to the theater, was mainly Polish. Even after the closing of the university after the uprising of 1831, the Polish language dominated in the city's (Gentile) cultural life, and Russian officials complained of its ubiquity even into the twentieth century.[16]

Churches and the Catholic hierarchy were overwhelmingly Polish, and until the last third of the nineteenth century, even when clerics were themselves of Lithuanian origin, their seminary training in many ways Polonized them. Even Motiejus Valančius (1801–1875), who spent the last 25 years of his life as bishop of Samogitia (the seat of his bishopric was Kaunas), often signed his letters "Wołonczewski" and was suspected of Polish sympathies by the Russian authorities after 1863.[17] Only in the first years of the twentieth century did young Lithuanian priests begin to insist on the use of their native language in prayers, songs, and sermons (the liturgy was, of course, in Latin).[18] This insistence led to clashes between Lithuanian and Polish speakers in churches, but these were limited mainly to the countryside, while Polish continued to dominate in Vilnius's churches.

The failed uprising of 1863 changed much in Vilnius and made the public use of Polish more difficult.[19] The Russian authorities did not give permission for the publication of Polish-language periodicals in the city until 1905. Still, despite these repressions, Poles continued to think of the city as "their own." More important than any specific existing reality was the myth of Polish Wilno. After all, this was where the Polish national poet, Adam Mickiewicz, had studied, published his first verses, and been involved in secret patriotic student groups, an involvement that led to his exile from the city in late 1824. But while Mickiewicz had never returned to his beloved city, his works did. In particular *Konrad Wallenrod* (1828),

Dziady (Forefathers' Eve, published in multiple parts throughout the 1820s up to1832), and *Pan Tadeusz* (1833–1834) are set in the poet's native "Litwa." *Dziady,* part III, presents a dramatic retelling of the investigation into secret student societies at Wilno University and the arrest of the young Polish idealists by the tyrannical Russian "Pan Senator" (N. Novosil'tsev). The combination of Polish Catholic culture, Polish language, and the cherished memory of Mickiewicz in the city came together in the myth of Polish Wilno, which in certain ways has survived to the present day.[20]

After the First World War, as we have seen, Vilnius came under Polish rule and the percentage of Poles in the city went up sharply, reaching for the first time in over a century (at least) an absolute majority. Even before the Germans withdrew from the city in late 1918 and early 1919, Poles were setting up schools and newspapers, and preparing the way for a reopening of the university, which, despite the chaotic political events of this period, occurred in autumn 1919.[21] During the next 20 years, the Polish authorities would make every effort to nurture the Polish character of the city. Even Czesław Miłosz describes the "city of his youth" as primarily Polish, mentioning Jews only in passing.[22] Indeed, as Lucy Dawidowicz mentions in her memoir of 1938–1939 in the city, Polish was increasingly common—at least as a second language—among the Jews of Vilnius by the late 1930s.[23]

In the nineteenth century, at least, the Russians also laid claim to the city. To be sure, they had a harder time of making a plausible case, given their small numbers in Vilnius and the obviously far greater present strength of Polish and Catholic culture. Thus Russians tended to take a different tack, emphasizing the past rather than the present. For example, a guide to "Russian Vilnius" published in 1865 consisted essentially of one Orthodox church after another, with the author noting at certain points that the church in question had been recently "returned" to Orthodoxy from the Uniates.[24] Here the general line runs that the city was *properly* Russian and that its present, unnatural Polish veneer (Jews disappear almost entirely in this discourse) needed to be "cleaned away" to reveal the true Russian and Orthodox nature of the city.[25] This Russian city was also celebrated in the monuments to Count Mikhail N. Murav'ev (known as the "hangman" for his vigorous suppression of the Polish "mutineers" in 1863–1865) and to Catherine the Great.[26] As the inscription on the latter monument read, "*Ottorzhennyia vozvratikh*"—"that which was torn away, now returned" (i.e., the originally Russian and Orthodox territory in which Vilnius is located, now "returned" to Russia along with the Polish partitions of the late eighteenth century).

Lithuanians had an even more difficult task in claiming Vilnius than the Russians. Not only were their numbers in the city small, they also lacked the political and military power that the Russians so manifestly enjoyed. Furthermore, until nearly the end of the nineteenth century Lithuanians were a mainly peasant people, with low levels of literacy and national identity. On top of all these disadvantages, from the mid-1860s the tsarist government had forbidden the printing of Lithuanian in Latin letters. This amounted to a total ban on publications in the language, as the mainly Catholic-clerical intelligentsia refused to consider using the Cyrillic alphabet for their language. And yet, from the beginnings of the Lithuanian national movement, Vilnius was claimed as the nation's capital. The reason for this was fairly simple: as a mainly rural people, the Lithuanians in the nineteenth century did not dominate in *any* city, though their numbers were greater in Kaunas (which was also situated in the middle of Lithuanian ethnic territory) than in Vilnius. But Kaunas lacked the historical importance of Vilnius, which, after all, had been founded by a demonstrably Lithuanian ruler as the capital of a Lithuanian state. By reinterpreting Gediminas and the medieval Lithuanian state as an *ethnic* entity, Lithuanian nationalists of the later nineteenth century laid claim to Vilnius as the past and future capital of their nation and (future) state.[27]

With the Lithuanian national movement committed to the idea of Vilnius as "their own," it was extremely important to establish at least a symbolic presence in the city. It is remarkable that despite their small numbers, Lithuanians had a daily paper in Vilnius before the Poles. To a great extent, this success and the appearance of *Vilniaus Žinios* from 10 December 1904 was the work of one man, the Lithuanian patriotic activist Petras Vileišis. Using his connections with the Russian bureaucracy—he had made a fortune as a successful engineer and builder within the Russian Empire—Vileišis convinced the local authorities to permit him to publish a daily newspaper in Vilnius. By mid-1905 periodicals were appearing not just in Lithuanian but in Yiddish and Polish as well, breaking the monopoly that the Russian language had held over the periodic press since the mid-1860s.[28] The second major event "laying claim" to Vilnius as the Lithuanian capital has already been mentioned in passing: the "Great Seimas" held in the city in late 1905. Bringing together representatives of the Lithuanian intelligentsia from throughout "Lithuania," the very presence of this gathering in Vilnius was a source of pride for this patriotic movement.[29]

Lithuanian claims on Vilnius were kept alive by the establishment of schools in that language in the city under German rule during the First World War, and it was not by chance that the Lithuanian declaration of independence was signed there on 16 February 1918. But all efforts by the newly-formed Lithuanian state to establish actual control over the city failed, and it was officially incorporated into Poland (over the fervent protests of Lithuania in the League of Nations) in 1922.[30] The Vilnius question would poison interwar Polish–Lithuanian relations; all constitutions of Lithuania claimed the city as its "real" capital (Kaunas being only the "provisional capital") and no diplomatic relations at all existed between the two countries until 1938.[31]

One remarkable feature shared by all of these national discourses claiming Vilnius is their near total silence regarding the city's Jewish population. While Russians and Lithuanians might refer to Poles (generally in the sense of "new arrivals" or the Polonized descendants of other ethnicities), Jews simply do not figure into their rhetoric. One may speculate as to why this should be so; I would suggest that while Poles were perceived as a real threat to Russian or Lithuanian claims for the city, Jews were not. Despite their numerical predominance and economic importance, Jews lacked political clout (past or present) and essentially resided on the periphery of Christian perceptions: present, but not "native." While Polish–Jewish relations in general deteriorated significantly between 1863 and 1914, this change was only marginally visible in Vilnius.[32] Only during and—especially—in the aftermath of World War I did antisemitic rhetoric (and action) become more prevalent.

Jewish Vilnius

As we have seen, Jews were a permanent presence in Vilnius from the late sixteenth century (1593), when King Sigmund III Vasa guaranteed their right to reside in the city.[33] As the Polish-Lithuanian Commonwealth declined in power during the subsequent two centuries, Jews suffered along with their Christian neighbors from economic dislocation, wars, and natural disasters like the frequent fires that periodically devastated the city. Vilnius was one of the largest Jewish communities in the region and a renowned center of Jewish learning. The most famous Jewish scholar of this period was Rabbi Eliahu ben Shlomo Zalman (1720–1797), the "Gaon"—"genius"—of Vilnius. The Gaon's fame and influence, both at the time and after his death, are all the more remarkable given his refusal to accept an official position (such as the head of a yeshivah) and the fact that he published almost nothing during his lifetime. His influence was apparently due to his brilliance as a scholar of Torah and Talmud, his exemplary moral character, and the position he assumed (in a sense, against his own will) as the figurehead of the struggle of the traditional Orthodoxy (the so-called *mitnagdim*) against the new, less scholarly, and for traditionalists alarmingly frivolous Hasidim.[34] The Gaon won the fight for Vilnius in the sense that Hasidism never gained a serious foothold in the city and indeed Lithuanian Jews ("Litvaks") retained into the twentieth century a reputation for scholarliness, tinged with humorlessness and lack of emotion.

The partitions changed little for Vilnius's Jewish community. Jews remained separate from their Christian neighbors in language, religion, and everyday life. To be sure, the Jewish domination of retail trade meant that Christians could not avoid some contact with Jewish neighbors. In any case, Jews were a constant presence in the city. A doctor and professor at Vilnius University, Joseph Frank, who arrived in the city from Vienna in October 1804, claimed that Jews made up one third of the city's total population (in fact the percentage was almost certainly higher) and described the city's Jewish residents as exotic but unhygienic. According to Frank, every noble house—including that of the bishop—had its *Żyd-faktor* or Jewish agent who would arrange every manner of commercial transaction.[35] Along similar lines, describing her youth in the 1820s among the wealthy Polish nobility, Gabrjela Puzynina z Güntherów noted that at a relative's lavish wedding, presents were given to peasants and Jews (presumably individuals connected with the household). She recalled sitting at her window, overlooking Niemiecka ("German") Street, watching Jewish funerals pass, and once even dancing with a certain Lewensztejn, a rich merchant from Riga, at a ball.[36] A few Jews also attended the mainly Polish Vilnius University, around 40 of them in the period up to 1824.[37] In other words, before the mid-nineteenth century Jews in Vilnius were at once ubiquitous and a curiosity (in particular when they ventured into Christian society).

Jews in the Russian Empire, as is well known, were subject to a number of legal disabilities. They could normally only reside in certain provinces (the so-called "Pale of Settlement"), could rarely obtain government employment, and in general were subject to harassment on the part of local authorities. While the long-held thesis that the tsarist government actively sponsored violence against Jews (pogroms) has largely been laid to rest, it remains clear that most tsarist officials—and indeed the tsars themselves—harbored judeophobic sentiments.[38] At the same time, from the 1860s—the era of the "Great Reforms"—more liberal sentiments were expressed within the Russian bureaucracy, seeing a gradual "rapprochement" between Russians and Jews as a possibility. While Jews in the Russian Empire received equal rights only after the Tsar's abdication in early 1917, in the 1860s various exceptions were made to allow some groups of Jews more freedom of movement and educational opportunity. Thus Jews with specific skills or education (including, for example, university students and those learning specific crafts) could reside outside the Pale of Settlement. More broadly, the Russian government set up schools aimed to teach Jews Russian and thereby integrate them into Russian society. Still, as Irvin Aronson has shown, in the 1880s attitudes toward the possibility of integrating Jews into Russian society within the bureaucracy remained at best ambiguous.[39]

Vilnius was of course located within the Pale and Jews could legally reside there. As the major town of the so-called "Northwest Provinces," it also served as the testing ground for Russian–Jewish rapprochement (or, more precisely, for bringing Jews into the Russian mainstream). In 1847 a state rabbinical school was set up in Vilnius with two main purposes: to provide Russian-speaking teachers for state Jewish schools and to provide crown rabbis (which the Russian authorities required of each Jewish community). In the second respect this school was a dismal failure: not a single graduate was accepted by a community as their rabbi. Most Jews in the region regarded the graduates as suspect in their religious and ritual observance and perhaps even government agents aiming to convert Jews to Orthodoxy. On the other hand, the school was more successful in spreading Russian among Vilnius Jews and even helping to create a Russian-speaking Jewish intelligentsia in the city. When the Rabbinical School was closed in 1873, it was transformed into a teachers' seminary which functioned to the end of the tsarist period.[40]

For Vilnius and its region, the most important event of the 1860s was not the Russian Great Reforms but the Polish (or Polish-Lithuanian) Insurrection that exploded in November 1863, partly in response to Tsar Alexander II's reform efforts. The insurrection was violently suppressed, and in Vilnius the figure of Count Mikhail N. Murav'ev, who did not shy from hanging priests to "encourage the others," exemplified the cruelty and brutality of Russian rule for Poles and Lithuanians. Murav'ev left Vilnius in 1866 but his spirit remained in place to the end of Russian rule; in 1898 a monument in his honor was erected in the city center. Obviously, Poles and Lithuanians, who had participated actively in the anti-Russian insurrection, saw the post-1863 period as one of brutal and unjust Russification. But what about Jews? First of all, it should be remembered that throughout the insurrection Vilnius remained firmly in government hands, a source of some embarrassment to Polish patriots later on.[41] As for Jews, some did side with the rebels against the Russian authorities but most simply tried to keep out of a struggle that did not concern them.[42] It is interesting to note that on the whole Murav'ev was less hostile toward Jews than toward Poles and even thought that Jews could be used as an ally and russifying element.[43] In the aftermath of the 1863 uprising, John Klier has argued that many among the Jewish intelligentsia in the western provinces (which of course included Vilnius) welcomed "Russification" as an opportunity to become fully-appreciated Russian citizens, at least in the long run.[44] It must be admitted, however, that even into the twentieth century, the great majority of Vilnius Jews remained religious, traditional, and Yiddish-speaking.

The pogroms that swept the Ukrainian provinces of the Russian Empire (and, at the end of the year, Warsaw) in 1881 did not spread to the Northwest Provinces of which Vilnius was the main city.[45] One possible factor in preventing the spread of pogroms to this region might have been the energetic response of Vilnius Governor-General Count Eduard Ivanovich Totleben. Upon learning of pogroms in the south in April 1881, Totleben dispatched orders to military and civilian authorities warning them to take all possible measures to prevent any clashes between Christians and Jews. A circular of 6 May 1881 to the governors of Vilna, Kovno, and Grodno provinces clearly stated measures to be taken. First, all false rumors and agitation among the people were to be "vigilantly pursued"; authorities were to pay "painstaking attention" to "unknown individuals." If a disturbance broke out, local authorities were ordered to suppress it immediately and inform local military units. If need be, these military units were to aid civilian authorities in re-establishing order.[46] The correspondence between Totleben, local authorities, and the Ministry of the Interior in Petersburg show that all were concerned with maintaining public order. In the end, despite alarming rumors and fears, Vilnius's Jewish community was spared.

A unique witness to the situation of Jewish Vilnius was Dr. I. Rülf, a rabbi from Memel who visited the city in late summer 1881. Disturbed by news of pogroms in the south and suspicious of the anti-Jewish attitude of the Minister of the Interior, N. P. Ignatiev, Rülf decided to visit Russia himself and spent a bit over a week in Vilnius and Minsk. As an acculturated but religiously Orthodox German Jew, Rabbi Rülf felt both alienated from and attracted to Vilnius's Jewish population. His commentary alternates between condescension, affection, and a sense of superior protectiveness.

On his first day in the city, Rülf rose early and set off for the main synagogue. Walking from "German Street" where his Jewish-owned hotel was located, he remarked that the court of the synagogue (*Schulhof*) took up a large area "cut through with different irregular streets running hither and thither, badly paved and not entirely clean." Houses crowded the street, some containing apartments and others housing different charities and associations (*khevros*). Each association had its own prayer house (*beyt midrash / kloyz*).[47] After breakfast at his hotel, Rülf received a guided visit to the city's charitable institutions (Talmud Torah, hospital, clinic, old folk's home) from the state rabbi, Dr. A. Gordon. Despite the large number of charities, the streets abounded in beggars, crying *zedoko tazil mimowes* (in Rülf's transcription: "charity saves from death"). Even on shabbes beggars were busy—though on this day accepting alms in the form of bread.[48]

Rülf noted that the Jewish community in Vilnius was not unified. Dozens of prayer houses and small synagogues existed, practically one for each Jewish association (*khevrah*), with only the Great Synagogue and the cemetery uniting all. Vilnius lacked a chief rabbi, though it did have a crown rabbi, Dr. A. Gordon. Most Jews did not consider such rabbis, trained at state institutions, their true spiritual leaders, but they depended on crown rabbis to carry out many functions, such as performing marriage ceremonies. Several different rabbinical courts existed in the city, each with its own "clientele." As the abundance of beggars suggests, most Jews in Vilnius were far from prosperous. Entire streets were lined with tiny Jewish shops, all competing with each other for their daily bread. Jewish artisans and workers were also prevalent in the city, and many artisans personally sold the goods they made.[49]

Rülf praised the "deep piety" (*Herzensfrömmigkeit*) of the Vilnius Jews. Rabbis and their families enjoyed great respect in the community. Unlike many traditional Orthodox Jews, however, the Vilners were "tolerant to the highest degree." Rülf noted that the process of acculturation had made some inroads in Vilnius. Most of the youth could at least understand Russian, and graduates of the state Rabbinical School and other state Jewish schools formed a small but growing Russian-speaking Jewish elite. Unfortunately, from the point of view of traditional Jews and the Russian authorities alike, the presence of radical ideas could be discerned among the younger generation. While admitting that among younger Jews there were some "nihilists," Rülf suggested that Vilnius's Jews would soon be patriotic Russian citizens, if only the government would change its ways. Along these lines Rülf remarked that Governor-General Todleben was known as a "order-loving, decisive, and just" administrator: "a real German man" (*ein wahrhaft deutscher Mann*).[50] Obviously, here was a model for less enlightened Russian administrators to emulate.

The spread of both Russian and radical ideas among Vilnius's Jews noted by Rabbi Rülf would increase in the next decades. In 1897 the Jewish Bund, the first Jewish party combining national (Yiddish) ideology and socialism, would be founded in the city. Five years later, the artisan and Bund sympathizer Hirsh Lekert shot at and wounded the city's governor-general, Victor von Wahl and was executed, thereby becoming a major Bund martyr.[51] At the same time, more affluent Jews who were likely to speak Russian at home or at least in their business dealings banded together to build the opulent "Choral Synagogue" which opened in 1903. The synagogue, the only one that has survived to the present day, was significantly located just outside the traditional Jewish district on the edge of the mainly Russian "new town," where more affluent and acculturated Jews tended to take up residence.[52] In the same year as the Choral Synagogue's opening, Theodor Herzl visited the city to the great jubilation of the local Jewish community.[53] And yet, for all the sympathy among the Jewish community for socialism and various forms of Jewish nationalism, the Russian governor of Vilna Province could still write in his 1903 report that if treated properly, the Jews could form a bulwark for Russian culture and patriotism in the city.[54] Thus as the new century dawned, the Vilnius Jewish community remained traditional in its majority, but also exhibited a number of diverse modern tendencies, from socialism to nationalism to acculturation.

All of these tendencies strengthened and accelerated in the decade before World War I. Jews were prominent among the demonstrators—and victims—of the strikes and police repressions that occurred during the turbulent year 1905.[55] Even after the tsarist regime had crushed or driven the revolutionary forces underground, the political landscape had already changed radically. For one thing, censorship was now considerably lightened, enabling a lively Polish and Yiddish press to arise in the city. Secondly, elections to the newly created legislature, the Duma, sharpened ethnic conflict as voting increasingly fell along ethnic lines. In 1906, the Zionist Shmariahu Levin succeeded in being elected to the first Duma with the help of the liberal Kadet party,[56] but no Jew was sent from the city or province of Vilnius to the remaining three Dumas (1907–1917). At the same time, relations between Poles and Jews became increasingly strained, the Poles often accusing (with some justice) their Jewish neighbors of not supporting the Polish national cause.[57] On the eve of World War I, the diverse national groups in Vilnius were aware of each other as seldom before, but this awareness exhibited itself more in friction (Polish–Russian, Polish–Lithuanian, Polish–Jewish) than in harmony.

The First World War was a disaster for all inhabitants of Vilnius, but hit the Jews hardest of all. During the war's first year, still under Russian rule, the economy was severely disrupted, with an especially negative impact on traders, artisans, and small merchants—mainly Jews in Vilnius. The Russian army's open suspicion of Jews as potential spies and the evacuation of many thousands of Jews to the Russian interior further disrupted life and strained relations with non-Jews. The fact that Russian officials were issuing these evacuation orders and specifically targeting Jews fanned accusations of antisemitism. In late summer 1915, with the fall of Kovno (Kaunas), Vilnius Jews lived in terror that they too would be forced to leave their homes. The rapid German advance may have prevented this tragedy.[58]

By chance, the Russians pulled out of Vilnius on the eve of the most important holiday in the Jewish calendar, Yom Kippur. Hirsz Abramowicz described the final day of Russian rule in this way:

> Almost no one had a thought of attending Kol Nidrei services. People were afraid to appear in the streets. . . . Everyone was so fed up with the persecution, libelous attacks, and high inflation that nearly all of Vilna wished to be rid of the Russians. . . . After midnight on . . . 17 September everything was closed tight. . . . The night passed almost without . . . incident, except for the fear generated by the terrible explosions when bridges and other military targets were demolished.[59]

While the Germans were welcomed into Vilnius, their entry did not improve conditions. In fact, as Abramowicz recounts, the German desire to control all economic transactions and their confiscations of everything from horses to grain to fruit from orchards further impoverished the local population. While German cultural and political policy was on the whole benevolent or at least neutral toward Jews, their economic measures were devastating. By 1917 most of Vilnius's inhabitants were going hungry.[60] Mortality rates shot up, especially among the youngest and oldest parts of the population.[61] Banditry increased, and it appeared that all semblance of law and order was breaking down. The German authorities seemed entirely incapable of dealing with the situation and matters were made worse by the terrible harvest of 1916–1917. At the very least, Vilnius had hoped that the Germans would succeed in maintaining order, but by late 1917 and 1918 chaos and lawlessness gave the lie to any pretense of German *Ordnung*.[62] Despite the Russian Revolution and harsh Treaty of Brest-Litovsk in spring 1918, life did not improve in the city. The German capitulation of November 1918 translated into chaos in Vilnius; during the next two years control over the city passed from Lithuanians to Soviets to Poles to Soviets and finally back to the Poles.

The end of the war brought no respite for the suffering population of Vilnius. Khaykl Lunski described 1919 as a year of epidemics and famine, even worse than the war years. In 1914, Lunski noted, one often heard cries and weeping, but by 1919 the misery and exhaustion was so great that no one could even cry any more.[63] Hirsz Abramowicz describes almost total desolation under Soviet rule in April 1919: "Hunger was pervasive. It was against the law to buy or sell anything. . . . Bread was difficult to find and a bowl of plain soup was also a rarity. . . . [A]nyone who was able to do so fled Vilnius."[64] The Polish seizure of the city from the Bolsheviks in April 1919 was accompanied by a pogrom in which dozens were killed.[65] Worse yet, in the long run, was the Polish (and later Lithuanian) identification of the Jewish population with the Bolsheviks and communist rule.

When General Lucjan Żeligowski took the city from the Bolsheviks in October 1920 and declared the state of "Middle Lithuania" (Litwa Środkowa), Jews had mixed feelings. On the one hand, Żeligowski's troops were relatively well-behaved and the general himself refrained from anti-Jewish statements. On the other hand, Vilnius' Jewish community feared for its future within a nationalist Polish state, which was clearly the direction in which Żeligowski was leading "Middle Lithuania." Jews, along with Belorussians and Lithuanians, did not participate in the elections to the Diet (Sejm) that, as all had expected, declared that "Middle Lithuania" was an integral part of the Polish Republic. Thus *de facto* from 1920 and *de jure* from 1925 Vilnius became a provincial city on the far northeast edge of Poland.[66]

Interwar Vilnius was a city both economically depressed and culturally vibrant. Jews were an integral part of the cultural ferment here, whether at the university, as pioneering scholars in the Yiddish language, writing poetry, plays, and fiction in modern Hebrew and Yiddish, or continuing the religious-scholarly tradition of the Gaon. Jewish students made up a significant percentage of those studying (in Polish) at Uniwersytet Stefana Batorego (USB), leading to calls as early as 1922 for a *numerus clausus* limiting Jewish enrollments.[67] In fact, the percentage of Jews enrolled at USB grew quite steadily until the 1930–1931 academic year (1,192 students or 35.5 percent of total enrollment) and thereafter fell off rapidly, down to only 400 Jewish students in 1938–1939.[68] Jews also ran not one but several school systems alongside the official Polish one.[69] Well over a dozen dailies and many more weekly and monthly periodicals were published in Yiddish, Hebrew, and Polish.[70] Yiddish theater and literature also prospered, perhaps most famously in the literary movement *Yung Vilne*.[71]

The stature of Vilnius as a center of Jewish—and especially Yiddish—culture certainly influenced the decision to locate the Jewish/Yiddish Scientific Organization—YIVO—there in 1925.[72] It is no accident that YIVO's founding year also saw the opening of the Hebrew University of Jerusalem, the first modern university using the Hebrew language in instruction. YIVO's dual nature and scholarly mission was reflected in first word in its title—both "Yiddish" and "Jewish." The institute aimed both to further Jewish learning (though in a mainly secular, modern spirit) and to do this in Yiddish. Linguistic, historical, sociological, and ethnographic research were encouraged and fostered by YIVO. The institute also published various monographs and scholarly journals. After World War II, YIVO continued its existence in New York.

The German writer Alfred Döblin visited Vilnius (and other Polish cities) in the mid-1920s and described the city's agitated, uneasy atmosphere. The newspapers, Döblin noted, were full of stories of Bolshevik plots and attacks by bandits. Passing a cinema, he noted that its advertisements were in both Polish and Yiddish. Throughout the city Döblin observed Yiddish signs, but noted that Vilnius's Jews were clad not in traditional kaftans but in European clothing. "All of them [dressed] European and yet—speaking no Polish. This is another kind of Jew from Warsaw."[73] Döblin visited the Jewish quarter, admired the heritage of the Gaon, met with both sides of the "Hebrew–Yiddish language battle." Even as some children were being taught in Hebrew and others in Yiddish, yet others learned their lessons in Polish, he recorded.[74] Döblin's account was purposely fragmentary and anecdotal, offering a series of images without detailed commentary, reaching no conclusion. One thing, however, remained clear: Vilnius's Jewish community under Polish rule was diverse: politically divided (Bund, Zionists, Socialists, etc.), using various languages, following Jewish religious law to varying degrees, attempting to eke out a living in a variety of ways, trying to survive in an unfavorable political and economic situation.

A 1931 article by a Jewish economist spoke of the "downfall of a Jewish city," referring to Vilnius. Tracing this economic decline from the devastations of World War I, Jakob Lestschinski pointed out that Jewish businesses in the city had shrunk by at least one third. For certain professions, such as tailors and seamstresses, the job loses were almost double (compared to 1914). The situation was hardly better among shoe and stocking manufacturers. The reasons for this extreme economic shrinkage were many. For one thing, the Polish government favored ethnic Polish artisans and businessmen, giving them cheap bank credits and encouraging Polish civil servants to patronize them.[75] Even more important, Vilnius was now an isolated outpost, cut off from trade with Lithuania and from the USSR alike. Given the generally backward condition of the Polish economy, Vilnius's peripheral position in the state only worsened its economic woes. For Jews, the general economic malaise was exacerbated by the fact that the Polish state almost entirely excluded non-Poles from government jobs. Thus in Vilnius in 1931 a single Jew worked in the state post and telegraph office (among almost one thousand employees) and only eight for the state railroad (of 2,883). In state administrative offices, schools, courts, and the like, the situation was only marginally better. The worsening economic situation may be gauged by the fact that in 1938, nearly half of the Jews in Vilnius applied for relief at Passover.[76]

In the 1930s, relations between Poles and Jews deteriorated. In particular, university students affiliated with the National Democrats (known as ND, or Endek) seem to have been among the leaders of the antisemitic movement. At the beginning of the 1931–1932 academic year the Endek student organization organized attacks on Jewish students throughout Poland, including Vilnius. Starting on November 8, 1931 these antisemitic activists prevented Jewish students from entering the university. Two days later a scuffle between the antisemites and Jewish students led to the death of the Pole Stanisław Wacławski. One Jewish student, Szmuel Wulfin, was sentenced to two years' imprisonment for participating in the stone-throwing that led to Wacławski's death.[77] After these incidents the Endek students demanded that Jews be segregated from Polish students and obliged to sit on separate benches on the left-hand side of lecture halls.

From the mid-1930s, amidst increasing economic misery and mounting political instability, antisemitism became ever more prevalent. The economic boycott campaign that had simmered from the 1880s gained strength as Jewish businesses found it harder and harder to stay afloat.[78] At the same time government measures against the Jews increased, including laws restricting and ultimately forbidding entirely kosher butcheries. Jews strolling in the city parks were attacked by antisemitic thugs and Jewish vacationers on the outskirts of the city were subjected to similar indignities.[79] The Polish government did not condone physical attacks on Jews, though it must be admitted that anti-Jewish policies created an atmosphere propitious to anti-Jewish violence. The official line after 1935 may be summed up in the words of a prominent politician, General Stanisław Skwarczyński, in 1938: "[Jews] pose an obstacle to the normal evolution of the masses of the Polish nation"; hence the Polish government should seek "a radical decrease in the number of Jews in Poland."[80] This reduction in Poland's Jewish population was sought primarily through emigration but by the later 1930s very few possibilities for legal emigration existed.[81]

In fairness it must be said that there were Poles who protested the short-sighted chauvinism of their government at the time, but one cannot deny that by the late 1930s many Polish Jews—including those in Vilnius—found it difficult to be optimistic about their future in the Polish state. On the other hand, emigration did continue—including to Soviet Birobidzhan and illegally to Palestine.[82] And life went on despite all difficulties. In the 1930s still around one quarter of the city's population was Jewish, running their own schools, publishing a number of newspapers and journals, writing poetry in a number of languages, producing plays in Yiddish (and, occasionally, in Hebrew). For all the difficulties and economic dislocation of the late 1930s, Jewish Vilnius was still full of life.

A unique witness of the last "normal" year of Jewish Vilnius comes from the American Yiddishist and historian Lucy Dawidowicz. Coming from New York, Dawidowicz spent the academic year 1938–1939 at YIVO in Vilnius, leaving the city only as war loomed on 24 August 1939. She describes a Vilnius in which observant, traditional Jews no longer dominated. In her words, "the upholders of the Gaon's tradition were embattled, even if they did not yet consider themselves beleaguered."[83] Middle-class Jews in Vilnius were generally bilingual, though perhaps speaking Polish with a Yiddish accent. The Jewish "upper crust" tended to speak Russian at home, considering that language and culture superior to either Polish or Yiddish.[84] Most Vilnius Jews in 1938 were trying to adapt to the modern world, "in search of ways to reconcile their dual identity as Jews and as Poles," in Dawidowicz's words.[85] Once can certainly dispute Dawidowicz's account as that of an outsider, but the contemporary photographs of Jewish groups included in Leyzer Ran's monumental *Jerusalem of Lithuania* seem to corroborate her words: aside from a few religious leaders, men are usually clean-shaven, dressed in jacket and tie; women wear frocks or skirts and blouses that exactly resemble those of their Polish contemporaries.[86] Vilnius's Jews were rapidly becoming Europeanized, more closely resembling their Christian neighbors in outward appearance and language.

The terrible events of the years 1939–1947 essentially emptied Vilnius of its original population. The Lithuanians finally received "their capital" from Soviet forces in October 1939 and rapidly began to Lithuanianize the city, closing the Polish university and dismissing Polish policemen, teachers, and other city employees. The initial Lithuanian government (1939–1940) did not, however, institute any anti-Jewish measures and indeed tended to see Jews as possible allies against the dominant Poles. The process of Lithuanization continued, though perhaps in somewhat more muted form, under Soviet (1940–June 1941) and Nazi (June 1941–July 1944) rule. While many ethnic Lithuanians suffered under initial Soviet rule, more Poles and Jews both in absolute terms and per capita were arrested, in particular because they were more likely than Lithuanians to belong to "suspect social classes" (capitalists, professionals) and to have political pasts (essentially, with any Polish or Jewish party) deemed threatening by the Soviet authorities.[87]

Violence against the city's Jews began with Hitler's attack on the USSR. Despite Lithuanian hopes for the return of independence or at least autonomy, the Germans refused to allow them more than a symbolic role in ruling Vilnius. At the same time, Lithuanians were allowed a privileged place in the Nazi racial and political hierarchy, above Poles and of course Jews. Still, the Germans made abundantly clear—astonishingly clear considering their own military objectives—their contempt for all local peoples and their regard of them merely as tools and servants for Nazi domination.[88]

Vilnius' Jewish community was of course in a category by themselves, slated for rapid liquidation. In September 1941, not three months after the entry of the Germans into the city, all Jews were forced into a ghetto. The Jewish population was reduced by hunger and systematic persecutions, and the ghetto was finally liquidated with most of its residents in September 1943.[89] When the Red Army liberated Vilnius in July 1944, only a handful of Jews had survived in hiding, and most subsequently left the city. Most of the Polish population had survived the war but were "repatriated" to Poland in the years 1944–1946.[90] By the late 1940s, Vilnius was again a multiethnic city, but one inhabited nearly completely by newcomers, and at least officially Lithuanian and Soviet. Postwar construction—and rhetoric—would emphasize the city's Lithuanian character and slight the city's Jewish and Polish pasts.[91]

Conclusion

The history of Vilnius as a multiethnic, multicultural city can be interpreted in different ways. It is tempting to see the centuries of coexistence in the city of diverse nationalities and religions as proof of the human ability to live in harmony with cultural difference. But another, rather darker, interpretation is possible. In particular, looking at the course of ethnic-religious relations in the first half of the twentieth century, one can discern a human tendency toward cultural uniformity, even if this means repressing, exiling, or murdering one's neighbors. Obviously neither this bleakly pessimistic nor the sunny "multicultural" explanation does justice to the complexities of human interaction and the role that ethnic/religious/linguistic difference plays in human relations. Looking at multiethnic Vilnius over a century and a half, one witnesses both interest, ignorance, and hatred applied to national "others." In the twentieth century, the tendency of political ideologies and groupings to "play the ethnic card" reduced toleration and exacerbated conflict. But we cannot forget that an outside force—the Nazis—took this conflict to its most murderous conclusion. While it is not possible honestly to portray multiethnic Vilnius as an example of mutual respect and toleration over the centuries, the passing of the city's cultural and human diversity represents a loss that perhaps only now we are beginning to appreciate.

Notes

1. In this paper, for the sake of simplicity and with apologies for the anachronism, I will refer to the city as "Vilnius." Obviously this does not mean any recognition of Lithuanian "claims" to the city in this period.

2. For more on Polish–Jewish relations in particular in the Russian partition, see Theodore R. Weeks, *From Assimilation to Antisemitism: The "Jewish Question" in Poland, 1850–1914* (DeKalb: Northern Illinois University Press, 2006).

3. On ethnic/religious diversity in the sixteenth and seventeenth centuries in Vilnius, see David Frick, "The Bells of Vilnius: Keeping Time in a City of Many Calendars" in *Making Contact: Maps, Identity, and Travel* (Edmonton, Canada: University of Alberta Press, 2003), 23–59.

4. According to Klausner, legend has it that the Jewish cemetery in Vilnius was founded in 1487, but the first concrete historical records from it date from a century later. Israel Klausner, *Korot bet ha'almin ha'yasan beVilnah* (Vilno: Hevrah l'historiah v'etnografiah a"sh Sh. An-ski, 1935 [5695 in the Jewish calendar]).

5. Israel Klausner, *Yerushalayim deLita: dorot rishonim, 1495–1881* (Tel Aviv: Bet lohame ha'getaot, 1988).

6. Algė Jankevičienė, *Vilniaus Didžiojo Sinagoga = Great Synagogue of Vilnius* (Vilnius: Savastis, 1996).

7. Theodore R. Weeks, "Population Politics in Vilnius 1944–1947: A Case Study of State-Sponsored Ethnic Cleansing," *Post-Soviet Affairs* 23(1) (2007): 76–95.

8. Michał Baliński, *Opisanie statystyczne miasta Wilna* (Vilnius: Józef Zawadzki własnym nakładem, 1835), 59–61, 153. The exact figures were: Clericals, 523 men and 188 women; *szlachta,* 3,289 and 3,369; *mieszczanie,* 2,424 and 2,506; serfs, 152 and 167; Jews, 10,040 and 10,606.

9. Juozas Jurginis, V. Merkys, et al., *Vilniaus miesto istorija nuo Spalio revolucijos iki dabartinių dienų* (Vilnius: Mintis, 1972), 304.

10. Petras Ruseckas, ed., *Lietuva Didžiajame Kare* (Vilnius: Vilniaus žodis, 1939), 16–23.

11. *Rocznik statystyczny Wilna 1937* (Vilnius: Skład Główny w centralnym biurze statystycznym m. Wilna, 1939), 9.

12. Stanisława Lewandowska, *Życie codzienne Wilna w latach II wojny światowej* (Warsaw: Wydawnictwo Neriton, 1997), 326. Slightly different figures are given after a registration in the city of Vilnius that took place from 14 August to 6 September 1944: 6,897 Lithuanians, 7,363 Russians, 81,966 Poles, 1,160 Jews, 419 Ukrainian, 1,261 Belarusians, and 269 "other nationalities" for a total of 99,335 persons. Lietuvos Centrinis Valstybinės Archyvas, Vilnius (LCVA), f. R754, ap. 13, b. 21, l. 40.

13. Jurginis et al., *Vilniaus miesto istorija,* 249.

14. For some of the classics of the study of nation/nationalism, see Ernest Gellner, *Nations and Nationalism* (Ithaca, N.Y.: Cornell University Press, 1983); Perry Anderson, *Imagined Communities: Reflections on the Origin and Spread of Nationalism* (London: Verso, 1991); Eric Hobsbawm and Terence Ranger, eds., *The Invention of Tradition* (Cambridge: Cambridge University Press, 1992).

15. See the hundreds of files on the Vilnius city magistrate and duma at Lietuvos Valstybinis Istorijos Archyvas, Vilnius (LVIA) in fondas 458 and fondas 937, respectively.

16. Małgorzata Stolzman, *Nigdy od ciebie miasto . . . Dzieje kultury wileńskiej lat międzypowstaniowych (1832–1863)* (Olsztyn, Poland: Pojezierze, 1987).

17. On this fascinating figure, see Vytautas Merkys, *Motiejus Valančius. Tarp katalikiškojo universalizmo ir tautiškumo* (Vilnius: Mintis, 1999).

18. For example, the "Great Seimas" held in Vilnius in late 1905 stated its support for those who struggled for Lithuanian in Catholic churches. "Pirmojo Lietuvių Tautos Atstovų susivažiavimo

nutarimai," *Vilniaus žinios* 1(276) (24 November/7 December 1905), 1–2. For a translation of these decisions, see Jonas Dainauskas, "Prelude to Independence: The Great Conference of Vilnius, 1905" *Lituanus* 11(4) (Winter 1965), 56–57.

19. Wanda Dobaczewska, *Wilno i Wilenszczyzna w latach 1863–1914. Dzieje ruchów społecznych i politycznych* (Vilnius: Nakład "Dziennik Urzędowy Kuratorium Okr. Szk. Wileńskiego," 1938).

20. For example, even in the very helpful conference articles collected by Elżbieta Feliksiak, Polish Wilno is described in loving detail while other nationalities, though not entirely neglected, receive far less attention. See, for example, E. Felisiak, ed., *Wilno-Wileńszczyzna jako krajobraz i środowisko wielu kultur* (Białystok, Poland: Towarzystwo Literackie im. Adama Mickiewicza, 1992), 4 vols.

21. Piotr Łossowski, *Konflikt polsko-litewski* (Warsaw: Książka i wiedza, 1996), 104–107.

22. Czesław Miłosz, *Native Realm* (London: Sidgwick & Jackson, 1981), 54–68. See also the section on Wilno in Czesław Miłosz, *Zaczynając od moich ulic* (Paris: Instytut Literacki, 1985).

23. Lucy Dawidowicz, *From that Place and Time: A Memoir 1938–1947* (New York: Bantam Books, 1989), 117.

24. *Russkaia Vil'na. Prilozhenie k puteshestviiu po sv. mestam russkim* (Vilnius: A. Syrkin, 1865).

25. See, for example, N. Batiushkov, *Belorussia i Litva* (St. Petersburg: Obshcestvennaia pol'za, 1890); I. Kornilov, *Russkoe delo v Severo-zapadnom krae* (St. Petersburg: A. S. Suvorin, 1908); and A. I. Milovidov, *K 50-letiiu russkoi Vil'ny* (Vilnius: "Russkii pochin," 1914).

26. Theodore R. Weeks, "Monuments and Memory: Immortalizing Count M. N. Muraviev in Vilna, 1898," *Nationalities Papers,* vol. 27, no. 4 (December 1999), 551–64.

27. On the medieval Lithuanian state, see S. C. Rowell, *Lithuania Ascending: A Pagan Empire within East-Central Europe, 1295–1345* (Cambridge: Cambridge University Press, 1994), and in particular about the early years of Vilnius, 67–73.

28. See, for example, the proliferation of titles—to be sure, often short-lived—listed in Jadvyga Kazlauskaitė, ed., *Vilniaus lietuvių periodiniai leidiniai 1904–1940* (Vilnius: LTSR Liaudies Švietimo Ministerija, 1988). Despite the title, this helpful bibliography includes titles in a variety of languages. See also, by the same author, *Vilniaus periodiniai leidiniai 1760–1918* (Vilnius: Mintis, 1988). On the Jewish press, see Susanne Marten-Finnis, *Vilna as a Centre of the Modern Jewish Press, 1840–1928: Aspirations, Challenges, and Progress* (Bern, Switzerland: Peter Lang, 2004).

29. Egidijus Motieka, *Didysis Vilniaus seimas* (Vilnius: Saulabolis, 1996); for the memoirs of a participant and major figure in the Lithuanian national movement, see Jonas Basanavičius (J. S-lius, pseud.), *Iš didžiojo Vilniaus Seimo istorijos* (Vilnius: "Ruch," 1925).

30. Piotr Łossowski, *Konflikt polsko-litewski 1918–1920* (Warsaw: Książka i Wiedza, 1996); Alfred E. Senn, *The Great Powers, Lithuania, and the Vilna Question 1920–1928* (Leiden, Netherlands: Brill, 1966).

31. A marvelous source for popular depictions of the Polish–Lithuanian conflict is Krzysztof Buchowski, *Panowie ir žmogusy. Stosunki polsko-litewskie w międzywojennych karykaturach* (Białystok, Poland: Instytut Historii Uniwersytetu, 2004). For a more sober diplomatic history: Piotr Łossowski, *Stosunki polsko-litewskie 1921–1939* (Warsaw: Instytut Historii PAN, 1997).

32. Weeks, *Assimilation to Antisemitism.*

33. Henri Minczeles, *Vilna, Wilno, Vilnius: La Jérusalem de Lituanie* (Paris: Éditions la Découverte, 1993), 35.

34. On these two major figures of eighteenth-century Jewish life, see Murray Jay ("Moshe") Rosman, *Founder of Hasidism: A Quest for the Historical Ba'al Shem Tov* (Berkeley: University of California Press, 1996); and Immanuel Etkes, *The Gaon of Vilna: The Man and his Image* (Berkeley: University of California Press, 2002).

35. Dr. Józef Frank, *Pamiętniki,* vol. 1 (Vilnius: Księgarnia Stowar. Naucz. Polskiego, 1921): 44–50.

36. Gabrjela Puzynina z Güntherów, *W Wilnie i w dworach litewskich. Pamiętnik z lat 1815–1843* (Krakow: Krajowa Agecja Wydawnicza, 1990 [originally published in Vilnius in 1928]), 44, 69, 201.

37. Klausner, *Yerushalayim deLita: dorot rishonim,* 134; Pinchas Kon, *Dawny Uniwersytet Wileński a Żydzi. Zabiegi uniwersytetu o utworzenie szkoły początkowej dla żydów w Wilnie w latach 1808–1820* (Vilnius: "Lux," 1926).

38. On pogroms in Russia and possible government participation in them, see the articles collected in Hans Rogger, *Jewish Policies and Right-Wing Politics in Imperial Russia* (Berkeley: University of California Press, 1986); and John D. Klier and Shlomo Lambroza, eds., *Pogroms: Anti-Jewish Violence in Modern Russian History* (Cambridge: Cambridge University Press, 1992).

39. Irvin Michael Aronson, "The Attitudes of Russian Officials in the 1880s toward Jewish Assimilation and Emigration" *Slavic Review* 34(1) (1975): 1–18; idem, "Russian Commissions on the Jewish Question in the 1880s" *East European Quarterly* 14 (1980): 59–74.

40. Verena Dohrn, "Das Rabbinerseminar in Wilna (1847–1873). Zur Geschichte der ersten staatlichen höheren Schule für Juden im Russischen Reich," *Jahrbücher für Geschichte Osteuropas* 45(3): 379–401; Klausner, *Yerushalayim deLita: dorot rishonim,* 330–46.

41. In general on the 1863 uprising in the region, see Dawid Fajnhauz, *1863. Litwa i Białoruś* (Warsaw: Instytut Historii PAN, 1999); A. Krzyszkowska, *Powstanie styczniowe na Wileńszczyźnie* (Vilnius: "Lux," 1934); Vida Girinkienė, ed., *1863–1864 metai Lietuvoje. Straipsniai ir dokumentai* (Kaunas: Šviesa, 1991).

42. Dawid Fajnhauz, "Ludność żydowska na Lićtwie i Białorusi a powstanie styczniowe," *Biuletyn ŻIH,* nos. 37–38 (1961): 3–34, 39–68.

43. O. N. Shteinberg, "Graf M. N. Murav'ev i ego otnosheniia k evreiiam g. Vil'ny v 1863–1864 gg," *Russkaia starina* 32(2) (1901): 305–320.

44. John Klier, "The Polish Revolt of 1863 and the Birth of Russification: Bad for the Jews?" *Polin* 1 (1986): 96–110.

45. It should be remembered that for all the violence and property damage caused by the 1881 pogroms, the number of deaths could be counted on one hand. I. Michael Aronson, "Geographical and Socioeconomic Factors in the 1881 Anti-Jewish Pogroms in Russia" *Russian Review* 39(1) (1980), 18–31; Omeljan Pritsak, "The Pogroms of 1881," *Harvard Ukrainian Studies* 11(1–2) (1987): 8–43. Semen M. Dubno and G. Ia. Krasnyi-Admoni, eds., *Materialy dlia istorii antievreiskikh pogromov v Rossii* (Petrograd, 1919–1923), 2 vols., must be used with caution as the editors take for granted that the government was behind the violence.

46. LVIA, f. 378, PS 1881, b. 52, ll. 10–13.

47. Dr. I. Rülf, *Drei Tage in Jüdisch-Russland. Ein Cultur- und Sittenbild* (Frankfurt am Main: Verlag von J. Kauffmann, 1882), 4–6.

48. Ibid., 10–24.

49. Ibid., 26–43. Other sources corroborate the high percentage of Jews among Vilnius's artisans: Israel Klausner, *Vilna, Yerushalayim deLita, Doroth Ahronim 1881–1939* (Tel Aviv: Bet lohame ha'getaot, 1988), 60–63; Leyzer Ran, *Yerushalayim de Lita / Jerusalem of Lithuania* (New York: Laureate Press, 1976), vol. 1, 187–96; A. Subbotin, *V cherte evreiskoi osedlosti. Otryvki iz ekonomicheskikh issledovanii v zapadnoi i iugo-zapadnoi Rossii za leto 1887 g.* (St. Petersburg: Izdanie "Ekonomicheskogo zhurnala," 1888), 77–81.

50. Ibid., 45–58.

51. G. Aronson et al., *Di geshikhte fun Bund* (New York: Farlag unzer tsayt, 1960), vol. 1: *Der heroisher akt fun Hirsh Lekert,* 107–32 (on the founding of the party); ibid., 232–40. See also Henry J. Tobias, *The Jewish Bund in Russia from its Origins to 1905* (Stanford: Stanford University Press, 1972).

52. G. Agranovskii and I. Guzenberg, *Litovskii Ierusalim. Kratkii putevoditel' po pamiatnym mestam evreiskoi istorii I kul'tury v Vil'niuse* (Vilnius: Lituanus, 1992), 35; Ran, *Yerushalayim de Lita,* vol. 1, 113–14.

53. Pinchas Kon, *Geheimberichte über Herzls Besuch in Wilno im Jahre 1903* (Vienna: s.n., 1928); Cohen, *Vilna,* 349–51.

54. *Tainaia dokladnaia zapiska Vilenskogo gubernatora o polozhenii evreev v Rossii* (Geneva: Bund, 1904), 57. The governor, Count K. K. Palen (Pahlen), did not deny the danger of the Bund but argued that its attractiveness would be considerably diminished if the Russian government were to abolish restrictive measures (the so-called "May Laws" of 1882). His liberal suggestions were not, it goes without saying, accepted by the Tsar.

55. Theodore R. Weeks, "The 1905 Revolution in Vilnius," in *Rewolucja 1905–1907 w Królestwie Polskim i w Rosji,* ed. Marek Przeniosła and Stanisław Wiech (Kielce, Poland: Wydawnictwo Akademii Świętokrzyskiej, 2005), 213–36.

56. Vladimir Levin, "Russian Jewry and the Duma Elections, 1906–1907" in *Jews and Slavs* 7, ed. Wolf Moskovich (Jerusalem: The Hebrew University of Jerusalem Center for Slavic Languages and Literatures: 2000), 238.

57. Some time earlier the socialist Stanisław Mendelsohn had warned Jews in Vilnius that by taking on Russian culture, they risked exacerbating Polish nationalist feelings. But in a city of mixed culture in the Russian Empire, it was not illogical that many Jews would choose to learn the Russian language. S. Mendelsohn, "Wobec grożącego u nas antysemityzmu," *Przedświt*, no. 39–40 (26 March 1892), 5–8.

58. On the mass evacuations of civilian populations during World War I, see Peter Gatrell, *A Whole Empire Walking: Refugees in Russia during World War I* (Bloomington: Indiana University Press, 2004). For the situation in the Polish provinces, see Konrad Zieliński, *Stosunki polsko-żydowskie na ziemiach Królestwa Polskiego w czasie pierwszej wojnie światowej* (Lublin, Poland: Wydawnictwo Uniwersytetu Marii Curie-Skłodowskiej, 2005).

59. Hirsz Abramowicz, *Profiles of a Lost World: Memoirs of East European Jewish Life before World War II* (Detroit, Mich.: Wayne State University Press, 1999), 178. This memoir was originally published as *Farshvundene gashtaltn* (Buenos Aires: Tsentral-farband fun poylishe yidn in argentine, 1958); the sections on World War I and its aftermath are found at 261–325 in the Yiddish edition.

60. On the situation in 1916 and 1917 see Liudas Gira, "Vilniaus gyvenimas po vokiečiais," *Mūsų senovė* 1(2) (1921): 21–38; and 1(3) (1922): 410–24.

61. According to Minczeles, mortality rates went up from 292 in 1916 to 548 in 1917 among those under five years of age, and from 227 to 621 among those 61 to 70 years old. Minczeles, *Vilnius*, 135.

62. Vejas G. Liulevicius, *War Land on the Eastern Front: Culture, National Identity, and German Occupation in World War I* (Cambridge: Cambridge University Press, 2000), 181–84.

63. Khaykl Lunski, *Mehaghetto ha Vilniusi: tipusim vetslalim* (Vilnius: Agudath hasofrim ve-hazhurnalistim haivrim, 1921), 7. On the author, best known as a librarian at the Strashun library, see Abramowicz, *Profiles*, 260–64.

64. Ibid., 209.

65. Minczeles, *Vilnius*, 150–52; Frank M. Schuster, *Zwischen allen Fronten. Osteuropäische Juden während des Ersten Weltkrieges (1914–1919)* (Göttingen: Böhlau, 2004), 445–48; Lietuvos Centrinis Valstybinis Archyvas, Vilnius (LCVA), f. 383, ap. 4, b. 31, ll. 25, 30–45 (report on Vilnius pogrom).

66. Cohen, *Vilna*, 382–87; H. Šadžius, R. Žepkaitė, J. Žiugžda, *Vilniaus miesto istorija nuo Spalio revoliucijos iki dabartinių dienų* (Vilnius: "Mintis," 1972), 32–51.

67. Czesław Miłosz, *Wyprawa w dwudziestolecie* (Krakow: Wydawnictwo Literackie, 2000), 278–79. Miłosz quotes an article from *Przegląd Wileński* (17 December 1922) arguing against Endek-inspired demands to limit Jewish enrollment at the university.

68. Klausner, *Yerushalayim deLita*, 288–89. See also Irena Sławińska, "Z życia naukowego akademików USB w Wilnie" in *Wilno i kresy północno-wschodnie*, ed. Elżbieta Feliksiak and Antoni Mironowicz (Białystok: Towarzystwo Literackie im. Adama Mickiewicza, 1996), vol. 2, 283–96. Jews had a number of student groups at USB and appear to have dominated in the university Esperanto club: LCVA, f. 175, ap. 15, b. 9 ("Stowarzyszenie wzajemnej pomocy stud. Żydów USB"); LCVA, f. 175, ap. 15, b. 35 ("Akademickie koło Esperantistów USB").

69. Mojżesz Heller, "Wilno jako ośrodek żydowskiego życia kulturalnego" in *Wilno i ziemia wileńska. Zarys monograficzny* (Vilnius: Wydawnictwo wojewódzkiego komitetu regionalnego, 1930), vol. 1, 263–68; Abramowicz, *Profiles*, 219–48 (on vocational education).

70. On the Vilnius Jewish press, see Ran, *Jerusalem of Lithuania*, vol. 2, 364–70; Minczeles, *Vilnius*, 304–10; and Susanne Marten-Finnis, "The Jewish Press in Vilna: Traditions, Challenges, and Progress During the Inter-War Period" in Marina Dmitrieva and Heidemarie Peterson, eds., *Jüdische Kultur(en) im Neuen Europa. Wilna 1918–1939* (Wiesbaden: Harrassowitz Verlag, 2004), 134–46.

71. Ibid., 312–13, 331–50; Elias Schulman, *Yung Vilne 1929–1939* (New York: Farlag Getseltn, 1946); Sima Kaganowicz, "Teatr żydowski w Wilnie" in *Wilno i kresy północno-wschodnie*, vol. 2, 255–68; Justin Cammy, "Tsevorfene bleter: The Emergence of Yung Vilne," *Polin* 14 (2001): 170–91.

72. *Das jiddische wissenschaftliche Institut (1925–1928)* (Berlin: Auslandszentrale des Jiddischen Wissenschaftlichen Instituts, 1929); Klausner, *Yerushalayim deLita,* 546–59.

73. Alfred Döblin, *Reise in Polen* (Walter-Verlag: Olten und Freiburg im Breisgau, 1968), 116–18.

74. Ibid., 132–49.

75. Jakob Lestschinski, "Wilna, der Niedergang einer jüdischen Stadt," *Jüdische Wohlfahrtspflege und Sozialpolitik* 2 (1931): 21–33.

76. Cohen, *Vilna,* 405. Cohen gives the figure of 25,000 out of 60,000 Jews in Vilnius applying for Passover assistance in 1938.

77. Klausner, *Yerushalayim deLita,* 291–95; Ran, *Jerusalem of Lithuania,* 40; "Ekscesy antysemickie w Wilnie," *Słowo,* no. 259, 260, 266 (November 1931).

78. Ibid., 41–43 gives several examples of Polish calls to boycott Jews, antisemitic election sloganeering, and the like.

79. Klausner, *Yerushalayim deLita . . . dorot aharonim,* 191–203.

80. Quoted in Edward D. Wynot, Jr., "'A Necessary Cruelty': The Emergence of Official Anti-Semitism in Poland, 1935–1939," *American Historical Review* 76(4) (1971), 1046–47.

81. In general on Jewish Vilnius under Polish rule, see Cohen, *Vilna,* 388–423.

82. Klausner, *Yerushalayim deLita . . . dorot aharonim,* 279–87; Ran, *Jerusalem of Lithuania,* 244.

83. Lucy Dawidowicz, *From that Place and Time: A Memoir 1938–1947* (New York: Bantam Books, 1989), 117.

84. Ibid., 106. A Polish contemporary corroborates Dawidowicz's remark that the Jewish intelligentsia often spoke Russian at home: Stanisław Mianowski, *Świat, który odszedł. Wspomnienia Wilnianina 1895–1945* (Warsaw: Oficyna wydawnicza Rytm, 1995), 172.

85. Dawidowicz, *From that Place,* 107.

86. A similar impression of "modern Jewish Vilnius" may be derived from Morits Grosman, *Yidishe vilne in vort un bild* (Vilnius: Farlag-drukeray Hirsh Mats, 1925). For a child's memoirs of the 1930s in Vilnius, see Samuel Bak, *Painted in Words: A Memoir* (Bloomington: Indiana University Press, 2001).

87. Theodore R. Weeks, "A Multi-ethnic City in Transition: Vilnius's Stormy Decade, 1939–1949," *Eurasian Geography and Economics* 47(2) (March–April 2006): 153–75.

88. On the situation of Lithuania (including Vilnius) in this period, see Liudas Truska, *Lietuva 1938–1953 metais* (Vilnius: Šviesa, 1995). For a mainly Polish-centered but still useful overview of World War II in Vilnius, see Stanisława Lewandowska, *Losy Wilnian. Zapis rzeczywistości okupacyjnej. Ludzie, fakty, wydarzenia 1939–1945* (Warsaw: Neriton, 2004).

89. The literature on the Vilnius ghetto is huge. A poignant memoir by a political leader who did not survive is Herman Kruk, *The Last Days of the Jerusalem of Lithuania,* ed. Benjamin Harkav (New Haven: Yale University Press, 2002). Two excellent and very different overviews are Yitshak Arad, *Ghetto in Flames: The Struggle and Destruction of the Jews in Vilna in the Holocaust* (New York: Holocaust Library, 1982); and Markas Zingeris, ed., *The Days of Memory / Atminties dienos. International Conference in Commemoration of the 50th Anniversary of the Liquidation of the Vilnius Ghetto* (Vilnius: Baltos Lankos, 1995).

90. Theodore R. Weeks, "Population Politics in Vilnius 1944–1947: A Case Study of State-Sponsored Ethnic Cleansing," *Post-Soviet Affairs* 23(1) (2007): 76–95.

91. Theodore R. Weeks, "Remembering and Forgetting: Creating a Soviet Lithuanian Capital; Vilnius 1944–1949," *Journal of Baltic Studies* 39(4) (December 2008), 523–39.

PART TWO
Imperial Borderlands

5

OUR LAWS, OUR TAXES, AND OUR ADMINISTRATION
CITIZENSHIP IN IMPERIAL AUSTRIA

GARY B. COHEN

Writing on the history of the Habsburg monarchy during its last century long focused on the ideological and political development of the national movements, their conflicts, and the seemingly ineluctable decline of a state unable to satisfy nationalist aspirations. If one focuses too narrowly, however, on the ethnic and national conflicts of the late nineteenth century and the dissolution of the monarchy, it is easy to ignore the changing relations between society and the state and the actual character of loyalties to the state. The powerful influence of nationalist narratives in Central and East-Central Europe on much of the historical scholarship has left readers to think that identification with one's nationality, whether defined primarily by language, religion, territory, or some combination of these, generally captured the popular political consciousness during the half-century before World War I and left little space for anything more than minimal loyalties to the Habsburg state and a formal respect for the long-ruling emperor, Franz Joseph.

It is hard to see beyond the conventional portraits of the increasing alienation of much of the population from the Habsburg state during the last decades before 1914. In the Kingdom of Hungary, the heavy-handed efforts of the dominant Hungarian political elites to Magyarize the population and create a Magyar nation state may have converted some. Otherwise, those policies presumably alienated the oppressed non-Magyar peoples from the Hungarian government and ultimately from the state. If the contending national loyalties became ever stronger in the Austrian half of the monarchy after the mid-nineteenth century, then there was little possibility for any overarching Austrian national identity or any significant positive popular loyalty to the Austrian imperial polity. According to conventional views, the great majority of the population and the political elites simply accepted the reality of that state and obeyed its laws, while the various national and class-based political formations competed ferociously with each other for ever greater power, privileges, and advantages. One might call that presumed minimal loyalty to the Austrian state a sort of a residual "real existing Austrian identity," given the presumed absence of any positively freighted Austrian national identity.

Over the last two decades historians have begun to present a much more dynamic and contingent account of the political, social, and cultural processes involved in the rise of the nationalist movements and how national identification developed in the population during the last century of the monarchy. This new understanding of how national loyalties were *constructed* perceives the persistence of uncertainty or indifference in parts of the population well into the early twentieth century.[1] Still, historians have made only a beginning at examining just what happened in the meantime to popular loyalties to the Habsburg state. Jeremy King, in his influential study of Budějovice (Budweis) in southern Bohemia, has argued that loyalty to the Austrian state continued as a significant, although mutable, element in popular civic consciousness during the late nineteenth century and should not be viewed simply as a steadily declining residue.[2] In this interpretation, citizens' loyalties to nationality and to the state must be understood as parts of a changing, complex matrix of loyalties to local community, region, historic land, and dynasty *as well as* to nationality. King grants that for many in Budějovice and in the Bohemian lands and Austria as a whole growing loyalties to nation and nationalist politics meant a gradual decline in loyalty to the Habsburg state. Nonetheless, he shows that many citizens still combined their national loyalties—or their national ambivalence or indifference—with continuing loyalties to the Habsburg emperor *and* to the Austrian state. For many Austrian citizens, as Maureen Healy has demonstrated in her study of the Viennese population, it was the privation and suffering of the last years of World War I and the rapid growth of ethnic and nationalist tensions during that period which finally caused public confidence and allegiance to the Habsburg state to disintegrate.[3]

It is important to take a fresh, systematic look at not only how popular loyalties to the Habsburg state actually developed but also at how the state changed over time its relationship to the citizenry and the nationalist political movements. After 1890 the Austrian government began to make increasing concessions to nationalist demands to recognize the reality of the national groups as collective political actors. The 1867 constitutional provisions recognized citizens' individual rights to their national languages and cultures and the group rights of each people (*Volksstamm*) to its nationality in Article 19 of the Basic Law on the General Rights of Citizens (*Staatsgrundgesetz über die allgemeinen Rechte der Staatsbürger*), but the Austrian parliament adopted little implementing legislation in the succeeding years. In practice during the next three decades, the language of Article 19 was understood to guarantee primarily the rights of citizens and nationalities to their national cultural rights, particularly language rights in public education and in the functioning of justice and public administration. A series of court decisions recognized the rights of associations and communal governments to bring claims on behalf of national interests for the protection of individual national rights. As early as 1873, though, the Bohemian Diet adopted a law which provided for separate Czech and German local school boards in places with mixed populations, marking the initial formal division of a public authority on national lines.[4]

The creation of nationally separate organs of governance gradually accelerated after the 1890s. After 1900 nationalist politicians and state officials worked out a series of compromises on nationality disputes, including one for Moravia in 1905, for Bukovina in 1910, and for Galicia and the city of Budějovice in 1914. These agreements gave legal recognition to the nationalities as political entities in elections and the representative bodies of those territories.[5] In the meantime the introduction of universal, equal, and direct male suffrage for the Austrian chamber of deputies in 1907 included deliberate efforts to redraw many constituencies along lines of nationality. All these developments pointed in the direction of government for each nationality by officials and institutions of its own in a sort of "national autonomy" under the Habsburg crown, as the eminent Austrian constitutional scholar Edmund Bernatzik termed it. Most of the nationalist parties had long pushed for this, but one cannot know, of course, how such arrangements might have developed had the monarchy survived World War I.[6]

Examining the development during the late nineteenth century of citizens' relationship to the state and their loyalties to it as compared to nationality, religion, and class is a critical part of understanding the evolution of modern political action and civil society in Habsburg Central Europe. The practices of citizenship must be considered as an everyday reality in the lives of the population. Historians' neglect, until recently, of the issue of citizenship in imperial Austria contrasts sharply with the substantial body of scholarship on evolving notions of citizenship for many modern nation states.[7] The imperial states of Central and East-Central Europe, in fact, developed new concepts of citizenship during the long nineteenth century as they moved away from the early modern social hierarchies of corporate privilege toward a direct relationship of citizens with the state, greater equality of legal rights, and gradually increasing participation in representative institutions. Since the Hungarian half of the Habsburg monarchy took a different path of political and constitutional development during the late nineteenth century, it is best to examine the development of citizenship and relations of citizens to the state separately in Austria and Hungary.[8] As this chapter will show, the relationship of the populace to the Austrian state changed significantly during the second half of the nineteenth century. Not only did citizens' civil and political rights advance, but society developed a significant active engagement—indeed, an investment—in the workings of the transnational imperial state. The growth of the population's engagement and investment in the state occurred in the same public sphere which saw the powerful advance of nationalist loyalties.

Law and governmental practice in early modern Austria defined the populace in each of the crown lands as subjects (*Untertanen*) of the Habsburg *Landesfürst.* Citizenship in the modern sense, in contrast, typically means the fixed, formal membership of individuals in a polity or state which guarantees all the protection of certain specified rights and entitlements. Given this definition, the closest thing to a more modern notion of citizenship in early modern Austria was the right of domicile in a particular locality, what was eventually termed *Heimatrecht,* and with it, entitlement to poor relief.[9] As the eighteenth and early nineteenth century absolutist Austrian state moved increasingly toward a *Rechtsstaat* and guarantees of uniform protection under the law for all inhabitants, modern notions of state citizenship emerged. The civil code which Emperor Joseph II promulgated in 1786 began the explicit legal definition of *Staatsbürgerschaft* in the sense of citizens' civic rights, although the monarchy's legal language continued to mix notions of citizens, subjects, and corporate estates (*Stände*) for some decades into the nineteenth century. The legal reforms of 1848 and the 1850s and then the emergence of full constitutional government in the 1860s completed the process of creating equality before the law for all individual citizens. Legal historians have traced the development of the laws defining the relationship of individuals to the state in both halves of the Habsburg monarchy, but scholars have not treated systematically the evolution of popular concepts of citizenship and the practical relationship of individuals to the state in everyday life during the long nineteenth century.[10]

A historical inquiry into changing concepts of citizenship must consider discursive expressions of political loyalties, formal political action, and the realm of informal everyday social and political relationships as well. The populace developed and expressed political loyalties and identities as a matter of practice in everyday life. Loyalties to the state, like those to nationality, were, after all, a matter of both ideas and what the sociologist Pierre Bourdieu termed *habitus,* "a system of durable, transposable dispositions" or structured orientations which shape social action and reproduce various patterns in everyday activity.[11] Studies of popular political loyalties and civil society need to borrow something from the methodologies and perspectives of *Alltagsgeschichte* if we are to understand the character of individuals' and groups' relations with the state and in connection with their other political loyalties and relationships. This chapter offers some suggestions as to what such research may reveal about the character and dynamics of the population's relations with the Austrian state and popular attitudes toward that state during the late nineteenth century.

It is perhaps a commonplace to say that the state or government authority in all its layers and guises was a near-omnipresent reality for the inhabitants of Austria during the last half-century of the monarchy. It would be an interesting exercise to map all the contacts with various agencies of government which a typical citizen might have had in the course of a day or week. In city and town situations, those contacts included most obviously the post office for mail services and postal savings accounts; various tax and customs offices; public schools operated by the commune, the crown land, or the Ministry of Religion and Instruction; the communal magistracy; the registry of domiciles (the *Meldeamt*); local police and courts; communal registries for military service and district conscription offices; local military bases; state railroad and municipal transportation services; local building and health inspectors; communally or provincially operated hospitals and clinics; and state-licensed notaries. Perhaps the most familiar point of interaction between citizens and a governmental institution—or at least a franchised agency of the state—was the local tobacco shop. The central Austrian state exercised a longstanding monopoly on the production and sale of tobacco products and franchised the ubiquitous privately operated local tobacco shops to represent the state, in effect, by selling not only cigarettes and cigars, but also postage and revenue stamps, state lottery tickets, official forms, and, in larger towns, tram tickets.

However much nationalist parties or radical labor or peasants' organizations might complain about inadequate representation and unfair treatment at the hands of Austrian governmental institutions and agencies, the institutions of government were very much part of everyone's daily life. The complaints almost always accompanied demands for a greater stake in the operations of government or a bigger share of the benefits of government services. Perceptive observers at the time understood that Austria's nationality conflicts were, in fact, in Karl Renner's famous phrase, a "struggle for the state" rather than against it.[12]

During the absolutist era of the eighteenth and early nineteenth centuries, the Habsburg government made a significant start in developing modern administrative, judicial, police, and educational systems, even if their evolution between 1815 and the 1840s failed to keep pace with the needs of a growing population, the early industrial economy, or even the state's own security interests. By the 1820s and 1830s, though, even without modern representative institutions, the Habsburg monarchy already had the framework of a well-regulated *Rechtsstaat.* The imperial government abolished the last vestiges of patrimonial justice after 1848 and separated the judiciary and judicial processes from the state administrative apparatus. The neo-absolutist reforms of the 1850s and then the new constitutional government of the 1860s and 1870s renovated civil administration, law codes and the justice system, public education, and regulations for industry and commerce. The advent of constitutional government in the 1860s added a broad range of legal protections for citizens' rights and liberties, comparable in many respects to the liberal legal standards of Western Europe in that era. The state also began to take a much more activist role than before 1848 in furthering economic development and dealing with the social problems of an increasingly urbanized, industrial society.

As in other western and central European states, the various layers of Austrian government greatly increased their presence in society during the late nineteenth century by adding a myriad of new duties and responsibilities. These included the regulation of manufacturing and commerce, public transportation, health services, the licensing of certain professions and occupations, and new forms of specialized public education, to name only a few examples. John W. Boyer and other historians have noted that the addition of new government services and responsibilities accelerated significantly after the late 1880s and early 1890s, as modern capitalist agriculture and industry matured, conurbations grew, and political parties and interest groups reacted to economic development and the laissez faire policies of the 1860s and early 1870s.[13]

How did the populace relate to government authority and to its growing administrative and regulative functions? The Habsburg state originated in the dynastic alliances and wars of the late medieval and renaissance eras. During the late seventeenth and eighteenth centuries, the increasingly bureaucratized absolutist government tried to impose a uniform, centralized administration over all of the crown lands, although important autonomous institutions remained in the historic diets and Hungary's county governments. With the development of constitutionalism and representative institutions during the late nineteenth century, one must ask to what extent the populace won some influence over the development of government, gained some purchase on government administration, and came to see it as theirs in significant ways.

The growth of government functions and services in Austria during the late nineteenth century was based in part, but not completely, on legislation passed under constitutional procedures after the early 1860s by the parliament and secondarily by the diets of the individual crown lands and elected communal councils. Much of the foundations for the late nineteenth century administrative and regulatory functions originated before the constitutional era in a rich body of imperial decrees and ministerial ordinances, sometimes ratified by the diets of the individual crown lands, but often not. Even during the constitutional era, the state bureaucracy interpreted and implemented parliamentary and diet legislation by means of myriad ordinances and regulations issued by the ministries and the governors of the crown lands, who were responsible to the Interior Ministry. The central government issued many of the most important measures over the signature of the emperor, including orders to dissolve the parliament or individual diets and to call new elections, in the form of imperial patents, or *allerhöchste Handschreiben* in the colorful terminology of Habsburg administrative tradition.

For the most part, the Austrian government enjoyed a high level of civil order and popular compliance with its laws and ordinances over the second half of the nineteenth century. Episodes of civil unrest were limited in duration and scope, but simple compliance, of course, does not necessarily mean genuine loyalty or positive, active popular engagement in the functioning of the state. Historians have written much on how during the constitutional era various political interests, particularly nationalist groups, challenged the legitimacy of Austria's representative bodies and various imperial and ministerial decrees. Voters elected deputies to the lower house of parliament in separate curia, all with limited suffrage until 1897, when a new curia based on universal male suffrage was added. After 1907 all members of the chamber of deputies were elected under universal direct and equal male suffrage, but to the end of the monarchy the provincial diets and communal councils generally retained stratified electoral systems with limited suffrage. During the first decades of the constitutional era, the ministerial leadership in Vienna, in collusion with the dominant party interests, added to the inequalities of the representative bodies by gerrymandering the electoral districts for the lower house of parliament and many diets.

Various nationalist forces, most notably the Czechs and later some Slovene and Ruthenian/Ukrainian politicians, agitated against the suffrage systems for the parliament and the diets. As early as the 1860s, Czech nationalist politicians began the practice of boycotting the parliament or the Bohemian Diet for shorter or longer periods to protest the electoral system or government policies. After 1890 the Social Democrats and eventually some nationalists like the Czech National Social Party, the Slovene Catholic People's Party, and the Ruthenian-Ukrainian parties in Galicia campaigned for universal suffrage and challenged the legitimacy of all legislative bodies elected by limited suffrage. Still, these parties typically sent representatives to those bodies whenever they could elect them.

Throughout the constitutional era various aggrieved parties periodically boycotted the parliament, individual diets, or communal councils, hoping to delegitimize those bodies in the eyes of their supporters. After the early 1890s politicians of nearly all stripes sharply criticized particularly unpopular ministerial and imperial decrees as undemocratic interventions in a civilized modern legal and constitutional order, although they were generally careful to avoid committing sedition or *lèse majesté*. Still, one should not conclude that such complaints signified *ipso facto* a fundamental rejection of the state's legitimacy. Conventional historical accounts emphasize that after the 1890s radical nationalists and more moderate politicians as well frequently obstructed legislative work in the Austrian parliament and various provincial diets as a form of protest. In an increasingly contentious political environment, such disruptive actions undermined public respect for particular ministers and the work of the state bureaucracy, the parliament, and diets. Nonetheless, the politicians generally used obstructionist tactics, as Lothar Höbelt has pointed out, both to demonstrate that they were doing at least something for their constituents and to strengthen their own hands in winning concessions from ministers, provincial governors, and other party leaders in the negotiations which invariably followed the moments of confrontation and crisis.[14]

Nearly all political interests acted to win advantages for their causes and constituencies within the various arenas of political action offered by the Austrian governmental structure, however contentious and exasperating political interactions might become. In the periods of greatest conflict, whether during sessions of the parliament or individual diets or during recesses, the political parties, major interest groups, and government officials typically engaged in intensive multilateral negotiations. Both the party leaders and state officials were happy to pursue such discussions, but during the greatest crises they had to conduct the negotiations in the glare of daily newspaper reports. Party politicians who loudly criticized unpopular officials such as the long-time Bohemian governor Count Franz von Thun-Hohenstein

(1889–96 and 1911–15) or the Austrian minister-president from 1911 to 1916, Count Karl Stürgkh, might also engage in extensive bargaining with those same officials in private, either directly or through intermediaries, no matter how improbable some of those conversations might seem.[15] Some of the most extreme Czech nationalists or Pan-Germans might hope for the ultimate disappearance of the Habsburg state, but, as historians have often noted, almost no large, significant political interests within the monarchy worked actively and consistently for the dissolution of the Habsburg polity before the outbreak of World War I. This rejection of radical anti-state politics had as its natural corollary the vigorous and, more often than not, positive engagement of nearly all interests in the political processes established and supported by the state.

Many in imperial Austria recognized that after the 1860s a growing part of governmental work went on in councils and agencies of the individual crown lands and communes, which enjoyed considerable legal and practical political autonomy.[16] The frequent obstruction of the parliament by nationalist parties after the mid-1890s resulted in a further strengthening of the crown lands and their diets in the making of public policy, despite some ministers' complaints about the autonomy of the diets.[17] That autonomy facilitated an increasingly intensive engagement of provincial and local political and economic interests in the formation and implementation of policy. In this sense political parties and interest groups representing significant segments of society had a growing purchase on certain functions of the government administration, particularly since the crown lands and communal governments accounted for a large part of the expansion of public services at the end of the century. Nationalist politicians after the 1880s viewed the extent of their influence or control over various parts of the government structure as vitally important elements of their respective groups' "national property" (*nationaler Besitzstand*), and they campaigned vigorously for the advancement of that influence and control over various parts of the governmental structure.[18]

After the early 1860s autonomous functions for the communal councils and for the diets and executive committees of individual crown lands became a fundamental feature of constitutional law and government administration. In both Austrian law and public discourse the "state" referred to the central administrative, legislative, and judicial bodies and their direct appendages. For analytic purposes here, though, the Austrian state, in the broader sense of all government authority, should be considered as including the diets of the crown lands, their executive committees, the communal councils, and their respective administrative structures as well as the organs of the central government.

The Stadion Law of 1849 established the principle of broad autonomy for communal and city governments under elected councils. This liberal reform sought to strengthen both society and the state by encouraging local interests to take responsibility for communal administration. Suspended under the neo-absolutism of the 1850s, communal self-government and autonomous communal authority developed quickly after the beginning of the constitutional era in the 1860s. Communal governments, working under statutes and the supervision of the crown land governments, had primary responsibility for funding and operating primary education; assuring the security of persons and property; granting local legal residency (*Heimatrecht*); registering young men for military conscription; maintaining streets, squares, and bridges; providing for local water supplies, sanitation, local poor relief, and some local public health services; and regulating local commerce, markets, labor matters, construction, and building standards. More significant police matters beyond the competence of the

Ortspolizei remained in the hands of the central state authorities, as represented by district administrations (*Bezirkshauptmannschaften*) under the Interior Ministry.

Local elites, political parties, and interest groups took charge of the communal councils and the communal officialdom, working within restricted, stratified suffrage systems until the introduction of broader suffrage rights in a few localities after 1897. Already by the late 1860s, this part of the government structure belonged in effect to local political interests. Masters of communal politics at the turn of the century such as Vienna's Karl Lueger, Josef Taschek in Budějovice, or Jan Podlipný in Prague took advantage of the autonomy granted the city governments under the Austrian legal and constitutional system to wield significant powers and to reward their supporters and constituents with privileges and communal services. The dominant forces in the communal governments used their powers not only to advance their own political causes but also to pressure the crown land and ministerial authorities to support local initiatives and interests. Strong popular interest in local government and hotly contested elections for communal councils bore witness to the deep engagement of significant portions of the population in this level of the state structure. The restricted suffrage notwithstanding, many in the local communities identified strongly with that part of the Austrian government administration represented by the communes and clearly saw communal self-government as *theirs*.

Believing in a centralized government, the German liberal reformers of the 1860s did not initially intend to give the crown lands any great autonomy, but the structures of the crown lands survived from the early modern era. The emperor's short-lived federalist October 1860 Diploma reaffirmed their place in the government structure, and over time their responsibilities advanced steadily. The crown lands supervised police authorities and primary and secondary education; operated hospitals and asylums; set standards for public and animal health; maintained roads and highways; regulated property rights, manufacturing, hunting, fishing, and forest, mineral, and water resources; operated provincial museums and theaters; and collected taxes to support all these functions. The governor of each crown land (the *Statthalter,* or in smaller crown lands, *Landespräsident*) and his officialdom represented the central state administration as an extension of the Interior Ministry; but the governor shared responsibility for the delivery and oversight of the crown land's public services with the diet and its executive committee (*Landesausschuss*). Leaders of the dominant political parties and factions in each diet held seats in the executive committee, and the committee in each crown land developed its own staff to administer programs and services created by the diets.[19]

The governors of the crown lands hemmed in somewhat the autonomous functions of the diets and their executive committees, but where the diets functioned well, the political discourse of the time suggests that the dominant political forces and their constituencies had considerable purchase on the legislative activity, the executive committee, and the officialdom dependent on the committee. This was surely true for the Polish conservatives who long dominated the Galician Diet; for the Slovene and German liberals and Slovene clerical nationalists who competed to control the Carniolan Diet; for the Christian Socials who led the Lower Austrian Diet after 1896; and for the German Liberals, later German Nationals, and Catholic politicians who contended for control of the Upper Austrian Diet. In 1910, for example, Albert Gessmann, who helped Karl Lueger build the Christian Social Party, returned happily, after a brief stint as a cabinet minister, to his long-time position on the Lower Austrian executive committee, where he could influence primary and secondary education and the hiring of school directors and teachers. After working to develop a new Austrian Ministry of Public Works in 1908, Gessmann apparently found the provincial executive committee a more rewarding base of operations.

Despite repeated boycotts and obstruction of the Bohemian Diet between the 1860s and 1914, Czech nationalists became deeply invested in the provision of many provincial services which the executive committee administered. Naturally then, Czech nationalist politicians loudly protested the action of the emperor and minister-president Count Karl Stürgkh in July 1913 (in the so-called *Annapatente*) to dissolve the Bohemian Diet and executive committee and put the administration of that crown land and its public services in the hands of an extraordinary administrative committee responsible to the central government. This action came after months of Czech–German wrangling had blocked all normal legislative business in the diet, including the approval of a budget for provincial services. Before the emperor issued the *Annapatente*, the Bohemian governor had consulted many of those same Czech politicians who then criticized the emergency measure. Most of them had reason to be relieved, though, that government operations and the delivery of services in Bohemia could resume under the new administrative committee, particularly when most of the same officials continued in place who were formerly employed by the provincial executive committee.[20]

The sense of popular purchase or investment in the work of the government administration also applied to state agencies under direct control of the ministries, where services were at stake which interested the public. State railroads, veterans' facilities, and forests were obvious examples, but so also were institutions of secondary and higher education. After the 1860s the Ministry of Religion and Instruction regulated all *Gymnasien, Realschulen*, universities, and technical colleges. From the early 1870s that ministry also directly funded and operated all higher education and most of the secondary schools, although communal and crown land governments could operate their own secondary schools subject to ministerial regulation. In theory and practice, the Austrian state intended the *Gymnasien* and *Realschulen* to serve a narrow elite of youth, preparing them with rigorous academic curricula for further study in the universities and technical colleges, but growing public demand for secondary education continually stretched those intended limits.

Throughout the constitutional era an ever-increasing public appetite for access to *Gymnasien* and *Realschulen* put pressure on the Ministry of Religion and Instruction to expand educational opportunities. Where the Ministry would not open more schools, authorities of the crown lands or towns started new *Gymnasien* and *Realschulen* on their own, hoping in time for the Ministry to provide subsidies or to take them over and fund them fully.[21] Nationalist politicians and voluntary associations such as the *Deutscher Schulverein* and the Czech *Matice Školská* saw primary and secondary schools as critically important agencies for advancing and protecting national loyalties, particularly in localities where members of a particular nationality were underserved by existing communal and state schools. Nationalist interests also pressed for greater opportunities for university and technical college education in their own mother tongues—or protection of them where they already existed—as significant tokens of their national rights as well as crucial to the welfare of their constituencies.

In imperial Austria wherever there were linguistically mixed populations, nationalist political forces treated the operation of schools teaching in their own mother tongues as a major political concern. After 1880 nationalist school societies established networks of local associations and vigorously campaigned for donations to support their own primary schools for minority populations too small to qualify for their own public institutions. Occasionally, private associations started their own secondary schools as well, although the higher costs than for primary schools made this rarer. High levels of public support in some regions for the nationalist school societies and for politicians who campaigned on the school issues indicate the strong investment by nationalist constituencies in the issue of education in the respective national languages. Schools became important trophies in the nationalist political contention. Here too, though, nationalist political agitation had as its practical goal capturing various public services of the Austrian state for a particular nationalist interest while retaining the fiscal and administrative benefits of the government system.

German nationalist politicians tried to defend the privileged position of German-language instruction in Austrian secondary and higher education and often after 1890 vigorously opposed establishment of new state institutions teaching in other languages. After the 1860s, though, demographic and political realities worked in the interests of Polish- and Czech-language education. When Polish conservatives in the Galician Diet established effective autonomy for provincial government there in the late 1860s and early 1870s, they made Polish the principal language of instruction in the universities of Kraków and Lemberg/ Lwów/L'viv. Polish dominated as the language of instruction in Galician state *Gymnasien* and *Realschulen* from the 1860s onward. In Bohemia and Moravia after the early 1860s, Czech nationalists won a gradual but steady increase in the number of secondary schools teaching in Czech as well as in Czech-language classes at the university of Prague and the technical colleges of Prague and Brno, leading eventually to dividing them into separate Czech and German institutions.

Public secondary and higher education in Ukrainian and Slovene developed more slowly than did that in Czech and Polish. After the 1890s Ruthenian/Ukrainian political interests increased their efforts to advance public secondary and higher education in Ukrainian in eastern Galicia and Bukovina, but institutions teaching in Ukrainian and enrollments of Ukrainian-speakers still lagged well behind the Ukrainian-speaking share of the population for the Austrian half of the monarchy. Slovene-speakers enjoyed a strong political position in Carniola and had a higher average standard of living than did the Ukrainian-speaking population, but Slovene-language secondary education still developed more slowly than that in Czech and Polish. In 1895, for instance, German nationalist interests noisily blocked the efforts of the Austrian government to establish Slovene-language parallel classes in the existing German *Gymnasium* in Cilli/Celje, southern Styria, helping to bring down the coalition cabinet of the day. In contrast, Italian long enjoyed a privileged position as the language of secondary instruction in the Adriatic coastal towns, but a government effort in 1904 to open an Italian-language law faculty in Innsbruck collapsed in the face of German nationalist protests. Nationalist campaigns during the last two decades before 1914 to win new state universities or faculties teaching in Ukrainian, Czech, Italian, and Slovene failed due to Polish and German nationalist opposition, fiscal constraints at the ministerial level, and government disinterest.[22]

Beyond the highly visible agitation of nationalist political parties and interest groups on educational matters, the public expressed concerns about public schools based on quite independent considerations. Many localities saw clashes between clerical and anticlerical interests over curriculum and the hiring of teachers and school directors.[23] Citizens' sense of their individual rights and entitlement to public education also came to the fore, sometimes conflicting with what nationalist parties and organizations wanted. This was clear in citizens' reactions to official efforts to control or limit enrollments in particular public schools.

During the constitutional era separate systems of public schools arose in linguistically mixed districts where there were sufficient enrollments to teach in the officially recognized languages. Parents conventionally had freedom to choose which schools their children attended, regardless of what was their mother tongue or the family's possible national loyalties. Under the liberal constitutional principles of the 1860s, individual declarations of nationality, mother tongue, or, in the censuses after 1880, language of everyday use (*Umgangssprache*) were a matter of free self-ascription. Government authorities only began to register nationality officially in some crown lands after 1900. Many Czech- and Slovene-speaking parents, for example, sent their children to German schools for a few years or more so that they might learn German well, but Czech and Slovene nationalists complained that this put the children on the path to Germanization and alienation from their own nation. Ruthenian and Ukrainian nationalists in Galicia made similar complaints against the sending to Polish-language schools of children whose mother tongue was not Polish.

The Moravian Compromise of 1905 required citizens to register their nationality officially so that they could be assigned to the appropriate national cadastre of voters. The legislation also included a provision urged by Czech nationalists, the so-called Perek Law (*Lex Perek*), which permitted school children in Moravia to attend only schools where they were proficient in the language of instruction. Following these measures, Czech and German district school boards began to "reclaim" children of their own nationality for their own schools if their parents chose to send them to the other schools. All this provoked loud complaints and legal challenges, not only from nationalist political groups but also from parents who wanted to send their children to the schools of their choice, regardless of considerations of nationality. In a closely watched 1910 ruling, the Austrian Supreme Administrative Court affirmed the right of school boards to engage in the national "reclamation" of children but permitted enrollment by children in Moravian schools who might not be competent in the language of instruction if that language corresponded to the child's nationality.[24] The controversies surrounding the Perek Law and other nationalist initiatives to control which public schools children of a given nationality might attend raised a fundamental conflict in popular notions of citizens' rights, as nationalists' concepts of their nation's collective rights to its own public schools collided with individuals' understandings of their rights and entitlements as parents, taxpayers, and citizens of the Austrian state to send their children to the public school they chose.

When the central government made efforts to restrict enrollments in secondary schools to stem what it saw as excessively rapid growth, it ran into similar popular beliefs in citizens' entitlement to access to public institutions. The central government, through the Ministry of Religion and Instruction, made the first attempt to slow the growth of *Gymnasium* and *Realschule* enrollments under the German Liberal ministry of Leopold von Hasner in 1870 with the introduction of written and oral admissions examinations.[25] Secondary enrollments only continued to increase thereafter, and in August 1880, soon after the conservative Count Eduard Taaffe became minister-president, the Ministry of Religion and Instruction ordered all state-accredited secondary schools to submit detailed annual reports on the admissions examinations.

The August 1880 ministerial order also mandated school directors to speak with new applicants and their parents about the purposes of academic secondary education. The directors were to "warn against attending a general educational institution those pupils whom one, from the outset, would not expect to want to use the secondary school to prepare for higher education or to be able to, and to warn those whom one, from experience, would not expect to be successful in a secondary school." The directors were to encourage such youth to enroll instead in an intermediate vocational school to learn industrial, commercial, or agricultural skills.[26] Nonetheless, neither this nor subsequent ministerial initiatives in the 1880s had much success in slowing the growth of secondary school enrollments or the admission of youth who were not likely to complete full courses of study. The school directors and crown land school committees (*Landesschulräte*) reported back to the ministry in late 1880 that many parents wanted to give their sons at least a chance to study in an academic secondary school before trying something else. Some simply wanted their children to complete the lower forms before transferring to a commercial school, so that they could qualify for one-year "volunteer" military service instead of normal conscription. Other parents wanted their children to study a few years in a *Gymnasium* or *Realschule* rather than going directly from the *Volksschule* to a *Bürgerschule* or vocational school, because they expected their children to develop better language and writing skills in an academic secondary school. This was particularly true for children whose mother tongue was not German but who enrolled in German-language *Gymnasien* and *Realschulen*.

According to the school directors' reports from 1880, some parents were outspoken in their resentment of the official efforts to discourage their children from attending a *Gymnasium* or *Realschule*. They considered the choice of a school to be a family matter and not the business of any official. A *Gymnasium* director in Graz reported the blunt statement of a parent that "I pay taxes, too, and therefore have the same entitlement (*Anrecht*) as others to the education of my son in a state *Gymnasium*."[27] Whatever the state's intentions in establishing and maintaining academy secondary schools to prepare a small number of qualified male youth for higher education, by 1880 parents across Austria considered the opportunity for their sons to study in a public *Gymnasium* or *Realschule*, even if only for a few years, as an entitlement for them as citizens and taxpayers. It took several decades before that sense of entitlement to secondary education began to extend to daughters. The long campaign for publicly supported secondary education for girls of equal status and quality to that for boys was just beginning in the 1870s and early 1880s, and given the lack of ministerial and provincial support, the first girls' secondary schools were generally private institutions.[28]

Popular interest and political agitation regarding the whole range of public services at the end of the nineteenth century showed that the populace saw themselves as citizens of the Austrian state who *ipso facto* were entitled to certain protections and services. Certainly, many segments of the population complained about the great powers of the ministerial bureaucracy, the lack of genuine democracy at the higher levels of government, and various policies of the central government and individual crown lands, including the privileging of certain groups and interests. Nonetheless, as an everyday reality, citizens were deeply enmeshed in the various layers of the government structure through its myriad functions and services. Citizens had a very real sense of ownership of parts of the government's services, particularly those provided by the autonomous communal and crown land authorities, but also many services provided by the ministries themselves—and not merely as consumers but increasingly also as participants in the processes of creating, administering, and changing those services.

Citizens apparently thought themselves entitled to efficient and effective government services, whether provided by communal magistracies, the post, state railroads, the courts, public hospitals, or schools. To be sure, they did not consider "Austrian" a national designation on a par with German, Czech, Pole, or Slovene, but their engagement in political agitation, lobbying, and litigation regarding public services as well as electoral politics demonstrated a strong practical sense of citizenship in the Austrian state. When individual citizens and political groups voiced their sense of legal rights and entitlements to public services under the laws of the central state and the crown lands, they communicated a consciousness that, despite their grievances and disappointments, the Austrian governmental structure in its various layers and services was theirs, whatever their particular loyalties to nationalist interests.

Numerous memoirs, works of contemporary fiction, and historical accounts testify to the particularly strong loyalty of the Jewish population to the Habsburg state during the constitutional era.[29] Jews in both the Austrian and Hungarian halves of the monarchy were well aware that they enjoyed a far-reaching civil and legal equality that was unknown in tsarist Russia and Romania, as well as occupational opportunities in parts of government service and the military officers' corps that were greater than in much of Imperial Germany. In 1883, Adolf Jellinek, the chief rabbi of Vienna, summed up well the feelings of Jews in many of the Austrian crown lands: "The Jews of Austria are Austrians first and last; they feel and think Austrian; they want a great, strong and mighty Austria. . . . They know and remember in boundless gratitude what the Emperor of Austria has granted them. . . . (I)n the Jewish prayer houses it is loudly proclaimed that Franz Joseph I made his Jewish subjects into real human beings and free citizens."[30] Affection for Emperor Franz Joseph as a protector of Jewish rights survived in Central European Jewish lore for decades after the dissolution of the monarchy.

The desire of Jews in the monarchy for emancipation from the legal and economic disabilities of the early modern era and achievement of full political and social equality motivated them during the early decades of the constitutional era to support the political forces which championed—or at least accepted—equality and welcomed Jewish adherents. From the 1860s to around 1890 the majority of Jews in Vienna, the Alpine crown lands, and the Bohemian lands supported the German liberal political cause and in the public sphere accepted its vision of a liberal German nationalism, even if low levels of conversion and intermarriage still kept Jews' private lives largely separate. In Galicia, where the great majority of Jews retained Yiddish as their first language and most remained religiously observant, Jews tended until the 1890s to support the conservative constitutional politics of the Polish landowners and intellectuals, led by the Stańczyks in the Galician Diet, even if few Jews identified with the explicitly Catholic Polish national cause.[31]

The rise of a more aggressive mass-based nationalism among most of the Austrian nationalities and of radical political antisemitism after the late 1880s made Jewish political loyalties to the older liberal or conservative political parties increasingly problematic. The election of the Christian Social Party leader Karl Lueger as mayor of Vienna in 1897, mob attacks on Jewish homes and businesses in Prague in December 1897, pogroms in western Galicia in 1898, and antisemitic political agitation in many places over the next 15 years created shockwaves among Jews throughout the Austrian crown lands. Nonetheless, identification with a Jewish national cause, either in the form of diaspora nationalism or Zionism, attracted only a minority of the Jewish population up to 1918.

Whatever the fluctuations in Austrian Jews' support for one or another political cause, whether liberal nationalist, social democratic, or Jewish nationalist, most continued until the end of World War I to express an unquestioning loyalty to the Austrian state, to its laws and administrative structures. If anything, the challenges posed by the growing radicalism and antisemitism of many nationalist parties reinforced many Jews' loyalties to the liberal Austrian state as a bulwark of their civil and economic rights.[32]

The growing engagement and indeed investment of individual citizens and societal interests in the institutions of the Austrian state structure, its legislative bodies, judicial processes, public services, and administrative apparatus surely sustained some level of loyalty to that state among diverse elements of the population. It is no easy task, however, to determine just what was the character and strength of that loyalty for particular groups at various times, especially when much of the testimony which one would naturally consider was written after the collapse of the Habsburg polity and its replacement by avowedly national states. We do know that from the end of the Napoleonic Wars until the last year or two of World War I, there were high levels of popular compliance with the laws, administrative regulations, and military service obligations. But for the upheavals of 1848–1849, few in the Austrian crown lands before late in World War I openly challenged the sovereignty and legitimacy of the Habsburg state; moments of civil unrest were limited in duration and extent.

Famously, the Austrian imperial authorities chose early in the nineteenth century to cultivate popular loyalties to the emperor and the Habsburg dynasty as symbols of the state, its laws and regulations, accepting that they could not superimpose an Austrian national identity over national loyalties based on language, culture, and regional history among the populace.[33] Throughout the late nineteenth century the central state authorities worked to encourage popular loyalties to the state, not only by the coercive means of law enforcement measures, but also through the public performance of such loyalties in state celebrations and formal visits around the monarchy by high state officials, the emperor, and other members of the imperial family, much as other European states did during this era. At moments when nationalist political passions were running high, the central Austrian authorities feared the possibility of hostile counter-demonstrations or massive abstentions, but more often than not the public observances went off without serious incident. Indeed, Daniel Unowsky and other historians have shown that many local and provincial politicians, including most conservative and moderate nationalists, were eager to use state holidays and visits by the emperor, the empress, or archdukes and archduchesses to display the importance of the autonomous provincial and communal bodies and the accomplishments of those bodies under their elected leaders.[34] Radical nationalists like the Pan-Germans or the Czech National Socials and State-Right Radicals might ostentatiously avoid singing the imperial hymn—or even attending—when the emperor and other members of the imperial family were saluted, but large segments of the population joined in such observances.

The efforts of local and provincial political figures to use public celebrations and observances to demonstrate their own roles in civil society and the work of governance showed that such events affirmed the functionings of the whole state structure and, implicitly or explicitly, a sense of loyalty to the state on the part of local officials and the public alike as a natural part of everyday life. This was more than simple affection or curiosity vis-à-vis the persons of the emperor and his family or a traditional loyalty to dynastic authority. It is true that for many citizens with strong nationalist sentiments during the last decades before World War I, loyalty to the Austrian state did not involve the strong affective bonds and vivid sense of personal belonging which they invested in their national loyalties. Still, as a matter of everyday reality, the practices of citizenship and compliance with the Austrian state's web of laws, ordinances, administration, fiscal requirements, and military obligations constituted a loyalty to the state which went beyond personal respect for the emperor and which crossed the divisions of language, religion, national allegiance, and distinctive local or regional histories. In a political order where the populace had strong expectations about the rule of law and constitutional principles, the state which provided guarantees of law and order, personal security, and opportunities for representation could command a considerable degree of allegiance from much of the population, even despite the inequalities and lack of full democracy which persisted. Loyalty to the state coexisted, of course, with vigorous criticism of its policies and with other loyalties—to local communities, religious denominations, political parties and movements, and national causes. The population and their local, provincial, and parliamentary leaders expressed their multiple coexisting loyalties in the elaborately staged state celebrations and imperial visits and in the causes which they worked to advance through the engagement of parties and interest groups in policymaking at all levels of governance during the last half-century before 1918.

Support for the state and its military effort was strong in all the Austrian territories during the first two years of World War I, even among radical nationalists like the Czech National Socials, despite the efforts of German nationalists to spread the myth of Czech disloyalty.[35] Loyalty to the Austrian state only disintegrated in the general population toward the end of the war, when the central state authorities proved no longer able to assure the basic welfare, security, and rights of the citizenry or even to uphold an independent Austro-Hungarian diplomatic and military stance vis-à-vis Germany.[36] Still, given the citizenry's strong engagement in the web of the Austrian state during the last decades before 1914, one should not be surprised that in autumn 1918 many ardent nationalist politicians were careful to preserve significant parts of the old legal and administrative systems in the newly independent successor states. They did this in part to assure civil order but also because they were so thoroughly habituated to those systems and considered important parts of them their own.

The prominent Czech politician and financial expert Alois Rašín expressed these sentiments notably when he drafted much of Czechoslovakia's first law, issued with the declaration of independence on October 28, 1918. The second paragraph declared simply that "all previous provincial and imperial laws and regulations remain for the time being in effect." Rašín explained candidly this insistence on continuity: "The basic purpose of this law was to prevent any anarchic situation from developing, so that our whole state administration [celá naše správa] would remain and continue on October 29 as if there had been no revolution at all."[37] For Rašín and many others like him, it was not simply a matter of convenience to preserve temporarily the old Austrian government administration, rather it was *their* administration.

Rašín's colleague, Tomáš G. Masaryk, who quickly assumed the presidency of the Czechoslovak Republic, raised deep concerns about the heritage of the Austrian state, its laws and practices, and the public's habituation to them. He was a keen observer of society's relationship to state authority and of long-ingrained popular attitudes toward government. Masaryk argued that if a new, more fundamentally democratic political culture were to develop under the Republic, with less dependence on the government bureaucracy and state initiative than under the monarchy, then the populace must make concerted efforts to "de-Austrianize" (*odrakouštiti se*) itself.[38] Given the strong legacy of the old state and the difficult contemporary circumstances, that was a great challenge for all the successor states of the Habsburg monarchy. Despite the intentions of political thinkers such as Masaryk, the traditions of strong bureaucratic authority in fact survived well in all the new states.

NOTES

1. See, for examples, Robert Nemes, *The Once and Future Budapest* (DeKalb, Ill.: Northern Illinois University Press, 2005); John-Paul Himka, *Socialism in Galicia: The Emergence of Polish Social Democracy and Ukrainian Radicalism (1860–1890)* (Cambridge, Mass.: Harvard Ukrainian Research Institute, 1983); Brian A. Porter, *When Nationalism Began to Hate: Imagining Modern Politics in Nineteenth Century Poland* (New York: Oxford University Press, 2000); Keely Stauter-Halsted, *The Nation in the Village: The Genesis of Peasant National Identity in Austrian Poland, 1848–1914* (Ithaca, N.Y.: Cornell University Press, 2001); Daniel Unowsky, *The Pomp and Politics of Patriotism: Imperial Celebrations in Habsburg Austria, 1848–1916* (West Lafayette, Ind.: Purdue University Press, 2005); Cathleen M. Giustino, *Tearing Down Prague's Jewish Town: Ghetto Clearance and the Legacy of Middle-class Ethnic Politics around 1900* (Boulder, Colo.: East European Monographs/Columbia University Press, 2003); T. Mills Kelly, *Without Remorse: Czech National Socialism in Late-Habsburg Austria* (Boulder, Colo.: East European Monographs/Columbia University Press, 2006); Jeremy King, *Budweisers into Czechs and Germans: A Social History of Bohemian Politics, 1848–1948* (Princeton, N.J.: Princeton University Press, 2002); Jiří Malíř, *Od spolků k moderním politickým stranám. Vývoj politických stran na Moravě v letech 1848–1914* (Brno, Czech Republic: Filozofická fakulta Masarykovy univerzity v Brně, 1996); John W. Boyer, *Political Radicalism in Late Imperial Vienna: Origins of the Christian Social Movement, 1848–1897* (Chicago: University of Chicago Press, 1981); idem, *Culture and Political Crisis in Vienna: Christian Socialism in Power, 1897–1918* (Chicago: University of Chicago Press, 1995); Laurence Cole, *"Für Gott, Kaiser und Vaterland": Nationale Identität der deutschsprachigen Bevölkerung Tirols 1860–1914* (Frankfurt: Campus 2000); Milan Hlavačka, *Zlatý věk české samosprávy* (Prague: Libri, 2006); Lothar Höbelt, *Kornblume und Kaiseradler: Die deutschfreiheitlichen Parteien Altösterreichs 1882–1918* (Vienna: Verlag für Geschichte und Politik/R. Oldenbourg, 1993); Pieter M. Judson, *Exclusive Revolutionaries: Liberal Politics, Social Experience, and National Identity in the Austrian Empire, 1848–1914* (Ann Arbor: University of Michigan Press, 1996); and idem, *Guardians of the Nation: Activists on the Language Frontiers of Imperial Austria* (Cambridge, Mass.: Harvard University Press, 2006). See also the accounts of the development of civil society in the second half of the nineteenth century in Helmut Rumpler and Peter Urbanitsch, eds., *Die Habsburgermonarchie 1848–1918, VIII: Politische Öffentlichkeit und Zivilgesellschaft*, 2 pts. (Vienna: Österreichische Akademie der Wissenschaften, 2006).

2. Jeremy King, *Budweisers into Czechs and Germans: A Local History of Bohemian Politics, 1848–1948* (Princeton, N.J.: Princeton University Press, 2002).

3. Maureen Healy, *Vienna and the Fall of the Habsburg Empire: Total War and Everyday Life in World War I* (Cambridge: Cambridge University Press, 2004), passim.

4. See the analysis of these constitutional and legal developments in Gerald Stourzh, *Die Gleichberechtigung der Nationalitäten in der Verfassung und Verwaltung Österreichs 1948–1918* (Vienna: Österreichische Akademie der Wissenschaften, 1985), 53–83, 189–213.

5. The compromises for Galicia and Budějovice could not be implemented because of the outbreak of World War I. On the various compromises, see King, *Budweisers*, 137–47; Robert A. Kann, *Das Nationalitätenproblem der Habsburgermonarchie*, 2nd ed., 2 vols. (Graz, Austria: H. Böhlau 1964) vol. 1, 199–200, 231, 331–35; and Stourzh, *Gleichberechtigung*, 213–40. On Moravia, see Horst Glassl, *Der mährische Ausgleich* (Munich: Fides-Verlagsgesellschaft, 1967); T. Mills Kelly, "Last Best Chance or Last Gasp? The Compromise of 1905 and Czech Politics in Moravia," *Austrian History Yearbook* 34 (2003): 279–303; and Tara Zahra, *Kidnapped Souls: National Indifference and the Battle for Children in the Bohemian Lands, 1900–1948* (Ithaca, N.Y.: Cornell University Press, 2008), 32–39. On Bukovina, see John Leslie, "Der Ausgleich in Bukovina von 1910: Zur Österreichischen Nationalitätenpolitik vor dem Ersten Weltkrieg," in *Geschichte zwischen Freiheit und Ordnung. Gerald Stourzh zum 60. Geburtstag*, ed. Emil Brix, Thomas Fröschl, and Josef Leidenfrost (Graz, Austria: Styria, 1991), 113–44; and Alon Rachamimov, "Diaspora Nationalism's Pyrrhic Victory: The Controversy Regarding the Electoral Reform of 1909 in Bukovina," in *State and Nation Building in East Central Europe: Contemporary Perspectives*, ed. John Micgiel (New York: Institute on East Central Europe, Columbia University, 1996), 1–16. On Galicia, see John-Paul Himka, "Nationality Problems in the Habsburg Monarchy and the Soviet Union: The Perspective of History and the Soviet Union," in *Nationalism*

and Empire: The Habsburg Monarchy and the Soviet Union, ed. Richard L. Rudolph and David F. Good (New York: St. Martin's Press, 1992), 79–93; and on Budějovice, King, *Budweisers,* 137–47.

6. See Stourzh, *Die Gleichberechtigung,* 200; and Edmund Bernatzik, ed., *Die Österreichische Verfassungsgesetze mit Erläuterungen,* 2nd exp. ed. (Vienna: Manz, 1911), 989, cited in Stourzh. On the Austrian electoral reform of 1907, see William A. Jenks, *The Austrian Electoral Reform of 1907* (New York: Columbia University Press, 1950).

7. For examples of the recent literature on citizenship in modern Europe, see Rogers Brubaker, *Citizenship and Nationhood in France and Germany* (Cambridge, Mass.: Harvard University Press, 1992); Geoff Eley and Jan Palmowski, eds., *Citizenship and National Identity in Twentieth-century Germany* (Stanford: Stanford University Press, 2008); Andreas Fahrmeir, *Citizenship: The Rise and Fall of a Modern Concept* (New Haven: Yale University Press, 2007); Daniel Gorman, *Imperial Citizenship: Empire and the Question of Belonging* (Manchester: Manchester University Press, 2006); Derek Heater, *Citizenship in Britain: A History* (Edinburgh: Edinburgh University Press, 2006); Theresa Ann Smith, *The Emerging Female Citizen: Gender and Enlightenment in Spain* (Berkeley: University of California Press, 2006); Judith Surkis, *Sexing the Citizen: Morality and Masculinity in France, 1870–1920* (Ithaca, N.Y.: Cornell University Press, 2006); John Torpey, *The Invention of the Passport: Surveillance, Citizenship, and the State* (Cambridge: Cambridge University Press, 2000); and Patrick Weil, *Qu'est-ce qu'un Français? Histoire de la nationalité française depuis la revolution* (Paris: Grasset, 2002).

8. On the contrasting development of civil society and government in the Austrian and Hungarian halves of the monarchy, see Gary B. Cohen, "Nationalist Politics and the Dynamics of State and Civil Society in the Habsburg Monarchy, 1867–1914," *Central European History* 40 (2007): 241–78; idem, *Die Habsburgermonarchie 1848–1918, VII: Verfassung und Parlamentarismus,* ed. Helmut Rumpler and Peter Urbanitsch, 2 pts. (Vienna: Österreichische Akademie der Wissenschaften, 2000); and idem, *Die Habsburgermonarchie 1848–1918,* vol. 8: *Politische Öffentlichkeit und Zivilgesellschaft* (Vienna: Österreichische Akademie der Wissenschaften, 2006).

9. On the development of *Heimatrecht* in imperial Austria, see Ludwig Spiegel, "Heimatrecht," in *Österreichisches Staatswörterbuch,* ed. Ernst Mischler and Josef Ulbrich, 2nd rev. ed., 4 vols. (Vienna: A. Hölder, 1906), vol. 2, 809–43. On *Heimatrecht* during the last decades of the monarchy, see Maureen Healy, "Becoming Austrian: Women, the State, and Citizenship in World War I," *Central European History* 35 (2002): 2.

10. On *Staatsbürgerschaft* in imperial Austria, see Josef Ulbrich, "Staatsbürgerschaft," in *Österreichisches Staatswörterbuch,* vol. 4, 312–14; Hannelore Bürger, "Zum Begriff der Österreichischen Staatsbürgerschaft: Vom Josephinischen Gesetzbuch zum Staatsgrundgesetz über die allgemeinen Rechte der Staatsbürger" in *Geschichte und Recht: Festschrift für Gerald Stourzh zum 70. Geburtstag,* ed. Thomas Angerer et al. (Vienna: Böhlau, 1999), 207–23; and idem, "Paßwesen und Staatsbürgerschaft" in *Grenze und Staat. Paßwesen, Staatsbürgerschaft, Heimatrecht, und Fremdengesetzgebung in der Österreichischen Monarchie (1750–1867),* ed. Waltraud Heindl and Edith Saurer (Vienna: Böhlau, 2000), 3–172.

11. On *habitus,* see Pierre Bourdieu, *Outline of a Theory of Practice* (Cambridge, U.K.: Cambridge University Press, 1977), 72–95; and idem, *The Logic of Practice* (Stanford, Calif.: Stanford University Press, 1990). On the need to see modern national loyalties as a *habitus,* see Gary B. Cohen, *The Politics of Ethnic Survival: Germans in Prague, 1861–1914,* 2nd rev. ed. (West Lafayette, Ind.: Purdue University Press, 2006), 10–11.

12. Rudolf Springer (pseud. of Karl Renner), *Der Kampf der Österreichischen Nationen um den Staat* (Leipzig: Deuticke, 1902).

13. See John W. Boyer, "Religion and Political Development in Central Europe around 1900: A View from Vienna," *Austrian History Yearbook* 25 (1994): 31–36; and Gary B. Cohen, "Neither Absolutism nor Anarchy: New Narratives on Society and Government in Late Imperial Austria," *Austrian History Yearbook* 29 (1998), pt. 1: 53–54.

14. See Lothar Höbelt, "Parliamentary Politics in a Multinational Setting: Late Imperial Austria," University of Minnesota Center for Austrian Studies, *Working Papers in Austrian Studies,* nos. 92–96 (1992): 4–6, 12–13; and idem, *Kornblume und Kaiseradler,* 180–87.

15. For examples, see Robert Ehrhart, *Im Dienste des alten Österreich* (Vienna: Bergland Verlag, 1958), 132–38, 144–45, 167–68, 175–85, 302–13; and Jan Galandauer, "Husův národ a most Františka Ferdinanda," *Historie a vojenství* 44 (1995): 3–20.

16. On the autonomous functions of provincial and communal governments during the late nineteenth century, see Hlavačka, *Zlatý věk české samosprávy;* Ernst C. Hellbling, "Die Landesverwaltung in Cisleithanien," and Jiří Klabouch, "Die Lokalverwaltung in Cisleithanien," in *Die Habsburgermonarchie 1848–1918, II: Verwaltung und Reschtswesen,* ed. Adam Wandruszka and Peter Urbanitsch (Vienna: Österreichische Akademie der Wissenschaften, 1975), 190–269, 270–305; Ludwig Spiegel, "Länder: Autonomie und Selbstverwaltung in der Gegenwart" in *Österreichisches Staatswörterbuch,* 2nd rev. ed., vol. 3, 395–430; and Oskar Gluth "Gemeinden" and "Gemeindeverwaltung," in *Österreichisches Staatswörterbuch,* 2nd rev. ed., vol. 2, 312–34.

17. See Wilhelm Brauneder and Friedrich Lachmayer, *Österreichische Verfassungsgeschichte* (Vienna: Manz, 1976), 177ff; Hans Peter Hye, *Das politische System in der Habsburgermonarchie* (Prague: Karolinum, 1998), 163–65; and Stourzh, *Die Gleichberechtigung der Nationalitäten,* 242. On ministerial objections to the autonomy of the provincial diets, see Alfred Ableitinger, *Ernest von Koerber and das Verfassungsproblem im Jahre 1900* (Vienna: Böhlau, 1973); and Fredrik Lindström, "Ernest von Koerber and the Austrian State Idea: A Reinterpretation of the Koerber Plan (1900–1904)," *Austrian History Yearbook* 35 (2004): 143–84.

18. See, for example, Heinrich Rauchberg, *Der nationale Besitzstand in Böhmen,* 3 vols. (Leipzig: Duncker und Humblot, 1905); and the discussion in Judson, *Exclusive Revolutionaries,* 203–204, 215–17, 219.

19. On the *Landesausschüsse,* see Ludwig Spiegel, "Länder: Autonomie und Selbstverwaltung in der Gegenwart," in *Österreichisches Staatswörterbuch,* 2nd ed., 3: 421–22.

20. On the *Annapatente,* see Jörg Hoensch, *Geschichte Böhmens von der slavischen Landnahme bis ins 20. Jahrhundert* (Munich: C. H. Beck, 1987), 405; Galandauer, "Husův národ a most Františka Ferdinanda," *Historie a vojenství* 44 (1995): 3–20; Otto Urban, *česká společnost 1848–1918* (Prague: Svoboda, 1982), 550–51; Lothar Höbelt, "Bohemia 1913—a consensual *coup d'état?,*" *Parliaments, Estates, and Representation* 20 (Nov. 2000): 207–214; Karel Kazbunda, *Otázka česko-německá v předvečer velké války,* ed. Zdeněk Kárník (Prague: Univerzita Karlova, 1995); and Gerald Stourzh, "Verfassungsbruch im Königreich Böhmen: ein unbekanntes Kapitel zur Geschichte des richterlichen Prüfungsrechts im alten Österreich," in *Staatsrecht und Staatwissenschaften in Zeiten des Wandels. Festschrift für Ludwig Adamovich,* ed. Bernd-Christian Funk et al. (Vienna: Springer-Verlag, 1992), 675–90.

21. On the growth of Austrian secondary and higher education after the 1860s, see Gary B. Cohen, *Education and Middle-class Society in Imperial Austria, 1848–1918* (West Lafayette, Ind.: Purdue University Press, 1996), 55–126; and Helmut Engelbrecht, *Geschichte des Österreichischen Bildungswesens,* 5 vols. (Vienna: Österreichischer Bundesverlag, 1982–88), vol. 4, passim.

22. On the nationalist contention regarding secondary and higher education, see Cohen, *Education and Middle-class Society,* 91–94, 112–13, 140–47, 157–59, 168–69; Engelbrecht, *Geschichte des Österreichischen Bildungswesens,* vol. 4, 295–319; and Hannelore Bürger, *Sprachenrecht und Sprachgerechtigkeit im Österreichs Unterrichtwesen, 1867–1914* (Vienna: Österreichische Akademie der Wissenschaften, 1995), passim.

23. On the clerical–anticlerical clashes, see Boyer, "Religion and Political Development in Central Europe around 1900: A View from Vienna," *Austrian History Yearbook* 25 (1994): 41–55; idem, *Culture and Political Crisis,* 46–55; and Engelbrecht, *Geschichte des Österreichischen Bildungswesens,* vol. 4, 16–18, 29–31, 177–78.

24. On the Lex Perek and nationalists' efforts to control parents' choice of schools for their children, see Zahra, *Kidnapped Souls,* 13–39; Stourzh, *Die Gleichberechtigung,* 216–21, 306–16; and Bürger, *Sprachenrecht und Sprachgerechtigkeit,* 190–94.

25. See Cohen, *Education and Middle-class Society,* 42–44; and Engelbrecht, *Geschichte des Österreichischen Bildungswesens,* vol. 4, 159.

26. Ministerium für Kultus und Unterricht (hereafter KUM), ministerial decree, 20 August 1880, Z. 12050; published in the *Wiener Zeitung,* 28 August 1880. See the discussion in Cohen, *Education and Middle-class Society,* 99–102.

27. Reports of local *Gymnasium* and *Realschule* directors and the governors of the crown lands to the Ministry of Religion and Instruction on secondary school admissions, in Allgemeines Verwaltungsarchiv Wien, KUM in gen., Z. 17460/1880, Z. 17623/1880.

28. On the beginnings of secondary education for girls, see Cohen, *Education and Middle-class Society,* 74–75; and Engelbrecht, *Geschichte des Österreichischen Bildungswesens,* 4: 282–92.

29. On Jews in imperial Austria during the half century before World War I, see William O. McCagg, Jr., *A History of Habsburg Jews, 1670–1918* (Bloomington: Indiana University Press, 1989); Marsha L. Rozenblit, *The Jews of Vienna, 1867–1914: Assimilation and Identity, 1867–1914* (Albany: State University of New York Press, 1983); idem, *Reconstructing a National Identity: The Jews of Habsburg Austria during World War I* (New York: Oxford University Press, 2001); Robert S. Wistrich, *The Jews of Vienna in the Age of Franz Joseph* (Oxford: Oxford University Press, 1989); and idem, ed., *Austrians and Jews in the Twentieth Century: From Franz Joseph to Waldheim* (New York: St. Martin's Press, 1992).

30. Quoted in Wistrich, *The Jews of Vienna*, 165.

31. On Jewish politics in Galicia, see McCagg, *History of Habsburg Jews*, 182–87; and Leila Everett, "The Rise of Jewish National Politics in Galicia, 1905–1907" in *Nation-Building and the Politics of Nationalism: Essays on Austrian Galicia*, ed. Andrei S. Markovits and Frank E. Sysyn (Cambridge, Mass.: Harvard Ukrainian Research Institute, 1982), 149–77.

32. See Rozenblit, *Reconstructing a National Identity*, 24–48; McCagg, *History of Habsburg Jews*, 161–200, passim; and Wistrich, *The Jews of Vienna*, 164–202, 238–69, 621–56.

33. For a good recent analysis, see Peter Urbanitsch, "Pluralist Myth and Nationalist Realities: The Dynastic Myth of the Habsburg Monarchy—a Futile Exercise in the Creation of Identity," *Austrian History Yearbook* 35 (2004): 101–42.

34. See Unowsky, *Pomp and Politics of Patriotism;* Laurence Cole and Daniel Unowsky, eds., *The Limits of Loyalty: Imperial Symbolism, Popular Allegiances, and State Patriotism in the Late Habsburg Monarchy* (New York: Berghahn Books, 2007); and Urbanitsch, "Pluralist Myth and Nationalist Realities," 101–42.

35. See Zahra, *Kidnapped Souls*, 83–85; and Richard Lein, "Das militärische Verhalten der Tschechen im Ersten Weltkrieg" (Ph.D. Diss., University of Vienna, 2009).

36. See Mark Cornwall, "Disintegration and Defeat: The Austro-Hungarian Revolution," in M. Cornwall, ed., *The Last Years of Austria-Hungary: A Multi-national Experiment in Early Twentieth-century Europe*, rev. and exp. ed. (Exeter: University of Exeter Press, 2002), 167–96; Healy, *Vienna and the Fall of the Habsburg Empire;* and Richard Georg Plaschka, Horst Haselsteiner, and Arnold Suppan, *Innere Front: Militärassistenz, Widerstand u. Umsturz in d. Donaumonarchie 1918* (Munich: R. Oldenbourg, 1974).

37. Alois Rašín, quoted in Věra Olivová, *Dějiny první republiky* (Prague: Karolinum, 2000), 67.

38. For an example of Masaryk's rhetoric on this point, see Tomáš G. Masaryk, *The Making of a State; Memories and Observations, 1914–1918* (New York: H. Fertig, 1969 [1927]), 432.

6

MARKING NATIONAL SPACE ON THE HABSBURG AUSTRIAN BORDERLANDS

1880–1918

PIETER M. JUDSON

Early in Fritz Mauthner's 1913 novel, *Der letzte Deutsche von Blatna*, the hero, Anton Gegen-bauer, remarks on a minor renovation to an arcade in the main square of his fictional small town, Blatna. For Mauthner and his protagonist, these external cosmetic changes reflect some much deeper transformations that have gradually overtaken the fictional Bohemian community.

> The words "Stephan Silber's Gasthaus"—"zum römischen Kaiser"—had decorated the middle arcade for 20 years. [As a child] Anton had first practiced his knowledge of spelling by reading those freshly gilded letters. Now the text had been whitewashed and the bright red letters that decorated the white background spelled out: "Stjepan Zilbr hostinec." The given name Stephan had been Czechified, the name "Silber" had simply been written using Czech orthography; "hostinec" basically meant the same thing as "pub," but sounded more patriotic than "Gas-thaus." This painting over, along with the changes inside that they reflected, symbolized the process by which the German town had slowly but surely been transformed into a Czech one.[1]

Mauthner, a German (nationalist) Jewish Bohemian sets this tragic tale of national de-cline on the language frontier, a kind of unofficial borderland within imperial Austria that was understood to separate the Czech and German nations. In this region, Mauthner tells us, the specific geographic feature that separated the two nations was the Bjelounka river. "From time immemorial, the Bjelounka had served as the sharp frontier between the Czech and the German people, between the Slavic lowlands and the [German] highlands." The tollhouse at the southern extreme of Blatna sat "on the last piece of German earth," and "even the [statue of] St. John Nepomuk on the bridge would have spoken Czech, if silence had not been his lot."[2] In the course of the nineteenth century, however, some alarming new developments had called the traditional certainties of this boundary into question. Czech families had crossed the Bjelounka in search of employment with the prosperous German artisans and manufacturers of Blatna. Gradually, Czechs too had bought property in the town, and soon "some houses on the [main street], some offices in the Town Hall and even the Church Sacristy" came into Czech hands. The language frontier had been breached, although much of this had happened without evidently affecting the surface character of the town. "In Blatna there were many people who spoke German with difficulty, but together they felt themselves to be part of a German town."[3] The national character of the town changed more visibly, however, as Czech nationalists began to assert their presence more publicly. The fearful German community, meanwhile, acquiesced to the new conditions, and bilingual opportunists like pub owner Stephan Silber (himself a Slovakian Jew, we learn) followed the new direction the wind was blowing. Only Anton, the last German in Blatna, manfully battled Czech trickery, Czech threats of boycotts, of violence, and even Czech attempts to use an innocent girl to seduce him, in order to maintain both his nation's honor and the German character of his hometown.

In the context of late Imperial Austria this term "borderland" rarely referred to a border between sovereign states. Instead, borderlands usually referred to internal national or cultural frontiers that allegedly separated—or conjoined—imagined nations, cultures, or even civilizations, along shared peripheries. In the 1890s the use of the term "borderland" to characterize a town like Blatna would have called to mind several powerful ideological images for a nationalist readership, some of which I will elaborate below. These images were produced thanks largely (and unintentionally) to decisions made by Austria-Hungary's demographers in the 1870s. They determined that starting with the decennial census of 1880, respondents in Austria would be asked to list their "language of daily use." Nationalists had increasingly used the census results to plot the territorial extent of their nations geographically. They produced maps and statistical studies that measured and depicted the geographic dispersal of the population that spoke the national language, along with its gains or losses from decade to decade. Because nations had no legally sanctioned existence in Imperial Austria and occupied no officially recognized administrative units of territory, activists viewed the mapping, marking, and defense of these national frontiers as all the more critical. And because nationalists in Austria tended to define their national cultures primarily in terms of language, the use of a given language became their primary measure of the nation's territorial spread.

The officially a-national and apolitical census, on which many of these presumptions about national territory rested, became an important political moment every ten years, when rival nationalists of all kinds struggled against each other to increase their numbers.[4] The frontiers in this case were the places where people who spoke different languages lived next to each other. Since the census did not measure the phenomenon of bilingualism, it was possible to imagine that the choice of one language excluded the potential choice of other languages, and thus in theory to map the geographic extent of a single language's use.[5] At the same time, although the census did not reflect the extent of bilingualism in multilingual regions, nationalist activists were well aware that in such regions they had to use every possible power of persuasion to attract as many people as possible to their side, and to diminish the threat of side-switching. The language frontiers where such switching was possible became critical sites for nationalist activism.

In a sign of their anxiety about demographic changes in these conceptually peripheral regions, nationalist activists painted them as wild, untamed, potentially violent rural
frontiers, lawless regions less cultivated and civilized than the national centers.[6] For many
nationalists, the geographic proximity of one national culture to another alone conjured
disturbing images of vulnerability to unspecified forms of social disorder, to a breakdown
of cultural norms, but also images of potential heroism. Not surprisingly, given these dynamics, nationalist attitudes about these frontiers betrayed a contradictory set of hopes and
fears. In terms of their hopes, nationalists understood the language frontier to be the site
of authentic national identity, of age-old struggle, of strong and fearless frontier guardians.
Nationalists depicted the hardy frontier people as more nationally authentic than the "lazy
cultural degenerates" who inhabited the unthreatened hinterland with its cities and cosmopolitan culture. According to this view, these frontier peasants acted as border guards for
the nation. Their experiences told a moral lesson. Their families had lived in such regions
for centuries where they had battled to maintain their national identity in the face of attacks
by devious enemies. Another frontier novel about the southern borderlands, Rudolf Hans
Bartsch's *Das deutsche Leid,* depicted the Styrian border Germans in ideal terms: "Only the
strongest hearts can survive here on the borderland. Men, for whom honor and duty come
naturally, whose hearts are filled with divine love and not the earthly variety, men who are
strong enough to remain steadfast, to be good friends to each other and a worthy enemy to
the opponent . . . We offer a strong example, we people of the borderlands, we are no flabby
half-breeds."[7] On Bartsch's frontier (as on Mauthner's), the very physical proximity to other
nations clarified the boundaries that supposedly separated Germans from their Czech or
Slovene neighbors. The virtues displayed by the frontier German not only differentiated him
from other Germans, but more importantly, these virtues delineated the ways he differed
from his Slavic neighbors.

In terms of fears, however, nationalists also worried that the frontier could be breached,
as in the case of Mauthner's Blatna. Clearly, the conception of the frontier peasant as a hardy
national hero coexisted uncomfortably and in tension with far less flattering depictions of
peasants in these border regions. Activists constantly found themselves battling against what
they considered to be national indifference among peasants and rural villagers based in stubborn ignorance or religious fanaticism. Rural villagers frequently had no idea that a national
battle raged around them. They accepted bilingualism as normal; they socialized regularly
and even intermarried with members of other nations. Nationalists worried about the reli-
ability of rural communities on these language frontiers, especially where cunning, trickery,
and aggression on the part of a national enemy replaced normal forms of social interaction,
and where only the strongest representatives of the nation could maintain a clear sense of
national loyalty. Any national indifference on the part of villagers might cause the nation
to lose numbers and territory to the enemy. According to this view, the best way to bolster
frontier people in this daily battle for national survival was to teach them about their national
identity. These fears made it possible for nationalist activists from Austria's cities to justify
setting up shop in rural regions. They simultaneously found reasons to praise the locals they
encountered even as they complained about the shocking levels of national indifference and
ignorance they encountered.

Projecting aggressive colonizing hopes and demographic fears onto Austria's language
frontiers, nationalist activists of all kinds in Imperial Austria, whether Czech, German, or
Slovene, struggled to push back the frontier. Strengthening or expanding the frontier re-

quired ingenuity, strategic thinking, and considerable resources, because, in theory at least, the national opponent on the other side of the frontier engaged in the same kind of zero-sum game. So while language frontiers provided compelling settings for nationalist propaganda and calls to arms such as Mauthner's novel, they also increasingly demanded real interventions by activists determined to save them for the nation. Nationalist ambitions for the frontiers were limitless. Activists spoke of securing regions through colonial settlements, of building population bridges between territories, and of pushing enemy nations back behind rivers or mountain ranges. The bulk of the work they actually took up in these language frontier regions, however, involved far less ambitious forms of daily activism. Instead, as mentioned above, activists on the frontier found that their biggest challenge was to teach locals about the primary importance of their relationship to their nation.

Instead of developing *in situ* out of local experiences with a multilingual society, beliefs about national difference actually had to be imported to regions where pluricultural practices characterized daily life well into the twentieth century.[8] Rural Austria had its share of social conflicts, but those conflicts did not usually develop out of a prior sense of belonging to one nation or another, or of using one language or another. Nor does the evidence suggest that local differences in language use had traditionally produced hostilities within communities in multilingual regions.[9] In fact, activists' assertions about the nationalist significance of linguistic differences did not reflect deeply rooted cultural conflict or significant power differentials between alleged national groups, especially in the rural world.[10] Their claims often ran counter to the logic of local social practice in such regions. Instead of giving political voice to existing social and cultural differences in rural Austria, as nationalists claimed they did, their rhetoric constituted a strategy designed to *create* new social boundaries in multilingual communities, precisely where few such boundaries had traditionally existed. In fact, as nationalists occasionally admitted in frustration, the people of the frontier sometimes simply refused to commit themselves to a nation or to recognize that their language-use gave them a distinct national identity. Like renegades in stories of wartime struggle, on occasion these people even appeared to betray the national cause. Villagers frequently defended their rights to a bilingual education for their children, for example, against the prescriptions of nationalists who saw in bilingualism the first step toward a child's denationalization. In other cases too, religious practice and village tradition often signified more to local people as markers of community than did the different languages they used in daily life.[11] In the rest of this chapter I will explore some institutions, ritual and symbolic practices, and strategies of persuasion nationalists developed in order to promote a greater sense of national identification among the inhabitants of borderland regions in Bohemia, Moravia, and Styria.

Nationalists—especially, in retrospect, after 1918—liked to portray their movements as spontaneous products of popular agitation. But in fact it was the ways state policy made particular issues available for debate and particular political or organizational institutions available for use that enabled nationalists to build their movements. It is important to note just how the institutional framework within which they operated shaped the issues around which nationalists built their programs and the specific organizational strategies they developed. The enormously creative forms of community activism national activists brought to villages, towns and cities throughout the Empire were shaped more than we realize by imperial institutions.

In terms specifically of *form*, the constitutional laws of 1867 that created a common Austrian citizenship guaranteeing the rights of free association, of political participation, of a relatively free press, and of communal autonomy provided activists with several possible opportunities and sites for organizing effective local or interregional movements. At the same time, the new laws influenced the particular developmental trajectories taken by nationalist movements. For example, because the constitution placed some limits on specifically political associations—barring women from membership and requiring the presence of a police deputy at public meetings—it makes sense that the rise of mass nationalist organizations in Austria preceded and overshadowed the rise of effective mass nationalist political parties. These nonpolitical self-help organizations could profit from the activist energies of a female membership and avoid close scrutiny by the police.[12]

In terms of ideological *content,* these self-help organizations took up issues that would give them the greatest return on their activist investment. Again, imperial laws and constitutional rights played a key role in determining activist programs. Although the constitution did not admit the existence of nations, for example, it did recognize individual Austrians' right to an education in their own language, and to be able to communicate with the civil service in their own language. These general (vague) constitutional goals of linguistic equalization (*Gleichberechtigung*) were confirmed and elaborated by an independent judiciary in the decades following the constitution's implementation.[13] If we examine the issues around which local nationalist activists built their organizational efforts, we find that they focused precisely on elaborating or expanding those constitutional rights and that they frequently used the courts to do so. The first successful mass organizations created in 1880 by Czech and German nationalists were school associations, the *Ústřední matice školská* (Central Mother School) and the *Deutscher Schulverein* (German School Association). Slovene nationalists established their school association, the *Družba Ciril-Metod* (Cyril and Metodius Association) in 1885, and Italian nationalists founded a *Lega Nazionale* (National League) in 1891. These interregional organizations used the constitutional recognition of the right to schooling in one's own language to force the administration to expand the rights of linguistic minorities.

Seeking to reverse alleged national decline in border regions, these school associations raised money to build so-called "minority language schools" in districts where not enough school-aged minority children lived to entitle them to a public school in their own language. Austria's Supreme Administrative Court ruled in 1884 that if a minimum of 40 children living within four kilometers desired schooling in another language, then the state would have to provide a community with such a school.[14] Thus, once a school association had established a private minority school in a community, it worked hard to entice 40 children to attend, so that the state would have to assume public funding of the school, and the association could use its funds to start the process all over again in another village. That was hardly the end of the story, however. Once one school association became involved in a local community, it did not take long before a rival school association came to the local defense of "its" minority or majority, thereby escalating a competition for local children. Access to education in a particular language became one of the most sensitive political issues in the Monarchy, often shaping the forms of activism and politics engaged in by local nationalists.

Probably the most visible and influential nationalist institution in any frontier community was the minority or national schoolhouse. The solid, often two-story modern school buildings with their high-pitched roofs and signs that announced the "Česke Škola," the "Slovenske Škola," or the "Deutsche Schule" often towered over the rural landscape and constituted an aggressive challenge by one nationalist group to the local hegemony of another. More than nationalist street names or even monuments commemorating nationalist heroes like Jan Hus or Emperor Joseph II, the schools constituted an unmistakable symbol of national difference on a contested frontier. Or did they? Nationalists in multilingual frontier regions wanted locals to see the world in terms of opposed national communities. But in order to make their schools succeed, local nationalists often had to abandon their ideological insistence on purity, on cultural—if not racialized—differences that allegedly separated nations. The very pervasiveness of the kinds of behaviors that nationalists deplored—bilingualism, so-called mixed marriages or other unseemly forms of fraternization among nations—forced them to compete for children of all kinds to populate their schools. While nationalists proclaimed visions of cultures separated by unbridgeable gulfs, they used every form of persuasion they could devise to persuade anybody to send children to their schools.

By the turn of the century, nationalists used gifts of clothing, shoes, books, or even money to persuade families to send their children to one school or another.[15] In one 1913 fundraising appeal, for example, the German School Association reminded members that its schools required increasing support in order to compete successfully with well-funded Slav alternatives for "children from mixed marriages or children of nationally hermaphrodite parents." Such parents might send their children to "whichever school was better equipped or organized" or whichever school provided material advantages such as "free books or other instructional materials or better presents at Christmas."[16] Local competition for children could become fierce not simply because of economic incentives, but also because local parents frequently had good reason to desire a bilingual education for their children. On a trip to investigate nationalist conflict in Bohemia during the First World War, Viennese socialist and education expert Robert Scheu observed that, "Some families send their children alternately to the Czech school one year and the German school the next." This practice, he noted, produced a situation in which, "Both nations attempt to win students over for their schools, and not always with the most honest methods."[17] In his memoir, Heinrich Holek, a working-class Bohemian, recalled how his father had decided to send him to a new minority school erected by the Czech matice školská both because of the promised gifts of clothing and shoes, but also because his father believed that "it could also be useful for me to learn to write properly in Czech."[18]

Similar situations obtained in other so-called frontier regions of the Empire. A German nationalist newspaper in 1905 reported from the Styrian village of St. Egydi/Šentilj, for example, that five pupils had withdrawn from the German minority school that year to attend its Slovene counterpart, allegedly because of "nationalist agitation." It accused local Slovene nationalists of spreading rumors that children at the Slovene language school would receive new clothing for Christmas as opposed to the "old rags" distributed by the German School Association. Furthermore, two German families had supposedly decided to transfer their children to the Slovene school because it had a better reputation than the German school. The German nationalist reporter alleged bitterly that the real reason for the popularity of the Slovene school might be the fact that in the previous year "not one pupil had been disciplined for poor attendance."[19]

If minority schoolhouse buildings marked nationalist claims to the landscape in stone and brick, their glass windows often made them attractive targets for vandalism and sometimes riots. After the turn of the century, many frontier minority schools repeatedly suffered on those occasions when local rowdies had too much to drink or when they perceived that the community the school symbolized had wronged them in some way. Although it would be difficult to attribute particular motives to the individuals who actually vandalized minority school buildings, the nationalist media had no doubt who was to blame. Newspapers took advantage of such incidents to promote the idea that serious nationalist conflict threatened the locality.[20] A vandalized school offered a stern warning to members of a national community that the other side would not shrink from using violence if necessary, to accomplish its goal of political or cultural transformation. A vandalized school also provided local nationalists with a more convincing argument that national conflict was real and that the national community was physically endangered. Broken windows offered an immediate example of that "breached frontier" that Mauthner's novel described.

Frontier minority schools offered nationalists other opportunities to engage the local community in nation-building activities that also made claims on public space. School festivals, for example, involved parents and their children in public celebrations that could easily become public enactments of national identity. Whether parents and children actually experienced these celebrations as exercises in national community, nationalists on all sides certainly interpreted them in this fashion. In 1906 German and Slovene activists interpreted a festival in the Styrian town of Lichtenwald/Sevnica in nationalist terms because of its association with the new German minority school there. It is not clear, however, whether the parents and children who participated felt themselves to be engaged in a national ritual or simply a school ritual. Census data for Lichtenwald/Sevnica suggests that because the German-speaking minority was very small, there can be little doubt that a majority of the children who attended this school, described by one nationalist newspaper as "the most beautiful building in Lichtenwald," came from Slovene-speaking families. (In purely nationalist terms they had been seduced by the enemy to become renegades). On the evening of 29 July, children and parents joined to celebrate the end of the school year. After the festivities, held on school grounds, the organizers gave the children Chinese lanterns for a parade to the town's main square. With a small band playing, the children sang and their parents marched with them to the center of town. There, however, they encountered a crowd of some 50 people standing outside an inn who yelled "*pfui,*" an expression of disgust, along with the Slovene greeting "*Na zdar.*" A small riot ensued. No children were hurt, but anarchy reigned for an hour until the local gendarmes arrived to enforce the peace.[21] Not all such school festivals and celebrations ended in violence. Nevertheless, the example demonstrates both the importance nationalists assigned specifically to schools as physical symbols of nationalist programs, and the importance of rituals that enacted ownership of public space for the nation.

The teachers in minority schools often constituted the most committed nationalists in many frontier villages and towns. Teachers' numbers had expanded rapidly, starting with the liberal Austrian school reforms of 1869 that required eight years' primary schooling for both boys and girls. Within five years in Bohemia alone, five hundred new schools had been founded; by 1914 that number had grown to two thousand. In order to accommodate this expansion, the state set up teacher training institutes, and for the first time accorded teachers a status similar to that of state civil servants.[22] This new status and the rights to social insurance programs it offered made teaching an attractive vehicle for ambitious students from *Mittelstand* backgrounds who hoped to achieve social mobility and financial security. Many teachers came from rural village or small town backgrounds, but their training had taken them to Prague, Graz, Brünn/Brno, or Vienna where they had often become exposed to nationalist movements. When they were posted to rural schools, they often brought with them new commitments and enthusiasms for the national idea. Teachers hired by the nationalist school associations to teach in minority schools had an even greater sense of national mission.

Teachers' roles in constructing local national society built on their core educational functions in the classroom. Czech and German nationalist teachers in Bohemia and Moravia, for example, also served as librarians for the local peoples' libraries that offered (nationalist) entertaining and educational fare to their clients. In some regions rural schoolteachers served as informal loan officers for local nationalist credit unions, or as the organizers of reading societies, discussion clubs, adult education groups, lecture series, and of patriotic nationalist public celebrations. As we will see below, when local nationalists raised a monument to Joseph II or Jan Hus, for example, the schoolteacher often led the consecration ritual, explaining to onlookers the significance of the national figure whose stone likeness would now dominate the village square. The teacher, counseled one German nationalist pamphlet, "should emphasize the German character and honorable German history of the community, perhaps by focusing on important German role models from the past that can evoke pride and emulation among contemporary rural people."[23] Many Czech, German, and Slovene nationalist associations also hired "travelling teachers," men who hiked regularly from village to village in a given region, holding lectures and workshops on both nationalist and economic themes, and reporting to their employers on the national conditions they encountered in each locality. All of these pedagogical exercises aimed to mobilize as many local villagers as possible for nationalist events, to reinforce fundamental concepts of national difference that allegedly separated peoples, and to make those differences visible in daily life. As one Czech nationalist association pointed out, "The local branches of our [Czech] nationalist associations owe their existence in the countryside mainly to teachers. . . . They work in every way possible for the awakening of the indifferent countryside."[24]

Besides school associations, several other kinds of mass nationalist associations also directed local efforts to define and protect the embattled frontier. These organizations generally tried to engage a broader range of aspects of people's public and even private lives. Both Czech and German nationalists founded regional nationalist defense organizations, starting in 1884 with the *Národní jednota pošumavská* and the *Deutsche Böhmerwaldbund,* respectively, in southern Bohemia. These were quickly followed by the founding of defense organizations for other regions of Bohemia and Moravia. To the south, German nationalists in Graz founded the *Südmark* in 1889, an organization meant to protect and expand the local hegemony of the German nation in Austria's southern borderlands.[25] These organizations swiftly gained tens of thousands of members generally organized in small local branches that were responsible for planning local activism and funding the central organization.[26]

If imperial institutions had shaped the structural particulars of mass nationalist associations, the budding consumer and advertising revolutions of the late nineteenth century also influenced many of the tactics with which nationalists experimented. From the start, nationalists sought strategies that would make a territory national in easily recognizable ways and that would also remind people of the importance of national identity to their local social life. Nationalists adapted a variety of imaginative consumption-related strategies along with countless symbols and ritual practices both to rally men, women, and children for the nation and to produce a local landscape that was legibly national. Their frequent assertion that national defense was primarily a family issue enabled them to mobilize around issues that would otherwise have been considered purely domestic. This redefinition of national politics to highlight the family made the mobilization of women an increasingly central aim after 1900, even as these organizations proclaimed their essentially nonpolitical character. Despite the fact that boycotts were formally illegal in Imperial Austria, for example, nationalist news-papers and pamphlets counseled women to shop for food at shops and market stalls run by their co-nationals, to hire co-nationals as domestic servants if possible, and to consider the nation in every question of domestic consumption and leisure. Women in these organiza-tions also proved themselves to be skilled organizers and especially impressive fundraisers, as Heidrun Zettelbauer and others have recently demonstrated.

An examination of their financial records shows that in the years after 1900, the mil-lions of crowns these organizations raised annually to fund their various projects derived less from membership dues and increasingly from lotteries, festive fundraising events, and especially from the sale of cheap nationalist-designed commodities such as postcards, stamps, stationary, official forms, soap, and kitchen matches. Their expanding endowments in turn helped the nationalists to build their minority schoolhouses, their libraries, social centers, museums of local history, and monuments, and also funded imaginative propaganda campaigns, economic improvement schemes, welfare programs, and in one case colonial settlements.[27] As this list suggests, restless nationalists constantly sought new sites for their activism. In particular, after 1910, nationalists developed a range of welfare programs and institutions directed especially at children that also sought to bind clients to one national community or the other.[28]

The combination of consumer appeals with nationalist activism was also key to activ-ists' efforts to organize nationalist tourism in language-frontier regions of Austria. Already in the 1890s many nationalist defense organizations commissioned cheap guidebooks about their regions that they advertised in the rest of Austria. These early efforts attempted to ad-dress dual concerns. In the first place, nationalists argued that other members of the nation ought to learn more about the existence of these peripheral frontier regions and to visit them in order to offer both moral and financial support to the threatened frontier people. In the second place, however, tourism in the 1890s often appeared to constitute a potentially lucra-tive addition to the local economy, especially in rural regions suffering economic decline. Tourism might help to support local people so that they could remain in their frontier re-gion instead of emigrating and making way for the national enemy to take over. Very few organizations managed successfully to popularize tourism to their regions, however, in part because a successful tourism industry required a level of planning, of infrastructure, and of experience with commerce that was not to be found in most such regions. Some local na-tionalists also complained about the alleged indifference of their fellow citizens to making their village attractive to visitors or to offering visitors a decent level of service (politeness and hygiene were usually at issue). Still, whether they pursued this strategy seriously or not, all nationalist organizations appear to have talked about it.[29]

Where the idea of tourism made more of a local impact seems to be in the more mod-est ways it could be harnessed to organize leisure activities for locals, and in the ways that locally produced guidebooks and tours framed local history and landscapes in nationalist terms, however rudimentary. The Czech and German nationalist organizations for South-ern Bohemia, (the *Národní jednota pošumavská* and the *Deutsche Böhmerwaldbund*) pur-sued opposite strategies in this regard. Both budgeted significant funds for tourism-related projects, but the Czech association funded trips to Prague for groups of school-age children or young adults, while the German nationalists focused on bringing urban dwellers to the region for rural vacations.[30] Both groups competed to create hiking routes in forests and mountains, to build competing huts for different groups of hikers, and to restore historic buildings and sites that brought alive their nation's history. Both sides organized holiday trips on foot or by wagon to local destinations where participants might relax in a Czech or German beer garden. After 1900 these groups and others annually produced a range of postcards that depicted tourist destinations in national terms, or scenes from the nation's history.[31] Visiting the same location, the rare bilingual tourist with no national preconceptions might have derived a completely schizophrenic view of the experience. How local inhabitants interpreted this competition over local public space is, of course, more difficult to determine.

Such competition often yielded more permanent attempts to mark territory. Starting in the 1880s, for example, local German nationalists, particularly in linguistically mixed regions of Bohemia and Moravia began raising money to erect statues to Habsburg Emperor Joseph II. As many historians have noted, Joseph II's popular significance changed considerably during the late nineteenth century, from a nationally unmarked symbol of freedom for the peasantry, to a hero of German nationalism.[32] Joseph statues appeared across Bohemia, starting with the centennial of his accession in 1880, and they gained an increasingly nationalist significance during this decade. By 1900 statues of Jan Hus also made their appearance in many parts of Bohemia, as this religious figure became a popular symbol for a largely secular Czech nationalist movement. As elsewhere in Europe, the existence of controversial monuments produced vandalism against them, but also a local set of ritual celebrations that incorporated monuments into the local landscape. Once town or village in Bohemia had erected a Joseph or a Jan Hus monument in its square, then local nationalist associations devised regular ritual festivals of commemoration both to control the meaning of the monument and to continue to use it to mark territory for the nation.[33]

This brief survey suggests that linguistic borderlands came to occupy a critically important place in the imaginations of nationalist activists in the last half-century of Habsburg Austria's existence. Unlike the situation in royal Hungary, for example, a state founded explicitly on the power of the official Magyar nation, nationalists in Imperial Austria had to build their own communities without the help of a state. The history of the Imperial Austrian state after 1867 therefore, offers an interesting example of state-building that took place separately from the kind of cultural and political practices of nation-building that characterized many other European states during the same period. Within the context of an empire that neither recognized nations in law, nor recognized particular territories as belonging to particular nations, nationalists worked hard to define and justify their territorial pretensions in historic and increasingly in demographic terms.[34] This dynamic almost guaranteed that those territories where different nations allegedly bordered each other would become key sites of nationalist agitation. These linguistic borderlands offered nationalists the tempting opportunity to expand their territory primarily by pushing back the demographic boundaries between nations, a tendency confirmed by the incessant colonizing rhetoric that may be found in Czech and German nationalist literature of the period.[35] Nationalists could as easily, however, project masochistic fears of their own victimization at the hands of a national opponent onto precisely the same regions. The very indeterminate nature of these borderlands and their inhabitants made it possible to view them simultaneously from both perspectives.

Whatever linguistic differences may in fact have characterized the populations of these regions, this diversity had not necessarily produced a perception of distinct cultures among the local inhabitants. Nationalists, therefore, sought to build loyalty to national communities on the borderlands by literally nationalizing every possible aspect of daily life. For nationalists, there could be no public or private space that remained outside the nation. Their ritual and symbolic practices sought to confirm this truth for the people of the frontier. Yet as Tara Zahra has argued recently, it was precisely this totalizing competition among nationalists for the loyalties of local people that often produced the very contemptible behaviors of national opportunism or indifference that nationalists deplored.[36] Indifference among local people was far more a product of this nationalist competition, a strategy, for example, to assert agency and gain material advantage, than it was an archaic or premodern quality of rural tradition or rural ignorance, as the nationalists tended to characterize it. Opportunism among local people, in turn, drove nationalists to occupy ever more radical positions. It is certainly the case that by 1914 far more inhabitants of these language frontier regions had a stronger sense of belonging to a national community than they had in 1880. Nevertheless, the history of these regions well into the twentieth century demonstrates that the logic of nationalism continued to promote an attitude of nationalist opportunism among noticeable segments of the population. Had this not been the case, the issue of side switching or of national opportunism could not have remained such a powerful concern for nationalists even after the creation of self-styled nation states after 1918. Nazi policies in the occupied Sudetenland, Bohemia-Moravia, or the Yugoslav sections of Styria (to name the regions I have cited in this chapter) also raised these issues all over again in new contexts, but the Nazis too could find no coherent way to address them adequately. Only the radical finality of the post–World War II expulsions from such regions resolved their instability by removing their qualities as borderlands.[37]

NOTES

1. Fritz Mauthner, *Der letzte Deutsche von Blatna* (Berlin: Ullstein & Co, 1913), 72–73. Although there is an important town called Blatna in Bohemia, Mauthner gives his town an entirely fictional location and geography.

2. Mauthner, *Der letzte Deutsche*, 22–23.

3. Mauthner, *Der letzte Deutsche*, 24.

4. The best account by far of the Imperial Austrian census, its history and its politicization, remains Emil Brix, *Die Umgangssprachen in Altösterreich zwischen Agitation und Assimilation. Die Sprachenstatistik in den zisleithanischen Volkszählungen 1880 bis 1910* (Vienna: Böhlau, 1982).

5. On bilingualism and the census, see Brix, *Die Umgangssprachen,* 77–96; Jeremy King, *Budweisers into Czechs and Germans: A Local History of Bohemian Politics, 1848–1948* (Princeton, N.J.: Princeton University Press, 2002), 57–59.

6. For depictions, see Pieter M. Judson, *Guardians of the Nation: Activists on the Language Frontiers of Imperial Austria* (Cambridge, Mass.: Harvard University Press, 2006). For a German East comparison, see Kristin Kopp, "Constructing Racial Differences in Colonial Poland" in *Germany's Colonial Pasts,* ed. Eric Ames, Marcia Klotz, and Lora Wildenthal (Lincoln: University of Nebraska Press, 2005), 76–96.

7. Rudolf Hans Bartsch, *Das deutsche Leid: Ein Landschafts-Roman* (Leipzig: Verlag von L. Staackmann, 1912), 433.

8. Anil Bhatti "Kulturelle Vielfalt und Homogenisierung" in *Habsburg Post-Colonial. Machtstrukturen und kollektives Gedächtnis,* ed. Johannes Feichtinger, Ursula Prutsch, and Moritz Csáky (Vienna: StudienVerlag Ges. m.b.H., 2003), 55–68. Bhatti defines pluricultural character in terms of the strategies, rather than the outcomes, of daily life interactions.

9. In the eastern crownlands of Imperial Austria (Galicia, Bukovina) religious differences created more of a sense of distinct local cultures, but even there, shared local cultural commonalities

may often have outweighed specific differences in language use or religious practice when it came to loyalty and self-identification.

10. For an insightful analysis of this point for the southern province of Carniola, see Joachim Hösler, *Von Krain zu Slowenien. Die Anfänge der nationalen Differenzierungsprozesse in Krain und der Untersteiermark von der Aufklärung bis zur Revolution, 1768 bis 1848* (Munich: R. Oldenbourg Verlag, 2006). Hösler demonstrates that the later conflation by Slovene nationalists of German language use with feudal large landowners and of Slovene language use with the peasantry did not reflect local social usage in Carniola. When revolution broke out in 1848, for example, peasant programs saw no connection between language-use, class, and nation.

11. For some examples, Judson, *Guardians,* 39–40; Tara Zahra, *Kidnapped Souls: National Indifference and the Battle for Children in the Bohemian Lands, 1900-1948* (Ithaca, N.Y.: Cornell University Press, 2008), especially 30–32. This phenomenon of indifference to nation should not be viewed as a marker of premodern or nonmodern attitudes, the way nationalists themselves conceived of it. Often, for example, people remained indifferent to the concept of nation, or wedded to practices of multilingualism and other strategies for improving their life chances, even under quite "modern" conditions.

12. On women's activism, Heidrun Zettelbauer, *"Die Liebe sei Euer Heldentum." Geschlecht und Nation in völkischen Vereinen der Habsburgermonarchie* (Frankfurt am Main: Campus, 2005).

13. Gerald Stourzh, *Die Gleichberechtigung der Nationalitäten in der Verfassung und der Verwaltung Österreichs 1848-1918* (Vienna: Verlag der Österreichischen Akademie der Wissenschaften, 1985).

14. Hannelore Burger, *Sprachenrecht und Sprachgerechtigkeit im Österreichischen Unterrichtswesen, 1867-1918* (Vienna: Verlag der Österreichischen Akademie der Wissenschaften, 1995), 100–113. This dynamic played out in almost every one of Austria's Western crownlands, but it did not apply as obviously to Galicia. The autonomy negotiated by Galicia's Polish nationalist rulers at the time of the writing of the constitution ensured for them a relatively selective enforcement of several imperial laws, especially the school laws. This ensured also that the rate of illiteracy in Galicia was dramatically higher than in most of the rest of Austria.

15. Zahra, *Kidnapped Souls,* 13.

16. *Der Kampf ums Deutschtum* (Vienna, 1913), vol. 2, 25.

17. Robert Scheu, *Wanderung durch Böhmen am Vorabend der Revolution* (Vienna: Strache, 1919), 200–201.

18. Heinrich Holek, *Unterwegs. Eine Selbstbiographie mit Bildnis des Verfassers* (Vienna: Bugra, 1927), 146, quoted in Zahra, *Kidnapped Souls,* 28. Zahra also documents concerns by Czech nationalists that this bidding for children bred materialism and opportunism among parents.

19. *Marburger Zeitung,* 9 May 1905, 5.

20. The nationalist newspapers reported one such incident in the Styrian town of Lichtenwald/Sevnica in 1908 as a nationalist outrage, although it involved three youths who had consumed an extreme amount of alcohol and whose nationalist motives were unclear. See Judson, *Guardians of the Nation,* 58–59

21. For census data see K. k. statistische Zentralkommission, ed., *Gemeindelexikon der im Reichsrate vertretenen Königreiche und Länder bearbeitet auf Grund der Ergebnisse der Volkszählung vom 31. Dezember 1900,* vol. 4: Steiermark, (Vienna: Hölder, 1904), 252; for an account of the incident, see *Marburger Zeitung,* 29 July 1906; Steiermärkisches Landesarchiv (archive), Präsidium der KK steierm. Statthalterei, 573, Betreff: Lichtenwald, Schutz für die deutsche Vereinsschule, 1906–1907.

22. Karl Hugelmann, ed., *Das Nationalitätenrecht des alten Österreich* (Vienna and Leipzig: Braumüller, 1934), 371–73; Burger, *Sprachenrecht,* 39–43.

23. *Mittheilungen des Deutschen Böhmerwaldbundes* 8 (1886), 100.

24. František Joklík, *O poměrech českého národního školství a učitelstva v kralovství českem* (Prague: Beaufort, 1900), 129.

25. Most of these organizations established separate women's branches in the 1890s.

26. While the membership numbers of these organizations are impressive, it is of course important to distinguish between local branches that actually organized events, erected monuments, and generally sought to galvanize local communities, and the branches that simply existed on pa-

per. It also is important to note, especially among the German nationalist organizations, that these groups did not always agree on the specific parameters of the nation, especially in the case of German and Czech nationalists with regard to the question of Jewish membership.

27. The *Südmark* was the only association to attempt a serious colonization scheme. In the last decade before World War I it resettled farming families, often from southern Germany, on land acquired in the region immediately to the north and west of the Styrian city of Marburg/Maribor. For detailed accounts, see Judson, *Guardians of the Nation,* 100–140; and Eduard Staudinger, "Die Südmark: Aspekte der Programmatik und Struktur eines deutschen Schutzvereins in der Steiermark bis 1914," in *Geschichte der Deutschen im Bereich des heutigen Slowenien, 1848–1941,* ed. Helmut Rumpler and Arnold Suppan (Vienna: Verlag für Geschichte und Politik, 1988), 130–154.

28. See, for example, Tara Zahra, "Each Nation Only Cares for its Own: Empire, Nation, and Child Welfare Activism in the Bohemian Lands, 1900–1918," *American Historical Review* (December 2006): 1378–1402.

29. Pieter M. Judson, "'Every German visitor has a völkisch obligation he must fulfill': Nationalist Tourism in the Austrian Empire, 1880–1918," in *Histories of Leisure,* ed. Rudy Koshar (New York: Berg, 2002), 147–68.

30. On expenditures for tourism-related activities for the two organizations, see annual financial reports and descriptions in *Zpráva o činnosti Národní Jednoty Pošumavské* and *Mittheilungen des Deutschen Böhmerwaldbundes.*

31. Rudolf Jaworski, *Deutsche und tschechische Ansichten. Kollektive Identifikationsangebote auf Bildpostkarten in der späten Habsburgermonarchie* (Wien: Studienverlag, 2005), especially 63–78.

32. Ibid., 58. Nancy M. Wingfield, "Statues of Emperor Joseph II as Sites of German Identity," in *Staging the Past: The Politics of Commemoration in Habsburg Central Europe, 1848 to the Present,* ed. Maria Bucur and Nancy M. Wingfield (West Lafayette, Ind.: Purdue University Press, 2001), 178–205.

33. Cynthia Paces and Nancy Wingfield, "The Sacred and the Profane; Religion and Nationalism in the Bohemian Lands, 1880–1920," in *Constructing Nationalities in East Central Europe,* ed. Pieter M. Judson and Marsha L. Rozenblit (New York: Berghahn, 2005), 107–25. The demand for the Joseph II statues was so great, that a special ironworks in Blansko Moravia mass-produced them; see Wingfield, "Statues," 183.

34. It is important to note that starting with the Moravian Compromise of 1905 (and subsequent compromises in 1910 in Bukovina and 1914 in Galicia), in an attempt to diffuse the power of political nationalism, the state agreed to recognize nations legally in particular provincial contexts. In Moravia, for example, the compromise dictated that citizens be divided largely between German and Czech cadastres, for the purposes of schooling and elections to the Moravian Diet and to the Parliament. The problem of how to determine to which cadastre someone belonged quickly arose, especially since some Moravians were loath to identify with either. Nationalists increasingly demanded objective external determinations of national belonging, while the imperial state preferred to leave the question to individuals. In terms of judicial rulings in Moravian disputes about categorization, the nationalists were beginning to win this battle against the rights of individuals by 1914. In successor states like Czechoslovakia or Yugoslavia after 1918, however, the balance tipped precipitously in the other direction, and individuals generally lost all ability to determine their own national identities. See Judson, *Guardians;* Zahra, *Kidnapped Souls.*

35. For Czech nationalist examples, see Peter Haslinger's magisterial *Nation und Territorium im tschechischen politischen Diskurs 1880-1938* (Munich: R. Oldenbourg Verlag, 2010); also idem, "Staatsrecht oder Staatsgebiet? Böhmisches Staatsrecht, territoriales Denken und tschechisches Emanzipationsbestreben 1890–1914," in *Reiche und Territorien in Ostmitteleuropa. Historische Beziehungen und politische Herrschaftslegitimation,* ed. Dietmar Willoweit and Hans Lemberg (Munich: Oldenbourg Wissenschaftsverlag, 2006), 345–58; and "Der Rand als Zentrum? Die deutsch besiedelten Grenzregionen der böhmischen Länder als Wertezentrum im tschechischen nationalen Diskurs (1880–1938)" in *Mythen der Mitte. Regionen als nationale Wertezentren Konstruktionsprozesse und Sinnstiftungskonzepte im 19. und 20. Jahrhundert,* ed. Monika Gibas (Weimar: Bauhaus-Universität Weimar, 2005), 287–301.

36. Zahra, *Kidnapped Souls,* 269–73.

37. Even the expulsion process raised thorny issues of national belonging and identity, especially in Czechoslovakia. See, for example, David Gerlach, "Working with the Enemy: Labor Politics in the Czech Borderlands, 1945–48," in *Austrian History Yearbook* 38 (2007), 179–207; Benjamin Frommer, *National Cleansing: Retribution Against Nazi Collaborators in Postwar Czechoslovakia* (New York: Cambridge University Press, 2005); Zahra, *Kidnapped Souls,* 253–64.

7

Travel, Railroads, and Identity Formation in the Russian Empire

Frithjof Benjamin Schenk

Historians often perceive railroads primarily as an infrastructure helping a state to consolidate its territory and to integrate distant regions into one economic and political space. This is also true for most of the literature on the history of railroads in nineteenth century Russia. Undoubtedly the steam engine was an important tool in the Tsarist Empire to link various geographical parts of the large country one with another and thereby to enhance the exchange of commodities and the mobility of the population. In the second half of the nineteenth century both the government and private investors helped to create an iron network, which was envisioned already by contemporary cartographers as a skeleton strengthening the cohesive forces within the huge polyethnic empire. But by increasing the mobility of a significant number of Russian subjects, railroads also opened new opportunities for people to experience ethnic and religious diversity. Contemporary travel accounts bear witness that travelers on Russian railroads perceived the empire less as a homogeneous space of communication than a fragmented territory inhabited by a great and sometimes uncomfortable variety of ethnic and religious groups. Moreover, the railroad proved to be an effective tool in the hands of those political actors who were trying to undermine political stability. In particular, in the western borderlands railroads repeatedly became a target of politically motivated violence and were used by militant groups to spread the seeds of ethnic hatred. The Russian example bears witness that the railroad, envisioned by its proponents as a golden path to social and spatial integration, in the immediate term enabled violence and contributed to developing social disintegration.

My essay may be read—in a more general sense—as a plea for the inclusion of railway history into the broader discourse on the history of the borderlands of European empires in the long nineteenth century. As a matter of fact historians have treated the history of infrastructure in general and of railroads in particular for a long time as an exclusive domain of scholars studying either economic or technical history. Railway historians, conversely, have often neglected the great cultural and social impact of the construction and the use of networks of modern infrastructure in the era of the steam engine, but in recent years there has been a "cultural turn" in railway history.[1] In this spirit, we have to bring the history of infrastructure back into the general narrative of the development of European societies in the era of industrialization. The history of the borderlands of the Romanov, Habsburg, Ottoman, and Hohenzollern empires in particular gains substantially from insight into the social and cultural impacts of the construction and the use of modern infrastructure in the era of the steam engine.

The construction of railway networks altered significantly the structures of social spaces within these contested regions of the continent's polyethnic empires. In the imperial capitals the invention of the railroads inspired far-reaching spatial fantasies by politicians, military experts, and geographers alike. Both the state and private actors made a strong effort to use the new means of transportation in order to transform geographically and culturally heterogeneous territories into politically and economically integrated spaces. But in the borderlands of the continental empires of Europe, populated by a variety of ethnic and religious groups, the introduction of networks of modern transportation had extensive and often unintended social and cultural side effects. On the one hand, railways became an effective tool of imperial rule, helping imperial administrations to exert political and military control more effectively over large territories at the empires' peripheries; construction of railroads thereby helped to integrate borderland areas into the political, economic, and cultural space of their respective empires. On the other hand, the construction of railroads led to a significant increase in human mobility in all countries encountering the process of modernization of their infrastructure. Increasingly mobile societies became a growing threat to the social and political order of the *anciens régimes* in the polyethnic empires for various reasons. The new means of transportation opened up new possibilities for an increasing number of people to explore the various geographical regions of the imperial territories personally and thereby to encounter the empires' ethnic and religious heterogeneity. It is an open question whether this confrontation between an increasing number of subjects and the "imperial characters" of their respective empires consolidated feelings of imperial identity or—on the contrary—enforced processes of increased national or ethnic alienation. As the Russian example shows, the new means of transportation were also used by proponents of national liberation movements in the borderlands, enabling them to build up their own networks of communication and to destabilize mechanisms of imperial rule by attacking railways and telegraph lines. This chapter will analyze the ambivalent impact of the modernization of networks of transportation in the western borderlands of the Russian Empire in the second half of the nineteenth century.[2]

In the following, I will provide some observations on the ambivalent impact of infrastructure building and use in imperial contexts in nineteenth century Europe. First, I will briefly outline the political debates among Russian bureaucrats in Saint Petersburg in the latter half of the nineteenth century concerning the construction of railroads in the western part of the Russian Empire, and describe the development of the rail network in this part of the country prior to World War I. Second, I will focus on the travel accounts of nineteenth century railroad passengers traversing the Western Empire, describing their encounters with multiethnicity inside and outside the railroad cars. Finally, I will reflect on the issue of railroads and politically motivated violence, focusing first on the anti-Jewish pogroms of the early 1880s and second on the train raids conducted by the Polish Socialist Party at the beginning of the twentieth century.

The term "western borderlands" is used in this context in a rather broad sense. It comprises a geographically large region that was extremely heterogeneous in both socioeconomic and cultural terms. "Western borderlands of the Russian Empire," as they are understood in this article, encompassed the so called "western region" (*Zapadnyi krai*), the territory of the Polish Kingdom, the provinces of "left-bank Ukraine" (Chernigov and Poltava), New Russia (*Khersonskaia guberniia, Tavricheskaia guberniia*) and the province of Ekaterinoslav in the southwestern part of the country.[3] Despite the mixed character of this large region, it was nonetheless shaped by a number of common historical and structural features.[4] To a large extent the western borderlands were parts of the Polish-Lithuanian Commonwealth before they were incorporated into the Russian Empire in the eighteenth and nineteenth centuries; other parts belonged until the eighteenth century to the Ottoman Empire. In the second half of the nineteenth century the density of population in this region was much higher than in any other of the border zones of the imperial realm. In terms of socioeconomic development the region—the Polish Kingdom in particular—toward the end of the nineteenth century surpassed not only the other peripheries but also the core area of imperial Russia. Finally, the population of the western borderlands comprised a large number of different ethnic and religious groups. Since the boundaries of the region were almost identical with the Jewish Pale of Settlement, the area was also the homestead of the majority of Russian Jews. Toward the end of the century the political development in the region was increasingly dominated by the conflicting agendas of the Polish, Lithuanian, Ukrainian, Jewish, and Russian national movements, along with various kinds of revolutionary parties that strove to extend their social bases.

Railroads and the Consolidation of Territory in the Western Borderlands

When the Russian administration started to debate the possibility and utility of building railroads in the Tsarist Empire in the 1830s, proponents of the steam engine argued from the very beginning that the new means of transportation might help strengthen the links between the Russian heartland and the politically troublesome periphery in the West. In his note for Tsar Nicholas I, Franz Anton von Gerstner, an Austrian entrepreneur who applied in 1835 for the concession to build an entire network of railroads in European Russia, deliberately alluded to the revolutionary events in the Kingdom of Poland in 1830–1831 in order to convince the Emperor of the necessity of covering his realm with railway lines. Gerstner informed Nicholas I that the British government had successfully applied the new means of transportation for the quick dispatch of troops to suppress a revolt in Ireland.[5] He argued, "if Petersburg, Moscow, and Grodno or Warsaw had been connected by rail, it would have been possible to subdue the Polish insurgents in four weeks."[6] Although Gerstner's reference to the Polish November uprising was a good example of the applicability of the steam engine for strategic purposes, a railroad from Petersburg or Moscow to Warsaw or Grodno was ironically not part of the rail network he suggested setting up in European Russia in 1835.[7]

A few years later, the construction of long-distance railroads in Russia began—in the Western part of the empire.[8] In 1839 Nicholas I approved the application of a group of private investors from Warsaw, who planned to connect the city with the Austrian capital by rail.[9]

The plan was initiated by the Russian viceroy of Poland, Count Ivan Paskevich, who wanted to deflect the flow of Polish trade from Prussia to the Habsburg Empire. When the private stock company went bankrupt in 1843 the Russian government took over and completed the line in 1848.[10] Just a few years later Nicholas I gave the go-ahead for the construction of the strategically important railroad from St. Petersburg to Warsaw. The head of the empire's Board [later Ministry] for Ways of Communication, Count Petr Kleinmikhel' and other leading bureaucrats had openly criticized this project because they doubted its economic usefulness. Nevertheless the Emperor ordered the erection of the line in February 1851, half a year before the first overland railroad in Russia from St. Petersburg to Moscow was officially inaugurated.[11] Nicholas I perceived the railroad to Warsaw as a means to tighten the bonds between the politically unreliable Polish Kingdom and the Russian heartland and to strengthen the western borderlands strategically.[12] He argued that "in case of a sudden outbreak of war with the present state of the rail network in Europe, Warsaw, and with it our entire west, could be overrun by enemy forces before our troops could succeed in getting from Petersburg to Luga."[13] Although the beginning of the Crimean War in 1855 interrupted the construction of the Petersburg–Warsaw railroad, work resumed in 1857 and the line opened in 1862. Soon after its inauguration the railroad to Warsaw proved its utility for imperial rule. In 1863 the line enabled the autocratic regime quickly to dispatch guard regiments to the western provinces and the Polish Kingdom to suppress the January uprising.[14] In the same fashion, some years earlier the railroad from Warsaw to Vienna had enabled the Russian government in 1849 to relocate troops to Hungary, helping to contain the revolutionary upheaval there.[15]

Throughout the second half of the nineteenth century the western borderlands of the Russian Empire remained in the focus of infrastructure politics for two reasons. First, leading strategists in the Russian Ministry of War predicted a future military confrontation between the Tsarist Empire and its neighboring countries in the West. Therefore they urged their government to follow the example of Prussia and the Habsburg Empire, which were developing their networks of modern means of transportation in quick pace, improving their abilities to dispatch their troops to the Russian border with rapidity in the case of war.[16] Second, the experience of the January uprising in 1863 seemed to underscore the need to consolidate further the empire's territory in the west with the help of railway lines. Many contemporaries were influenced by the idea that a network of modern means of transportation would not only integrate a country economically but in the meantime would help overcome cultural and ethnic borders.

A good example of this way of thinking is the lecture that General of Infantry Sergei Buturlin gave in 1865 at the Imperial Society for History and Archaeology in Moscow.[17] This presentation was part of a larger campaign by the Ministry of War against the plans of the Board of Ways of Communication for the development of Russia's network of railroads, drafted by the administration's head Pavel Mel'nikov in 1862–1863.[18] Mel'nikov, a representative of the first generation of Russian engineers of transportation, perceived railroads first and foremost as an instrument to integrate the territories of the Tsarist Empire economically. His aim was primarily to connect the centers of Russian agricultural (and to a lesser extent industrial) production with the highly populated areas in European Russia and with the empire's harbors at the Baltic and the Black Seas. In earlier years Mel'nikov had openly criticized the construction of a strategic railroad from St. Petersburg to Warsaw. Therefore it was not surprising that he included in his 1862 master plan just one more railway line crossing the western borderlands (from Briansk to Odessa via Chernigov, Kiev, and Balta). Mel'nikov's draft was published in 1863 and ignited a large public debate about the principles of Russia's future railway policy. Proponents of an economically sustainable network argued with advocates of strategic railroad building; supporters of regional business interests were confronted with activists seeking to serve the interests of the empire as a whole; adherents of a state-funded railroad were facing experts reminding them of the limited resources of the government's budget and arguing for cooperation with private investors. Sergei Buturlin represented the camp of railway politicians promoting the construction of *strategic* railways in general and in the western borderlands of the empire in particular.[19]

Referring to a possible scenario of a war of defense (*voina oboronitel'naia*) against Russia's Western neighbors, Buturlin reminded his listeners in 1865 of the fact that Warsaw was located 200 *versts*[20] closer to the river Rhine than to Moscow and that the distance between the Polish capital and Moscow was in fact even larger due to the poor state of the roads in Russia. The countries of Europe, having built a dense network of railway lines in the last 20 or 30 years, had accordingly succeeded in "shortening the distance between themselves and Russia" significantly, whereas the distance between Russia and the West had remained almost the same.[21] Buturlin argued that Russia must not stand idle facing this problem. Instead he formulated a detailed plan for the construction of approximately 6,095 versts of new railway lines in the western part of the country. The author, who wisely did not touch the difficult question of costs and funding for his ambitious project, planned not only to strengthen Russia's military potential against attacks from her Western neighbors, but also to crisscross Russia's western borderlands from the Baltic Sea to the Crimea with a network of strategic railroads as an answer to separatism and revolutionary movements in this region. Alluding openly to the January uprising of 1863 Buturlin stated:

> Railroads have a great strategic importance as a means of national defense [*oborony kraia*] against enemies both from outside and from inside. [This is particularly true] in that case when a state has integrated by force territories inhabited by tribes [*plemena*] of different ethnic origin which have not merged yet morally with the conquering people. Integration and acculturation [*sliianie*] can be and must be reached with the help of legal and political measures. . . . But if there exist elements which openly or secretly obstruct the moral integration of all parts of the political body to which they belong . . . , the government has to ground its regime in the revolting areas on the basis of military institutions. These include, among others, the permanent presence of armed forces, the building of fortifications and the construction of ways of communication serving the army to move easily and quickly to any destination in order to prevent or to suppress internal disorder or to throw back an assault from outside.[22]

Buturlin argued that it would serve Russia's strategic interests better if one built railroads "which join the Western parts of the empire with the country's core area" than railways connecting Russia's periphery with the country's Western neighbors or improving the mutual exchange and traffic between the various parts of the western borderlands.[23] That's why Buturlin identified the city of Brest-Litovsk as the most Western outpost of Russia's strategic railway system. According to his plan the territory of the Polish kingdom should not be further developed by a network of modern infrastructure.[24]

Buturlin's outline reflected almost perfectly the main features of the Ministry of War's official railway policy in the 1860s. Three years later, in 1868, Minister of War Dmitrii Miliutin urged Tsar Alexander II in a memorandum to make further investments in strategic railway building in Russia's western borderlands.[25] He reminded the Tsar of the superiority of Russia's Western neighbors in terms of infrastructure development. Both Prussia and the Habsburg Empire could rely on more railway lines leading to the common border than the Tsarist Empire, enabling them to dispatch troops more quickly to the front in a future war. Like Buturlin, Miliutin made a strong argument for the construction of strategic railroads from the Russian heartland to the western borderlands and agreed that Poland should *not* be part of the program of railway construction in the future.

In fact the question whether the Tsarist administration should encourage the construction of railroads in the Kingdom of Poland remained disputed within the Ministry of War until World War I. After the Franco-Prussian War of 1870–1871, which Prussia managed to win in large part due to the quick movement of troops and armaments on strategic railroads, Miliutin himself looked at the issue of railroad building in Russia's Western periphery from a different perspective. In 1873 the Minister of War demanded at an official meeting on national security affairs the construction of 5,000 versts of new strategic railway lines in the Western part of the country, 1,000 within the borders of the Polish Kingdom. But due to a lack of sufficient funding none of the 11 lines he demanded were constructed until 1881 and only three until 1888. After a new shift in strategic planning at the beginning of the twentieth century, the Ministry of War in 1910 again opposed the construction of new railroads in the Polish Kingdom, on the grounds they could help a future aggressor quickly to invade the Russian heartland.[26]

The repeated shifts in railway policy by Russia's Ministry of War clearly illustrate the undecided attitude of the Tsarist elite toward the issue of infrastructure building and its possible impact in the western borderlands in the second half of the nineteenth century. Already in December 1861 the General-Governor of the northwestern region (*Severo-Zapadnyi krai*), General V. I. Nazimov, had warned of the "ambivalent attitude of the administration of the newly opened [St. Petersburg–Warsaw] railroad and the personnel of the line who are almost exclusively Poles and foreigners."[27] Nazimov apparently was afraid of the regime's dependence on the loyalty of the representatives of national minorities who were running the new system of transportation. The experience of the January uprising would soon show that Nazimov's fears were not at all ill-founded. When the national revolt began, Polish insurgents not only burnt several railway bridges and cut the wires of the strategically important telegraph; they found active supporters among the staff of the privately run railroad company who were happy to further obstruct the quick dispatch of loyal Tsarist troops by rail to the revolting provinces.[28] After the uprising's suppression the railwaymen who had collaborated with the insurgents were harshly punished and the Tsarist administration made a strong effort to enhance its control over the strategically important network of railway lines in the Western districts.[29] In 1880s Warsaw Governor-General I. Gurko even advocated that Poles not be employed in the railway sector any longer. Subsequently it was decided to ban Polish staff from the most important strategic railway lines. But this decision remained difficult to implement as there simply were not enough qualified Orthodox technical and engineering specialists to substitute for the professionals of Catholic backgrounds.[30] The Tsarist administration was not only afraid of disloyal Polish railwaymen. Bureaucrats in the administration of the General-Governor of Vilna had warned back in 1867 against further consolidating the regional railway network between the *Zapadnyi krai* and the Polish Kingdom. In a letter from August 23rd the official A. P. Storozhenko reported that the construction of the railroad from Vil'na to Warsaw had significantly increased the reach of Polish nationalist propaganda in the province of Grodno. The local bureaucrat lamented that the railroad brought not only pork salesmen from Mazuriia but also "agents of the Polish cause" "spreading unrest" in the region.[31]

Notwithstanding these misgivings, neither the Minister of War, who was afraid of further developing the network of modern infrastructure in the Polish Kingdom, nor the local representatives of the Tsarist regime in the western borderlands who warned of the unintended political effects of railway building at the empire's periphery could stop the process of modernization and industrialization that Russia in general and her western borderlands in particular were experiencing in the second half of the nineteenth century.[32] Between 1868 and 1872 the Tsarist Empire encountered its first boom of railroad building, with a second one coming in the 1890s. During these periods the western borderlands became the region with the best developed regional railway network in the entire empire.[33] Already the public debate about the construction of the so-called "Southern Line" had shown in the 1860s that the arguments of those political forces stressing the importance of the steam engine for the *economic* development of the country often exceeded those of the representatives of the national security agencies.[34] Despite the hesitant attitudes of several agencies regarding the modernization of the region's infrastructure, it was the western borderlands that experienced the quickest development of railroad networks, and consequently the greatest increase in passenger mobility, of any region of the Russian Empire toward the end of the nineteenth century.[35]

The Railway Journey and the Experience of Ethnic Diversity

Despite the fact that railway passengers traveling from the Russian heartland to the Habsburg Empire had to change trains in the city of Warsaw due to different gauges on the tracks eastward and westward of the Vistula River, cartographers of the nineteenth century envisioned the vast expanses of the Tsarist Empire as a single, homogeneous space structured and bound together by a integrated system of black, iron arteries.[36] From the 1880s on every waiting room of the first two classes in Russian railway stations had to be equipped with such a map of Russian networks.[37] But it is an open question whether cartographical artifacts of this kind had an enduring effect on the mental maps of Russia's railway passengers. Did, one may ask, passengers traveling by rail in the western borderlands experience the space outside the railway car really as an integral part of one national or imperial space? Was the image of an iron network holding together the various parts of the multiethnic empire only a product of the wishful thinking of engineers and cartographers, or did it also have a significant impact on the patterns of spatial perception of Russian railroad passengers? The analysis of a small number of randomly selected travel accounts by Russian railway passengers who visited the western borderlands during the last decades of the nineteenth century make a different hypothesis more likely. Apparently the new possibilities for easy travel from one part of the country to another in the railway age did not consolidate images of territorial integrity but, on the contrary, strengthened the awareness of the multiethnic and multi-religious character of the huge country. Different ethnic and religious groups came into focus in these travelers' perceptions according to the geographical regions they covered. When taking a closer look at travel accounts from Russians who made their trip to or through the western borderlands of the empire in the late nineteenth century, one is repeatedly surprised by the omnipresence of anti-Jewish stereotypes and detailed descriptions of Jews as embodiments of the internal "other." Apparently many Russian railway travelers perceived these regions mainly as a "Jewish" space that differed significantly from the Russian heartland.

For travelers in railway cars in late nineteenth century Russia, experiencing the internal borders of the empire was first and foremost a matter of acoustic perception. Aleksandr Klevanov, a historian and translator of ancient literature, made a trip in 1870 from St. Petersburg to the German lands, crossing the Western periphery in a first-class carriage of the St. Petersburg–Warsaw line.[38] In the city of Dünaburg/Dvinsk, at the intersection with the railway line to Riga, Klevanov noticed a large number of Germans entering the train who accompanied the traveling society to Vilna. Getting closer to the empire's western border he remarked that he had left the Russian heartland acoustically: "the employees of the railways are without exception Polish. The sound of the Russian language can't be heard anywhere except from travelling passengers."[39] After he had gone through passport control at the Russian checkpoint, which was conducted by a Polish border guard, he stated: "In general the last impressions of my fatherland [*rodiny*], at least those of the Polish borderland [*okrainy*], were not too pleasant." In order to illustrate his estrangement in the borderzone, he added that a Jew addressed him at the station, offering to change his Russian money into Austrian currency.[40]

The encounter with the Jews in the western borderlands left a deep impression on most of the Russian railway voyagers who gave an account of their travel experiences in this region. This was also true for those Russians who lived in the western part of the empire and who in principle were well acquainted with the polyethnic reality of social life in these regions. For example, Vasilii Liakhotskii, an Orthodox priest from the city of Kholm/Chełm, made a roundtrip from his Polish/Ukrainian hometown through the Russian Empire by train in 1898 and published his travelogue two years later.[41] At the railway station of Kovel' in Volhynia, where Liakhotskii and his fellow passenger came into contact with Jews offering them accommodation in a local hotel, the author made fun of the "*zhidki*" and their Russian accent.[42] Two years later Liakhotskii left again his hometown for a journey to the southern Caucasus, documented in another travel account.[43] This time he bought a ticket for a third-class carriage, which took him from Kholm via Kovel' southwards to Berdichev, Kazatyn and further to Rostov na Donu. On the first part of his journey his carriage was almost completely populated by Jewish passengers. In his travelogue Liakhotskii frankly reveals his feeling of discomfort in this situation:

> This tribe [*plemia*] stands out because of its [extraordinary—FS] forbearance, which can be studied particularly on journeys like this. In order to travel as cheap as possible a Jew [*zhid*] is even happy to sleep the whole way underneath an ordinary bench. Since there were so many Jews in the car (it was after Saturday), many of them had almost to sit down on somebody else.[44]

Liakhotskii did not hide his anti-Jewish sentiments when he called the city of Berdichev a *zhidovskaia stolica* (capital of Jews) and described Jewish passengers on their way to Kiev in the following strongly derogatory terms: "This tribe, repudiated by God and other people, strives to the capital, to the mother of Russian towns, the sanctuary of Rus', meanwhile our folk are wandering from the North to the South and the way back just in order to make a living."[45] Obviously Liakhotskii perceived the western borderlands as an integral part of an all-embracing imperial space of communication. Nevertheless, he interpreted the increasing mobility of the different ethnic and religious groups less as an indicator of growing spatial cohesion and more as an erratic and ominous development.

Despite the increasing density of the local network of railroads in the western border-lands of the Russian Empire before World War I, the region did not lose its image as a sphere of political unrest and instability. This spatial stereotype was based not only on the percep-tion of the polyethnic composition of the region's population but also on the imagination of its landscape. The report of Vasilii M. Sidorov, who traveled in the late 1880s by train from Vilna to Kiev, is a lucid example of this kind of mental mapping.[46] Sidorov, who had a choice between a rail connection via Brest and one via Gomel, chose the latter option and got stuck in the swamps of Pripiat. After days of rain the river had flooded wide areas of the embank-ment and train traffic was stopped in order to avoid serious accidents. After having passed "endless forests" Sidorov got "deeper and deeper into the land of nowhere, into the woods, into the horrible marshes of Pinsk." In his train that could move neither forward nor backward he experienced the "feeling of absolute loneliness [*chuvstvo polneishago odinochestva*], . . . of horrible depression [*strashnoi toski*] and alienation of everything familiar [*otchuzhdennosti ot vsego blizkogo*]."[47] There were almost no other passengers in the train, except three huntsmen in the second class and some peasants in the third. On the railway stations he met just "crowds of Jews [*zhidy*], who curiously stared at me without understanding what I am doing in this soli-tude."[48] After having arrived in the city of Gomel he was shocked by the "filthy hotel room in the provincial town that was crowded with Jews."[49] When he finally got to Kiev, two days later than originally planned, he felt as if he "saw the light again" after a journey through the darkness.

The Russian perception of the western borderlands in late nineteenth century was af-fected both by patterns of ethnic diversity in general and the Jewish population in particular. This becomes even more obvious if one takes a closer look at the memoirs of a Jewish writer who reported on a railway journey from St. Petersburg to Moscow in the 1860s.[50] Vladimir Garkavi, a son of a wealthy Jewish family in Vilna, moved to Moscow in 1864, in order to start his studies in law at the city's university. Garkavi went first to St. Petersburg, from where he took the train to his new hometown. Traveling in a cheap third-class carriage, the young student was surrounded by Russian peasants, women and children who were sitting on the "benches and on the floor." Every passenger carried a lot of luggage; people drank tea, sang songs, slept on the floor and underneath the settees. Garkavi was surprised that during the whole journey, which lasted about 36 hours,

> nobody pronounced the word "*zhid*." I became acquainted with almost every passenger and—what seems to me quiet naïve and funny from today's perspective—I read loudly poems of Nekrasov and Nikitin to the peasants [in the train]. The peasants listened attentively, giving a deep sigh from time to time, and I realized that I was in touch with the essence of [Russian] folk life. In the carriage I made first acquaintance with an educated Russian woman. . . . We talked about literature, about Belinskii, Dobroliubov, Pisarev, Chernyshevski, and about the female protagonists in Turgenev's novels. From my accent and manner of speech she recog-nized that I was a "foreigner" [*inorodets*]. But when I told her that I was a Jew, she was more than surprised.[51]

Garkavi's travelogue is a fascinating source. It illustrates that the railways as a modern means of communication could open up new spaces of social integration and interethnic communi-cation. But this was apparently true to a larger extent for the railways in the heartland of the Russian Empire than for its western borderlands.

The perception of the western borderlands of the Tsarist Empire by Russian railway passengers as a "Jewish" space corresponds in an interesting way with the patterns of description of trains and railway stations in this region in Yiddish literature at the turn of the century. Analyzing novels and short stories by Elyokum Zunser, Sholem Abramovitsh, Sholem Aleichem, and David Bergelson in which railroads play an important role both as settings for the story and/or as a signifier of modernity, Leah Garrett writes of a tendency to "Judaize" Russian railroads in the Yiddish literature of the time.[52] Contemporary Jewish writers repeatedly depicted the railroads as a means of helping Jews either to escape or to pull them out of the narrow world of traditional shtetl life. Although Jews were neither allowed to work for the telegraph service of the Russian railroads (decree of 1875) nor to rent restaurants and buffets at railway stations (decree of 1894) and were not even allowed after 1897 to practice their religion openly in train compartments or the waiting rooms of Russian railway stations, Jewish writers developed various imaginative techniques to appropriate these public spaces.[53] Garrett unveils an ambivalent mode of perceiving the railroads in Yiddish literature in the second half of the century.[54] Zunser, Abramovitsh, and other Yiddish authors depicted the railroads in the Pale of Settlement as a space of social encounter where Jews got in touch with men and women from different parts of the country and representatives of other religious and ethnic groups. Whereas Zunser praised the steam engine in his poem "Der ayznban" ("The Railroad"), written in 1865, as a "democratic, positive force to literally transport the Jews into the modern world," Bergelson depicted a Ukrainian railroad depot in his 1909 novel *Arum vokzal* (*At the Depot*) as a location of complete stagnation and social desperation.[55] Overcrowded compartments in third-class railway cars inspired both Sholem Abramovitch's short story "Shem un Yefes in a vogn" ("Shem and Japheth on a Train") in 1890 and Sholem Aleichem's *Ayznban-geshikhtes* (*Railroad Stories*), written between 1902 and 1909.[56] Abramovitsh uses this framework to tell a mythical story of reconciliation and fraternization between a Jewish tailor and a Polish shoemaker during a time of modern ethnic persecution, while Aleichem depicts crowded railway cars as an almost ideal site for the exchange of information, gossip, and Jewish storytelling.

Railroads and Politically Motivated Violence

Aleichem's *Railroad Stories,* though they have to be treated of course primarily as literary fiction, give us a good impression of the extent to which the steam engine altered social life in the Jewish Pale of Settlement at the beginning of the twentieth century.[57] From his narrative we learn a lot about the narrowness and noisiness of overpopulated third-class carriages, and about Jews ignoring the law prohibiting prayers in the public sphere. Aleichem depicts the ceremonial welcome of trains by the populace of small towns in the western borderlands, and the increased mobility of Jewish traders and salesmen. Vicariously, we experience the encounters and conflicts between different religious and ethnic groups in trains and railway stations. Moreover, Aleichem's stories can be read as an attempt "to explore a new kind of Jewish experience and to describe a Jewish society that had reached a new level of development or of disintegration."[58] His tale, "The Wedding That Came without Its Band," written in 1909, is of particular interest in our context.[59] In this short story Aleichem treats the subject of railroads and their role in anti-Jewish pogroms in early twentieth century with a hearty dose of black humor. The population of a small Jewish settlement called Heysin is informed about a group of Ukrainian roughnecks planning to conduct a pogrom in their shtetl. As the Ukrainians approached the settlement by train, the Jews, aware of the impending catastrophe, alarm a Russian prefect and plead for his help. In return for a large payment or bribe the representative of the Tsarist authorities orders a company of Cossacks from a nearby city to protect the Jews from the pogromists. But when the Cossacks, the Jews, and other residents from Heysin gather at the railway station awaiting the train's arrival they find out that the drunk driver of the steam engine had forgotten to connect it to the passenger cars at the point of departure. Thus the locomotive arrives at Heysin while leaving the cars with their precarious passengers on its way. The Jews are saved from another wave of ethnic hatred thanks to the stupidity of Russian railwaymen.

Although Aleichem's story about the impeded pogrom at Heysin is purely fictitious, it nevertheless consists of historically reliable elements.[60] It is particularly interesting that Aleichem was aware of the fact that the construction of railroads in the western borderlands contributed to the increased regional mobility both of ordinary salesmen and workers and of perpetrators spreading hatred and ethnic violence from one part of the country to the other. This observation was later affirmed by the studies of Michael Aronson, Omeljan Pritsak, and other historians who analyzed the origins of the anti-Jewish pogroms of the 1880s in the western borderlands of the Tsarist Empire.[61] Aronson convincingly demonstrated the high degree of involvement of railway employees and workers in the riots of 1881; he also pointed out the importance of railway lines in enabling militant groups to move easily from one location to the other and to conduct their destructive activities in the whole region. Despite the fact that the government later tried to blame Ukrainian peasants for the outburst of ethnic and religious violence, the pogroms had their origins less in rural than in urban contexts. The critical role railwaymen, who were suffering from bad working conditions and alienation from their home regions, played in the pogroms of the 1880s brings Aronson to the conclusion that "the pogroms were more the result of Russia's modernization and industrialization process than of age-old religious and national antagonisms."[62] Already fearful of pogroms in the early 1880s, the inhabitants of Jewish settlements were well aware of the dangerous potential of the railroads as a network for the spread of ethnic violence. As John Klier has shown, in some Jewish towns in the western borderlands in 1881 and 1882 the populations set up armed self-defense units, which made rounds by night and tried to stop potential perpetrators from disembarking trains at railway stations.[63]

As the example of militant destruction of railway bridges and telegraph lines during the January uprising in 1863 has shown, railroads and other strategically important infrastructures were used by militant groups to spread ethnic violence and were identified as highly sensitive targets of politically motivated criminal acts. Further examples of this often neglected side of railway history in the western borderlands of the Russian Empire are found in the attempts of political underground movements in late nineteenth and early twentieth centuries to target sites of Russian infrastructure like trains and railway stations. In this context one may point, for example, to the attempt of the terrorist organization "People's Will" (*Narodnaia volia*) to blow up the train of Tsar Alexander II near Odessa on its way from the Crimea to Moscow in November 1879.[64] Due to changes in the Emperor's travel route, the Populist activists quickly halted their preparations at the site near Odessa and shifted their activities to two other spots on the road. When one of the bombs finally exploded underneath the railway track near Moscow, the Emperor escaped the attempt at his life only by chance.

But the railroads in the western borderlands remained in the following decades a contested space in the struggle between the Tsarist authorities and various political underground movements. On 26 September 1908, the Revolutionary Faction of the Polish Socialist Party under the leadership of Józef Piłsudski committed an armed train raid at the small railway station of Bezdany (Lithuanian: Bezdonys) 25 km. from Vilna. The rebels had learned that every Saturday the government sent tax money with the night train from Vilna to St. Petersburg. The train was identified as an ideal target for an action of expropriation to fund the party's militant activities and to equip the newly founded Union of Active Struggle (*Związek Walki Czynnej*) with weapons. Nineteen activists carried out the operation, planned in detail one year in advance. When the train reached the station, a bomb was thrown under the postal coach and the door of the carriage was opened by force. The rebels started shooting at the escort and left one Russian soldier dead and five seriously injured. Within 45 minutes the rebels succeeded in capturing more than 200,000 rubles. The police detained only four of the 19 raiders; they received lifelong prison sentences.[65] It was obviously difficult or almost impossible for the administration to find adequate measures to meet this form of revolutionary attack, reminiscent of partisan war. The authorities had to realize again and again that the network of railways they had created in the western borderlands, imagined and constructed not least to politically consolidate and stabilize the periphery of the Tsarist Empire, were also being used by the opponents of the autocratic regime for quite the opposite purpose.

Conclusion

The construction of railroads in the western borderlands of the Russian Empire had different and to a certain extent contradictory effects. On the one hand, the Polish Kingdom and other parts of the region possessed toward the end of the nineteenth century one of the densest rail networks in the entire Russian Empire. Run by both private and state-owned companies, Russian railroads helped to develop the country economically and to consolidate the multi-ethnic empire as one political space. On the other hand, the development of Russia's infrastructure led to a significant increase in geographical mobility that opened up for many people new possibilities for encountering the large variety of the country's ethnic and religious groups and to experience the empire less as a homogeneous and more as a highly fragmented space of communication. Railway passengers who were Gentiles perceived the region primarily not as a Russian but a Jewish space, a reaction that corresponds, interestingly enough, with similar forms of imagination in the Yiddish literature of the time. Jewish writers depicted the railroads in the western borderlands as a space of both communication and estrangement that confronted the Jews with new challenges of modernity. The victims of anti-Jewish pogroms in the 1880s as well as the Jewish writers at the turn of the century realized that the railroads brought to their traditional habitat not only blessings but also the violence of the modern era. The traditional master narrative of railway history, which has emphasized the integrative force of the new means of transportation, has failed to take into account its impact on the modes of perception among polyethnic populations. The intensification of ethnic and politically motivated violence on the Russian railroads, in the empire in general and its western borderlands in particular, is a case that points to the darker effects of railroad development.

NOTES

1. Michael Freeman, *Railways and the Victorian Imagination* (New Haven: Yale University Press, 1999); Ian Carter, *Railways and Culture in Britain: The Epitome of Modernity* (Manchester: Man-

chester University Press 2001); *The Railway and Modernity: Time, Space, and the Machine Ensemble,* ed. Matthew Beaumont and Michael Freeman (Oxford: Lang, 2007). Most of these works, which can all be considered parts of a "New Railway History," are still inspired by Wolfgang Schivelbusch's trailblazing study *The Railway Journey: The Industrialization of Time and Space in the Nineteenth Century* (Berkeley: University of California Press, 1986) (originally published in German in 1977).

2. On the Russian case from a general perspective see Frithjof Benjamin Schenk, "Mastering Imperial Space? The Ambivalent Impact of Railway Building in Tsarist Russia," in *Comparing Empires: Encounters and Transfers in the Long Nineteenth Century,* ed. Jörn Leonard and Ulrike von Hirschhausen (Göttingen: Vandenhoeck & Ruprecht, 2011), 60–77.

3. *Zapadnyi Krai* covered the territory of the provinces (*guberniia*) of Kovno, Vitebsk, Vilna, Grodno, Minsk, Mogilev, Volhynia, Podolia, and Kiev. The Polish Kingdom was subdivided into the provinces of Suwałki, Łomża, Płock, Kalisz, Warsaw, Siedlce, Piotrków, Radom, Lublin, and Kielce.

4. Mikhail Dolbilov and Aleksei Miller, eds., *Zapadnye okrainy Rossiiskoi Imperii* (Moscow: Novoe Literaturnoe Obozrenie, 2006), 13–14.

5. "Zapiska glavnoupravliaiushchego putiami soobshcheniiami gr. K. F. Tolia, 17 fevralia 1835 g.," in *Krasnyi Arkhiv* 3(76) (1936): 90–98, here 90.

6. Quoted in Walter McKenzie Pinter, *Russian Economic Policy under Nicholas I.* (Ithaca, N.Y.: Cornell University Press, 1967), 137.

7. Gerster suggested building three trunk lines in European Russia: 1) St. Petersburg–Moscow; 2) Moscow–Nizhnii Novgorod–Kazan´; 3) Moscow–Taganrog.

8. Russia's first railway line for public use was a 27 km.–long connection between St. Petersburg and the Tsarist residences of Pavlovsk and Tsarkoe Selo, inaugurated in 1837 and built by a private stock company founded by Franz Anton von Gerstner.

9. On the history of railroads in the Polish Kingdom, see Stanisław M. Koziarski, *Sieć kolejowa Polski w latach 1842–1918* (Opole: Państwowy Inst. Naukowy–Inst. Śląski, 1993); Zbigniew Taylor, *Rozwój i regres sieci kolejowej w Polsce* (Warsaw: Polska Akad. Nauk, Instytut Geografii i Przestrzennego Zagospodarowania im. Stanisława Leszczyckiego, 2007), 25–46.

10. Richard Haywood, *The Beginnings of Railway Development in Russia in the Reign of Nicholas I., 1835–1842* (Durham, N.C.: Duke University Press, 1969), 193–200; *150 lat drogi żelaznej Warszawsko-Wiedeńskiej* (Warsaw: Centralna Dyrekcja Okręgowa Kolei Państwowych, 1995).

11. Pavel Mel´nikov, "Svedeniia o russkikh zheleznykh dorogakh," in *P. Mel´nikov. Inzhener, uchenyi, gosudarstvennyi deiatel´,* ed. Mikhail I. Voronin (Saint Petersburg: Gumanistika, 2003), 223–398, here 345–47; Vladimir Verkhovskii, *Istoricheskii ocherk razvitiia zheleznykh dorog v Rossii s ikh osnovaniia po 1897 g. vkliuchitel´no,* vol. 1 (Moscow: Tip. Ministerstva putei soobshcheniia, 1898), 72; Richard Haywood, *Russia Enters the Railway Age, 1845–1855* (New York: Columbia University Press, 1998), 536–44; Aida Solov´eva, *Zheleznodorozhnyi transport Rossii vo vtoroi polovine XIX v.* (Moscow: Nauka, 1975), 59–60.

12. Nikolai A. Kislinskii, ed., *Nasha zheleznodorozhnaia politika po dokumentam arkhiva Komiteta ministrov, Istoricheskii ocherk,* pod redakcii A. N. Kulomzina, (Saint Petersburg: n.p., 1901), vol. 1, 53. In 1851 Nicholas also abolished the tariff border between the Polish Kingdom and the Russian heartland. This measure was perceived as a means to further integrate Poland economically into the imperial realm. Rosa Luxemburg, *Die industrielle Entwicklung Polens* (Leipzig: Duncker & Humblot, 1898), 9–10.

13. "Imperator Nikolai v soveshchatel´nykh sobraniiakh iz sovremennykh zapisok shtatssekretaria barona Korfa," in *SIRIO* 98 (1896), 125–27, quoted after Alfred Rieber, "The Rise of Engineers in Russia," in *Cahiers du Monde Russe et Soviétique* 31(4) (1990): 539–68, here 562.

14. L. G. Zakharova, ed., *Vospominaniia general-fel´dmarshala grafa Dmitriia Alekseevicha Miliutina. 1863–1864* (Moscow: ROSSPEN, 2003), 46, 54–58.

15. M. Annenkov, "Voennaia sluzhba zheleznykh dorog," *Voennyi sbornik* 19 (1876): 112–42, 115–16; Regierungsrat Wernekke, "Die Mitwirkung der Eisenbahnen an den Kriegen in Mitteleuropa," *Archiv für das Eisenbahnwesen* (1912): 930–58, esp. 930; W. Baumgart, "Eisenbahnen und Kriegsführung in der Geschichte," *Technikgeschichte* 38 (1971): 191–219, 202.

16. In fact the difference of density of the networks of railroads in the Polish partition zones between Prussia and Austria at the one hand and the Russian Empire on the other was appalling. See the map of Polish railroads in 1914 in Taylor, *Rozwój i regres,* 37.

17. Sergei Petrovich Buturlin, "O voennom znachenii zheleznykh dorog i osobennoi ikh vazhnosti dlia Rossii. S proektom seti sikh putei i kartoiu," *Chteniia v imp. o-ve istorii i drevn. ross. pri Mosk. u-te* 4 (1865): 1–62.

18. Pavel Mel'nikov, "Set' glavnykh linii zheleznykh dorog Evropeiskoi Rossii, sostavlennaia v Glavnom upravlenii putei soobshcheniia i publichnykh zdanii," *Zhurnal Glavnogo upravleniia putei soobshcheniia i publichnykh zdanii* 41(5) (1863): 22–34.

19. Representatives of the conflicting camps clashed for the first time in 1863–64 during the public debate about the so-called Southern Line, a dispute analyzed in detail by Alfred Rieber in his "The Debate over the Southern Line: Economic Integration or National Security?," in *Synopsis: A Collection of Essays in Honour of Zenon E. Kohut,* ed. Serhii Plokhy and Frank Sysyn (Toronto: Canadian Institute of Ukrainian Studies Press, 2005), 371–97.

20. 1 verst = 1.07 km.

21. Buturlin, "O voennom znachenii zheleznykh dorog," 13.

22. Buturlin, "O voennom znachenii zheleznykh dorog," 2.

23. Buturlin, "O voennom znachenii zheleznykh dorog," 48.

24. Buturlin, "O voennom znachenii zheleznykh dorog," 16. Similar ideas were articulated in 1868 by General Nikolai N. Obruchev, a professor at the Academy of the General staff. Cf. A. Zaionchkovskii, *Voennye reformy 1860–1870 godov v Rossii* (Moscow: Izd-vo Moskovskogo universiteta, 1952), 120–24; Jacob W. Kipp, "Strategic Railroads and the Dilemmas of Modernization," in *Reforming the Tsar's Army: Military Innovation in Imperial Russia from Peter the Great to the Revolution,* ed. David Schimmelpenninck van der Oye and Bruce W. Menning (Cambridge: Cambridge University Press, 2004), 82–103, here 92.

25. *Nasha zheleznodorozhnaia politika,* vol. 1, 333–34.

26. William C. Fuller, *Strategy and Power in Russia, 1600–1914* (New York: Free Press, 1992), 295–98, 305, 339, 440.

27. Rieber, "The Debate over the Southern Line," 377.

28. Vospominaniia general-fel'dmarshala grafa Dmitriia Alekseevicha Miliutina, 46, 54–58; *Dnevnik A. Valueva, Ministra vnutrennykh del v dvukh tomakh* (Moskva: Izd-vo Akademii nauk SSSR, 1961), vol. 1: *1861–1864,* 202–204; Mikhail N. Katkov, *1863 god. Sobranie statei po pol'skomu voprosu pomeshavshikhsia v Moskovskikh Vedomostiakh, Russkom Vestnike I Sovremennoi Letopisi* (Moscow: n.p., 1887), vol. 1, 10 (reprint of Katkov's editorial in *Moskovskie vedomosti,* 16 January 1863); "Obshchii Ustav Rossiiskikh Zheleznykh Dorog. Sankt Peterburg," (n.d.) in *Rossiia. Gosudarstvennyi Sovet. Materialy* 158 (1885): 525 (Russian National Library, Saint Petersburg, call number 135/286.158).

29. V. A. D'iakov, V. D. Koroliuk, and I. S. Miller, eds., *Russko-pol'skie revoliutsionnye sviazi 60-kh godov i vosstanie 1863 goda. Sbornik statei i materialov* (Moscow: Izd-vo Akademii nauk SSSR, 1962), 253; *Sbornik svedenii o zheleznykh dorogakh v Rossii, 1867, otdel III, Vysochaishiia poveleniia, ukazy pravitel'stvuiushchago senata i ministerskiia postanovleniia,* ed. Departament zheleznykh dorog (Saint Petersburg: n.p., 1867), 613–17.

30. A. Chwalba, *Polacy w służbie Moskali* (Warsaw: Wydawn. Nauk. PWN, 1999), 214.

31. Michail Dolbilov, "'We are at one with our tsar who serves the Fatherland as we do': The Civic Identity of Russifying Officials in the Empire's Northwestern Region after 1863," (unpublished paper, 2004), 11.

32. W. L. Blackwell, "The Historical Geography of Industry in Russia during the Nineteenth Century," in *Studies in Russian Historical Geography,* ed. James H. Bater and R. A. French (London: Academic Press, 1983), vol. 2, 387–422, here 390–96, 402–10; Ezhi Edlitskii, "Gosudarstvennaia promyshlennost' v Tsarstve Pol'skom v XIX v.," in *Genezis kapitalizma v promyshlennosti,* ed. S. D. Skazkin (Moscow: n.p., 1963), 278–304; Arcadius Kahan, "Kongreßpolen," in *Handbuch der europäischen Wirtschafts- und Sozialgeschichte* (Stuttgart: Klett-Cotta, 1985), vol. 5, 584–600.

33. "Raspredelenie seti russkikh zheleznykh dorog po guberniiam," in *S. Iu. Vitte, Sobranie sochinenii i dokumental'nykh materialov,* vol. 1: *Puti soobshcheniia i ekonomicheskoe razvitie Rossii,* book 2, pt. 1 (Moscow: Nauka, 2004), 531–33.

34. Rieber, "The Debate over the Southern Line."

35. It's difficult to determine exactly the increase of regional mobility on the railroads in the western borderlands in late nineteenth century. The increase of the number of passengers of

those railway companies operating in the region gives a first impression of this process. Southwestern Railroad: in 1883, 3.05 million; in 1912, 15.23 million. Warsaw–Vienna: in 1883, 1.87 million; in 1912, 11.49 million. Privislinskaia zheleznaia doroga: 1883, 0.95 million; 1912, 11.78 million. *Statisticheskii vremennik Rossiiskoi Imperii,* series 3, vol. 8; Tsentral'nyi statisticheskii komitet, ed., *Sbornik svedenii po Rossii za 1883 god* MVD (Saint Petersburg: n.p., 1886), 228; *Statisticheskii sbornik Ministerstva Putei Soobshcheniia,* vol. 131, pts. 2–3, (Saint Petersburg: n.p., 1916), chart 7.

36. In addition to the trunk line from Warsaw to Vienna, the spur from Lobkowicz to Bromberg in Prussia (inaugurated in 1863) and the railway linkage to Łódź (put into operation in 1866) were also built on European standard gauge (1435 mm). Only in the late 1860s did the Tsarist government decide that all future railway lines in the Empire should be built on Russian regular gauge (1524 mm). Richard M. Haywood, "The Question of a Standard Gauge for Russian Railways, 1836–1860," *Slavic Review* 28(1) (1969), 72–80, 79.

37. *Sistematicheskii sbornik deistvuiushikh na russkikh zheleznykh dorogakh uzakonenii i razporiazhenii pravitel'stva,* ed. Nikolai L. Briul' (Saint Petersburg: n.p., 1889), pt. 1: *S 1860 g. po 1 iiuniia 1889 g.,* 63.

38. Aleksandr Semenovich Klevanov, *Putevyia zametki za graniceiu i po Rossii v 1870 godu* (Moscow: Tip. A.I. Mamontova, 1871).

39. Klevanov, *Putevyia zametki,* 46.

40. Klevanov, *Putevyia zametki,* 49.

41. Valentin Kantelinenko (Vasilii Fedorovich Liakhotskii), *Pervoe moe puteshestvie po Rossii* (Cholm: n.p., 1900).

42. Ibid., 6. On the pejorative *zhid,* see John Klier, "Zhid: The Biography of a Russian Pejorative," *Slavonic and East European Review* 60(1) (1982): 1–26.

43. Valentin Kantelinenko (Vasilii Fedorovich Liachotskii), *Vtoroe moe puteshestvie po Rossii* (Cholm: n.p., 1903).

44. Ibid., 10.

45. Ibid., 11, 45.

46. Vasilij Mikhajlovich Sidorov, *Okol'noi dorogoi. Putevye zametki i vpechatleniia* (Saint Petersburg: n.p., 1891).

47. Ibid., 25–26.

48. Ibid., 27.

49. Ibid., 30–31.

50. Garkavi, Vladimir Osipovich: "Otryvki vospominanii," in *Perezhitoe* 4: 270–87.

51. Ibid., 279.

52. Leah Garrett, "Trains and Train Travel in Modern Yiddish Literature," *Jewish Social Studies,* New Series 7(2) (2001): 67–88; idem, *Journeys beyond the Pale: Yiddish Travel Writing in the Modern World* (Madison: University of Wisconsin Press, 2003), 90–122.

53. "Tsirkuliar tekhnichesko-inspektorskogo komiteta zheleznykh dorog, Nr. 4926, 22 avgusta 1875" in *Sbornik ministerskikh postanovlenii i obshchikh pravitel'stvennykh rasporiazhenii Ministerstva Putei Soobshcheniia po zheleznym dorogam* (Saint Petersburg: n.p., 1877), vol. 2, 124; "Tsirkuliar po eksploatatsionnomu otdelu, Nr. 21839–45," 12 June 1896, cited in *Sistematicheskii sbornik uzakonenii i obshchikh rasporiazhenii, otnosiashchikhsia do postroiki i ekspluatatsii zheleznykh dorog kaznoiu i posledovavshikh v period vremeni s nachala 1881 g. po 31 maia 1898 g. vkliuchitel'no* (edition of laws) (Saint Petersburg: n.p., 1900), 650. On the ban on Jewish prayers in railroad cars and stations: "Tsirkular Departamenta Zheleznykh dorog, Nr. 11592, 5 Iiuliia 1897 g.," quoted in Otton Fomich Glinka, *Mery k sobliudeniiu passazhirami v poezdakh ustanovlennykh dlia nikh pravil* (Kiev: n.p., 1901), 12; *Die Welt* 1(12) (1897): 7; Aleksandr Vasil'evich Anisimov, "Palomnichestvo na russkii Sever," in *Dushepoleznoe chtenie* 1(1) (1903): 97.

54. Garrett, *Trains and Train Travel,* 67.

55. Garrett, *Trains and Train Travel,* 69, 81–85.

56. Sholem Yankev Abramovitsh, "Shem and Japheth on the Train," in *The Literature of Destruction: Jewish Responses to Catastrophe,* ed. David G. Roskies (Philadelphia: Jewish Publication Society, 1989), 123–36; Scholem Alejchem, *Eisenbahngeschichten,* 2nd ed., ed. Gernot Jonas, (Frankfurt am Main: Jüdischer Verl., 1996).

57. On Aleichem's *Railroad Stories,* see also Dan Miron, *The Image of the Shtetl and Other Studies of Modern Jewish Literary Imagination* (Syracuse, N.Y.: Syracuse University Press, 2000), 256–334.

58. Miron, *The Image,* 278.

59. Alejchem, *Eisenbahngeschichten,* 108–15. Cf. Garrett, *Trains and Train Travel,* 80; idem, *Journeys beyond the Pale,* 111–12; Miron, *The Image,* 333. This story was published for the first time in the Warsaw newspaper *Di naye velt* (*The New World*) in 1909.

60. According to Miron this story (among others) is based on a detailed description of Jewish life in a small town in Podolia at the beginning of the twentieth century, provided by a stranger to Aleichem during his stay in a sanatorium in the Black Forest resort St. Blazyenne in 1909. Miron, *The Image,* 260.

61. Michael Aronson, "Geographical and Socioeconomic Factors in the 1881 Anti-Jewish Pogroms in Russia," *Russian Review* 39 (1980): 18–31; idem, *Troubled Waters: The Origins of the 1881 Anti-Jewish Pogroms in Russia* (Pittsburgh, Pa.: University of Pittsburgh Press, 1990), 108–24; Omeljan Pritsak, "Pogroms of 1881," *Harvard Ukrainian Studies* 11 (1987): 8–41; John D. Klier, "What Exactly Was a Shtetl?" in *The Shtetl, Image and Reality,* ed. Gennady Estraikh and Mikhail Krutikov (Oxford: Legenda, 2000), 23–35, here 31–32.

62. Aronson, *Geographical and Socioeconomic Factors,* 31.

63. Klier, *What Exactly Was a Shtetl?* 31. On attempts of Jewish self-defense in the town of Berdichev, see Simon M. Dubnow, *History of the Jews in Russia and Poland: From the Earliest Times until the Present Day, vol. 2: From the Death of Alexander I. until the Death of Alexander III. (1825–1894)* (Philadelphia: Jewish Publ. Soc. of America, 1918), 256–57.

64. Vera Figner, *Memoirs of a Revolutionist* (DeKalb: Northern Illinois University Press, 1991), 77–80. For greater detail, see Frithjof Benjamin Schenk, "Attacking the Empire's Achilles Heels: Railroads and Terrorism in Tsarist Russia," *Jahrbücher für Geschichte Osteuropas* 58(2) (2010): 232–53.

65. Wacław Jędrzejewicz, *Piłsudski: A Life for Poland* (New York: Hippocrene Books, 1982), 41–43; Andrzej Garlicki, *Jozef Piłsudski, 1867–1935* (Warsaw: Czytelnik, 1990), 128–30; Heidi Hein, *Der Piłsudski-Kult und seine Bedeutung für den polnischen Staat 1926–1939* (Marburg: Herder-Institut, 2002), 38; Wladyslaw Pobog-Malinowski, *Akcja bojowa pod Bezdanami 26.9.1908* (Warszawa: Główna Księg. Wojskowa, 1933); P. Zavarzin, "Rabota tainoi politsii," *Okhranka. Vospominaniia rukovoditelei politicheskogo syska,* ed. A. I. Reitblat, (Moskva: Novoe Literaturnoe Obozrenie, 2004), vol. 1, 409–508, esp. 459–62.

8

Germany and the Ottoman Borderlands

The Entwining of Imperial Aspirations, Revolution, and Ethnic Violence

Eric D. Weitz

The borderlands of Eastern Europe into the eastern Mediterranean, from the Baltic to the Black Sea, constituted the prime area of German imperial ambitions. The interlocking German elite of bureaucrats and businessmen, officers and diplomats, intellectuals and pastors, kaisers and chancellors, had their gaze fixed tightly on Eastern Europe and the Ottoman Empire. Through all the political upheavals of modern German history, the German elite thought of Eastern Europe as the place for German territorial expansion and population settlement and the Ottoman Empire as the prime site of German imperial influence abroad. The widely strewn territory of the Empire, including its European, Anatolian, and Middle Eastern lands, would provide investment opportunities and markets for the German economy and, no less important, a place for Germany to assert its Great Power stature and contest British, French, and Russian power.

In seeking to exert its influence in the Ottoman Empire, Germany confronted two pressing, interlocked problems: the ambitions of other powers and the political and national conflicts that increasingly dominated domestic Ottoman politics. Germany had to contend, first of all, with the aspirations of the other powers, great and minor, in the eastern Mediterranean. In the nineteenth century and into World War I, Britain, France, Russia, and Austria-Hungary, along with a dozen minor countries from Bulgaria to Italy, had each their own claims on Ottoman territory, their own desires to exercise powerful influence in the region. Germany sought to block all of them and become the only foreign state on which the Ottoman rulers, sultans, colonels, or pashas, could rely. It deployed a combination of classic Great Power diplomatic chess moves complemented by eminently modern cultural and economic politics designed to demonstrate to the Ottoman elite the superiority of German ways of waging war, business, and science.

Second, Germany had to contend with the internal, domestic conflicts within the Ottoman Empire. Germany wanted, above all else, stability in the Empire, a prerequisite to the pursuit of its imperial aims. In the late nineteenth century and into the twentieth, it had to face the political discontent that led to the Young Turk Revolution of 1908 and to conflicts among the myriad ethnicities and religious groups within Ottoman territory. In the heyday of Ottoman power and of empires generally, managing diversity was not a terribly difficult problem. Like most empires and in line with general Muslim political practice, the Ottomans granted Christians and Jews a great deal of autonomy in their communal affairs. Jewish life in particular thrived in the Ottoman Empire, especially in comparison with Europe. However, in the age of nationalism and imperialism, with activists of various population groups staking out national claims and demanding independence or at least autonomy, population diversity became a huge problem for Ottoman rulers and, in turn, their German suitors.

The international and domestic issues that Germany encountered were, in fact, inextricably entwined, so much so that they made large swaths of the borderlands very dangerous and violence-prone in the modern era. In this meeting place of the Russian, Habsburg, Ottoman, and German empires and their successor states, international conflicts tended to heighten communal tensions and make regimes more suspicious of populations that might be linked to compatriots across their borders. At the same time, ethnic violence often provoked the intervention of the Great Powers. Every move for national independence by, say, Bulgarians or for the expansion of national territory by, say, Cretans and Greeks became an international crisis that sometimes erupted in warfare. Every land grab by Imperial Russia or countless others invoked the response of the Ottoman military and then the other powers. Often social grievances, those of Serbian or Bulgarian or Armenian peasants, for example, took on national hues, resulting in an explosive mix of social, national, and imperial conflicts. Almost invariably, this entwining of international and domestic factors had disastrous consequences for minority populations, whether Christians in predominantly Muslim lands or Muslims in predominantly Christian lands.

Germany encountered, utilized, and exacerbated this maelstrom of imperial, national, and social conflicts. The one constant was Germany's determination that the Ottoman Empire be a site where it could exercise its power and reap strategic, economic, and cultural benefits. Germany's abiding commitment to the exercise of imperial power in the eastern Mediterranean ran together with the determination of the Ottoman rulers—both sultans and, after 1908, Young Turks—to maintain and even expand the territorial integrity and Great Power stature of the Empire. Ultimately, this conjoining of Ottoman and German interests fed a recklessness and radicalism on both sides that led both countries into World War I. The result was the devastation of total war experienced by Germans and Ottomans, the demise of both empires and, more importantly and most tragically, the decimation—with German complicity—of the Armenian and Assyrian populations of the Ottoman Empire.

In the following chapter, I examine German policy toward the Ottoman Empire, with some particular attention to the crisis year 1908, the year of the Young Turk Revolution, and, not coincidentally, of renewed efforts by European states to seize Ottoman territory coupled with outbreaks of social and ethnic violence. The events in and around 1908 demonstrate the entwining of national claims, imperial ambitions, and social grievances—in short, of international and domestic factors—in the making of the history of the borderlands.

In following the course of German–Ottoman relations, I want to make two larger historical points. First, the focus on *either* domestic *or* international politics is shortsighted and misses the profound interplay between the two. This point may be commonplace, even a truism that describes almost any historical event. But the entwining of the domestic and the international was a *defining feature* of the borderlands precisely because this is where competing empires, national movements and states, and profound social grievances met and intersected with a population characterized by great diversity. Geography mattered. Demography mattered. This is not to say that these factors prescribed the history of the borderlands in the modern era. There are always choices in politics. But the history of this area, which so profoundly shaped the course of the twentieth century in Europe, Eurasia (including, of course, the Middle East), and beyond, with effects that continue to reverberate into the twenty-first century, can only be written with profound attentiveness to the structural features of the region. Over the course of the modern period, the violence of war, ethnic cleansing, and genocide radically transformed the political geography and demography of the borderlands, resulting in a region in which states presided over populations that had become far more homogeneous than ever before.

By making these arguments about the nature of Ottoman–German relations in the borderlands, I am also challenging the significance of the German colonial empire for the larger course of German and European history. Germany became a colonial power in 1884 at the Berlin West Africa Conference, where its claims to four African territories were confirmed; soon it would add Samoa in the Pacific.[1] It also shared in the establishment of European claims in China. Germany's chancellor Otto von Bismarck was a reluctant colonizer, but he understood that Great Power stature at the end of the nineteenth century rested at least in part on the possession of overseas colonies.[2]

In the last 15 years historians and literary scholars have rediscovered German colonialism.[3] The outpouring of books and articles and dissertations have all revolved around the simple but important claim: colonialism mattered. The encounter with the larger world decisively influenced German culture and society, and proved fatal for twentieth century politics, or so goes the argument. In its most forceful version, articulated by Jürgen Zimmerer and others, Nazism and the Holocaust can be traced to the exercise of unbridled violence against the Herero and Nama of Southwest Africa, where the German military between 1904 and 1908 committed the first genocide of the twentieth century. "A taboo was broken," Zimmerer contends; from Windhoek, the capital of Southwest Africa, runs the line to Auschwitz.[4]

Certainly, Germany's colonial empire had an important impact on German social and political history. But the rush of scholarship on German colonialism is overdrawn. All the clamor for colonies propagated by the German Colonial Society and many other associations pales in comparison to the concentration on the Ottoman Empire, whose core territory and borderlands (in part, the same thing, given the centrality of the Balkans to Ottoman rule) constituted places critical to German political and strategic thinking. Not the colonial empire but its European and Eurasian designs drove Germany into World War I, with all of its reverberations through the twentieth and twenty-first centuries. Notably, the centrality of the Ottoman borderlands (and later, Republican Turkey) to German imperial ambitions prevailed through all the various regime and territorial changes that both countries experienced: Imperial, Weimar, and Nazi Germany; and the sultanate, the Unionist period from 1908–1918, the interregnum of 1919–1923, and the Republic of Turkey.

* * *

Germany's major involvement in southeastern Europe began at the Congress of Berlin in 1878. The Congress, convened by Bismarck to settle the Russo-Turkish War of 1877–1878, rolled back Russian territorial acquisitions and recognized four new states—Serbia, Romania, Montenegro, and Bulgaria—out of lands that had been Ottoman since the fifteenth century. As the price of recognition, the new states reluctantly agreed to constitutions that established civil and political liberties. But that was not the end of the story. The famous Article 61 established international supervision over the treatment of Armenians in the Ottoman Empire. It would rarely be enforced, but it entangled Germany in southeastern Europe (where the Ottoman Empire retained a foothold) and Anatolia despite Bismarck's well-known warnings against such involvements. Moreover, the Ottoman state had gone bankrupt in 1875, leading to supervision over Ottoman finances by the Great Powers. In 1881, they established the Ottoman Public Debt Administration, a classic means of exercising imperial power.[5]

Through the 1880s, German economic investment expanded. The tiny but influential number of Germans interested in the Ottoman Empire also increased. Some were looking for business opportunities, others proselytized Protestantism, and still others sought in the sedimentary layers of Ottoman lands the traces of classical Greek civilization.[6] Perhaps most important, the German army was present, beginning in 1883, in the form of advisors, who would gradually supplant the role played by the French since the Napoleonic period. Major (later Field Marshall) Colmar Freiherr von der Goltz was the key figure here. An officer in the classic Prusso-German mold, he learned Turkish and seems to have been revered by his Ottoman counterparts. Hundreds of officers of the Ottoman army were trained by Goltz. German contracts followed the army: Krupp, the major armaments producer, with very close ties to the very top of the German power structure, became the major supplier to the Ottoman army.[7] The other powers took notice of Germany's enhanced position in the Ottoman Empire, and worried.

Germany was well poised to expand its influence in the Ottoman Empire when Kaiser Wilhelm II ascended to the throne in 1888. His two visits to Istanbul, in 1889 and 1898, were themselves signs of Germany's serious interest in Anatolia and the Middle East. The Kaiser's proclamation in 1897 of Germany's *Weltpolitik* signaled even more forcefully that Germany would not rest until its stature rivaled that of the older European states and their exercise of power on the continent and around the world.[8]

The Baghdad railway project, unveiled with great pomp in 1903, was to be the main avenue of German imperial influence. The Deutsche Bank provided the major portion of the capital and controlled the project. The engineering and business expertise and all the goods required for the construction of the railroad came from Germany. Work began that same year. Deutsche Bank was skittish about the project because of the great risks involved. It had tried (unsuccessfully) to bring in British co-investors on smaller railway constructions in Anatolia. But now, politics emanating from the very top of the German system drove the project. Kaiser Wilhelm II was determined to use the railroad as a vehicle to establish Germany's predominant role in Ottoman lands and wanted no other countries involved. Sultan Abdul Hamid II also viewed the railroad almost completely in political, not economic terms: the railroad would permit the rapid movement of troops to quell both internal disturbances and external threats.[9]

However, the Kaiser had to concede somewhat to economic realities. The capital requirements were so great that Deutsche Bank needed co-investors. It managed to secure some collaborators, though not London banks, and German domination of the project remained secure. The Kaiser's ambassador in Istanbul, Baron Marschall von Biberstein, was a most effective advocate and jealously guarded Germany's primary role. When Abdul Hamid's brother-in-law, Mahmoud Pasha, sought to enhance his own influence in the palace by promising the English a significant share of the Baghdad railway, the Foreign Office and the embassy in Istanbul reacted with vehemence. The Kaiser went so far as to write that English involvement in the railway project would be a "cause for war."[10]

German plans, however, were continually confronted by the unanticipated moves of other countries and movements with their own designs on southeastern Europe, Anatolia, and the Middle East. Their provocations (as they clearly were) challenged the deftness of German diplomacy, but also created opportunities for Germany to display its "friendship" with the rulers of the Ottoman Empire. At the same time, every seizure of Ottoman territory by another European power endangered the fate of Muslim and Christian populations when they lived outside the territory of their titular states, or, in the case of Armenians and Assyrians, had no state at all. Crisscrossing crises complicated immensely Germany's dealings with the Ottoman elite. In this way, international developments became inextricably entwined with Ottoman domestic politics.

Just a few years into the construction of the Baghdad railway, as German personnel, investment, and goods poured into the Ottoman Empire, the maelstrom hit. In July 1908, political discontent erupted in the Young Turk Revolution. Powers both great and minor and social movements seized the opportunity to assert their respective imperial and national ambitions. Ethnic violence took on dangerous proportions. Now Germany would be put to the test.

The Young Turks (more formally known as Unionists, from their party, the Committee of Union and Progress, or CUP) pioneered what would become a classic form of twentieth century politics: the colonels' revolt.[11] They drew on a variety of oppositional movements in the Ottoman Empire dating back to the 1890s. Their leading members constituted that classic in-between group—ambitious social and political climbers, they found their aspirations blocked by a stultifying regime and system; young and often from middling backgrounds, they had become educated and were conversant in the main currents of European thought. Many hailed from the borderlands, places like Albania, Salonika, or the Caucasus, a feature of their biographies that was substantively and symbolically significant.[12] Their ideology was highly mobile (as we shall see in more detail). In the first blush of revolution, they restored the constitution of 1876 and proclaimed the equality of all citizen-subjects of the Empire. Their seizure of power inspired enthusiasm and popular demonstrations all over Ottoman territory.[13] Quite quickly, however, their political goals became more exclusively Turkic in character, a result especially of the series of foreign policy and military catastrophes the Empire suffered. As Ottoman territory shrunk at the hands of European powers great and minor—including the loss of the birthplaces of many leading Young Turks—their distrust of the remaining Christian populations of the Empire became ever greater. They began to conceive of and implement a demographic restructuring of the Empire, with few objections from the one power—Germany—that had never seized Ottoman lands and that was forging an ever-tighter bond with the CUP.

*   *   *

In 1908, within weeks of the Young Turk Revolution, Germany's closest ally, Austria-Hungary, annexed Bosnia-Herzegovina. It had administered the province, its prize at the Berlin

Congress, since 1878. But it had been explicitly barred from completely absorbing Bosnia-Herzegovina into the Habsburg Empire. Bulgaria followed in turn and absorbed Eastern Rumelia (Thrace). Within days, Greek nationalists on Crete and in Greece joined the trend with efforts to unite the island, Ottoman territory since the seventeenth century, with Greece. Austrians, Bulgarians, Greeks—they all took advantage of the perceived weakness of the Ottoman Empire in the wake of the Young Turk Revolution to take Ottoman lands and assert their own regional and international power. They all unleashed new episodes of ethnic violence. The entwined crises of imperial competition, national claims, and ethnic violence created grave problems, but also opportunities, for Germany.

The preemptive and provocative moves by Austria, Bulgaria, Crete, and Greece caused a profound crisis in Istanbul and threatened German–Ottoman relations. Probably every member of the Ottoman elite believed that Austria-Hungary would only have acted with Germany's support. In fact, Germans straight up to the Kaiser were as surprised as anyone by the annexation. At the embassy in Istanbul, Marschall, the long-serving and very knowledgeable German ambassador, was furious. He feared, correctly, that Germany would be blamed, and called for a firm stance against the annexation. But he would not prevail. The alliance with Austria-Hungary was too important for Germany, and after all sorts of diplomatic deliberations, Germany ultimately decided not to pursue any measures against its ally.

Chancellor Bernhard von Bülow underscored the importance of friendly relations with Turkey, but said that Marschall:

> goes too far, when he proposes to us that we sacrifice or risk our alliance with Austria-Hungary for the friendship relationship [with Turkey]. . . . Our ambassador in Constantinople must be able to explain that we cannot act against a neighbor with whom we have had an alliance for thirty years and whose existence is in good part responsible for the long years of peace that Europe has had.[14]

According to Bülow, the Turks (the word the Germans always used, never saying Ottomans) had to realize that in reality, Bosnia-Herzegovina had long been under Austro-Hungarian rule. Bülow also expressed the fantasies of German statesmen who believed that England would "understand" the importance of the German–Austrian alliance.[15]

Kaiser Wilhelm also accepted this reality, though he was not pleased with the situation. He was quoted in one diplomatic report as saying, "after 20 years of my friendly policies [toward Turkey], my best ally [Austria-Hungary] is the first to give the signal for the partition of European Turkey." Sarcastically he added, "a pleasant situation for us in Istanbul."[16] But he would not take a stand against the Austrians.

Marschall continually pointed out that the Young Turks had come to power only weeks before, so they naturally viewed the Austrian and Bulgarian moves as blows against the new regime.[17] The Kaiser demanded that his ambassador energetically protest to the Ottoman government the widespread view that Germany had planned or knew in advance of the annexation.[18] Marschall communicated that the Grand Vizier said he had received messages of support from London, Rome, Paris, and St. Petersburg, "'but not a word from Berlin.' . . . I said to him that Germany through its actions has given Turkey so much proof of its friendship that words were not necessary to prove it."[19] The next day, the ambassador telegrammed that the Grand Vizier expressed his joy concerning Marschall's protest that Germany had not been involved.[20] Leading Young Turks, who had heard of the ambassador's entreaties to the Grand Vizier, visited him also to express their joy and "their deep thanks to His Majesty the Kaiser . . . who repeatedly in times of the greatest need had shown himself as a friend of Turkey."[21]

Marschall had exerted all of his efforts to win back the loyalty of the Ottoman government, now dominated by the Young Turks. He succeeded. But the public reaction was not so positive. In one of the first truly popular movements in the Ottoman Empire, a boycott of German and Austrian goods and businesses spread throughout the realm. On 10 October 1908, Marschall was reporting with worry the placards that had sprouted up around Istanbul calling for the boycott of German and Austrian businesses. Newspapers condemned Germany's "low" role in the events.[22] Meanwhile, thousands of Muslim refugees fled Bosnia-Herzegovina for Anatolia, accelerating a process that had begun during the Russo-Turkish War of 1877–1878.

Friendly relations with Turkey were critically important, but they would not be allowed to surmount the alliance with Austria-Hungary. Yet at the same time, German support for its Habsburg ally was limited. A few years later, Marschall's successor as ambassador in 1912, Baron Hans von Wangenheim, argued internally that Germany had to partially distance itself from its Austrian ally, whose expansionist aims were not in accord with German interests. Even worse, Austria was not always honest and upright in its dealings even with Germany—"in Vienna another conception of Nibelungen loyalty reigns than in Berlin."[23] During World War I, when the Kaiser read a report that an Austrian had developed a project for bridging the Bosporus and that this might be built with Austrian capital, he wrote in the margins, "This is our affair!" [*Das ist unsere Sache!*].[24]

Despite official and public outrage, Austrian actions actually provided Germany with the opportunity to prove its loyalty to the new rulers. Germany managed to contain the ramifications of the Bosnian crisis and convince the Ottoman rulers of its friendship. When diplomatic crises emanated from Britain and Greece, it was even easier for Germany to cultivate its ties with both the palace and the Young Turks.

* * *

Crete is one of those historical topics little remembered today, except by specialists of Ottoman and Greek history. But the events that transpired on the island had a profound impact on the course of European and Eurasian politics. Through the nineteenth and into the twentieth century, Greek nationalist activism in Crete threatened to undo the balance of power in the eastern Mediterranean.[25] As mentioned, Crete had been Ottoman since the seventeenth century, its population predominantly Greek Orthodox but with a large Muslim contingent as well. Greek nationalists wanted Crete to be a part of the Greek state. The European powers were continually divided over the matter. When yet another revolt broke out on the island in 1897 and Greece sent troops in support, Germany sided strongly with the Ottoman Empire. In fact, Kaiser Wilhelm II's disdain for the Greeks was so great that he demanded that they "beg" for protection from the Ottoman army, which had launched a retaliatory campaign.[26]

Sultan Abdul Hamid had only a temporary victory over Greece on the battlefields of Eastern Rumelia and in Crete. After some more unrest and the killing of a few British diplomats and consuls in 1898, the British effectively occupied the island (along with other European powers in particular sectors). Britain evicted Ottoman troops and officials. Technically, Crete remained Ottoman territory; in reality, the Sultan lost sovereignty over the island. The

British were hardly intent on fostering Cretan unity with Greece. Their goal was stability in the eastern Mediterranean. With the opening of the Suez Canal, Crete had become even more critical to British strategic interests, and successive British governments claimed they had to maintain the peace on the island between the Greek Orthodox majority and the Muslim minority. Hence, British imperial interests led to effective occupation of the island, but no settlement of the larger political conflicts and ethnic rivalries.

The Bosnian annexation and the assertion of full Bulgarian sovereignty over Eastern Rumelia gave another opening to Greek nationalists on Crete. The autonomous administration in Crete, set up under British supervision, declared a union with Greece, thus fomenting another international crisis. The British overlords were not pleased, and forced Greece to pull back from its expression of support for unity. But the British, as usual, played a double game. The Young Turks had come to power and were an unpredictable antagonist. Moreover, they were determined to assert Ottoman sovereignty on the island. But they could not do so in the face of British power. Britain remained in control, and countered the efforts of Greek nationalists for union, thereby antagonizing both parties. Meanwhile the tensions between the two predominant religious communities only intensified, with back-and-forth provocations and killings—yet another manifestation of the intertwining of international crises and ethnic violence in the borderlands. Meanwhile, German representatives watched contentedly as Ottoman hostility to Britain intensified, and noted every signal of good will toward Germany.[27]

Close on the heels of the Young Turk Revolution, the Austrian and Bulgarian annexations, and Cretan attempts at union with Greece, came, in April 1909, the great pogrom against Armenians in Adana. Probably some 20–30,000 Armenians were massacred.[28] The pogrom seems not to have been organized from the center of power in Istanbul, either by the sultan or by the CUP, but at the same time local CUP officials and armed units also became involved in the depredations against Armenians.

The Adana events took place alongside an attempted counterrevolution by more conservative, religious forces in the Ottoman Empire. The activists opposed the liberal proclamations issued by the Young Turks, which seemed to herald the end of Muslim predominance in the Empire. Rumors circulated that Armenians had slaughtered Muslims and had desecrated Adana's major mosque. Underlying all this were longstanding prejudices against Christians, the increasing wealth and stature of some Armenians over the course of the nineteenth and into the twentieth century, and the strong current of suspicion that Armenians were always allied with the European powers, now an even more incendiary sentiment in the wake of the territorial losses of 1908. In this way, too, international and domestic factors played off against one another.

None of the international conflicts or the related ethnic violence caused any rethinking of the German commitment to the Ottoman rulers, whether sultans or Young Turks. The Kaiser did, finally, protest the Adana killings, and other Germans in the Empire also voiced their displeasure. But that was it. Certainly, German embassy officials were cautious, to say the least, about the Young Turks. They were always unnerved by the secrecy of "the Committee," the sense that there was a shadow government operating to which they had only limited entrée after years of easy access to the Sublime Porte (the seat of government) and the palace. For their part, the Young Turks were highly suspicious of Germany because of its close ties to Abdul Hamid. But cool-headed interests—and Marschall's adept diplomacy—prevailed. The Unionists needed a strong supporter among the Great Powers, and Germany was prepared to accept any authority that promised to establish stability in the Empire.[29]

At the time of the Young Turk Revolution in 1908, Ambassador Marschall was in Germany for his annual summer vacation. He had left Istanbul in June, and only returned at the beginning of September. He began his first report to Chancellor Bülow since the Revolution in expansive terms. It is worth quoting at length for what it reveals about German interests and perceptions.

> The violent transformation that has occurred in the last weeks in the Turkish Empire and the manner in which it came to life is almost without precedent in history. When I left the Turkish capital at the beginning of June, the Sultan possessed in his hands a power that hardly any other monarch could match. All the threads of the state ran together in the palace. Without an imperial decree hardly a stone could fall to earth in this immense empire. The system of centralization was developed in the most thorough manner. And to maintain it, the Sultan wanted to know what went on among the people. He wanted to know not just the ideas and sentiments of a variety of circles, he wanted to know what went on with the single individual. From this attitude arose the espionage system, whose net covered the entire empire. Thousands upon thousands of people were deployed as spies. Immense sums were spent. Reports and denunciations by the hundreds flowed into the palace on a daily basis. Countless innocent people became victims of denunciations, which ever more degenerated into a lucrative means of earning a living. It is one of the tragedies that this espionage system, which was supposed to firm up the autocratic system, became the basis for the gradual destruction of the sultan's power because of the bitterness it created in wide circles of the population. And in the decisive moment, it failed to be the source of the information that was most necessary. There is no doubt that a few weeks before the catastrophe, the Sultan knew that *something* was underway, but *what* that was he only learned when it was too late. Over night . . . the Sultan's system broke into pieces. . . . Today the Sultan *has nothing more to say* in his empire. That is completely true, and is no exaggeration.[30]

Marschall went on to describe the inner workings of the system—how the Sultan's edicts were now only formalities; how power had shifted from the palace to the Porte; the palace secretariat, the center of the system, had become desolate; the telegraph bureau of the palace, which earlier ran day and night, had been removed; the receiving hall in which the grand viziers, ministers, and all sorts of others had waited for an audience was empty. Seven of eight hundred cooks had been dismissed; the horses from the imperial stalls had been largely taken over by the army.[31]

But what did this all mean for Germany? For over a decade Marschall had cultivated close ties with Abdul Hamid. Despite reservations concerning some of his policies, Marschall supported the sultanate as a bastion of stability in the Empire. The army was the other critical factor, and it had now rebelled. Nonetheless, Marschall was impressed that a military revolt had occurred in a largely bloodless fashion.

> The movement led by the officers was directed against the autocracy of the monarch. Its goal was the restoration of civil liberties on the basis of a constitution. This fact alone . . . signifies a sharp indictment of the Sultan. He failed to grasp the sense of the moment, what we call the "spirit of the army."[32]

Except for a few loyal corps, the army became estranged from the sultan, and the espionage system worked everywhere except in the army. Indeed, the Sultan's failure to reform the army, or his success in doing the opposite—from the systematic blockages of all earnest efforts to make the army war-ready, the dismissal of good elements of the officer corps, and the promotion of poor and unqualified candidates—was perhaps the Sultan's greatest failure.

> More than a hundred, in part excellent officers have served in the German army. They have there brought to fulfillment their military knowledge. They have also absorbed that spirit that has made the German army the first in the world, that spirit of loyalty to the crown, of discipline, of the sense of honor. And when these officers returned to their country with the hope to make useful for their own army all that they had learned, they experienced the most bitter disappointment. The Sultan, whose mistrust and fear were nourished by an unscrupulous circle, thrust aside precisely these officers who could have been of great service to him personally and to his army. In deep anguish they had to watch the decline of the Turkish army. And when the catastrophe came, the *revolutionary* committee brought these "German" officers to the fore and entrusted them with the leading military positions in the country. Today, the officers who served in Germany have in their hands positions as minister of war, undersecretary of state in the war ministry, chief of the general staff, commander of the guard corps, and other important commands. Truly, Turkey is rich in strange paradoxes.[33]

A strange paradox perhaps, but that was also always the hope—an Ottoman Empire dominated by officers who had served in Germany, knew Germany, and, in a few crucial cases, like the later Minister of War Enver Pasha, were fluent in German. More than that: the goal was a Muslim-defined Empire ruled by Germanophiles. Always the prescient observer, Marschall argued that the Committee would only reach its goal when it had firm support among the Muslim population, for whom Marschall had some sympathy in the face of the depredations it had suffered in Greece and Bulgaria.[34] Indeed, Marschall believed that the CUP could only rule with the pronounced support of the Muslim majority.

Hence, Germany supported Muslims (albeit ignoring the differences among them and homogenizing them) and largely discounted the entreaties of Armenians, Greeks, and Assyrians, even though these Christians also had a number of powerful supporters among the German elite. Indeed, Marschall underscored (and exaggerated) the Muslim character of the Young Turk rebellion, which he described as a "national-Turkish-Islamist movement. "I underscore the word 'islamist' [*islamitisch*]," he wrote.[35]

> In the first days of celebration, with their shouts of joy, the streets crowded with people, flags flying and everywhere music blaring, when "equality, freedom, and brotherhood" were proclaimed and everyone wore a cockade and everything previously forbidden was allowed, Turks and Armenians, Bulgarians and Greeks exchanged brotherly kisses. But after the Tuesday night party comes Ash Wednesday, and after the full moon comes the earnestness of life with its real factors. And with that the phantom came to an end. . . . Up until now the Christians in the Turkish Empire have played the role of helots who groaned under Turkish oppression and wanted nothing other than equal rights. Now that the equality of all races and religions constitutionally guaranteed, they cry for *their old privileges*.[36]

Marschall, like all Germans active in the Ottoman Empire, feared the complete fragmentation of the land along ethnic and religious lines, and watched internal developments very carefully. He and his colleagues reported attacks on Christians; the fear of pogroms against Jews; riots by traditional Muslims when a local CUP chapter used a mosque for a political rally; hues and cries against the emancipation of women; the lynching of a Greek Christian romantically involved with a Muslim woman.[37] Marschall knew that international crises only exacerbated these tensions and conflicts, which always threatened to spin out of control. As the solution, he promoted an authoritarian, Turkic, and Germanophile solution for all the crises besetting the Ottoman Empire. Marschall and many other Germans articulated precisely the entwining of domestic and international factors. They pursued Germany's imperial ambitions in the Ottoman Empire, supported the Young Turks despite initial hesitancies, and sought, if not demographic homogeneity, at least the clear domination of Muslim Turks (no matter that the real ethnic background of the individuals in question might be Albanian or Circassian) in the Empire.

This concept of politics as defined by ethnic or national exclusivity would have fatal consequences. Alongside their pro-Turkic positions, many leading Germans typically disparaged Armenians and Greeks as the "Jews of the Orient," a phrase that appears again and again in the archives.[38] The expression was not meant as a compliment. It meant that in German eyes, the Christians of the Empire were exploiters and usurers, and politically disloyal, especially since their ties were to France, Russia, or England, or all three. Many others supportive of the Ottoman–German alliance, like Goltz, the mercurial intellectual Ernst Jäckh, and the later German commander of Ottoman forces in World War I, General Hans von Seeckt, articulated also a racial understanding of the Turks—they were the Prussians of the East, the disciplined, martial race who would necessarily prevail because of the disposition of their blood.[39]

By 1910, within two years of the Young Turk Revolution and the series of foreign policy disasters for the Ottomans, German officials were gloating about their successes with the CUP. "Since the Revolution, the entire situation has shifted in our favor," noted Miquel, temporarily in charge of the embassy, in June 1910 in a dispatch to Chancellor Bethmann-Hollweg.[40] "A real bitterness exists against England," he was told by the Khedive, and "great joy that many German officers work for the progress of the Turkish army."[41] The Cretan question had emerged again, and in this matter especially England was the "enfant terrible" for Turkey. Germany had won great support by not intervening in the Cretan matter.[42] Germany had checked British and French influence, and was widely seen by the Ottoman rulers as a reliable ally. As a bonding gift, Germany sold two war ships to the Ottomans at a very low price. The ceremony on board was lavish—the decoration of German naval officers, a sumptuous banquet at which the German representative sat next to the Sultan, well wishes all around, expressions of gratitude to the Kaiser and to Ambassador Marschall.[43]

Bosnia-Herzegovina, Eastern Rumelia, Crete—the succession of Ottoman disasters did not end there. In 1911, Italy provoked a war with the Ottomans over Tripoli. The British blocked the advance of Ottoman troops through Egypt, while the superior (though hardly great) Italian navy prevented the Ottoman fleet from attacking from the sea. The Ottoman Empire lost its last North African territory when Libya for all intents and purposes became an Italian colony.[44] Italy also seized the Dodecanese Islands. Germany stood by and reaped the political benefits of its noninvolvement.

Hard on the heels of the North African defeat came the still greater disaster of the Balkan Wars of 1912–1913. The loss of so much Ottoman territory and population, almost the last footholds of a once-great European, as well as Asian and Middle Eastern, empire—and, not insignificantly, also the homelands of some of the Young Turk leaders—was a huge blow. As M. Şükrü Hanioğlu writes: "For centuries, the empire had rested on two central pillars, Rumelia [Thrace] and Anatolia, between which nested the imperial capital [Istanbul]. Suddenly, the Arab periphery became the only significant extension of the empire outside its new Anatolian heartland."[45] The Balkan Wars demonstrated that Britain and France would do nothing to prevent the seizure of Ottoman territory, while Russia was an even greater threat than the small Balkan states. Of the Great Powers, that left only Germany as the one country that had not sheared off Ottoman territory.

The Balkan Wars were astoundingly brutal on all sides, as many contemporary observers commented.[46] The reasons have little to do with "primitive" violence. In fact, the wars were eminently modern affairs. The Balkan states were trying to make more homogeneous populations as supposedly befitted nation states. Bulgarians in Greece and Greeks in Bulgaria now became outsiders that needed to be expunged from their homelands. Muslim populations suffered terrible violence. Tens of thousands fled for Anatolia, adding to the streams of refugees that had developed since the 1860s and 1870s.[47] The Ottomans, in turn, exacted vengeance and sought to populate the approaches to Istanbul with more reliable Turkic (and not just Muslim) peoples.[48] After the war, various bilateral agreements established "population exchanges" as a popular policy choice of both local governments and the international community.[49]

And on Crete, once again imperial conflicts elsewhere gave on opening to Greek nationalists on the island and their mainland supporters. This time they were successful. The major leader on Crete, soon to be the most formidable Greek political leader of the twentieth century, Eleutherios Venizelos, triumphantly left the island and assumed the leadership of Greece. In 1913, at the peace negotiations, Venizelos pushed hard for Cretan union with Greece. The British, worn down by the unending crises and tensions in the eastern Mediterranean, finally relented. The Treaty of London that ended the Balkan Wars provided for Crete becoming a part of Greece. The Greek Orthodox celebrated; the Muslim population on the island became a beleaguered minority. Germany watched all this from the sidelines, gave moral encouragement to the Porte, and reaped the benefits.

The foreign policy and military defeats in 1908, 1911, and 1912–1913 made the CUP leadership ever more antagonistic toward the Great Powers. Nonetheless, the Unionists understood the weaknesses of the Ottoman Empire and continually hunted for a protector among the Great Powers. Shortly after taking power, the CUP had floated the idea of an alliance first to Britain and then to Germany. Both powers rebuffed the untested leaders of the CUP. It tried again in the years just on the eve of World War I. It had not yet fully ruled out the possibility of an accommodation or alliance with Britain, Austria-Hungary, France, or even its greatest antagonist, Russia. It was rebuffed by each of them, and by Germany as well, which was cautious about being too tightly tied to its erstwhile friend.

Meanwhile, the Young Turks had become more fearful of the remaining substantial Christian populations in the Empire, i.e., Greeks (on the southern shore of the Black Sea and on the Aegean coast) and Armenians. In 1913 the Young Turks began deporting Aegean Greeks, an operation that we would now dub an ethnic cleansing.[50] The economic exploitation and sheer physical violence visited upon Armenians in Eastern Anatolia and Cilicia had become epidemic. Armenian activists raised demands for political reform, autonomy or even independence, and pleaded with the Great Powers to act upon Article 61 of the Berlin Treaty. Russia especially pressured for improvement in the conditions of Armenians in the six eastern provinces, and found support among all the Great Powers including Germany. In the spring of 1914, the Ottoman government reluctantly acceded to a reform program and the establishment of a commission to implement the changes manned by a Dutchman and a Norwegian.

All the leading Germans with experience in the Ottoman Empire had promoted a strong central state with a powerful role for the military. Those institutions would, it was hoped, secure the stability that German imperial interests required. But in the last year and a half before the war, in the face of all the losses the Ottoman Empire had suffered and the specter of continued national conflict, German officials began rethinking their political options. Some of them, including the ambassador, Wangenheim, began to promote cultural autonomy—basically a Habsburg model—for the Armenian population.[51] For this reason, Germany supported the establishment of the reform commission in spring 1914.

Ottoman officials placed many roadblocks in the path of the commission. Then came the July crisis following the assassination in Sarajevo of Archduke Franz Ferdinand and the ramp-up to war. Germany now courted the Ottoman Empire for the alliance to which it had earlier been unwilling to commit. Kaiser Wilhelm, overruling the reservations of many officers and diplomats, ordered the alliance signed on 2 August 1914.[52] Germany promised the CUP that it would fight the war until the Ottoman Empire had recovered the territory it had lost in the preceding decades. It also agreed to suspend the hated capitulations, the privileges accorded Europeans who resided in Ottoman lands. Germany's clean hands in regard to Ottoman territory gave the CUP triumvirate—Enver, Talaat, and Djemal—confidence in their new ally. But they were not alone. On the eve of World War I and into its first months, broad segments of the Ottoman elite had come to support war and the alliance with Germany.[53] Meanwhile, the clash of armies made the work of the reform commission impossible, and the two officials were forced to depart the Ottoman Empire, crushing any hope that the condition of Armenians could be improved through diplomacy.

For the Young Turks, World War I followed quickly on the humiliating losses of the Bosnian and Bulgarian annexations, Libya, the Dodecanese Islands, the Balkan Wars, and Crete. Their German ally promised them the restoration (and more) of their losses. A few of the Young Turks began thinking in even more grandiose terms, of extending the territory into Central Asia and of reconstructing the empire internally to guarantee the unquestioned predominance of Turks. Armenians sat in the middle of this grand vision, their ancestral settlement in Eastern Anatolia threatening (in the eyes of some Unionists) a contiguous empire through the Caucasus and beyond. Smaller Christian populations, like the Assyrians, were of less concern to the Ottoman rulers, but would be caught up in the maelstrom of events.[54] The exigencies of warfare, the ultimate form of international conflict, enabled the Young Turks to envision resolving the domestic conflicts of the Empire once and for all. Through the massive exercise of violence, they would annihilate Armenians and Assyrians.

For two decades, the stage had been set for German complicity in the genocidal program of the CUP. This is not to say that massacres were inevitable. Political choices are always available, in this case, for Germany and for the Unionists. But the entwining of domestic and international factors made German accommodation likely. Germany was determined to establish its preeminent position in the Ottoman Empire, which necessarily meant conflict with the other Great Powers. With the outbreak of war, it was also determined to fight the war to complete victory.[55] The pursuit of victory meant, in German military thinking, no toleration of supposedly disloyal elements behind front lines, and that came to mean the Armenian population *in toto*. Moreover, the ethnic conception of politics meant that a strong, Turkic-inclined government was needed for the pursuit of victory, especially with an army that had been trained by and was now even being commanded by German officers. The hostility to the national aspirations of Armenian activists, the pursuit of imperial interests, and military strategy all combined to make German officials either largely indifferent to or outright supportive of the genocide of the Armenians and Assyrians. In this way, international factors and domestic Ottoman politics became inextricably entwined.

Germans were well informed about the massacres of Armenians that began in spring 1915 (and to a lesser extent of the Assyrians, who typically lived in more isolated regions and were much fewer in number and even less well organized than the Armenians). The consuls in Trabzon, Erzerum, and other places protested in vain to Ambassador Wangenheim, pleading with him to intervene both with the Ottoman leadership and the German government in Berlin. Wangenheim did nothing until early July 1915, and even then his protest was couched in the most moderate language. Chancellor Bethmann Hollweg and Kaiser Wilhelm II rejected these entreaties. They claimed that "military necessity" required Germany to support its Ottoman ally.[56] To the very end, German officials supported the Young Turks even though the alliance was riven by all sorts of conflicts.[57]

Talaat Pasha, Minister of the Interior and from 1916 also Grand Vizier, the major architect of the Armenian Genocide, expressed perfectly the entwining of domestic and international factors that characterized both CUP and German policies. Prince Said Halim, Grand Vizier until he was deposed and replaced by Talaat, related a conversation in which Talaat said: "We must create a Turkish bloc that is free from foreign elements, who will no longer in the future give the great European states the opportunity to intervene in the internal affairs of Turkey."[58] In such a "Turkish bloc," there could be no room for Armenians, who were indeed often connected to the European powers, or even for the small, more dispersed Assyrian population.

To be sure, there were CUP members and Germans who opposed the violent policies of the triumvirate. Said Halim was one of them.[59] Leading German figures, like the Catholic Center leader Matthias Erzberger, the missionary Johannes Lepsius, and the Social Democrat Karl Liebknecht, were appalled at Young Turk policies and German complicity. They attempted a rearguard defense of the Ottoman Christians, but could not prevail.[60]

But mostly, German officials shed crocodile tears. After Wangenheim's death in autumn 1915, a couple of outspoken ambassadors served in Istanbul. Paul Wolff-Metternich antagonized the Young Turk leaders so much with his criticism that he was recalled after nine months.[61] His successor, Richard von Kühlmann, returned the embassy to business as usual. Kühlmann heaped praise on Talaat when he became Grand Vizier, since Talaat viewed "the cultivation and extension of intimate relations with Germany as his most important task."[62] In contrast, Kühlmann had nothing but contempt for Talaat's predecessor, the prince who had opposed the destruction of the Armenians. Kühlmann described the "rich prince" Said Halim as a "small man with prominent, lively saucer eyes and the scrubby white beard of conservative, gentlemanly, orthodox elements in a government of new men." He had played a "decorative" role.[63] For Kühlmann, the future undoubtedly lay with the "new men."

Kühlmann, astonishingly, claimed that Talaat would now pursue a moderate course, away from the excesses of radical nationalism and the murderous policies against Armenians and Greeks. Yet Kühlmann could not resist the charge that Armenians were a treacherous element in the Turkish body politic. Turkey presents an "essentially different picture [than the European countries]" because of the many "foreign elements in its midst," he said, as if national homogeneity rather than diversity were a natural state of affairs. Under Abdul Hamid, Kühlmann continued, the attempt to develop a policy of reconciliation and an Ottoman patriotism continually alternated with efforts of oppression and eradication through which the state compelled the necessary unity.[64] The Young Turks tried to bring together all the different elements of Ottoman society. But:

The constant revolutionary-separatist efforts of the Armenians, especially during the Balkan Wars, when Turkey appeared to be near the collapse, and the newly emerging and treasonous [*vaterlandsverräterische*] sentiments of wide circles of the Armenian and Greek populations led to a reversal and the complete victory of the Turkish-nationalist direction in the Committee.

The annihilation of the Armenians, carried out to a very great extent [*im großen Umfange durchgeführte Armeniervernichtung*] and the varied, individual efforts along the same lines that are taking place today, including ruthlessly in regard to Greek elements, are the result of this political tendency.[65]

Kühlmann claimed that the extermination of the Armenians had gone too far and had drastically weakened the country.

I believe that the total result of the eradication policy has harmed the Turkish Empire. The cruelty of the Armenian campaign will long burden the Turkish name and will give a poison weapon to those who deny Turkey the characteristics of a cultured state and demand the removal of Turkey from Europe. Also internally the country is weakened by the demise and banning of a physically strong, productive, and thrifty population, especially since the poverty of the people constitutes one of the greatest obstacles to the rapid development of Turkey's resources.[66]

Somehow, Kühlmann believed that the Ottoman Empire under Talaat would now shift course, that Armenians would be allowed to return and all nationalities would have equal rights.

But something else may have been motivating Kühlmann's self-contradictory expressions and the fantasy (or self-deception) that Talaat would steer a moderate course. Russia, Britain, and France had issued a note to the Ottoman government in May 1915 in which they coined the term "crimes against humanity."[67] For these crimes, the massacres of Armenians, the Allies said they would hold responsible the Ottoman government and its agents. Talaat's new course, Kühlmann wrote, was a great benefit for the cause of the German–Turkish alliance, because Germany's enemies attempted to make it responsible for the "bloody excesses of Turkish nationalism."[68] Turkey's actions had also compelled Germany to make a variety of humanitarian expressions which had caused continual irritations with the Turkish government. An alliance with a modern, moderate, law-abiding Turkey would be much easier to defend to the German public and to maintain than an alliance with a Turkey that had an explicit Ottoman-nationalist character.[69]

These were all fantasies. Kühlmann was trying to wash the blood off German hands. Maybe he did really fear that an Allied victory would mean a new standard of international law and the prosecution of Germans for their complicity in the annihilation of the Armenians and Assyrians. Maybe the Allies were groping their way toward a new practice of intervening in support of endangered populations. Perhaps Kühlmann was articulating a new way that the domestic and international would become entwined.

*   *   *

Of course, World War I ended in disaster for both Germany and the Ottoman Empire. But illusions died hard. Well into the late spring and summer of 1918, German officials were arguing among themselves and with their Ottoman allies about what precisely would be the territorial gains the Ottomans would have upon victory—where the border would be drawn with Bulgaria; whether the Ottomans could legitimately claim the Dodecanese Islands and other Mediterranean islands, some of which were Greek but currently under English occupation; where the Turkish border in the Caucasus would lie, especially as Enver tried to determine the facts on the ground in violation of the Brest-Litovsk Treaty.[70] Leading officers like General Hans von Seeckt repeated the old lines. They argued for "the deepening of the German-Turkish alliance. . . . Turkey can trust and rely on the single friend that has shown itself as unselfish as is possible in politics and, in contrast to the other powers, has never intervened in internal [Ottoman] questions."[71]

All through summer 1918, as the Caucasus unraveled in the wake of the Bolshevik Revolution and German–Ottoman relations became increasingly tense, German officials were still trying to figure out how Germany could exercise predominant influence in the Ottoman Empire. Bernstoff, exasperated, claimed that "Turkey receives everything from us and gives as good as nothing."[72] But he also claimed that the Empire could repay its debt to Germany by making the country "an almost exclusively German field of activity."[73] Even when some Germans recoiled at the massacres of Armenians, they worried about the thousands upon thousands of Armenian refugees sprinkled throughout the Caucasus. An Armenian state might be a possibility, but Armenians had to be kept in their place because they were too adept at commerce and would come to dominate the region economically.[74]

After the signing of the Modros Armistice that ended Allied hostilities with the Ottoman Empire, a lone German official stayed at his post in the embassy in Istanbul. British, French, Italian, and Greek ships sailed up the Bosporus, and their crews (except for the Greeks) occupied Istanbul. The Entente flags flew over the capital—the Greek one more than any other. As a clear sign of the disarray at home in the chaotic days after the war ended, the telegram Waldburg sent on 19 November 1918 only arrived at the foreign ministry one month later! The new government, he wrote, is composed of "old Turks," men who had occupied positions of influence before the war, and was certainly quite weak and would not last long. The English were clearly the dominant power in the Ottoman capital, and a certain tension existed between them and the French. The embassy itself was in dire straits, unclear about whether Sweden would represent Germany's interests, and unsure whether German citizens would even be allowed to remain there in safety, and, if not, how they were to be transported back to Germany.[75]

It was a most inglorious end to both Imperial Germany and the Ottoman Empire. Neither had been able to master the conflicts it faced except in one disastrous sense: the Armenians and Assyrians had been annihilated, and the Republic of Turkey that would emerge after five more years of conflict and warfare would preside over a more homogeneous population than had ever existed previously in Anatolia.

War and genocide drastically altered the political geography and demography of the once-proud Ottoman Empire. These events were far more fateful for the course of twentieth century history than were Germany's involvements in Africa, as brutal as they were, especially for the populations of Southwest and East Africa. Undoubtedly, a colonial culture emerged in Germany, especially after it was stripped of its overseas possessions through the Versailles Treaty. That culture, together with the revanchist colonial claims against the Allied powers and the Weimar Republic, contributed to the dissemination of racial ideology and the growth of the extreme right in Germany. But how weighty those factors were in the rise to power of the Nazi Party is doubtful. The Nazis focused their attention on Europe and on their cosmic enemy, the Jews.

Almost two decades before the Nazis seized power, Germany had become a co-player in the genocide of the Christian populations of Anatolia. Determined to assert its imperial ambitions, it became embroiled in the domestic policies of successive Ottoman governments. The domestic and international converged, with devastating consequences for Armenians and Assyrians and profound impact on the political geography of the Middle East, Anatolia, and Europe.

NOTES

I would like to thank the Harry Frank Guggenheim Foundation and the Arsham and Charlotte Ohanessian Chair in the College of Liberal Arts, University of Minnesota, whose support made possible the research for this chapter.

1. See especially Stig Förster, Wolfgang J. Mommsen, and Ronald Robinson, eds., *Bismarck, Europe, and Africa: The Berlin Africa Conference 1884–1885 and the Onset of Partition* (Oxford: Oxford University Press, 1988).

2. Hans-Ulrich Wehler's *Bismarck und der Imperialismus* (Cologne: Kiepenheuer and Witsch, 1969). Wehler's argument that colonization was driven by domestic considerations (i.e., was a means to divert the working class from socialism) has not stood the test of time. "Social imperialism," as Wehler dubbed Bismarck's rather sudden adoption of colonialism in the mid-1880s, constituted only a part of Bismarck's rationale.

3. Just two examples from a now quite substantial literature: Sara Friedrichsmeyer, Sarah Lennox, and Susanna Zantop, eds., *The Imperialist Imagination: German Colonialism and its Legacies* (Ann Arbor: University of Michigan Press, 1998), and the excellent synthesis of Sebastian Conrad, *Deutsche Kolonialgeschichte* (Munich: Beck, 2008). See also, George Steinmetz, *The Devil's Handwriting: Precoloniality and the German Colonial State in Qindao, Samoa, and Southwest Africa* (Chicago: University of Chicago Press, 2007).

4. Jürgen Zimmerer, "Krieg, KZ und Völkermord in Südwestafrika: Der erste deutsche Genozid," in *Völkermord in Deutch-Südwestafrika: Der Kolonialkrieg (1904–1908) in Namibia und seine Folgen,* ed. Jürgen Zimmerer and Joachim Zeller (Berlin: Ch. Links, 2003), 45–63, quote 62.

5. In the Politischen Archiv des Auswärtigen Amts (the German Foreign Office archive), the files on the Public Debt Administration alone run to about 50 fat volumes.

6. See especially Malte Fuhrmann, *Der Traum vom deutschen Orient: Zwei deutsche Kolonien im Osmanischen Reich 1851–1918* (Frankfurt am Main: Campus, 2006); Suzanne L. Marchand, *Down from Olympus: Archaeology and Philhellenism in Germany, 1750–1970* (Princeton: Princeton University Press, 1996); idem, *German Orientalism in the Age of Empire: Religion, Race, and Scholarship* (Cambridge: Cambridge University Press, 2009).

7. On Goltz, see, Carl Andrew Krethlow, "Colmar Freiherr von der Goltz und der Genozid an den Armeniern 1915–1916," *Sozial.Geschichte* 21(3) (2006): 53–77, and F. A. K. Yasamee, "Colmar Freiherr von der Goltz and the Rebirth of the Ottoman Empire," *Diplomacy and Statecraft* 9(1) (1998): 91–128. Despite its exaggerated interpretation, significant information can also be gleaned from Vahakn N. Dadrian, *German Responsibility in the Armenian Genocide: A Review of the Historical Evidence of German Complicity* (Watertown, Mass.: Blue Crane, 1996), 7, 124–32.

8. See John C. G. Röhl, *Wilhelm II: Der Aufbau der Persönlichen Monarchie, 1888–1900* (Munich: Beck, 2001), 153–54, 1042–44, 1050–60.

9. On the Baghdad Railway, see especially, Lothar Gall et al., *The Deutsche Bank, 1870–1995* (London: Weidenfeld and Nicolson, 1995), 67–77, and Jonathan S. McMurray, *Distant Ties: Germany, the Ottoman Empire, and the Construction of the Baghdad Railway* (Westport, Conn.: Praeger, 2001). Older works, e.g., John B. Wolf, *The Diplomatic History of the Bagdad Railroad* (Columbia: University of Missouri Studies, 1936), are still valuable. But note also M. S. Anderson, *The Eastern Question, 1774–1923: A Study in International Relations* (London: Macmillan, 1966), 264–68, which shows that imperial rivalries over the railroad eased on the eve of World War I and argues effectively

that its role in imperial competition has often been overdrawn. The major powers reached agreement on the completion of the line from Baghdad to Basra on the Persian Gulf. But then World War I broke out, scuttling all the deals.

10. Marschall to Auswärtiges Amt (hereafter AA), 27 December 1899, Politisches Archiv des Auswärtigem Amtes (hereafter PAAA)/R14155/A15307/No. 392, with marginal notations of Kaiser Wilhelm II.

11. On the Young Turks, see M. Şükrü Hanioğlu, *The Young Turks in Opposition* (New York: Oxford University Press, 1995), and idem, *Preparation for Revolution: The Young Turks, 1902–1908* (New York: Oxford University Press, 2001).

12. Erik Jan Zürcher, "The Young Turks: Children of the Borderlands?" *International Journal of Turkish Studies* 9(1–2) (2003): 275–85.

13. See, for example, Michelle U. Campos, "Between 'Beloved Ottomania' and 'The Land of Israel': The Struggle over Ottomanism and Zionism among Palestine's Sephardi Jews, 1908–13," *International Journal of Middle East Studies* 37(4) (2005): 461–83.

14. Bülow to AA, Nordeney, 5 October 1908, PAAA/R13746/A16145/No. 111. See also Marschall to AA, Therapia, 4 October 1908, PAAA/R13746/A16073/No. 322; Marschall to AA, Therapia, 7 October 1908, PAAA/R13746/A16278/No. 336.

15. Bülow to AA, Nordeney, 5 October 1908, PAAA/R13746/A16145/No. 111.

16. Jenisch to AA, Rominten, 6 October 1908, PAAA/R13746/A1521/No. 158.

17. See the comments in Marschall to AA, Therapia, 8 October 1908, PAAA/R13746/A16384/No. 339.

18. Jenisch to AA, Rominten, 8 October 1908, PAAA/R13746/A16387/No. 171.

19. Marschall to AA, Therapia, 8 October 1908, PAAA/R13746/A16431/No. 341.

20. Marschall to AA, Constantinople, 9 October 1908, PAAA/R13746/A16519/No. 347.

21. Marschall to AA, Therapia, 11 October 1908, PAAA/R13746/A16687/No. 355.

22. Translation of *Tanin* article, Botschaft, Pera, 5 November 1918, PAAA/R13746/A18657/No. 279.

23. Wangenheim to Staatssekretär, Therapia, 3 September 1912, PAAA/R137 49/A.15460.

24. Marowitz [?] to Bethmann Hollweg, Pera, 6 November 1916, B.Nr.I.3617, PAAA/R13197/146.

25. See, generally, Robert Holland and Diana Markides, *The British and the Hellenes: The Struggles for Mastery in the Eastern Mediterranean, 1850–1960* (Oxford: Oxford University Press, 2006), 81–161.

26. Quoted in Holland and Markides, *The British and the Hellenes*, 95.

27. Miquel to Bethmann Hollweg, Therapia, 16 June 1910, PAAA/R13747/A10721/Nr. 200.

28. On the Adana massacres, see Matthias Bjørnlund, "Adana and Bexond: Revolution and Massacre in the Ottoman Empire Seen Through Danish Eyes, 1908/9," (ms., 2009), cited by permission, and Vahakn Dadrian, "The Circumstances Surrounding the 1909 Adana Holocaust," *Armenian Review* 41(4) (1988): 1–16. Dadrian points out that in Istanbul, Armenian revolutionaries came to the defense of the Young Turk Revolution.

29. For more on this, see Eric D. Weitz, "Germany and the Young Turks: Revolutionaries into Statesmen" in *A Question of Genocide: Armenians and Turks at the End of the Ottoman Empire,* ed. Fatma Müge Göçek, Norman Naimark, and Ronald Grigor Suny (New York: Oxford University Press, 2010).

30. Marschall to Bülow, Therapia, 3 September 1908, PAAA/R13181/A.14516/1–2 (of report).

31. Ibid., 2–3.

32. Ibid., 4.

33. Ibid., 5–6.

34. Ibid., 6.

35. Ibid., 9–10.

36. Ibid.

37. On these incidents, see Konsulatsverweser (Helle) Baghdad to AA, Baghdad, 14 October 1908, PAAA/R13181/Nr. 11; Marschall to AA, Therapia, 18 October 1908, PAAA/R13181/Nr. 200; Marschall to AA, conveying report from the vice consul in Samsun, 25 October 1908, PAAA/

R13181/No. 412 (and numerous other documents in this file); and Marschall to AA, Constantinople, 14 April 1909, PAAA/R14160/A6579/No. 123.

38. For just one example, see Marschall to Bethmannn Hollweg, 13 May 1911, Constantinople, PAAA/R14160/11–12, 16–17.

39. See, for example, Yasamee, "Colmar Freiherr von der Goltz."

40. Miquel to Bethmann Hollweg, Therapia, 25 June 1910, PAAA/R13747/A11134/No. 316.

41. Miquel to Bethmann Hollweg, Therapia, 11 June 1910, PAAA/R13747/A10436/No. 193, quoting the Khedive. The latter also said that there was joy at Goltz's expected return to Constantinople in the fall.

42. Miquel to Bethmann Hollweg, Therapia, 25 June 1910, PAAA/R13747/A11134/No. 316.

43. Miquel to Bethmann Hollweg, Therapia, 8 September 1910, PAAA/R15060/A7407/No. 280. (Marschall was away on vacation.) However, the signs of close relations with Germany also led to attacks on Germany in the press. Marschall to Bethmann Hollweg, Pera, 8 November 1910, PAAA/R13747/A18813/No. 346.

44. On these developments, see M. Şükrü Hanioğlu, *A Brief History of the Late Ottoman Empire* (Princeton: Princeton University Press, 2008), 167–70.

45. Hanioğlu, *Brief History of the Late Ottoman Empire,* 173.

46. *Report of the International Commission to Inquire into the Causes and Conducts of the Balkan Wars* (Washington, D.C.: Carnegie Endowment for International Peace, 1914), and the chapters by Eyal Ginio (15) and Keith Brown (16) in this volume.

47. See Kemal H. Karpat, *Ottoman Population, 1830–1914: Demographic and Social Characteristics* (Madison: University of Wisconsin Press, 1985).

48. Fikret Adanir and Hilmar Kaiser, "Migration, Deportation, and Nation-Building: The Case of the Ottoman Empire," in *Migrations et migrants dans une perspective historique: Permanences et innovations,* ed. René Leboutte (Brussels: Peter Lang, 2000), 273–92.

49. Stephen Ladas, *The Exchange of Minorities: Bulgaria, Greece, and Turkey* (New York: Macmillan, 1932). Generally on this phenomenon, see Eric D. Weitz, "From the Vienna to the Paris System: International Politics and the Entangled Histories of Human Rights, Forced Deportations, and Civilizing Missions," *American Historical Review* 113(5) (2008): 1113–43.

50. See chapter 14 by Taner Akçam in this volume.

51. See Wangenheim's account of his conversation with the "liberal" Ismail Bey, Wangenheim to Bethmannn-Hollweg, Korfu, 2 April 1912, PAAA/R14161/A6382/No. 4; and Wangenheim to Bethmannn Holloweg, Therapia, 20 October 1913, PAAA/R14161/A21246/No. 304.

52. Hanioğlu, *Brief History of the Late Ottoman Empire,* 174–75.

53. This is the conclusion of the most recent research that challenges the older, standard view that Enver, Talaat, and Djemal dragged a reluctant Ottoman society into war on the side of the Central Powers. For the new interpretation, see Mustafa Aksakal, *The Ottoman Road to War in 1914: The Ottoman Empire and the First World War* (Cambridge: Cambridge University Press, 2008), and Michael A. Reynolds, *Shattering Empires: The Clash and Collapse of the Ottoman and Russian Empires, 1908–1918* (Cambridge: Cambridge University Press, 2010). For one retrospective observation that Germany had never taken Ottoman territory, see Bernstoff to Hertling, Pera, 5 August 1918, PAAA/R1375/190–91, quoting from a report of General Hans von Seeckt to the Supreme Army Command (OHL).

54. See chapter 17 by David Gaunt in this volume.

55. See Isabel V. Hull, *Absolute Destruction: Military Culture and the Practices of War in Imperial Germany* (Ithaca, N.Y.: Cornell University Press, 2005).

56. On the development of the Armenian Genocide and the German response, see Taner Akçam, *The Young Turks' Crime against Humanity: The Armenian Genocide and Ethnic Cleansing in the Ottoman Empire* (Princeton: Princeton University Press, 2012); idem, *A Shameful Act: The Armenian Genocide and the Question of Turkish Responsibility* (New York: Metropolitan Books, 2006), 111–204; Donald Bloxham, *The Great Game of Genocide: Imperialism, Nationalism, and the Destruction of the Ottoman Armenians* (Oxford: Oxford University Press, 2005), 115–33; Hull, *Absolute Destruction,* 271–90; and Ulrich Trumpener, *Germany and the Ottoman Empire, 1914–1918* (Princeton: Princeton University Press, 1968), 200–70.

57. On the conflicts between Ottoman and German officers and rivalries within the German camp, see Trumpener, *Germany and the Ottoman Empire,* and for some particularly striking complaints, Wangenheim to an unnamed "Dear Friend," Pera, 30 December 1914, PAAA/R13263/AL46, concerning Wangenheim's difficulties with the head of the German military mission, Liman von Sanders; Metternich to AA, with a long quote from Liman, Pera, 24 February 1916, Nr. 297, PAAA/R13799/n.p.; von Massow to OHL, Sofia, 9 December 1917, PAAA/R13820/n.p.; and Oberndorff (Kaiserlicher Gesandte) to AA, Sofia, 25 June 1918, Nr. 437, PAAA/R13820/n.p.

58. Neurath to Bethmann Hollweg, Pera, 5 November 1915, Nr. 654, PAAA/R13799/n.p.

59. Ibid.

60. See, for example, Matthias Erzberger, "Bericht über meine Reiseeindrücke in der Türkei," 5–13 February 1916, PAAA/R13750, 87–94, here 1, 7–8 (of report). On the same trip, Reichstag deputy Gustav Stresemann reached similar cautionary conclusions about the situation in the Ottoman Empire and the strong reaction against Jäckh among German businessmen. See his report, "Türkei," 14 March 1916, in ibid., 121–41. Jäckh defended himself in a secret report, "Bericht von Dr. Jäckh über Konstantinopel im März und April 1916," Berlin, 20 April 1916, PAAA/R13751/ A12238, 46–48, in which he complains about Germans who come to the Ottoman Empire with no knowledge and no experience and presume to comment on the situation.

61. See, for example, Metternich to Bethmannn Hollweg, on journey form the Dardanelles to Constantinople, 15 December 1915, PAAA/R13750/A36980/No. 722.

62. Kühlmann to AA, Konstantinopel, 5 February 1917, Nr. 155, PAAA/R13820/n.p.

63. Kühlmann to Bethmann Hollweg, Pera, 5 February 1917, No. 88, PAAA/R13820/n.p.

64. Kühlmann to Bethmann Hollweg, Pera, 16 February 1917, No. 112, PAAA/R13820/n.p.

65. Ibid.

66. Ibid.

67. For the most thorough analysis of the origins of the term, see Peter Holquist, "The Origins of 'Crimes against Humanity': The Russian Empire, International Law, and the 1915 Note on the Armenian Genocide" (paper presented at the Harvard International and Global History Seminar, Harvard University, 24 February 2010), cited by permission.

68. Kühlmann to Bethmann Hollweg, Pera, 16 February 1917, No. 112, PAAA/R13820/n.p.

69. Ibid.

70. Kühlmann to Berckheim (AA), Berlin, 27 May 1916, PAAA/R13757/Nr. 1087/56–57; Ludendorff to Seeckt, with instructions to relay to Enver Pasha, Hauptquartier Seiner Majestät (Freiherr von Berckheim), 6 June 1918, PAAA/R13757/Nr. 1347/67; Ludendorff to Seeckt with instructions to relay to Enver, Hauptquartier (Breckenheim), 8 June 1918, PAAA/R13757Nr. 1363/74.

71. Bernstoff to Hertling, Pera, 5 August 1918, PAAA/R13757/Nr. 206/190–91, quoting from a report of Seeckt's to the OHL.

72. Bernstoff to Hertling, Pera, 11 May 1918, PAAA/R13757/II.2720/9–20, quote 2.

73. Ibid., 11.

74. See the long, well-informed, and interesting report, Kaiserliche Deutsche Delegation im Kaukasus to Reichskanzler Hertling, Tiflis, 18 July 1918, PAAA/R13757/J. Nr. D. 156/168–72.

75. Waldburg [Geschäftsträger] to AA, 19 November 1918, A. 53235, PAAA/R13820/n.p. The arrival of the telegram is recorded as 17 December 1918.

9

THE CENTRAL STATE IN THE BORDERLANDS

OTTOMAN EASTERN ANATOLIA IN THE LATE NINETEENTH CENTURY

ELKE HARTMANN

The borderlands paradigm offers a way of understanding the mass violence that characterized especially the borderlands or shatterzones of the German, Russian, Habsburg, and Ottoman Empires from roughly the mid-nineteenth to the mid-twentieth century, when these multi-ethnic, multiconfessional, and multilingual empires underwent massive modernizing and homogenizing transformation processes. The borderlands paradigm perceives the violence in these regions as concomitant to, and a consequence of, this fundamental political, social, and cultural change which accompanied modernization.[1] The borderlands paradigm further assumes that "ethnic violence in the modern period has become so much more frequent, systematic, and deadly precisely because of its dual character, that is, fomented by states and enacted by significant segments of the population at large."[2] This points to the problem of central state control, which was fundamental for the eastern borderlands of the Ottoman Empire, i.e. the Kurdish and Armenian provinces in the eastern parts of Asia Minor.

Rather than looking at ideological and intellectual or cultural developments in this connection, this chapter will adopt a pragmatic perspective, focusing on the shifts in Ottoman power structures and examining the changing nature of power within the Empire in the late nineteenth century. It will be argued that during that century a constantly widening gap opened between the postulated ideal of a modern central state exercising exclusive control over its provinces and guaranteeing public order on the one hand, and the real political desiderata and the applied practice on the other, especially in the provinces of Eastern Anatolia. It will further be argued that, under these conditions, the fragmentation and above all the delegation of power contributed considerably to the escalation of violence in the Eastern Ottoman borderlands.

*   *   *

Eastern Asia Minor shares important characteristics with other borderlands. The first among them is the geographical position between two great empires. In this case, the Ottoman lands bordered on Russia, and, in the south, on Persia. A second main characteristic was the extremely heterogeneous population: in addition to the fact that it was populated by relative majorities of (Christian) Armenians and (Muslim) Kurds, both of which groups were further subdivided into different confessional denominations, Eastern Asia Minor was inhabited by a multitude of ethnic and linguistic groups, among whom the growing proportion of *muhaci-run*, Muslim refugees from the Crimea, the Caucasus, and the Balkans, deserve special mention.[3] A third common characteristic of borderlands is the interaction of a single population group that lives on both sides of the border. Most important for Asia Minor was the migration of Kurdish tribes fleeing Ottoman state control, and the activities of Armenian revolutionaries who came to the Ottoman lands from Russian Armenia.[4] Most of them were caught by Ottoman frontier guards; all told, these revolutionaries were few in number and hardly represented a real threat to the Ottoman state. Indeed, it seems that the revolutionary parties found comparatively little support among Ottoman Armenians.[5] The central authorities nevertheless registered their border violations as anxiously as they did the tribal border crossings.[6]

The specific situation in Eastern Asia Minor resulted mainly from the weakness of the Ottoman central state in the region and from the way central state control was achieved and practiced there. Since the idea of central state control and the establishment of a central state monopoly on violence are specific for the *modern* state, the question of how and under what conditions modernizing reforms were conceived and carried out in the Ottoman Empire—and especially in its Eastern borderlands—is crucial in this context.

*   *   *

At the core of the Ottoman modernization process, known as *Tanzimat* (reorganization), stood the problem of centralization, the question of how to strengthen a central state confronted with regional power centers—local notables, *de facto* autonomous tribal chiefs, and its own provincial governors—who had steadily loosened their ties to the capital during a long process of decentralization and whose unauthorized actions and claims to power in the late eighteenth and early nineteenth centuries called the persistence of the Ottoman state much more seriously into question than the secessionist movements that had arisen in the Balkans in the same period.[7] In 1833 and 1839, the situation had become especially dangerous when only European intervention against the rebellious governor of Egypt saved the empire's integrity. This so-called "Mehmed Ali crisis" marked the beginning of the "Eastern Question," the basic European foreign policy question of the "long nineteenth century": how to deal with the disintegrating Ottoman Empire, which had through its weakness become a danger for the European state system and its order of peace.[8]

In the age of the advancing colonization of Africa and Asia, the Ottoman Empire, which was geographically still huge, defied the logic of colonial distribution of the non-European world. Its immediate proximity to Russia and Austria-Hungary precluded an all-

European agreement on the partition of the Ottoman territories. Thus Great Britain, France, Russia, Austria-Hungary, Germany, and partly also Italy had a genuine interest in guaranteeing the continued existence of the Ottoman Empire and defending and protecting it against the danger of disintegration by pressing for modernizing reform and even intervening militarily.[9] In so doing, the European Powers became active participants in shaping Ottoman domestic policy. Their relations to the Ottoman state were, however, ambivalent, since they were at the same time competing to achieve indirect, semi-colonial penetration of the Ottoman Empire by means of commercial treaties, advisory missions in support of reform in administration, education, and the organization of the army, navy, police, and the like, but also by advancing claims that they had to protect the various non-Muslim Ottoman communities. Until the end of the Empire, European politics maintained two kinds of impact on the Ottoman reform process: they constituted an important motor for Ottoman modernization and stabilization on the one hand, but often favored reform measures more closely in line with their own imperial interests than with Ottoman priorities. The opening of the markets and the envisaged equality of Muslims and non-Muslims, especially, were constant sources of fear and humiliation for the Muslim Ottomans.[10]

A third characteristic of Ottoman modernization was that it comprised a reform "from above," initiated by few high-ranking state officials. The major advances here—the decrees of 1839 and 1856 and the 1876 constitution—came about only under heavy European pressure, amid an existential crisis; sufficiently large indigenous groups in favor of reform were lacking. Except for a constantly growing new Muslim elite in the military and administration, itself a product of the new schools and institutions, it was mainly the non-Muslims who supported the reform efforts. They made—at least in those fields that were open to them—considerable and even disproportionally large contributions to Ottoman modernization,[11] and, at the same time, reaped much greater benefits from the radical changes of the eighteenth and nineteenth centuries than their Muslim counterparts.[12] The promise of equality, proclaimed since the mid-nineteenth century, aroused the non-Muslims' hopes that they would be able to participate in political life in a way that would also reflect their role in economic life and the modernizing efforts of the Ottoman Empire—a state that they had begun to regard as theirs, as much as the Sultan's Muslim subjects did. Proportionate participation, including leading positions in the police and provincial administrations, would also have been the strongest guarantor of their safety in the Ottoman Empire.[13] Leaders and representatives of the non-Muslim communities were well aware of this. It is precisely because of the close connection between participation and safety that Armenian politicians, especially, advocated the inclusion of non-Muslims in the armed forces as well.[14] To note the prominent role of the Armenian deputies in the Ottoman parliament in this connection is also to underscore the necessary differentiation between the Empire's various non-Muslim groups: more than other communities, it was the Anatolian and Arab Christians, for whom political independence from the Ottoman Empire was never a realistic political option, who had to pin their hopes on the Ottoman will to, and capacity for, reform.[15]

In contrast, many Muslim Ottomans were more skeptical, disapproving and even opposing modernization. Traditional elites had to fear for their privileges, and the prospect of integration into the reformed structures was not likely to make all their members enthusiastic supporters of modernization.[16] Radical economic change and closer integration into the world economy caused, in many cases, stiffer competition and growing uncertainty. Many Muslims consequently felt that they were losers in the ongoing modernization process. The impression that the reforms favored the traditionally disdained nonbelievers among all Ottoman subjects, while their own social fabric and value system had begun to unravel, only increased reservations about the reforms.[17] Finally, for any Muslim, Europe's ambivalent role in the Ottoman modernization process made the reforms seem alien and hostile, and made their Ottoman advocates seem to be enemy agents. That all leading *Tanzimat* reformers were addressed as "*gavur* (infidel, heretic) *pasha*" during their careers[18] is just one indication of this attitude. There was now a yawning gulf between Muslim worries and fears on one hand and Christian expectations on the other, with the European interest in Ottoman reform as an exacerbating factor.

* * *

Under the conditions just sketched, the conception and realization of reform in the Ottoman Empire also had a number of special characteristics. First, it should be mentioned that, for most Ottoman reformers, for a long time—probably down to the Young Turk coup—the imagined model was *not* European modernity, despite the many Western techniques and institutions that the reformers adopted and the orientation, advice, and support they sought from their European neighbors. Their ideal remained their own, the Ottoman-Islamic state as it had been in its heyday, for which the long reign of Sultan Süleyman Kanuni (1520–1566) stood as both symbol and model.[19] Accordingly, early Ottoman reform plans always stressed the importance of restoring the ideal order of the sixteenth century; indeed, the first important reform decree of 1839, generally seen as the starting point for Westernizing reform in the Ottoman Empire, was inspired mainly by Islamic-Ottoman tradition. The Decree of Gülhane, even as it proclaimed the most fundamental changes, always referred to Islamic tradition. It consequently located its promise of equality for the non-Muslim subjects strictly within the limits of the sharia (*hüküm şer'i iktizasınca:* "according to the requirement of the sharia order"), i.e. it promised equal protection for all subjects regardless of confession, but certainly not equal participation or equal rights, as a modern European reading would assume.[20] Only the second reform decree, the Hatt-ı Hümayun (or Islahat fermanı) of 1856— under heavy pressure from the European powers and with European diplomats taking an active part in the formulation of the text itself—went further and proclaimed full equality for Muslims and non-Muslims. From that date on and throughout the entire reform process, it seems that the European powers accorded special attention to the realization of this promise, taking it in general as an acid test for the Ottoman state's willingness and ability to modernize.[21] However, this proclamation of 1856 was, for the first time, an overt and very radical break with the Ottoman Empire's Islamic traditions. For the Ottoman state and its Muslim society, the *millet-i hakime* ("ruling nation"), it was simply impossible to fulfill this promise of unrestricted equality without fundamentally calling the Islamic character of the state into question, and, ultimately, abandoning Islamic Law—and thus a conception of just rule based on the inequality, not the equality of the different religious and social groups[22]—as the foundation of the state order. The more Muslims felt themselves disadvantaged and weakened by the implications of modernization and reform, the less they were willing to consider giving up a core element of their own political tradition and identity. On the contrary: defending the Islamic foundations of the state seemed to be that last nucleus of Ottoman identity which was, in the final analysis, the sole objective of reform. Hence, Ottoman policy found itself caught on the horns of an irresolvable dilemma: reforms that could only be judged altogether insufficient for non-Muslim Ottomans (as well as the European powers) already represented too great a concession for the Muslim Ottomans. Implementation of this reform promise was correspondingly cautious, indeed, hesitant and faltering. Thereafter, even more moderate reform proposals to ensure Christian security, even when they were in full accord with tradition, all too easily came under suspicion of challenging the basis of Ottoman statehood.

*   *   *

Because it was impossible to fulfill mutually exclusive expectations, Sultan Abdul Hamid II, in particular, perfected a strategy intended essentially to gain time and keep the whole empire in a constant state of expectation: he put off major decisions as long as possible so as to continue to sustain contradictory hopes and hold all options permanently open. In the meantime, he could gently introduce changes wherever possible, preparing the ground for a future that would perhaps—thanks to changes in the international or domestic political constellation—offer greater room to maneuver. Not surprisingly, Abdul Hamid's most important reforms were in the field of education, civil and military; they aimed to prepare a new generation for that future. This strategy of foot-dragging, procrastination, and delay sought to take deliberate advantage of the gap between the announcement of reforms and their enactment. Such delaying tactics—promising without fulfilling, decreeing without applying—allowed the Sultan simultaneously to yield to demands for reforms, which had become inevitable, and to ward off the most dreaded measures. The gap between promise and execution opened up a space for Ottoman agency. This practice was not restricted to the most sensitive reform measures, those that favored non-Muslims. It was observable in every field of modernization, wherever the rift between the diverging expectations of the parties involved was especially wide.[23]

*   *   *

The weakness of the Ottoman central state, which had initially triggered the reform process, left its mark on the course, character, and shape of modernization in different ways. At no stage did the central government in Istanbul have sufficient power resources at its disposal to enforce drastic changes against larger-scale resistance. To be implemented, therefore, reforms had to be negotiated with those opposed to them. Elites hostile to reform could not be easily ignored or replaced, but had to be integrated into the new system by means of incentives.[24] In other cases, an explicitly Islamic terminology and legitimation was used to win wider acceptance for a reform.[25] In other cases still, the authors of a reform simply steered clear of conflict by establishing parallel structures, creating new institutions alongside the existing ones, which remained in place.[26]

One consequence of these reform strategies was that many reforms had to be partly rescinded in the course of implementation.[27] Another, perhaps more momentous result was that the old elites did not lose their positions of power and influence, but kept and in some cases even strengthened them, albeit sometimes under a new name. This held especially for the provincial notables. To enforce government action in the provinces, the Porte and the Sultan were dependent on the mediation of local leaders and dignitaries. Thus, paradoxically, flying in the face of the core objective of centralization and direct control, which was supposed to eliminate all local intermediaries, provincial notables emerged from the modernization process more influential than ever.[28] Like the notables' position in the provinces, the structures of the religious communities (*millets*) were consolidated during the nineteenth century reform process rather than being abolished as they strengthened their function as representatives of autonomous community rights.[29]

In an increasingly confusing tangle, old and new elites, and competing households persisted as rival political forces that were able to acquire or keep power bases in the multitude of traditional and modern structures, institutions, and commissions. Often, at the political level, the particular interests of rival factions or households prevailed over a sense of common affiliation to, and responsibility for, the Ottoman state, even when the state faced fundamental crisis and existential danger.[30] As Ottoman modernization progressed, a progression that, not least, implied mass mobilization, the question as to what could provide the unifying bond to integrate the host of different ethnic, linguistic, religious, and social groups, differently socialized elites, and rival political factions and households became more and more pressing. In the Western European states, the ideology that offered such identification to a majority of subjects and secured their active support was the notion of "nation." In the Ottoman Empire, one of the greatest ideological challenges was the almost impossible task of finding an equivalent to fulfill the same function.

During the reform period, three ideas emerged to fill this blank. Each of these three partly concordant concepts was also connected to the government of its day and to the specific external conditions that would favor it. The Ottomanism of the *Tanzimat* reformers came too late and too hesitantly to win over the important Christian populations of the Balkan provinces to the Ottoman state.[31] The policy of Islamic unity pursued by Abdul Hamid II was very much a reaction to the loss of most of the Balkans in 1878 and the attendant immigration of hundreds of thousands of Muslim refugees.[32] The Turkish nationalism of the Young Turks by no means suppressed Islam as factor of integration, but included the confession of Sunni Islam in its definition of Turkishness[33]—even at the price of marginalizing non-Sunni Turks or Turkomans. Turkism also shared common ground with the Ottomanism of an earlier day, since even the most open-minded and liberal advocates of Ottomanism seemed always to have left the dominance of the Turkish element unquestioned. The transition from Ottomanism to Islamism, and, finally, Turkism was thus less the replacement of one ideology by another than a shift in priorities. In the end, however, none of these models was able to include all Ottoman subjects in practice, so that the modern reconceptualization of the Ottoman state necessarily and by definition meant the exclusion of larger segments of the population.

* * *

Like the 1839 events that shaped the agenda of Ottoman policy for decades, the existential crisis of the years 1875–1878 also constituted a major turning point in modern Ottoman history, one that fundamentally reshaped Ottoman policy. The bankruptcy of the state in 1875, the inauguration of three Sultans in one year (1876), the Balkan crisis that had prevailed since 1875, and, finally, the lost war against Russia in 1877–1878, all demonstrated the problems of the Ottoman Empire far too clearly. It was not least in light of his experience of these years of crisis that Abdul Hamid II, who became Sultan in August 1876, determined the principles and strategies of his policy: always to give due consideration to the rivalries among the Ottoman elites; to avoid war and direct confrontation with his European neighbors at all costs;[34] and—rather than to seek an inevitably unequal alliance with one European power—to maintain strict neutrality, which would make it possible for him to offer different forms of cooperation, railway concessions, commercial agreements, or the admission of advisory missions to the Empire to all powers, thus playing one European state off against the other and benefiting both from their competition for influence in the Ottoman Empire and, more generally, their political maxim of maintaining the "balance of power."[35]

In the domestic sphere Abdul Hamid II mobilized the same strategy to play rival actors against one another and induce them to hold each other in check. This compensated, at least to some extent, for the weakness of the central state vis-à-vis the various political, social, and regional forces.[36] Finally, the Sultan fell back on the same principle in his attempt to control the provinces as well; here it was backed up by the venerable strategy of "divide and rule." This held especially for the eastern borderlands, where central state control was particularly new and weak.

*   *   *

Nominally, Eastern Asia Minor had been under Ottoman dominion since the early sixteenth century. In fact, however, the Kurdish tribes and also a few small Armenian enclaves (in particular, Zeytoun in Cilicia and Sasoun in the province of Bitlis) remained autonomous until the mid-nineteenth century.[37] Mahmud II (1808–1839) was the first sultan to try to subdue the tribes in the empire's periphery and subject them to direct central administration.[38] The difficult terrain, but mainly the lack of reliable and loyal troops in the area, made the campaigns in the East arduous. The conscription of soldiers was possible only with massive use of force, and mass desertions took place despite the close guarding of the army camps.[39] Even after the suppression of the Kurdish principalities, subjugating the tribes and establishing immediate control of the region still involved numerous obstacles. The problems with which the whole empire was confronted in establishing modern statehood were multiplied here.

The population was not only extremely heterogeneous as far as ethnic, linguistic, or confessional identities were concerned; their way of life and social organization also confronted the central government with serious challenges. The Eastern Anatolian Turkomans, Kurds, and Arabs were predominantly tribal populations until the nineteenth century; a significant proportion of them lived nomadic or semi-nomadic lives. These groups evaded administrative control almost completely, which is why the government made a special effort to settle them in the nineteenth and early twentieth centuries.[40] Infrastructure in the region was poor; the situation here did not change substantially down to the end of the Ottoman Empire. Some mountain regions were almost inaccessible.[41] These provinces could hardly be governed by state officials sent directly from Istanbul. At the same time, all representatives of the central state in the provinces, i.e. the organs of the provincial administration and the military, soon became part of the local political fabric and could easily develop their own aims and interests and act according to them rather than on behalf of the Porte—as Ottoman experience in the past had all too often showed. Provincial notables, many of whom had found an additional field of action in the provincial and municipal councils created by the *Tanzimat,* were an additional factor in local politics. A third important force was constituted by tribal leaders, who could only be integrated and at least partly controlled if they were allowed to retain certain privileges and liberties. The foundation of the Hamidiye cavalry in 1890–1891, an irregular force recruited mainly from Sunni Kurdish tribes of Anatolia under the command of their own tribal chiefs, was presented as an attempt to win the cooperation of the tribes through incentives in a first stage, and gradually to integrate them thereafter into the regular administrative and military structures.[42] In the face of this weakness of the central state in the borderlands region, the politics of balance became all the more important, i.e. the strategy of ruling through the fragmentation and instrumentalization of local forces, with an eye to the reciprocal limitation of their power. Alongside the *valis* (provincial governors), the local military commanders were vested with powers of their own. The influence of urban notables was curbed through tribal leaders.[43]

Initially, the suppression of the Kurdish principalities failed to reinforce public order. To the contrary, it led to greater anarchy.[44] The old order and the existing balance of local powers was destroyed; yet, for the nonce, no new stable order took its place. Every community, grouping, and political actor had to redefine and reassert its place and power base. In this reshuffling of forces, violence did not diminish, but rather increased. Since, after its conquest of the Eastern provinces, the Ottoman army was able neither to disarm the tribes nor to fully subdue them, many of the protagonists on the scene remained armed, further intensifying the violence. Times of crisis aggravated the situation. Especially during and in the aftermath of wars, vendettas flared up among the tribes and threatened to escalate out of control. In the year of the Russo-Ottoman war, 1877–1878, the central government in Istanbul registered an alarming number of murders in the province of Bitlis and its environs, meticulously recording each one.[45] Moreover, after the destruction of the Kurdish Emirates, Armenian complaints about violent infringements commenced, especially in the 1860s, when the settlement of *muhacirun* as well as government programs for the sedentarization of nomads aggravated conflicts over farmland and pastures.[46]

Whenever the central state saw its interests in danger, it intervened and suppressed local unrest, dispatching military forces.[47] Documentation by the Ottoman Ministry of Finance, however, shows how much these military actions strained Ottoman financial, material, and personal capacities. The 1904 campaign against the small Armenian mountain region of Sasoun may serve as an instructive example.[48] The province of Bitlis, where the region was situated, lacked the soldiers needed to carry out the expedition and had to request reinforcements from the neighboring provinces. A lengthy discussion started among the provinces involved about who was to pay for the soldiers' rations and equipment. Bitlis was unable to shoulder the financial burden alone, yet the other provinces' situation was equally dismal. They accordingly agreed to send troops, but expected the province of Bitlis to pay for the soldiers it had asked for. This example, far from unique, leads to the conclusion that the region could not be controlled with the means available locally.[49] A long-term occupation with forces from distant provinces was so costly that the Ottoman government obviously shied away from the expenditure in material and personnel, opting for other, innovative methods of indirect rule over these provinces. The developments of the 1890s, in particular, make this clear.

*   *   *

With the state's key ruling strategy being *divide et impera,* the playing of political actors off against one another, by the 1890s not only state officials and local notables but also the different population groups—whether ethno-confessional groupings or rival tribes—were turned against each other and were mutually weakened as a result. *Muhacirun* were deliberately settled not only at points of strategic importance but also in dominantly Christian regions. They were often not given enough land or tools for agricultural production, so plundering the local peasants became an indispensable means of survival for these refugees. At the same time, *muhacirun* were scattered among the local population to assimilate them faster.[50]

Controlling the provinces by skillfully playing rival forces off against each other apparently proved simpler and more cost-effective in the short and middle term than attempts to achieve lasting, direct control. Kurdish tribal leaders' power was not broken by Ottoman soldiers, but by other Kurdish tribes. The Armenians, whose plight inspired European demands for reform and threats of intervention, were not suppressed by central army units but by local forces. The central government was able to limit its role to manipulation of the local balance of power in its own interests through different means of support and punishment. In particular these included strengthening the sedentary Sunni stratum of the population at the expense of heterodox Muslims (especially Alevites) and nomad tribes and intimidating the non-Muslims enough to keep them from appealing to the European Powers for reform and help.[51]

The 1891 foundation of the Hamidiye cavalry, named after Sultan Abdul Hamid, took to a new level the dual policies of divide and rule on the one hand and what can be labeled a modern policy of indirect rule on the other. In this irregular military formation (which in practice remained restricted mostly to the Kurdish tribes of Eastern Asia Minor) only Sunni tribes and a small minority of Yezidis were included, excluding the Alevi segment of the Kurdish population.[52] Smaller tribes would join the Hamidiye cavalry to strengthen their position vis-à-vis the more powerful tribes of their region.[53] With the establishment of the Hamidiye cavalry, a new dimension was added to the policy of divide and rule. Rather than simply failing to disarm the population, this time, one specific segment of the population was deliberately armed to the detriment of the other groups in the region. The central government handed over modern weapons to the Hamidiye regiments but—in violation of the law—did not demand that they be returned after the campaign or maneuver was over. In this way, the Hamidiye regiment remained permanently armed during the long years of peace. Being part of an official military unit and keeping their arms, the Hamidiye tribes had, compared to their local adversaries, a considerable technical advantage as well as an additional claim to legitimacy for their actions.[54]

By equipping the—irregular!—Hamidiye regiments in this way, the central state effectively abandoned its monopoly on power and violence, surrendering its ability and right to use force in the region to the Hamidiye cavalry. Rather than achieving a central state monopoly of power, a system of delegation of power to local forces was instituted; state-supported local action against rebellious tribes, heterodox Muslims, or Armenians in fact took the place of central state intervention through military or military police. Against this background, it becomes understandable that the violence of local actors in the eastern borderlands—up to and including violent excesses that could even take the form of large-scale massacres—went unpunished. These violent acts were tolerated and even sympathetically accepted as long as they did not offend central state interests or disturb civil life, especially agricultural and economic production, too much.

A number of indications suggest that the Hamidiye regiments were created not least as a counterweight to, and means of exerting pressure on, the large Armenian population.[55] During the large-scale massacres of Armenians in 1895–1896, the Hamidiye regiments played a significant role, even if—as we now know—their contribution should not be overestimated.[56] After the massacres, the expansion of the organization, which had previously been fostered with great zeal, essentially came to an end.[57]

Thus the end result of this *de facto* delegation of power to local actors was not only, and not even primarily, that regular army resources and personnel did not have to be mobilized for the "pacification" of the Eastern provinces. Much more important was the fact that this delegation of power opened up new room for action in a grey area that was not at all, or at least not in the same unquestioned manner, at the disposal of the central state's regular organs. Recruiting and arming the Hamidiye troops allowed the central government to make use of local forces to pursue its own goals without assuming responsibility for their actions. Even more, it made possible the use of massive violence as a policy instrument in times of peace. It allowed the state, whose first duty was the protection of its subjects, to implement an indirect policy of violence against its own subjects, without engineering a provocation, alleging a rebellion, or making a fundamental threat out of a minor incident like a harmless border violation or the discovery of a few hunting weapons—in short, without the strategies of legitimation a state needs to carry out domestic mass violence.[58] Tolerating the—sometimes massive—violence of irregular troops opened up additional possibilities of action in the paradoxical *entre-deux* of doing and not doing something at the same time. As we have seen in the case of the reforms that were difficult to negotiate, the government could profit from the existence of a gap between promising and carrying out a measure; it could both initiate and block a reform, taking credit for initiation while blaming subordinate bodies for delaying it. Similarly, by means of the Hamidiye regiments, the government was able to allow the use of violence and simultaneously reject responsibility for it.

This policy, however, was linked to the government's assertion that it could not control the actions of its irregular troops. That gaining permanent control over the entire borderlands region would have brought the Ottoman Empire up against the limits of its personnel and financial capacities can hardly be disputed. Nevertheless, this image of the powerless state is exaggerated. As the punitive expeditions to the regions confirm, despite temporal and spatial limitations, the central state *was* able to execute its control and put local forces in their place at any time and in any place in the Eastern borderlands. Reports about successfully completed censuses in remote, barely accessible districts are another proof of the state's effective reach.[59] Thus, the violent acts of *muhacirun,* Kurdish chieftains, or Hamidiye regiments certainly could have been consistently and systematically punished if the political will to do so had been sufficiently strong.

* * *

The problems of the Ottoman modernization process, and, above all, the question of how modern central state power could be achieved and permanently established after 1878 were especially conspicuous in the Empire's eastern borderlands. After the loss of the Balkan provinces, the "Eastern Question" was narrowed and at the same time aggravated due to the new conditions. The Muslim *muhacirun* had suffered considerable violence in their native regions and were all the more sensitive and ready to commit violence in response to Christian emancipation in their new homes.[60] After being a neglected periphery over centuries, the region now became increasingly central, especially on the maps and political agenda of rising Turkish nationalism. Most importantly, in contrast to the Balkan provinces, secession from the Ottoman Empire was never a realistic Armenian policy option, even if the utopia of a "Free Armenia"—where the Muslim Kurdish elements of the country would simply disappear as a result of peaceful assimilation into the Armenian population!—was sketched in the nationalist Armenian literature of the time.[61] The commitment to Armenian well-being in the European cabinets was, beyond popular polemics, too feeble, the Armenian population of the Ottoman state was too widely dispersed, the Muslim presence even on the Armenian plateau was, by the beginning of the nineteenth century too strong, to admit the possibility of a homogeneous Armenian nation state in the Ottoman provinces "inhabited by the Armenians." This may also be the reason for the high level of Armenian integration into Ottoman-Turkish society; in Cilicia, it went so far that many Armenians were linguistically assimilated and Turkish had become the *lingua franca* of the community.[62] Seeing their place as being in the Ottoman state, hoping for its reform, modernization, and consolidation and contributing as much as they could to it was, *a fortiori,* the only viable alternative for the Armenians. This explains the pioneer role that Armenians played in some fields of the Ottoman reform process.[63] It also explains the political aims of the Western Armenian revolutionaries, whose actions were—in conjunction with those of the Young Turks—directed against the authoritarian regime of Abdul Hamid II, but never against the Ottoman state as such.[64] The countless petitions that the Armenian Patriarchs sent to the Porte and the Sultan point in the same direction. These petitions invariably appealed to the Ottoman state to fulfill its protective role in a reliable manner, yet never incited the Armenian population to revolt against that state. To the contrary, the Armenian *millet* establishment consistently condemned revolutionary action. At the same time, even when they appealed to the European powers to press for reform, they always refused to be instrumentalized in any way by foreign interests.[65]

Not surprisingly, the Ottoman Armenians' nation-building process was still only in a rudimentary stage; an Armenian national consciousness, to say nothing of an Armenian national movement, had hardly developed even by the turn of the twentieth century.[66] Most notable in this regard is the fact that, to the very end, no Armenian uprising of significant proportions ever occurred. Armed resistance remained a narrowly limited, local affair with exclusively local focuses and ends.[67] In the end, in 1895–1896 as well as in 1915–1816, mass violence and genocide against the Armenians were largely possible only because the Ottoman Armenians in their overwhelming majority were not armed and not rebellious.[68]

The Turkish rulers of the late Ottoman Empire were very well aware of the Armenian *millet*'s special attachment and loyalty to their state. Not for nothing were they in the habit of calling the Armenian community the *millet-i sadika* (the loyal nation)—right down to the eve of the genocide. After the disastrous defeat at Sarıkamış in January 1915, where Enver Pasha carelessly sacrificed the lives of 90,000 Ottoman soldiers, the Ottoman Minister of War explicitly confirmed the absolute loyalty of the Anatolian Armenians, even in this situation of extreme threat to the empire and in the face of the Russian advance on the Ottoman domains.[69] It seems, however, that this Armenian devotion and the concomitant Armenian demands for reform were a much greater challenge for the Muslim Turkish elites of the Ottoman Empire than the Armenians' alleged separatism, because pressing for equal participation in their state and its organs meant nothing less than, first, putting an end to the Islamic foundation of the state, and second, finding a way to accept plurality in a modern state—doubtless the most problematic aspects of all Ottoman modernization efforts. Not without reason were the Hamidian massacres of 1895–1896 as well as the Young Turk genocide of 1915–1916 triggered by urgent, powerfully presented demands for Armenian reforms.

* * *

The empire-wide massacres of the years 1895–1896 are a showpiece of Abdul Hamid II's political strategy; at the same time, they are the most extreme example of his policy of delegating power and thus also delegating the execution of violence. The European Powers' insistence on reforms for the benefit of Ottoman non-Muslims were a double-edged sword as long as the reform proposals were connected with European aspirations to extend their influence. All too easily could Christians, in particular, be stigmatized as protégés of foreign powers, even as their agents, and, ultimately, as domestic foes, always suspect because of their appeals for reform, and more so as they raised the issue before not only the Ottoman government but also "Europe."[70] After 1878, the Armenians were particularly vulnerable to this kind of prejudice and enmity against a foreign-imposed reform that was projected onto them. At the same time, because of the ban on carrying arms to which non-Muslims were subject, they were in their great majority completely defenseless as long as no other force intervened militarily to protect them.[71]

The peace treaty of San Stefano, dictated by the Russians after their rout of the Ottomans in 1878, had for the first time introduced the issue of Armenian reforms in an international treaty. The revision of the relevant article in the Treaty of Berlin later that same year, and, in particular, the other powers' rejection of the Russian claim to protect the Armenians and its replacement by a vague guarantee to be executed by all the signatory powers, showed all too clearly that the European powers were, after the independence of great parts of the Balkans, not willing to tolerate the extension of Russian influence in Eastern Asia Minor.[72] Abdul Hamid II could foresee that the Europeans would steadily demand reforms for the benefit of the Armenians, but would never back up their demands with economic or military sanctions.

In the course of the 1880s, violent acts against Armenians occurred more and more frequently; the perpetrators went unpunished in most cases. The abduction, in 1889, of an Armenian girl named Giulizar from the province of Muş by a Kurdish tribal chief by the name of Musa Bey attracted particular attention. Her fate, however, unlike that of many other victims of similar cases of violence, became known to the European general public. Abdul Hamid II reacted by organizing a trial, which, however, turned into a farce; Musa Bey got off scot-free.[73] The countless Armenian petitions accompanying other instances of abduction, robbery, and murder went unheeded. These events must have strengthened Abdul Hamid II in the conviction that the European powers—despite the shock waves in their public opinion, as reflected in many articles in the European press—would not agree to intervene in concerted fashion to protect the Ottoman Armenians, however serious the atrocities against them, but would restrict themselves to mere protest.

In the 1890s, demands for reforms in the Armenian provinces were again on the agenda; this time they were more insistent, more vehement. Ultimately, Abdul Hamid II consented to the European reform proposals. The subsequent, empire-wide massacres of the Armenians show his calculations. They were as cynical as they were successful. Direct involvement of the state organs in the massacres can hardly be proved. But Abdul Hamid had made it all too clear to the European delegates that if they imposed far-reaching Armenian reforms he would not be able to contain the rage of his Muslim compatriots.[74] An announcement of the kind was in fact nothing less than a barely veiled threat of massacres—not a direct call for violence, but a license to murder and a guarantee of impunity. Like the policy of delegating violence, the conjuration of popular wrath via the public announcement that it might erupt allowed the Ottoman government indirectly to employ and reap the benefits of violence, in this case mass violence, without having to carry it out itself or order it explicitly.

The calculation proved correct. Up to 300,000 Armenians fell victim to the massacres; the European powers protested but did not intervene. The massacres of 1895–1896 diminished the weight of the Armenians in the region, but, above all, they were a clear warning to Armenians and Europeans alike not to press too hard for reforms in the Eastern borderlands. They had the desired effect: until the eve of World War I, the issue of Armenian reforms was never again raised in the same way. Unpunished violence in the provinces' everyday life, and, now, even massacres had become an instrument of Ottoman administration in the borderlands.

* * *

Violence, however, and, all the more, mass violence, does not occur in the absence of certain basic conditions. Massacres of such a large scale as in 1895–1896 cannot be explained with reference to the Hamidian policy of delegation of power alone. In addition, a mobilization of the masses had to take place. In general, there are two important prerequisites that are causally related to the emergence of mass violence and broad participation by the local population in it. Both of them existed in the late Ottoman Empire. One is a situation of political uncertainty, a power vacuum or a war or civil war that could temporarily suspend universal moral commandments and inhibitions on killing and allow perpetrators to hope for impunity. The second is a perceived existential threat. Obviously, nothing is more conducive to large-scale readiness to use violence than a feeling of fear that does not correlate with a real position of weakness, but rather with a situation of relative strength—such as that of the Muslims of Asia Minor (and, even more so, the Ottoman state) vis-à-vis the Armenians living in the same region.

The Armenian genocide occurred in the shadow of World War I, and there are many indications that the Young Turks led their country into the Great War, among other reasons, in order to achieve their goals—expansion to the East, annihilation of the Armenians, and Turkification of the economy—much more radically and rapidly than could be imagined in times of peace.[75] The extensive massacres of the Armenians of Cilicia took place amid the turmoil of revolution and counterrevolution. The Hamidian massacres, however, took place in the middle of a long period of peace. In this case, it was the delegation of power and the announcement of a temporary withdrawal of central state authority through the conjuration of popular wrath that simulated a power vacuum and thus allowed for the transmission of the exceptional situation of war and revolution to peacetime.

The picture of a situation of existential danger was not difficult to paint in the Ottoman Empire, given the constant possibility of foreign intervention and sometimes even scenarios of dismemberment of the empire. The European presence hovering over the empire, the permanent fear of intervention, eventually evolved into a veritable neurosis—one which completely ignored the fact that the European interest in the Ottoman Empire under the conditions of the European policy of balance was, precisely, also the best guarantee for the preservation of the Empire, which, without European intervention, would already have collapsed in 1839. Also repressed was the fact that even the loss of another borderland province did not mean the end of the empire.

In this atmosphere of latent threat, uncertainty, and humiliation that European policy toward the Ottoman Empire signified in the view of many Muslims, the modernization process and, especially, the call for equal status for Muslims and non-Muslims appeared as yet another element of fundamental threat: by demanding equality non-Muslims had "moved out of [the] place"[76] that had been assigned to them by traditional Islamic law, a move that undermined the very foundations of the Ottoman state. Beyond ideology and abstract state conceptions, Anatolian Muslims, as far as their everyday life was concerned, had good reason to fear the restriction of their present status, prerogatives, and privileges in any scenario of change for the benefit of the Armenians, whether it took the form of partial autonomy under a Christian governor or only a greater Armenian share in the provincial administration and police.

Obviously the flames of these fears were deliberately fanned. Prior to the Hamidian massacres of 1895–1896, fearful images of the loss of the country to the Armenians were whipped up during Friday prayers in the mosques.[77] There was a general atmosphere of fear of loss, frightening rumors, and scenarios of European colonization. Hostile stereotypes and prejudices were cultivated.[78] However, to mobilize a sufficiently large number of Muslims to kill Armenians these had to be combined with more concrete local fears directed to focus on the local Armenian population. The "popular rage" that Abdul Hamid II had called up in 1895/96 was there to be tapped and could be channeled in the requisite direction only because it had already been created and stoked long enough through this politics of fear.[79]

In the end, in conjunction with the discord and irresolution of the European powers, the Hamidian strategy of refusing to make decisions of general principle, of maintaining the whole empire in a state of vacillation, certainly intensified existing fears and uncertainties. Together, European and Hamidian policies undoubtedly prolonged the life of the Ottoman Empire for decades. On the other hand, these policies did not at all resolve existing tensions and conflicts, but on the contrary, multiplied them infinitely. In this situation, permanent insecurity and fear became the crucial variables that Ottoman policies made use of in the Eastern borderlands.

*　*　*

In sum, the central significance of the borderlands paradigm seems to lie in its comparative approach, which allows us to put the findings of a regionally limited case study in a broader context. This makes it possible to differentiate between the more general structures of central state control and occasions for mass violence in borderland regions and the specific way Ottoman rulers in the last decades of the Empire dealt with the weakness of their central state. By fragmenting and delegating power to local actors who escaped effective control and were not systematically held responsible for their actions, the central state opened up spaces for violence. The violence that became endemic in the Ottoman Eastern borderlands, especially in the latter half of the nineteenth century, was not always the unwanted outcome of a tense atmosphere and feelings of uncertainty and fear resulting from the radical challenges and changes of the time, but was often enough tolerated and encouraged by the central authorities. It was perpetrated, if not in their name, then in their place.

Notes

Key To Archival Citations

AA-PA: Auswärtiges Amt–Politisches Archiv [Archive of the German Foreign Ministry]
BOA: Başbakanlık Osmanlı Arşivi [Ottoman Prime Minister's Archive, Istanbul]
BOA sections consulted:

A} MKT.MHM.: Sadaret Mektubi Mühimme Kalemi
DH.EUM.EMN.: Emniyet-i Umumiye Müdüriyeti Emniyet Şubesi Evrakı
DH.MKT.: Dahiliye Nezareti Mektubi Kalemi
Y.EE.d.: Yıldız Esas Defterleri
Y.PRK.ASK.: Yıldız Perakende Evrakı Askeri Maruzatı
Y.PRK.DH.: Yıldız Perakende Evrakı Dahiliye Nezareti Maruzatı
Y.PRK.MYD.: Yıldız Perakende Evrakı Maiyyet-i Seniyye ve Yaveran Dairesi Maruzatı

1. http://www.watsoninstitute.org/borderlands/ (accessed 20 March 2012).

2. Ibid.

3. For a detailed discussion of the different estimates and statistics of the population of Eastern Asia Minor as well as their political implications, see Raymond Kévorkian, *Le génocide des Arméniens* (Paris: Odile Jacob, 2006), 331–344; Fuat Dündar, *Modern Türkiye'nin Şifresi* (Istanbul: İletişim, 2008), 85–115.

4. For a description from an Armenian perspective, see Roupen [Minas Der Minasian], *Hay Heghapokhagani me Hishadagnere* (Beirut: Hamazkaine Vahé Sethian Press, 1983), vol. 1, 127–35, 327–39, passim.

5. Cf. Elke Hartmann, "'Havadarim Azke' ou Anor Yerespokhannere," *Datev Hayakidagan Darekirk* 1 (2008): 144–206, see esp. 204.

6. Cf., for example, BOA, DH.MKT. 1505/70 of 2 May 1888, BOA, A.}MKT.MHM. 750/12 of 9 August 1894; BOA, A.}MKT.MHM. 638/15 of 26 October 1895; BOA, DH.EUM.EMN. 58/3 of 3 March 1914; BOA, A.}MKT.MHM. 545/43 of 21 March 1901; BOA, A.}MKT.MHM. 665/6 of 13 November 1895; BOA, A.}MKT.MHM. 622/14 of 24 June 1903; BOA, Y.PRK.MYD. 15/27 of 16 August 1894 et al.

7. For a general overview, Robert Mantran, "L'Etat ottoman au XVIIIe siècle: la pression européenne" in *Histoire de l'Empire ottoman*, ed. Robert Mantran (Paris: Fayard, 1989), 65–287.

8. On the "Eastern Question," see Malcolm E. Yapp, *The Making of the Modern Near East 1792–1923* (London: Longman, 1987), 47–96, esp. 70–72 on the Mehmed Ali crisis. Cf. Matthew S. Anderson, *The Eastern Question 1774–1923* (London: Macmillan, 1966), 77–109.

9. On the European economic interest—in addition to political and strategic considerations—in maintaining the Ottoman territory in the form of one undivided market, see Donald Quataert, "The Age of Reforms, 1812–1914" in *An Economic and Social History of the Ottoman Empire 1300–1914*, ed. Halil İnalcık and Donald Quataert (Cambridge: Cambridge University Press, 1994), 759–943, esp. 761–62.

10. On the interrelation of the great reform decrees (1839, 1856, and the constitution of 1876) with existential crises and massive European pressure, see Roderic H. Davison, "Tanzīmāt" in *Encyclopedia of Islam*, 2nd ed. (hereafter EI²), vol. 10, 201–209, esp. 204, 208; cf. Erik J. Zürcher, *Turkey: A Modern History* (London: Tauris, 1993), 53, 59. About the Ottoman resistance against the abuse of the "capitulations," see Halil İnalcık, "İmtiyāzāt II. The Ottoman Empire," EI² 3: 1179–89, esp. 1185–88.

11. On the new Muslim elites, see the study of Fatma M. Göçek, *Rise of the Bourgeoisie, Demise of the Empire* (New York: Oxford University Press, 1996). On the role of non-Muslims as agents of reform, see Roderic H. Davison, "The *Millets* as Agents of Change in the Nineteenth-Century Ottoman Empire," in *Christians and Jews in the Ottoman Empire*, ed. Benjamin Braude and Bernard Lewis (New York: Holmes & Meier Publishers, 1982), vol. 1, 319–37.

12. Especially about the Armenians, who were most relevant in the Eastern borderlands, see Salahi R. Sonyel, "The Socio-Economic Development of the Armenian *Millet* in the Ottoman Empire after the Tanzimat Reforms" in *Histoire économique et sociale de l'Empire ottoman et de la Turquie (1326–1960)*, ed. Daniel Panzac (Louvain, Belgium: Peeters, 1995), 471–83.

13. On the Armenian presence in the Ottoman administration and police forces, mostly restricted to lower posts, see the case study by Mesrob K. Krikorian, *Armenians in the Service of the Ottoman Empire 1860–1908* (London: Routledge, 1977); more generally, for the non-Muslims, cf. Carter V. Findley, "The Acid Test of Ottomanism: The Acceptance of Non-Muslims in the Late Ottoman Bureaucracy" in *Christians and Jews*, ed. Braude and Lewis, vol. 1, 339–368.

14. See *Meclis-i Mebusan 1293 Zabit Ceridesi,* ed. Hakkı Tarık Us (Istanbul: Vakit Gazete Matbaa Kütüphane, 1939), 173–74, 178; Moushegh Srpazan Seropian, *Inknagensakroutiun* (unpublished manuscript), vol. 4, January 1916–May 1917, 947 (entry of 25 March 1917 citing his diary of 1909), archive of the Bibliothèque Nubar, Paris; Krikor Zohrab, *Collected Works* [in Armenian], vol. 5: *Speeches, Memoranda, Draft Bills, etc.,* ed. by Albert Sharourian (Yerevan, Armenia: Kraganoutian yev Arvesdi Tankarani Hradaragtchoutiun, 2004), 195, 252–54, 263, 272–75, 431–32, 436–37; cf. Elke Hartmann, "The 'Loyal Nation' and Its Deputies: The Armenians in the First Ottoman Parliament" in *The First Ottoman Experiment in Democracy,* ed. Christoph Herzog and Malek Sharif (Würzburg, Germany: Ergon, 2010), 187–222, esp. 220.

15. On the attitude of Arab Christians, see for example, the 25 April 1877 debate in the Ottoman parliament on the Russian declaration of war on the Ottoman Empire: *Meclis-i Mebusan 1293,* ed. Us, 172–80, esp. 173–74; on the "Ottomanist" attitude of the Greeks of Asia Minor, cf. Vangelis C. Kechriotis, "The Greeks of Izmir at the End of the Empire" (Ph.D. Dissertation, University of Leiden, Netherlands, 2005); on the Armenians, see below.

16. For example on the integration of the Janissaries into the reformed army of Mahmud II, see Avigdor Levy, "The Officer Corps in Sultan Mahmud II's New Ottoman Army, 1826–39," *International Journal of Middle East Studies* 2 (1971): 21–39.

17. On the idea of cultural superiority, Bernard Lewis, *The Emergence of Modern Turkey* (Oxford: Oxford University Press, 1965), 34–36; on the traditional position of non-Muslims in Muslim societies, see as a short introduction Claude Cahen, "Dhimma," *EI²* 2: 227–231; cf. Mihran Dabag, "Katastrophe und Identität" in *Erlebnis—Gedächtnis—Sinn,* ed. Hanno Loewy and Bernhard Moltmann (Frankfurt: Campus Verlag, 1996), 177–235, esp. 190. Dabag in this connection coins the expression of a "despising toleration" (*verachtende Duldung*) of the non-Muslims in the Ottoman Empire.

18. Roderic H. Davison, "Turkish Attitudes Concerning Christian–Muslim Equality in the Nineteenth Century," *American Historical Review* 59 (1954): 844–64, esp. 859.

19. On the perception of Süleyman Kanuni's reign as a "golden age," see Cemal Kafadar, "The Myth of the Golden Age" in *Suleyman the Second and his Time,* ed. Halil İnalcık and Cemal Kafadar (Istanbul: Isis Press, 1993), 37–48.

20. Butrus Abu-Manneh, "The Islamic Roots of the Gülhane Rescript," *Welt des Islams* 34 (1994): 173–203; cf. the text of the decree in *Düstur,* series 1 (Constantinople: Dâr ül-tibâat ül-âmire, 1289–1295 H. [1872–1878), vol. 1, 4–7; quotation on 6.

21. Text of the *ferman* in ibid., 7–14, see esp. 8.

22. On the Islamic notion of just rule based on the concept of *adalet* (justice), cf. E. Tyan, "'adl" in *EI²* 1: 209–210; Lawrence Rosen, "Concepts of Justice" in *The Oxford Encyclopedia of the Modern Islamic World* (Oxford: Oxford University Press, 1995), vol. 2, 388–391; for the Ottoman Empire, cf. Halil İnalcık, *The Ottoman Empire: The Classical Age, 1300–1600* (London: Weidenfeld & Nicolson, 1973), 65–69.

23. On the 1882 German military mission to the Ottoman Empire as a good example, see Jehuda L. Wallach, *Anatomie einer Militärhilfe* (Düsseldorf: Droste, 1976); Merwin A. Griffiths, "The Reorganization of the Ottoman Army under Abdul Hamid II. 1880–1897" (Ph.D. Diss., University of California, Los Angeles, 1966). On German officers' complaints about the stonewalling of reforms, see Radowitz to Bismarck 25 December 1882, appendix 1: report of General Kaehler, 23 December 1882, AA-PA, Türkei 142, vol. 1; Colmar Freiherr von der Goltz, *Denkwürdigkeiten* (Berlin: Mittler, 1929), 109. On Abdul Hamid II's appeasing moves, see, for example, Radolin to Caprivi, 31 May 1893, AA-PA, Türkei 142, vol. 7 (notes exorbitantly high payments to the German officers); Thielmann to Bismarck, 30 July 1885, AA-PA, Türkei 142, vol. 1; Wallach, *Anatomie einer Militärhilfe,* 104–107; İlber Ortaylı, *Osmanlı İmparatorluğu'nda Alman Nüfuzu* (Istanbul: İletişim, 1998), 119–21 (notes sale of huge amounts of German weaponry to the Ottoman army).

24. Cf., for example, on the military, Avigdor Levy, "Military Reform and the Problem of Centralization in the Ottoman Empire in the Eighteenth Century," *Middle Eastern Studies* 18 (1982): 227–49; idem, "Officer Corps," 21–39.

25. For an example of the modern army Mahmud II created under the name of "muallem asakir-i mansure-i Muhammadiye" ([well] trained, victorious Muhammadan soldiers), see Stanford J. Shaw and Ezel Kural Shaw, *History of the Ottoman Empire and Modern Turkey* (Cambridge: Cambridge University Press, 1977), vol. 2, 19–24, 28; Levy, "Officer Corps," 21, 27.

26. Davison, "Tanzīmāt," 202; for example, on the new secular schools founded alongside the traditional *medreses*, see Selçuk A. Somel, *The Modernization of Public Education in the Ottoman Empire 1839–1908* (Leiden, Netherlands: Brill, 2001), esp. chapter 1.

27. Cf. Davison "Tanzīmāt," for example, on the principle of merit-based promotion of army officers, which had soon to be in large measure reversed; cf. Levy, "Officer Corps," 30–31.

28. Albert Hourani, "Ottoman Reform and the Politics of Notables," in *The Modern Middle East: A Reader*, ed. Albert Hourani, Philip S. Khoury, and Mary C. Wilson (London: I. B. Tauris, 1993), 83–109.

29. Cf. Davison, "Tanzīmāt."

30. Levy, "Officer Corps," 36–38 discusses one example.

31. Davison, "Tanzīmāt," 209.

32. Cf. Azmi Özcan, *Pan-Islamism: Indian Muslims, the Ottomans, and Britain (1877–1924)* (Leiden, Netherlands: Brill, 1997); Stephen Duguid, "The Politics of Unity," *Middle Eastern Studies* 9 (1973): 139–156; on specific aspects of the Hamidian policy of Islamization see Selim Deringil, *The Well-Protected Domains* (London: Tauris, 1998), 68–84; Benjamin C. Fortna, "Islamic Morality in Late Ottoman 'Secular' Schools," *International Journal of Middle East Studies* 32 (2000): 369–393; Dündar, *Modern Türkiye'nin Şifresi*, 41–52.

33. On the emergence and development of the Young Turkish movement, see especially the studies of M. Şükrü Hanioğlu, *The Young Turks in Opposition* (New York: Oxford University Press, 1995); and idem, *Preparation for a Revolution* (Oxford: Oxford University Press, 2001).

34. On Abdul Hamid II's refusal to declare war on Bulgaria in 1885, despite his formal right to do so, see Shaw and Kural Shaw, *History of the Ottoman Empire and Modern Turkey*, vol. 2, 196–99.

35. On the often praised diplomacy of Abdul Hamid II, see Feroze A. K. Yasamee, *Ottoman Diplomacy: Abdul Hamid II and the Great Powers 1878–1888* (Istanbul: Isis Press, 1996).

36. On the confusing system of commissions Abdul Hamid II created in his palace, leading to the establishment of a virtual parallel government paid from the civil list, see François Georgeon, *Abdul Hamid II* (Paris: Fayard, 2003), 147–69.

37. On the Kurdish principalities, see David McDowall, *A Modern History of the Kurds* (London: I. B. Tauris, 1997), 38–48.

38. Metin Heper, "Center and Periphery in the Ottoman Empire," *International Political Science Review* 1 (1980): 81–105.

39. See the report of the Prussian military advisor Helmuth Graf von Moltke, who had participated in the campaigns against the Kurds: *Briefe über Zustände und Begebenheiten in der Türkei aus den Jahren 1835 bis 1839* (Berlin: Mittler, 1893), letter no. 43.

40. A short overview can be found in Fuat Dündar, *İttihat ve Terakki'nin Müslümanları İskân Politikası (1913–1918)* (Istanbul: İletişim, 2001), 52–56 for the period until 1908; with reference to more recent studies, see ibid., *Modern Türkiye'nin Şifresi*, 50–52.

41. On the futile attempts of the Ottoman general staff to create a railway connection from Ankara to Erzurum and on the isolation and difficulties in provisioning the Fourth Army stationed in Eastern Asia Minor, see Griffiths, "The Reorganization of the Ottoman Army," 81–82, 125–16, 182; cf. Zürcher, *Turkey*, 81–82.

42. Bayram Kodaman, "Hamidiye Hafif Süvari Alayları," in: *İstanbul Üniversitesi Edebiyat Fakültesi Tarih Dergisi* 32 (1979): 427–80, esp. 452–459; Osman Aytar, *Hamidiye Alaylarından Köy Koruculuğuna* (Istanbul: Medya Güneşi Yayınları, 1992), 75–81.

43. On the Hamidian policy in the Eastern Anatolian provinces, see Duguid, "The Politics of Unity," 139–56.

44. Martin van Bruinessen, *Agha, Sheykh, and State* (Utrecht, Netherlands: Rijksuniversiteit, 1978), 228–29; Robert W. Olson, *The Emergence of Kurdish Nationalism and the Sheikh Said Rebellion 1880–1925* (Austin: University of Texas Press, 1989), 4.

45. BOA, Y.EE.d. 297, 23 Ca. 1295 H. For similar incidents at a later date, see, among others, BOA, Y.PRK.DH. 5/76, 20 C. 1310 H.

46. Garo Sasouni, *Kiurd Azkayin Sharjoumnere yev Hay-Krdagan Haraperoutiunnere* (Beirut: Hamazkayin, 1969), 130–37 (with longer quotations from petitions and reports by the Armenian Patriarchate).

47. For example, on the punitive expedition against Sheikh Ubeydullah and his "Kurdish League" in 1881, see BOA, Y.PRK.ASK. 14/7, 6 L. 1299 H.; Olson, *The Emergence of Kurdish Nationalism*, 6–7.

48. For the following example, see BOA, A}MKT.MHM. 623/1, 21 Za. 1321 H. (8.2.1904).

49. Cf. BOA, A.}MKT.MHM 638/2, 25 Ra. 1313 H.; BOA, A}MKT.MHM 638/30, 16 Ca. 1313 H. etc.

50. Dündar, *Modern Türkiye'nin Şifresi*, 45–46.

51. On the increasing violence caused by the Hamidiye cavalry, see Aytar, *Hamidiye Alaylarından*, 62–63, 69. On the effect of strengthening the Sunni Muslims at the expense of other groups, see Dündar, *Modern Türkiye'nin Şifresi*, 43–52; cf. Aytar, *Hamidiye Alaylarından*, 14, 24, 55–56. On the mobilization of Kurdish tribes against European attempts at exerting influence, see Olson, *The Emergence of Kurdish Nationalism*, 5–6; Kodaman, "Hamidiye Hafif Süvari Alayları," 436. On the issue of Armenian reforms, see below.

52. Aytar, *Hamidiye Alaylarından*, 14, 24, 55–56. On the history of the Hamidiye cavalry, cf. Kodaman, "Hamidiye Hafif Süvari Alayları," 436; and Janet Klein, *The Margins of Empire: Kurdish Militias in the Ottoman Tribal Zone* (Stanford: Stanford University Press, 2011).

53. Aytar, *Hamidiye Alaylarından*, 16; cf. Griffiths, "The Reorganization of the Ottoman Army," 121.

54. On the arming of the Hamidiye regiments, see Kodaman, "Hamidiye Hafif Süvari Alayları," 447; on their legitimation, cf. Aytar, *Hamidiye Alaylarından*, 54–62, 325; Olson, *The Emergence of Kurdish Nationalism*, 9.

55. See for example BOA, Y.PRK.MYD 19/99, 17. Ra. 1315 H.

56. Jelle Verheij, "'Les frères de terre et d'eau': Sur le rôle des Kurdes dans les massacres arméniens de 1894–1896," *Cahiers de l'autre Islam* 5 (1999): 225–76.

57. Kodaman, "Hamidiye Hafif Süvari Alayları," 463–71; Duguid, *The Politics of Unity*, 144–51; Aytar, *Hamidiye Alaylarından*, 97–103, cf. also 151–64; Raymond H. Kévorkian and Paul B. Paboudjian, *Les Arméniens dans l'empire ottoman à la veille du genocide* (Paris: ARHIS, 1992), 48–51.

58. On the propaganda effort to portray the Armenians as traitors that accompanied the genocide of 1915–1916, see Kévorkian and Paboudjian, *Le Génocide des Arméniens*, 214–15, 218–23, 268–69, 289–90, 299–301, 307.

59. See for example BOA, DH.MKT. 1478/53, 4 Ca. 1305 H. for the district of Hakkari.

60. Cf. *Doksanüç muhacereti 1877–1878*, ed. Bilal Şimşir, (Ankara: Türk Tarih Kurumu Yayınları, 1989); Justin McCarthy, *Death and Exile* (Princeton: Darwin Press, 1996).

61. See for example "Vartan's dream" in Raffi's best-selling novel *Khente [The Fool]*. English translation: Raffi, *The Fool*, trans. Donald Abcarian (Princeton: Gomidas Institute, 2000), 206–217, esp. 210–11.

62. For the disproportionate number of Armenian teachers in the new Ottoman secular school system, see, for instance, Somel, *The Modernization of Public Education*, 129. On the Armenians' significance for the Ottoman press, theater, and photography, see Suraiya Faroqhi, *Geschichte des Osmanischen Reiches* (München: C. H. Beck, 2000), 107–108. On linguistic assimilation: Vahé Tachjian, "Une reconstruction nationale: réinsertion des filles et des femmes arméniennes après 1918," in *Trames d'Arménie, Catalogue Museon Arlatan* 2007, 107–115, esp. 110; cf. Findley, "The Acid Test of Ottomanism," 350.

63. See for example the important role of Midhat Paşa's advisor Krikor Odian: Davison, *Reform in the Ottoman Empire*, 115, 289–90, 369; and idem, "The Millets as Agents of Change," 330. On the Armenian *millet* constitution and its significance, cf. Vartan Artinian, *The Armenian Constitutional System in the Ottoman Empire 1839–1863* (Istanbul: n.p., 1988).

64. Georgeon, *Abdul Hamid II*, 390, 391.

65. See for example *Masis*, 26 April 1877; *Masis*, 28 April 1877, etc.; cf. also *Meclis-i Mebusan*, ed. Us, 174–75. On the Armenian demands at San Stefano, cf. Hagop Dj. Sirouni, *Bolis yev ir Tere*, vol. 3 (Antelias, Lebanon: Dbaran Gatoghigosoutian Hayots Medzi Dann Giligio, 1987), 537–43. For the memorandum the Armenian Patriarchate presented at the Congress of Berlin, see Marcel Léart [a.k.a. Krikor Zohrab], *La Question arménienne à la lumière des documents* (Paris: Augustin Challamel, 1913); cf. Sirouni, *Bolis yev ir Tere*, vol. 3, 544–61 (based on the minutes of the Armenian *millet* parliament).

66. Vahé Tachjian, "Azkaynaganoutiunn ou Serayin Khdroutiunè Tseghasbanoutian Verabradz Ginerou ou Aghtchignerou Verahamargman Kordzenatsin Metch," *Bazmavep* 165 (2007): 229–58, esp. 229–35; Ronald G. Suny, "Religion, Ethnicity, and Nationalism; Armenians, Turks, and

the End of the Ottoman Empire" in *In God's Name: Genocide and Religion in the Twentieth Century,* ed. Omer Bartov and Phyllis Mack (New York: Berghahn, 2001), 24–61, esp. 32–38, 40, 42.

67. On the Zeytoun and Sasoun events, see Louise Nalbandian, *The Armenian Revolutionary Movement: The Development of Armenian Political Parties Through the Nineteenth Century* (Berkeley: University of California Press, 1963), 74–78, 120–22, 126–28.

68. Cf. also Kévorkian and Paboudjian, *Le Génocide des Arméniens,* 302.

69. *Osmanischer Lloyd,* 26 February 1915; cf. Johannes Lepsius, *Der Todesgang des Armenischen Volkes* (Potsdam, Germany: Missionshandlung und Verlag, 1930), 161–62; Taner Akçam, *Armenien und der Völkermord* (Hamburg: Hamburger Edition, 2004), 58; Kévorkian and Paboudjian, *Le Génocide des Arméniens,* 278.

70. On "appealing to Europe" as an analytical framework for similar situations all over Eastern Europe since the eighteenth century, cf. *Europäische Öffentlichkeit. Transnationale Kommunikation seit dem 18. Jahrhundert,* ed. Jörg Requate and Martin Schulze Wessel (Frankfurt am Main: Campus, 2002).

71. On the close interconnection between European imperialism and the genocide of the Armenians, see Donald Bloxham, *The Great Game of Genocide* (Oxford: Oxford University Press, 2005); Manug J. Somakian, *Empires in Conflict* (London: Tauris, 1995).

72. Cf. Anderson, *The Eastern Question,* 206; on the Armenian reform issue in the treaty of San Stefano (Art. 16), see *Der Berliner Kongreß 1878,* ed. Imanuel Geiss (Boppard am Rhein: Boldt, 1978), 19 (English version quoted in Vartan S. Kasparian, "The Historical Roots of the Armenian Question, 1878–97," [Ph.D. Diss., University of Utah, 1977], 126). On the Congress of Berlin (Art. 61): *Der Berliner Kongress,* ed. Geiss, 405 (English version cited in *The Great Powers and the Near East 1774–1923,* ed. Matthew S. Anderson [London: Arnold, 1970], 112).

73. Georgeon, *Abdul Hamid II,* 257–59; cf. Musa Şaşmaz, *Kürt Musa Bey Olayı (1883–1890)* (Istanbul: Kitabevi, 2004) (which includes long extracts from the trial transcripts); Armenouhi Der Garabedian, *Kiulizar* [the memoirs of Giulizar, as written down by her daughter] (Paris: Imprimerie A. Der Agopian, 1946).

74. Georgeon, *Abdul Hamid II,* 289, 293; cf. Engin Akarlı, "The Problem of External Pressures, Power Struggles, and Budgetary Deficits in Ottoman Politics under Abdul Hamid II" (Ph.D. Diss., Princeton University, 1976), 130.

75. Akçam, *Armenien und der Völkermord,* 44.

76. Cf. Gudrun Krämer, "Moving out of Place" in *The Urban Social History of the Middle East, 1750–1950,* ed. Peter Sluglett (Syracuse, N.Y.: Syracuse University Press, 2008), 182–223.

77. Georgeon, *Abdul Hamid II,* 294.

78. On the intensification of anti-Armenian stereotypes in the late Ottoman Empire, cf. Stephan H. Astourian, "Modern Turkish Identity and the Armenian Genocide," in *Remembrance and Denial,* ed. Richard G. Hovannisian (Detroit, Mich.: Wayne State University Press, 1999), 23–49.

79. Cf. Akçam, *Armenien und der Völkermord,* 22 on the Young Ottomans' warnings about violent Muslim reactions and possible bloodshed in the case of equalizing reforms.

PART THREE

Nationalizing the Borderlands

10

BORDERLAND ENCOUNTERS IN THE CARPATHIAN MOUNTAINS AND THEIR IMPACT ON IDENTITY FORMATION

PATRICE M. DABROWSKI

The Carpathian Mountains historically have been a genuine—perhaps even the quintessen-tial—borderland, this despite the fact that they rather neatly bisect what was once called Eastern Europe. Besides being a part of this multiethnic and multidenominational region, the mountain range has comprised the border of numerous states, in both their historic and present-day incarnations. Whereas today one finds the arc of the mountains running along or through countries such as Slovakia, Poland, Ukraine, and Romania, in the deeper past it demarcated—at least, for a significant stretch—the border between the lands of the multi-ethnic Polish-Lithuanian Commonwealth and Hungary. As of the last third of the nineteenth century, this same stretch of the Carpathians came to mark the internal Habsburg frontier: it separated "Austria" (more exactly, the Austrian province of Galicia) to the north from Hungary to the south.[1] While this beautiful and diverse mountain range has been the most prominent physical feature of this part of Europe, it thus has also been oddly peripheral.

Yet this is true more literally than figuratively. Studying a somewhat similar mountain frontier, albeit on the other side of Europe, Peter Sahlins observed that "frontier regions are privileged sites for the articulation of national distinctions."[2] This claim seems to apply even better to the Carpathians than to Sahlin's Pyrenees, given the wealth of ethnic groups that has historically inhabited the former. For, in addition to the nations one associates with the present states in the region—Slovaks, Poles, Ukrainians, Romanians, and the Hungar-ians and Germans who also dwelled in the vicinity—various other peoples could be found in the mountains.[3] These were people generically known as highlanders. Some went solely by that name, as in the case of the *Górale* (the Polish term for highlanders) who inhabited the northern slopes of the Tatra Mountains, the highest segment of the Carpathian range. Others who may have thought of themselves primarily as highlanders had other names bestowed upon them by their neighbors. Such was the case of the Lemkos further east (in the region of the Low Beskids and Bieszczady Mountains) and the Hutsuls of the Eastern Carpathians (also known as the Eastern Beskids).[4] Each of these groups could equally well have been termed, simply, *horiany* (the Ruthenian/Ukrainian term for highlanders).

The ethnic composition of these highland frontier regions was further complicated by the mixing of peoples. Some of this mixing took place over the centuries, in the form of migration into the mountains and piedmont. It also took place in interesting larger spurts that we might identify more with the development of tourism than with true migratory patterns, spurts that are the focus of my own research on the "discovering" of the Carpathians.[5] The highlands were penetrated by lowlanders from the immediate environs as well as lands somewhat further removed; in the latter case, the encounter proved more of an out-of-the-ordinary experience. Many of these lowlanders were nationally conscious individuals, members of what in this part of the world was known as the intelligentsia. They were the bearers of the national idea. The same could not be said for the highlanders, who tended to have a more localized, even tribal, identity—not a modern, national one. What, then, transpired when a critical mass of such nationally conscious individuals came into contact with Carpathian highlanders?

This is where Sahlins' dictum seems pertinent. This encounter amounted to more than an infatuation with a newfound tourist destination. It was potentially transformative, and not just in the sense of *terra incognita* becoming tourist destination. Rather, the encounter had implications for the way the peoples involved—lowlanders as well as highlanders—saw themselves. In some cases, non-national peoples might begin to think of themselves in national terms, while the nationally inclined might see in the other something of value for a given nation. Indeed: instead of a clash of cultures, one finds in some cases a reconfiguring of identities, with each side both contributing to and partaking of the mix. Such an outcome I have termed elsewhere to be a genuine "discovery."[6]

Here we will examine encounters with the mountains and mountain folk on the part of various lowlanders at several different points in history. The initial period of encounter took place prior to World War I, under Habsburg rule, in areas that today belong to Poland and Ukraine. We will consider aspects of the "discovery" of the Tatra highlanders (the so-called Górale) by Poles in the last third of the nineteenth century, then examine a no less interesting episode of "discovery"—this time, of the Hutsul highlanders—by nationally conscious Ukrainians in the early decades of the twentieth century. Finally, we will see how the same Hutsuls, as well as other highlanders, were being "discovered" by Poles after World War I. In this final episode, both Hutsuls and Poles found themselves living no longer in the Habsburg province of Galicia but rather in the new, interwar Polish state, the so-called Second Republic (the first having been the early modern state partitioned by Russia, Prussia, and Austria at the end of the eighteenth century).

What we will see is that there is a qualitative difference between the "discoveries" that took place in the two very different time periods. The period preceding World War I provided scope for genuine nation-building in the mountains. The advent of Polish sovereignty in the period between the two world wars changed the situation dramatically. It ultimately fostered not nation-building (certainly not in the integral nationalist sense) but state-building projects in the mountains. That is, Polish lowlanders—represented by new and influential organizations—sought to establish a Polish civic identity among the various highland populations. Yet this did not mean the end of highland distinctiveness: for at the same time, the Polish organizations not only tolerated but indeed sought to reinforce the local, regional, or even tribal identities of the highlands. This approach would nonetheless have interesting implications for the development in the region of what we would recognize as modern national identities.

Poles and Górale

The Carpathian highlanders of the Tatra Mountains (now part of both Poland and Slovakia; in the late nineteenth century situated along the internal Habsburg border separating Austria [Galicia] from Hungary) represented a mix of many peoples who had traipsed through the region. In ethnic terms, we would identify these highland colonists today as Poles, Slovaks, Ukrainians, Hungarians, Germans, even Romanians. While many engaged in pastoral pursuits best suited to the rocky and barren highland terrain, some settlers came to work in the mines and the lumber industry. With time many melded into the people known as Górale, Poland's most famous regional group. As Timothy J. Cooley has rightly pointed out, this transformation of the Górale into an ethnicity was to a great extent facilitated by lowland incursions into the region in the form of tourism.[7]

Despite the fact that the Górale consisted of an amalgam of peoples, they paradoxically came to be perceived as a pure primeval Polish type by the upper-class Poles who penetrated the mountains in the last third of the nineteenth century. The latter were people who came to the region to hike as well as to regain their health in the fresh alpine air found in the highland village of Zakopane, nestled at the foot of the Tatra Mountains. Many of these nationally conscious Poles hailed from Warsaw or other locales in what was then the Russian Empire. Encouraged by Doctor Tytus Chałubiński to travel to the highland borderland, this group included such luminaries as the novelist Henryk Sienkiewicz and the writer, artist, and activist Stanisław Witkiewicz. To them, the highlanders were an exotic native people inhabiting the southern frontier of the historic Polish lands. As such, the Górale were understood to be undeniably Polish, albeit in an attractively primitive sort of way.

This perception was reinforced by the lowlanders' encounters with this fascinating highland folk. Lowlanders surmised that the Górale differed in striking ways from the peasants of the lowlands, the latter only recently liberated from serfdom and generally still thinking like serfs. By contrast, the Górale were distinguished by their proud demeanor, feisty nature, and, above all, by their love of freedom. They thus were considered to be the most attractive of the peasant populations to be found in the former Polish lands. The attractiveness of the highlander was "discovered" at a time when the nationally conscious (upper-class) Poles became more cognizant of the need to join forces with the peasantry, to think of themselves as one people. That is, the Polish nation, formerly the purview of the nobility, needed to embrace the masses of peasants in order to become a modern nation.[8]

In the process, the Górale became not only the most attractive, newest members of a modern Polish nation; they were seen as ur-Poles. Influential Polish intellectuals who became enamored of the Tatra highlanders imagined them to be authentic primitive Poles possessing attributes of value to the nation. The Polish novelist (and later Nobel laureate) Henryk Sienkiewicz was so taken with the Górale that he wrote them into his historical novel, *The Deluge:* in a rousing yet historically inaccurate scene, highlanders come to the defense of a seventeenth-century Polish king. In this way, the Tatra Mountain highlanders were being written into Polish history, a history that traditionally had been monopolized by the nobility. In yet another work, Sienkiewicz used the highland dialect to approximate medieval Polish speech. The Polish novelist, the most popular writer of his time, thus allowed readers of his *Teutonic Knights* to imagine, as they hiked in the mountains under the tutelage of Górale guides or visited the village of Zakopane, that what they were hearing was medieval Polish.[9]

In turn, the Polish writer and artist Stanisław Witkiewicz was struck by the artistry of the Górale, who went to great lengths to decorate their wooden homes, furniture, and utensils with fanciful carvings. He thought that "perhaps the mountain people, locked in the depths of the valleys, cut off from the world, have preserved longer than anywhere else the most ancient general form specific to the mountainous regions of Poland."[10] In other words, he suspected—indeed, believed—that the highland style of architecture and decorative arts had once flourished throughout the entire Polish state. Updating this folk style for modern, upper-class, use, Witkiewicz created the so-called "Zakopane Style," a style the artist thought of as, simply, "Polish style."[11] This was yet another contribution of the highlanders to the Polish nation—another way in which folk motifs were incorporated into an all-Polish culture.

These contributions, although in their own ways significant, might have had less of an impact had there not been a challenge to Polish control over these mountains at this time—a challenge that summoned forth a Polish response. For a border dispute flared up, in which a landowner from the Hungarian side laid claim to the beautiful highland lake known as Morskie Oko (Eye of the Sea), the destination of many a Polish hiking expedition in the mountains. The story is a fascinating, if complicated one.[12] Suffice it here to say that a number of highlanders as well as nationally conscious Poles fought—some literally (in border skirmishes with Hungarian gendarmes), others figuratively (in archives seeking proof of Polish possession)—to keep the lake Polish. In 1902, the dispute was resolved in the Poles' favor. This border dispute resulted in the transformation of Morskie Oko from just another alpine lake into an outright symbol of Polishness. Generations of Poles would henceforth consider it their patriotic duty to make a pilgrimage to Morskie Oko. In turn, their sense of being Polish was strengthened by this and other highland experiences. Indeed, it has been argued that those who scaled the peaks or skied in the mountains found themselves under the natural conditions most conducive to the strengthening or even the embracing of a genuine national identity, thus making the mountains *the* place for personal discoveries of this kind.[13]

Ukrainians and Hutsuls

Outside interest in the Carpathians was not limited to the Tatra Mountains. In the early years of the twentieth century, members of the nascent Ukrainian intelligentsia (many of whom, like the Poles, also lived under Habsburg rule in Galicia) began to make their own kind of summer pilgrimage to what they considered to be *their* native mountains, the Eastern Carpathians. There they encountered the fascinating highland folk known as the Hutsuls. The Hutsul village of Kryvorivnia (Polish: Krzyworównia) proved to be the destination of choice for many Ukrainian writers, artists, and thinkers. Kryvorivnia was akin to a Ukrainian Zakopane, and has been called the Ukrainian Athens. Galician Ukrainian luminaries of the likes of writer and activist Ivan Franko, ethnographer Volodymyr Hnatiuk, historian

Mykhailo Hrushevsky, and others summered in the region.[14] Yet, as in the case of the Poles, some of the more significant visitors to the highland region came from across the border, in the Russian Empire.

When it comes to demonstrating the potential impact of the Hutsul highlanders on the Ukrainian nation (and vice versa), one case is especially telling. It involves one of those "Russian" Ukrainians, a Ukrainian from Kharkiv (Russian: Kharkov). A veritable Jack-of-all-trades now remembered primarily as a writer and a minstrel (he played the traditional Ukrainian bandura), Hnat Khotkevych came to the Hutsul region after ending up in Galician exile after the Revolution of 1905. He was advised to spend the summer in Kryvorivnia, like many members of the Ukrainian intelligentsia. Some of them—much like the Poles in the Tatras—engaged in ethnographic studies, collecting songs and tales as well as sketching the beauties of the region. Yet Khotkevych seemed even more taken with the Hutsuls and their region than most of his co-nationalists. Khotkevych claimed "there is nothing more beautiful . . . on earth," adding, "As I, having arrived in the Hutsul region, opened my mouth wide with amazement, thus with mouth agape I went about for six years."[15]

Khotkevych did more than just go about the Hutsul region for six years. He studied the Hutsul dialect, which he termed "a fresh stream of highland water" in comparison to the way Ukrainian was spoken back home—a dialect that hearkened back to its proto-Slavic roots.[16] He came to know the Hutsuls as a people, traveling high up into the alpine pastures known as *polonyny* where Hutsul shepherds took their animals to graze in the summer. And Khotkevych wrote about the Hutsuls and their life (his most famous novel being *Heart of Stone,* which dealt with a famous Hutsul brigand from the beginning of the nineteenth century and his lover).[17] The Ukrainian author did not shy away from writing dialogue in the Hutsul dialect, which apparently he did with greater success than did the more renowned novelist Mykhailo Kotsiubyns'kyi, whose 1912 novel *Shadows of Forgotten Ancestors* was famously made into a film in Soviet times.[18]

All of this knowledge and these (and other) talents would lead Khotkevych to play the crucial role in the founding of a Hutsul theater in 1910. Essentially he took a group of Hutsuls in the village of Krasnoïla, some literate, some not—members of a population that had never even seen a play—and transformed them into a theatrical troupe. This the Ukrainian writer (and sometime thespian and director) accomplished, despite his project being mocked by a number of his colleagues, who could not imagine that such an endeavor could succeed.[19] Yet Khotkevych saw in the Hutsuls—dramatic, energetic, crafty—born actors. Of course, they could only play themselves, Hutsuls, but, given the right dramatic vehicle, they could do that on stage convincingly, with verve and aplomb.

Khotkevych's ambitions for the Hutsul theater extended far beyond the Hutsul region. Serving as impresario for the troupe, he organized a theatrical tour through the entire Habsburg province of Galicia. His Hutsul troupe performed to acclaim, with audiences marveling at their self-assuredness and bold acting—not what one would expect of illiterate peasants. The Hutsul theater went on several tours in the province. But Khotkevych was not content to show off his Hutsuls and their vivid culture (featured in a number of plays he later wrote especially for the troupe as well as in Józef Korzeniowski's *Carpathian Highlanders*) to Galicians. He set about organizing a miniature troupe that would perform back in his homeland, part of the Russian Empire at this time. Together they traveled to his hometown of Kharkiv, then through the Ukrainian lands more broadly, even to Moscow. Thus Russians as well as Ukrainians were exposed to Hutsuls and their culture, and they took an interest in the troupe. However, further development of this fascinating undertaking was cut short by the outbreak of war in 1914.

Khotkevych's Hutsul theater accomplished much in its short lifespan. It reinforced the pride of the Hutsuls in their culture, which was appreciated far and wide by audiences of different nationalities, who also came to see the Hutsul as a particularly colorful and attractive highland folk. In some ways, the similarities of this "discovery" of the Hutsuls of the Eastern Carpathians to that of the Górale of the Tatra Mountains are quite striking, with both the seemingly ancient provenance of the highlanders and their vigorous dialect appreciated by the discoverers. In introducing his Hutsul troupe to audiences in the Russian empire, Khotkevych emphasized that the remote, inaccessible mountains "made them perhaps the only Slavic tribe that had preserved the patriarchal way of life and even pagan rites."[20] He also believed that the vigor of their dialect could infuse the Ukrainian language with new life. Were they, then, *ur*-Ukrainians? Khotkevych seemed to think they represented a particularly attractive regional variant of the Ukrainian nation. He expected that, with time and with the right conditions, "the Hutsul theater could create in the bosom of the Ukrainian theater an original and colorful phenomenon no less interesting than the Sicilian theater in Italy or the Tyrolean theater on the German stage."[21]

These two episodes of "discovery," thus, suggest how important these encounters could be for shaping national, regional, and local identities. Poles and Ukrainians from the Russian Empire as well as the Habsburg province of Galicia were captivated by the Carpathian highlanders they encountered, whether they be Górale or Hutsuls. These nationally conscious members of their respective intelligentsias—writers, artists, and the like—took inspiration from the highlanders, who represented useful characteristics for modern nations in the making, the most important of these, perhaps, being the highlanders' love of liberty as well as the fact that they seemed to be remnants of an archaic past. Each group of highlanders was being claimed by its respective nation as a regional—and by extension, national—treasure. Furthermore, as lovers of freedom and putative preserves of ancient language and ways, highlanders were considered excellent candidates for membership in nations that sought not only to increase and/or consolidate their ranks but also, eventually, to gain independence.

In turn, this encounter with the lowlanders reinforced the innate dignity and confident demeanor of both Górale and Hutsuls, who learned that outsiders appreciated their unique qualities. It also inspired some highlanders to think more in national terms, as seen from the fact that some members of both highland populations elected to fight in their respective national units—the Polish Legions or Ukrainian Sich Riflemen—during World War I.[22]

Interwar Poles and the Highlanders

A new configuration of power in the region after World War I brought the situation of the Carpathian highlanders into new relief. The land previously known as Galicia came to be part of the new interwar Polish state, and all Carpathian highlanders within the borders of the country were transformed from subjects in a multiethnic empire to citizens of a putative nation state. Of course, as is well known, interwar Poland was hardly a state of only Poles: minorities made up a significant percentage of the population.[23]

What would the attitude of Poles be to their minorities, especially their highland compatriots? By World War I, as mentioned earlier, the Górale had found a place of honor within the Polish nation. No one who believed that the Polish nation was more than the sum of the Polish nobility saw them as being anything but Polish, if still somewhat exotic. At the same time, the Tatra Mountain region had become the premier "domestic" vacation destination of Poles in winter (for the new and increasingly popular sport of skiing) as well as summer (for hiking).

Yet Poles also laid claim to the central and eastern Carpathians—indeed, to the entirety of Galicia, with its Carpathian borderland. These lands were considered part of the patrimony of the former Polish-Lithuanian Commonwealth. Poles had believed them to be theirs under Habsburg rule; they were all the more convinced of this once they regained their independence in 1918 and once the borders of the state in the region of the eastern Carpathians were determined in their favor.

The situation of the highlanders in the central and eastern Carpathians, as well as those territories, was less certain. These minority populations—the Hutsuls discussed above as well as the Lemkos and Boikos—were Eastern Slav peoples of Eastern-rite Catholicism or Eastern Orthodoxy, not the Poles' Roman Catholicism. Were they to become "nationalized," they might identify, instead, with Ukrainians, who saw them as part of their Ukrainian nation—and indeed, strove during the interwar period to convince these highlanders that they were Ukrainian. Whether the highlanders would come to see themselves as Poles, broadly defined—that is, as loyal citizens of the interwar Polish state while retaining their local identity—or meld into the Ukrainian nation (and perhaps join in opposition to Polish rule) was a burning question for interwar Poland.

In the interwar period Poles addressed the question of highlanders' national allegiance. Various Polish organizations strove to turn the highlanders across the length of the Carpathians (whether Górale, Lemkos, Boikos, or Hutsuls) into loyal Polish citizens while at the same time—interestingly—making room for continued or even increased ethnic/local/regional distinctiveness. This move toward a Poland of regions, with a slogan of "unity in diversity," gives the lie to views of the new Polish state as striving above all to become a pure nation state, although the push for a civic understanding of Polishness was doubtless less benign than it may seem at first glance. The rest of this chapter will present the projects of two of these organizations, the Society of Friends of the Hutsul Region (Towarzystwo Przyjaciół Huculszczyzny) and the Union of Highlands (Związek Ziem Górskich) and draw some conclusions about this interwar "discovery" of the Carpathians.

The Society of Friends of the Hutsul Region

The Society of Friends of the Hutsul Region was far from a typical alpine club. Founded in 1933, it had at its head a highly placed military officer, Brigadier General Tadeusz Kasprzycki. An official within the Ministry of Military Affairs, Kasprzycki was undoubtedly close to Marshal Józef Piłsudski. As a 23-year-old he had been entrusted by Piłsudski with the command of the first military incursion of Polish forces (the so-called First Brigade of the Polish Legions) into the Russian empire in August 1914.[24] That there was a military connection here should perhaps come as no surprise during the period after Piłsudski's coup d'état in 1927, when many Polish generals came to occupy positions within the government; yet the Society of Friends of the Hutsul Region was ostensibly a non-governmental organization. What this connection did mean was that the Society had many influential friends and unquestionably better access to funding than many similar organizations.

How these not-so casual "friends" intended to support the Hutsul region and people says much about their vision of the highland region. The main aims of the Society were four: 1) to coordinate the methodical economic and cultural development of the Hutsul region; 2) to protect those characteristics of the region that comprised its distinctiveness; 3) to utilize the "climatic values" of the Hutsul region to improve the "social hygiene" of the State; and 4) to oversee and rationally develop the Hutsul region as a center for tourism, summer resorts, and health spas.[25] Given its Warsaw connections and home base, the Society planned to coordinate the work of all institutions and individuals seeking to improve the Hutsul region and assist in its development, serve as an intermediary to the authorities and advocate on the region's behalf, and generally promote the "Hutsul question" in myriad ways.[26] The wording of the Society's statute makes clear the special value that the Hutsul region had for the interwar Polish state: it was a "valuable component in the sum of the natural and spiritual riches of the Polish Republic."[27] In other words, this was to be no simple "Polska B"—no second-class Poland. Rather, this periphery of the interwar Polish state had much to offer in the way of cultural distinctiveness, a restorative climate, beautiful landscapes, and opportunities to profit from them. It was the goal of the Society of Friends of the Hutsul Region to encourage those outside the region to avail themselves of this unique reservoir of values: physical, climatic, even spiritual.

To that end, an increased and active Polish presence in the region was desired. One of the ways in which the aims of the Society were to be met was through the activities of its branches and clubs. Indeed, it would be hard for a Warsaw-based organization to exert influence on this remote region without deputies in the field to do its bidding. Thus, from the very outset, branches, sections, and clubs were envisaged as the backbone of the Society. The main branch (*ekspozytura*) of the Society was located in the provincial capital of Stanisławów; it was the formal conduit for communication between center and periphery. There likewise existed a plethora of specialized sections, which gathered together experts in specific fields who could bring their expertise to bear on the challenges that faced this remote region. One of the initially more active sections was a Hygiene Section; it was designed not only to determine the best location for spas and health resorts but also to help restore the health of the Hutsuls and improve the hygiene of existing villages, as syphilis was endemic to the region.[28] Economic and Propaganda Sections helped to funnel financial assistance as well as popular interest, respectively, into the Eastern Carpathians; a Tourism Section featured prominently, given that the Society thought that tourism would be the salvation of the Hutsul region.

Nor were questions of identity ever far removed from the Society's interests. One of the most fascinating sections was the so-called Section for the Preservation of Nativeness (*Sekcja obrony swojszczyzny*). Preserving the authentic distinctiveness of the region was seen as something that had to be done consciously. Awareness of this issue was reportedly indebted to the bad example provided by the Tatra region, where foreign influences in the period before World War I had distorted its unique highland style. One important (if not the only) reason for this interest in authenticity concerned the Hutsuls' own self-awareness. If Poland was to be a composite of little homelands, comprised of a mosaic of peoples who acknowledged Polish statehood while maintaining their own distinct identity, then peoples like the Hutsuls would have to maintain their traditional ways. Thus, over the next years the Society underscored the value of Hutsul distinctiveness by mandating that participants in the various contests and festivals appear in proper Hutsul dress and on traditional Hutsul horses. Among its varied projects, the Society produced a periodical, calendars, and almanacs in Hutsul dialect (the first ever such published) as well as built a Hutsul Museum in the village of Żabie (today's Verkhovyna). Hutsuls were taught that their way of life was unique and exotic, and that only by maintaining their traditional dress, habits, and speech could they expect to attract tourists to the region.

Polish–Hutsul relations were likewise furthered by those members of the Society, such as the scouts and Legionnaires, who conducted direct work in the field. The second of these groups played a key role. The Legionnaires' Club of Friends of the Hutsuls consisted of former soldiers of the Second "Iron" Brigade, part of the Polish Legions that fought on the side of Austria during World War I. They had seen battle in the Hutsul region in 1914–1915. If Hutsuls were to be written into Polish history, the World War I connection was the most promising way to do so. As a report on the Society stated, "The history of the Second Brigade—in its most essential moment . . . through battles, fights, through the graves of Carpathian soldiers . . . [—]is connected with the Hutsul land and with the Hutsuls, who in a . . . relatively significant number served in the Second Brigade."[29] Indeed, a company of some hundred Hutsuls had been assembled at that time; Hutsuls, thus, fought alongside Poles during the war, trying to repel the Russian forces that had moved into the region.[30]

The existence of a Legionnaires' Club hints at the unique connection of Hutsuls to the interwar Polish state. That Hutsuls had actually been part of the fight for Polish independence—for that is how their presence in the Second Brigade was interpreted by the Poles—made it easier for the authorities as well as organizations such as the Society of Friends of the Hutsul Region to imagine them as part of the solution to the multiethnic interwar state's ills rather than part of the problem. In other words, Hutsuls needed to be distinguished from the Ukrainians of the lowlands, to be encouraged to see themselves as a distinct people with their own separate history. In the 1930s, the authorities and the Society would try to capitalize on this positive experience from the past, hoping thus to reinforce the somewhat tenuous relationship of Poles and Hutsuls and turn the latter and their region into one of the brightest pieces of the ethnic mosaic that was interwar Poland. The result was the main annual event of the region, a three-day competitive cross-country ski march that commemorated Hutsul–Polish cooperation during World War I. It was known as the March along the Hutsul Route of the Second Legionnaire Brigade. Piłsudski himself sponsored the March, and one of the trophies was given in his honor. The Hutsul Route March was the major annual public event sponsored by the Society.

There is much more that could be said about the organization, its aims, and its projects, many of which—like the Hutsul Museum—were ambitious and expensive. This attention and investment was summed up by Kasprzycki: "The whole action is being led in a strictly social dimension with conspicuous support on the part of practically all governmental agencies, for it is a fragment of a creative state and economic work, conceived on a large scale, on the territory of the Hutsul region."[31] The Society, thus, could be seen as doing the government's bidding by integrating the region further into the Polish body politic and economy. Highlanders were encouraged to consider themselves full-fledged and valuable citizens of the interwar Polish state. The Society was also to ensure that economic development in the region was powered by a Polish, not Ukrainian, engine—a matter of extreme importance in this borderland, for reasons of state security as well as national politics. The task of the Society was made easier in that this was one part of the borderlands where Poles and the highland folk had once worked together (even though the Hutsuls surely thought they were fighting for Emperor Franz Joseph, not for Polish independence).

The Society of Friends of the Hutsul Region also sponsored a major summer event, intended to be comparable to the Hutsul Route March. First held in the summer of 1933 (before the organization was founded, *nota bene*), the Hutsul Holiday was designed to draw in crowds interested in experiencing this exotic corner of interwar Poland, its beauty and highland culture. This event appeared to inspire yet another highland holiday that soon would reshape general attitudes toward highlanders and the highlands as well as the attitudes of the highlanders toward the Carpathian Mountain region (and, by its extension, the rest of Poland). This was the aptly named Highland or Mountain Holiday (*Święto Gór*).

The first Highland Holiday was originally slated to take place in Zakopane in the summer of 1934. However, destructive floods in the highlands rendered those plans untenable, and the holiday was postponed until the following summer. Behind the event stood two organizations: that of the Tatra Mountain highlanders as well as the Society of Friends of the Hutsul Region. Brigadier General Tadeusz Kasprzycki, newly promoted to Deputy Minister of Military Affairs, headed the organizational committee, and reportedly the military was of assistance during the event as well. Yet that is not the main reason for our interest. Featured at the Highland Holiday was a much-anticipated folk song and dance competition, with highlanders from throughout the Carpathian Mountain region of Poland taking part. Participants included Tatra Mountain highlanders, Lemkos, and Boikos, not to mention several groups of Hutsuls, whose dancing was considered most impressive. Indeed, one of the Hutsul troupes won the competition.[32]

Several purposes seemed to underlie the event. The first echoes the aims of the Section for the Preservation of Nativeness of the Society of Friends of the Hutsul Region: for the competition—for best performance by a highland group—encouraged the highlanders to maintain their colorful manner of dress and their highland traditions. Indeed, some regional groups may even have been encouraged to resurrect or reconstruct them—revive old songs, sew anew traditional highland garb, and the like—if they had fallen out of style (which by this time was true of some regions, where highlanders, encountering a modernizing world, had sought rather to assimilate to it and downplay their folk origins). Second, by bringing representatives of the various highland peoples together at one event, the organizers hoped to foster a sense of brotherhood across the Carpathian region. (They also sought to strengthen the highlanders' sense of belonging to the Polish state: all highlanders participating in the Highland Holiday were escorted on a free trip around Poland after the event.) They seem to have succeeded. While still present at the Highland Holiday in Zakopane, leaders of the regional groups resolved to create an organization that would work toward the "unification [*zespolenie*] and elevation—ideologically, culturally, and economically—of all the highland areas of Poland."[33]

Union of Highlands

This resolution would result in the establishment of the Union of Highlands. Although proposed the previous year in Zakopane, its founding formally took place at the Highland Congress in Sanok 15–17 August 1936—a slightly smaller affair (by design) but one no less significant. There the folklorization of the highland folk proceeded apace—again, in competitive fashion. But this was not the only thrust of the event: as in the case of the Highland Holiday, the congress was likewise intended for those interested in the region's development, and various talks and reports were presented to those assembled.[34]

The most lasting accomplishment of the Highland Congress in Sanok, nonetheless, was the establishment of the Union of Highlands. Heading the organization was the by now familiar figure of Brigadier General Tadeusz Kasprzycki. His three deputies encapsulated in their own persons the main directions of the Union of Highlands: the organization's desire to attract summer and winter guests to the mountain in a modern way (Aleksander Bobkowski); the value of tourism, nature preservation, and scholarly study of the Carpathians and their inhabitants (Walery Goetel); and the need for improved animal husbandry and dairy production (Janusz Rudnicki).[35] As stated by Walery Goetel, the goal of the Union of Highlands was to "connect the Carpathians with the rest of Poland economically and culturally."[36] Speaking at one of the Union's conferences, Goetel implied that this would not be as difficult as some might think. The outcomes of the highland congresses in Zakopane and Sanok were encouraging. There, he said, one could see that the various highlanders had much in common with each other, and that they saw that Poland had their best interests at heart.[37]

Another scholar developed further a picture of the Carpathians and their role within the Polish state. Professor Jerzy Smoleński said that this territory of nearly 30,000 square kilometers—about 8 percent of the territory of the Second Republic—differed in manifold ways from the rest of Poland, the quintessential lowland. (For those unfamiliar with the etymology of "Poland," the toponym comes from the word *pole,* implying fields and plains, not mountains.) The Carpathian Mountains' inhabitants were different, too, having—according to Smoleński—a "completely different material culture and even a [different] spiritual one."[38]

Yet—notably—this was not seen as a drawback but as a reflection of the very nature of Poland. Poland was a state characterized by diversity and known historically to integrate varied lands into one whole (in contrast to Russia, Smoleński asserted).[39] Although no direct reference was made, this suggested that there were still Poles who saw their country as the heir to the multiethnic and multidenominational Polish-Lithuanian Commonwealth, that premodern entity that encompassed much of Central and Eastern Europe before 1795. Poland, thus, was no regular nation state but a state of regions, each potentially with its own distinct profile and making unique contributions to the whole.

Further statements provide evidence of this new interwar regional approach to Poland. Smoleński touted the highland region's promise as a producer of energy, to come from waterpower (and, potentially, natural gas). The country's electrification would rest, he said, on the southern borderlands.[40] Yet this was not the only strength of the region. One could not forget its vivifying climate, curative mineral springs, and the beauty of the landscape. These qualities would make it, according to Goetel, the country's rest region, a region that would "regenerate the strength of the citizen."[41]

And, indeed, the question of summer resorts and tourism was among the most important for both the highland region and for the Union of Highlands. The distinct cultural qualities of the local population would be another draw. Such tourism and vacationing likewise could have a great impact on the Carpathian highlanders across the region, who would be exposed to all manner of Poles—especially, it was hoped, Polish workers, who most needed to regenerate their strength (and were least accustomed to taking such vacations). The potential for such development was great.

Yet the Carpathian Mountain region had its own regional differences, and they were much discussed within the Union of Highlands. The central Carpathians were seen as being particularly well situated for tourism—this despite the fact that the western and eastern Carpathians actually needed to rely most heavily on the tourist industry, given their lack of fertile soil. Located to the south of the Sandomierz industrial region, the locus of much development during the interwar period, the central Carpathians would be most accessible to the workers.

The decision to develop tourism in the relatively populous central Carpathians was also a strategic one. As Smoleński noted, "the turning of the mass movement of the Polish worker toward the central Carpathians would have a great significance from a nationalities point of view."[42] For the region was inhabited by Lemkos and Boikos. They were the most impoverished highland populations, living in a region where little had been done to foster tourism. In fact, one might think of the central Carpathians as essentially a touristic blank spot during this period. No regional organization had yet taken responsibility for its development. All focus had been on the Tatras and the Hutsul region. But of course a huge swath of the Carpathians separated the two: the Sącz Beskids, Low Beskids, Bieszczady, even the Gorgany (although the last lay along the border of the Hutsul region, where tourism and health resorts were developing apace). At any rate, it was thought that the Union of Highlands must see to it that the central Carpathians were given the requisite attention: "Our postulate must be that the necessary connection of the west and east segments of the Carpathians take place as fast as possible."[43] Poland's Carpathian Mountain borderland, thus, was to become a unified entity, its segments equally well studied, analyzed, and developed in rational fashion.

This new approach to the Carpathians proved to be Janus-faced—looking backward as well as forward. As yet another influential Union of Highlands member put it, "Individuality and improvisation are our national characteristics, all the more so the axis of our state must be planning and organization."[44] Poles like Colonel Tadeusz Grabowski, the General Secretary of the Union of Highlands, were all too aware of the historic faults identified with their self-perceived national character: individualism leading to near anarchy as well as a kind of spontaneity that belied a lack of foresight, and was often followed by a lack of constancy in pursuit of goals. Such negative national attributes would not facilitate the running of a modern state. Thus, interwar Poland, at least in the instances we have seen, was trying to right itself. It strove to become a less improvisational, haphazard place as well as one that exerted some degree of control over all its borderland regions. Yet that did not mean that it sought outright homogenization. At a certain level, it apparently was trying to become a country where regions retained their distinctive identity, where each contributed something different to the good of the whole.

Such at least appeared to be the thrust of the Union of Highlands, as seen through the discussions that took place during its spring 1937 Congress. One wonders whether this organization and the state authorities behind it were consistent in their application of the earlier expressed slogan of "unity in diversity," as well as whether highlanders responded favorably to continuing developments—both subjects that await further research.[45] What surely can be said is that this ambitious project for the Carpathian mountain region was never fully realized, Polish efforts being interrupted within the space of several years by the outbreak of World War II.

Nonetheless, some conclusions can be drawn from this and the previous examples. Despite the borderland status of the Carpathian Mountains, the highland regions proved important for national as well as state development. The highlands and, especially, the highlanders played a crucial role for the Poles. The encounter helped to shore up the development of the Polish nation from a noble one to one that would encompass the full spectrum of society. In the case of the Ukrainians, the encounter with the Hutsuls seemed to have less of a direct effect on the general shape of the nation, although it clearly touched individuals such as Hnat Khotkevych and the members of his Hutsul troupe, in part nationalizing the latter.

In the interwar period, a lack of Ukrainian statehood essentially nixed further lowland Ukrainian moves in the highlands or rendered them subject to official Polish approval. At the same time, Poles—certainly after the ascent to power of Józef Piłsudski—redoubled their efforts in the Carpathian borderlands, which they hoped to make secure as well as integrate into a properly run modern state. In the process, they appeared to value the diversity of the borderland—indeed, to foster it through the varied projects of organizations such as those initiated by the Society of Friends of the Hutsul Region and the Union of Highlands. Of course, this appreciation of diversity—or was it a mere folklorization of the highlanders?—was likewise colored by the fact that the maintenance of traditional local and regional identities might keep highland populations such as the Hutsuls, Lemkos, and Boikos from becoming "national"—that is, from becoming nationally conscious Ukrainians.

Although styled as a modern, rational project, this Polish approach to the highland borderlands was at the same time anachronistic. It is certainly redolent of premodern, Polish-Lithuanian Commonwealth–style ideas about the nature of states and nations, ideas that have proven to be on the losing side in the modern race to "reconstruct" nations in the region.[46] The fostering of regionalism and diversity, after all, cuts across the grain of modern nation formation, which tends to seek homogeneity within a nation state and place allegiance to the nation first and foremost. A modern edition of Poland, or something approximating it, would emerge only after the conflagration that was World War II.

Epilogue

World War II profoundly affected what had until then been a rich mosaic of peoples. The annihilation of the region's Jews in the Holocaust was but one significant alteration of what had been a multiethnic landscape. It was further "homogenized" in the years 1944–1946, which witnessed the deportation (so-called "repatriation") of most Lemkos and Boikos from the new postwar Polish state, one whose borders were shifted westward.[47] As a result of this shift, Hutsuls and many Boikos found themselves living in the Ukrainian Socialist Soviet Republic, which declared them to be Ukrainians. Considered Ukrainians as well by the postwar Polish state, the remaining 30 percent of Lemkos were likewise expelled from their central Carpathian homeland and scattered in settlements in the west and north of Poland as a result of Operation Vistula in 1947; in that way, these remaining East Slavs were to be lost in a sea of Polishness and perhaps lose their ethnic identity in the process.[48] What ultimately resulted, however, starting in 1989 after decades of quietude, was a resurgence of their identification as Lemkos and—for some[49]—a sense of Rusyn brotherhood with the Carpatho-Rusyns on the southern slopes of the Carpathians.

In today's Europe, a Europe of Euroregions as well as states, the idea of transnational and multiethnic entities gaining ascendancy seems less farfetched. Euroregions encompassing segments of the Carpathian highlands already exist, although at present they seem to be languishing rather than thriving.[50] Whether these might ultimately encourage the highlanders of the region to see that they have more in common with each other than with their lowland compatriots (who continue to claim the highlanders for their respective nations) nonetheless remains to be seen.

Notes

1. Following customary practice, I use the term Austria as shorthand for the "Kingdoms and Lands represented in the Imperial Council."

2. Peter Sahlins, *Boundaries: The Making of France and Spain in the Pyrenees* (Berkeley: University of California Press, 1989), 271.

3. It should be noted that Jews, Armenians, and Roma also lived in various segments of the Carpathian highlands. The fascinating subset of "mountain Jews"—that is, Jews who ended up working as shepherds—has been little researched and begs further investigation.

4. Lemkos are also sometimes referred to as Rusnaks, which—in distinction to the ascriptive term "Lemko"—is what they had called themselves until the early twentieth century. More recently, Lemkos have also been included, or chosen to include themselves, within the ranks of the people known as the Rusyns or Carpatho-Rusyns—a people (inhabiting above all the southern slopes of the Carpathians) that has declared itself to be a nation distinct from the Ukrainian. See, for example, Helena Duć-Fajfer, "Lemkos," in *Encyclopedia of Rusyn History and Culture,* ed. Paul Robert Magocsi and Ivan Pop (Toronto: University of Toronto Press, 2002), 280–82; and chapter 24 by Paul Robert Magocsi in this volume.

5. I am presently working on a book tentatively entitled *"Discovering" the Carpathians: Episodes in Imagining and Reshaping Alpine Borderland Regions.* In it, I disagree with Timothy J. Cooley, who argues (in his *Making Music in the Polish Tatras: Tourists, Ethnographers, and Mountain Musicians* [Bloomington: Indiana University Press, 2005]) that the influx of tourists into the Tatras amounted to a migration. If anything, it was originally a seasonal migration, in that families spent their summer vacations there.

6. Patrice M. Dabrowski, "'Discovering' the Galician Borderlands: The Case of the Eastern Carpathians," *Slavic Review* 64(2) (Summer 2005): 380–402, esp. 380–81.

7. Cooley, *Making Music,* 8 and passim.

8. For the connection between the Polish positivists of this period and Zakopane, see, for example, David Crowley, "Finding Poland in the Margins: The Case of the Zakopane Style," *Journal of Design History* 14(2) (2001): 105–16 or Patrice M. Dabrowski, "Constructing a Polish Landscape: The Example of the Carpathian Frontier," *Austrian History Yearbook* 39 (2008): 51–53.

9. For more on these examples, see Dabrowski, "Constructing a Polish Landscape," 54–55.

10. Stanisław Witkiewicz, cited in Zbigniew Moździerz, ed., *Stanisław Witkiewicz: Człowiek—artysta—myśliciel* (Zakopane, Poland: Tatra Museum, 1997), cited in Edward Manouelian, "Invented Traditions: Primitivist Narrative and Design in the Polish Fin de Siècle," *Slavic Review* 59(2) (2000): 393.

11. Zbigniew Moździerz, "Z dziejów 'Koliby,' pierwszej willi w stylu zakopiańskim," *Wierchy* 59 (1993): 166.

12. See Jerzy M. Roszkowski, "Towarzystwo Tatrzańskie wobec sporu o Morskie Oko w latach 1873–1902," in *Spór o Morskie Oko: Materiały z sesji naukowej poświęconej 90 rocznicy procesu w Grazu, Zakopane 12–13 września 1992 r.,* ed. Jerzy M. Roszkowski (Zakopane, Poland: Wydawnictwo Muzeum Tatrzańskie, 1993), for the intricacies; or my own—briefer—remarks in Dabrowski, "Constructing a Polish Landscape," 60–63.

13. This is the thrust of Nikodem Bończa-Tomaszewski's argument in chapter 14 of his pathbreaking *źródła narodowości: Powstanie i rozwój polskiej świadomości w II połowie XIX i na początku XX wieku* (Monografie Fundacji na Rzecz Nauki Polskiej) (Wrocław, Poland: Wydawnictwo Uniwersytetu Wrocławskiego, 2006).

14. On Kryvorivnia, see, for example, Petro Arsenych, *Kryvorivnia v zhytii i tvorchosti ukrains'kykh pys'mennykiv, diiachiv nauky i kul'tury* (Ivano-Frankivs'k, Ukraine: "Nova zoria," 2000).

15. Hnat Khotkevych, "Spohady," in *Tvory v dvokh tomakh,* vol. 2 (Kiev: Dnipro, 1966), 544–45.

16. Ibid., 544.

17. This was *Kaminna Dushia* (alt. *Dusha*), first published in 1911.

18. Khotkevych himself criticized Kotsiubyns'kyi's work (Tsentral'nyi Derzhavnyi Istorychnyi Arkhiv v Ukraïny u m. L'vovi 688/1/89: 5), while his own has been praised as "so Hutsul, that the most Hutsul of Hutsuls could envy it" (words of Ulas Samchuk, *Zhyvi struni: Bandury i bandurysty*

[Detroit, Mich.: Vyd. Kapeli Bandurystiv im. Tarasa Shevchenka, 1970], 57, cited in Ol'ha Shlemko, "Mystets'ki zasady "Hutsul's'koho teatru" Hnata Khotkevycha," in *Dyvosvit Hnata Khotkevycha: Aspekty tvorchoï spadshchyny,* ed. Petro Cherems'kyi [Kharkiv, Ukraine: "Fort," 1997], 74).

19. For an example of the reactions to his project, see Khotkevych, "Spohady," 550.

20. Dmytro Mynailiuk, "Teatral'ni spomyny," in Vasyl' Stef'iuk, *Kermanych Hutsul's'koho teatru: Narys zhyttia i tvorchosti H. Khotkevycha; Spohady pro n'oho* (Kosiv, Ukraine: Pysanyi Kamin', 2000), 165.

21. Khotkevych, "Spohady," 576. The reference to the relatively new nations of Italy and Germany seems quite apt here, given the nation-building efforts of the Ukrainians.

22. See, for example, Tadeusz Krawczak, "Udział chłopów galicyjskich w ruchu niepodległościowym, 1912–1918" (Master's Thesis, Warsaw University, 1976), as well as the brief biography of Petro Shekeryk-Donykiv in Petro Arsenych and Ihor Pelypeiko, *Doslidnyky ta kraieznavtsi Hutsul'shchyny: Dovidnyk* (Kosiv, Ukraine: Pysanyi Kamin', 2002), 244.

23. According to the 1921 census, Ukrainians comprised 14 percent of the population, with Jews amounting to 8 percent and Belorussians and Germans each at 4 percent (Rogers Brubaker, *Nationalism Reframed: Nationhood and the National Question in the New Europe* [Cambridge: Cambridge University Press, 1996], 86). I cite Brubaker, as on the same page he claims that "in eastern rural districts the aim was to nationalize the borderland East Slav population." While their nationalization might have been possible, I would like to argue that the approach taken by the authorities was somewhat more complex than Brubaker suggests.

24. For more on this incursion and its significance, see, for example, Patrice M. Dabrowski, *Commemorations and the Shaping of Modern Poland* (Bloomington: Indiana University Press, 2004), 206–209.

25. From Paragraph 4 of the statute, Derzhavnyi Arkhiv Ivano-Frankivs'koï Oblasti (henceforth DAIFO), 370/1/42: 1.

26. DAIFO 370/1/42: 2.

27. DAIFO 370/1/42: 1, also cited (without attribution) by Jan A. Choroszy in his postscript to Jerzy Kolankowski, *Gdzie szum Prutu, Czeremoszu* (Wrocław, Poland: Wydawnictwo Dolnośląskie, 1989), 112.

28. DAIFO 370/1/42: 19.

29. DAIFO 370/1/42: 23.

30. On the Hutsul company, see, for example, *Huculskim szlakiem II Brygady Legjonów Polskich* (Warsaw: Wydawnictwo Towarzystwa Przyjaciół Huculszczyzny, 1934), 25, or *Szlakiem II Brygady Legionów Polskich w Karpatach Wschodnich* (Warsaw: Wojskowy Instytut Naukowo-Oświatowy, 1937), 207–208.

31. DAIFO 370/1/18: 12.

32. Among the numerous accounts of the event is Walery Goetel, "Święto Gór," *Turysta w Polsce* 1(7) (1935): 6–7.

33. Ibid.

34. Archival material on this event is found in the archive of the Muzeum Historyczne w Sanoku: collection 21a. Zjazd Górski w Sanoku. See also the article by Edward Zając, "Zjazd Ziem Górskich w Sanoku, 14–17 sierpnia 1936 r.," *Płaj* 8 (Spring 1994): 102–109.

35. For biographical information on each, see (respectively) Wojciech Szatkowski, "Hej kolejka, kolejka . . . rzecz o powstaniu i początkach kolejki linowej na Kasprowy Wierch," http://www.naszkasprowy.pl/artykuly,1,Hej_kolejka_kolejka_rzecz_o_powstaniu_i_poczatkach_kolejki_linowej_na_Kasprowy_Wierch.html (accessed 5 October 2008); "Walery Goetel: Geologist, Ecologist, Conservationist," http://info-poland.buffalo.edu/classroom/goetel.html (accessed 5 October 2008); Marek Gajdziński, "Janusz Rudnicki, Harzmistrz," http://www.16wdh.pl/panteon/Rudnicki Janusz.htm (accessed 26 June 2008).

36. Minutes from the ZZG Congress, April 1937, 23–24 in the Centralne Archiwum Turystyki Górskiej PTTK Kraków: Zwiazek Ziem Gorskich (ZZG), 1937.

37. Ibid., 24.

38. Ibid., 2.

39. Ibid, 2.

40. Ibid, 2.

41. Ibid., 6.

42. Ibid., 8.

43. The words of Walery Goetel, in ibid., 24.

44. Ibid., 38.

45. For the slogan, see Walery Goetel, "Zagadnienia regjonalizmu górskiego w Polsce," *Wierchy* 14 (1936): 164.

46. See Timothy Snyder's excellent *Reconstruction of Nations: Poland, Ukraine, Lithuania, Belarus, 1569–1999* (New Haven, Conn.: Yale University Press, 2003).

47. See, for example, Orest Subtelny, "Expulsion, Resettlement, Civil Strife: The Fate of Poland's Ukrainians, 1944–1947," in *Redrawing Nations: Ethnic Cleansing in East-Central Europe, 1944–1948,* ed. Philipp Ther and Ana Siljak (Harvard Cold War Studies Book Series) (Lanham, Md.: Rowman & Littlefield, 2001), 155–72.

48. Details of Operation Vistula are presented by Marek Jasiak, "Overcoming Ukrainian Resistance: The Deportation of Ukrainians within Poland in 1947," in Ther and Siljak, *Redrawing Nations,* 173–94. This labeling of Boikos and especially Lemkos as Ukrainians by the new Polish state clearly marked an about-face from the policies of the interwar state in the region, as discussed earlier in this chapter and also in chapter 24.

49. Others consider themselves to be part of the Ukrainian nation. On this, see, for example, Karen M. Laun, "A Fractured Identity: the Lemko of Poland," *Central Europe Review* 1(24) (6 December 1999).

50. Of especial note here are the Carpathian Euroregion (established 1993) and the Tatra Euroregion (established 1994). For some of the problems faced by these transnational regional entities, see Wojtek Kość, "Not That Easy," *Central Europe Review* 3(14) (23 April 2001).

11

Mapping the Hungarian Borderlands

Robert Nemes

Austria-Hungary typically merits one or perhaps two maps in most modern European history textbooks. Almost invariably, one of them shows a multicolored Austria-Hungary fractured into a dozen small regions, each occupied by a discrete nationality.[1] That no other European states have comparable maps is unsurprising, since maps of the modern world usually represent states as "more integrated, distinct, and centralized than was and in fact is the case."[2] Austria-Hungary stands as a distinct exception to this cartographic rule, and it requires no great imagination to see in these maps not only the diversity and decentralization of Austria-Hungary, but even foreshadowing of the assassination at Sarajevo, the disappearance of the empire, and the century of ethnic tensions and national conflict that followed. Such maps draw upon models created in the last decades of Austria-Hungary, and they have been a feature of scholarship on the region ever since. The spread and survival of these nationalities maps thus raise historical and historiographical questions. What explains their creation and dissemination around 1900? Why do historians continue to reproduce them?

To begin to answer these questions, we must recognize that maps contain interpretations, arguments, and messages about the political systems they depict. For Austria-Hungary, the multicolored maps just described reflect a distinctly nationalist worldview, according to which Austria-Hungary was hopelessly divided into a limited number of bounded, permanent, and antagonistic national groups. In recent decades, however, scholars have begun to draw a very different picture of Austria-Hungary, emphasizing the state's resilience and resourcefulness in an era of mass politics; the expansion and professionalization of its public administration; and the emergence of a broad, vibrant civil society.[3] Particularly in the Austrian half of the monarchy, traditions of liberalism and legal equality tempered the state's response to the "national question." This is not to deny the salience of nationhood (a sense of national belonging) and nationalism (a means of political mobilization) in Austria-Hungary in the decades around 1900. As elsewhere in Europe, the wider processes of state building, mass education, and economic modernization contributed to the emergence of a political culture in which national activists could and did play a prominent role. But prominence rarely meant dominance, and the citizens of Austria-Hungary often greeted nationalist agitation with indifference or only short-lived support.

This revisionist scholarship is crucial to reconceptualizing the multicolored map of Austria-Hungary, with its thick lines separating different national groups. So too is a growing literature on borderlands, which has shifted the spotlight from the imperial centers to the edges of empires. This work has drawn attention to the processes by which boundaries are imagined and constructed, as well as to the movements of peoples, goods, and ideas across real and imagined borders. Such approaches can illuminate the role of the state and its practices of cartography and classification (censuses, passports, schools, and so on). Scholars have also emphasized the importance of Europe-wide ideologies, and in particular the model of the nation state and of territorial citizenship, in redefining the meaning of boundaries and border regions. Thinking about borderlands thus encourages us to ask how states went about making borders; to look closely at the posture of state officials and at power relations on the ground; and to understand the ways in which borders did—and did not—become rooted in everyday social practices.[4]

The focus of this chapter is not an existing international boundary, the starting point for much scholarship on borderlands. It instead examines one of Austria-Hungary's "national borderlands," as I call regions of ethnographic diversity contested by competing national activists. Its subject is Bihar/Bihor County, a region today divided between Hungary and Romania.[5] A century ago, Bihar/Bihor was a rather unremarkable corner of the Hungarian Kingdom, one situated far from international boundaries. Its population was almost equally split between ethnic Hungarians and ethnic Romanians, a fact of little consequence until the last decades of the nineteenth century, when a number of local middle-class national activists began to emphasize the region's status as a national borderland and worked to define and defend the Hungarian–Romanian border they saw running through it.

This case study demonstrates the many consequences of political mobilization around national borderlands in the last decades of the nineteenth century. It is organized around two distinct interpretative frameworks, which the geographer John Agnew has identified as "cross-border othering" and "cultural-symbolic borrowing."[6] Put differently, it asks what it means to think of this region first as a "barrier" and then as a "bridge." My primary aim is to show that the sharp lines on the textbook maps of Austria-Hungary, far from being fixed and timeless, emerged in a particular historical context and required a great deal of intellectual labor and cultural work. At the same time, I argue that much of the impetus for "border-making" in this case came from local actors rather than from outsiders and state officials, as is often suggested in recent writing on Central and East European borderlands. Last, I show that the agitation over national borderlands helped reveal and redefine competing symbolic geographies: the creation of one new border made it possible to imagine many more.

Border Making

Geographers have shown how the making of international boundaries in modern Europe was an evolutionary process, one that required the allocation, delimitation, demarcation, and administration of physical borders. State functions in border zones also changed over time, as did the meanings different social groups attached to specific borders.[7] The creation of national borderlands within the state (rather than between states) involved several related processes. First, nationalists measured the limits of the "national territory" and drew borders through ethnically mixed regions; importantly, such lines rarely followed historic boundaries (between provinces, counties, and bishoprics). Second, nationalists worked to mobilize political energies both on the ground and in the center toward these "threatened borderlands." In this way, nationalists attempted to politicize everyday behaviors and social tensions. Third, nationalist agitation on one side of a perceived border frequently brought forth a response from nationalists on the other side. It also forced other locals to respond, although it is worth underlining that national borderlands often mattered more to some social groups than to others.

On the surface, late nineteenth-century Hungary presented a surprisingly inhospitable environment for the emergence of national borderlands. This point is often obscured in writing about the region. It is true that Hungary had a multiethnic population, barely half of whom listed Hungarian as their "mother tongue" in censuses and many of whom lived in large, relatively homogeneous ethnic blocs. Yet the Hungarian political leadership, firmly in power after the Compromise of 1867 created the Dual Monarchy of Austria-Hungary, was wholly committed to the historic borders of the Hungarian Kingdom. This applied especially to Hungary's external frontiers, but also to its internal administration, the key unit of which was the county (Hungarian *vármegye*, Romanian *judeţ*). "The county, and nothing else, was the unit and motive force of this old Hungary," wrote a contemporary historian.[8] Balancing the needs of rationalization with the claims of Hungarian nationalism, the government redrew a number of county lines in 1876, leaving Hungary with 71 counties including Croatia-Slavonia, or 63 without it.

Challenges to these internal boundaries came primarily from Slavic and Romanian nationalists, who resented what they saw as the Hungarian state's nationalizing policies (which expanded the use of the Hungarian language in schools, courts, and local administration). In this they received encouragement from outside Hungary: in Bucharest, for example, the Romanian government, members of parliament, and cultural associations all provided meaningful support to their fellow Romanians within Hungary.[9] The increasingly assertive non-Hungarian nationalists attempted to gain political control of the counties and, when that strategy failed, called for county borders to be redrawn along ethnic lines. At the same time, a growing number of Hungarian nationalists, alarmed at the activities of their opponents and the seeming passivity of the ethnically Hungarian population, likewise began to focus on what they saw as contested national borderlands. Herein lay the seeds of a challenge to Hungary's historic borders.

In places like Bihar/Bihor County, nationalists confronted remarkable diversity. Contemporaries proudly described Bihar/Bihor as "Hungary in miniature," pointing to its varied topography, sharp urban/rural divide, and mixture of peoples. Like much of Hungary, the region was a mixture of broad, treeless plains and high hills, through which swift rivers flowed. Its county seat, Nagyvárad/Oradea (also known by its German name Grosswardein), was one of the most economically dynamic and culturally vibrant cities in Hungary. The surrounding countryside was much poorer and long plagued by bad transportation, low literacy, and banditry in the highlands. Bihar/Bihor County had more than 600,000 inhabitants, who spoke a number of languages (Hungarian and Romanian were the most common); belonged to six major religions; and pursued a wide range of occupations. For many locals, this diversity was a source of great pride: the writer Pál Szabó later claimed that many people in his native village had had "pure Mongolian features," making them the presumed descendants of nomadic horsemen who had overrun Hungary in 1241.[10]

Not all locals shared Szabó's enthusiasm. In the last decades of the nineteenth century, a small but vocal number of national-minded officials, lawyers, writers, and newspapermen began to describe the region in very different terms: as a contested borderland containing two discrete and hostile national groups. The idea of Bihar/Bihor County as a borderland was not implausible. Indeed, historian R. J. W. Evans has observed that the Hungarian word for "border" (*határ*, from which the Romanian word *hotar* derived) long retained a flexible and imprecise meaning, and could apply either to a specific boundary or to a shifting no-man's land.[11] For Bihor/Bihar, one could make an argument for its "border" status based upon its topography, which forms a natural divide between the vast Hungarian plains and the Transylvanian highlands. Alternately, one could observe that the county stood on the frontier of Eastern and Western Christianity, a fact attested by the large number of Greek Catholics (so-called Uniates), members of Eastern Orthodox churches that had accepted communion with the Vatican in the late seventeenth century. Finally, one could argue from history, noting that Ottoman, Habsburg, and Transylvanian rulers had all controlled Bihar/Bihor at various points in the past, creating uncertainty about whether the region belonged to Hungary proper or to Transylvania.

Nineteenth-century nationalists instead seized on the Hungarian–Romanian language frontier, which ran through the county. In newspaper articles and scholarly works, Hungarian nationalists worried aloud about the "infiltration" of ethnic Romanians and described their towns as "border fortresses"; for their part, Romanians despaired of living on the "extreme margins of the Romanian element" and thus subject to strong pressures of linguistic Hungarianization.[12] Nationalists on both sides spoke and acted as though an actual border existed in the county, and they worked to map, police, and, when possible, shift it. Statisticians, mapmakers, and amateur ethnographers helped define the border, as did historians, who inventively used place names and other sources to establish that their national group had been the first to settle the region. As a result, the nationalists' border often overlapped with other forms of difference, and the dichotomies just described (plains/mountains, Western/Eastern Christianity, and Western/Eastern polities) were frequently superimposed onto the Hungarian/Romanian divide. By looking closely at the strategies nationalists pursued in one borderland, we can see clearly the extent of their ambitions, the relative strength of the two sides, and the outcomes of their activity. Briefly, we can identify four processes at work.

POLITICIZATION

Creating borderlands in regions not previously seen as such required a great deal of intellectual work. The borderlands had to be mapped, their inhabitants counted and classified, and the wider public convinced that this was an issue worthy of attention and in need of decisive action. National activists in late nineteenth-century Hungary faced additional challenges in their attempts to mobilize the population around national borders. Most obviously, formal political life in these regions was stubbornly oligarchic: only a small fraction of the population had the vote on the state and county levels, which limited nationalists' financial resources and access to the coercive power of the state. To be sure, officials in both Budapest and Bihar/Bihor County broadly supported the Hungarian national movement and, at the same time, monitored Romanian associations and students, noted visits of Romanian national leaders from outside the county, and openly interfered in elections to ensure the defeat of Romanian nationalist candidates.[13] But it is important to recall that the Hungarian administration had a limited reach outside the realm of elections and education, and that local officials often took a pragmatic approach when confronted with nationalist claims. Liberal ideology also encouraged officials in Bihar/Bihor to tolerate initiatives that did not appear to threaten the public order, including journals, savings banks, reading societies, and choirs.

This points to another challenge nationalists faced on the local level: the strength of non-national civic life in provincial Hungary. The decades around 1900 were a golden era for coffeehouses, clubs, newspapers, and voluntary associations. Although nationhood clearly mattered to the participants in these institutions, it usually overlapped with—and was often subordinate to—other social and political interests. That the working language of most of Bihar/Bihor County's associations and newspapers was Hungarian thus says more about Hungarian-speakers' relatively high social status, level of education, and rate of urbanization than about the strength of Hungarian nationalism. For educated Romanians, nationalism was a much more salient feature of public life, in large part because of the disparities in social position and political power between them and leading Hungarians. To borrow the words of sociologist Rogers Brubaker, Romanianness was "marked" (meaning "different" or "other"), whereas Hungarianness was "unmarked" ("the normal, default, taken-for-granted category").[14] Yet local Romanians had to balance their ambitions against the reality of a poor, rural society, which provided limited resources and a narrow social base for their undertakings.

For a small number of cultural associations, nationalism trumped all other concerns. On the Hungarian side, the most important was the Bihar County Society for Popular Education (*A Biharvármegyei Népnevelési Egyesület*, or BNE), which began operations in Nagyvárad/Oradea in 1884.[15] For national-minded Romanians, the four chapters of the Transylvanian Association for Romanian Literature and the Culture of the Romanian People (*Asociația Transilvană pentru Literatura Română și Cultura Poporului Român*, or ASTRA), the largest and most active Romanian cultural association in prewar Hungary, had the greatest significance.[16] The Hungarian and Romanian nationalist associations shared much in common. First, they drew upon the same social groups, with clergymen, teachers, and urban professionals comprising the largest part of their memberships. Second, the Hungarian and Romanian cultural associations pursued nearly identical aims, including the spread of popular education through literacy campaigns, public lectures, and support for teachers in village schools; in this way, both sides linked their national goals (the cultivation of national awareness among the lower strata of society) to a liberal vision of progress (economic change and social mobility through self-improvement). Last, both Hungarian and Romanian national activists focused their energies on linguistically mixed areas. According to one of its leaders, the BNE had as its mission the rescue of ethnic Hungarians living on "contiguous borders" with Romanians. These Hungarians, he explained, had thrown off their "national customs, racial virtues, most characteristic good features, and indeed, in place of their mother tongue had begun to bring the neighboring language [Romanian] into the domestic hearth."[17] The same author justified these efforts with the assertion that this was a life-and-death struggle: "Our enemies' numbers, strength, and power are greater than we believe. Perhaps they are closer than we to forcing the final battle."[18] The nationalists' language, with its images of battles, fronts, fortresses, and enemies, reveals how associations dedicated to popular education could take on a militaristic aspect in regions viewed as contested borderlands.

DIVIDING

The semi-official encyclopedia of Bihar/Bihor County, published in Hungarian in 1901, contained several detailed maps. One, a large foldout map of the county, was richly drawn and colorfully illustrated. It carefully displayed the county's rivers, mountains, roads, and railroad lines, as well as the names of all large settlements and the boundaries of the county's 17 electoral districts. The empty spaces beyond the county's borders emphasized the historic boundaries of the county, just as the exclusive use of Hungarian versions of place names misleadingly depicted the region as linguistically homogeneous.[19] A second map told a different story. Entitled "Nationality Map of Bihar County," it showed areas occupied by Hungarian, Romanian, German, Slovak, and mixed Hungarian/Romanian populations. With the exception of a limited number of settlements and the electoral boundaries, all other distinguishing features were removed from the map. What remained showed Bihar/Bihor to have a solid Hungarian mass in the west, a solid Romanian block in the east, and a mixed zone running through the middle of the county. Historic and homogeneous in the first map, Bihar/Bihor County was now shown to contain a national borderland. The *Enciclopedia română* (*Romanian Encyclopedia*), published three years later in Transylvania, included a similar map. Strikingly, in the copy I consulted, someone had noted the new international borders drawn in 1919–1920 and traced a thick red line around the farthest reach of Romanian settlement in Bihar/Bihor and the surrounding counties, and then a thick blue line beyond that, thereby erasing any doubt that this region was a borderland.

How did mapmakers define nationality? In late nineteenth-century Hungary, as in much of Europe, language use and religion were widely understood to be the primary markers of national belonging. In Bihar/Bihor County, Hungarian nationalists tended to give primacy to language in ascribing nationality, particularly since it allowed them to claim, among other groups, the many Jews and Greek Catholics who listed Hungarian as their "mother tongue" in the decennial census. Romanian scholars in contrast emphasized religion, asserting that all Eastern Orthodox and Greek Catholics were nationally Romanian (thereby putting Hungarian-speaking Greek Catholics back into the Romanian column). This allowed Romanian writers to reinterpret the official census figures: according to one estimate, ethnic Romanians (defined by religion rather than mother tongue) comprised 45 percent of the population of Bihar/Bihorand Hungarians just 47 percent (instead of the 41 and 57 percent figures based on "mother tongue").[20] Both sides agreed, however, that all residents of the county should be assigned to one national category. This left little room for the many villagers and townspeople who spoke two or more languages, and it also disregarded the ways in which centuries of migration, religious conversion, and "mixed" marriages had unsettled the categories of language and religion in this region.[21]

Nationalists employed ethnography to accentuate further the sharp divisions they saw between local Hungarians and Romanians. Anthropologist Tamás Hofer has demonstrated that around 1900 scholarly, professional traditions of ethnography, which stressed the diversity of the Hungarian homeland and used historical, evolutionary models to explain differences among ethnic groups, were increasingly eclipsed by more popular, amateur forms of ethnography, which asserted the superiority of Hungarian folk culture and emphasized the great disparity among different peoples.[22] The 1901 encyclopedia of Bihar/Bihor County reflected the latter tendency. It highlighted the many differences between Hungarian and Romanian folk practices, including costumes, wedding rituals, domestic architecture, and religious holidays. The encyclopedia also drew a clear divide between the morals of the two groups. It thus lavished praise on the Hungarian peasants of the plains, who were extolled as religious, law-abiding, sober, and loyal, whereas the highland Romanians were dismissed as dissolute, illiterate, unclean, and politically unreliable. It warned, however, that looser morals were to be found among Hungarians who lived "adjacent to or among Romanians."[23] Ethnographic diversity again emerges as a problem in need of a solution. The county encyclopedia did not suggest one, but a regional association devoted to tourism did. It argued that Hungarian tourism to these mixed areas would bring the "strong Hungarian feeling of the Great Plains" into this region "where we struggle with the [Romanians'] unjust claims and terrorism."[24] Once more, an ostensibly apolitical activity (here tourism) took on political dimensions in the context of a national borderland.

REMEMBERING

Like many counties in Hungary, Bihar/Bihor County had a historical society and a local history museum. The historical society's leadership comprised county officials and high clerics, including a large number of Roman and Greek Catholic prelates (but no rabbis, since the historical society did not accept Jewish members). The history museum in Nagyvárad/Oradea held a modest and eclectic collection, in which visitors could find Roman antiquities, old weapons, watches, keys, portraits of local luminaries, and the leather cigar case of a Hungarian general executed at the end of the 1848–1849 revolution.[25] As Celia Applegate has written of similar provincial German museums, the display of such quotidian objects sought to make whole a fragmented past, to sustain the local community in an era of significant socioeconomic change.[26] In Bihar/Bihor, the historical society and museum presented what might be considered the official version of local history, in which the county's different ethnic and religious groups played different roles (with some much more visible than others) yet coexisted peacefully for centuries. In different forms, this story of local patriotism and ethnic harmony was told again and again at public holidays and in local historical works.

Both Hungarian and Romanian nationalists challenged this narrative, although from very different perspectives. That educated Hungarians and Romanians possessed competing conceptions of history is not surprising. The anthropologist Katherine Verdery has argued that middle-class Hungarians and Romanians "inhabited the same space and participated in many of the same events, but each group saw those things through lenses specific to itself and its past. Any given occurrence meant different things to each, for their experiences differed from one another, they saw differing things as significant, and their hopes and expectations were not the same."[27] Nor, it is worth stressing, were their relations to political power and thus their ability to display their version of history. Hungarian nationalists could raise money for statues of Lajos Kossuth, the hero of the 1848–1849 revolution, and call on villages to adopt more Hungarian-sounding names. Romanian nationalists in contrast had few public opportunities to celebrate their heroes. When rumors spread that several villages in Bihar/Bihor had gathered money for a statue to Avram Iancu, the Romanian hero of 1848–1849, the Hungarian authorities reacted with alarm. Describing the plan as "treasonous," one official called for the removal of a Greek Catholic priest who had organized a collection for the statute, reasoning that his punishment would serve as a warning to other Romanian-speaking villages.[28]

Hungarian and Romanian nationalists competed on more even terms when it came to the distant past. And the distant past mattered greatly to them both. Historian Sorin Mitu has observed that educated Romanians stressed their Latin origins in part because the present "seemed to offer so little satisfaction" and because Latin descent moved Romanians "from the bottom to the top of the list in terms of civilization, freedom, political development, and national-self-assertion."[29] In Bihar/Bihor County, national-minded Romanians asserted that that the Romanian people had occupied the region continuously since the time of the Romans. The *Enciclopedia română* stated that local Romanians had defended themselves first against Attila the Hun and later against Árpád, the leader of the Hungarian tribes who settled in the Carpathian Basin.[30] Hungarian scholars tirelessly rejected the Romanians' claims to primacy, citing chronicles, manuscripts, place names, and linguistic evidence. For the canon and historian János Karácsonyi, it was simply impossible that "before 1235 a single Romanian lived in Bihar County."[31] Echoing a common argument, he claimed that only the devastation wrought by the Mongols and later the Ottomans had allowed significant numbers of Romanians to immigrate into the region. Karácsonyi thus counted more than 50 villages in the county that had once been wholly Hungarian but were now Romanian. In this reading of history, national groups have existed—and stood in conflict with one another—for millennia. At the same time, by claiming that the "other side" was wrongly occupying "national territory," activists could justify their own actions in defense of the national borderland.

Closing Ranks

Much of the nationalists' work in the borderlands was directed at their "co-nationals," and especially at locals who were seen as insufficiently demonstrative in their national commitments or even in danger of "switching sides." The Hungarian-language press in Nagyvárad/Oradea, for example, denounced the local Chevra Kadisha, or Jewish burial society, for using only Hebrew—and not Hungarian—letters on Jewish gravestones; after a long debate, the society relented and allowed Hungarian and German inscriptions to appear alongside Hebrew ones.[32] This small anecdote underscores the highly symbolic nature of nationalist politics in the borderlands. Both Hungarian nationalists and their opponents attached great importance to flags and monuments, place and personal names, ritualized demonstrations and crowd activities, and everyday behaviors and speech. The Chevra Kadisha's concession was, however, a rare (and partial) victory for nationalists in Bihar/Bihor County. For all their sound and fury, nationalists' attempts to "police" the borderland often met with only limited success, particularly in the countryside.

Both Hungarian and Romanian activists faced sizeable obstacles in taking their campaigns into rural areas. Most obviously, the rhetoric of both Hungarian and Romanian cultural associations habitually outran their resources. When it was reported in 1892, for example, that the Hungarian residents of one small village were in danger of losing both "their language and patriotic feeling" (that is, of becoming Romanian), the BNE immediately voted funds to send them "good Hungarian reading materials," a symbolic but hardly decisive intervention.[33] The larger truth is that peasants in Bihar/Bihor, like their counterparts across much of Europe, were only partially integrated into the wider political culture. What Eugen Weber has written about rural France could be applied equally to rural Hungary, where poor roads, bad school, and widespread poverty insulated the mass of the rural population from newer political ideologies.[34] Few peasants had the vote, and both state and local authorities were ready to quash rural political organizations. In 1897 and 1898, agricultural workers in eastern Hungary struck at harvest time and spontaneously seized land on larger estates; the authorities responded with martial law, mass arrests, and the so-called "slave law," which banned strikes and strengthened the employers' position, even as it provided minimal protection for agricultural workers.[35] Middle-class nationalists, with their emphasis on language and national symbols, had few answers for the problems faced by poor villagers living on the plains and in the mountains of Bihar/Bihor County.

But the nationalists' attempts at policing were not without effect. Arguably, such efforts made the greatest impression not on poor peasants and craftsmen but on nationalists from the "other side." The case of the BNE is again instructive. In the late 1880s, the BNE attempted to branch out from its base in Nagyvárad/Oradea and create local chapters throughout the county. Three soon formed in small towns with mixed Hungarian and Romanian populations. According to the BNE's newspaper, the chapter in Bél/Beliu attracted members of the local Romanian intelligentsia, who had earlier kept their distance from the BNE but now seemed willing to accept its offer of aid for schools and teachers. To the BNE, this was nothing less than a "triumph of Hungarian–Romanian brotherhood," particularly since this town was known as a "border fortress of Daco-Romanian ideas."[36] The Romanian-language *Tribuna* responded quickly, denouncing locals for "allowing themselves to be seduced" and for joining an organization "diametrically opposed to the goals of the Romanians." It noted that the BNE only supported teachers and schools which visibly demonstrated their commitment to the Hungarian cause and cited the worrisome example of Romanian teachers who now used Hungarian to greet their Romanian students in the street. Local Romanians, it concluded, should not make this "national sacrifice" (*jertfă națională*).[37] The BNE's paper in turn denounced *Tribuna*'s "limitless audacity" and scolded it for stirring up local Romanians. But *Tribuna* had the last laugh, as none of the BNE's local chapters lasted for very long.

This was typical. Although nationalism was a key ingredient of the political culture of prewar Hungary, most nationalist initiatives in the provinces proved remarkably short-lived. This was certainly true of Bihar/Bihor. By the late 1890s, the BNE had lost momentum, leading one of its members to write bitterly that the BNE "had always scraped along under unfavorable circumstances, obtaining only negligible support from the wider public and barely counting enough members to secure its existence."[38] The BNE survived into the twentieth century, but in a different form: the bulk of its membership (and teachers in particular) wanted to focus more on pedagogical and professional issues than on the loud but often ineffective national agitation of its early years. On the Romanian side, none of the four chapters of ASTRA remained active for more than a few years. Official harassment played an important role here, as did the obstacles outlined above: the narrow social basis and limited resources for nationalist projects, as well as the frequent indifference of villagers.

It would be a mistake to dismiss the nationalists' efforts entirely. Writing about similar events in the Austrian half of the Monarchy, Pieter Judson concluded that "nationalists succeeded brilliantly in nationalizing perceptions of the rural language frontier by 1914," even as they "largely failed to nationalize its populations."[39] In Bihar/Bihor County, local and state officials increasingly saw dangers in undertakings formerly judged useful: thus the authorities long refused to approve the by-laws of associations formed by local Greek Catholic and Eastern Orthodox teachers, leaving both societies in limbo for the better part of a decade.[40] Over the long term, nationalists popularized a set of images in which the Hungarian-Romanian borderland appeared as a site of anxiety, conflict, uncertainty, and loss. Such images would prove enduring, and they took on new meanings when a state border was drawn through the county in 1919. Writing in the 1930s, a Hungarian geographer described the residents of his home village (now part of Romania) as "border guards" defending a "marchland" against the surrounding Romanians.[41] In the space of just a few decades, nationalists in Bihar/Bihor County, as well as in other regions of the Hungarian Kingdom, succeeded in superimposing national borderlands onto the historic borders of Hungary. Many locals may not have taken notice, but officials, scholars, and mapmakers did.

Border Crossing

This section draws upon a growing body of literature that views borderlands in terms of mixing and hybridity, rather than solely as sites of opposition and othering. In works on diverse regions, scholars have shown how exchanges among people far from the centers of power have produced accommodations of difference, syncretic cultures, social fluidity, and a blurring of administrative borders.[42] In such studies, tensions between the borderlands and the center are often more pronounced than among different groups living on the periphery. This scholarship has been especially sensitive to everyday practices of ethnicity and nationhood, which can reveal the ways in which ordinary people often deflected the arguments of national activists. To highlight the complexities of the case of Bihar/Bihor County, the following section looks at three key areas: language use, cultural practices, and regional loyalties.

BORROWING WORDS

In studies of Habsburg Austria, bilingualism is often seen as evidence of—or at least a factor increasing the likelihood of—national indifference. The situation in late nineteenth-century Hungary was different. Bi- and multilingualism were on the rise before 1914, largely because of the gains made by the Hungarian language among non-native speakers. This process was often politicized, and the advance of Hungarian was loudly debated at home and abroad. Crucially, both Hungarian nationalists and their many critics saw bilingualism not as an end in itself, but rather as an interim stage between one form of monolingualism (speaking Romanian, Serbian, or Slovak) and another (speaking Hungarian). Patterns of language use and change varied greatly across different ethnic and religious groups, as well as across different regions, with the result that some social groups (German-speaking Jews in western Hungary, for example) were much more likely to learn Hungarian than others (such as Romanian-speaking Eastern Orthodox in Transylvania). Scholars have also emphasized the role of urbanization and social mobility in the acquisition of a second language, thereby downplaying the role of nationalist pressures and the Hungarian state. Yet, in itself, bilingualism did not pose a direct challenge to nationalism. As historian R. J. W. Evans has written, "*functional* polyglossia was in all likelihood still growing" through 1914, but "it lacked more and more the *ideological* commitment in official, establishment, and intellectual circles."[43]

Many residents of Bihar/Bihor County knew more than one language. As elsewhere in Hungary, bi- and multilingualism was most common in cities and towns. In the county seat, for example, nearly 70 percent of the city's 3,000 Romanian-speakers claimed knowledge of Hungarian in the 1900 census. In the countryside, where the bulk of ethnic Romanians lived, the figure was 16 percent.[44] Unsurprisingly, few Hungarian peasants knew languages other than Hungarian. These broad patterns added weight to nationalist claims that Bihar/Bihor was divided into Hungarian-speaking and Romanian-speaking halves, with a thin borderland in between. Such arguments obscured important sociological factors, and most obviously, the relative isolation of many peasants, who had few incentives or opportunities to learn a second language. Nationalist views of language use also sat uneasily with evidence of linguistic borrowing. In making the case that Hungarian-speaking peasants spoke a unique dialect, the county encyclopedia observed that "many foreign, Romanian- and German-sounding expressions" had influenced the Hungarian spoken in Bihar/Bihor.[45] Similarly, to one disapproving Romanian journalist, the residents of the county spoke a Romanian that was "ancient and invaluable to philology," but added that "they do not have in their speech the flashes of spirit that peasants in other regions have. . . . The language is mottled with Hungarian words."[46] Other writers stressed the diversity of language use, noting that each village had its own vocabulary and distinct pronunciation of certain words. Such assertions may tell us more about regional pride (or its absence) than about local linguistic practices, yet they serve as a further reminder of the inadequacies of nationalist categories.

The interplay of language use, nationalist politics, and local practices can be seen in the case of the Greek Catholic *Gymnasium* in Belényes/Beiuş, a small town in the highlands. The *Gymnasium*'s origins went back to 1828, when the Greek Catholic Bishop Samuil Vulcan had established a secondary school for local Romanian-speakers. By the late nineteenth century, the school had expanded to eight grades and nearly 400 students. In 1888, during a visit of the Roman Catholic Bishop, the Hungarian flag was taken down from the roof the *Gymnasium* and thrown into a nearby canal. The event attracted statewide attention, and in the ensuing crackdown the responsible student was expelled, three teachers lost their posts, and the Education Ministry pressured the school into increasing the number of subjects taught in the Hungarian language. As a result, the *Gymnasium*'s teachers used both Romanian (primarily in the lower grades) and Hungarian (in the upper grades) as languages of instruction. The school's balancing act pleased neither Hungarian nor Romanian nationalists. To national-minded Hungarians, the fact that many courses were taught in Hungarian was of little consequence: in their eyes, the students and staff of the institution lacked patriotism; only Hungarian-language instruction for all classes and all grades could remove the stain of suspicion.[47] Romanian national leaders were no kinder. Writing in 1892, Aurel Popovici denounced the growing use of Hungarian: "Had Bishop Vulcan known that the gymnasium dedicated to the education of his people would be transformed into an instrument of denationalization, he would certainly have preferred to throw his money into the waters of the Criş!"[48]

From our perspective, what is most striking is how cautiously the schools' leaders responded in the face of nationalist provocations (the muddied flag) and counterattacks (accusations of treason in the Hungarian press). Indeed, the leaders of the school (if not all their students) attempted to avoid demonstrating an unambiguous national affiliation in the following years. For example, the school's holidays in the early twentieth century commemorated events whose orientations included the broadly secular and "Hungarian" (the return of Ferenc Rákóczi's remains from Turkey to Hungary), the Greek Catholic and "Romanian" (the death dates of the schools founder and a recent Greek Catholic bishop), and "Habsburg" (the emperor-king's birthday and his late wife's name day). It is also worth noting that the student body was far from homogeneous: the vast majority of students were Greek Catholic and Eastern Orthodox, yet they also included a surprising number of Hungarian-speaking Roman Catholics, Calvinists, and Jews (nearly 13 percent of the total). Clearly, for many local families the promise of social mobility and an acceptance of bilingualism trumped nationalist considerations. At a minimum, such evidence suggests the complexity of the relationship between nationalism on the one hand and religion, education, and language use on the other.

MIXING CULTURES

The example of the Greek Catholic *Gymnasium* may serve as a warning against drawing a firm line between "Hungarian culture" and "Romanian culture." So too does the example of Iosif Vulcan, who edited an influential Romanian-language journal in Nagyvárad/Oradea and tirelessly campaigned to create a standing Romanian-language theater in Transylvania. Yet Vulcan was also a member of the BNE and had his plays performed in Hungarian in the local theater. But for every writer who could, when he chose to, cross cultural boundaries, one can find many examples in the sources of cultural divisions among the county's many ethnic and religious groups. The memoirs of Margit Imrik Benda, who grew up in a middle-class Catholic family, contain the revealing observation that polite society in town "would rather have accepted a Jew than a Romanian," a point driven home with a further anecdote about a clumsy Romanian military officer whose spurs tore his partner's dress.[49] Descriptions of village culture similarly emphasize the many differences between ethnic Hungarians and ethnic Romanians, although they also provide examples of shared cultural practices, such as the pilgrimages taken by ethnic Hungarian Roman Catholics and ethnic Romanian Greek Catholics to the nearby shrine of Máriapócs/Pociu. The purpose here is not to map the many cultural fault lines in Bihar/Bihor, but to examine the wider meanings attached to cases of cultural "boundary crossing."

Local cultural life was defined by obvious asymmetries between Hungarian-language and Romanian-language culture. Hungarian was not just the language of power: it was the language of the theater, sports, and scholarship. By 1900 the county had more than a dozen Hungarian-language journals and newspapers, including several dailies, but only two Romanian-language periodicals, both of them weeklies. This imbalance created a dilemma for educated Romanians, who had to choose between engaging with the wider Hungarian-speaking world (which could lead to greater professional success) and ignoring it altogether (which had its own costs and benefits). Romanian nationalists strongly advocated the latter course. Denouncing the lack of a Romanian public life in Bihar/Bihor County, a newspaper wrote that "the educated class prefers Hungarian culture rather than Romanian and prefers to speak the Hungarian language instead of the national language."[50] Only an education with a stronger national spirit, the paper continued, would bring an end to this "non-Romanian politics." For their part, educated Hungarians had little incentive to pay attention to Romanian-language culture. Few of them knew Romanian, fewer still attempted to familiarize themselves with Romanian literature, poetry, and music. Sándor Márki, a university professor and author of a Hungarian-language book about Romanian writers in Bihar/Bihor, admitted that he had embarked upon his research with an uncertain grasp of the Romanian language.[51] This did not prevent him from denouncing Romanian claims to primacy or from calling the Daco-Romanian idea a "hallucination." Márki's survey of Romanian-language literature is often condescending: Romanian short stories and novels are dismissed as "weak and undeveloped." The book concludes with the observation that Romanian writers should follow the example of local Hungarians and concentrate on just a few genres, instead of trying unsuccessfully to master them all.

Certain individuals nonetheless worked to cross cultural boundaries, and their efforts at times produced remarkable local understandings. Perhaps the best-known example is Béla Bartók, who collected nearly 700 Romanian folksongs in Bihar/Bihor County in the first decades of the twentieth century. Bartók was drawn to the region because of its proximity to his hometown in nearby Békés County and because its highlands were removed from the urban culture that corrupted the Romanian "peasant music" he sought to record. Lengthy stays brought Bartók into contact with a number of educated Romanians, including several teachers at the Greek Catholic *Gymnasium*. In an extended correspondence with one teacher, Ioan Bușița, Bartók at one point both essentialized cultural differences and expressed his desire to move across the boundaries that separated them. "I wish I knew more Romanian," he stated in an early Hungarian-language letter to Bușița. Bartók wrote his next letter in Romanian, and in it he approvingly described a poem of Endre Ady, which, Bartók explained, "says that the Hungarians, Romanians, and Slavs in this country should all be united, since they are kindred in misery."[52] Bartók's first scholarly publication was a collection of Romanian folksongs from Bihar/Bihor, in which he identified examples of melodic borrowings between Hungarian and Romanian traditions. With Bartók, then, we can see evidence not just of an imagined cultural kinship between ethnic Hungarians and ethnic Romanians, but a political outlook at odds with more intolerant forms of nationalism in Bihar/Bihor County and beyond.

THINKING REGIONALLY

Traditionally, regional diversity in prewar Hungary has been the concern of folklorists, musicologists, and ethnographers (many of whom, Tamás Hofer has shown, have given primacy to ethnic-national categories and thereby reinforced the view that regional diversity is subordinate to national divisions). In contrast, comparatively few Hungarian historians have shown interest in the regional dimensions of nineteenth-century political life. One has to look hard to find work comparable to that done in recent decades on Imperial Germany, Habsburg Austria, and post–World War I Romania, in which regions and provinces appear as an organizing principle of political life and civic activity. There are obvious reasons for this: after 1867 the government in Budapest systematically undermined the autonomy and administrative functions of the counties and provincial cities. The result, historian Károly Vörös argued, was widespread apathy and indifference toward local politics. But to end the story here, as most scholars do, is to ignore important changes reshaping the political culture of the provinces. Counties and cities may have ceded important functions to Budapest, but they nonetheless continued to add officials (who were more professional than their predecessors), increase their budgets, and take on additional responsibilities. This was especially true of provincial towns, which often owned waterworks, gasworks, distilleries, and savings banks. Many Hungarian counties also witnessed an upsurge in local patriotism: county politics may not have stirred passions, but local history and civic pride apparently did. The result was an explosion of provincial museums, statues of local luminaries, associations dedicated to regional tourism, and catalogues of native flora and fauna.[53]

The signs in the provinces thus point in different directions. Even as centralizing, standardizing decrees emanating from Budapest stripped local political institutions of much of their authority, local boosters catalogued, commemorated, and celebrated every aspect of their beloved counties. In Bihar/Bihor County, the encyclopedia, museum, and tourist associations described above typified this local pride, as did repeated declarations that this was a region of great ethnic and religious diversity, but one whose residents had always lived in peace and rallied together at times of crisis. Typical was the speech of Mayor Károly Rimler at the dedication of the new City Hall building in Nàgyvárad/Oradea. Outlining the city's history, Rimler emphasized the unity and determination of the city's multiethnic, multiconfessional population during the 1848–1849 revolution, its common response to natural disasters such as fires and floods, and its luminous future.[54] Similar chords were struck in 1896 by Iosif Goldiş, vicar and head of the Eastern Orthodox community in Bihar/Bihor. In a well-publicized speech, delivered first in Hungarian and then in Romanian, Goldiş attempted to find middle ground between the two camps by invoking their common history (he cited Lajos Kossuth as well as Andrei Şaguna), common interests, and common enemies (Pan-Slavs in particular).[55] With their language of civic pride and local fraternity, leaders such as Rimler and Goldiş offered a different vision of national belonging, one that emphasized coexistence and downplayed conflict.

Declarations of local patriotism thus suggested impatience with the nationalists' warnings about a threatened borderland. So too did local alternatives to the historic borders of the county. Residents often referred to the region as "Bihar/Bihor Land" (*Bihar ország* in Hungarian, *ţeara Bihor* in Romanian), a name that was less a description of a specific geographic area than a poetic evocation of the region's storied history, natural beauty, and rural inhabitants—in short, it conveyed the same sense of local belonging that the German term *Heimat* did. Other options existed as well: both Hungarian and (to a lesser extent) Romanian historians emphasized that Bihar/Bihor had once been included in the Partium (or "parts"), a string of eastern counties that had changed hands several times in the Ottoman era (indeed, since 1990 there has been a "Partium Christian University" in Nagyvárad/Oradea). Local Romanians also referred to this region as Crişana, after the three branches of the Criş River that flowed through the area (the Hungarian equivalent, *Körösköz,* was less widely used). These different symbolic geographies—Bihar/Bihor Land, the Partium, and Crişana—are examples of what historian Fridrik Lindström has called "spatial remnant structures," regions "that were still relevant and could be activated politically."[56] That such "remnant structures" did not serve as a framework for widespread political mobilization or economic activity points to the tenacity of historic boundaries within the Kingdom of Hungary, as well as to the general absence of regionalism from prewar Hungarian political culture (this would soon change: after 1918 Crişana would take on a new importance in the Romanian Kingdom, just as the Partium has for Hungarians after 1989). Yet they matter for our purposes, because in references to Bihar/Bihor Land, the Partium, and Crişana, one can detect not just local pride, but alternate symbolic geographies to the national borderland described by many contemporaries.

The varied local practices examined here—bilingualism and linguistic exchange, cultural boundary crossing, and regional pride—did not rewrite the rules of Hungarian political life. The compromises described here were too confined, improvised, and fleeting to form the basis of a sustained challenge to existing political structures and ideologies. Sorin Mitu, an incisive observer of Hungarian–Romanian relations in Transylvania, has observed that "whatever more or less invented historical traditions of Transylvanian particularism may claim, the Romanian and Hungarian residents have, since the beginning of the modern period, preferred a separate to a common political existence, and have preferred to be closer to Bucharest or to Budapest than to each other."[57] In Bihar/Bihor County in the nineteenth century, the local accommodations and varied borrowings described above suggest that there was substantial common ground in everyday life between ethnic Hungarians and Romanians. In themselves, however, such practices could not counteract the gravitational pulls of Bucharest and Budapest.

Local practices still mattered in at least two ways. First, the residents of regions such as Bihar/Bihor County served an important role in defining the "other side." As historian

Peter Thaler has observed, "The border populations *understood* their neighbor; they learned from them, transmitted this knowledge on to other members of their respective cultural communities, and thus contributed to a constant flow of information between larger cultural spheres."[58] This is not to say that stereotypes and ignorance were absent from the local knowledge that emanated from places like Bihar/Bihor County—the county encyclopedia and Sándor Márki's survey of Romanian-language writers show this plainly. But other publications (such as the pamphlet containing Rimler's speech) and Bartók's music presented a different image of Romanians to Hungarian audiences, just as the Greek Catholic *Gymnasium* helped create an image of Hungarians for the wider Romanian community.

Second, local practices of bilingualism, cultural borrowing, and regional boosterism held the potential to redefine what it meant to call Bihar/Bihor a borderland, creating an experience of the region defined not by conflict and tension, but by cultural contact and mutual recognition. In this telling, Bihar/Bihor is a bridge, not a battle zone. Some residents of Bihar/Bihor County embraced this alternate meaning of the borderland at key moments during the twentieth century, and the bridge metaphor has gained new currency again today with the establishment of several Euroregions across Bihar/Bihor. Although regional cooperation has a poor track record in Eastern Europe, the larger point here is the continued existence of multiple, competing symbolic geographies, even in unexceptional places like the one examined here.[59]

Conclusion

The First World War brought Austria-Hungary to an end, and a state border was drawn through Bihar/Bihor County in 1919. It is no small irony that the new international boundary had less to do with the linguistic frontier—the central preoccupation of national activists on both sides for decades—than with railroads: Nagyvárad/Oradea, it happened, was located on an important regional railroad line and was thus assigned to Romania. This new state border had profound consequences for local residents. Even Béla Bartók turned down an invitation from his friend Ioan Bușița to collect folk songs in Bihar/Bihor, noting that the authorities would not allow him to bring phonographs or notebooks across the border. "No, the curtain has been drawn over that work," wrote Bartók.[60] The state border changed symbolic geographies as well. The local writer Géza Tabéry noted in the 1930s that Nagyvárad/Oradea had become a different kind of border fortress, one now defending the region against the West.

Not everything changed with the new border. Both Hungary and Romania, for different purposes, maintained the historic borders of the county. And beneath the stormy Hungarian-Romanian relations of the interwar period, patterns of ethnic interaction and accommodation continued. As Tabéry tartly put it, many local Hungarians understood "from where the sun now shone" and, as they had much earlier under the Ottomans, oriented themselves to the new regime.[61] On the Romanian side, local elites looked to the new Romanian state for answers to many of their problems. Its nationalizing policies had broad support among educated Romanians in Bihar/Bihor. Yet their broad liberalism and local patriotism also countered, at least partly, some policies emanating from Bucharest.

The state borders established after World War I thus have a kinship to the national borderlands described in this chapter. In tracing the genealogy of one borderland, this chapter has highlighted the many ways in which nationalist ideology and ethnographic diversity animated local activists, who formed associations, pored over census returns, erected statues, and issued warnings to wayward co-nationals. Importantly, such activities took place within an imperial framework. Indeed, the tools employed by national activists to create borders—censuses, maps, history books, and so on—closely resemble those employed by nineteenth-century European imperial "cores" in their administration of a wide range of "peripheries," including rural hinterlands and overseas colonies. As Benedict Anderson has observed, in their repeated classification and categorization of local populations, ostensibly anti-national empires helped create a world in which everyone belonged to one—and only one—ethnic, racial, and national group.[62] The imperial framework mattered for Hungary in a second way as well: in the radial administration of power. Alexander Motyl once described an empire as a "hubless structure—a rimless wheel—within which a core elite and state dominate peripheral elites and societies by serving as intermediaries for their significant interactions."[63] This chapter has attempted to show that "peripheral elites" possessed much more agency than Motyl's definition might allow, but his observation that empires lack "rims"—that is, meaningful links among peripheral regions—can help us understand the relative weakness of regionalism in prewar Hungary and in the states that emerged from it after World War I.

The mobilization around national borderlands met with significant resistance, as the chapter has also shown. It was not that locals were unresponsive to political appeals. Many of them, in fact, were eager to engage in civic activity and public rituals; they were simply unwilling to let their actions be guided solely by nationalist considerations. The result was practices that called into question the argument that Bihar/Bihor County was a contested borderland and that the lines on a map could—or should—separate local Hungarians from local Romanians. This brings us back to the issue raised at the outset of this chapter: the inadequacy of many maps of Austria-Hungary, which more often than not, uncritically reproduce a nationalist symbolic geography. In recent years, scholars have done much to hammer away at the foundations of nationalist myths. They have been much slower to reflect upon how their findings should be represented visually. The time may be right, then, for scholars and students to think more critically about the maps they use and the messages they convey.

NOTES

I would like to thank Dan Bouk, R. M. Douglas, James Niessen, John Swanson, Alexander Vari, and my colleagues at Colgate University for their many useful comments and suggestions. Grants from Colgate University made possible my research in Hungary and Romania.

1. For recent examples, see John McKay et al., *A History of Western Society*, 10th ed. (Boston, Mass.: Houghton-Mifflin, 2011), 690; and John Merriman, *A History of Modern Europe: From the French Revolution to the Present*, 3rd ed. (New York: W. W. Norton & Company, 2010), 674. The best source of maps for the region remains Robert Paul Magocsi, *Historical Atlas of Central Europe*, rev. and expanded ed. (Seattle, Wash.: University of Washington Press, 2002), which offers multiple perspectives onto Habsburg Central Europe.

2. Jeremy Black, *Maps and Politics* (London: Reaktion Books, 1997), 112.

3. See Gary B. Cohen, "Nationalist Politics and the Dynamics of State and Civil Society in the Habsburg Monarchy, 1867–1914," *Central European History* 40 (2007): 241–78, with previous bibliography.

4. For innovative studies of the borderlands of the Habsburg Monarchy and its successors, see Peter Thaler, "Fluid Identities in Central European Borderlands," *European History Quarterly* 31(4)

(2001): 519–48; Tara Zahra, "Looking East: East Central European 'Borderlands' in German History and Historiography," *History Compass* 3(1) (2005): 1–23; Hans-Christian Maner, ed., *Grenzregionen der Habsburgermonarchie im 18. und 19. Jahrhundert. Ihre Bedeutung und Funktion aus der Perspektive Wiens* (Münster, Germany: LIT Verlag, 2005); Pieter Judson, *Guardians of the Nation: Activists on the Language Frontiers of Imperial Austria* (Cambridge, Mass.: Harvard University Press 2006); and Jessica Alina-Pisano, "From Iron Curtain to Golden Curtain: Remaking Identity in the European Union Borderlands," *East European Politics and Societies* 23, no. 2 (2009): 266–90.

5. Because different people had different names for many of the places described here, I have chosen to present the Hungarian form followed by its Romanian equivalent (except in quotations, where I retain the original). The one shortcut I have taken is to use "Hungary" to mean the Hungarian half of the Dual Monarchy.

6. John Agnew, "No Borders, No Nations: Making Greece in Macedonia," *Annals of the American Association of Geographers* 97(2) (2007): 398–422.

7. J. R. V. Prescott, *Political Frontiers and Boundaries* (London: Allen and Unwin, 1987), 58–92; and Hastings Donnan and Thomas M. Wilson, *Borders: Frontiers of Identity, Nation, and State* (Oxford: Berg, 1999).

8. Henry Marczali, *Hungary in the Eighteenth Century* (Cambridge: Cambridge University Press, 1910), 142.

9. On the wider political context, see Keith Hutchins, *Romania 1866–1947* (Oxford: Oxford University Press, 1994), 202–30.

10. Pál Szabó, *Szülőföldem, Biharország* (Budapest: Panoráma, 1968), 30.

11. R. J. W. Evans, "Essay and Reflection: Frontiers and National Identities in Central Europe," *International History Review* 14(3) (1992): 480–502 (here 481).

12. The image of Romanian "infiltration" appears in Samu Borovszky, ed., *Bihar Vármegye és Nagyvárad* (Budapest: Apollo, [1901]), 212; "border fortresses" (*végvárak*) from "Valász," *Belényesi Ujság*, 25 September 1910, 1; and "extreme margins" from Iosif Vulcan, "Salutăm asociaţiunea în Bihor!" *Familia*, 16/28 August, 1898, 391.

13. On elections in Bihar/Bihor County, see Ioan Tomole, *Românii din Crişana, Sălaj şi Sătmar în luptele naţional-electorale de la începutul secolului al XX-lea* (Baia Mare, Romania: Editura Gutinul, 1999), 90–112.

14. Rogers Brubaker et al., *Nationalist Politics and Everyday Ethnicity in a Transylvanian Town* (Princeton: Princeton University Press, 2006), 211–12. The perceived reversal of these marking relationships on Austria-Hungary's language frontiers helped make them sites of nationalist anxiety.

15. Orbán Sipos, *A Biharvármegyei Népnevelési Egyesület története. Huszonöt éves fennállása megünneplésének alkalmára* (Oradea, Romania: A Biharvármegyei Népnevelési Egyesület, 1909).

16. On Romanian initiatives, see Viorel Faur, "Aspecte ale luptei românilor din Crişana pentru afirmare culturală între 1848–1919," *Revista de Istorie* 33(5) (1980): 873–87; Ioan Bolovan, "Regional Cultural Associations Among the Romanians of Transylvania, 1861–1914," *Romanian Civilization* 4(2) (1995): 61–69; Keith Hitchins, *A Nation Affirmed: The Romanian National Movement in Transylvania, 1860–1914* (Bucharest: The Encyclopaedic Publishing House, 1999); and Ion Zainea, *Aurel Lazăr (1872–1930). Viaţa şi activitatea* (Cluj, Romania: Presa Universitară Clujeană, 1999), 22–54.

17. Sipos, *A Biharvármegyei Népnevelési Egyesület története*, 4. For a similar and much earlier statement from the Romanian side, see Ioan Munteanu's letter in Sorin Mitu, *National Identity of Romanians in Transylvania*, trans. Sorana Corneanu (Budapest: Central European University Press, 2001), 167.

18. Orbán Sipos, *Biharvármegye a népesedési, vallási, nemzetiségi közoktatási statisztika szempontjából* (Oradea, Romania: Szent László, 1903), 203.

19. For the roots of such practices, see Irina Popova, "Representing National Territory: Cartography and Nationalism in Hungary, 1700–1848," in *Creating the Other: Ethnic Conflict and Nationalism in Habsburg Central Europe*, ed. Nancy Wingfield (New York: Berghahn Books, 2003), 20–38.

20. Valeriu Popa and Nicolae Istrate, *Situaţia economică şi culturală a teritoriilor româneşti din Ungaria: Transilvania, Banatul, Crişana şi Maramureşul* (Bucharest: F. Göbl, 1915), 25–27. For the wider context of these claims, see James Niessen, "Vallás és nemzetiség Erdélyben a századfordulón," *Regio* 2(3) (1991): 38–64.

21. A typical example: the village of Magyarcséke/Ceica was populated in the sixteenth century by Hungarian-speaking Roman Catholics. They were later joined by Romanian-speaking Eastern Orthodox and Greek Catholic Ruthenians (as colonists settled by the Greek Catholic bishop). By the mid-nineteenth century, the Roman Catholics had left or converted, leaving the vast majority of villagers Romanian-speaking Greek Catholics and Orthodox. But this too changed rapidly in the following decades, as the booming forestry sector drew Hungarian-speaking Calvinists to the village, with the result that by 1900, the population was divided into three confessions (Calvinist, Greek Catholic, Eastern Orthodox) and into two ethnic groups (Hungarian, Romanian) of equal size. See István Györffy, "Dél Bihar népesedési és nemzetiségi viszonyai negyedfélszáz év óta," *Földrajzi Közlemények* 43(6–7) (1915): 281.

22. Tamás Hofer, "Construction of the 'Folk Cultural Heritage' in Hungary and Rival Versions of National Identity," *Ethnologia Europaea* 21(2) (1991): 145–70.

23. Borovszky, *Bihar Vármegye*, 215.

24. Ioan Popovici et al., eds., *Bihor: Permanenţe ale luptei naţionale româneşti, 1892–1900. Documente* (Bucharest: Directia Generala a Arhivelor Statului din Republica Socialista România, 1988), doc. 60.

25. János Karácsonyi, ed., *Emlékkönyv a Biharvármegyei és Nagyváradi Régészeti és Történelmi Egylet múzeum-épületének s a benne levő kettős gyüjteménynek megnyitó ünnepéről* (Oradea, Romania: Szent László, 1896).

26. Celia Applegate, *A Nation of Provincials: The German Idea of Heimat* (Berkeley: University of California Press, 1990), 52.

27. Katherine Verdery, "On the Nationality Problem in Transylvania until World War I: An Overview," *East European Quarterly* 19(1) (1983): 15–30 (here 26).

28. Popovici, *Bihor*, doc. 104.

29. Mitu, *National Identity of Romanians in Transylvania*, 178, 192.

30. Corneliu Diaconovich, ed., *Enciclopedia română*, vol. 1 (Sibiu, Romania: W. Kraft, 1898), 484.

31. János Karácsonyi, *Százezer baj, millió jaj egy tévedés miatt* (Oradea, Romania: Szent-László, 1911), 8.

32. Dezső Schön, ed., *A tégnap városa: A nagyváradi zsidóság emlékkönyve* (Tel-Aviv: Kiadta a Nagyváradról Elszármazottak Egyesülete Izráelben, 1981), 69.

33. "A révi magyarság," *Népnevelési Közlöny*, May 1892, 70.

34. Eugen Weber, *Peasants into Frenchmen: The Modernization of Rural France, 1870–1914* (Stanford: Stanford University Press, 1976).

35. László Kontler, *A History of Hungary* (New York: Palgrave: 2002), 293.

36. *Népnevelési Közlöny*, 25 March 1887, 58–59; and *Népnevelési Közlöny*, 31 March 1887, 99.

37. "De pe malul Crişului-negru," *Tribuna*, 13/25 April 1887.

38. Ödön Rádl, "Népnevelési egyletünk," *Népnevelési Közlöny*, 15 May 1898, 9–11.

39. Judson, *Guardians of the Nation*, 5.

40. Popovici, *Bihor*, doc. 119; and Faur, "Aspecte ale luptei românilor din Crişana," 880–81.

41. Ferenc Fodor, *Az elnemsodort falu* (Budapest: Athenaeum, 1942), 49.

42. For Central and Eastern Europe, see Mark von Hagen, "Empires, Borderlands, and Diasporas: Eurasia as Anti-Paradigm for the Post-Soviet Era," *American Historical Review* 109(2) (2004): 445–68; Kate Brown, *A Biography of No Place: From Ethnic Borderland to Soviet Heartland* (Cambridge, Mass.: Harvard University Press, 2004); and Judson, *Guardians of the Nation*.

43. R. J. W. Evans, "Language and State Building: The Case of the Habsburg Monarchy," *Austrian History Yearbook* 35 (2004): 1–23 (here 22).

44. *A magyar szent korona országainak 1910. évi népszámlálása*, vol. 6: *Végeredmények összefoglalása*. Magyar Statisztikai Közlemények, új sorozat, 64 (Budapest, 1920), 102–103, 116–17.

45. Borovszky, *Bihar Vármegye*, 231.

46. E. Dăianu, "Dela Beiuş," *Tribuna*, 26 August/7 September 1898, 742. The Nagyvárad/Oradea-based journal *Familia* allowed that Romanians who had frequent contact with Hungarians used a number of Hungarian words, but downplayed the importance of such borrowings, stressing that languages "are judged by the speech of the community, not by some adoptions on the margins." See "Noul debut al dlul Moldován Gergely," *Familia*, 27 May/9 June 1901, 250.

47. For the Hungarian perspective, see Imre Sipos, "A belényesi gymnázium," *Nagyvárad*, 28 August 1893, 3. On the school more generally, see Traian I. Farkas, *Istoria gimnasiului gr. cat. de Beiuş (1828–1895)* (Beiuş: Aurora, 1896); and [Antal Huszár], *A magyarországi románok egyházi, iskolai, közművelődési, közgazdasági intézményeinek és mozgalmainak ismertetése* (Budapest: Uránia, 1908), 197–223. On school holidays, see Joachim von Puttkamer, "Alltägliche Inszenierungen. Kirchliche und nationale Schulfeste in Ungarn 1867–1914," in *Nationalisierung der Religion und Sakralisierung der Nation im östlichen Europa*, ed. Martin Schulze Wessel (Stuttgart, Germany: Franz Steiner, 2006), 141–52.

48. Aurel C. Popovici, *La question roumaine en Transylvanie et en Hongrie* (Lausanne, Switzerland: Payot, 1918), 109.

49. Magda Sebős, ed., *Egy váradi úrilány. Benda Gyuláné Imrik Margit emlékezése* (Budapest: Noran, 2006), 51.

50. Popovici, *Bihor*, doc. 144.

51. Sándor Márki, *Bihari román irók* (Oradea, Romania: Holósy, 1880), 4, 153, 160.

52. Bartók cited in János Demény, ed., *Béla Bártok Letters*, trans. Péter Balabán et al. (New York: St. Martin's Press, 1971), 113. Also see Ion Bradu, "Bartók Béla népdalkutató tevékenysége Biharban," in *A Népdalkutató Bartók Béla, Békés, Arad és Bihar megyékben*, ed. Béla Csende (Békéscsaba, Hungary: Rózsa Ferenc Gimnázium, 1981), 122–41.

53. On local administration and regionalism in Austria-Hungary, see Peter Haslinger, ed., *Regionale und nationale Identitäten. Wechselwirkungen und Spannungsfelder im Zeitalter moderner Staatlichkeit* (Würzburg, Germany: Ergon, 2001); Fridrik Lindström, "Region, Cultural Identity, and Politics in the Late Habsburg Monarchy," in *Regions in Central Europe: The Legacy of History*, ed. Sven Tägil (West Lafayette, Ind.: Purdue University Press, 1999), 115–46; and Károly Vörös, "Die Munizipalverwaltung in Ungarn im Zeitalter des Dualismus," in *Die Habsburger Monarchie 1848–1918*, vol. 7: *Verfassung und Parlamentarismus*, ed. Helmut Rumpler and Peter Urbanitsch (Vienna: Verlag der Österreichischen Akademie der Wissenschaften, 1990), pt. 2: 2345–82.

54. *Ünnepi beszéd felolvasta Nagyvárad-város uj székházának megnyitási ünnepélyén Rimler Károly polgármester* (Oradea, Romania: Boros Jenő, 1904).

55. On Goldiş and the context of his speech, see Neş, *Oameni din Bihor 1848–1918* (Oradea: Diecezană, 1937), 214–18; and Hitchins, *A Nation Affirmed*, 152–58. Romanian nationalists loudly denounced Goldiş: see "Vicarul apostat," *Tribuna*, 26 July/7 August, 1896, 653; and "Caterisirea lui Goldiş," *Tribuna*, 28 July/9 August, 1896, 662.

56. Lindström, "Region, Cultural Identity, and Politics," 117.

57. Sorin Mitu, "Illusions and Facts About Transylvania," *The Hungarian Quarterly*, 39, no. 152 (1998), 64–74 (here 72).

58. Thaler, "Fluid Identities in Central European Borderlands," 541. Italics in the original.

59. Sorin Antohi, "Habits of the Mind: Europe's Post-1989 Symbolic Geographies," in *Between Past and Future: The Revolutions of 1989 and Their Aftermath*, ed. Sorin Antohi and Vladimir Tismaneanu (Budapest: Central European University Press, 2000), 61–77.

60. Demény, *Béla Bártok Letters*, 154.

61. Géza Tabéry, "Nagyvárad," in *Erdélyi városképek*, ed. Béla Pomogáts (Bratislava, Slovakia: Madách-Posonium, [1934] 1994), 84–120 (here 115).

62. See "Census, Map, Museum," in Benedict Anderson, *Imagined Communities: Reflections on the Origins and Spread of Nationalism*, 2nd ed. (London: Verso, 1991), 163–85.

63. Alexander Motyl, *Imperial Ends: The Decay, Collapse, and Revival of Empire* (New York: Columbia University Press, 2001), 4.

12

A STRANGE CASE OF ANTISEMITISM
IVAN FRANKO AND THE JEWISH ISSUE

YAROSLAV HRYTSAK

In the Ukrainian intellectual tradition, there is no other author who has written as extensively on the Jewish issue as Ivan Franko (1856–1916). He turned to this issue in various ways: in his poetry and prose, as a political leader and a journalist, and through his research in the Biblical tradition. The volume and richness of Franko's production stands in stark contrast to the rather modest amount of research devoted to it by scholars.[1] This paucity may be partly explained by the Soviet tradition of eliminating Jewish topics from public and academic discourse. In Soviet Ukraine, this tendency seemed to take a more extreme form than in any other Soviet republic.[2] In the case of Franko, it led to the passing over in silence of his writings on the Jewish issue, some of which were considered covert propaganda for Zionism.[3]

There is yet another difficulty in studying Franko's attitudes toward Jews, and that is the ambivalent and sometimes controversial character of his statements. Indeed, Franko's writings may be read sometimes as philosemitic, sometimes as antisemitic. There has been a telling discrepancy between Ukrainian and non-Ukrainian authors: while the former explored Franko's positive statements on Jews,[4] the latter often speak of him as another Ukrainian antisemite.[5] The following paper seeks to analyze these two controversial facets of his lore as an expression of an essential controversy within his ideology. In a broader comparative context, the paper addresses the issue of antisemitism and its various historical expressions, using case of Franko as an interesting case study for late nineteenth century Central and Eastern Europe.

Setting the Context: A Borderland on the Threshold of Modernity

Franko's lifetime was distinctive as the period during which there emerged modern movements and ideologies that shaped the whole of twentieth-century European history. At the time he started his career (1870s), there emerged all the possible new words—nihilism, materialism, socialism, assimilation, antisemitism, decadence, and others—that by the time of his death (1916) already dominated the political and intellectual scene of his native Habsburg Galicia.[6] Franko himself was very instrumental in spreading these modern concepts and ideas—to the extent that he was regarded as "an epitome of modernity" by his numerous followers and as a "great demoralizer" by his no less numerous foes.[7] Like most East European intellectuals, he faced, however, a great challenge: *how* to implement these modern concepts that emerged from outside of his region and had little relevance to the local social and cultural circumstances? For one thing, modern ideologies required from their adherents clear-cut loyalties and identities. Galicia was, however, a typical borderland marked by wholesale confusion of identities. Until the very final days of Habsburg rule, two major local ethnic groups, the Ruthenians and the Jews, were engaged in debates about to which nation they belonged: Polish, Russian, Ukrainian, or a separate Ruthenian nation in the first case,[8] or German, Polish, or Jewish in the latter case.[9] The third major group, the Roman Catholic Poles, was saved from these debates due to the existence of a heavily populated stratum of intellectuals and politicians with a strong feeling of their Polish identity. Polish elites strove to establish their political dominance in the province. Polish nationalism faced, however, a problem similar to the one that confronted both Ukrainian and Jewish nationalisms: how to integrate into the single body of a modern nation a largely illiterate and traditional population who were either apathetic or sometimes even hostile to nation-building projects.

The Galician situation was hardly unique. It was rather typical for the whole of Eastern Europe, where large expanses of space without internal geographical divisions and with a diverse population led to contests over the definition of territorial and ethnic boundaries.[10] Galicia was distinctive, however, in one sense: the ways in which the local crisis of identities might be resolved had a major impact on neighboring Russian provinces that were populated by the same set of ethnic and religious groups. The importance of Galicia was further aggravated by the fact that when the Polish and Ukrainian movements were repressed in the Russian empire in the 1860s, they shifted the center of their activity to the Austro-Hungarian empire, with its more liberal political regime. Each of them saw the region as their "Piedmont," that is, an embryo of their future national state. Their ambitions were treated as a threat of irredentism by the Russian imperial regime. Small wonder that Galicia became a major *casus belli* between the Austro-Hungarian and Russian empires during World War I and between the newly emergent Polish, Ukrainian, and Soviet regimes in 1918–1920.[11]

Galicia was a modern society in the making, or, as some economic historians prefer to name it, a "post-traditional society."[12] This point has to be especially emphasized to counterbalance the stereotyped image of Galicia as the epitome of a traditional society barely touched by modernization[13] To be sure, Galicia was an overwhelmingly agrarian province. Truth is, however, that Habsburg rule introduced here a peculiar kind of modernization—"modernization through bureaucratization"—in which the main agents of change were not entrepreneurs or bankers, but state clerks.[14] Among other things, Habsburg bureaucrats turned L'viv (Lwów/Lemberg), the administrative capital of Galicia, into a modern metropolis. This Galician capital became one of the few *really* modern cities in Central and Eastern Europe, if judged by the criteria of maximum use of city infrastructure for the needs of everyday life and the support of urban culture.[15] Due to its modern metropolitan character, L'viv had become a major center of a highly modern, flourishing urban culture that radiated throughout all of Central Eastern Europe.[16]

Since the mid-nineteenth century, the region had been gradually losing its insular character as radical modern changes made deep inroads into Galician society. The last feudal restrictions were lifted: the serfdom was abolished (1848), and Jews were finally granted equal rights (1867–1868). The first elements of a capitalist economy, such as industry and railways, were introduced. Even though Galicia remained a province with a high level of illiteracy and a short life expectancy, new demographic and cultural processes—similar to those that were underway in Western Europe—slowly but surely transformed the local lifeways.[17] Social changes were accompanied by political modernization. A series of international defeats in wars with Prussia and Italy pushed the empire toward constitutional experiments. In 1869, two years after the Compromise with Hungary and the reorganization of the empire as the Dual Monarchy of Austria-Hungary, Galicia was granted a broad autonomy. Galician autonomy and further reforms opened new avenues for public activity and mass politics.

Under the pressure of demographic and economic changes, the Christian (Polish and Ruthenian) and Jewish communities started to lose some of their traditional features (such as their total dependence on meager natural resources). In order to survive, many migrated to neighboring provinces of the Austro-Hungarian, Prussian, and Russian empires; some went overseas to North and South America. The most active portion of those who stayed looked for ways either to intensify old or to explore new realms of economic activity.

Like Jews everywhere, Galician Jews tended to establish themselves as an exclusively commercial class when they entered a country less developed economically. Traditionally, they were involved in trade, handicraft, and small industry. The lifting of anti-Jewish restrictions allowed them to acquire new social roles; for example, they played an important part in the development of the Galician oil industry in Boryslav. And, most significantly, they became increasingly visible in the agricultural sector, where they bought lands from impoverished landlords and peasants. But there they clashed with emerging Ukrainian and Polish peasant cooperatives, which considered agriculture as their legitimate field of activity.[18] This created new tensions. Each group felt increasingly endangered by the other. On the Christian part, there were talks about the gradual disappearance of peasants (and, in the Polish case, land aristocracy) as a result of "subversive" Jewish activities. Among Jews, there were fears of anti-Jewish violence; especially after the 1881 pogroms occurred in Russian provinces relatively nearby.

And above all, there was a feeling of a gradual disintegration of traditional society, with its classes and ethnic groups. Socialists and liberals applauded these changes; conservatives abhorred them. There was, however, a broad consensus that the current situation was not tenable anymore, and political programs had to be brought in line with the new circumstances. For rival political movements, it was important to respond to changing circumstances in a way that might increase their chances to win in the contested region. Under these conditions, for the Polish and Ruthenian-Ukrainian parties the Jewish issue was increasingly becoming a point of reference without which it was very hard, if impossible, to imagine their own class or nation.

It could scarcely be otherwise: with the exception of a few towns that had the medieval privilege *de non tolerandis Judaeis*, Jews were omnipresent in Galicia. The ratio of Jews to non-Jews there was 1:9 compared to 1:26 in the Austro-Hungarian Empire as a whole.[19] Throughout his life Franko lived in precisely the localities that had the largest numerical presence of Jews. He was born in the Eastern (Ukrainian) part of Galicia, in village of Nahujevychi was a few miles away from the county seat of Drohobych/Drohobycz. In the local antisemitic literature, this town was nicknamed "the capital of Galician onion-eaters" (a derogatory term for Jews).[20] Here Jews made up over 50 percent of the population. By the time he was a successful adult, the 1900 census recorded that the region held three-quarters of all Galician Jews. In neighboring Boryslav, a center of the Galician oil industry, their share exceeded 75 percent.[21] In 1875, Franko moved to L'viv, which, until the early 1900s, was the city with the largest Jewish population in the Habsburg monarchy (it was then overtaken in this respect by Budapest).[22] Galician Jews suffered from a bad public image: they were considered dirt-poor, barely literate, and arrogant. *Ein typischer Galizianer* was one of the nastier insults that a Western or Central European Jew might direct at an East European Jew.[23] The poverty of Galician Jews was striking: despite inroads into trade and agriculture, half of them were *Luftmenschen,* people devoid of any stable means of life and who lived on the charity of the Jewish community. The bitter irony was that in Eastern Galicia they faced Christian peasants who were likewise poor and, most often, even more illiterate. Despite their common poverty, Jews and local peasants rarely empathized with each other.

This is attested by, among other things, a rich collection of Galician Ruthenian proverbs that Franko compiled and edited.[24] It presented an overabundance of Judeophobic stereotypes: Jews were shown as cowards and imbeciles, deceitful and impure, a source of contagious diseases. Jews were represented as a caste of untouchables, worthy of contempt only. But, in the imagination of Ruthenians, this was a caste of untouchables of a peculiar kind, since in the social hierarchy they stood above, and not below, the Christians: they exploited the latter and brought them to ruin. Jews were presented as absolute "others," alien and hostile in every possible way. They were not deserving of sympathy in this world and would not be saved in the next. By this token, these proverbs specifically condemned those Christians who helped or served Jews.[25]

Franko and his Writings in *Dilo* and *Zerkalo*

A large number of these proverbs Franko collected in his own village and vicinity. But it seems that he himself was not affected by Judeophobism as a child. As he explained in his memoirs, it was because of his mother, Maria Kulczycka, a woman from a petty noble family, who taught her children not to believe in stories about Jews.[26] Jews were among the best friends of his childhood, his classmates in the Drohobych *Gymnasium* and the L'viv universities, and among his colleagues when he participated in the Galician socialist movement. Paradoxically, during the time of his socialist youth (the 1870s–80s) Franko had more contacts with the world of the impoverished Jewish artisans and workers than his colleagues, socialists of Jewish origin. Through his numerous contacts with Jews in his childhood and adolescence, he was very well informed on many aspects of Jewish life and had a good command of Yiddish. His knowledge was reflected in his numerous stories, novels, and verses on Jewish topics. Among these writings was a novel, *Boa Constrictor* (1878), a story told from the point of a view of a Jew—something quite exceptional for non-Jewish East European literature.[27]

Franko was exceptional in another way: his Judeophilic attitudes stood in contrast with the prevailing mood among Galician literati. Franko's youth was a time when, in the words of a Jewish publicist, antisemitism was present "in all walks of life."[28] As a student in Drohobych, he witnessed a three-day anti-Jewish pogrom (1863) initiated by students of the local *Gymnasium*.[29] He started his literary and political activity in L'viv in milieus that were overtly Judeophobic. Leaders of rival trends within the Ruthenian camp shared a common view that in the Ruthenian–Jewish relationship the survival for Ruthenians as a group was at stake: Jews were blamed for the impoverishment and demoralization of local peasants and for bringing them to the brink of disappearance as a social and national group.[30] This mood mirrored largely peasant attitudes. Galician Ruthenian peasants were expecting a major war that would erase Jews from the face of the earth. They placed their hopes on the "White Tsar"—the Russian monarch—who was supposed to come to Galicia to expel all the Polish landlords and Jews.[31]

This mood reached a climax in the aftermath of the Russian pogroms of 1881. There were both fears and expectations that something similar might occur in Galicia. Franko recorded and translated local Jewish songs that emerged after pogroms. Reflecting his fears, his own verses on that subject were full of sympathy toward Jewish victims and condemnation of the irrational and senseless character of the pogroms.[32] Again, Franko's attitudes toward this issue stood in contrast to the position taken by some socialists (Ruthenian-Ukrainian socialists included), who saw in the Russian pogroms a beginning of the great socialist upheaval for which they were waiting.[33]

Franko must be given credit for his distance from these plans. In general, he had many chances and occasions to become more antisemitic. He was often harshly criticized for his philosemitism—to the extent that some of his critics believed that he was a Jew himself. Nonetheless, he was not consistent in his attitude toward Jews. In 1883, he wrote a long article titled "Pytannia zhydivske" ("The Jewish Question") that was published as an unsigned editorial piece in the leading Ukrainian newspaper *Dilo*. It marks a clear departure from everything that Franko wrote before—or for that matter after—to the extent that Pavlo Kudriavtsev, a leading expert on the topic of "Franko and Jews," has refused to believe that this piece belongs to Franko at all.[34]

In "Pytannia zhydivske," Franko claimed that antisemitism had become a universal phenomenon. As such, it could not be relegated to the social or religious realm only. The roots of antisemitism, according to him, were deeper and therefore much more dangerous. He saw them in the "demoralizing supremacy of Jewish capital and Jewish exploitation" and in "Jewish impudence and provocation." Franko wrote that in many cases it was the Jews who were to blame for the eruption of violence: they were provoking pogroms to get direct profits, he alleged. As proof, he referred to the fact that perpetrators of pogroms—"simple" Christian workers and peasants—suffered much more than their victims. While the former were caught, shot at by the army and punished, the latter stayed safe and were given compensation by Jewish organizations (such as Alliance Israélite) and the state.

Franko suggested a program for averting pogroms in the future. Some of his suggestions were in a tune with his socialist spirit: he recommended workers to create self-reliance organizations and cooperatives in order to fight back against the exploitations of the Jewish capitalists. But some of Franko's points sounded strikingly non-socialist. For example, he called upon Christian priests to do their best to ensure that "Christians would not serve Jews and by that token [not be] alienated from their religion and their folk."[35]

The strange case of Franko's antisemitism did not finish there. The next year (1884), he published the poem "The Travels of Schwindeles Parchenblütt from the Village Derychlop to America and Back" ("Швинеделеса Пархенблита вандрівка з села Дерихлопа до Америки і назад").[36] Here he made maximum use of several Jewish stereotypes—the Jew as a leech, parasite, exploiter. This was not a poem of great artistic value, to say the least. What is also worth nothing is his emphasis on the solidarity of Jews versus their victims.

Jews were exploiting peasants because Talmud permitted them to do so. So exploitation of Christians, according to him, was at the core of Jewish identity. Franko implicitly extends responsibility for this exploitation to the whole Jewish community.

The poem was published in the Ukrainian satirical magazine *Zerkalo* (later *Nova Zerkalo*). This publication waged a systematic literary war against the "three best friends of Ukrainian peasants" (using ironic names for the three alleged worst enemies of the Ukrainian people), as embodied in the symbolic figures of "Us" (the Russophile hierarchy of the Greek Catholic Church), the "Patriots" (Polish nobility), and the "*Schwindeles Parchenblütt*" (Jews). It is unclear whether Franko invented the latter image himself. But he definitely exercised a certain influence on the editorial politics of *Zerkalo*: the chief editor Vasyl' Nahirnyj was his friend, and he had published extensively there and even came up with ideas for some cartoons.[37] In any case, Franko's poem enjoyed enormous popularity—to the extent that when the editor advertised for subscriptions for the next year, he referred to new installments of the poem as a "real jewel" awaiting readers.[38]

Among his works, Franko's article on the Jewish issue and his poem on Parchenblütt can hardly be classified as of marginal importance. Both were published in leading Ukrainian periodicals, and had all the formal appearances of important publications: the article was an editorial printed on the front page, and the poem was highlighted as a main attraction for readers. The question is: does it suffice to identify those two pieces as a programmatic statement of Franko's antisemitism? Or were they just an accident in his biography?

The Debates in *Przegląd Społeczny* (1886–1887)

This question can be answered by referring to Franko's later (1886–1887) writings, when he tried to bring his ideas on the Jewish issue into a certain system. An occasion was provided by a debate that was held in the L'viv-based journal *Przegląd Społeczny*. In the stifling intellectual atmosphere of Austrian Galicia of the 1880s, the journal was really an outstanding phenomenon. It was a truly international magazine that brought together Polish, Ukrainian, Jewish, and Russian authors of leftist trends from both empires.[39]

In 1886, a young Jewish intellectual by the name of Alfred Nossig published in this journal a long essay entitled "An attempt to resolve the Jewish issue" ("*Proba rozwiazania questiji Zydowskiej*"). It was one of the earliest political manifestos of Zionism. The publication made a splash: for years, Nossig had been a leader of the Polish assimilation movement, and now he was declaring that assimilation was not tenable and the only viable solution to the Jewish question was Zionism.[40] Nossig became a subject of attacks from assimilationists; Franko intervened to support him, and thus drew sharp criticism toward himself. He responded to his critics with the article "Semitism and Antisemitism in Galicia" ("Semityzm i antysemityzm w Galicji") published in *Przegląd Społeczny* (1887). This essay could be considered as programmatic: in many ways, his later writings would mostly continue to repeat and elaborate on the points that he made here.

Much of what Franko said during this discussion was a reiteration and support of Nossig's statements. Both stated explicitly that the Jewish Question was neither a racial nor a religious issue: for them, it was a *national* issue. Jews were supposed to be recognized as a separate nation with all the necessary cultural and political implications. Above all, Jews were entitled to make their own decisions as to their future and were expected to recognize the same rights for other nondominant ethnic groups, such as Ukrainains in Galicia. This was quite an original idea whose importance could hardly be underestimated. According to the Habsburg legislature, Jews were considered to be a religious group, not a nation, and this view also prevailed among local politicians and intellectuals. So by their recognition of Jews as a *nation,* both Nossig and Franko made quite a revolutionary statement.

Nor did either writer stop there. They went on by formulating their vision of how the Jewish issue was to be solved. Their solution suggested two major options for Galician Jews: 1) a voluntary assimilation into the local non-Jewish population; 2) for those who were not willing to assimilate, emigration to a land where they could live as an independent nation. For those Jews who would not be willing to accept either of these solutions, Franko suggested a third option: to remain in Galicia, but with the legal status of "aliens" (deprived of certain political and civic rights).

Intellectual historians have been intrigued by the second point of Franko's program: the emigration of Jews to a land where they could live as an independent nation, seeing here the embryo of Zionism.[41] They have generally ignored, however, the fact that it was not Franko's own original idea; rather, Franko reiterated the concept already articulated by Nossig and *Przegląd Społeczny.* It seems that, for Franko at that time, the Zionist option was actually of marginal importance—most likely because he did not believe in the plausibility of its implementation. On one occasion, he referred Zionism as the "most dangerous" political trend among Galician Jews and mocked their ideal as "childish dreams."[42] Franko's personal contribution—as distinct from Nossig's—was the idea of granting some Jews the legal status of "aliens." But then again, he was not completely original in that: such a solution was widely discussed by Jewish newspapers in the Russian empire in the wake of the 1881 pogrom. Franko explicitly referred to these discussions in laying out his "alien" option.

The true originality in Franko's approach is found in his understanding of assimilation. He does not see it as "baptization and consumption of pork." Quite to the contrary, Franko stood for a preservation of the Jewish religious rite and was against the conversion of Jews into Christians.[43] He also opposed the pattern of assimilation suggested by Moses Mendelssohn,[44] that is, assimilation into the "high culture" of the countries where Jews lived, but without denial of Judaism. He feared that the Mendelssohn formula might alienate the Jewish intelligentsia from the poor classes—both their own and those of other nondominant ethnic groups—which made up a bulk of the population in the borderland provinces of the Austrian and Russian empires. He envisioned assimilation as granting Jews all political rights, but on the condition of Jewish "solidarity with [working] people's ideals and working towards their implementation."[45] This conditional understanding of assimilation turned Franko's proposal into a social utopia: for most of the Jews, solidarity and assimilation with "working people" (i.e., local peasants) was out of the question. It also eroded the very concept of assimilation to the extent that, as an analyst noted, "there was nothing left of it."[46] Even though Franko placed assimilation "in first place in our Jewish politics,"[47] he made it practically impossible.

There were further problems with the translation of Franko's preferred program into a language of pragmatic solutions. He stated that the political emancipation of Jews must be accompanied by the economic emancipation of Gentiles. There had been a certain asymmetry in Jewish–Gentile relations—while Jews were denied rights in the political realm, they dominated in economics, holding control over 60 percent of the industry and 90 percent of the trade in Galicia. Therefore, not only did Jews require legal protection, but Gentiles had to be defended, too.

Following this line, Franko argued for certain anti-Jewish restrictions. First, he demanded that Jews be legally stripped of their right to buy land. According to him, by acquiring lands, Jews were aggravating a severe land hunger that had already been plaguing Ukraianian and Polish peasants. He also believed that Jews could not handle agricultural households efficiently and that they did not possess adequate skills in farming. Secondly, Franko proposed introducing a law that would prohibit rabbis from excommunicating any Jew from the Jewish community. He was inclined to think that rabbis were abusing this right in order to support economic exploitation under the disguise of confessional solidarity. On this point he was supporting a program proposed by Galician Polish liberal Teofil Merunowicz. He believed, however, that such changes in law had to be initiated not by Gentiles, but by those educated Jews who sought to get equal rights.

Franko's views of the Jewish issue were full of ambivalence and contradictions. On the one hand, he suggested granting Jews large-scale political rights to the extent of recognizing them as a separate nation; on the other, he was willing to impose on them certain restrictions. No wonder the latter part was read as antisemitism. Dr. Karl Lippe, a Zionist from Romania, went so far as to name Franko's program one of numerous "manifestations of mental disease" (that is antisemitism) that were plaguing Europe in the 1880s.[48]

To be sure, to call Franko an antisemite was not doing him full justice: it implied ignoring his positive program and his usually sympathetic attitudes toward Jews. In contrast to the 1883 article and poem, his publications in *Przegląd Społeczny* did not exploit overt antisemitic stereotypes. All of the three publications contained, however, one common topic that could be read, at least implicitly, as antisemitic. This was a statement on the inner solidarity of Jews vis-à-vis Gentiles. Franko believed that Jewish solidarity was a major source of Jewish domination in certain sectors of the Galician economy.

A Comparative Context: The Case of France

Antisemitism, like any other "ism," is a very broad phenomenon that eludes a clear-cut definition.[49] There is no consensus over whether all Judeophobic violence can be defined as antisemitism, and whether and to what extent nineteenth-century antisemitism is ontologically connected with the ugliest and most criminal forms of it in the twentieth century.[50] Some antisemitic statements of Franko's seem to fall into the category of so-called "progressive antisemitism." This is a brand that seeks to instrumentalize the Jewish issue for revolutionary moods and actions. In contradiction to "conservative" antisemitism, the "progressive" form opposes chauvinism and racism, and also stands against any attempts to use antisemitism for the defense and legitimization of *anciens régimes*. Even though such a classification of antisemitism implies a clear-cut division between "progressive" and "reactionary" types, in the political history of East-Central Europe there are not that many cases when public figures had positioned themselves only in one or another way. There was, however, a minimum program that no progressive antisemite would ever violate under any circumstances: support of Jewish assimilation combined with programmatic resistance to any "reactionary" (conservative, Christian, right-wing) antisemitism.[51]

Franko's antisemitism arose from his experience in the socialist movement. Beginning in the late 1870s and early 1880s, he was actively involved in the creation of an international (Ukrainian/Polish/Jewish) socialist party ("commune") in Galicia. It was supposed to unite peasants, artisans, and members of the intelligentsia regardless of their ethnic origin. He and his colleagues succeeded in establishing the editorial boards of the socialist newspaper *Praca* and, later, *Przegląd Społeczny,* as prototypes of such a commune. But, on the level of mass politics, their attempts proved to be a major failure. To a certain extent, this was because of the repression and harassment by local authorities of the socialist movement and its leaders (Franko himself was jailed in 1877–1878 and again in 1880). Harassment and repression could not, however, disguise the basic fact that Galician socialists were not able to find larger support among the "toiling masses" whom they sought to represent. Especially depressing for them was the behavior of the Jewish poor, whom they considered to be their "proletariat." In Franko's understanding, it was a strange kind of a proletariat: even though it was often starving, it still looked for means of survival through the exploitation of "alien elements."[52]

There is a striking similarity between the image of Jews in Ruthenian folklore and the one that was provided by Franko and Nossig. Both believed that "on average, a Jewish type is stronger in the struggle for survival, but morally stands lower than a non-Jewish type; he displays more flexibility and endurance, but also more arrogance, ambition and unscrupulousness."[53] Stripped of antisemitic overtones, this image reflects a certain type of social reality that cannot be adequately understood only as something exclusive to Galician Jews and their relations with local gentiles. A broader treatment was suggested by Aleksander Hertz in his *The Jews in Polish Culture.* As a Polish social scientist of Jewish origin who emigrated to the U.S., he managed to combine several cultural perspectives. A comparison of the Jewish community of Central Eastern Europe with African American communities helped him to introduce the sociological concept of a caste. This concept, he argued, was central for understanding relations between Jews and non-Jews. Jews made up a caste, that is, a closed group with a number of strict rules which, among other things, imposed a certain solidarity, and which were very hard, if impossible, for any individual to break. These rules persisted even when class distinctions began to be more pronounced. The Jewish community functioned as a caste, not a national group in the modern sense of the world, until the end of the nineteenth century, and in some regions until World War II.[54]

Following the Hertz interpretation, one can identify a source of Franko's caustic remarks on Jews. He and his fellow socialists believed in an overwhelming social progress that was about to bring radical changes. Jews, as well as other traditional groups, were to undergo rapid transformation. They were supposed to evolve into "modern" classes and nations. When this did not happen, Franko blamed not his utopian beliefs, but certain social strata for resisting progress: authorities, aristocracy, priests, rabbis—and last but not least, the Jewish proletariat, who failed to exhibit class solidarity with the poor of other nationalities.[55] Franko defended poor Jews against any kind of oppression, but he blamed the whole Jewish community, the paupers included, for their collective solidarity in exploiting Ukrainian peasants rather than joining forces with them.

It took him a long time to reconsider the critically socialist ideals of his youth. His long and complicated ideological evolution can be presented as one from socialism to nationalism. The climax of that evolution was an acceptance, after long hesitations and inner struggle, of an ideal of an independent Ukrainian state, which he had originally opposed as a right-wing invention.[56] It may be expected that along with this evolution, Franko's antisemitism should increase, not decrease. This did not happen. Quite to the contrary: among the works that he produced during this stage of his thought, like those written in the years of his youth , one can hardly find any antisemitic statements. Moreover, there are strong reasons to believe that his evolution occurred under the influence of Zionism. A telling illustration was his enthusiastic reaction to Theoder Herzl's *Judenstaat* in a review that he wrote immediately after the book had been published.[57]

Franko's case particularly, and the Galician Ukrainian case in general, seems to defy a conclusion by Peter Pulzer in his comparative study of political antisemitism that "it was stronger among 'unhistorical' nations than among 'historical' ones."[58] This is more in tune with his other observation that antisemitism was weaker in ethnically "mixed" regions, where the need for allies counterbalanced the sharper tempers and greater mutual suspicions.[59] This observation, however, has to be adjusted: besides pragmatic calculations of "counterbalancing," there were ideological considerations that could hardly be ignored.

For a comprehensive evaluation of Franko's views, it makes sense to compare them with the attitudes of other Central European intellectuals toward the Jewish issue, especially those whom he personally knew, corresponded or exchanged ideas with, and so on. I will choose three examples: Viktor Adler, leader of the Austrian social-democrat party; Eliza Orzeszko, Polish poetess; and Czech President Tomáš G. Masaryk. Each of them, in a way, relates to a part of Franko's versatile personality: Viktor Adler as a socialist, Eliza Orzeszko as a writer, Tomáš G. Masaryk as an ideologue on the "nonstate" nation.

Viktor Adler was Jewish by origin, and his marriage was held according to Orthodox Jewish ritual. His three children were, however, baptized. On this occasion, Adler used to quote Heinrich Heine that "*[d]er Taufzettel ist das Entréebillet zur europäischen Kultur*" ("Baptism is an entry ticket to European culture"). Like many other Jews of their generation, he and his wife Emma fell under the spell of socialism while it promised emancipation not only of the proletariat, but specifically of Jews as well. Jewish leftist intellectuals saw themselves as leaders of the exodus of their compatriots from traditional society into a modern world. In Viktor Adler's case, this implied national and religious assimilation. His socialist views were accompanied by a racist antisemitic mood, which he openly revealed—to a great dismay of his wife—in private conversations in a circle of his closest friends.[60]

Eliza Orzeszko was, in a sense, Franko's *alter ego*: she was the first Polish writer who treated the Jewish issue systematically. She saw some similarities in the historical fate of Poles and Jews. As in the Franko's case, her works are full of very sympathetic descriptions of Jews and Jewish life (the similarity was accentuated by the fact that both displayed a very strong moralistic and didactic tone). Orzeszko consistently condemned antisemitism—an act that required courage, given the rampant antisemitic mood among Polish intellectuals (exemplified in Bolesław Prus's *Lalka* (*Doll*, 1890) or Władysław Reymont *Promised Land* [1897–1898]). Like young Franko, she denied the practical value of Zionism, and considered assimilation to be the most efficient way to release tensions between Jews and non-Jews. The similarity of their views was further illustrated by the fact that she—unlike Adler—was against religious conversion of Jews to Christianity. A major difference was that she understood assimilation as the integration of Jews into the Polish nation only. She denied their right to be a separate modern nation while they did not possess their own modern national language.[61]

And finally: Tomáš G. Masaryk was born in a village where, like Franko, he heard and learned a lot of anti-Jewish stories. He could not overcome some of the Judeophobic bias and superstitions that he inherited during his early years. His intellectual magnitude could be measured by the fact that, despite these biases, he combated antisemitism. In 1900, he raised his voice in defense of a Jew accused of a ritual murder and wrote a book to that effect—and was ostracized, as a result, by his colleagues, professors, and students at the Czech university in Prague.[62]

A comparison with Adler and Orzeszko helps to identify the position of Franko within the trend of "progressive antisemitism." Two moments make his views distinctive: the first is opposition (in contrast to Adler) of Jewish assimilation in a national or religious sense; the second is recognition (in contrast to Orzeszko) of Jews as a separate nation. An analogy with Masaryk suggests another perspective: both were raised and acted in milieux where it was much easier to become an antisemite than a philosemite. Like Masaryk, Franko was criticized by his compatriots for his sympathy toward Jews.[63] The fact that Franko wrote a pamphlet that explained to rank-and-file members of Ruthenian-Ukrainian Radical Party— a party of which he was the leader—his attitude toward Jews makes us think that even his closest milieu of Ukrainian socialists was not immune to the antisemitic mood.[64]

Conclusion

The case of Ivan Franko serves as an illustration of the fact that the various manifestations of antisemitism in the nineteenth century cannot be that easily classified and generalized. It seems to undermine the views of those historians who draw a direct line between the antisemitism of 1870–1914 and the antisemitic manifestations after 1914, especially in the 1930–40s.[65] From the perspective of studies on Franko, a much more productive approach for an evaluation of antisemitism was suggested Peter Gay. In a series of essays on German antisemitism of the nineteenth century, Gay criticized the image of German history "as a prologue to Hitler." He stated, "Nineteenth-century German antisemitism, however unpalatable even at the time, however pregnant with terrifying future, was different in kind from the twentieth-century variety. . . . It was a culture in which clusters of ideas we would regard as grossly contradictory co-existed without strain in the same person."[66]

Franko's attitudes toward Jews were very ambivalent. But so were his attitudes toward Marxists, feminists, peasants, priests, and, for that matter, Ukrainian nationalists. This is neither to excuse nor to eulogize him. It is just to call attention to the fact that there was more in his attitudes toward Jews than antisemitism. To discredit any nineteenth-century intellectual on the basis of his or her antisemitism is an approach that smacks of teleology. The victims of this misplaced historical hindsight might include Marx, Dostoyevsky, and Freud, to mention the most famous historical figures only.

The nineteenth-century antisemitism seemed to be universal phenomenon, and even the most "enlightened" intellectuals were not immune to it.[67] In this sense, the case of Franko is hardly unique. Therefore it is not enough to state that Franko was an antisemite—it is no less important to explore what he did with his antisemitism. Did he make it the core of his intellectual and political activity? The analysis of this chapter demonstrates that in fact Franko juggled various attitudes, and in his body of work as a whole the most antisemitic of them were marginalized.

Notes

1. The few exceptions are: Pavlo Kudriavtsev, "Yevreystvo, yevreï ta yevreys'ke sprava v tvor-akh Ivana Franka," *Zbirnyk prats' yevreys'koï istorychno-arkheohrafichnoï komisiï,* vol. 2, ed. A. I. Kryms'kï (Kiev, 1929), 1–81; Volodymyr Poliek, "Ivan Franko ta yevrei (Odna storinka z litopysu

ukrainsko-yevreyskykh zviazkiv)," *Halychyna* 1 (1992): 93–98. See also my earlier publications on that subject: "A Ukrainian Answer to the Galician Ethnic Triangle: The Case of Ivan Franko," *Polin: Studies in Polish Jewry*, vol. 12: *Focusing on Galicia: Jews, Poles, and Ukrainians 1772–1918*, ed. Israel Bartal and Antony Polonsky (London: The Littman Library of Jewish Civilization, 1999), 137–46. "Między filosemityzmem i antysemityzmem—Iwan Franko i kwestia żydowska" in *Świat Niepożegnany. Żydzi na dawnych ziemiach wschodnich Rzeczypospolitej w XVIII-XX wieku*, ed. Krzysztof Jasiewicz (Warsaw: Instytut Studiów Politycznych PAN: Oficyna Wydawn, 2005), 451–80; idem, *Mizh semityzmom j antysemityzmom: Ivan Franko ta jevrejs'ke pytannia* (Drohobych, Ukraine: Kolo 2005); idem, *Prorok u svoïy vitchyzni: Ivan Franko ta yoho spil'nota* (Kiev: Krytyka, 2006).

2. Zvi Gitelman, "Soviet Reactions to the Holocaust, 1945–1991," in *The Holocaust in the Soviet Union: Studies and Sources on the Destruction of the Jews in the Nazi-Occupied Territories of the USSR, 1941–1945*, ed. L. Dobroszycki, and J. S. Gurock (Armonk, N.Y: M. E. Sharpe, 1993), 3, 9–11.

3. On 12 March 1953, at the height of Soviet antisemitic politics, Glalvit (General Directorate for the Protection of State Secrets in the Press, the highest censoring committee of the Ukrainian RSR) wrote a report "On pernicious practices of the Ukrainian Literature Institute, Academy of Sciences, Ukrainian SSR." The report forbade, among other things, publication of the second volume of Franko's collected works. The reason was that the volume had his poem "Moses," which, according to the Glavlit, "eulogized the 'promised land' of Jewish people of Palestine, nostalgia of Jews for Palestine, which is for them their native home, etc." (Tsentral'nyy derzhavnyy arkhiv derzhavnykh hromads'kykh ob'yednan' Ukraïny, f. 1, op, 24, spr. 2712, ark. 162). For a list of Franko's works on the Jewish issue that were never published under the Soviet regime see: Zinoviya Franko, "50-tomne zibrannia tvoriv I. Franka v otsintsi s'ohodennia," *Suchasnist'* 10(342) (1989): 113–14; idem, "Peredmova" in *Ivan Franko. Mozaïka. Iz tvoriv, щo ne vviyshly do Zibrannia tvoriv u 50 tomakh*, ed. Z. T. Franko, M. H. Vasylenko (L'viv: Kameniar, 2001), 10–12.

4. For their bibliography see: Myroslav Moroz, ed., *Zarubizhne Frankoznavstvo. Biblografichnï pokazhcyk* (L'viv: Naukova dumka 1997), 41, 56, 63–64.

5. Leila Everett, "The Rise of Jewish National Politics in Galicia, 1905–1907," in *Nationbuilding and the Politics of Nationalism: Essays on Austrian Galicia*, ed. Andrei S. Markovits and Frank E. Sysyn (Cambridge, Mass.: Harvard University Press, 1982), 166–67; Kerstin S. Jobst, *Zwischen Nationalismus und Internationalismus. Die Polnische und ukrainische Sozial-demokratie in Galizien von 1890 bis 1914. Ein Beitrag zur Nationalitätenfrage im Habsburgreich* (Hamburg: Dölling und Galitz, 1996), 82–83; Ezra Mendelsohn, "From Assimilation to Zionism in Lvov: The Case of Alfred Nossig," *The Slavonic and East European Review* 49(117) (October 1971): 531. The only exception to this tendency is: Asher Wilcher, "Ivan Franko and Theodor Herzl: To the Genesis of Franko's Mojsej," *Harvard Ukrainian Studies* 6 (1982): 238–43. This article treats Franko's attitudes toward the Jews positively and in detail. But again, this article was published in a Ukrainian academic magazine.

6. Maria Kłańska, *Aus des Schtetl in die Welt 1772 bis 1938. Ostjüdische Autobiographien in deutscher Sprache* (Vienna: Böhlau Verlag, 1994), 215; Peter Pulzer, *The Rise of Political Anti-Semitism in Germany & Austria*, rev. ed. (London: Peter Halban, 1988), xi; Norman Stone, *Europe Transformed, 1879–1919* (Cambridge, Mass.: Harvard University Press, 1984), 13.

7. For details see my *Prorok u svoïy vitczyzni*, especially chapters 8 and 16.

8. John-Paul Himka, "The Construction of Nationality in Galician Rus': Icarian Flights in Almost All Directions," in *Intellectuals and Articulation of the Nation*, ed. Ronald G. Suny and Michael D. Kennedy (Ann Arbor: University of Michigan Press, 1999), 109–54. In order to represent adequately the complicated and fluid character of identities, throughout this article I use "Ruthenian" as an ethnic term and "Ukrainian" as a national choice. Therefore, the local folk culture should be branded as Ruthenian, while Franko identified himself as Ukrainian, or Ruthenian-Ukrainian.

9. Jerzy Holzer, "Vom Orient die Fantasie, und in der Brust der Slawen Feuer . . ." Jüdishes Leben und Akkulturation im Lemberg des 19. und 20. Jahrhunderts" in *Lemberg—Lwów-L'viv. Eine Stadt im Schnittpunkt europäischer Kulturen*, ed. Fäßler, T. Held, and D. Sawitzki (Cologne: Böhlau Verlag1993), 75–91.

10. Mark R. Bessinger, "The Persisting Ambiguity of Empire," *Post-Soviet Affairs* 11(2) (1995): 180.

11. Klaus Bachmann, *Ein Herd der Feindschaft gegen Russland: Galizien als Krisenherd in den Beziehungen der Donaumonarchie mit Russland (1907–1914)* (Vienna: Verlag für Geschichte und

Politik, 2001); Maciej Kozłowski, *Mię dzy Sanem a Zbruczem: walki o Lwów i Galicję Wschodnia 1918–1919* (Krakow: Znak, 1990).

12. Jacek Kochanowicz, *Spór o teorię gospodarski chłopskiej. Gospodarstwo chłopskie w teorii ekonomii i w historii gospodarczej* (Warsaw: Wydawnictwo Uniwersytetu Warszawskiego, 1992), 156–57.

13. This image has been forged in the literature of that time, and persists in academic discourse to the present time. For its origins, see: Stanisław Szczepanowski, *Nędza Galicï w cyfrach i program energicznego rozwoju gospodarstwa krajowego* (L'viv: Gubrynowicz i Schmidt, 1888); Leszek Kuberski, "'Nędza Galicji' Stanisława Szepanowskiego i jej odbicie w ówczesnej prasie polskiej" in *Kraków-Lwów. Książki czasopisma biblioteki XIX I XX wieku*, vol. 5, ed. Jerzy Jarowiecki (Krakow: Wydawnictwo naukowe Akademii Pedagogicznej, 2001), 427–39. For a critique of this stereotype see: Helena Madurowicz-Urbańska, "Perspektywy nowych badań nad społeczeństwem galicyjskim," *Pamiętnik XIII Powszechnego Zjazdu Historyków Polskich*, vol. 1 (Wrocław, Poland: Zakład Narodowy, 1986): 139–49.

14. Waltraud Heindl, *Gehörsame Rebellen. Bürokratie und Beamte in Österreich 1780–1848* (Vienna: Bohlau Verlag, 1990); idem, "Modernizatsiia ta teoriii modernizatsii: pryklad Habsburz'koï biurokratiï," *Ukraïna moderna* 1 (1996): 89–100.

15. Krzysztof Pawłowski, "Miejsce Lwowa w rozwoju urbanistyki europejskiej przełomu XIX i XX wieku" in *Arkhitektura Halychyny XIX–XX st. Vybrani materialy mizhnarodnoho symposium 24–27 travnia 1994, prysviachenoho 150-richchiu zasnuvannia Derzhavnoho universytetu*, ed. Bohdan Cherkes, Martin Kubelik, and Elizabet Hofer (L'viv: L'viv'ska politekhnika, 1996), 125–30; idem, "Narodziny nowoczesnego miasta" in *Sztuka drugiej połowy XIX wieku* (Warsaw: PWN, 1973), 57–58, 61–68.

16. Suffice it to say that in the 1880s, L'viv had more newspapers and magazines per capita than Moscow, the second largest city of the Russian empire—see: Korneli Heck, "Bibliografia Polska z r. 1881 w porównaniu z czeską, wegierską i rossyjską," *Przewodnik naukowy i literacki. Dodatek miesięczny do, Gazety Lwowskiej* 10 (1882): 1097.

17. Krzysztof Zamorski, "Zasadnicze linie przemian demograficznych Galicji w drugiej połowie XIX wieku i na początku XX wieku" in *Galicja i jej dziedzictwo*, vol. 2, ed. Jerzy Chłopcki and Helena Madurowicz-Urbańska (Rzeszów, Poland: Wydawn. Wyższej Szkoły Pedagogicznej w Rzeszowie, 1995), 102.

18. Alison Fleig Frank, *Oil Empire: Visions of Prosperity in Austrian Empire* (Cambridge, Mass.: Harvard University Press, 2003); John-Paul Himka, "Ukrainian–Jewish Antagonism in the Galician Countryside during the Late Nineteenth Century" in *Ukrainian-Jewish Relations*, ed. Potichnyj and Aster (Edmonton: CIUS Press, 1988), 111–58; Slawomir Tokarski, *Ethnic Conflict and Economic Development: Jews in Galician Agriculture 1868–1914* (Warsaw: Trio, 2003).

19. Ivan Franko, *Zibrannia tvoriv,* 50 vols., vol. 44/1 (Kiev: Naukova Dumka 1984), 478; Alfred Nossig, *Materiallen zur Statistik des Jüdischen Stammes* (ViennaWien: C. Konegen, 1887), 38, 59.

20. Józef Rogosz, *W piekle Galicyjskim. Obraz z życia* (Gródek, Poland: Nakładem i drukiem J. Czańskiego, 1896), 5.

21. Zbigniew Fras, *Galicja* (Wrocław: Wydawnictwo Dolnośląskie, 2000), 75.

22. Piotr Wróbel, "The Jews of Galicia under Austrian-Polish Rule, 1869–1918," *Austrian History Yearbook* 25 (1994): 106; Robert S. Wistrich, "The Jews and Nationality Conflicts in the Habsburg Lands," *East European Politics and Societies* 9(2) (Spring 1995): 119.

23. Istvan Deak, *Essays on Hitler's Europe* (Lincoln: University of Nebraska Press, 2001), 47.

24. Ivan Franko, ed. *Halyts'ko-rus'ki narodni prypovidky,* vols. 1–3 (*Etnohrafichnyi zbirnyk,* published by the Ethnographic Commission of the Shevchenko Scientific Society, vol. 23. Originally published in L'viv, 1901–1909.)

25. *Halyts'ko-rus'ki prypovidky,* vol.1, 106–16. See also: Kai Struve, "Gentry, Jews, and Peasants: Jews as Others in the Formation of the Modern Polish Nation in Rural Galicia during the Second Half of the Nineteenth Century" in *Creating the Other: Ethnic Conflict and Nationalism in Habsburg Central Europe,* ed. Nancy M. Wingfield (New York, Oxford: Berghahn Books, 2003), 103–26. To be sure, resentments and stereotypes were mutual—see: Henry Abramson, *A Prayer for the Government: Ukrainians and Jews in Revolutionary Times, 1917–1920* (Cambridge, Mass.:

Harvard University Press, 1999), 6; Mark Zborowski and Elizabeth Herzog, *Life is With People: The Culture of the Shtetl* (New York: International University Press, 1964), 67, 144, 148, 152.

26. Franko, *Mozaika,* 338. Rumor had it that Ivan Franko himself was an illegitimate son of a Jew with whom his mother fell in love. Ludwik Krzywicki, *Wspomnienia,* vol. 1: *1859–1885* (Warsaw: Czytelnik, 1947), 265; Volodymyr Doroshenko, "'Ivan Franko' (zi spomyniv avtora)," *Svoboda* no. 145 (6 June 1957).

27. Aleksander Hertz, *The Jews in Polish Culture,* trans. Richard Lourie (Evanston, Ill.: Northwestern University Press, 1988).

28. Quoted in Ezra Mendelson, "Jewish Assimilation in L'viv: The Case of Wilhelm Feldman" in *Nationbuilding and the Politics of Nationalism: Essays on Austrian Galicia,* ed. Andrei S. Markovits and Frank Sysyn (Cambridge, Mass.: Harvard University Press, 1982), 107.

29. Franko, *Mozaika,* 340–42; Ždisław Kultys, *Historya Gimnazyum Drohobyckiego* (Drohobycz, 1908), 60–61; *L'vivska naukova biblioteka im. V.Stefanyka, viddil rukopysiv,* f.41 (Hrushkevych), spr. 6/1, 28–29.

30. Ivan Naumovych, "O Halitskoi Rusi," *Slavianskï Sbornik* 1 (1875): 33–40; Nykola Zahors'kï [Stepan Kachala], *Polityka rusyniv* (L'viv, 1873), 23; *Perepyska Mykhaila Drahomanova z Mykhailom Pavlykom* (1876–1895), vol. 2 (Chernivtsi, Ukraine: Tovarystvo "Rus'ka Rada" 1910), 28.

31. *Perepyska Mykhaila Drahomanova,* 28, 354.

32. Franko, *Mozaika,* 27–32; ibid., 27, 31; ibid., 32.

33. M. Hrushevskï, *Z pochyniv ukrainskoho sotsialistychnoho rukhu. Mykh. Drahomanov i zhenevskï sotsialistychnï hurtok* (Vienna: Institut sociologique ukrainien, Zakordonye [sic] biuro i sklad, 1922), 86–87.

34. Kudriavtsev, "Yevreystvo," 72 (footnote).

35. Ivan Franko, "Pytannia zhydivske," *Dilo* no. 94 (20 August 1884): 1–2.

36. The low artistic value of the poem was admitted by some of Franko's friends. See Doroshenko, "Ivan Franko."

37. Omelian Ohonovsky, one of Franko's professors at university, claimed that Franko was the "soul" of the magazine. Omelian Ohonovskii, *Istoriya literatury ruskoï,* vol. 3, pt. 2 (L'viv: Nakl. T-va im. Shevchenka, 1893), 1069.

38. "Ot redaktsiï," *Nove Zerkalo* 2(24) (15 [27] December 1884), 4.

39. Krzywicki, *Wspomnienia,* 258–65; *Przegląd Społeczny 1886–1887. Wstęp i antologię opracował Krzysztof Dunin-Wąsowicz. Bibliografię opracowała Jadwiga Czachowska* (Wrocław: Zakład im. Ossolińskich, 1955).

40. On Nossig see: Samuel Almog, "Alfred Nossig: A Reappraisal," *Studies in Zionism* 7 (Spring 1983): 1–29; Mendelsohn, *From Assimilation,* 521–53; Janina Kulczycka-Saloni, *Na polskich i europejskich szlakach litteracikch. Z pism rozproszonych 1985–1998* (Warsaw: Antyk, 2000), 198–213; A. Rieber, "Alfred Nossig," *Polski Słownik Biograficzny,* vol. 23 (Wrocław: Zakłład Polskiego Słownika Biograficznego Instytutu Historii im. Tadeusza Manteuffla Polskiej Akademii Nauk, 1978), 236–38.

41. Ivan Lysiak-Rudnyts'kyy, *Istorychni ese,* vol. 1 (Kiev: Osnovy, 1994).

42. In a later (1893) article, he defined Zionism as the "most dangerous" political trend among Galician Jews and mocked its ideal as "childish dreams": Iwan Franko, "Żydzi o kwestji żydowskiej," *Tydzień* no. 12 (20 March 1893): 93.

43. Franko, *Mozaïka,* 326.

44. See Franko's article on Moses Mendelssohn: Ivan Franko, "Zhydy v zhyttiu i literaturi. I. Moses Mendelssohn reformator zhydivs'ki," *Zoria* no. 7 (1 [13] April 1886): 114–15.

45. Franko, *Mozaïka,* 328.

46. Kudriavtsev, "Yevreystvo," 79.

47. Franko, *Mozaïka,* 328.

48. *Der Israelit* 19(21) (26 November 1886): 1–2; K. Lippe, *Symptome der anti-Semitische Geisteskrankheit* (Jassy, Romania: H. Goldner, 1887).

49. Pulzer, *The Rise,* 9.

50. See: Michael Brown, ed., *Approaches to Anti-Semitism: Context and Curriculum* (New York: American Jewish Committee and International Center for University Teaching of Jewish Civilization, 1994).

51. Theodore R. Weeks, "Polish 'Progressive Anti-Semitism,' 1905–1914," *East Eureopean Jewish Affairs* 25(2) (1995): 49–67.

52. Franko, *Mozaïka,* 324.

53. *Przegląd Społeczny,* vol. 2 (1886), 232.

54. Hertz, *The Jews,* 59–62, 84, 131.

55. Franko was especially frustrated by industrial developments in Boryslav, which at some point brought about a large confrontation between Christian and Jewish workers (see my article: "Franko's Boryslav Cycle: An Intellectual History," *Journal of Ukrainian Studies* 20(1–2) (Summer–Winter 2005): 169–90.

56. For details see: Yaroslav Hrytsak, "Ivan Franko pro politychnu samostiynist's Ukraïny," in *Zeszyty Naukowe Uniwersytetu Jagiellońskiego.Prace Historyczne.-Z.103/Ukraińska myśl polityczna w XIX wieku. Materiały z międzynarodowej konferencji naukowej . . . 28–30 maja 1990* (Krakow, 1993), 45–53.

57. Wilcher, *Ivan Franko,* passim.

58. Pulzer, *The Rise,* 136.

59. Ibid., 135–36.

60. *Emma Adler* (Vienna: Verein für Geschichte der Arbeiterbewegung, 1989), 2–3, 10, 14. This is an excerpt from the unpublished memoirs of Emma Adler.

61. Ursula Philipps, "The 'Jewish Question' in the Novels and Short Stories of Eliza Orzesz-kova," *East European Jewish Affairs* 25(2) (1995): 69–90.

62. Karel Čapek, *President Masaryk Tells His Story* (London: G. Allen & Unwin, Ltd., 1934), 29; Wistrich, "The Jews and Nationality Conflicts," 129, 136.

63. See: Ivan Franko, *Radykal'na partiya,* vol. 2: *Radykaly i zhydy* (L'viv: n.p., 1899), 9–11.

64. Ibid.

65. Pulzer, *The Rise,* passim.

66. Peter Gay, *Freud, Jews, and Other Germans: Masters and Victims of Modernist Culture* (Oxford: Oxford University Press, 1978), 15.

67. Heiko Haumann, one of the best experts on history of Eastern Jews, has reached a similar conclusion—see his *"Wir waren alle ein klein wenig antisemitisch." Ein Versuch über hisstorische Massstäbe zur Beurteiling von Judengegnerschaft* [separatum].

13

NATION STATE, ETHNIC CONFLICT, AND REFUGEES IN LITHUANIA
1939–1940

TOMAS BALKELIS

Introduction

Hitler's attack on Poland in September 1939 following the Molotov-Ribbentrop Pact destroyed the last illusions of peace and stability in Europe. The rapid two-pronged destruction of the Polish state by the Nazi and Soviet armies precipitated a humanitarian crisis which spilled over into neighboring East European states. Hundreds of thousands of Polish civilians, government officials, and military fled the path of the invading armies into neighboring Slovakia, Romania, Hungary, and Lithuania in the hope of finding a safe haven. The first weeks of the war thereby rendered them homeless refugees.

This chapter explores the refugee crisis in eastern Lithuania, where around 27,000 refugees from Poland sought sanctuary.[1] For the small and truncated Lithuanian state—in March 1939 Germany had annexed the region of Klaipėda (Memel)—the influx of so many refugees presented a considerable challenge.[2] The government in Kaunas faced a humanitarian crisis because these refugees had to be fed and accommodated. It had to deal simultaneously with international pressure from the Polish government-in-exile and its Western allies, and from Germany. While the allies demanded full protection for the refugees, Germany wanted to curb all anti-German political and military activities among the Polish population in Lithuania.[3]

Having emerged as an independent state from the mayhem of World War I, Lithuania had inherited an ethnically mixed population. During the interwar years its two largest ethnic minorities, Jews and Poles, officially had been protected by the minority protection regime imposed by Versailles. Yet by the mid-1920s their minority rights were being seriously eroded by the country's swing toward right-wing politics and the growing competition between ethnic Lithuanian and Jewish economic interests.[4] Meanwhile, the relations with Poles remained poisoned by the conflict with Poland, a hostility derived from the military coup led by Lucjan Żeligowski in October 1920 and Poland's occupation of Vilnius. Lithuania never recognized this annexation, which damaged relations between the two states throughout the interwar years.

Lithuanians based their claims to Vilnius on its role as the historical capital of the medieval Grand Duchy of Lithuania, whereas Poland staked its claim on the grounds that the city and surrounding area were predominantly ethnically Polish. The two states failed to develop diplomatic relations, attempts to settle the Vilnius dispute internationally having come to nothing.[5] Throughout the interwar and early war years, the Vilnius region, traditionally a multiconfessional and multiethnic area, thus, remained a borderland of encounter where competing political interests clashed with each other (see chapter 4). Needless to say, these conflicts had a destabilizing effect on the states involved and forms of coexistence in the region.

After the Soviet-backed transfer of the Vilnius region from Poland to Lithuania in October 1939, the Lithuanian government attempted to integrate the region politically, economically, and culturally. This was marked by a sustained campaign of Lithuanization, requested by many members of the Lithuanian public. The Lithuanian government attempted to steer a course through this volatile domestic and international situation. However, the unpopular authoritarian regime, seriously weakened by the Polish ultimatum of March 1938 and the loss of Klaipėda in March 1939, was able to produce only a series of short-lived governments. The government attempted to regain its popularity by claiming the return of Vilnius as a diplomatic victory, but the refugee crisis contributed to further destabilizing the political scene. Lithuania embarked on contradictory policies that ranged from attempts to assist the refugees by involving international relief agencies to measures to control their movement. Refugees were enumerated, classified, controlled, isolated, forcibly employed, resettled, or even jailed. In other words, compulsory "rooting" and "sifting" of the population went hand-in-hand with relief efforts. In practice, as we shall see, the relief measures also served to achieve the state's political objectives.

Yet the refugee crisis provided the backdrop to a new critical development in the region, which is another focus of this chapter. For those Polish citizens who fled into Lithuania the onset of war entailed physical displacement. For the many thousand Poles who lived in the Vilnius region and found rather that borders had shifted, the onset of war brought about their political disenfranchisement. In March 1940, Lithuania denied citizenship rights to around 83,000 Poles who had settled in the Vilnius region between 1920 and 1939. This group of people became officially labeled as "newcomers" (Lithuanian: ateiviai). From now on their status was made similar to that of the war refugees. Not surprisingly, the political loyalties of local Poles were significantly affected by this decision, which swelled the number of the displaced to more than 100,000, created serious unrest among them and produced a negative reaction from the Polish government-in-exile and its Western allies.[6] Since almost every fourth person in the Vilnius region now could be regarded as a refugee, the situation spelled a long-term predicament.[7] The crisis only exacerbated the existing tensions between Poles and Lithuanians. Ultimately it provided the backdrop to the expulsion of more than 196,000 Poles from Soviet Lithuania to Poland in 1945–1946.[8]

The Birth and Scale of the Refugee Crisis

Polish war refugees found their way into Lithuania as early as the first week of September 1939. The first refugees, mostly well-to-do members of the Polish community, arrived from Gdańsk and received warm support and help from Polish residents of Vilnius who saw them as the first "heroic victims" of the local Nazi takeover.[9] By mid-September Lithuanian border guards reported that Polish army units had begun crossing into Lithuania, where they were immediately disarmed and interned. In total, Lithuania received about 9,500 Polish military personnel. They were placed in six special camps administered by the Lithuanian army.[10]

The largest wave of refugees, mostly civilians with their families and small children, poured into Vilnius in the last days of September. They were destitute and hungry people who had been on the march for more than two weeks from western Poland. Their arrival changed the face of the city: as one contemporary noted, "the prices of property shot up, while scores of the people slept on the street."[11] The local population was shocked by their appearance and mood; the refugees' sense of panic finally destroyed their hopes that the Polish army could withstand the invaders. As a result, the refugees were received coldly. Their numbers induced what one contemporary described as the "warsawization" of the city: "Vilnius started to 'warsawize,' and city cafés became totally 'warsawized.'"[12]

By early December there were about 18,000 registered war refugees in Vilnius, among them 7,700 Poles, 6,860 Jews, and 3,700 Lithuanians.[13] Adult men formed the highest percentage. But these numbers underestimated the real total. An early attempt by the Lithuanian government to count the refugees revealed that "the majority of the registered are only those who are in need of relief. Those who can support themselves avoid the registration, since they are afraid that the registration lists could end up in the hands of the Soviets."[14]

From the perspective of refugees and local Poles alike, the destruction of Poland and the subsequent transfer of the Vilnius region by the Soviets to Lithuania on 10 October 1939 were not permanent developments but rather a temporary outcome of the war that would be rectified by the Allies in due course. Certainly the refugees (as well as most local Poles) did not welcome the Lithuanian army that marched into the city in full military gear and with great pomp on 28 October.[15] In the minds of the refugees, Vilnius still remained a little unoccupied island of Poland.[16] Local people looked upon the symbols of Lithuanian power as unfamiliar and regarded as alien the Lithuanian language that was spoken by a minority of the city's population.[17]

The final official count of refugees in February 1940 gave a total of around 27,000 registered refugees. Among them there were 12,000 Poles and Belorussians, 11,000 Jews, and 3,700 Lithuanians.[18] In all likelihood the total number exceeded 30,000, because some refugees still refused to register. Most Lithuanian refugees were farmers, while Jews were largely merchants, artisans, and professionals. The Poles were reportedly "for the most part former government officials with their family members, while some were public figures and people of free professions."[19] The steady growth of the registered refugee population reflected government efforts to control refugees. Those who failed to register before the deadline of 20

January 1940 faced imprisonment for up to six months. The increasing numbers also implied a worsening of the refugees' material condition: only those registered could expect any help.[20]

Relief as a State Strategy?

After their abrupt arrival, refugees found themselves in a humanitarian crisis. With a pre-war population (in 1937) of about 210,000, Vilnius could not absorb the intake of 30,000 refugees, given the disruption of the local economy.[21] Although well-to-do refugees might survive on their savings, the majority faced serious deprivation because of the depreciation of the currency. Around 12,000 refugees depended totally on assistance of one form or another.[22] In November 1939, a representative of the American Joint Distribution Committee (JDC) noted that half of the 12,000 Jewish refugees were being fed in kitchens operated by various Jewish relief organizations.[23] The refugees were also in dire need of winter clothing. "Today one can practically identify the refugees in Vilna by the fact that they wear raincoats," he noted. He concluded that the local relief agencies would not be able to support the refugees without external funds.

At first the relief effort took on an informal and largely decentralized character. The Soviet Military Council of the Vilnius Region attempted to house the first group of refugees in September, while local Jewish, Polish, and Lithuanian organizations tried to provide emergency aid for their ethnic compatriots. The most efficient and largest of these organizations was the left-wing Polish *Komitet Pomocy Uchodźców* (Committee for Aid to Refugees), which had about 60 employees and was led by a well-respected lawyer named I. Zagórski.[24] This was the only relief agency that took care of all refugees regardless of their ethnicity and included representatives of all the city's major ethnic groups. In addition, several large international relief agencies, notably the International Red Cross, the JDC, and the Hoover Committee sent representatives to Vilnius. They began negotiations with the Lithuanian government.[25]

The Lithuanian government did not expect a humanitarian crisis on such a scale. Its main priority was to carry out a rapid administrative and economic integration of the region. This was evident in the decision to move some government offices into Vilnius as early as October and November 1939 and in the establishment of local branches of Maistas and Pieno Centras, the largest state food-processing companies, whose task was to ensure a steady supply of food for the local residents.[26] Having seen the lengthy queues in front of the shops in Vilnius, the government introduced food rationing.[27]

Notwithstanding the economic hardships which did little to ensure its popularity, the Lithuanian government tried to gain the political loyalty of the local population during the first two months of its rule in Vilnius. Many Jews and Belorussians viewed the appearance of Lithuanian troops in the city as a welcome relief from the rigid policies pursued by the Soviets in late September–early October 1939. During the All Souls Day celebrations on 1 November, Lithuanian troops even placed a guard of honor at the tomb of Józef Piłsudski. According to one Polish observer, this gesture was intended "to win over Polish society."[28]

The serious challenge posed by the refugee crisis was reflected in the creation of a Department of War Refugees in the Ministry of the Interior.[29] In the middle of December the Lithuanian Foreign Ministry urged the government to assume full control of the relief work as "a pressing matter."[30] Against this background the government welcomed the offer made by the International Red Cross, JDC, and Hoover Committee to provide altogether about \$100,000 per month, on condition that Lithuania add \$50,000 from its own funds for the relief of refugees.

What motives led the government to accept this offer of international aid? According to one official report, "the government does not regard the proposal as a matter of funding refugee relief, but as a very useful economic deal, which might be compared to an export premium. Even the possibility of obtaining 7.2 million litai in hard currency annually would be of great significance for our economy."[31] Furthermore, Lithuania's acceptance of the deal "would be politically advantageous for our international prestige and reputation." Besides humanitarian reasons, then, economic and political considerations were seen as significant.

The international credibility of Lithuania was soon put to a test when the existence of concentration camps for refugees came to light. The Lithuanian Refugee Law of 9 December 1939 envisaged these camps as a means of controlling "refugees who are a danger to public order."[32] The camps, such as that in Žagarė, became an embarrassment for the government.[33] British radio reported that "Lithuania is preparing to force all its Polish refugees into concentration camps," a view that the government found disturbing.[34] In April 1940 the Polish government-in-exile concluded that the Polish population in the Vilnius region faced a "tragic" situation. Max Huber, the secretary of the International Red Cross, even accused Lithuania of conducting a "policy of terror against its refugees."[35]

The Lithuanian Red Cross expressed its concern about the one-sided publications in the local press, which devoted more attention to punitive aspects of the Refugee Law than to the government's relief efforts.[36] It urged the government to bring into line those who advocated giving support exclusively to Lithuanian refugees and advised that "building refugee concentration camps should be halted for the time being."[37] The government responded to these suggestions by curbing anti-Polish propaganda in the press and by relabeling the camps as "forced labor camps."[38] This shift in policy came as a result of accepting international assistance and agreeing to an increased monthly contribution of \$75,000 to the relief of refugees.[39]

By July 1940 the Lithuanian Red Cross, which in January became the central relief institution administering the war refugees, received 8 million litai (\$1,360,000) in total, of which the American JDC contributed around 3 million, the Hoover Committee 800,000, and various British agencies 1.2 million litai. The Lithuanian government provided over 2.5 million litai for the relief effort.[40]

Thus, economic and international political considerations prompted the Lithuanian government to permit external participation in the relief of Polish refugees. The internationalization of the relief effort earned Lithuania some international credibility, though it was short-lived. It confirmed Lithuania's neutrality and helped maintain an uneasy balance between its aggressive neighbors and Poland's allies in the West.

The Deepening Crisis: Newcomers

For the Lithuanian political elite the refugee crisis constituted one element of a much broader project. Throughout the interwar years Lithuanian politics and international relations had been shaped and permeated by the threat from Poland. On the diplomatic level, the Lithuanian attitude was expressed by the refusal to accept Poland's occupation of Vilnius. At a local level, it found expression in the struggle against the attempted Polonization of Lithuania. Accordingly, efforts were made to curb Polish cultural and linguistic influences throughout Lithuania and also to destroy the social basis for Polish influence.[41] Not surprisingly, the fortunes of successive governments between the wars depended on how far they could mobilize public opinion against the Polish cause. The public campaign to regain Vilnius became a cornerstone of interwar policy; typically it found expression in the popular slogan, "*Mes be Vilniaus nenurimsim!*" ("We will not rest until Vilnius is ours!")

There was thus little doubt that the government would attempt to integrate the Vilnius region into Lithuania. In terms of the refugee issue, this meant making a clear distinction between potentially loyal citizens on the one hand and those who could not be integrated on the other. Only people deemed to be loyal nationals would be accepted as full citizens. Having arrived in Vilnius in November 1939, the chief representative of the Lithuanian government noted that: "We inherited a very difficult legacy. Here, in Vilnius, there is a mixture of everything: demoralized soldiers of the former Polish army, partisans, freed criminals, various refugees from everywhere without any future, adventurers, foreign agents . . ."[42] An editorial in the government daily *Lietuvos žinios* (*Lithuanian News*) offered a similar assessment and proposed a program of action:

> Eventually we need to clarify who is a local resident and who is a stranger. We have to treat differently the locals whose biographies will need to be checked by the state and the newcomers, namely the war refugees, imported from the Polish interior. . . . The people of this kind have to be . . . isolated from local life . . . because they are a foreign element that might be very dangerous.[43]

The public campaign went hand-in-hand with the rapid Lithuanization of Vilnius. Lithuanian became the sole official language. Polish social and educational institutions were closed down, including Stepan Bator University, where several hundred Polish professors and staff lost their jobs. Polish street and shop signs were removed and property requisitioned by the Lithuanian government.[44] The municipal police force was disbanded and Polish officials were replaced by ethnic Lithuanians. Particularly at risk were former Polish officials who had settled in Vilnius following Želigowski's coup in October 1920. They became a new target of the Lithuanian press exhilarated by the takeover of Vilnius. As *Lietuvos Žinios* wrote, "it is not only refugees who create a difficult problem. Vilnius has so many so-called newcomers, who, according to Lithuanian law, are foreigners."[45]

It did not take long for the government to impose restrictions on Poles who had settled in the Vilnius region between 1920 and 1939. Officially these settlers were now described as *ateiviai* or "newcomers." The law of 20 March 1940 denied them any prospect of Lithuanian citizenship. They were obliged to register as war refugees, but, unlike others in this category, their residence permits debarred them from receiving official assistance.[46] In addition, they were prohibited from traveling freely, buying property, working (except in agriculture and the forest industry), and joining any political organizations.

According to the Lithuanian Red Cross, in February 1940 these "newcomers" numbered around 150,000 in the entire Vilnius region, including 83,000 in Vilnius itself.[47] Around two fifths were workers, one quarter were former Polish government officials and members of the free professions, and the remainder were Polish ex-employees or pensioners of the railway, schools, and post office.[48] The government dismissed approximately 7,000 former state employees while 12,000 lost their jobs "for various reasons." On the eve of the Soviet annexation of Lithuania, Vilnius alone was home to around 100,000 newcomers, including 85,000 Poles, 10,000 Jews, and 5,000 Belorussians and Russians.[49]

According to international law, the imposition of these disabilities on people who had resided for more than ten years in the same location constituted an illegal act. However, the government took no notice. A confidential report prepared by the Lithuanian Red Cross claimed that:

> The sudden addition [of 100,000 newcomers] to our somewhat disloyal Poles or the Polonized [Lithuanians] is a heavy burden to Lithuania. If Lithuania were a larger, richer and stronger state, then it could absorb this element which is unpleasant, hungry, totally unproductive and unstable. . . . They are a well-known and absolutely harmful element, which the Lithuanian nation should avoid as much as it can.[50]

Evidently, the government believed the newcomers to be a much more serious danger than the war refugees, whom it perceived as unorganized, homeless, and rootless victims of war, whereas the newcomers formed a "rooted" and tightly knit community which included members of the Polish intelligentsia known for their political disloyalty to Lithuania. According to a secret report, "the Polish newcomers feel already at home here. Many of them believe that they are on a great mission on Poland's behalf."[51]

The Lithuanian Secret Service (*Saugumas*) closely followed the political mood and activities of the Poles in Vilnius. It identified four major political groupings among the local Poles. The first group was the largest and included people who had no serious ties with the former Polish state. They were represented by such newspapers as *Gazeta codzienna* (10,000 subscribers) and *Nowe słowo rolnicze* (12,000). According to Saugumas, these people comprised "the central objective of our policy." The second, smaller group, represented by the paper *Kurjer wilenski,* included former Polish university teachers and government officials. They were "politically unreliable." The newcomers constituted a third grouping, "politically the most disloyal to Lithuania." The report continued that "under certain conditions this element can form itself into an anti-Lithuanian military organization. Therefore they must be controlled not by political, but by police means." The last and smallest group was that of the Polish war refugees who "are not a political object and can be dealt with solely by technical and police means."[52]

Vilnius's political life in early 1940 included a small group formed around Professor Michał Römer, who was well known for his loyalty to the Lithuanian state as well as his sympathies toward Lithuania's Polish population. He convened a small discussion club of intellectuals, including some old Vilnius autonomists (*krajowcy*) and Lithuanian intellectuals. They argued that local Poles had a separate local identity (*tutejszosc*) and that "the aim of state policy should not be segregation along ethnic lines but rather to give a chance for all to become Lithuanians in the civic sense of the word." Unfortunately, this group had a very limited popular following.[53] The government took no serious notice of their proposals to tackle the refugee crisis by a more liberal approach.

By the beginning of 1940 the material conditions of the newcomers had become critical. Having lost their jobs and property and exhausted their savings, they turned increasingly to various relief agencies. According to the Lithuanian Red Cross:

> The condition of the newcomers is far more critical than that of the Polish war refugees. . . . More than 65,000 of the newcomers need food, housing, clothing or medical care. Belorussians and Russians fare no better. Jewish refugees are doing somewhat better since they had worked as artisans and traders, not as state officials. . . . The Jews also receive . . . much more help from abroad.[54]

The Lithuanian Red Cross tried to help the Polish newcomers through a special "Supervisory Committee for the Polish Newcomers" which received most of its funds from various British relief agencies and from the Polish government-in-exile via the Hoover Committee. In total, the Committee received 1.5 million litai ($255,000): 500,000 litai from the Lithuanian Red Cross, 800,000 from the Hoover Committee, and 200,000 from the Polish-British Relief Agency.[55] Even so, the relief effort suffered from a shortage of funds: Jurkūnas-Šeinius warned that at least 300,000 litai per month were needed to avoid a worsening of the crisis.[56]

Lithuania's decision to segregate and disenfranchise the long-term Polish residents in the Vilnius region greatly inflamed the refugee crisis there. By 1940 Lithuania was home to more than 100,000 refugees. For a small state with a fragile economy this was a heavy burden. Furthermore, the government's decision to remove their citizenship rights and social security was a hostile act that only served to foster their mistrust and political disloyalty. This, in turn, allowed local right-wing extremists to accuse the government of insufficient energy in dealing with the Poles.

Ethnic Conflict and Refugee Relief

After October 1939, the Polish–Lithuanian ethnic conflict in the Vilnius region was transformed from an interstate and minority–majority conflict into a clash between the Lithuanian state and the Polish newcomers and war refugees. The state gave the refugee crisis a clear ethnic overtone: the Poles were targeted as a disloyal element, while the Jewish refugees were seen as politically neutral.

Without a doubt Lithuanian public opinion played an important part in pouring oil on the fire and bringing about a gradual change in official policy. The government found it increasingly difficult to control radical voices. The Lithuanian Red Cross pointed out that many Lithuanian officials who moved from Kaunas into the Vilnius region in 1939 lacked any understanding of its multicultural character. They were inclined to embrace radical slogans and policies.[57]

The most radical attack against the local Poles, refugees included, came from Lithuanian nationalists. As early as October 1939, the newspaper *Lietuvos aidas* (*Lithuania's Echo*) warned that "Vilnius's Poles have already received orders 'from the top' and they hope according to the old Klaipėda recipe to organize a separate Polish community in Lithuania."[58] Public organizations such as the Society of the First Lithuanian Army Volunteers openly urged the government to incarcerate refugees in labor camps or to employ them on public works.[59] Not surprisingly, the most vehement view was expressed by right-wing youths. The newly reopened Vilnius University became a hotbed of radical student societies such as Ramovė, Neo Lithuania, and Geležinis vilkas (Iron Wolf) which conducted "patriotic" activity designed "to spread Lithuanianness in those areas most damaged by the propaganda of the occupiers."[60] On 7 April 1940 these societies staged a riot and carried out attacks on Poles in city cafés and streets.[61] Even moderate Lithuanian Social Democrats wrote of the refugees that "this element, having lost its equilibrium, is irreparably terrorist [*diversiškas*]. At the current time it is ready to take any risks."[62]

Although the government refused to cave in to radical opinion, it was difficult to ignore the calls to Lithuanize. The tensions were most evident in the state's efforts to organize relief work by giving preference to those agencies that seemed to be politically most loyal and by putting pressure on those seeking to pursue a more independent-minded agenda.

The main attack came against *Polski komitet ofiarów wojny* (the Polish War Victim Relief Committee), which included several leading Polish intellectuals and had 25 branches in the Vilnius region.[63] One official observed that "in (the Polish Committee) there are people who aim not only to help the needy, but also . . . to conduct Polish propaganda in order to keep all the Poles together and . . . to strengthen their spirit."[64] The government tried to take control of its administration and funding by including a number of pro-Lithuanian officials in its structure, but the Polish Committee refused to accept them and protested not only to the central authorities in Kaunas but also to international bodies.[65] Eventually the government agreed not to close it but reduce the number of local branches and insisted on taking full control of its finances. Official support was given instead to the aforementioned *Komitet pomocy uchodźców,* run by Polish liberals who (as one official put it) "seemed to be totally loyal people."[66]

The second target of the state's attempt to take full control of relief became the Polish Red Cross in Vilnius. This was one of the oldest institutions in the city involved in the refugee relief work. Polish activists in the city lobbied the international relief agencies to give the Polish Red Cross full responsibility over the ethnically Polish refugees, but the Lithuanian government refused to accept this proposal, preferring instead to concentrate relief efforts in the hands of the Lithuanian Red Cross. Eventually the Polish community had to accept the closure both of the Polish Red Cross and the *Polski Komitet Ofiarów Wojny.*[67]

Understandably, in the minds of local Poles the legacy of the interwar conflict remained very much alive. According to the Polish historian Lewandowska ". . . the Poles did not understand the intentions of the new government and viewed it with . . . disdain."[68] On 31 October 1939 Vilnius witnessed street riots that involved refugees. The Lithuanian police reported that some Jewish food stores were sacked by a hungry mob. Twenty-three people were wounded and three arrested.[69] It was described as a full-scale anti-Jewish pogrom; according to one Polish observer, it was prompted by the desire of Poles to seek revenge against pro-Soviet Jews.[70] Another plausible explanation is that many local Jews welcomed the Lithuanian takeover, which produced anger among the Poles. The Lithuanian police reacted sharply to the pogrom and also forcibly dispersed the Poles who gathered the following day to commemorate All Soul's Day and march to the tomb of Piłsudski.[71]

One Polish observer summed up the political situation in Vilnius as follows: "Lithuanians do not feel strong enough to conduct a decisive policy in Vilnius, but at the same time they feel uncomfortable about the strongly patriotic mood of the Polish city populace."[72] Some 40 Polish organizations worked on behalf of Polish interests in Vilnius. They included organizations such as *Koła Pułkowe* (Regimental Circles), *Komisariat rządu* (Government Council), *Związek Bojowników Niepodległośći* (The Union of Independence Fighters) and many others covering the entire spectrum of interwar Polish politics. At least one of these, the socialist *Wolność* (Freedom), was established entirely by Polish refugees from central Poland.[73]

Refugees were actively recruited by Vilnius-based Poles, who regarded them as a reliable and politically loyal element. Polish radicals and others conducted a propaganda campaign among the refugees and took it upon themselves to speak on their behalf in politics. In January and February 1940, the Lithuanian Secret Service arrested 168 members of the semi-military Polish Fighting Organization (PFO, Polish: *Organizacija Polska Wojskowa*), but this formed only part of the Polish resistance to Lithuania. The PFO was well organized, with separate sections devoted to intelligence, surveillance, recruitment, radio contacts, and technical support. The Lithuanian historian Aldona Žepkaitė has claimed that it had ties with the Polish government-in-exile in Britain and France.[74]

Thus, between November 1939 and January 1940, official policy toward the refugees started to shift from one of broadly humanitarian assistance to one of strict control and "security." Although the government tried to steer a middle way between a radicalized Lithuanian public and an increasingly angry Polish population, its policy toward the Vilnius Poles, refugees included, became increasingly repressive. This change was reflected in the replacement of Antanas Merkys by Kazys Bizauskas as the chief Government Representative in Vilnius at the end of November 1939.[75]

Lithuania sought to obtain international support from the Western allies for its tough policy. Lithuanian diplomats lobbied embassies and international relief agencies in order to put pressure on the Polish government-in-exile and the Polish underground in Vilnius. A spokesman for the Polish Relief fund, H. F. Anderson, addressed a meeting of Polish refugee journalists and intellectuals and urged them "to stop any activities that could be harmful to the Lithuanians. The sole aim of the refugees should be to survive and find shelter."[76] He claimed British support for Lithuania's refugee policy on the grounds that the Kaunas government sought primarily to alleviate the plight of the refugees. A Lithuanian diplomat in London also reported that Britain supported Lithuania's efforts to strengthen its position in the Vilnius region.[77]

The hardening of Lithuanian policy was also inspired by pressure from Nazi Germany, which became increasingly hostile to the pro-Polish underground movement in Vilnius. The Nazi governor of East Prussia, Erich Koch, expressed his displeasure at the Polish organizations in Vilnius that were also active in occupied Poland.[78]

Anderson urged Lithuania to use refugees as cheap labor in public works programs. In a meeting with an official Lithuanian representative in Vilnius, he noted "this would be useful to Lithuania because you can build more good roads using their cheap labour, while the *newcomers* will be kept busy and quiet and will earn some cash for their tobacco." He even offered to provide food for the forced laborers from the funds of the Polish Relief Fund so long as Lithuania supplied tools and technical equipment.[79]

In due course the government introduced a forced labor scheme. A labor camp was established in Pabradė, north of Vilnius, housing refugees who had been arrested or deported from Vilnius for their political activities.[80] In Žagarė, too, thousands of refugees were put to work digging dolomite, clearing stones from fields, and repairing roads. They were also graciously "loaned" to the other Baltic states; Estonia, for instance, received 1,500 refugees from Vilnius for agricultural work.[81]

The End of the Crisis

The government's policy toward refugees, including newcomers, besides having as its main aim the wish "to neutralize refugees politically and to reduce economic costs of their support," was also designed to reduce their numbers.[82] The government attempted to achieve this by their repatriation, emigration, and a systematic transfer from Vilnius to the surrounding province. To be sure, Vilnius was overcrowded with refugees, making relief work difficult, while living costs were lower in the Lithuanian countryside. The unemployment rate was high and refugees were expected to find better employment opportunities outside the city. The dispersion of the newcomers was also regarded as a means to improve "security."[83]

Ultimately the government established more than 50 refugee camps to which refugees were transferred. Žagarė alone housed about 2,000 refugees. The transfer of people started in the middle of March 1940. Those who refused forfeited support from the Lithuanian Red Cross and could be jailed for up to six months.[84] However, the forceful relocation had only limited success, insofar as only 5,200 refugees had been moved to the camps by June.[85]

Not surprisingly, the policy provoked a harsh reaction from the refugees as well as from the international press. Most refugees tried to evade the roundup by hiding or changing their place of residence. Staying in the city at least provided a modicum of anonymity and freedom as well as strengthening a sense of community. Thus the refugees tried to circumvent the repressive government measures designed to create a controlled contingent of purely passive recipients of relief.

Trying to reduce further the number of refugees, Lithuania decided in March 1940 to free interned soldiers who were residents of the Vilnius region and to return to the USSR and Germany those who had lived in those countries before the war.[86] This repatriation was coordinated with the Western powers, which agreed in principle but in practice would repatriate only those who wished to leave. Britain and France objected to the return of those who could be used as soldiers or forced laborers by the Wehrmacht. Nevertheless, Lithuania went ahead and shipped to Germany about 5,000 refugees, among them 1,500 of the internees.[87] The government also tried to return Jews to Nazi-occupied Poland but the German representative in Kaunas replied that their return "is out of the question" (*kommt nicht in Frage*). The Soviet Union accepted about 3,000 refugees and internees. Finally, Lithuania tried to convince the U.S.A., Sweden, Norway, and Argentina to accept some of its refugees, but these countries turned down the offer, referring the government to their immigration restrictions.[88]

The government also promoted the voluntary emigration of the refugees by providing them with necessary visas. Some Jews managed to leave Lithuania via Latvia and Scandinavia to the West or to Palestine. For the majority of the Polish refugees, however, travel through Scandinavia became impossible because the Scandinavian countries agreed to a German request not to allow their transfer to the West.[89]

On 8 May 1940, the pro-government *Lietuvos žinios* reported that "there are no more refugees in Vilnius . . . Some left for the provinces, others were repatriated, while others have gone to Estonia."

The final chapter of the refugee crisis took place with the Soviet occupation of Lithuania on 15 June 1940. Many refugees received permission to return to Vilnius, while others moved to the Soviet interior. According to the new refugee registration by the Soviet Lithuanian government, 18,000 refugees still remained in Lithuania.[90] Most of these were offered Soviet citizenship. Those who refused for various reasons were arrested and deported.[91] The Soviet authorities continued to select and sift the refugees by refusing citizenship to those deemed to be "class enemies." Thus ethnicity gave way to class as a means of drawing distinctions between citizens and noncitizens.

Conclusion

The influx of refugees from Poland into Lithuania in 1939 created a humanitarian crisis which coincided with other dramatic developments such as the loss of Klaipėda in March 1939 and the unexpected acquisition of Vilnius in October 1939. The refugee crisis put a heavy burden on Lithuania that could be alleviated only with foreign help. By making the crisis an international issue, Lithuania tried not only to resolve the humanitarian problem, but also to gain international credibility and economic advantage. The Lithuanian government saw refugee relief as a profitable and risk-free venture that could improve the struggling national economy.

However, refugee relief was only of secondary importance for the Lithuanian government, whose first priority was to incorporate the Vilnius region, a contested borderland between Poland and Lithuania. Social and cultural integration entailed de-Polonization and Lithuanization of the ethnically mixed territory. The old Polish–Lithuanian ethnic conflict provided an additional dimension to the refugee crisis insofar as refugees and the largest ethnic minority, the Poles, were regarded as people from a historically alien state.

The government's decision to isolate those who had come to Lithuania between 1920 and 1939 (the so-called newcomers) greatly expanded the refugee crisis. In brief, the government used the arrival of war refugees to settle political scores with the local Poles. In this way, the refugee crisis became a political instrument for staging ethnic conflict. More than 83,000 Poles became "newcomers" after their residence and political rights were removed in the Vilnius region in March 1940. By this move, the government virtually transformed this large group of local population into refugees.

Against this background, the Lithuanian public and government singled out the refugees of the Polish ethnicity as an "uprooted," "disloyal," and "unreliable" element that had to be "rooted down": registered, controlled, filtered, isolated, forcibly employed, and either resettled or repatriated. The mass uprooting of the population further fostered discontent and political activism among them, which eventually led the authorities to adopt a more repressive policy. Thus between December 1939 and May 1940 Lithuania pursued a radical policy whose purpose was to contain, neutralize, and repatriate the refugees.

If initially the refugee relief was a matter of international reputation, in due course state-led humanitarian intervention came to be used largely as a smokescreen for the mass uprooting of a civilian population perceived as politically disloyal. The refugees' political loyalties were verified and tested by state-controlled relief agencies led by the Lithuanian Red Cross. The centralization and bureaucratization of the relief were seen as prerequisites that could help control the refugees and increase security. Independent relief work was seen as a potential danger to the state. Nevertheless, it was more tolerated in regard to the Jewish refugees, who were largely perceived as politically neutral, unlike the Poles.

Meanwhile, the Polish refugees as well as most of the indigenous Poles in the region refused to recognize the new political reality. In their eyes, Lithuania's presence in Vilnius was only a temporary episode brought about by the war and to be rectified by the victory of the Western allies. Local Polish anti-government radicals spoke and acted on behalf of Polish refugees and tried to recruit them into their secret organizations. The Polish government-in-exile eagerly conducted anti-Lithuanian propaganda both internationally and locally. Meanwhile, the Lithuanian radical right exerted pressure on the government, calling for open attacks against the disloyal Polish element in the region. In this situation, the scope of the government's choice of policy became limited. Overall, the refugee crisis weakened the state politically and economically.

The collapse of independent Lithuania in June 1940 alleviated the refugee crisis. By this time thousands of them had been repatriated or deported to the Soviet Union and Germany, while others left for the West or were granted Soviet citizenship. As a result of changes brought about by the Second World War, the Vilnius region gradually became absorbed into Lithuania. However, the "unmixing" of the ethnically diverse population in the borderland region occurred at great cost. The first drastic step in this process was almost a complete annihilation of Lithuanian Jewry by the Nazis and their Lithuanian collaborators during 1941–1944. Meanwhile, the convergence of the refugee crisis and the ethnic conflict in 1939–1940 provided the backdrop to the subsequent mass expulsion ("evacuation") of Poles from Soviet-occupied Lithuania in 1945–1946. Despite the fact that their expulsion formed only part of the broader process of the Soviet postwar redrawing of Eastern Europe, the Soviet Lithuanian government was able to achieve what the interwar state had failed to do—to create a more ethnically homogeneous Lithuania.

NOTES

1. Regina Žepkaitė, *Vilniaus istorijos atkarpa, 1939–1940* (Vilnius: Mokslas, 1990), 110. Hereafter Žepkaitė, *Atkarpa*.
2. According to the Lithuanian census of 1923, Lithuania had a population of 2 million (without the regions of Klaipėda and Vilnius). In late 1939, after the loss of Klaipėda and acquisition of the region of Vilnius, Lithuania had a population of 2.9 million. See *Lietuvos statistikos metraštis* [*Statistical Yearbook of Lithuania*], vol. 12 (Vilnius: Centrinis statistikos biuras, 1939), 13.
3. Žepkaitė, *Atkarpa*, 118–19. The population of the Vilnius region was 482,500 by the end of 1939. See *Statistical Yearbook of Lithuania*, vol. 10, 4.
4. Formal national autonomy granted to the local Jews after the Great War was revoked by the closure of the Ministry of Jewish Affaires and the Jewish National Council in 1924. Yet the Jews were able to retain their cultural autonomy including a vast network of state-sponsored Jewish schools. See: Alfonsas Eidintas, ed., *Lithuania in European Politics: the Years of the First Republic, 1918–1940* (New York: St. Martin's Press, 1998), 134.
5. On the Polish–Lithuanian dispute see Timothy Snyder, *The Reconstruction of Nations: Poland, Ukraine, Lithuania, Belarus, 1569–1999* (New Haven, Conn.: Yale University Press, 2003); Eidintas, *Lithuania*.
6. Žepkaitė, *Atkarpa*, 111.
7. The implications for the Jewish population of Vilnius are considered by Šarūnas Liekis in "The Transfer of Vilnius District into Lithuania, 1939," *Polin: Studies in Polish Jewry* 14 (2001): 212–22.
8. Jerzy Kochanowski, "Gathering Poles into Poland" in *Redrawing Nations: Ethnic Cleansing in East-Central Europe, 1944–1948*, ed. Philippe Ther and Ana Siljak (Oxford: Rowman, 2001), 138.
9. *Lietuvos žinios* [*Lithuanian News*], 9 January 1940, 4.
10. Lietuvos centrinis valstybinis archyvas (Central State Archive of Lithuania), Collection 923, Subsection. 1, File. 1033, 327. Hereafter, LCVA, Collection Nr., Subsection (S.), File (F.).
11. *Lietuvos žinios*, 9 January 1940, 4.
12. *Lietuvos žinios*, 9 January 1940, 4. "Warsawization" most likely meant overcrowding of the city.
13. LCVA 317, S. 1, F. 2, 151.
14. LCVA 317, S. 1, F. 2, 151.
15. Stanisława Lewandowska, *Życie codzienne Wilna w latach II wojny światowej* (Warsaw: Neriton, 1997), 28–9.
16. A Report of the Lithuanian Secret Service (*Saugumas*), 23 February 1940, LCVA 383, S. 7, F. 2234, 69–75.
17. According to the Polish census of 1931, 66 percent of the city population were Poles, 28 percent Jews, 4 percent Russians, 1 percent Lithuanians, and 1 percent Belorussians. However, in the census the Polish authorities replaced the question of nationality with two separate questions of "religion worshipped" and "language spoken at home." This fact led to numerous protests by Lithu-

anians and Jews that their actual numbers were misrepresented. See *Drugi Powszechny Spis Ludności z dnia 9 XII 1931 roku* (Warsaw: Główny Urząd Statystyczny, 1931), 34.

18. LCVA 317, S. 1, F. 2, 33.

19. LCVA 317, S. 1, F. 10, 37.

20. "Karo atbėgėliams tvarkyti įstatymas," *Vyriausybės žinios* [*Government News*], 9 December 1939.

21. Žepkaitė, *Atkarpa,* 49. M. W. Beckelman noted that about 10,000 of the city population left Vilnius during the Soviet evacuation of the city in late October. See LCVA 317, S. 1, F. 2, 191.

22. LCVA 317, S. 1, F. 2, 114.

23. The number of 12,000 also included those Jewish refugees who did not register with the Lithuanian government. See LCVA 317, S. 1, F. 2, 192.

24. Žepkaitė, *Atkarpa,* 50. An official report described I. Zagórski as a highly popular activist of the PPS (*Polska Partia Socjalistyczna*). It also noted that he was a loyal supporter of the Lithuanian government. See LCVA 393, S. 1, F. 1033, 307.

25. LCVA 393, S. 1, F. 1033, 307; LCVA 317, S. 1, F. 2, 152.

26. Gediminas Vaskėla, *Lietuva 1939–1940 metais* (Vilnius: Lietuvos istorijos institutas, 2002), 63.

27. Vaskėla, *Lietuva,* 63.

28. Longin Tomaszewski, *Wileńszczyzna lat wojnych i okupacji, 1939–1945* (Warsaw: Rytm, 1999), 4.

29. Gintautas Surgailis, "Lenkai, antrojo pasaulinio karo atbėgėliai Lietuvoje, 1939 m. rugsėjis–1940 m. birželis" ("Polish Refugees of Second World War in Lithuania, September 1939–June 1940") in *Rytų Lietuva: istorija, kultūra, kalba,* ed. K. Garšva (Vilnius: Mokslas, 1992), 107.

30. LCVA 923, S. 1, F. 1065, 318.

31. LCVA 317, S. 1, F. 2, 109.

32. "Karo atbėgėliams tvarkyti įstatymas," *Vyriausybės žinios,* 9 December 1939.

33. LCVA 317, S. 1, F. 2, 113.

34. LCVA 317, S. 1, F. 2, 114.

35. "E. Turauskas, Pro memoria, 28 January 1940," LCVA 393, S. 1, F. 1033, 308; Žepkaitė, *Atkarpa,* 125.

36. LCVA 317, S. 1, F. 2, 110.

37. LCVA 317, S. 1, F. 2, 116.

38. LCVA 317, S.1, F. 2, 113–14. It is not clear though whether this minor change of name assuaged the international critics.

39. LCVA 923, S. 1, F. 1033, 287.

40. LCVA 757, S. 9, F. 6, 68; Surgailis, "Lenkai," 110; Vaskėla, *Lietuva,* 59, 70.

41. During the Land Reform of 1922–1926, 77 percent of the land owned by Polish landlords went into the hands of landless Lithuanian peasants and small and medium-sized landholders. See Gediminas Vaskėla, "The Land Reform of 1919–1940: Lithuania and the Countries of East and Central Europe," *Lithuanian Historical Studies* 1 (1996): 116–32.

42. *Lietuvos žinios,* 2 November 1939, 1.

43. *Lietuvos žinios,* 3 November 1939, 2.

44. Lewandowska, *Życie,* 39–41.

45. *Lietuvos žinios,* 13 December 1939, 6.

46. "Karo pabėgėlių komisaro įstatymas," LCVA 317, S. 1. F. 10, 16.

47. LCVA 393, S. 1, F. 1033, 299; LCVA 379, S. 1, F. 293, 390.

48. The data includes all family members. See "The problem of the newcomers of the Vilnius region: what is to be done by Lithuania? 5 February 1940," LCVA 379, S. 1, F. 293, 363–64.

49. Surgailis, "Lenkai," 113; LCVA 757, S. 9, F. 5, 36–7; "Pro memoria, 20 March 1940" LCVA 317, S. 1, F. 2, 13.

50. LCVA 379, S. 1, F. 293, 390.

51. LCVA 379, S. 1, F. 293, 373.

52. "V. Čečeta. Pro memoria. 13 April, 1940," LCVA 393, S. 11, F. 1033, 235–36.

53. "V. Čečeta. Pro memoria. 13 April, 1940," LCVA 393, S. 11, F. 1033, 237. On Vilnius' autonomists before 1939 See Rimantas Miknys, *Lietuvos demokratų partija 1902-1915 metais* (Vilnius: Vilniaus universiteto leidykla, 1995).

54. "Lenkų ateivių būklė. 12 July 1940," LCVA 379, S. 1, F. 293, 358.

55. "Atbėgėliams šelpti komiteto apyskaita, June 1940," LCVA 379, S. 1, F. 293, 433.

56. LCVA 379, S. 1, F. 293, 360.

57. "Dar ir dar dėl nusiskundimų, 15 January 1940," LCVA 317, S. 1, F. 2, 119-23.

58. *Lietuvos aidas,* 11 October 1939; Lewandowska, *Życie,* 34.

59. LCVA 923, S. 1, F. 1032, 22. The Polish historian Stanisława Lewandowska has also claimed that "Lithuanians from the very beginning formed a negative attitude towards refugees." See Lewandowska, *Życie,* 34.

60. Žepkaitė, *Atkarpa,* 115. *Ramovė* (literally "imperturbability") is a pagan place of worship.

61. Žepkaitė, *Atkarpa,* 115. Žepkaitė quotes secret data collected by the Lithuanian Secret Police. See also, LCVA 378, S. 10, F. 225, 428, 462, 479.

62. *Mintis* [*The Thought*], November 1939, No. 10, 333.

63. "Komitet Polski bandymai kištis į lenkų pabėgėlių šelpimo darbą. 13 March 1940," LCVA 317, S. 1, F. 2, 18-19.

64. "Komitet Polski bandymai kištis į lenkų pabėgėlių šelpimo darbą. 13 March 1940," LCVA 317, S. 1, F. 2, 18-19.

65. "Komitet Polski bandymai kištis į lenkų pabėgėlių šelpimo darbą. 13 March 1940," LCVA 317, S. 1, F. 2, 18-19.

66. "Pabėgėlių šelpimo reikalai Vilniuje. 6 December 1939," LCVA 317, S. 1, F. 2, 152.

67. LCVA 317, S. 1, F. 2, 118.

68. Lewandowska, *Życie,* 31.

69. Lewandowska, *Życie,* 31.

70. Tomaszewski, *Wileńszczyzna,* 52.

71. Tomaszewski, *Wileńszczyzna,* 53.

72. *Armia Krajowa w dokumentach, 1939-1945,* vol. 1 (London: Studium Polski Podziemnej, 1970), 68.

73. Tomaszewski, *Wileńszczyzna,* 74.

74. Žepkaitė, *Atkarpa,* 114. Among those arrested were 11 Polish war refugees and more than 40 newcomers.

75. Tomaszewski, *Wileńszczyzna,* 55.

76. "Trimako pasikalbėjimas su Linskiu, 7 February 1940," LCVA 317, S. 1, F. 2, 82.

77. LCVA 383, S. 7, F. 188, 532.

78. Žepkaitė, *Atkarpa,* 119; LCVA 383, S. 7, F. 2244, 11-12.

79. "Pro memoria: Trimako pasikalbėjimas su Andersonu, 2 March 1940," LCVA 393, S. 1, F. 1033, 242.

80. Surgailis, "Lenkai," 108.

81. Surgailis, "Lenkai," 112.

82. LCVA 393, S. 1, F. 1033, 288.

83. "Pabėgėlių dislokacijos klausimu, 20 March 1940," LCVA 317, S. 1, F. 2, 13.

84. Surgailis, "Lenkai," 113-14.

85. LCVA 757, S. 9, F. 5, 242.

86. "Pro memoria: internuotųjų ir pabėgėlių reikalu. 29 March 1940," LCVA 393, S. 1, F. 1033, 282.

87. "Pro memoria: internuotųjų ir pabėgėlių reikalu. 29 March 1940," LCVA 393, S. 1, F. 1033, 283.

88. "Pro memoria: internuotųjų ir pabėgėlių reikalu. 29 March 1940," LCVA 393, S. 1, F. 1033, 283.

89. "Pro memoria, 7 February 1940," LCVA 317, S. 1, F. 2, 83.

90. Surgailis, "Lenkai," 114.

91. Surgailis, "Lenkai," 115.

14

THE YOUNG TURKS AND THE PLANS FOR THE ETHNIC HOMOGENIZATION OF ANATOLIA

TANER AKÇAM

The French historian F. Braudel notices: "first one encounters the question of borders . . . everything else is derived from this. In order to draw a border, it is necessary to define it, to understand it, and reconstruct what that border means; beyond that it means to claim for itself a certain historical aspect."

—Hagen Schulze

Introduction

Turkey's borders have changed dramatically over the last two centuries—swelling and shrinking as the Ottoman Empire rose and then declined, and as different national states emerged in the empire's regions. This change in geographical borders necessitated a shift in thinking in Turkey. The logic of nation states is in total contradiction to the idea of empire. For a nation state you need, ideally, a homogeneous population, and a defined territory. This can be created only with a clear knowledge of what this homogeneity consists and who belongs to it. As a natural consequence of the logic, what follows is the "purification" of those who do not belong to that collective in the defined region.

In the process of nation building, it is not enough to have a territory and homogeneous population. In addition to these two criteria, which are called ethno-cultural or religiously "objective" criteria, a nation needs also a common memory. A collective memory is one of the building blocks of the "imagined" nation and the ensuing nation state. To achieve this, the history of the nation has to be rewritten in a unique way so as to create a common reflection of the group through time, a collective memory. In other words, the people must *remember* themselves as being one.

Two different "borders" are critical to forge a definition that clearly solves the questions of what and who constitute a nation. First, how is cultural identity to be defined? Second, how are the boundaries of the nation state to be drawn? The thesis that there must somehow be a relation between the borders of cultural identity and the state emerges as something new in the nineteenth century. Nationalists argued that both identities are somehow identical and this is the reason why "the people" have to establish their own state within supposedly natural borders.

Turkish national identity has been shaped gradually through the tension of these two different border issues. The homogenization of Anatolia was a response to this tension. In that sense my approach can also be described as an attempt to understand nationalism from a different angle. Throughout previous decades of research, scholars tended to define nationalism mostly as fixed, objective, and primordial. They now agree that nationalism is mostly the product of hard work on the part of intellectuals, political actors, and propagandists, who have applied their energies to the mapping of differences and boundaries. Turkish nationalism must be conceived as a "being" process. There were no clear-cut definitive objective or subjective determinants defining the nation. Rather, the pragmatic necessities of saving the state were important for the nationalists. In essence, the state made the nation.

The boundaries of the Turkish national identity moved and changed parallel to the shrinking borders of the Empire. When the Committee of Union and Progress (CUP, or, informally, the Young Turks) came to power in 1908, the party at first intended to preserve the Empire's multiethnic character. The Young Turks combined the principle of universal citizenship with a cultural identity that could be defined as Ottomanism, but which in practice was a mandate for an Islamic-Turkish identity. They claimed Ottomanism was an overarching identity that also covered the Christians of the Empire. However, popular resistance to this policy, and the loss of several territories before World War I (see chapter 8), gradually led the CUP to narrow the scope and so the borders of this definition. After 1913, the party adopted the concept of a Turkic-Islamic synthesis as its official ideology and implemented it to exclude religious and ethnic minorities within the Empire and to include Muslims and Turkic peoples outside the country's borders.

Another important characteristic of the CUP was its highly pragmatic attitude in regard to ideology. While Ottomanism, Islamism, and Turkism were the main intellectual currents of the day, the CUP used these terms interchangebly.[1] This pragmatism allowed the leaders to jump from one ideology to another in order to best serve their purposes. Ziya Gökalp articulated the theoretical framework for this pragmatism. He developed an ideology based on an "Islamic-Turkish-Western" synthesis that became the official Unionist rhetoric, and was produced and repeated according to occasion and need.[2]

The Young Turks were true social engineers in that they moved populations of non-Turkish Muslims around the region in order to keep them from forming a critical mass and to facilitate their assimilation. However, outwardly they were Islamist, considering their non-Turkish Muslim citizens inside their borders (and also including those outside their borders) to be their brothers. This tension stemmed from the desire to keep the Empire extant, and it naturally disappeared when the Republic came into being, because the idea of a nation state superseded the need to keep the Empire intact.

During the nineteenth and early twentieth centuries, territories were lost at the fringes of the Ottoman Empire, mostly due to the nationalist movements of Christian subjects of the Empire, which were supported by the Great Powers (Britain, France, Germany, and Russia). As a consequence, Christian subjects began to be identified as "Others" and excluded from the Ottoman identity. This was followed by expulsions of Christians from certain regions. As the loss of territories from the fringes toward the center of the empire accelerated, so did this process of the exclusion of "Others." The Christians located in the center of the region, such as the Greeks and Armenians, were regarded as much more dangerous than those living in the fringe regions. For this reason, the violence they experienced was more severe.

The loss of territories with the concomitant shrinking of geographical borders was crucial for the emergence of Turkish national identity. In order to grasp the extent of this shrinking, imagine an Ottoman Empire that maintained about 100 square kilometers of territory throughout nearly the entire eighteenth century. Between the beginning of the nineteenth century and the Balkan War, a mere one hundred years, this mini-Empire would have lost 60 square kilometers., and between the Balkan War and the end of World War I, it lost an additional 35 square kilometers, a 95 percent loss since its height. Indeed, in 1919 only five percent of the former Ottoman Empire was controlled by Turkey (although a few square kilometers were added during the Independence/National Liberation War of 1919–22). This is today's Turkey.[3] The speed of this loss was as extravagant as its extent. For example, in 1912, within one or two weeks 83 percent of the European territories (69 percent of the population) were lost.[4] Calculated another way, between 1878 and 1920, the Ottomans lost 85 percent of their territory and 75 percent of their population.[5]

This steady and speedy loss of land determined, for the most part, the debate around both the geographical and identity aspects of the newly defined borders. As land was lost, the idea developed among the Young Turk leadership that an expansion of the Empire could occur by including other Muslim peoples while at the same time excluding those who were considered to be responsible for the loss. The idea of Turkism or Pan-Islamism emerged as a core ideal, originating from a defensive goal of keeping the Empire as big as possible.

In this chapter I will deal with only one aspect of the above described theoretical framework; namely the plans to homogenize Anatolia. I will try to show how the Ottomon authorities used population policy to create and redefine their new "borders," and in two senses. First, in terms of geography, they defined Anatolian core lands as the "center of the Empire," and, second, in terms of culture they drew a new border between Muslims and Christians as We/Other. As a result of this dual process of redefinition, Christians were expelled from and killed in Anatolia.

The CUP Population and Resettlement Policy: Some Principal Characteristics

All the available Ottoman sources demonstrate that even before the onset of World War I, the Young Turks devised and implemented a plan to "free [ourselves] of non-Turkish elements" in the Aegean region.[6] Then, under the cover of war, the CUP expanded this plan to include all of Anatolia. The primary goal of this project, which can be described as an ethno-religious homogenization of Anatolia, was a conscious reshaping of the region's demographic character on the basis of its Turkish Muslim population. The two main pillars of the government's "population and resettlement policy" entailed a "cleansing" of Anatolia of its non-Muslim (which basically meant Christian) population, seen as a mortal threat to the continued existence of the state and even described as a "cancer" in the body of the empire, and the assimilation (read: Turkification) of all of Anatolia's non-Turkish Muslim communities.[7]

As of 1913 these policies were put into place through the exercise of the dual mechanism of parallel official and unofficial tracks, of which I shall give various examples below. The government issued orders that amounted to an official policy of expulsion and forced emigration. This policy was officially decided upon and implemented either within the ambiguous framework of "population exchanges" with other countries, such as Greece, Serbia, and Bulgaria, or as one of unilateral expulsion and deportation, such as in the case of the Armenians. At the same time, various covert, extra-legal but state-sponsored acts of terror were undertaken under the protective umbrella provided by the "official" state policies.

The CUP created an organizational structure well suited to this dual mechanism. In the main indictment against the CUP Central Committee members in their 1919 trial in Istanbul's court martial, the prosecution stated that, in line with the Unionist party's structure and working conditions, a "secret network" had been formed to carry out the CUP's illegal actions. The CUP itself, the indictment said, was an organization that "possessed two contradictory natures: the first, a visible and public [one] based on a [public] program and internal code of regulations, the other based on secrecy and [operating according to unwritten] verbal instructions."[8]

By means of these policies, which were put into practice between 1913 and 1918, the ethnic character of Anatolia was thoroughly transformed. The population of Anatolia was so completely disrupted over this six-year period that almost one-third of the total population (estimated in 1914 to be around 17.5 million people) were displaced, expelled, or annihilated.[9]

Although the Ottoman Empire (and others) possessed a lengthy history of devising and implementing population and resettlement policies, by the second half of the nineteenth century it was forced to contend with a totally new problem.[10] Large numbers of Muslims—both those from recently lost Ottoman territories and those forcibly expelled from other countries—began to flood across the now shrinking borders of the Ottoman state, many continuing well into the imperial hinterlands. In this regard, the 1912–1913 Balkan Wars must be considered both as the climax of this phenomenon and as an important turning point. Before this time, the Ottoman authorities had always attempted to solve the problem of immigration and resettlement on a reactive, ad hoc basis; now, however, the question would be considered and resolved in a systematic fashion, as a part of the overall plan for the Turkification of Anatolia. The principal characteristics of this population and resettlement policy were: ethnic censuses and map-making, registries of the assets of minority populations, assimilation of non-Turkic Muslims, deportations, and, ultimately, annihilation.[11]

I. Population Counts and Maps based on the Ethnic Construction of Anatolia

In order to be able to implement these policies properly, it was necessary first to restructure the Ottoman bureaucracy, and the Interior Ministry in particular. As a result of the forced migrations that followed the Balkan Wars the Ottoman government published, on 13 May 1913, its "Code of Regulations for the Settlement of Emigrants." The responsibility for the implementation of these regulations was left to the Interior Ministry, and, in particular, its Office of Tribal and Immigrant Settlement (*Dahiliye Nezareti İskân-ı Aşair ve Muhacir'in Müdüriyeti,* hereafter İAMM or "Settlement Office"), founded in December 1913. It went through a number of reorganizations; finally, on 14 March 1916, the government established the General Directorate of Tribal and Immigrant Settlement (*Aşair ve Muhacirin Müdiriyeti Umumiyesi,* hereafter AMMU).[12]

In parallel with these efforts at greater organization, censuses were undertaken to provide the authorities with a clearer picture of the ethnic and social makeup of Anatolia, after which demographic maps were drawn up. As is well known, the basic category of classification in Ottoman censuses was religion; as a result, the empire's Muslim population appeared as a single group. Although no official census was undertaken during the Unionist period (1908–1918), on the basis of previous counts (1882, 1895, 1905) the government further divided and reclassified the Muslim population into ethnic categories. Ottoman census officials who traveled to the empire's different provinces recorded the numbers given them by the elders of different neighborhoods and areas and the leaders of the different religious communities. In addition, every three months the central government received regular reports from the provincial counties on such statistics as births, deaths, and in- and out-migrations. On the basis of this information statistical lists and tables were prepared, even at the county level, on changes in the Muslim and non-Muslim populations. The Interior Ministry's Office of Population Registry then updated its information accordingly and passed it on to the government.[13]

Various documents show that Unionist efforts aimed at acquiring an accurate picture of the ethno-religious demographics of Anatolia preceded even the Balkan War.[14] Right afterward, by 1913 at the latest, the movements of the non-Muslim population—and in particular that of the Greek and Armenian communities—had been placed under tight control and monitoring. The communities' respective religious and local secular authorities were made responsible for "reporting to the [office of] population registry . . . [all] weddings and divorces of non-Muslims . . . [all] births, deaths and changes of locale."[15] It was also demanded that those persons in authority not carrying out their entrusted duties be punished.[16]

Moreover, the Interior Ministry sent cables marked "top secret" to various provinces requesting of the local officials that they compile "in a highly secret manner" and forward to the ministry lists of the wealth, education, and social status of the Christians in these regions, as well as of the prominent or influential members of their communities.[17] Special importance was given to the documentation of businesses and moveable and immovable property belonging to this population.

The information compiled through these efforts would become the basis for both the prewar and wartime policies of forcible removal and annihilation of Anatolia's Christian population and the settlement of Muslims in their place. Even during the tumultuous periods of forced expulsion and deportations the government expected daily reports on the changing demographics of various regions.

On the basis of these local reports officials recorded overall population changes, which served as the basis of new ethnographic maps of the empire's remaining provinces. An example of this policy in practice can be seen in the telegram, sent on 20 July 1915 by Interior Minister Talât Pasha to all provincial and district governors. In it, Talât instructs the officials to

> send, within one month, without exception, a complete and comprehensive map showing [all of] the administrative units and divisions within the province, down even to the village level, including two compiled lists containing the figures for existing [populations], both earlier and currently, on the basis of the [respective] nationalities of the population in the various towns and villages.[18]

The purpose of the "two lists" was to be able to assess the extent of demographic changes so as to better monitor and control the process of ethnic restructuring.

Even after the Armenian deportations were concluded, the Ottoman government continued to track internal population movements throughout the course of the war. For example, in an August 1916 cable to many different regions, marked "urgent and secret" and with instructions to "resolve this matter personally," Talât Pasha ordered his provincial subordinates to "quickly prepare and send a list showing separately the population figures [for] existing Greek[s] in each and every village and town within the province."[19]

II. Registries Concerning the Ethno-Social-Cultural Composition of the Population

These population reports and registries prepared by the various local officials also contained information on the socioeconomic construction of each and every major ethnic group, along with descriptions of the character of their language and culture, their manner and level of education, and their relations with the other groups. In an April 1916 cable sent by the İAMM to the province of Trabzon, the latter was asked to report on "how many Kurds were living in the province, where they were residing, the status of their relations with the Turkish population, and whether or not they were preserving their own traditions and language."[20]

An Interior Ministry cable sent to the Baghdad Governor's Office on 1 May 1916 offers some insight into just what sort of information was being gathered. After stressing the extreme importance for the government's policy of having sound and accurate information "regarding the number and social condition of the those Turks who are considered to be among the long-settled population in Iraq," the telegram went on to request the provincial officials to provide answers to the following questions:

> [H]ow many Turks are there in the other areas of the province? . . . how many Turks are there [total], [and] in which provinces, districts and counties are they registered? Are they in a comfortable majority in relation to the Arab and Kurdish population of the areas in which they live? Have they been at all influenced by the languages and customs, and if so, to what extent? What language is spoken within the family and, in regard to the local elements, to what extent are their relations with the government related to their economic status? What sort of education do they give to their children, and what language is it given in at the [educational] institutions? Are there [Turkish] families who, in their inner workings, have either come to resemble those of the Arabs or Kurds or who lean in this direction?[21]

III. Registries Regarding the Economic Conditions of the Christian Populations

Officials also requested data on the economic status and situation of the Christian communities, including reports on the occupations, workplaces, and immovable property of the individual members of these groups. Even before the outbreak of the First World War, the state gathered detailed information on the property and possessions in the hands of the empire's Christians. An Interior Ministry cable sent on 5 September 1914 to the Aydın and Trabzon provinces and the provincial district of Canik (Samsun)—all areas with sizeable Greek communities—asked for "the preparation and sending of a report clarifying the value and owners, including type and quantity, of all property and covered buildings [such as houses, business centers, shops, etc.] belonging to the Greek community."[22] Ten days later, a similar request was sent to almost all of the provinces of the empire.[23] It is clear that these orders from the central government were indeed followed in the various provinces, and that the requested reports were prepared and sent to Istanbul.[24]

It should be added here as a side-note that this detailed information gathering—particularly regarding the Greek population—was undertaken in parallel with the ongoing efforts of a commission studying the possibility of a Turkish–Greek population exchange. From different documents we can infer that these lists were being prepared for just such a contingency.[25] In a similar vein, detailed 16-point sets of instructions on how such lists should be prepared, "Instructions for Completing the Lists Regarding the Exchange of Immigrants," were sent to all of the provinces.[26]

Similar lists were prepared for the Armenian population. During the Armenian deportations the central government demanded detailed lists containing information on businesses that were either controlled or administered by Armenians, or belonged to either Istanbul Armenians or foreigners:

> [Please] report speedily, clearly and explicitly ... whether or not in Istanbul and the provinces from which the Armenians have yet to be transported there still exist Armenians merchants, or houses of commerce, real estate, factories and such that are run by Armenians, either or as local representatives of or partners in institutions owned by other Ottoman citizens or by foreigners; if so, then [also provide] the names of those who have been deported from there, as well as the names of the owners and businesses both here and abroad.[27]

The practice of keeping detailed records of Christian property and possessions continued even after the Armenian deportations. For example, a coded telegram from the İAMM's Bureau of Statistics to various provinces and districts in the Aegean region calls for

> an investigation to be conducted and information gathered on the number of farms and large land tracts in the province [district] in the hands of non-Muslims, along with their estimated size and value and the names and reputations of those with the right to them; upon the completion [of this task] and the writing of [this information] in a detailed report for each and every county, it should be sent with all haste [to the bureau].[28]

IV. The Drive to Assimilate All the Empire's Muslims

Many of the empire's Muslims had also been uprooted for a variety of reasons and forced to relocate. The main and ultimate goal of the Unionist government's population and settlement policies vis-à-vis its non-Turkish Muslim communities was one of assimilation. In order for these groups fully to meld into the Turkish majority, the logic went, they would first have to abandon their own languages and cultures. Unlike the efforts vis-à-vis the Christian communities, the government openly and clearly stated its assimilationist motive behind gathering detailed information on the social and cultural characteristics of the empire's Muslim groups.

In the event that the refugees could not be assimilated into the new communities into which they were sent, it was explained, it would be necessary to find an alternative location. The Turkish refugees and migrants being relocated, however, wanted to preserve their language and culture.

The frequent use of the terms *temsil* and *temessül,* meaning to "come to resemble" or "assimilate," makes it clear that this was indeed the primary aim of the government's Muslim settlement policy. In a coded telegram, dated 23 January 1916, to the province of Suriye, for instance, the government stated:

> As it has been communicated to the Province of Syria that it is seen as appropriate to resettle in widely dispersed manner and assimilate the Tripolitanian and Algerian immigrants who were sent to and now reside in Syria, information should be provided regarding the here-tofore-taken necessary steps for the resettlement of the aforementioned immigrants to the greatest possible extent, the undertaking of communication with the aforementioned prov-ince, the securing of their [re-]settlement and its results.[29]

In order to be able to attain its assimilationist goals, the government first had to de-termine the actual number of Muslim refugees who had fled from the combat regions of World War I and their social and cultural backgrounds. The government sent frequent cables to these regions requesting such information.[30] The investigations and inspections focused on the ethnic identities of those Muslims fleeing the war zones. In numerous telegrams, the central government asked such questions as "What is the number of Kurdish refugees fleeing the war zones? What are the names of the tribes to which they belong? How many youths or orphans are there traveling among them? Please report . . ."[31] Or: "Of those refugees coming into the province from the war zones, which cities or tribes are they Turkish, Kurdish or Ira-nian, and as for the Iranians: what city or tribe do they come from? Are they Shi'ite or Sunni [Muslims]? What language [do they speak]? To what tribe do the Kurds belong? Where [are they from], how many are they, and to where have they been sent?"[32]

Another problem that had to be resolved was to determine whether or not it was pos-sible to designate separate areas in which the Turkish and non-Turkish Muslims could be resettled. For this purpose specific questions were asked of each of the potential areas of re-settlement. Officials hoped, for example, to send Turkish refugees to the Baghdad region, and to this effect a cable was sent to the provincial administration in June 1916 asking whether or not Turkish refugees, if sent to the area, would be able to preserve their own language and national identity.[33]

The government's actions in regard to the Kurdish population demonstrate its as-similation policies toward non-Turkish Muslims. On the basis of the detailed information that has been gathered on the ethnic and cultural makeup of Central and Western Anatolia, the authorities viewed these areas as suitable for resettling some of the indigenous Kurd-ish population in order to facilitate its assimilation. In a January 1916 cable to the empire's western provinces, the İAMM stated that it has been considering "the deportation of those Kurds who have fled to the interior due to the wartime conditions to the western provinces of Anatolia." After then reporting the need for "information regarding the Kurds and Kurd-ish villages who are now in the [respective] inner province[s as a result of] earlier orders," the telegram goes on to ask "where the Kurdish villages are [and] how many there are; how many persons there are? Do they preserve their original language and customs? What are their relations like with the Turkish villagers and villages with whom they associate? Com-mence immediately with an investigation and provide a detailed report, including [personal] assessment."[34]

After areas of settlement were found that were seen as amenable to the assimilation of Muslim refugees, care was taken not to send different ethnic groups to the same loca-tions. For the displaced Kurds, for example, "The provinces of Konya, Ankara, Kastamonu and districts of Niğde, Kayseri, Kütahya, Eskişehir, Amasya and Tokat" were chosen.[35] If the number of refugees exceeded the predetermined absorptive capacity of a given province or district, the excess refugees were to be sent to other regions, not randomly but according to set criteria as to the ethnic makeup of both the refugees themselves and the destinations chosen.[36] It was prohibited to send Kurdish groups into areas of Arab or Kurdish predominance since it was understood that their assimilation into broader Turkish society would be nearly impossible within such a milieu. In situations where this had already been done or was still underway, officials ordered the process to cease immediately. The AMMU even sent such notice to War Minister Enver Pasha in a 3 May 1916 cable, informing him that "it did not appear suitable to resettle those displaced Kurds from the Eastern Provinces in districts in which there were already Kurds and Arabs present," and that the decision had therefore been rendered to "send them from the war zone into the Anatolian interior."[37]

Officials sought to keep displaced persons slated for assimilation from settling together in large groups so as to ensure that they fully abandoned their nomadic lifestyles, languages, and customs. The Kurdish refugees in particular were targeted for broad dispersal—and their traditional leaders, both religious and secular, were separated from and settled apart from their communities. In fact, this policy of "separating the nomads' leaders (sheikhs, beys, aghas) from the main group of nomads and then settling them in cities and towns"—"detaching the head from the body," as Kemal Karpat has characterized it—had actually been in existence since the nineteenth century.[38]

The principal lines of the government's Kurdish resettlement policy were stated openly in various cables sent to the provinces in May 1916. A cable sent on 4 May to the provincial districts of Urfa, Marash, and Antep, for example, states that:

> [I]t is absolutely necessary that if there are Kurdish refugees who were previously sent the members of these tribes should be separated from their leaders, with the leaders being settled in the towns and the [other] individual [member]s being dispersed in the Turkish villages that are scattered throughout the southern part of the district, two or three households per village, so that they will not all be resettled together as a group in one place; this, in order that they abandon the nomadic lifestyle that they have lived [until now], as well as their language and customs. . . .[That t]he sheikhs and imams be settled separately from the [other] members of the tribe, and that other members of the tribe should likewise be resettled in a dispersed manner and that relations between the tribal leaders, the sheikhs and the individual members should not be allowed to continue.[39]

V. IMPLEMENTING THE 5–10 PERCENT RULE

The government also sought to ensure that the Kurdish population in the new places of settlement not exceed five percent of the total population. This concern is expressed, openly and repeatedly, in many of the communications sent out to the provinces,[40] and applied equally to all non-Turkish groups without any distinction for religion. One order, for example, emphasized that "the Albanians and Bosnians [being sent to the region] be placed in a dispersed fashion among the Turkish population at ratio of 1:10."[41]

Similar actions were carried out vis-à-vis the Greek population of Bursa and its environs. In July 1916 the governor ordered the Greek immigrants in Bursa to be dispersed among the Turkish villages at a proportion not to exceed 10 percent of the total population. A subsequent report by the Greek Orthodox Church claims that [t]he governor "was simply carrying out an organised plan by the CUP, having as an object to convert them to Mohammedanism."[42]

The 5–10 percent criterion was also put in place for the Armenians. Noteworthy, however, are the differences in implementation between western and eastern Anatolia. During the period of "emptying out" Anatolia of its Armenian population, this criterion was not applied in the eastern provinces where Armenians were thick on the ground. All of the Armenians in these regions were deported without any attempts at separation or dispersion. A cable from Interior Minister Talât to the governor of Erzurum in May 1915, when the first mass deportations took place, explains this situation clearly: "since the province is on the border with Russia, according to the principle that we follow not a single Armenian is to be allowed to remain there."[43]

Similarly, another telegram to the governors' offices of the eastern provinces on 20 June 1915 informed them that "all Armenians living in the towns and villages in the province are to be deported along with their families, and without exception, and sent to the province of Mosul and the regions of Urfa and [Deyr-i] Zor."[44]

In the western provinces of Anatolia, however, where the Armenian population was not as concentrated, the policy that was followed tended to be either to leave them where they were or to subject them to an "internal dispersion" within the same province where they lived according to the 5–10 percent rule. An August 1915 coded telegram from the Security Directorate to the provincial district of Antalya, for instance, informed the local officials that "in light of their small numbers, there is at present no need to deport the Armenians from there."[45] The directorate sent another cable to the district of Çanakkale in early June advising that "if a suitable destination for deportation and resettlement within the district can be found [send them there], but if such a place cannot be found, send them to Karesi [Balıkesir]."[46]

In an August 1915 cable to the district governor of İzmit, the Security Directorate granted permission for some of the local Armenians to remain in the area on the condition that they be dispersed into the Muslim villages in the region.[47] A follow-up cable on the same day reads that "it has been reported to the High Command that the Armenian workers whose continued service at the felt factory in İzmit is currently necessary should, in light of their deportation, be settled in Muslim villages [so as to constitute no more than] five percent [of the total population] and in a manner that will not prevent their continued employment."[48]

In numerous cables, sent to the provinces at regular intervals, central government functionaries asked for current population figures for Christian communities—distinguishing Catholics from Protestants, and those slated for deportation but not yet sent from those having newly arrived after being deported from other areas. Beyond simple population counts, one of the main bits of information the authorities wished to learn was the exact percentages of the population that these various groups comprised—especially in relation to the Muslims. For example, a telegram from the Security Directorate, dated 25 August 1915 and sent to almost all of the provinces of Anatolia asked the following questions:

> How many Armenians are left within the province/provincial district who are currently being deported[?] How many Armenians are currently present there who are to be deported from the other areas to the designated regions, and where are they located[?] How many Armenians currently being deported are there on the roads, at the [train] stations and in the villages? How many Catholic and Protestant Armenians are there within the province/provincial district[?] Of these how many have already been deported and how many are there at this moment? What are the separate percentages of remaining Protestant and Catholic

[Armenians] vis-a-vis the Muslim population[?] It is of urgent import that a reply [to these questions] be sent off within no later than three days.[49]

At the outset of the mass deportations, a decision was made to ensure that the 5–10 percent rule was adhered to in the newly resettled areas. The Ottoman Ministry of War, in a memo to the Interior Ministry on 26 May 1915, stated that "the Armenian population must not exceed 10% of the number of [nomadic] tribal and Muslim inhabitants of the place to which they are sent."[50]

Orders were subsequently sent to the provinces along the lines of this decision. Cables relayed to a great number of provincial and local administrative officials on 5 July 1915 defined the borders of the new areas designated for the resettlement of the Armenians, then added the reminder that the Armenians should be settled in these areas at a level of 10 percent of the [total] Muslim population."[51]

Special care would continue to be given to the question of population ratios in the resettlement of Armenian deportees. In a cable to the province of Aleppo on 8 September 1915 the Security Directorate advised that

> the wholesale acceptance of [all] the Armenians sent there from various locales and their resettlement in the [provincial] center and periphery is not acceptable since it will subsequently result in them forming a relative majority in this area," and therefore, "they should be constantly monitored from this consideration and all of those [Armenian deportees] apart from those who have arrived already should not be sent to the interior of the province and instead be sent to the area around Urfa.[52]

Information regarding the 5–10 percent criterion for resettlement can also be found in the German and American documentation. In his report of 30 December 1915, the American Consul in Harput, Leslie Davis, states that "of nearly a hundred thousand Armenians who were in this Vilayet a year ago, there are probably not more than four thousand left. It has been reported recently that not more than five per cent of the Armenians were to be left. It is doubtful if that many remain now."[53]

Rössler, the German Consul in Aleppo, gave similar information in a report from 27 April 1916. Regarding the provincial district of Deyr-i Zor, he wrote that

> according to what I have learned from a Turkish officer who arrived from Deyr-i Zor on 20 April 1916, the District Governor of the Deyr-i Zor provincial district received orders to leave [only enough] Armenians so that they would make up [no more than] 10% of the [total] local population while the rest should be sent further on to Mosul. The population of Deyr-i Zor can be estimated at about 20,000 souls. It is said that at least 15,000 of these are Armenians who were sent there, meaning that at least 13,000 of them will have to be deported [to somewhere else].[54]

In his report of 29 July 1916 Rössler informed the German Embassy that on the seventeenth of the month the Armenians in the Deyr-i Zor district had received the order to leave the region, since the central government had decided that Armenians should comprise no more than 10 percent of the district's population. The consul added that "it would be necessary to annihilate those who were left over." In line with this goal the then-district governor of Deyr-i Zor, Suad Bey, was removed from his post and transferred to Baghdad and in his place the district "received a merciless successor."[55]

Indeed, Suad Bey was removed and Salih Zeki was appointed as new official to the region with the basic task of eliminating the Armenians in the Deyr-i Zor region. According to different sources the number of Armenians massacred during the 1916 summer months was around 200,000.[56]

VI. One Important Result of the 5–10 Percent Policy

In and of itself, this decision to ensure that the number of deported and resettled Armenians would not exceed a level 5–10 percent of the local population of their new locale provides ample indication that the aim of the government's policy was the annihilation of the Armenians. The number of Armenians deported from their ancestral lands was, according to Ottoman statistics, more than one million. This number is almost equal to the Muslim populations of the areas chosen for their resettlement. These areas were defined initially in one Interior Ministry telegram of 24 April 1915 as "the southeastern portion of [the province of] Aleppo, and the vicinities of [Deyr-i] Zor and Urfa."[57] On 5 July 1915 the area designated for resettlement was expanded somewhat and the government informed the relevant districts and provinces with a cipher cable. It read:

> As it has appeared necessary the areas set aside for the resettlement of Armenians have been changed and expanded. They will be settled in the existing towns and villages at a rate of no more than 10 percent of the Muslim population in: 1–The southern and western portions of the province of Mosul, including the towns and villages of the provincial district of Kirkuk that lie 80 kilometers from the Iranian border; 2–The eastern and southern [parts of the] provincial district of [Deyr-i] Zor, including 25 kilometers of border with Diyârbakır and the settled areas in the Khabur and Euphrates river valleys. 3–In all the towns and villages in the eastern, southern and southwestern portions of the province of Aleppo (but not in the northern part) which are within 25 kilometers of the rail line, including the provincial districts of Havran and Kerek in the province of Syria.[58]

Assuming that the number of Armenians who were to be resettled was nowhere to exceed 10 percent of the local Muslim population, we will first need to learn the figures for the Muslim population in a given area in order to learn its "capacity" for absorbing Armenians. If we calculate the total population for the provinces where Armenians were to be settled, we attain a total number of 1,892,393, of whom 1,680,721 were Muslims.[59] The emerging picture is very simple: the total Armenian population designated to be settled (in keeping with the Ottoman government's 10 percent ceiling) was not supposed to exceed a figure of approximately 168,000.

The American Consul in Aleppo, J. B. Jackson, reported that he had learned from reliable sources that since 3 February 1916 some 486,000 Armenians were living in the environs of the Aleppo and Damascus (Şam) region and along the Euphrates River as far as Deyr-i Zor.[60] In other words, this figure was far above—at least 220,000 persons above—the 10 percent maximum ordered by the government. Such calculations might help us to understand the reasons for the second wave of massacres in Syria (at Res ül-Ayn İntilli and Deyr-i Zor) in the spring and summer of 1916, in which around 200,000 Armenians lost their lives. To put it in the terms of cold calculation, the number of Armenians who arrived safely in the region was seen as much too high for its absorptive capacity, and thus needed to be reduced.[61]

According to Ottoman figures, the prewar Armenian population of Anatolia was 1.3 million; according to the Armenian [Gregorian] Church, the figure was 2.1 million. All estimates fall somewhere between these numbers.[62] For example, according to some Ottoman documents, even the Ottoman authorities admitted that their official numbers were low and at least 30 percent must be added on top.[63] The figures that one arrives at of Armenians subjected to deportation will vary widely depending on which of these two numbers one uses as a starting point. Whichever figure we use, a safe estimate is that somewhere in the vicinity of one million Armenians were deported.[64]

Murat Bardakçi, a Turkish writer and journalist of popular histories, recently published a book which includes some documents he calls "the daily journal of Talât Pasha," actually a report, commissioned by Pasha in his capacity of Grand Vizier, showing the distribution of Armenians in Ottoman provinces. There are two very important documents in this publication. One is about the population of Armenians before and after the deportations and is probably from 1918; it claims that there were 1,256,403 Armenians living in Anatolia. The document also says that "it is appropriate to add 30 percent on top of this number" and to estimate the number of Armenians around 1.5 million. According to the same document, after the deportations the number of Armenians who survived was officially 284,157, and again 30 percent must be added on top of this number. Hence, we have a figure of approximately 350,000 Armenians who survived.[65] If we take this number as a basis and deduct the number of Armenians who escaped to Russia, which is estimated between 200,000 and 300,000, we can arrive at the number of Armenians who perished during the Genocide, around 900,000 to one million. This is very close to the official Ottoman number, 800,000.

In the second document, we find the numbers of deported Armenians for each city, which allows us to estimate the total number of deported Armenians. According to Talât Pasha's personal papers, the number of Armenians subjected to forced emigration was 924,158.[66] Of course we have to add 30 percent to this number too, and we then arrive at a figure of 1.2 million deported Armenians. But this figure can easily be shown to be mistaken. If we look the list of provinces and villages from which the Armenians were deported, we will see that a great many provinces from which we have decisive proof that Armenians were also deported are missing from this list.[67] As one can easily see from the list of "missing" locations—Istanbul, Edirne, Aydın, Bolu, Kastamonu, Van, parts of Syria, Antalya, Biga, Eskişehir, İçel, Kütahya, Menteşe, Çatalca, and Urfa—many were far from inconsequential areas of Armenian settlement.[68] Thus, if we take the both documents as our foundation, we can confidently say that the number of deported Armenians were around 1.3 or 1.4 million. The British historian Toynbee estimated the number of deported Armenians as 1.2 million, which is the closest estimate of the time.[69]

The question that cannot be answered—or perhaps can be, but only indirectly—is how 1.2 million Armenians were to be made into only 10 percent of a Muslim population of just under 1.7 million?

VII. Muslim Refugees Denied Permission to Settle Where They Wish

One of the most significant pieces of evidence that the settling of deportees and refugees was done according to a prearranged plan is the simple fact that they were forcibly settled in designated areas and most definitely not wherever they wished. The government sent a detailed communiqué to all of the relevant provinces and provincial districts on 25 August 1915 that listed the steps to be followed in the process of resettlement.

From this circular it is clear that some of the refugees did not go to the areas to which they had been directed, choosing instead to flee to other places. The determination to prevent the free movement of peoples occupied a large part of the government's concerns and efforts. Numerous telegrams to the provinces testify to this fact. One sent to Urfa on 15 April 1916, for instance, states that "it is entirely unacceptable that the deportees should go to other destinations instead of to their [designated] places of resettlement," and demands that "the deportees not be allowed to sneak off and that measures be taken to prevent this."[70] Another document further orders that those displaced persons who did not go to the destinations that had been determined for them in advance were to be forcibly sent there. In the telegram it was ordered that they were to be sent off "to their designated place of resettlement without any opportunity whatsoever being given for them to run off or flee elsewhere."[71]

In some regions, even after being resettled, the refugees continued to flee from their new homes; in response, the government imposed harsh measures to prevent this. An Interior Ministry cable to Bursa on 31 December 1917 said:

> Reports have been received from the province of Hüdavendigâr (Bursa) that a large number of deportees from Batum has arrived in Bursa, and that many of these ran off or disappeared over the course of the journey. Although they claim that this province was not, in fact, their [correct] area for resettlement . . . absolutely no deportee should be allowed to escape in such a fashion . . . [and] any [official] who shows complacency or negligence [in this matter] will be severely punished.[72]

This prohibition and strict enforcement also covered the Turkish refugees. A telegram from January 1918 to the province of Adana gives some idea of just how close the monitoring was in this matter.

> Of those [Muslim] refugees who fled Rumelia after the Balkan War[s] and those Turkish and Kurdish refugees that left the provinces of Van, Bitlis, and Erzurum for Adana, the Kurds have been registered to be resettled in certain areas and absolutely no permission whatsoever will be given for them to go to any other place, whereas with the Turks, when the registries will be sent to the province's office of immigration they will have to be registered in the registry of "foreigners" and their registration in the basic registries will be marked and papers drawn up.[73]

This firm—even harsh—attitude toward all Muslim immigrants, Turkish and non-Turkish, is another clear indication that the government's population and settlement policies were being undertaken according to a comprehensive plan possessing clearly defined criteria for resettlement.

Conclusion

Not all of the deportations and relocations that are claimed to have taken place between 1913 and 1918 were the result of a centrally planned population and settlement policy for which all the details had been worked out in advance. But that such a policy existed is clear. From the existing documents from the Interior Ministry's Cipher Office we can see that there were five main reasons for the movement of populations during this period.

First, those groups of Christians whose presence was considered to be a threat (in particular, the Greeks in the Aegean coastal regions, the Syriac Christians in the Mardin-Diyarbakır area, and all Armenian citizens) were to be removed from Anatolia through forced emigration or expulsion, and Muslims were to be resettled in these areas in their place.

In the case of the Aegean Greeks, this removal was accomplished in the spring and summer of 1914 partially through forced deportation to Greece, but in greater measure through a campaign of threat, intimidation, looting, and a limited number of killings. The Armenians, on the other hand, were deported beginning in May 1915 and many were massacred on the way or left to die in the desert wastes. In addition to the Armenians, a significant number of the Syriac Christians were also massacred (see chapter 17).

In tandem with the removal of undesired populations, the Muslim population arriving from the Balkans and Caucasus regions was systematically resettled in the Christian villages that had been emptied out. These resettlement efforts, which began in the Aegean region in 1913, would reach a new level with the wholesale evacuation of the Armenian villages in 1915 and continue on through much of the war. The Prime Minister's Archives in Istanbul are replete with documents describing plans for relocating these populations.[74] In general, the government attempted to ensure that the new immigrants would have their material needs met through the "abandoned property, existing provisions, clothing and other possessions" left behind by the departing Armenians and Greeks; in fact, the various "Liquidation Commissions," which were originally formed in order to monitor abandoned Armenian properties, were eventually entrusted with the task of providing for the immigrants' needs.[75]

Second, a great many more Christian citizens of the empire were deported or otherwise forcibly displaced at various times for military reasons. In October 1914 the decision was taken for military reasons to remove from the area of the Iranian border those "Nestorians [Christians] who were susceptible to foreign incitements," and to resettle them in places in the center of Anatolia such as Ankara and Konya.[76] The forcible removal of Greek Orthodox Christians—especially those situated along the Black Sea and Aegean coasts—and their relocation in the Anatolian hinterlands grew considerably in scale at the end of 1916 and into 1917, and is another example of the Ottomans' policy of directed population transfers.

Third, in large measure the forcible deportation and resettlement actions were the result of political concerns: into this category we can place the first deportations that were directed at the Armenian community, which occurred in the Çukurova region between February and April 1915. Since it was feared that the Armenians of the region would receive military assistance from abroad and revolt, they were first deported from the İskenderun and Dörtyol areas and resettled in Adana.[77]

In similar fashion—and for similar reasons—some prominent Arab leaders and families in Syria who were thought capable of leading a revolt against the Ottoman regime were deported to the Anatolian interior by Fourth Army Commander and Unionist Triumvir Cemal Pasha. Documents dealing with the subject openly state that the action was taken "for political reasons."[78] Another such politically motivated deportation was the one against many of the members of the new Jewish *Yishuv* (settlement) in Palestine. In August 1915, for example, the interior minister sent a message to the Fourth Army Commander demanding that "those Jewish citizens of the enemy states who are in the lands of Palestine and who are hostile to the Ottomans be deported to Çorum."[79] We may even add to this list the deportation to the middle of Anatolia of some of the more problematic Kurdish tribes that the state had had difficulty controlling.[80]

Fourth, the forcible resettling of Muslim populations fleeing the war zones in the Anatolian interior was not planned in advance, but rather was the result of a necessity born of war. This applies, in particular, to the attempts to resettle the massive and unexpected wave of refugees that appeared in the wake of military setbacks on the Caucasian Front. The Muslim refugees were also settled in the now-empty Armenian and Greek towns and villages and thus became a part of the government's concrete population and settlement policies.[81] According to some sources, there were some 702,900 Muslims who fled before the advancing Russian armies in the years 1915 and 1916 alone; these were largely resettled in central and western Anatolia (see chapter 18).[82]

Finally, there were deportations that were carried out by the local authorities without either consultation or notification of the central government. An example of this type can be seen in a December 1914 telegram to the provincial district of Jerusalem, which indicates that "evictions" were already being carried out long before the central government instituted any wide-ranging deportation operations.[83] In another cable sent by Talât to the provincial district of Jerusalem on 6 February 1915, the interior minister complained about this situation and demanded that no further persons be deported without prior permission.[84] Certain Druze families were also deported, in one instance from Havran to the county of Osmaniye in the Adana region.[85] Even Italian citizens were deported from Jerusalem, as Talât would also learn after the fact.[86]

As this chapter has shown, the breakup of an empire into nation states involves much more than geographic realignments or simple redrawings of borders. It also signals the emergence of an exclusivist national identity that stands in tension with the social dynamics of an empire that transcends national identities. Emerging in a period of dramatic territorial losses, Turkish identity was defined in two ways: exclusively, in relation to the country's native Christians, and inclusively, in relation to the non-Turkic Muslim peoples of Anatolia. The first group faced deportations and, sometimes, mass killings, the second, assimilation into a loosely defined Turkish-Islamic ideology. Both the fear of geographical extinction and the tension between exclusion and inclusion persist in Turkish national identity to this day.

NOTES

KEY TO ARCHIVAL CITATIONS
BOA: Prime Ministerial Ottoman Archive [Başbakanlık Osmanlı Arşivi]
DH.SN.THR: Dahiliye Nezareti Sicill-i Nüfus Tahrirat Kalemi [Ministry of the Interior, Secretariat of Population Registry]
DH.ŞFR: Dahiliye Nezareti Şifre Kalemi [Ministry of the Interior, Cipher Office]
DH.EUM. 3.Şube: Dahiliye Nezareti Emniyet-i Umumiye Üçüncü Şube [Ministry of the Interior, Third Department of General Security]

The epigraph is from *Gibt es überhaupt eine deutsche Geschichte?* (Berlin: Corso, bei Siedler, 1989), 20

1. For this pragmatic attitude toward the deployment of different ideologies by CUP, see J. M. Landau, *The Politics of Pan-Islamism: Ideology and Organization* (Oxford: Oxford University Press, 1990); idem, *Pan-Turkism: From Irredentism to Cooperation* (Bloomington: Indiana University Press, 1995), 7–74; Taner Akçam, *A Shameful Act: The Armenian Genocide and Turkish Responsibility* (New York: Metropolitan, 2006), 39–46.

2. A large portion of Gökalp's articles, in which he outlines the fundamental ideological directions of the Union and Progress movement, were published in the journals *Türk Yurdu* and *İslam* between the years 1913 and 1914. These were subsequently collected and published in book form in 1918 under the title *Türkleşmek, İslamlaşmak, Muasırlaşmak* [*Turkification, Islamification, Modernization*]. Regarding Ziya Gökalp and his ideas, see Uriel Heyd, *The Foundations of Turkish*

Nationalism (London: Luzac, 1950); Niyazi Berkes, *Turkish Nationalism and Western Civilization: Selected Essays of Ziya Gökalp* (London: George Allen & Unwin, 1959); and Taha Parla, *The Social and Political Thought of Ziya Gökalp, 1876–1924* (Leiden, Netherlands: Brill, 1985).

3. Murat Paker, "Egemen Politik Kültürün Dayanılmaz Ağırlığı," in *Birikim* 184–185 (Ağustos-Eylül, 2004), 66, n5.

4. Stanford Shaw, *Osmanlı İmparatorluğu ve Modern Türkiye*, pt. 2 (Istanbul: E Yayınları, 1983), 359.

5. Ertuğrul Zekai Ökte, ed., Ottoman Archives, Yıldız Collection, *The Armenian Question*, vol. 1 (Istanbul: Historical Research Foundation, Istanbul Research Center, 1989), xii.

6. Quoted from the memoirs of Eşref Kuşçubaşı, one of the leading members of Teşkilat-ı Mahsusa, in *Celal Bayar, Ben de Yazdım* (Istanbul: Baha Matbaası, 1966), vol. 5, 1574.

7. As mentioned above, even though "Turkification" was used by the CUP as a general ideological formulation, the party never clearly defined the term. The CUP used outward expressions of Islam as an important component of its Turkish ideology. As we will show below, the CUP also deployed the term "assimilation" to define its policy toward non-Turkish Muslim groups who were ordered to settle in the regions where the other inhabitants were Turks. The meaning of Turkification is discussed by some scholars, e. g., Erol Ülker, "Contextualising 'Turkification': Nation-building in the Late Ottoman Empire, 1908–18," *Nations and Nationalism* 11(4) (2005): 613–36.

8. *Takvim-i Vekayi*, no. 3540 (5 May 1919). The first session of the trial was held on 27 April 1919.

9. According to the 1914 Ottoman census, the population of the empire, including the Arab provinces, was around 18.5 million. If we exclude the latter, the population of Anatolia would have been somewhere between 15 and 17.5 million. In his studies of the empire's population Kemal Karpat estimates the Anatolian population at about 15 million (*Osmanlı Nüfusu (1830–1914), Demografik ve Sosyal Özellikleri*, [Istanbul: Tarih Vakfı Yayınları, 2003], s. 226). On the basis of several upward corrections of these figures Justin McCarthy puts the figure for Anatolia alone at 17.5 million in *Muslim and Minorities: The Population of Ottoman Anatolia and the End of the Empire* (Istanbul: İnkılap, 1998), s. 110.

10. For Ottoman settlement policies before the nineteenth century, the reader is advised to refer to the following works: Cengiz Orhonlu, *Osmanlı İmparatorluğunda Aşiretlerin İskânı* (Istanbul: Eren, 1987); Yusuf Halaçoğlu, *XVIII. Yüzyılda Osmanlı İmparatorluğu'nun İskân Siyaseti ve Aşiretlerin Yerleştirilmesi* (Ankara: Türk Tarih Kurumu, 1988); Karpat, *Osmanlı Nüfusu*, 1–36, 102–121, 300–311.

11. I would stress that I have approached this subject within the framework of the 1915 deportation and annihilation operations against the Armenians, not as a general discussion of Ottoman expulsion, migration, and settlement policies. The subject of Ottoman population and (Muslim) resettlement policies in the period after 1913 have been covered in two comprehensive works: Fuat Dündar, *İttihat ve Terakki'nin Müslümanları İskân Politikası (1913–1918)*, (Istanbul: İletişim Yayınları, 2001); and the same author's doctoral thesis: "L'ingenierie ethnique du Comité Union et Progrès et la turcisation de l'Anatolie (1913–1918)" (EHESS Paris, 2006).

12. For its initial charge and more details on its organization, see Fuat Dündar, *İttihat ve Terakki'nin . . .* , 60–61.

13. For more information see: ibid., 84–85.

14. See, for example, BOA/DH.SN.THR., 68/676 (200/1–A/90/1328.RA.9/1), communication from the Interior Ministry to the counties of Sındırgı, Bilecik, and İnegöl, dated 14 September 1910; BOA/DH.SN.THR., 48/75, 564–71; BOA/DH.SN.THR., 42/58; Fuat Dündar, *İttihat ve Terakki'nin . . .* , 85.

15. BOA/DH.SN.THR., 2517/55/23, from a request by the Armenian Patriarch for instructions on how to put the relevant statutes into practice, dated 6 September 1914.

16. BOA/DH.SN.THR., 49/39, written reply (dated 19 February 1914) of the Interior Ministry's Legal Advisor to the telegram (dated 16 February 1914) from the Office of the District Governor of İzmit to the Interior Ministry.

17. BOA/DH.ŞFR., nr. 58/42, coded telegram from the Interior Ministry's Directorate-General of Security to the Office of the District Governor of Teke, dated 17 November 1915.

18. BOA/DH.ŞFR., nr. 54–A/51, coded telegram, from the Interior Ministry's Directorate-General of Security to the governors of the provinces of Edirne, Erzurum, Adana, Ankara, Aydın, Bitlis, Basra, Bağdat, Beyrut, Hicaz, Halep, Hüdâvendigâr, Diyarbakır, Suriye, Sivas, Trabzon, Kastamonu, Mamûretü'l-Aziz, Musul, Van, Yemen, and the provincial district governors of Urfa, İzmit, İçel, Niğde, Maraş, Bolu, Canik, Çatalca, Zor, Asir, Kudûs-ü Şerif (Jerusalem), Kal'a-i Sultaniye, Menteşe, Teke, Medîne-i Münevvere (Medina), Eskişehir, Kütahya, and Karahisar-ı Sahib, dated 20 July 1915.

19. BOA/DH.ŞFR., nr. 52/188, coded telegram from Interior Minister Talât to the governors of the provinces of Edirne, Diyarbakır, Adana, Sivas, Konya, Ankara, Trabzon, Aydın, Kastamonu, Mamuretülaziz, Hüdâvendigâr and the governors of the districts of Bolu, Canik, Çatalca, Kudüs-i Şerif, Kala-i Sultaniye, Menteşe, Teke, Kayseri, Maraş, İzmit, Niğde, Eskişehir, İçel, Kütahya, Karahisar-ı Sahib, dated 9 August 1915.

20. BOA/DH.ŞFR., nr. 62/188, coded telegram from the Interior Ministry's Office of Tribal and Immigrant Settlement to the province of Trabzon, dated 1 April 1916.

21. BOA/DH./ŞFR., 63/151, coded telegram from the Interior Ministry's General Directorate of Tribal and Immigrant Affairs to the Governor of the Baghdad Province, dated 1 May 1916.

22. BOA/DH.ŞFR., nr. 45/200, coded telegram from the Interior Ministry's General Director-ate of Security to the provinces of Aydın and Trabzon and the provincial district of Canik, dated 5 September 1914.

23. See, for example, BOA/DH. EUM. 3.ŞB., 2/24, cable from the Interior Ministry to the provinces of Edirne, Adana, Aydın, Trabzon, Kastamonu, and the provincial districts of İzmit, Bolu, Canik, Karesi, Antalya, and Menteşe, dated 15 September 1914; and BOA/EUM. 3.ŞB., 2/31, coded telegram from the Interior Ministry's General Directorate of Security to the provinces of İzmir and Trabzon and the provincial district of Canik, dated 6 October 1914.

24. BOA/DH. EUM. 3.ŞB., 2/24. Reports prepared in the Trabzon and Aydın provinces, for example, where there were sizeable Greek populations, were sent to Istanbul on 24 December 1914. In his reply cable sent on the same day the governor of Trabzon claims that it is "a reply to the [Interior Ministry]'s cipher telegram no. 45, received on 23 Eylül [1]330 [7 October 1914]" and reports that "the three separate notebooks that are enclosed contain the number, type, monetary value and names of the owners of the properties and covered structures owned by [members of] the Greek community in the towns of Trabzon, Ordu and Giresun" (BOA/EUM. 3.ŞB., 2/31).

25. Here are some examples: DH.EUM. 3.ŞB, 1/32, a telegraph sent by provincial district governor of Izmit to Interior Ministry, dated 13 August 1914; DH. EUM. 3.ŞB, 1/34, a telegram sent by Aydin Province to the Interior Ministry dated 7 August 1914; and DH. EUM. 3.SB, 2/41/1 a telegraph sent by Interior Ministry to the provinces of Edirne and Hüdâvendigâr and the provincial districts of Kale-i Sultaniye, Karesi, Çatalca, İzmit.

26. For the full text of the instructions see: BOA/DH. EUM. 3.ŞB, 2/26–A.

27. BOA/DH.ŞFR., nr. 57/24, coded telegram from the Interior Ministry's Office of Tribal and Immigrant Settlement to the President of the Commissions on Abandoned Property for the provinces of Adana, Erzurum, Bitlis, Halep, Maraş, Hüdâvendigâr, Diyarbakır, Sivas, Trabzon, Canik, Mamuretü'l-Azîz, Konya, and the provincial districts of İzmit, Eskişehir, Niğde, Kayseri, Karahisar-ı Sâhib, dated 1 November 1915.

28. BOA/DH.ŞFR., nr. 65/140, coded telegram from the Bureau of Statistics of the Interior Ministry's Office of Tribal and Immigrant Settlement to the provinces of Hüdâvendigâr, Aydın, Adana, Edirne, and the provincial districts of Menteşe, Antalya, İçel, Karesi, İzmit, dated 2 July 1916.

29. BOA/DH.ŞFR., nr. 60/93, coded telegram from the Interior Ministry's Office of Tribal and Immigrant Settlement to the province of Suriye, dated 23 January 1916.

30. BOA/DH.ŞFR., nr. 53/26, coded telegram from the Interior Ministry's Office of Tribal and Immigrant Settlement to the provinces of Erzurum, Van, Bitlis, Trabzon, Sivas, Ankara, Kastamonu, Edirne, and Hüdâvendigâr, and the provincial districts of Canik, Karesi, and Kale-i Sultaniye, dated 17 May 1915; BOA/DH.ŞFR., nr. 62/268, coded telegram from the Interior Ministry's General Directorate of Tribal and Immigrant Affairs to the Director of the Committee of Inspection (*Hey'et-i Teftişiye Müdüriyeti*) in the provinces of Sivas, Diyarbakır, Trabzon, and the provincial district of Tokat, dated 7 April 1916.

31. BOA/DH.ŞFR., nr. 60/136, coded telegram from the Interior Ministry's Office of Tribal and Immigrant Settlement to the provinces of Bitlis, Diyarbakır, Musul, Mamuretü'l-Aziz, and Erzurum, dated 26 January 1916.

32. BOA/DH.ŞFR., nr. 63/224, coded telegram from the Interior Ministry's Office of Tribal and Immigrant Settlement to the province of Mosul, dated 6 May 1916.

33. BOA/DH.ŞFR., nr. 65/30, coded telegram from Interior Minister Talât to the province of Baghdad, dated 18 June 1916.

34. BOA/DH.ŞFR., nr. 60/140, coded telegram from the Interior Ministry's Office of Tribal and Immigrant Resettlement to the provinces of Konya, Kastamonu, Adana, Ankara, Sivas, Aydın, and others, and to the provincial districts of Kayseri, Canik, Eskişehir, Karahisarı, and Niğde, dated 26 January 1916.

35. BOA/DH.ŞFR., nr. 63/215, coded telegram from the Interior Ministry's Office of Tribal and Immigrant Resettlement to the province of Mosul, dated 6 May 1916.

36. BOA/DH.ŞFR., nr. 64/93, coded telegram from the Interior Ministry's Office of Tribal and Immigrant Resettlement to the province of Mamuretü'l-aziz, dated 21 May 1916; and BOA/DH.ŞFR., nr. 67/49, coded telegram from the Interior Ministry's General Directorate of Tribal and Immigrant Affairs to the provincial district of Kayseri, dated 19 August 1916.

37. BOA/DH.ŞFR., nr. 63/190, coded telegram from the Interior Ministry's General Directorate of Tribal and Immigrant Affairs to Minister of War Enver Pasha, dated 3 May 1916.

38. Karpat, Osmanlı Nüfusu, 19.

39. BOA/DH.ŞFR., nr. 63/187, coded telegram from Interior Minister Talât to the provincial districts of Urfa, Marash, and Antep, dated 4 May 1916.

40. BOA/DH.ŞFR., nr. 63/188, coded telegram from the Interior Ministry's General Directorate of Tribal and Immigrant Affairs to the provinces of Ankara, Konya, Hüdâvendigâr, and Kastamonum and the provincial districts of Kütahya Kayseri and Niğde, dated 2 May 1916.

41. BOA/DH.ŞFR., nr. 56/290, coded telegram from the Interior Ministry's Office of Tribal and Immigrant Settlement to the province of Ankara, dated 5 October 1916.

42. Greek Patriarchate, Persecution of the Greeks in Turkey, 1914–1918 (Istanbul: The Hesperia Press, 1919), 56.

43. BOA/DH.ŞFR., nr. 53/129, coded telegram from the Interior Ministry's General Directorate of Security to the province of Erzurum, dated 27 May 1915.

44. BOA/DH.ŞFR., nr. 54/87, coded telegram from the Interior Ministry's General Directorate of Security to the provinces of Trabzon, Ma'mûretü'l-azîz, Sivas, and Diyarbakır and the provincial district of Canik, dated 20 June 1915.

45. BOA/DH.ŞFR., nr. 55/59, coded telegram from the Interior Ministry's General Directorate of Security to the provincial district of Antalya, dated 17 August 1915.

46. BOA/DH.ŞFR., nr. 53/289, coded telegram from the Interior Ministry's General Directorat of Security to the provincial district of Kale-yi Sultâniye, dated 8 June 1915. Other examples in BOA/DH.ŞFR., nr. 54/335 ve 336, coded telegram from the Interior Ministry's Office of Tribal and Immigrant Settlement to the province of Hüdâvendigâr and the provincial district of Karesi, dated 7 July 1915; and BOA/DH.ŞFR., nr. 53/246, coded telegram from the Interior Ministry's General Directorat of Security to the provincial district of Kayseri, dated 5 June 1915.

47. BOA/DH.ŞFR., nr. 54–A/293, coded telegram from the Interior Ministry's General Directorat of Security to the provincial district of İzmit, dated 7 August 1915.

48. BOA/DH.ŞFR., nr. 54–A/294, coded telegram from the Interior Ministry's General Directorat of Security to the provincial district İzmit, dated 7 August 1915. It is highly probable that this cable and the one in the previous note relate to the same events. The subject under discussion is the temporary delay in deporting the Armenian workers. From the wording of both communications ("until they are replaced") there is nothing to preclude the possibility that these Armenians were in fact subjected to deportation at a later date.

49. BOA/DH.ŞFR., nr. 55/208, coded telegram from the Interior Ministry's General Directorat of Security to the provinces of Erzurum, Adana, Ankara, Bitlis, Halep, Hüdâvendigâr, Diyarbakır, Sivas, Trabzon, Konya, and Mamuretülaziz and the provincial districts of İzmit, Canik, Karesi, Karahisâr-ı sahib, Kayseri, Maraş, Niğde, and Kütahya, dated 25 August 1915.

50. İhsan Sakarya, *Belgelerle Ermeni Sorunu* (Ankara: Genelkurmay Başkanlığı, 1984), 224; Kamuran Gürün, *Ermeni Dosyası* (Ankara: Bilgi Yayınevi, 1988, dördüncü basım), 277.

51. BOA/DH.ŞFR., nr. 54/315, coded telegram from the Interior Ministry's Office of Tribal and Immigrant Settlement to the provinces of Adana, Erzurum, Bitlis, Halep, Diyarbakır, Sûriye, Sivas, Trabzon, Mamûretü'l-azîz, and Mosul; to the President of the Commission on Abandoned Property in Adana and Aleppo; and to the provincial districts of [Deyr-i] Zor, Maraş, Canik, Kayseri, and İzmit Halep, dated 5 July 1915.

52. BOA/DH.ŞFR., nr. 55–A/145, coded telegram from the Interior Ministry's General Directorate of Security to the province of Aleppo, dated 8 September 1915.

53. NA/RG59/867.4016/269, report by Harput Consul Leslie Davis to Ambassador Henry Morgenthau in Constantinople, dated 30 December 1915; reprinted in: Ara Sarafyan, ed., *United States Official Record on the Armenian Genocide 1915–1917* (Princeton, N.J.: Gomidas Institute, 2004), 473.

54. PA-AA/R14091, report, dated 27 April 1916, from Aleppo Consul Rössler to [German] Reichskanzler Bethmann Hollweg.

55. PA-AA/R14093, report, dated 29 July 1916, from Aleppo Consul Rössler to [German] Reichskanzler Bethmann Hollweg.

56. During the Military Tribunal in Istanbul there was a trial against Zeki Bey, who was a fugitive at the time of the trial. He was charged of the crimes of murder, annihilation, and seizure of property of deported Armenians in the region of Zor. The trial was quite short and resulted in the issuance of a death sentence on 28 April 1920. This decision was based on the testimony of both Muslim and non-Muslims under oath (Vakit, 30 April and 2 May 1920).

57. BOA/DH.ŞFR., nr. 52/93, coded telegram from the Interior Ministry's General Directorate of Security to Fourth Army Commander Cemal Pasha, dated 24 April 1915. For further elaborations, see: BOA/DH.ŞFR., nr. 53/94, coded telegram from Interior Minister Talât to the Command of the Fourth Imperial Army, dated 23 May 1915. Another coded telegram with the same information was sent on the same day to the provinces of Erzurum, Van, and Bitlis; see: BOA/DH.ŞFR., nr. 53/93; and memorandum from the Interior Ministry to the Office of the Grand Vizier, dated 26 May 1915. For the full text, see: *Ati,* 23 February 1920.

58. BOA/DH.ŞFR., nr. 54/315, coded telegram from the Interior Ministry's Office of Tribal and Immigrant Settlement to the provinces of Adana, Erzurum, Bitlis, Halep, Diyârbekır, Sûriye, Sivas, Trabzon, Ma'mûretü'lazîz, and Musul, to the provincial districts of [Deyr-i] Zor, Mar'aş, Canik, Kayseri, İzmit and the Presidents of the Commissions on Abandoned Property in Adana and Aleppo, dated 5 July 1915. The same information is repeated, along with a reminder of the 10 percent rule, in: BOA/DH.ŞFR., nr. 54/308, coded telegram from the Interior Ministry's General Directorate of Security to the provincial district of [Deyr-i] Zor, dated 5 July 1915.

59. Karpat, *Osmanlı Nüfusu,* 214–15.

60. NA/RG59/867.48/271, report, dated 8 February 1916, from Aleppo Consul Jesse B. Jackson to Ambassador Henry Morgenthau. Reproduced in: Sarafyan, ed., *United States Official Record,* 489–90.

61. Raymond H. Kévorkian has written several works on the subject of the 1916 Deyr-i Zor massacres in Syria that are based predominantly on eyewitness accounts. See, for instance: Raymond Kévorkian, "L'extermination des déportés arméniens ottomans dans les camps de concentration de Syrie-Mésopotamie (1915–1916)," *Revue d'histoire arménienne contemporaine* 2, Special Issue (1998). For further information, see the following pages at www.imprescriptible.fr: http://www.imprescriptible.fr/cdca/kevorkian.htm, and http://www.imprescriptible.fr/rhac/tome2.htm (both accessed 20 March 2012); and Hilmar Kaiser, *At the Crossroads of Der Zor: Death, Survival, and Humanitarian Resistance in Aleppo, 1915–1917* (Princeton, N.J.: Gomidas Institute, 2002).

62. The purpose here is not to debate the question of Armenian population figures and their losses. Rather, it is simply to shed some light on one of the reasons behind the second wave of large-scale massacres that took place in Syria in 1916. In regard to the subject of Armenian population figures within the Ottoman Empire, in addition to the aforementioned works by Kemal Karpat and Justin McCarthy, a good, general distillation of the available sources can be found in: Hikmet Özdemir, Kemal Çiçek, Ömer Turan, Ramazan Çalik, and Yusuf Halaçoğlu, *Ermeniler: Sürgün*

ve Göç (Ankara: Türk Tarih Kurumu, 2004), 5–53. For Armenian sources see: Kevork Pamukci-yan, "Zamanlar, Mekânlar, İnsanlar," *Ermeni Kaynaklarından Tarihe Katkılar,* vol. 3 (Istanbul: Aras Yayıncılık, 2003), 289–92; and Levon Marashlian, *Politics and Demography: Armenians, Turks, and Kurds in the Ottoman Empire* (Toronto: Zoryan Insitute 1991).

63. Murat Bardakçı, *Talât Paşa'nın Evrak-ı Metrukesi, Sadrazam Talât Paşa'nın özel arşivinde bulunan Ermeni tehciri konusundaki belgeler ve hususi yazışmalar* (Istanbul: Everest Yayınları, 2008), s. 109.

64. According to some Turkish sources the number of Armenians deported was in the area of 450,000; the Turkish Chiefs of Staff give the figure of 413,067. See: Genelkurmay Başkanlığı, *Arşiv Belgeleriyle Ermeni Faaliyetleri 1914–1918,* vol. 1, (Ankara: Genelkurmay Basım Evi, 2005), 147–58 and 439–56. In his work *Ermeni Tehciri ve Gerçekler (1914–1918),* (Ankara: Türk Tarih Kurumu, 2001), Yusuf Halaçoğlu uses the number 438,758 (p. 76). Various Armenian sources put the number of deportees at anywhere from 800,000 (Kevork Pamukciyan) to 1,600,000 (Raymond Kévorkian). Johannes Lepsius would later give the figure of 1.4 million at the trial of Talât Pasha's young Arme-nian assassin, Sogomon Tehliryan. See: Doğan Akhanlı, *Talât Paşa Davası Tutanakları* (Istanbul: Belge Yayınları, 2003), 87.

65. Bardakçı, *Talât Paşa'nın,* 109.

66. Murat Bardakçı, "İşte Kara Kaplı Defterdeki Gerçek," *Hürriyet,* 25 April 2006; Bardakçı repeats the same information in an article from 2006, "Savaş Sırasında 93 bin 88 Rum Başka Viláy-etlere Nakledildi," *Hürriyet,* 26 April 2006.

67. The document which gives the number of Armenian deportees at 924,000 contains the names of only 18 provinces and towns, see: Bardakçı, *Talât Paşa'nın,* 77.

68. For a complete list of the provinces and provincial districts of the period, see: Dahiliye Nezâreti İdare-i Umumiye-i Dahiliye Müdüriyeti, *Teşkilât-ı Hâzıra-i Mülkiyeyi ve Vilâyet, Livâ, Kazâ ve Nâhiyelerin Hurûf-i Hecâ Sırasıyla Esâmîsini Hâvî Cedveldir* (Istanbul: Matbaa-i Âmire, 1331[1915]).

69. Arnold Toynbee and James Bryce, *The Treatment of Armenians in the Ottoman Empire: Documents Presented to Viscount Grey of Fallodon, Secretary of State for Foreign Affairs By Viscount Bryce* (Princeton: Gomidas Institute, 2005), 646. This same number was published in several con-temporary Arab-language newspapers. In the 30 May 1916 edition of the daily *el-Mokattam* the fig-ure 1.2 million is given for the number of Armenians deported (cited in: Faız El-Ghusein, *Martyred Armenia* [New York: Tankian Publishing Corporation, 1975], 58).

70. BOA/DH.ŞFR., nr. 63/9, coded telegram from the Interior Ministry's General Directorate of Tribal and Immigrant Affairs to the provincial district of Urfa, dated 15 April 1916.

71. BOA/DH.ŞFR., nr. 55/256, coded telegram from the Interior Ministry's General Direc-torate of Security to the provinces of Erzurum, Bitlis, Diyarbakır, Kastamonu, Adana, Ankara, Ha-lep, Sivas, Mamuretülaziz, Hüdâvendigâr, Trabzon, and Van, and to the provincial districts of Urfa, İzmit, Karesi, Kütahya, Eskişehir, Canik, Kayseri, and Marash, dated 25 August 1915.

72. BOA/DH.ŞFR., nr. 72/131, coded telegram from the Interior Ministry's General Director-ate of Tribal and Immigrant Affairs to the provinces of Sivas and Kastamonu, dated 31 December 2005.

73. BOA/DH.SN.THR nr. 1857/77/47 (52. Dosya), cable from the Interior Ministry to the province of Adana, dated 7 January 1918.

74. BOA/DH.ŞFR., nr. 54/246, coded telegram from the Interior Ministry's Office of Tribal and Immigrant Settlement to the province of Konya, dated 30 June 1915.

75. BOA/DH.ŞFR., nr. 61/120 ve 61/122, coded telegrams from the Interior Ministry's Office of Tribal and Immigrant Settlement to the provinces of Bitlis, Trabzon, and Sivas, dated 26 February 1916, can be shown as examples of the commission's functioning.

76. BOA/DH.ŞFR., nr. 46/78, coded telegram from Interior Minister Talât to the province of Van, dated 26 October 1914.

77. More detailed information will be given on this subject in the later sections. Additionally, for a broader discussion of the February 1915 deportations from Dörtyol, İskenderun and the later ones from Zeytun and Marash that occurred in March and April, see Taner Akçam, *A Shameful Act: The Armenian Genocide and the Question of Turkish Responsibility* (New York: Metropolitan Books, 2006), 146–47, 159–61.

78. BOA/DH.ŞFR., nr. 72/66, coded telegram from Interior Minister Talât to the provinces of Edirne, Adana, Ankara, Aydın, Hüdâvendigâr, Sivas, Kastamonu, Konya, İzmit, Eskişehir, Bolu, Karesi, Menteşe, Teke, Kayseri, Karahisar-ı Sahib, Kütahya, Maraş, and Niğde, dated 22 January 1917.

79. BOA/DH.ŞFR., nr. 55/235, coded telegram from Interior Minister Talât to the Fourth Army Command, dated 25 August 1915.

80. The deportation to Konya of the Ciranlı tribe, which had "destroyed and looted property [?] and goods" in Urfa in July 1917 and "attacked the detachment of gendarmes sent [to the scene], causing the deaths of four gendarmes" is an example of this type of action. BOA/DH.ŞFR., nr. 79–A/173, coded telegram from the Interior Ministry's General Directorate of Tribal and Immigrant Affairs to the provincial district of Urfa, dated 27 September 1917.

81. One example can be seen in: BOA/DH.ŞFR., nr. 61/120, coded telegram from the Interior Ministry's Office of Tribal and Immigrant Settlement to the province of Bitlis, dated 26 February 1916. To give two additional examples: BOA/DH.ŞFR., nr. 53/26, coded telegram from the Interior Ministry's Office of Tribal and Immigrant Settlement to the provinces of Erzurum, Van, Bitlis, Trabzon, Sivas, Ankara, Kastamonu, Edirne, and Hüdâvendigâr, and to the provincial districts of Canik, Karesi, and Kale-i Sultaniye, dated 17 May 1915; and BOA/DH.ŞFR., nr. 62/268, coded telegram from the Interior Ministry's General Directorate for Tribal and Immigrant Affairs to the provinces of Sivas, Diyarbakır, and Trabzon and the Committee of Inspection in Tokat, dated 7 April 1916. See also, BOA/DH.ŞFR., nr. 63/261, coded telegram from the Interior Ministry's Office of Tribal and Immigrant Settlement to the provinces of Ankara, Adana, Halep, Hüdâvendigâr, Diyarbekir, Kastamonu, Ma'muretü'l-azîz, Sivas, and Trabzon, and to the provincial districts of İzmit, Eskişehir, Urfa, Canik, Karesi, Kayseri, and Niğde, dated 6 May 1916.

82. One document in which the Interior Ministry explains the current migration and immigration situation is published in: *Askeri Tarih Belgeleri Dergisi* 31(81) (December 1982): 223–34; Document No. 1845.

83. BOA/DH.ŞFR., nr. 48/110, coded telegram from Interior Minister Talât to the provincial district of Jerusalem (Kudüs), dated 22 December 1914.

84. BOA/DH.ŞFR. nr. 49/216, coded telegram from Interior Minister Talât to the Provincial District Governor of Jerusalem, Midhat Bey Efendi, dated 6 February 1915.

85. BOA/DH.ŞFR., nr. 56/237, coded telegram from the Interior Ministry's General Directorate of Security to the 4th Army Command, dated 30 September 1915.

86. BOA/DH.ŞFR., nr. 62/28, coded telegram from the Interior Ministry's General Directorate of Security to the provincial district of Jerusalem, dated 16 March 1916.

PART FOUR
Violence on the Borderlands

15

PAVING THE WAY FOR ETHNIC CLEANSING

EASTERN THRACE DURING THE BALKAN WARS (1912–1913) AND THEIR AFTERMATH

EYAL GINIO

On 13 March 1913 the newly established Special Office (*Kalem-i Mahsus*) in the Ottoman Ministry of Internal Affairs issued a ciphered telegram to the governor of Karesi (present-day Balıkesir, Turkey) in northwestern Anatolia. The official, who signed the telegram in the name of his Minister, appealed to the local authorities to prevent any obstacle to the emigration of Bulgarians who were gathering in Istanbul (Karesi province included the harbor of Bandırma, from which vessels could transport the emigrants to Bulgaria). The official informed the governor that he had recently learned that the Bulgarians' emigration was being hampered by demands for the remittance of various debts and that the Bulgarians were prevented from selling their belongings. He emphasized that everything should be done in order to assist the Bulgarians with their swift emigration.[1] Similar telegrams were sporadically dispatched during the months of March and April 1914 to various provinces in eastern Thrace and northwestern Anatolia. They were all in the same vein: local officials should assist the fleeing Bulgarians (and, sometimes, also the Greeks) to emigrate from the country.

An unequivocal explanation for this policy appeared in another telegram that was sent to the governor of Karesi by the Ministry of Internal Affairs. In this telegram, the subject was the status of the Bulgarians who were indebted to the Ottoman Agricultural Bank (*Ziraat Bankası*). It was stated that the immovable properties they would leave behind would suffice to repay their debts to the bank. It was forbidden, the telegram reiterated, to prevent those Bulgarians who wished to leave the country from doing so on the grounds of their failure to settle their debts. Furthermore, "the acceleration and assistance for [the Bulgarians'] emigration correspond better with the state's interests" ("*tesri ve teshil-i azimetleri menafi-i devlet daha muvafıktır*").[2] At the same time, several religious leaders of the non-Muslim inhabitants of these areas dispatched petitions to the Ministry of Internal Affairs to complain about the harassment endured by the non-Muslims in their residences and during their emigration. They all spoke of an unprecedented atmosphere of disorder, hatred, and revenge that was reigning in eastern Thrace.[3]

Erik Jan Zürcher argues that the transfer of the Bulgarian population following the Balkan Wars was "strictly on a voluntary basis."[4] While it is true that at least during the months of March and April 1914 we cannot speak yet of a general and state-sponsored policy to transfer the Bulgarian population, it is clear from the above-mentioned telegrams and many others kept in the Ottoman Archives of the Prime Ministry (*Başbakanlık*) in Istanbul that the Ministry of Internal Affairs approved of the Bulgarians' emigration and did all it could to encourage and to carry out the immediate removal of its own citizens to the land of its enemies. This new type of exclusion that targeted a section of Ottoman society was an innovation in state policy toward religious minorities.

What began as sporadic cases of harassment and deportation received international recognition as early as 29 September 1913 when the Ottoman Empire and Bulgaria included in their peace agreement a clause that sanctioned the mutual transfer of populations from the new border between the two states in Thrace and mutual compensation for those who chose to emigrate permanently from one county to the other. The treaty envisioned the exchange of about 50,000 people from each side of the border and therefore was limited in its scope. However, the cases presented above indicate that Bulgarians living in areas relatively distant from the newly drawn border were compelled to emigrate. Similar discussions on population exchange took place between the Ottomans and the Greek government. The outbreak of World War I hindered the conclusion of a similar pact.[5] The principle of population transfer was therefore legitimized and became an accepted method of solving what was considered at times to be "a problem of alien minorities." Indeed, Norman Naimark states that "as result of the Balkan Wars, massive population transfers and ethnic separatism became part of modern European conflict and made their way into the vocabulary of peacemaking."[6]

The Balkan Wars (October 1912–August 1913) can serve as a case study to explore changing Ottoman ethnic policies, as well as to discuss the different meanings of collective identities during this period in Ottoman history. Furthermore, as will be demonstrated in this chapter, following the Ottoman defeat in the Balkan Wars, the process of exclusion began its most earnest phase in the recently reshaped borderlands of the Ottoman State: eastern Thrace. I will claim that fear of what was seen as a treacherous fifth column inhabiting the sensitive border of the defeated Empire, as well as calls for vengeance, played a major role in implementing such a discriminatory policy. Therefore, I will argue that the Balkan Wars redirected the formation of the Ottoman nation according to religious lines. It was mainly in eastern Thrace that the fiery debates that took place in the capital regarding the external and internal borders of the national community turned into concrete actions targeting those who were now pushed outside of the nation.

This chapter aims to explore the development of an excluding discourse in the policy of the Ottoman Empire toward its non-Muslim populations, as it appeared in the press, in the memoir literature, and in various other publications during the Balkan Wars and their aftermath. I will argue that Ottoman policy toward its minorities at the outbreak of hostilities in October 1912 began to take a very different path, as we will see clearly after first looking at the relatively inclusive discourse (and practice) that prevailed with regard to the non-Muslims in the Ottoman nation during the first weeks of the first Balkan War. After briefly demonstrating this, I will present the narratives of total rout that quickly appeared during and following the first Balkan War and their emphasis on the role assigned to the non-Muslims (mostly Greeks and Bulgarians) in the military debacle and the ensuing atrocities against local Muslim populations. I will show how these narratives contributed to the singling out of non-Muslims as traitors and to their subsequent exclusion from the imagined Ottoman nation. These changes, I will argue, make the Balkan Wars the true watershed in the way the Ottoman state perceived its non-Muslim populations. The first who suffered from this new exclusionist approach were the Christians who inhabited the European area later known as eastern Thrace that remained under Ottoman sway following the Balkan Wars. It was in these borderlands that Ottoman non-Muslims fell victim to a nascent nationalist movement that perceived them as aliens and as a threat on the national community and its cohesion.

Eastern Thrace as a Borderland

The mostly flat area of eastern Thrace was the major front of the Balkan Wars. Known to contemporaries as the "Eastern Front," it separated Bulgaria from the Ottoman capital of Istanbul. Indeed, in Thrace it was mainly the advancing Bulgarian Army that bore the brunt of the fighting against the Ottoman Eastern Army. Following the outbreak of hostilities in this area on 18 October, the first major military encounter took place in Kırkkilise (Kırklareli). Over the course of three days (22–24 October) the invading Bulgarian army fought the Ottomans along a 36-mile front stretching from Kırkkilise to Edirne. Suffering from heavy casualties and the loss of military equipment, the demoralized Ottoman army hastily retreated. After a few days' break in the hostilities the two armies met again in Lüleburgaz. Following a four-day battle (29 October–1 November) in which the Bulgarian attack benefited from very effective artillery use, the victorious Bulgarian army was able to further advance as far as the defense line of Çatalca, only 20 miles away from the center of Istanbul.

On their way to Istanbul, the Bulgarians were able to lead a siege on the fortified city of Edirne. Under the command of Ferik Mehmet Şükrü Paşa, manned by a garrison of about 52,500 soldiers, and supported by mighty fortifications, the city was able to endure a siege of about five months until its capitulation on 26 March 1913. The Bulgarians were therefore able to establish their control over the whole of Thrace.

By the spring of 1913 the debate between the Balkan allies with regard to the division of the gained territories quickly deteriorated into military confrontation. Convinced of the righteousness of its claims in Macedonia and the strength of its army, isolated Bulgaria attacked its former allies, Serbia and Greece, on the night of 29–30 June. The Bulgarian army evacuated the Ottoman front to face its new adversaries. The collapse of the Balkan League offered the Ottomans the opportunity to regain some of their lost territories. The Ottomans ignored the European protests, and Ottoman units, under the command of Enver Bey, retook Edirne without firing a shot (23 July), as well as most parts of eastern Thrace. The inclusion of Edirne within Ottoman borders was secured in the ensuing peace accord signed with Bulgaria in Istanbul on 30 September 1913.[7]

The civilian populations of eastern Thrace—Muslim and non-Muslim—present an illuminating case study of the deterioration of ethnic relations in the Late Ottoman period and during the first decades of the Turkish Republic. During the Balkan Wars, this region became the main battlefield in which the Ottoman state faced its major routs, but it also was the scene of the Ottomans' most decisive attempts to survive against their Bulgarian foes and their allies.[8] Prior to the Balkan Wars eastern Thrace had a large population of Muslims and non-Muslims: Bulgarians, Greeks, Jews, and Armenians. Their exact numbers are hard to determine, as eastern Thrace was a new administrative concept that emerged only following the territorial losses of the Balkan Wars and encompassed most of what was left of the European provinces of the Ottoman state. Therefore, we do not have any Ottoman official assessments of the region's population prior to the Balkan Wars. Prior to the outbreak of the Balkan Wars, eastern Thrace was to a large extent part of Edirne province (*vilayet*). The population of the province was estimated in the 1887/88 census at 200,808, of which 39.3 percent were Muslims, 38.4 Greeks, 15.9 Bulgarians, 0.04 Jews, and 0.02 Armenians.[9] However, as Zürcher estimates, most of the Muslim population inhabited the western parts of the provinces that were allocated to Bulgaria following the Balkan Wars (and later, in 1919, to Greece), while the population of eastern Thrace was mainly non-Muslim.[10] Edirne (Greek: Adrianopole; Bulgarian: Odrin; Ladino: Andrinópoli), the administrative centre of the province, represented this ethnic diversity. It harbored prior to the first Balkan War a population of about 90,000 people—47,000 Turks, 20,000 Greeks, 15,000 Jews, 4,000 Armenians, 2,000 Bulgarians, and others.[11]

For most of its Ottoman history, this region, "the gates to Istanbul," was in the very heart of the Ottoman state. Edirne served as the second Ottoman capital ca. 1365–1453 and thereafter as a popular retreat for the sultans and their households. This prestigious position ensured the patronage of the ruling dynasty, which was manifested in the construction of large religious and imperial complexes. These impressive sets of buildings were rivaled only by those of the capital, Istanbul.

However, following the debacle of the Balkan Wars, eastern Thrace became a sensitive borderland adjacent to the Bulgarian border (and after World War I also to the Greek border). This area's final shape was determined in 1915 in the accord in which the Ottoman state had to surrender Dimetoka (Greek: Didymoteicho) to Bulgaria in order to secure Bulgaria's entry into World War I on the side of the Central Powers. Furthermore, the area of eastern Thrace became a clear example for the process of ethnic homogenization that took place in many parts of the post-Ottoman lands during the first half of the twentieth century; its varied population of Turks, Greeks, Armenians, and Jews lost its multiconfessional and multiethnic characteristics due to a continuous process of intimidating and transferring large segments of the population. The Bulgarians' swift victories in October–November 1912 allowed them to conquer most of the area up to the Çatalca line. Following the advance of the Bulgarian army and the subsequent atrocities against the local Muslim population, many of the Muslim inhabitants hastily fled to Istanbul where they were able to find a temporary shelter.[12] A vivid description of the Bulgarian atrocities can be found in the Carnegie Endowment report published in 1913.[13] During the brief Second Balkan War (July–August 1913), the Ottoman army was able to conquer the area without firing one shot. It was now the turn of the Bulgarian civil population to suffer from reprisals. The Greeks and the Armenians left the province following the Treaty of Lausanne (1923) and the retreat of the Greek army from the province following a brief Greek occupation (1920–1922); finally, the Jewish population of the province largely left it during the first two decades of the Turkish republic in the face of official and popular pressure exerted on it, the last remaining minority population. The demise of the Ottoman Empire and the foundation of the Turkish republic put unprecedented pressure on all the Jewish communities of Turkey. They were required to assimilate linguistically and culturally into Turkish society. This pressure must be seen as part of the overall anti-minority attitude that prevailed in public opinion in the Republic's first years. It seems that the lot of the Jewish community in Thrace (including Edirne) was the harshest. Living on a sensitive border area and becoming the only non-Muslim minority following the departure of the Bulgarian, Greek, and Armenian populations, the Jews of Edirne suffered from verbal and occasional physical assaults as well as from legal restrictions on their economic activities. These assaults reached their peak with the attacks on Jews in the major towns of eastern Thrace in 1934. The agitation of mobs in Edirne that involved some physical attacks on Jews and multiplying threats against the community spread panic among the members of Edirne Jewry. Thousands of them immigrated permanently to Istanbul, although the government intervened to stop the attacks and assured the Jews of their safety. The community never recovered from this blow.[14]

Turkish Thrace became a religiously and ethnically homogeneous region with no minorities. Similar results occurred during this period in all the new nation states that were established in the Balkans in which the state demanded the assimilation of its minorities into the mainstream. Those who were reckoned to be unfit for assimilation were marginalized and sometimes persecuted by various means and techniques. However, in the Ottoman case of eastern Thrace, this process had already begun under the authority of the still multiethnic and multiconfessional Ottoman state. The following parts of this chapter will attempt to offer an explanation for this new Ottoman policy.

"The War against the Ottoman Nation"

On the eve of the outbreak of the military offensive about to be launched by the Balkan states, the daily paper *Tanin* (*The Echo*), an organ of the Committee of Union and Progress (CUP) or the Young Turks, then an opposition party, reported on the patriotic demonstrations that took place in the city of Yanya (Greek: Ioannina). According to the enthusiastic reporter, Muslims and Christians gathered together in the streets of the city to demonstrate their loathing of the quarrelsome Balkan states and to protest against the imminent war.[15] Another reporter, from Salonica, informed his readers about an initiative of local Jews to form a regiment of volunteers to fight the enemies of the Ottoman fatherland.[16] Similar reports arrived from all corners of the Ottoman state. While we cannot today assess the full truth behind these optimistic reports, we can still argue that such accounts clearly reflected the official discourse that prevailed during the first weeks of the Balkan War about the ongoing fighting and its aims: the war that was launched by the Balkan states was described as an anachronistic and bigoted religious war about to be waged against the Ottoman nation. The origins of this conflict could be traced back to the Crusades. The response of the Ottoman nation to this obsolete challenge was portrayed as a total mobilization of all segments of the Ottoman nation: soldiers and civilians, Muslims and non-Muslims, men and women, adults and children. This discourse was promoted in official ceremonies, military parades, and popular gatherings. However, it was the thriving Ottoman press (including the minorities' press) that had the greatest power to diffuse these messages and shape an image of a general mobilization.

The daily press published enthusiastic reports about the war and military operations. The texts were accompanied by abundant photographs and detailed maps. The various journalists and reporters in the press attempted to explain the official stand of the Ottomans in the war and to instill in the soldiers' and civilians' minds a deep belief in the impending Ottoman victories on the various fronts. One finds in the press pictures of leading army officers, scenes from ongoing battles, reports on new weapons, accounts of heroic deeds performed by individual soldiers. All of these images and texts meant to glorify the Ottoman cause to promote the all-inclusive Ottomanist discourse.

The Balkan Wars required the embracing of widely accepted identities and the invention and adoption of symbols that would be meaningful to all sections of Ottoman society. The press was responsible for their transmission and dissemination to varied broad strata of the population. It devoted large sections of the news to demonstrate the general mobilization by producing a new set of heroes who could reflect the diversity of the Ottomans, yet simultaneously emphasize the common goal of the Ottoman nation. The Ottoman authorities had to take recourse to common symbols that would be attractive to large and diverse target groups. The war was depicted and envisioned through the prism of Ottoman patriotism and shared citizenship. In the various speeches delivered to the soldiers and the citizens, high officials employed terms implying Ottoman identity: "the Ottoman nation" (*millet*), "the Ottoman fatherland" (*vatan*), "the national mission," "the sacred obligation toward the Ottoman motherland," etc.[17] The formal use of Islamic symbols was limited.

A major indication of this inclusive policy was that the incumbent sultan, Mehmed Reşad V (reigned 1909–1918), in his capacity of caliph (the spiritual leader of the Muslim community), did not proclaim a *jihad* (holy war)[18] against the Christian Balkan states. This omission was not a coincidence; the Ottomans made an effort to depict themselves as struggling for a noble cause that represented the interests of all populations in the Empire. However, this discourse of a joint effort to safeguard the future of the shared motherland was soon to be replaced with another that put forth the treason of the non-Muslims. For the Turkish-speaking press and other publications, eastern Thrace became the main arena in which this alleged treachery took place. The loyalty of its non-Muslim populations was repeatedly debated and questioned in the press. Most writers believed that they had enough proofs to indicate the non-Muslims' betrayal and enmity toward their Muslim neighbors.

The Evolution of the Discourse of Non-Muslims' Treason

Defeated nations often trade the sword for the pen.[19] In a similar manner, the Ottoman debacle during the Balkan Wars triggered the appearance of various publications that provide insight into the contemporary debate about the defeat's causes, the ensuing internal crisis, and the possible new directions that could be taken to achieve transformation, revenge, and regeneration. This Ottoman "culture of defeat"—to use Wolfgang Schivelbusch's term[20]—represented the complete crushing of Ottoman self-confidence and the deep disillusionment of long-held convictions, but also evoked hope for crucial reforms, change, and national renewal.

Within a few weeks after the first Balkan War had begun, the dimensions of the crucial defeat became very clear to the Ottomans. A public discussion ensued around this military breakdown and its causes and culprits. A straightforward debate appeared first in the press and soon later in various publications. People began to ask blunt questions, to look for remedies and for new directions. Some of the debated issues were the set of symbols with which the Ottoman soldiers had marched into battle and the implementation of the general conscription that included non-Muslims. The scale of the war literature that appeared during the year that separated the Balkan Wars from the outbreak of World War I is impressive in its size, diversity, and openness. A major place in this "culture of defeat" was given to eastern Thrace and its diversified populations. Many Turkish-speaking publicists and authors perceived this area as the main representation of Ottoman military feebleness and of civil sufferings in the face of unprecedented Bulgarian atrocities. The alleged cooperation of the Christian population of eastern Thrace with the Bulgarian army was often mentioned.

The turning of the area into a borderland did not imply its remoteness. On the contrary, the proximity of eastern Thrace to the capital, its accessibility and its significant place as the cradle of the Ottoman presence in the Balkans, located eastern Thrace as a major symbol of the Balkan Wars. The region's transfer into a sensitive borderzone and the understanding that along this front line the future of the Ottoman state was to be determined, placed it in the major spotlight of the Ottoman press. The reconquest of the area by the Ottoman army during the brief Second Balkan War enabled the Ottoman press (and Ottoman officials) to survey the region and to fully report to their readers about the atrocities that took place in it; these reports contained frequent mentions of the alleged behavior of the Christian population and the Bulgarian policy of scorched earth.[21]

One major genre that characterizes the Ottoman war literature of the Balkan Wars is the memoirs written by military commanders. The traumatic events of the Balkan Wars prompted some of its senior participants to publish their diaries and to expose their experience of the war. Many of them endeavored to provide their readers with rational explanations for the defeat. Probably writing under the urge to establish their own blamelessness, they described the war as a major watershed in the history of the Ottoman nation, a complete catastrophe that could be repaired only if the Ottoman state would draw the right conclusions and implement the needed crucial reforms. As firsthand eyewitnesses to the military catastrophe, their testimonies dominated the public debate. They first appeared in the daily press; some of them were later published in separate books. These memoirs disclose a profound debate about the validity of the current symbols and about the future character of Ottoman identity. Against the background of total defeat and confusion, the different authors suggest an assortment of explanations. However, all of them asserted that one of the main problems was the low morale and the lack of a clear and meaningful ideological message that would unite soldiers and civilians alike around well-defined aims. Many authors pondered the non-Muslims' role in the defeat.

Some of the authors of these articles and booklets questioned the general loyalty of the non-Muslim population. Poor performance of the non-Muslim soldiers in battle and hostile behavior by the non-Muslim population that inhabited the areas in which the confrontations with the enemy took place were brought up as evidence for the non-Muslims' infamous treachery. Mehmut Muhtar Paşa, the commander of the Third Corps, claims to have concluded his memoirs in the terrible days when Edirne finally capitulated to the Bulgarian army (March 1913). His accounts and explanations for the defeat are illuminating, as he stood at the head of the Eastern Front and oversaw, quite desperately, the panicky retreat of his troops from the Bulgarian border to the outskirts of Istanbul. His book was published later that year and thus was one of the first that dealt with the military rout. It is filled with scenes of failure and incompetence. The routed commander repeatedly searched for explanations concerning the inadequate military preparations, the poor preparation of the reserve soldiers, and the huge number of exemptions from military service granted to students in Islamic institutions. Other perceived hindrances to victory were the lack of infrastructure, the politicization of the officers' ranks, the absence of modern and adequate weapons, and the soldiers' incompetence in using the weapons at their disposal. Mehmet Muhtar Paşa even attributed his forces' defeat to turbulent weather.

However, an alarming thought permeates all his writing: the severely low morale among the Ottoman soldiers. The Christian soldiers and civilians receive several sporadic references in his book, emphasizing their hostility toward the Ottoman nation. Consequently, one senses that Mehmet Muhtar Paşa actually regarded them as being situated outside the boundaries of the Ottoman nation. He suggested as a most probable possibility, for instance, that the Greeks and Bulgarians who inhabited Kırk Kilise (Kırklareli) informed the Bulgarian army about the Ottomans' ongoing disorderly retreat from the front.[22] Likewise, he justified the hastiness of the retreat toward Vize on the grounds that local Christians had informed the enemy about it.[23] He further mentioned that while preparing for action in Vize he found it difficult to organize supplies, as Christians inhabited all the neighboring villages. He claimed that the villagers murdered soldiers and officers who looked for provisions.[24]

For Mehmet Muhtar Paşa, the reference group was the Ottoman nation, and morale coincided with national strength. However, the Christians did not appear to be part of this collective any longer. Their desertion during battle proved their treachery. He wondered, for example, whether the desertion of the Christians enticed other soldiers to desert. Though he acknowledged that the answer was not clear, he noted that it was well known that most of the Greeks deserted to the enemy with the first retreat; during the second battle—he continued—not one Christian soldier was to be found.[25]

Halil Bey Efendi, the governor of Edirne during the Bulgarian siege on the city likewise referred to the assistance provided by the local non-Muslims to the advancing Bulgarian army. In an interview given to *Tanin* following the surrender of Edirne, he revealed that local non-Muslim bandits—Bulgarians and Greeks—played an important role in cutting off Edirne from Istanbul and the major military headquarters, thus condemning the city to a long siege. They were able to sever the railway tracks and telegraph lines during the crucial days of October. He further claimed that following the retreat of the Eastern army from Kırk Kilise those bandits terrorized the Muslim civilian population in different surrounding locations, such as Baba Eski, Dimetoka, and Sofulu (Soufli).[26]

The alleged disloyalty of the non-Muslim population, or at least its general indifference to the Ottoman cause, seems to be a recurring accusation in the accounts of the Balkan Wars. However, a more severe accusation sometimes accompanied the writing on the Christian population of the Balkans: its alleged participation in the Bulgarians' atrocities against the non-Muslim population of eastern Thrace.

The Evolution of the Discourse of *Mezalim* (Atrocities)

In the beginning of August 1913, *Tanin* published a report compiled by Mehmet Celal, the head of a gendarmerie unit from Gelibolu (Gallipolli) that took part in the liberation of eastern Thrace. In the center of the report appears a poignant description of the atrocities that took place in the village of Ada, not far from the town of Sofulu (Greek: Soufli). His report describes scenes of plundering, rape, and murder of innocent local Muslims and refugees at the hands of Bulgarian and Greek bandits and villagers. The prosperous village of Ada was notable for the silk industry and trade that flourished there prior to the Balkan Wars. It included about 1,900 inhabitants, from babies in their cradles to old women. After the outset of the war, the local population was augmented by a large number of refugees fleeing surrounding villages in search of a shelter in this relatively well-off community. Following the Ottoman retreat from the area, Bulgarian gangs and Greek villagers assembled in the neighboring town of Sofulu and from there launched a murderous assault on Ada. The reporter estimated that about 1,800 of the original inhabitants and 200 refugees were killed during these assaults. The reporter was able to find in the village only 16 men, 25 women, and 55 children, 96 people altogether, who survived this massacre by taking refuge in the surrounding fields. Some of them, however, suffered from appalling wounds. Similar cases of mass killings took place in neighboring Muslim villages[27]

This horrendous report represents another major genre of publication that proliferated during the Balkan Wars and in their aftermath. This genre refers to what we can describe as the documentation of *mezalim* or atrocities. This sort of publication aimed to describe bluntly the Balkan States', especially Bulgaria's, atrocities perpetrated against Muslim civilians. It sometimes also referred to the participation of local Greeks and Bulgarians in these deeds. Furthermore, as the dimensions of defeat became clearer, the documentation of the Balkan Armies' atrocities developed to become one of the main issues discussed in the press. The suffering and victimhood of the Muslim population of eastern Thrace became one of the major icons of this war literature. Testimonies of their anguish and calls to revenge their torments often appeared in the general press, in plays, and in journals designated for women or children.

At the beginning of the hostilities, only small announcements that appeared under the title "Searching for. . . ." (*aranıyor*) briefly hinted at the ordeals of the refugees who arrived in the capital from Thrace.[28] These desperate calls for assistance in locating lost members of refugees' families who disappeared in the hasty escape toward Istanbul could provide the readers with some information on the Muslims' conditions in the areas that came under Bulgarian control. However, as the war continued, the refugees' plight was considered to be one of the main arguments that could serve the Ottoman cause, and consequently it began to receive much more attention in the press and elsewhere. By providing horrible images that presented acts of sheer cruelty and violence, the Ottoman press and propaganda aimed to spread feelings of horror and revenge among the Muslim population against the Balkan states, "those twentieth-century crusaders" (*yirminci asırın ehl-i salibi*). These accusations came mainly from the ranks of semi-autonomous charitable associations that were founded during the Balkan Wars, but also from the reports of foreign journalists.[29]

Indeed, one of the major outcomes of these prolonged conflicts was a proliferation of philanthropic associations, many of them headed by politicians and bureaucrats or their female relatives, who aimed to popularize the war and to mobilize large segments of the Ottoman population for the war effort. These associations took it upon themselves to mobilize the civilian population for humanitarian, military, and political causes and thereby to fill gaps not covered by the state. While regarding themselves as "national associations" they were nevertheless equally dependant upon state funds and upon donations from benevolent individuals and fundraising campaigns. Two of these associations are pertinent to our discussion at this stage: The Association for the Muslim Refugees from the Balkans (*Rumeli Muhacirin-i İslâmiye Cemiyeti*) and The Association for Publishing Documents (*Neşr-i Vesaik Cemiyeti*). The latter provided the press with documentation of the enemy's cruelty against Muslim civilians.[30] Its honorary secretary, the famous poet Ahmet Cevat (a.k.a. Emre) (1876–1961), published in 1912/13 a book under the title of *Kırmızı Siyah Kitab* (The Red-Black Book) in which he described the Bulgarian and Greek atrocities that took place in Thrace and Macedonia. Probably in order to provide his book with credibility, the author chose to rely on oral testimonies and photos—many of which had appeared previously in the Western media. He also supplemented the coverage with calls for revenge and rejuvenation—which for him were clearly intertwined.[31]

The Association for the Muslim Refugees from the Balkans endeavored to assist the thousands of Muslim refugees who congregated in Istanbul in a desperate search for temporary housing and work. This association became most active in disseminating a discourse on the refugees' plight, albeit one that clearly attended only to the Muslim refugees. Meanwhile, independent Jewish associations were founded in Istanbul to assist the Jewish refugees from eastern Thrace.[32] While it seems that the plight of refugees was shared, their treatment was differentiated according to communal boundaries.

In order to entice the general public to assist these refugees, The Association for the Muslim Refugees emphasized the refugees' desperate plight and the atrocities that they faced in their places of origin in eastern Thrace. While at first the reports mainly referred to atrocities that had been inflicted upon civilians, it subsequently also discussed the atrocities inflicted upon Ottoman POWs who were captured in the province. The Association was the main organ that spread these particular accusations in the press and in an assortment of publications. The Association also printed booklets that were distributed to the general public in return for modest donations. One example of this literature is a booklet that appeared under the title *The Atrocities in the Balkans and the Bulgarians' Barbarism* (*Rumeli Mezalimi ve Bulgar Vahşetleri*), which provided terrifying accounts of the Bulgarian army's atrocities accompanied by graphic images depicting the victims' ordeals.[33]

One of the association's interesting initiatives was to produce a documentary film abut the refugees' plight; Hüsamettin, the association's general secretary, sent a telegram in November 1913 to the Ministry of Internal Affairs asking Talât Bey for permission to produce a film that would present the injustice, humiliation, atrocities, and tortures with which the Muslim population of the Balkans had to cope. His request emphasized the advantages of the new medium for propagating clear and poignant messages to large and varied audiences throughout the entire state. The aim was to incite a general repugnance and outrage about the Balkan atrocities and their perpetrators.[34] If completed, this would have been the very first Ottoman film, but apparently the initiative did not go anywhere.

The atrocities accusations were mainly raised against the Bulgarian army. However, the Bulgarian army and the Christian civilian population of the conquered areas in Thrace seem to blur together in various reports. A three-way correspondence between a bereaved Turkish mother from Plovdiv, Bulgaria, the Ottoman consulate in the city, and the army authorities gives us an example of one case in which there is no distinction between Bulgarian paramilitary groups and collaborating local villagers. The mother reported to the consulate that her son, Hasan, a soldier in the gendarmerie of Kırk Kilise, was murdered while in office by irregular "bandits" (*eşkiya*).[35] It is worth noting that this infamous term in Ottoman parlance connoted local outlaws who purportedly conducted life beyond the pale in the mountainous areas of the Balkans, persons who were implicitly subject to total exclusion and persecution. This case of murder was not rare. Indeed, the press reported on Christian villagers who were put on trial for participation in atrocities against Ottoman soldiers. Three Greeks from Mytilene, for example, were caught in Izmir and were tried on the grounds of murdering Turks and using weapons against Ottoman soldiers during the Greek attack against the island. The military court found them guilty and sentenced them to death.[36]

The Bulgarian atrocities against non-Muslim civilians in the name of Christian bigotry typify the Ottoman discourse on the Balkan Wars. This discourse places the non-Muslim population of eastern Thrace as putative collaborators who took an active part in these atrocities. How did the Ottoman press and public perceive the outcome of these alleged deeds of non-Muslims against the Ottoman state? Can we draw a direct line linking the calls for wreaking vengeance on Balkan states and their local non-Muslim collaborators with the non-Muslims' growing marginalization?

The Exclusion of the Non-Muslims: First Steps

Hüseyin Cahid (a.k.a. Yalcin) (1875–1957), an eminent writer and a member of the literary school known as the *Edebiyat-i Cedide* (New Literature)[37] published an editorial article in the *Tanin* in April 1913 that clearly reflects part of the new atmosphere toward non-Muslims following the experience of the First Balkan War. Under the title "The Military Service of the Non-Muslims" (*Gayri Müslimlerin Askerliği*),[38] he questioned the concept of general conscription. For him, general mobilization without any exception reflected the ideal of a joint motherland in which both Muslims and non-Muslims were equal members. The alleged behavior of non-Muslims in battle and their overwhelming desertion of the battlefield proved the futility of this hope of blending all segments of Ottoman society into one nation. For the author of this article, the conclusion was clear: the nation would not need those who were clearly not attached to the motherland. Therefore, he suggested military service should become voluntary for the non-Muslims; all those who preferred to be exempted from this national duty should pay a tax in lieu of military service.

This suspicion stirred up against the non-Muslims was further developed following the second Balkan War and the liberation of eastern Thrace. In this area, the Ottoman press found what it considered to be proof of the true scale of collaboration between the local Christian population and the Bulgarian army. At first, the press endeavored to differentiate between the acts of individuals and the attitude it ascribed to the majority of local Christians. It explained, for example, the flight of Bulgarian villagers from the liberated lands as a result of a Bulgarian wave of intimidation and incitement, and refuted any allegation of general flight; on the contrary, it claimed that most of the Christian population remained in the province and complained about the Bulgarian atrocities.[39] However, reports of Ottoman citizens of Bulgarian descent who assisted the Bulgarian army recurred in the press. It is clear from these reports that the local Bulgarians were not portrayed as part of the liberated population, or part of the Ottoman nation.[40]

A further dilemma for judging the period is precisely how to evaluate the Muslim population's responses to the alleged betrayal of the non-Muslims. One can argue that a few excerpts of journal articles constitute but impressionistic evidence and that they do not prove a general trend. Yet, it is clear, for example, that the non-Muslims were very much excluded from the accounts of the general suffering caused by the war. I have already mentioned above that the refugees' misery was perceived in the press very much as a Muslim tragedy in which the Ottoman non-Muslims had no part. It seems that the non-Muslims were absent as well in the commemoration of those who fell in battle. The ceremonies for the fallen soldiers began during the first Balkan War. Here, again, we can demonstrate that the initiative was taken from below—it was mainly the bereft families who shaped the first ceremonies. Though these private ceremonies were dedicated to specific soldiers, they nevertheless envisioned a general community as well. The purpose, we can assume, was to unite private grief with general mourning. We learn about these gatherings of grief from small announcements that appeared in the daily press inviting the public to attend commemoration ceremonies on behalf of those who had fallen in battle. The semi-private community of grieving was thereby extended to a general public, but since the ceremonies were religious and took place in neighborhood mosques, the public was envisioned as a religious one. Through these gatherings, individual tragedies were extended to include all the Muslim victims of the ongoing war. The ceremony included the reading of the *Mevlûd-i Şerif*, the traditional holy text to be read in such occasions, mentioning the divine reward awaiting the souls of the Muslim martyrs (*şüheda-yi Müslimin*). The expected reward was to be bestowed upon the soldier's soul, as well as upon other Muslim martyrs. The family of Captain (Yüzbaşı) Muhyüldin Bey, for example, who was killed during the battle of Kırk Kilise, organized a public reading of the *Mevlûd-i Şerif* in the so-called Arab mosque in the Galata quarter of Istanbul to commemorate their son and other Muslim martyrs. This form of commemoration prevailed through much of the Balkan Wars.

The exclusion of the non-Muslims was manifested in other arenas. Thus, for example, another result of the Balkan Wars was a new emphasis on what was described as "the shaping of a national economy." Policies that opposed the consumption of imported products had been implemented during previous international crises, following the Balkan Wars, the slogan was directed also against local non-Muslims with the aim of shaping a new Muslim class of merchants and entrepreneurs who would implement the new national economy. In this field of consumption, a major role was bestowed on women, who could now demonstrate their patriotic devotion toward the motherland by consuming local products. Women's associations exhorted other women to adhere to the new policy of "National Consumption" (*milli istihlâk*) of local products.[41] Here again, we can detect a new discourse that explicitly excluded non-Muslims from national interests and visions.

The Balkan Wars represent a clear watershed in the relations between the Ottoman political elite and the Empire's non-Muslim citizens. Following the development of a new discourse of Muslim Ottoman identity, the non-Muslims were excluded from the national community. The exclusion of the non-Muslims was perceived by many Ottomans who belonged to the political and cultural elite as a legitimate response to non-Muslim betrayal during the Balkan Wars. The new prevailing discourse portrayed the non-Muslims as disloyal to the national cause; the response was non-Muslims' exclusion from the major symbol of national pride and sacrifice—the army. This exclusion also implied their marginalization in the national memory of the war effort, and in the economic sphere.

Conclusion

Selânikli Fatma İclâl, a leading female author from Salonica who took refuge in Istanbul, wrote a book in March 1913 under the title *A Warning out of a Disaster* (*Felâketten İbret*). She claimed in her introduction that those who were looking at the Ottoman state might assume that they were watching an exhibition of one man with many different characters. However, she argued, this Ottoman body was actually built out of many Muslim peoples and equally diversified Christian elements, as well as Jews. However, she lamented, one could not find among these various elements one general sense of patriotism or national love that could unite all them. On the contrary, each segment of the population had its own language, vision, and religion. She compared Ottoman society to a harmony played by a broken *saz* (a stringed musical instrument) in which no order could be found. Her only conclusion was that the Turkish nation should be built from scratch; a vital role in this process would be bestowed on women in their capacity as mothers and educators.[42]

This brisk "awakening" from the Ottoman "dream" characterized much of the writing on the Balkan Wars. The Balkan Wars proved the frailty of secular Ottoman identity. The failure of an Ottoman collective identity spelled the end of the imagined secular Ottoman Nation. The Bulgarians who lived in the war-torn region of eastern Thrace and many of the Greeks who dwelled in western Anatolia were among the first victims of this new apprehension. Living in what became sensitive borderlands, many of them were forced starting in 1913 and 1914 to abandon their homes and to take refuge in the neighboring states. The wars also emphasized the vitality of Islam and its fundamental role in the Ottoman dynasty. The Ottomans entered World War I well acquainted with this inspiration. The proclamation of *jihad* at the outset of that war and the extended use of Islamic symbols in the years that followed demonstrate the importance accorded to Islam as the major characteristic of the Ottoman state. The Balkan Wars brought about an awakening from secular Ottomanism, but they did not bring about the disappearance of Ottoman ideology. Rather, the all-inclusive Ottomanism was replaced with a more Islamic Ottomanism, an ideology from which non-Muslims were excluded. They were no longer regarded as trusted members who could contribute to the task of preserving the Ottoman state from further internal fragmentation and foreign encroachment. For the Ottoman official mind, the experiment of absorbing the non-Muslims into the Ottoman nation had totally failed; the figure of the unfaithful non-Muslim prevailed in the official discourse and thence in the authorities' actual treatment of minorities.

However, for the non-Muslim population of eastern Thrace, now a vulnerable borderland, this new suspicious attitude toward the non-Muslim caused the implementation of a formal and unprecedented policy that encouraged the emigration of the Christian populations from the area. It was mainly Ottoman horror resulting from the military defeat and the Bulgarian atrocities and an ensuing resolution to preempt future debacles that prompted the adoption of harsh measures against civilian populations. This exclusion of a segment within Ottoman society and the determination to remove ostensibly alien yet still Ottoman citizens from the region set a dangerous precedent. Ethnic cleansing of unwanted ethnic and religious minorities became an acceptable practice.

NOTES

Key to Archival Citations:
The Ottoman Archives of the Prime Ministry (Başbakanlık Osmanlı Arşivi—hereafter BOA):
BOA, DH.KMŞ: The Archive of the Ministry of Internal Affairs—Special Office
BOA, DH.MTV: The Archive of the Ministry of Internal Affairs—Various Topics
BOA, DH.ŞFR: The Archive of the Ministry of Internal Affairs—Cipher
BOA.HR.HMŞ: Archives of the Ministry of Foreign Affairs—Legal Advice

This research was supported by The Israel Science Foundation (grant no. 609/04).

    1. *Serian hicretlerini te'min için kendilerine her suretle teshilât iraesi ve müşkilât ika edenlerin hemen bildirilmesi.* Başbakanlık Osmanlı Arşivi (hereafter BOA) DH.ŞFR 39/152, 20 Mart 1330 [2 April 1914].

2. BOA, DH.ŞFR 40/89, 13 Nisan 1330 [26 April 1914].

3. See, for example a petition that recounts the misery of Greeks in Vize, Lüleburgaz, and some neighboring villages, DH.ŞFR 39/163, from Talat to Edirne *vilayeti*, 22 Mart 1330 [5 April 1914].

4. Erik-Jan Zürcher, "Greek and Turkish Refugees and Deportees 1912–1924," *Turkology Update Leiden Project Working Papers Archive* (January 2003), 2 (available through the Leiden University website, www.let.leidenuniv.nl).

5. Stephen Ladas, *The Exchange of Minorities: Bulgaria, Greece, and Turkey* (New York: Macmillan, 1923). Recent studies of the transfer of the Bulgarian and Greek populations of eastern Thrace and Western Anatolia in 1913–1914 drew their arguments mainly from the archives of the Greek Ministry of Foreign Affairs. See Yannis G. Mourelos, "The 1914 Persecutions and the First Attempt at an Exchange of Minorities between Greece and Turkey," *Balkan Studies* 26 (1985): 389–413; Elizabeth Kontogiorgi, "Forced Migration, Repatriation, Exodus: The Case of Ganos-Chora and Myriophyto-Peristasis Orthodox Communities in Eastern Thrace," *Balkan Studies* 35 (1994): 15–45.

6. Norman M. Naimark, *Fires of Hatred: Ethnic Cleansing in Twentieth-Century Europe* (Cambridge, Mass.: Harvard University Press, 2002), 17.

7. For a general history of the two Balkan Wars, see Richard C. Hall, *The Balkan Wars 1912–1913: Prelude to the First World War* (London: Routledge, 2000). For a detailed description of the Ottoman army during the Balkan Wars, see Edward J. Erickson, *Defeat in Detail: The Ottoman Army in the Balkans, 1912–1913* (Westport, Conn.: Praeger, 2003).

8. On the area's historical significance as perceived during the Balkan Wars, see Mehmet Ali Nüzhet, *1912–1913 Balkan Harbi* (Istanbul: Karagöz Gazetesi, 1913?), 30–31.

9. Yonca Köksal, "Reform in the Province of Edirne: Ottoman Archives on Local Administration during the Tanzimat Period (1839–1876)," *Peri Thrakis* 2 (2002): 177. See also Kemal Karpat, *Ottoman Population 1830–1914: Demographic and Social Characteristics* (Madison: University of Wisconsin Press, 1985); Alexis Alexandris, "The Greek Census of Anatolia and Thrace (1910–1912): A Contribution to Ottoman Historical Demography," in *Ottoman Greeks in the Age of Nationalism*, ed. Dimitri Gondicas and Charles Issawi (Princeton, N.J.: The Darvin Press, 1999), 45–76.

10. Zürcher, "Greek and Turkish Refugees," 2.

11. A. Yerolympos, "A Contribution to the Topography of 19th Century Adrianople," *Balkan Studies* 34(1) (1993): 52.

12. Ahmet Halaçoğlu, *Balkan Harbi Sıranda Rumeli´den Türk Göçleri (1912–1913)* (Ankara: Turk Tarih Kurumu Basımevi, 1995); Justine McCarthy, *Death and Exile: The Ethnic Cleansing of Ottoman Muslims, 1821–1922* (Princeton, N.J.: The Darvin Press, 1995).

13. George Kennan, *The Other Balkan Wars: A 1913 Carnegie Endowment Inquiry in Retrospect with a New Introduction and Reflection on the Present Record* (Washington, D.C.: Carnegie Endowment for International Peace, 1993), 109–35. Also see chapter 13 this volume.

14. Avner Levi, "The Anti-Jewish Pogrom in Terakia, 1934," *Pe'amim* 20 (1984): 111–32 [in Hebrew].

15. *Tanin*, 26 Eylül 1328 [9 October 1912].

16. *Tanin*, 26 Eylül 1328 [9 October 1912].

17. See, for example, the declaration given by Nâzim Paşa, the war minister, to the Ottoman soldiers at the beginning of hostilities, quoted in Aram Andonyan, *Balkan Savaşı*, trans. Zaven Biberyan (Istanbul: Aras, 1999), 237–38.

18. On the meaning and use of *jihad* in modern times, see Rudolph Peters, *Islam and Colonialism—The Doctrine of Jihad in Modern History* (The Hague: Mouton, 1979).

19. W. Schivelbusch, *The Culture of Defeat: On National Trauma, Mourning, and Recovery,* trans. by J. Chase (New York: Picador, 2003), 4.

20. Ibid.

21. See, for example *Takvim-i Vekayi* [the Ottoman official gazette], 28 Temmuz 1329 [8 August 1913].

22. Mahmud Muhtar Paşa, *Üçüncü Kol Ordusu ve İkinci Şark Ordusu'nun Muharebât* (Istanbul: Kannat Kütübhanesi, 1331 [1915/16], 34–5.

23. Ibid, 48.

24. Ibid, 56.

25. Ibid.

26. "Edirne'nin Muhasarasının Tarihçesi," *Tanin,* 17 Nisan 1329 [30 April 1913].

27. "Mühim bir Vesika," *Tanin,* 26 Temmuz 1329 [8 August 1913].

28. See, for example *Tanin,* 4 Nisan 1329 [17 April 1913]; *Takvim-i Vekayi,* 10 Kânun-ı Sâni 1328 [23 January 1913].

29. The first Ottoman book that was dedicated to the fall of Salonica and the ensuing atrocities used British, German, and Belgian reports that appeared in the European press. See Sadık Alevi, *Tahsin Paşa Ordusu ve Selânik Teslimi* (Istanbul: Meşrutiyet Kütübhanesi, 1332 h. [1914/15]).

30. See, for example *Tanin,* no. 1499, 20 Kânun-ı Sâni 1328 [3 February 1913].

31. Ahmet Cevad [Emre], *Kırmızı Siyah Kitab—1328 Fecayi* (Istanbul: s.n., 1329 [1913–14]).

32. On their activities in accommodating Jewish refugees from eastern Thrace, see my article "'Ottoman Jews! Run to Save our Homeland!'—Ottoman Jews in the Balkan Wars 1912–1913," *Pe'amim* 105–106 (2005–6): 14–16 [in Hebrew].

33. *Rumeli Mezalimi ve Bulgar Vahşetleri* (Istanbul: Mahmud Bey Matbaası, 1328 [1912/1913]).

34. BOA, DH.KMŞ. nr.63/69. Also quoted in Ali Özuyar, *Babiâli'de Sinema* (Istanbul: İzdüşüm, 2004), 37–38.

35. BOA, HR.HMŞ, 246/89, 5 Temmuz 1330 [18 July 1914].

36. *Tanin,* 23 Mart 1329 [6 April 1913].

37. David Kushner, *The Rise of Turkish Nationalism 1876–1908* (London: Frank Cass, 1977), 82–84.

38. *Tanin,* 14 Kânun-ı Evvel 1328 [27 December 1913].

39. *Tanin,* 8 Temmuz 1329 [21 July 1913].

40. See, for example *Tanin,* 22 Temmuz 1329 [4 August 1913]; 23 Temmuz 1329 [5 August 1913]; 24 Temmuz 1329 [6 August 1913].

41. See, for example *Tanin,* 2 Mart 1329 [15 March 1913].

42. Selânikli Fatma İclâl, *Felâketten İbret* (Istanbul: Keteon Bedrosyan Matbaası, 1331 [1915/1916]).

16

"Wiping out the Bulgar Race"

Hatred, Duty, and National Self-Fashioning in the Second Balkan War

Keith Brown

Introduction

This paper attempts an anthropologically informed reading of Greek military conduct toward Bulgarian civilians during the Second Balkan War of 1912–13. It draws on a set of accounts of atrocities allegedly authored by their Greek perpetrators, captured by Bulgarian forces, and reproduced and analyzed in the Carnegie Inquiry set up to investigate the causes and conduct of the Balkan Wars.[1] Greek and pro-Greek scholars at the time strenuously denied the authenticity of the sources, in addition to accusing Bulgarian regular and irregular forces of worse atrocities over a longer period; outside observers found the soldiers' narratives persuasive evidence of the region's primitive passions.[2]

The incidence of contested narratives is, of course, hardly rare, in the Balkans or elsewhere. Nonetheless, this case—which, in the words of one recent commentator, "still awaits its modern scholarly researcher"—invites a treatment that draws on, and hopefully advances, ongoing and vibrant debates at the intersection of anthropology and history which stress the importance of critical and reflective attitudes toward both the particular facticity of documentary sources and the explicatory power of theoretical categories of ostensible sociocultural regularities.[3]

In that spirit, the reading offered here is "anthropological" not in the sense presumed by historian Jacob Gould Schurman, who made reference to the fluid connections between "anthropological" and "linguistic or political" units in the Balkans as one cause of the region's turbulence, nor in the sense more recently invoked by military historian John Keegan, who in the early 1990s argued that the break-up of Yugoslavia was "a primitive tribal conflict only anthropologists can understand."⁴ These authors see anthropology's contribution to histori-cal debates as limited to the so-called "primordial attachments"—what Clifford Geertz re-ferred to as the "congruities of blood, speech, custom, and so on, [which] are seen to have an ineffable, and at times overpowering coerciveness in and of themselves."⁵

What I offer here instead is an anthropological reading in the spirit of the interpretive turn that Geertz himself pioneered in that 1973 volume, where he emphasized that both the coerciveness of such attachments, and indeed the attachments themselves, are not simply "given": their givenness is the product of cultural and/or historical processes which them-selves demand interrogation. And this same spirit, I suggest, infuses recent anthropological work in and on archival material in which, in Ann Stoler's words, "distinguishing fiction from fact has given way to efforts to track the production and consumption of facticities as the contingent coordinates of particular times and temperaments, places and purposes."⁶

Here, then, I revisit and revivify a charged debate that was waged over and through a set of written materials produced in 1913, during the Second Balkan War, specifically letters purportedly written by Greek soldiers and captured by Bulgarian forces, which are preserved in the 1913 Carnegie Endowment Inquiry in the form of reprinted English translations, along with a facsimile of one of the original letters and its envelope.⁷ The letters describe a campaign of extermination by the Greek Army against Bulgarian civilians, in which soldiers violate girls, kill prisoners, and burn houses, all to try and "wipe out the race."⁸

This paper explores previous readings of this material, moving beyond an investment in distinguishing "fact" from "fiction" to analyze their facticities and the different discursive domains within which they can be placed. The more familiar readings, as one might expect, serve to buttress well-rehearsed arguments about the Balkan Wars in particular, and Balkan character in general. I hope that the more ambitious readings here offer something new to the debate over the nature of Balkan history in highlighting the relationship between ongo-ing processes of nation formation in the region and ideas about warfare and racial hierarchy circulating elsewhere in Europe and North America at the time. A key trope, I suggest, is the concept of national duty: and I conclude by arguing that a focus on this aspect of the Balkan Wars offers a pathway out of an unproductive, continuously adversarial and predominantly "groupist" debate which spirals around ideas of ethnic hatred and claims of genocide.⁹

The Sources and Their Context

The First Balkan War began in the first week of October 1912, when Montenegro, Serbia, Bulgaria, and Greece all declared war on the Ottoman Empire and launched their armies against Turkish forces in "Turkey-in-Europe," a swathe of land from the Adriatic to the Black Sea coast, including modern day Albania, Kosovo, the Republic of Macedonia, a substan-tial part of northern Greece, and western Bulgaria. Montenegro's ambitions were limited, and Greece's participation only confirmed relatively late: at the heart of the alliance was a Serb-Bulgarian agreement on the deployment of forces and the division of Macedonia. The investment was substantial: both countries, as well as Greece and Turkey, had spent signifi-cant sums on European weapons systems, and drawn on Western experience and expertise to train and build their armies. Although British Foreign Office assessments rated the Greek army as inferior to that of its allies, all three deployed large conscript armies. Bulgaria boast-ed the highest mobilization rate—a Bulgarian general in 1910 proclaimed "we have become the most militaristic state in the world—putting over 350,000 men into the field."¹⁰

The First Balkan War saw the allies gain ground on all fronts. In the west, Greece and Serbia faced relatively little resistance after the first month of fighting, and annexed or occupied substantial territory in Albania, Kosovo, and Macedonia. In Thrace in the east, by contrast, closer to the Turkish capital of Constantinople (Istanbul), Bulgarian forces were drawn into extended siege warfare against a stubborn defense. That disparity of effort and spoils generated friction between the allies: a death-blow to their solidarity was struck by the internationally brokered Treaty of London of May 1913, which created an autonomous Albania and thereby deprived Serbia of territory it had expected to gain. Instead of withdrawing from northern Macedonia to make way for Bulgaria to take control, Serbian forces stayed in place as occupiers: Greek forces did the same in southern Macedonia. Bulgaria's leaders decided to seek further gains through military action against their former allies, launching the Second Balkan War in late May of 1913. The initiative failed, as Bulgarian troops found themselves fighting not only Greek and Serbian, but also Turkish and Romanian forces. Entirely isolated—and effectively blockaded, with active hostilities against all neighbors—Bulgaria eventually sued for peace, having lost 44,000 dead and 102,000 wounded in the two wars. Serbia's losses were reported at around 12,000 dead and 48,000 wounded; Greece's around 6,000 dead and 45,000 wounded.[11]

Besides military losses, what caught international attention at the time, and in subsequent writing, was the civilian toll of the wars. The military campaigns were waged across a civilian landscape which all three states claimed to be liberating or reclaiming, but where lines of loyalty were far from clear, and where at least some of the locals had been waging irregular warfare for the past decade or longer, complicating the civilian/soldier divide. Historian Alan Kramer provides figures for civilian casualties reported—Greece, for example, claimed that the Bulgarian army massacred between 220,000 and 250,000 civilians—and also notes the contemporaneous press coverage of atrocities in newspapers across Europe.[12] In Kramer's view, the atrocities were "part of a longer-term project of nation-state construction on the basis of the chimera of 'ethnic' purity." As hundreds of thousands of people were displaced, observers witnessed what Mark Mazower has described as the first attempt by states to use military conflict "to pursue long-term demographic goals."[13]

Some of the most horrifying accounts came from Leon Trotsky, traveling as a correspondent with the Serbian army in "Old Serbia," Kosovo, and Albania, who heard first-hand accounts of casual brutality against "Arnaut" [Albanian] prisoners and civilians by Serbian irregular and regular soldiers.[14] The *Frankfurter Zeitung* indicated that Serbian atrocities against Albanians were the worst, and had as their goal extermination: the Carnegie Inquiry reported Greek and Bulgarian violence against Muslim civilians, and also a trend for those civilians to flee ahead of the advancing (Christian) armies.[15]

Contemporary observers did not find these stories surprising or puzzling. There was general consensus that that antipathy between Serbs and Albanians ran deep, that Christians had suffered under Muslim rule, and that the First Balkan War was infused by a spirit of revenge, as armed Christian forces sought retribution for the infamous "five hundred years under the Turks."[16] What attracted more attention as both more shocking and more puzzling was the "fratricidal" behavior of the second war that was labeled by d'Estournelles De Constant, the Commission's head, as the "more atrocious of the two."[17]

Indeed, the Carnegie commission was formed only in July 1913, after the commencement of the Second Balkan War, and calls from the Greek King Constantine for the international community to acknowledge and address the unlawful behavior of Bulgaria's army. The commission traced how tensions between the allies, and their incompatible agendas, shaped developments on the ground. They documented, for example, how in Vodena (modern Edhessa) the atmosphere changed from the early enthusiasm expressed by the "Bulgarian" population toward their Greek "liberators." The Greek army began requisitioning food and valuables, arresting notables, and erasing Slavic inscriptions.[18] When fighting between the former allies began in earnest in early July, the situation in places like Voden escalated: large numbers of young men were jailed as alleged *komitadjis*—a term discussed further below—while communities were compelled to sign declarations declaring that they were Greek. In other towns and villages, according to the Carnegie Inquiry, these national conversions were enforced at bayonet-point.[19] Similar measures were reportedly taken by Serbian forces in Western Macedonia against residents who identified themselves as "Bulgarian."[20]

It was on the battlegrounds of Thrace and eastern Macedonia, though, where Greek and Bulgarian forces clashed, that the Carnegie Commission found its most disturbing data. The fighting lasted only a month: in that time, the front line moved back and forth over a landscape still occupied by civilians, and in the maneuvering came the events at the heart of this paper. The Carnegie Inquiry reported in the following terms:

> It happened that on the eve of the armistice (27 July) the Bulgarians captured the baggage of the Nineteenth Greek infantry regiment at Dobrinichte (Razlog). It included its post-bags, together with the file of its telegraphic orders, and some of its accounts. We were permitted to examine these documents at the Foreign Office at Sofia.... The file of telegrams and accounts presented no feature of interest. The soldiers' letters were written often in pencil on scraps of paper of every sort and size. Some were neatly folded without envelopes. Some were written on souvenir paper commemorating the war, and others on official sheets. Most of them bore the regimental postal stamp. Four or five were on stamped business paper belonging to a Turkish firm in Serres, which some Greek soldier had presumably taken while looting the shop. The greater number of the letters were of no public interest, and simply informed the family at home that the writer was well.... We studied with particular care a series of twenty-five letters which contained definite avowals by these Greek soldiers of the brutalities which they had practiced.[21]

Among the phrases the commissioners quoted from these letters were the following:

> "We picked out their eyes while they were still alive."
> "We killed them like sparrows."
> "Everywhere we pass, not even the cats escape. We have burnt all the Bulgarian villages that we have traversed."
> "We have turned out much crueler than the Bulgars—we violated every girl we met."
> "We are burning villages and killing Bulgarians, women and children."
> "Wherever there was a Bulgarian village we set fire to it and burned it, so that this dirty race of Bulgars couldn't spring up again."
> "This is something like real war, not like that with the Turks. We fight day and night and we have burned all the villages."
> "We shoot all the Bulgarians we take, and there are a good number of them."

These eyewitness testimonies were a key resource for the Commission's overall argument, and prompted bitter exchanges between advocates of the different states involved.

Believing the Sources, Diagnosing the Sentiments

The Commission members saw in the diversity of the letter stock, the variety of handwriting, and the range of expression, evidence of the letters' authenticity: other commentators agreed.[22] They therefore included them in an assemblage of data points from which they diagnosed the condition of wider Greek society. They were especially struck by prints they saw on sale on the streets of Salonika depicting Greek soldiers gouging out the eyes of Bulgarian soldiers, or in one case included in their report, "holding a living Bulgarian soldier with both hands, while [the Greek] gnaws at the face of his victim with his teeth, like some beast of prey."[23] And finally, the Commissioners also include the entire text of a telegram sent to Greek diplomatic staff across Europe by King Constantine on 12 July 1913, which concluded by stating "the Bulgarians have surpassed all the horrors perpetrated by their barbarous hordes in the past, thus proving that they have not the right to be classed among civilized peoples."[24] On this evidence the Commission reached the following verdict on the roots of Greek conduct in the Second Balkan War:

> Day after day the Bulgarians were represented as a race of monsters, and public feeling was roused to a pitch of chauvinism which made it inevitable that war, when it came, would be ruthless. In talk and in print one phrase summed up the general feeling of the Greeks toward the Bulgarians, "Dhen einai anthropoi!" (They are not human beings). In their excitement and indignation the Greeks came to think of themselves as the appointed avengers of civilization against a race which stood outside the pale of humanity.[25]

The commissioners thus made clear their condemnation of the Greek way of war, and what they saw as the deliberate deployment of stereotypes in order to whip up sentiments among soldiers as well as civilians. They saw the letters as documentary proof that the various representations had an effect on people's thoughts and actions. They went on to suggest that the effectiveness of such representations owed something to the characteristics of Greeks in general, which they describe in these terms:

> When an excitable southern race, which has been schooled in Balkan conceptions of vengeance, begins to reason in this way, it is easy to predict the consequences. Deny that your enemies are men, and presently you will treat them as vermin. Only half realizing the full meaning of what he said, a Greek officer remarked to the writer, "When you have to deal with barbarians, you must behave like a barbarian yourself. It is the only thing they understand."[26]

The conduct of the Greek soldiers, then, attested in these letters, is in this reading a function of larger forces—most notably a propaganda campaign in which the commander-in-chief participated, and an inherent "excitability" which combined to bring about breaches of the law of war.

Denying the Sources, Justifying the Actions

Even before the Carnegie Commission published its findings, Greek and pro-Greek authors had challenged the authenticity of these sources, which were originally made public by the Bulgarian government. The tone of the Inquiry sparked further polemical responses, as some readers argued that the letters in fact said more about Bulgarian behavior than about Greek conduct or, indeed, excitability. The arguments in this line were multiple, and not necessarily consistent with one another. In the first case, they suggested Bulgarian perfidy in forging the documents. Responding to specific assertions in the Carnegie report, for example, Demetrius Cassavetti took the approach of disproving the veracity of two of the 25 letters—in one case, on the basis of the author's name matching a soldier who actually served on a different front, and in another on a point of internal fact with regard to a claim that a set of prisoners were all killed, whereas Cassavetti claimed to know from a personal friend that they were not. He then argued from these two cases to the whole set, stating that "if two (or even one) of these letters be proved by external evidence to be forgeries, then the remainder would hardly be looked on as genuine."[27] Not content with this, he then additionally pointed to discrepancies in their form: the texts are reproduced only in fragments, in which academic handwriting is combined with illiterate spelling, and many accents are missing. For Cassavetti, these were clear signs of Bulgarian forgery.

A number of pro-Greek authors also saw mischief at work in the Commission's readiness to accept the letters. Cassavetti and others were particularly critical of the role played by H. N. Brailsford and Paul Milioukov in the Commission's work: Milioukov, a Russian, was considered pro-Bulgarian because of his nationality, and Brailsford, a British journalist and academic, was considered pro-Bulgarian on the basis of his most recent authoritative work on the region.[28] They were the two commission members who had read and partly translated the Greek letters, and their integrity was directly impugned in rebuttals published in Greece and distributed widely in Europe and North America.[29]

Cassavetti's dogged detective work, though, as well as the focus on the bad faith of the sources' handlers, is a departure from his overall argument, as well as the more general trend of philhellene interpretation. For the most part, the evidence of the letters was put to one side in a focus on the brutal or savage characteristics of Bulgarians—as a race, or people, and not only as an army. Cassavetti cited as authority the *Daily Telegraph*'s Captain Trapmann, who enrolled Bulgarian soldiers in a cast list of historical infamy, shrilling that "Tipoo Sahib, Nero, Robespierre, Catherine of Russia and the Borgias were but mildly oppressive and unkind as compared with the lustful brutes who wear the uniform of King Ferdinand of Bulgaria."[30] Other authors devoted their labor to highlighting Bulgarian misconduct.[31] The highest-profile figure identified with this view, though, was King Constantine himself, who had claimed the right to enforce the rules of war and prevent further "abominations" through "... reprisals, in order to inspire their authors with a salutary fear, and to cause them to reflect before committing similar atrocities."[32]

All this, in some sense, undercut the efforts by Cassavetti to prove that the letters were forged. For these data indicate that the commander-in-chief of the army declared publicly a willingness to respond to unlawful killing—itself a function of deep-rooted Bulgarian character—with violence of the kind that the letters describe. The overall effect is to say both "Greek soldiers did not commit any crimes or atrocities" and also "Greek soldiers would be fully justified had they committed such crimes, because Bulgarians had already done worse"—a two-pronged argument in which each blunts the force of the other.

Common Ground: The Mutual Constitution of "Greeks" and "Bulgarians"

What the different sides in the debate over the authenticity of the letters and the driving factors behind atrocities share is what Rogers Brubaker recently diagnosed as "groupism," or "the tendency to take bounded groups as fundamental units of analysis (and basic constituents of the social world)."[33] They differed on the genealogy and membership of those named groups. Greek sources tended to suggest a centuries-old antipathy between the peoples, while at the same time denying that residents in Greece or Thrace were "really" Bulgarians and deploring Bulgarian efforts to encroach on communities which were "really" Greek. The Carnegie commission, by contrast, focused on the novelty of the extreme violence, linking it to a contemporary, deliberate, and top-down process of creating an inhuman enemy on the part of Greek leaders.

More recent scholarship, as well as some other work of the period, cuts through the rhetoric of timeless ethno-national groups and emphasizes instead the mutual constitution of the two identities as each went through a wrenching and far-reaching transformation in the late nineteenth century. The endpoint—the Second Balkan War of 1913—was a full-fledged interstate rivalry or antipathy that shaped subsequent decision-making for both countries, playing a part in their choice of sides in the First World War. Both "Greek" and "Bulgarian" emerged from that process far closer kin to European models of belonging than Greek sources acknowledged for Bulgaria, or than the Carnegie commission acknowledged for Greece. They remained throughout, in Peter Loizos's apposite term, "culturally intimate."[34] The identity work of the late nineteenth century, culminating in the violence of 1913, reinscribed intimacy within national frontiers, while creating distance at those frontiers.

As this language indicates, a key component of this process was the making of claims over territory. For Bulgaria, one of the fundamental resources in this regard was the map of "greater Bulgaria" produced in the late 1870s, which showed the country extending to the shores of Lake Ohrid, on the modern border between Albania and the Republic of Macedonia. This map was reproduced by the Carnegie Commission in their report.[35]

A Greek counterpart from the early twentieth-century is described by an English author sympathetic to the Greek cause as "one insignificant but widely circulated document of the time."

> It is an Easter card, with "Christ is risen" printed across it, and is a "memento from Macedonia." Macedonia lies enclosed in the red crescent of Ottoman rule, and in it is a heart, with the red blood of the "Greek spirit" flowing from it. The shears of Panslavism are cutting it, and the Austrian snake is making through it to Salonica, and the arrows of Bulgarian propaganda and Servian propaganda and Roumanian propaganda are piercing it. And in the centre of the heart is a cross, and the words "Mother Church, help me!" To the average Greek this was not insincere or sentimental; it was as true an expression of national emotion as that which inspired Holland against Spain, or Italy against Austria, or the Boers against ourselves.[36]

This image offers a number of modalities of attack on the "true faith" of Orthodoxy. First, two great powers—Austria and Russia—respectively penetrate and cut, in imagery that can be read as highly gendered, assaulting both Greek (feminine) virtue and Greek (male) vigor. But the primary cast is religious: (Greek) Macedonia is within the (Islamic) crescent, but its vitality is being sapped as a set of rival and expanding Christian religious movements, each with national and territorial dimensions (Bulgarian, Servian, and Roumanian respectively), launch their own assaults.

The image comes from a time in which "Greekness" was synonymous with Christian Orthodoxy, with the Patriarch in Constantinople as unquestioned spiritual leader of the geographically dispersed community that constituted the Rum millet—a millet being a protected minority community under Ottoman law. From the mid-eighteenth century until the end of the nineteenth century, "Greeks" had a spiritual monopoly in this domain, so Orthodox

Christians, whatever their mother tongue, worshipped in Greek. "Greekness" also signaled a position of power or influence in the commercial realm: Greeks represented a middleman minority, in which role they competed directly with other non-Muslim groups, most notably Jews.[37] This second component of Greekness remained a permeable category, into which upwardly mobile Orthodox Christians of other walks of life could be assimilated, and to which it was expected that such individuals aspired. As a shared (though not necessarily understood) language of worship Greek did have the status of "truth-language," but it was also a marker of socioeconomic status gained in the marketplace and passed on in the schools.[38]

There was, therefore, both a universalist aspect to Greekness (in that it was attributed to all members of the Rum millet) and a particularistic aspect, in that it was a property of a professional, commercial elite. Only in the latter sense was there room for the term "Bulgar," which generally referred to less wealthy, less sophisticated rural folk who were nonetheless still members of the Rum millet. It was not that all Greeks were merchants and Bulgars peasants, but rather that merchants were Greeks, and peasants Bulgars. Alongside the work of Stoianovich and Karakasidou, this argument has been made convincingly by Hans Vermeulen and is also at the heart of work by Laurie Kain Hart, who terms it a "linguistically coded caste structure."[39]

Scholarly consensus also indicates the historical significance of 1870, when the Ottoman Sultan recognized the Exarchate, with its head in Constantinople, as a distinct Christian church structure, the principal novelty of which was that the language of worship was not Greek, but literary Bulgarian. This represented innovation in two ways: not only was the language different, but so was the register. Where the Patriarchate liturgy continued to employ the classically derived *katharevousa* as opposed to everyday spoken Greek, the Exarchate broke down the diglossic divide between "high" and "low" registers (available also in the Slavic languages, which each had their own vernacular but traced origins to Old Church Slavonic) and preached a more populist form of religion. Where the Patriarchate emphasized the crucial role of the church as intermediary between worshipper and God, the Exarchate created conditions in which lay members could shape their own relationship with the Almighty.

The Sultan granted the Exarchate authority over religious communities in the territory which now constitutes Bulgaria. The greater threat to "Greek" unity and influence, though, was the provision in the law that congregations elsewhere could vote whether to remain under the authority of the Patriarch or transfer to the Exarchate. Greek historian Evangelos Kofos has argued that a key moment in the transformation of the force of Hellenism came in 1872, when the membrane separating religion and politics was breached as the Patriarchate leadership declared the Exarchate schismatic.[40] That decision raised the stakes for Christian communities all across Macedonia, contributing to the hardening of the lines of allegiance, as "Exarchist" and "Bulgarian" increasingly came to be considered synonymous, as did "Greek" and "Patriarchist."

Projects of national unity and mobilization adopted religious trappings, in a move that much of modern scholarship has tended to accept as inevitable. That it was not necessarily so at the time is clear not only from Kofos's careful reconstruction of efforts to mend the schism, but also from accounts like the following consular report by a British diplomat describing the activities of a Greek (state) official in the area of Gevgelija, at the modern Greek-Macedonian border.

> No one can contest the right, and even duty, of the Œcumenical Patriarchate to organize and encourage its adherents to resist the aggression of the Exarchists by every legitimate means. But the participation of Hellenic officials in the struggle would at once transfer it openly to

the political and racial arena; and however much that policy might commend itself to the partisans of the "Great Idea," it would inevitably introduce a new and powerful element of discord into this disturbed province.[41]

This British official notes the phenomena that Kofos describes—that the creation of the Greek (or in his terms "Hellenic") nation state, and its efforts to intervene outside its borders, impinged upon the wider sense of Greekness represented by the Patriarchate's religious leadership. What both Graves and Kofos, diplomat and historian respectively, recognize and describe is analyzed in theoretical terms by Laurie Kain Hart in work on Epirus, a city on the Greek-Albanian border. There, Hart juxtaposes "civilization" and "culture" as two modes of Greek national identity: the first, an open and expansive conception, which recruits and assimilates potential others, and which is rooted in language: the Greek term is *politismos*. The second is less porous and relies more on a notion of shared blood or descent. Hart ties it to a late-nineteenth century German model of *kultur*, acknowledging that it can manifest itself in aggression and preemptive action against perceived "others."

This contextual knowledge makes another reading of the letters, not offered at the time, plausible. The letters could be seen as evidence as to how this debate by Greeks over the nature of "Greekness" had worked itself out by 1913. The soldiers, in this view, had risen to the specific challenge that Greek intellectuals and activists had been posing ever since the establishment of the Exarchate, and with added force in the period since 1903, the year of the Ilinden Uprising, which most Greeks saw as a Bulgarian enterprise. In 1904, George Ditsias, a resident of the mountain town of Krushevo, had written an account of how his town had been seized by Bulgarian insurgents—and its Greek population, as a result, subjected to violence both by the invaders and then by Ottoman forces. In the main text, published in Athens in 1904, Ditsias describes the development of Krushevo's prosperity as a Greek community that prided itself on its culture, toleration, and peaceful, lawful character. In the afterword, Ditsias urged the imperative that Greeks begin to think of themselves as a threatened community. The Bulgarians had "unanimity of purpose, and brotherly co-operation": they represented a determined and extremist minority which recruited new members.[42] Their solidarity was rooted in the present and in collective action, and Ditsias called on his Hellenic readers to meet this determination with their own. His call was heeded, as the so-called *Makedonomachoi*, Greek paramilitaries (including many army officers), crossed into Ottoman Macedonia in the years 1903–1908, using the same violent methods as their adversaries.[43]

Ditsias's perspective was shared by writers across different genres of Greek literature in the same period who all painted an increasingly hostile view of Bulgarians as posing a particular threat. The poet Kostis Palamas, for example, stressed the Greek need for a "fighting leader" and a "more militant stand toward life," while authors Ion Dragoumis, Penelope Delta, and A. N. Kyriakou mobilized the story of Basil the Bulgar-Slayer and linked it to present struggles.[44] Basil's symbolic importance was such that one Greek professor, writing of Bulgarian atrocities, included the reported desecration of his tomb. Meanwhile, a pro-Bulgarian author noted that Constantine was granted the epithet "Bulgar-killer" in a triumphal arch erected in Salonika.[45]

Hierarchy Out of History: The Slavic Menace

The Bulgarian national project of the late nineteenth century, then, mobilized linguistic and religious solidarity to threaten Greek hegemony. The project also involved physical violence—manifested most dramatically in the Ilinden Uprising of 1903, but also in a longer campaign of intimidation and assassination of representatives of the status quo. One part of the Greek response, as described above, was to adopt the same tactics—becoming, effectively, more like Bulgarians in so doing. This pragmatic reorientation in turn demanded a renewed project of ideological distance-making, which took the form of a sustained effort to draw moral distinctions and inscribe an ordered hierarchy of races. The earlier, Ottoman-era "caste structure" identified by Hart served as a key resource; so too, though, did contemporary scholarly ideas about the people of "the East."[46]

In this regard, Greek propagandists and political and religious leaders were in the mainstream of Western European ideas. As Larry Wolff argues in *Inventing Eastern Europe,* the Slavic East had long been seen as exotic and backward, a place where Asiatic influences were dominant, and where travelers found confirmation of ideas regarding racial hierarchies.[47] In a work published in 1878, Edson Clark paraphrased Cyprien Robert, writing "Nothing is more like a group of savages' huts than a cello [*sic*], or Bulgarian village." Earlier, American explorer John Ledyard had seen connections between "Tartars" and Africans, widely perceived as symbols of the primitive.[48] With the growth in Russian ambition and capacity in international relations, and the presumption that other Slavic states would be natural allies or clients to the new power, nineteenth-century alarmists saw the potential for this human mass to be put to work in conquest.

As late as World War II, as Omer Bartov points out, racist ideas about Slavs could be mobilized in German propaganda, as for example in the second of the *Kampfparolen,* or battle slogans, of 1945: "A rule of the Asiatic Untermenschen over the West is unnatural and goes against the sense of history."[49] A similar sense of world order was already being expressed at Greek universities as early as 1879 (in the immediate aftermath of Russian intervention in support of a "greater Bulgaria"), when Professor Neokles Kazazis wrote, "the Cossack in the East, at Constantinople or near it, signifies nothing else but an entire and immediate overthrowing of the European equilibrium and of modern civilization." In the same vein, Cassavetti wrote in 1914 that the Bulgarian was ". . . only a rustic Tartar with the thinnest veneer of civilization and education," with "savage and primitive instincts . . . repulsive to the mind and feeling of the average Hellene."[50]

As these citations suggest, Bulgarians, or Bulgars, represented a particularly fertile space in the late nineteenth century for the fusion of ideas of cultural and racial backwardness. Still subject to Ottoman rule, their language was often viewed as simpler and less rich than that of other peoples—as a patois, for example, "at the level of the lowest intelligences," or, in a 1912 United States congressional document prepared for the Dillingham Commission on Immigration, as "the most corrupt of all Slavic languages at the present time."[51] Claims of Bulgarian linguistic inferiority also found confirmation in the head-measuring practices of physical anthropology. In fact, Bulgars emerged even more stigmatized, as it was reported that they were in fact of "Asiatic" or "Mongol" origin, and elsewhere as "less Slavs than Huns."[52] Thus, in Folkmar's terms, Bulgarians represented an oddity, being "physically of one stock and linguistically of another."[53]

This kind of rigid, categorical thinking is easy now to disown, dismiss, or ridicule. But the particularly close correspondences between the language of Demetrius Cassavetti and Daniel Folkmar, as well as that of the Greek and other European university teachers and scholars cited here, and their capacity to influence policy and opinion, demand greater attention. Given the debates over "race-suicide" and the "white man's burden" of this period,

associated most closely with the U.S. Presidency of Theodore Roosevelt but extending further in time and space, it certainly seems plausible that ideas about racial inferiority more
familiar from Western colonial projects were harnessed to mobilize public opinion for war
in Greece. The Macedonian Bulgars, with their hybrid ethnological roots, recent religious
apostasy, and their perceived backwardness, seem cut from the same cloth as their colonized
brethren, described in Rudyard Kipling's "The White Man's Burden" as "new-caught sullen
peoples, half-devil and half-child."[54]

The Horror of Modern War: What the Soldiers Say

All this looks like corroboration of the conclusion reached by the Carnegie commission on
the significance of the Greek soldiers' letters: that they represent evidence both of atrocities
being committed, and of a singular Greek view of Bulgarians as at best inferior, and at worst
sub-human. The rank-and-file in the Greek army killed Bulgarian civilians, in this view, because they knew, or at least believed, it was the right thing to do. Certainly, the snippets
noted above, with their reference to the "dirty race," could easily be supplemented by linked
references to "this dishonest nation [Bulgaria/Bulgarians]," or to determination to "leave not
a root of this race," that make it sound as if the soldiers were on message.

That is, though, cut-and-paste and uncritical cherry-picking. When we look more
closely at the letters, this interpretation looks more controversial. There is, for example, a
mismatch between the Commission's reading that the letters were "avowals of atrocity" and
the fact that only three of the 28 use the first-person singular "I" as the agent of the actions
they describe: the rest use instead the collective "we" which represents a weaker form of
ownership of actions and may, in fact, describe observer rather than participant status for
the writer. Of the three who use the first person singular, two declare their participation in
shooting prisoners, and one specifies that the prisoners in question were *komitadjis*—that is,
guerillas and terrorists of the kind who had operated in Macedonia over the past decade, targeting civilians who opposed their agenda. The examples of explicit avowal, then, are against
past or present armed enemies, all male.

Describing the burning and pillaging of villages and the rape and murder of civilians,
we could compile from the letters the following judgments or commentaries:

> "This war has been very painful . . ."
> ". . . the places will stay in my memory for ever."
> "God only knows what will come of it."
> "God knows where this will end."
> ". . . you cannot imagine what takes place in a war."
> "How cruel!"
> ". . . impossible to describe. . . . it is butchery."
> ". . . an inhuman business."

This simple, and deliberately fragmentary exercise reveals that at least a third of the letter-
writers include editorial commentary that is rather different in tone from the sentiments
which the Carnegie Inquiry emphasized. This strand depicts the war as painful and cruel,
and their actions against people and property as "butchery" or "an inhuman business." Several of the writers explicitly state that they cannot describe what they have witnessed. One
soldier writes "these places will stay in my memory for ever," while two others use variants on

the sentiment "Only God knows where this will end." These, then, are not readily recognizable as the men who, in the words of the Carnegie Endowment Inquiry, "wished to believe that they and their comrades perpetuated bestial cruelties."[55]

What can we make of this? These aspects were highlighted neither by the commission, who read the letters in the light of their own ideas about the Balkans, nor by Greek interpreters, who sought to move the discussion to focus on Bulgarian conduct, and so did not engage with the content of the letters. One regrettable advantage of rereading these letters a century later is that we now have a greater pool of eyewitness testimony of military violence in civilian contexts with which to compare their tone and phrasing, and from which to better understand the particular stresses that their authors confronted. German atrocities in Belgium during World War I, for example, were attested in captured soldiers' diaries, first analyzed by Joseph Bedier, and also mobilized by Gustave Le Bon, who picked out language that is strikingly similar to that of the Greek soldiers. Among the excerpts Le Bon presents are the following:

> "Not a single living man will be left behind us."
> "The sight of the corpses of the inhabitants who had been killed beggars description. Not a house is left standing. We took all the survivors from . . . a convent which we burnt, and shot them all."

Le Bon also reports that German officers at Louvain gave the order "kill everyone and burn everything."[56]

Similar language can also be observed across the Atlantic, just before the Balkan Wars, in the U.S. occupation and "pacification" of the Philippines. A member of an artillery unit wrote "We bombarded a place called Malabon, and then we went in and killed every native we met, men, women and children. It was a dreadful sight, the killing of the poor creatures."[57] In December 1901, 12 years before King Constantine's telegram, General J. Franklin Bell went on record with plans to violate "accepted tactics of civilized warfare," and in the course of reprisals for a successful surprise attack on a unit in Balangiga, another U.S. general issued to a subordinate the order "Kill and burn! The more you kill and burn the better you will please me!"[58]

The language of both Greek soldiers and their commanders, then, was hardly exceptional at the time, nor were their actions. From the German testimony of conduct in Belgium, Bedier drew out two strands of conduct and attitude: "the cold premeditated authoritarianism of the High Command and the undisciplined license of a brutal soldiery."[59] Le Bon notes the similarity of the testimony to that of the Balkan Wars, and appears to point to the poverty of the argument that atrocities are perpetrated only by "semi-savage races": for, he concludes, "even the highest form of civilization does not make men less barbarous."[60]

Both these French scholars, then, read in these accounts humanity gone awry—or perhaps, revealed for the façade that it is. That strand of argument remains alive in more recent scholarship that seeks to explain systematic violence, from its early twentieth century forms through more recent cases of ethnic cleansing or genocide. Mark Osiel, for example, indicates that some atrocities are fostered when passions are stimulated from below, and Daniel Pick points to the particular way in which anthropological and "medico-biological" diagnoses served to stimulate those passions while shrouding them in scientific authority during the Franco-Prussian War, as well as in subsequent conflicts.[61] Daniel Goldhagen's account of German complicity in the Nazi project of genocide is perhaps one of the best known versions of this approach: John Dower's use of American combat soldiers' views of the Japanese other during World War II also fits this mold.[62]

An alternative strand, though, emphasizes not atavistic hatred, but bureaucratic routines and the obedience they engender as a key factor in the generation of atrocities. Discipline, in this interpretation, is not an unqualified virtue or universal remedy: especially in its modern, bureaucratic form it organizes, orchestrates, and amplifies violence rather than limiting it.[63] A key dimension in this interpretation of human willingness to inflict harm, laid out by Stanley Milgram in his classic study, is the surrender of autonomy and the adoption of what Milgram calls the "agentic state."[64] What Milgram notes in particular is how this self-transformation is accompanied by the allocation of responsibility to the victim of the violence—that they deserve punishment and, with that moral judgment made, the perpetrator of violence becomes a dutiful instrument of a larger, already determined set of causes and consequences.[65]

Milgram's insights have informed subsequent analyses of obedience—lying at the heart, for example, of Christopher Browning's study of a German reserve police battalion during World War II.[66] Milgram's own immediate point of reference was American military experience in Vietnam. But his work also illuminates aspects of early twentieth-century military behavior. Alongside Bedier and Le Bon's reading of German atrocities in Belgium, for example, stands Van Langenhove's nuanced account of the central importance of the idea of the *franc-tireur*—the irregular warrior, concealed in the civilian landscape, who poses a deadly threat to the individual soldiers in an advancing army.[67] Tracing the history of the figure back to the Franco-Prussian War, van Langenhove describes how the rank-and-file of the German army became convinced that almost any civilian might be a *franc-tireur* and grew willing to use preemptive, disproportionate violence against civilians, justifying it to themselves as a defensive tactic. In Milgram's terms, the *franc-tireur* became for German officers and enlisted men the prime mover of the violence in which they were engaged, and as such the deserving victim of their righteous retribution: by eradicating these duplicitous enemies, they would restore order.[68]

Figures with the *franc-tireur*'s core characteristic of duplicity and mystery, who blur the line between active and passive resistance among civilians, can be found in a host of other historical settings including, most recently, the Iraq of 2003, where Saddam Hussein's Fedayeen threatened to derail the anticipated speed and smoothness of the U.S. military's advance. Ottoman Macedonia was also home to a figure of this kind, most often called by their Bulgarian or Macedonian name, *komitadji* . . . and I conclude this paper by suggesting that a focus on the figure of the *komitadji* as a variant on the *franc-tireur* provides the basis for a fuller analysis of the Greek soldiers' conduct and testimonies, and a definitive judgment on their facticity.

As noted above, it was only in those cases where either prisoners or *komitadjis* were being executed that the Greek letters contain avowals of personal agency. Irregular forces, comprised of locals and some nationals from neighboring states, had been operating on Ottoman territory for at least a decade, sometimes targeting civilians for assassination or terror attacks, and sometimes engaging each other. By far the most numerous and locally embedded were those associated with the Macedonian Revolutionary Organization, which looked to Bulgaria for support.[69] As the Carnegie commission reported, the Balkan Wars were marked by cases in which local communities welcomed the allied armies as liberators and took up arms against Turkish forces or civilians. As tensions between the allies arose, and liberators became occupiers, these irregulars harassed or at times even confronted the regular armed forces of Greece, Bulgaria, and Serbia. The Greek and Serbian fears of *komitadji* actions in the areas they controlled, then, were not wholly fabricated, but were an acknowledgment of the reality: their campaigns in Macedonia and Thrace were those of foreigners, and once they broke with Bulgaria, goodwill was lost. But there was a spiraling and rumor-driven element to this as well, as, like German soldiers in Belgium, or U.S. soldiers in Iraq, they found it impossible to distinguish between civilians and potential enemies.

And at the same time, it was this very context—where their self-image as liberators did not match the way they were perceived, as occupiers—that led to the kinds of atrocity that were witnessed. Louvain in Belgium, Malabon in the Philippines, and Haditha in Iraq all demonstrate the same kind of reaction by military units to unanticipated resistance, or perceived duplicity, that we see in the Greek letters. The issue in all cases is not the level of barbarism or civilization of one army or people as opposed to another: it is the breakdown of easy distinctions between civilian and military in contested spaces, and the blurring of the categories of occupation, liberation, and collaboration that define the limits of what is acceptable conduct.

Such comparison from beyond the region, across space and time, weighs in to suggest that these letters were genuine, not forged. They also point to the importance of understanding that there was indeed a fundamental difference between the Greek and Bulgarian enterprises in Macedonia and Thrace. This was not racial, or civilizational, but rather organizational. Although both armies were equipped with similar hardware from the armories of Europe, they were built for very different kinds of war. The Greek military was built on the German or Prussian model; later this was complemented by a French military mission.[70] The Hellenic Army had sent selected military cadres to operate in Macedonia in the period 1903–1908, but they operated strictly against Macedonian and Bulgarian *komitadjis* and their sympathizers. They were counterinsurgents, rather than insurgents: in military parlance, holding the field, preparing it for the main attack by Greece's regular army. During the Balkan Wars, the use of such tactics reportedly continued, with advance emissaries "fixing" enemy targets (which included uncooperative civilians) so that the main force could then operate directly against them.[71] Greece's irredentist agenda was to be realized, in standard Clausewitzian terms, by the application of maximal force—represented by the army, operating outside national borders—at the enemy's center of gravity.

The Bulgarian army, by contrast, looked to Russian doctrine for its roots.[72] It was built to wage wars of national liberation for the Bulgarians in Macedonia: its strategy was to operate alongside irregulars, paramilitaries, or insurgents on "foreign" territory, as part of a mass national movement.[73] As such, it was closer in orientation to concepts of "people's war" that have become more familiar in the course of the twentieth century. When Bulgarian generals prided themselves on their level of militarization, it can be argued that they referred to something more than sheer numbers of conscripts. To a far greater extent than Greece, Bulgaria had sponsored and nurtured ideas of local autonomy in Macedonia, and Bulgarian officers had spent far more time working directly with inhabitants of the region, diffusing both the hardware and the ideas necessary for violent revolution. The goal was a "nation under arms" that stretched across Macedonia, and that would exact an unacceptable cost from any foreign occupying army.

The Greek soldiers of the Nineteenth Infantry, then, found themselves fighting a war they did not understand. Their leaders, military and civilian, were little better off. But the front-line troops and their commanders dealt with the difficulties posed by this particular challenge to their doctrines and procedures in different ways. It is at a distance from the battlefield that ideas—and especially dangerous ones—work most effectively. As noted in Bartov's account of Germany's World War II invasion of Russia, "the dehumanization of the enemy, which is at the core of the process of barbarization, hinges upon the enemy's anonymity, facelessness . . . best achieved when he is part of a mass, and most difficult when it is reduced to two individuals facing each other."[74] King Constantine's response to obstacles in Thrace and Macedonia, and that of his general officers—as with General Smith in the Philippines, or General Moltke in World War I, frustrated by the slow advance of his army through Belgium—was informed by a dangerous mix of second-hand experiences, theories of the behavior of "others," and somewhat Manichaean conceptions about the mission of civilization or culture. Thus, in the terms used by Sir Edward Grey in the British parliament, the war began as liberation, turned to a struggle for conquest, then ended as war of extermination.[75]

The reactions of Greek soldiers on the front line were rather different, and the letters bear witness to their distress. As such, they resonate with the conclusions reached by two of the foreign commentators cited earlier. H. N. Brailsford, who translated the letters and worked most closely with them as a member of the Carnegie commission, published a book of his own one month after the release of the *Inquiry*. *The War of Steel and Gold* is a radical, anti-imperialist work: among its targets were British jingoism and chauvinism more generally. Brailsford included his own front-line testimony from his experience as a volunteer in the Greco-Turkish War of 1898.

> I had not known I was firing at simple peasants. I had been firing at "the enemy," "the Turks," "the Sultan's brutal soldiery," the "forces of Oriental barbarism," and other names, phrases and abstractions . . . I understood at length that the military discipline which I had been proud to obey myself, and to impose on others, was the necessary condition of this criminal stupidity called war.[76]

Russian war correspondent (and future Red Army Commander) Leon Trotsky offered a different, but equally scathing commentary on the international order's ultimate responsibility for the violence he witnessed in the Balkans, writing:

> We have learned how to wear suspenders, to write clever leading articles, and to make milk chocolate, but when we need to reach a serious decision about how a few different tribes are to live together on a well-endowed European peninsula, we are incapable of finding any other method than mutual extermination on a mass scale.[77]

I conclude with these citations, and the suggestion that they came out of what could be termed an ethnographic sensibility on these authors' part to the realities of asymmetrical warfare among civilians, wherever it occurs. They resonate, I suggest, with the content and form of the Greek soldiers' testimony from 1913, suggesting that the systematic slaughters of the Balkan Wars should be attributed not to the mentality of an "excitable southern race" but to the reach and impact of European-style military loyalty, duty, and discipline—terms that, as Stanley Milgram argued, are "heavily saturated with moral meaning," and which underpin the kind of groupist thinking that was so much a part of national self-fashioning across the continent.[78] In this reading, the Greek soldiers' testimonies from the borderlands of Europe register not atavistic hatred, but flickers of human resistance to the modern, totalizing project of which their authors were an unwilling part. The Balkan Wars, perhaps, were not as Balkan as we have come to believe.

Notes

1. George Kennan, ed., *The Other Balkan Wars: A 1913 Carnegie Endowment Inquiry in Retrospect with a New Introduction and Reflections on the Present Conflict* (Washington, D.C.: Carnegie Endowment, 1993).

2. See for example Anonymous, *Les Cruautés bulgares en Macédoine orientale et en Thrace, 1912–1913; faits, rapports, documents, temoignages, officiels* (Athens: D. Sakellarios, 1913); Demetrius Cassavetti, *Hellas and the Balkan Wars* (London: T. F. Unwin, 1914); Z. Duckett Ferriman, *Greeks, Bulgars, and English Opinion* (London, 1914); Theodore Zaimis, *The Crimes of Bulgaria in Macedonia* (Washington DC, 1914; available as an e-book through Kessinger publishing company, www.kessinger.net).

3. Alan Kramer, *Dynamic of Destruction: Culture and Mass Killing in the First World War* (Oxford: Oxford University Press, 2007), 136. Recent anthropological and historical works operating at this intersection would include Ann Laura Stoler, *Along the Archival Grain: Epistemic Anxieties and Colonial Common Sense* (Princeton: Princeton University Press, 2009); Brian Keith Axel, ed., *From the Margins: Historical Anthropology and its Futures* (Durham, N.C.: Duke University Press, 2002); Penelope Papailias, *Genres of Recollection: Archival Poetics and Modern Greece* (New York: Palgrave, 2005); Omer Bartov, *Germany's War and the Holocaust: Disputed Histories* (Ithaca, N.Y.: Cornell University Press, 2003).

4. Jacob Gould Schurman, *The Balkan Wars 1912–1913* (Princeton: Princeton University Press, 1914), 89. John Keegan, cited in Mark Mazower, "Ethnicity and War in the Balkans" 1997, online at: http: //nationalhumanitiescenter.org/publications/hongkong/mazower.htm (accessed 20 March 2012).

5. Clifford Geertz, *The Interpretation of Cultures* (New York: Basic Books, 1973), 259.

6. Stoler, *Along the Archival Grain,* 33.

7. Kennan, ed., *The Other Balkan Wars,* 307–315: figures 50, 51.

8. Ibid., 311ff.

9. The concept of groupism is taken from Rogers Brubaker, *Ethnicity Without Groups* (Cambridge, Mass.: Harvard University Press, 2004).

10. Jonathan Grant, *Rulers, Guns, and Money: The Global Arms Trade in the Age of Imperialism* (Cambridge, Mass.: Harvard University Press, 2007); Misha Glenny, *The Balkans 1804–1999: Nationalism, War, and the Great Powers* (London: Granta, 1999), 222; James Sheehan, *Where Have all the Soldiers Gone? The Transformation of Modern Europe* (Boston: Houghton and Mifflin, 2008), 12; Glenny, *The Balkans,* 219.

11. Figures for Bulgarian and Serbian casualties are taken from Kennan, ed., *The Other Balkan Wars,* 378, 395. Figures for Greek casualties are from Hellenic Army General Staff, "The Hellenic Army from Independence to the 1920s," in *Essays on War and Society in East Central Europe, 1740–1920,* ed. Stephen Fischer-Galati and Béla K. Király (Boulder, Colo.: Social Science Monographs 1987), 159.

12. Kramer, *Dynamic of Destruction,* 13637; Zaimis, *The Crimes of Bulgaria,* 5.

13. Kramer, *Dynamic of Destruction,* 136; Mark Mazower, *The Balkans: A Short History* (New York: Modern Library, 2000), 117. See also Richard Hall, *The Balkan Wars, 1912–1913: Prelude to the First World War* (London: Routledge, 2000), 124.

14. Leon Trotsky, *The Balkan Wars 191213: The War Correspondence of Leon Trotsky,* trans. Brian Pearce (New York: Pathfinder Press 1980), 266–72.

15. Kramer, *Dynamic of Destruction,* 137; Kennan, ed., *The Other Balkan Wars,* 151.

16. Hermenegild Wagner, *With the Victorious Bulgarians* (London: Constable and Company, 1913), 255; see also Mazower, *The Balkans,* 118.

17. In Kennan, ed., *The Other Balkan Wars,* 1.

18. Ibid., 198–200.

19. Ibid., 197.

20. D. Mikoff, *Le Calvaire d'un people: A propos de l'anniversaire de la guerre entre les allies* (Sophia, Bulgaria: The Royal Court, 1914).

21. Kennan, ed., *The Other Balkan Wars,* 104.

22. See for example H. M. Wallis, "The Devastation of Macedonia," *The Quarterly Review* 220 (January and April, 1914): 520.

23. Kennan, ed., *The Other Balkan Wars*, 97. The images are reproduced on 96 and 98.

24. Ibid., 300. The telegram is also referenced at a number of points in the main text, including 96 and 214.

25. Ibid., 95.

26. Ibid., 95.

27. Cassavetti, *Hellas*, 348.

28. H. N. Brailsford, *Macedonia: Its Races and Their Future* (London: Methuen and Co. 1906). Ironically, earlier in his career Brailsford had fought as a volunteer on the Greek side in the Greco-Turkish War, an experience he documented in his first book, *The Broom of the War God: A Novel* (London: William Heinemann, 1898).

29. Anonymous, *Les Cruautés bulgares*, vol. 6. I take the presence of the 1913 volume in Brown University's library, with a bookplate indicating that it was a gift from the Greek government, as one data point for the reach of the Greek propaganda effort.

30. Cited in Leland Buxton, *The Black Sheep of the Balkans* (London: Nisbet and Co, 1920), 95n.

31. Anonymous, *Les Cruautés bulgares*; Zaimis, *The Crimes of Bulgaria*.

32. Kennan, ed., *The Other Balkan Wars*, 300.

33. Brubaker, *Ethnicity Without Groups*, 2.

34. Peter Loizos, "Intercommunal Killing in Cyprus," *Man* (ns) 13(4) (December 1988): 639–53. This is a slightly different usage from Michael Herzfeld, *Cultural Intimacy: Social Poetics in the Nation-state* (London: Routledge, 1997).

35. Kennan, ed., *The Other Balkan Wars*, 32.

36. Ronald M. Burrows, "The New Greece," *The Quarterly Review* 220 (January and April 1914), 489.

37. Trajan Stoianovich, "The Conquering Balkan Orthodox Merchant," *Journal of Economic History* 20 (1960): 234–313.

38. Anastasia Karakasidou, *Fields of Wheat, Hills of Blood: Passages to Nationhood in Greek Macedonia, 1870–1990* (Chicago: University of Chicago Press, 1997).

39. Hans Vermeulen, "Greek Cultural Dominance Among the Orthodox Population of Macedonia during the Last Period of Ottoman Rule," in Anton Blok and Henk Driessen, eds., *Cultural Dominance in the Mediterranean Area* (Nijmegen, Netherlands: Katholieke Universiteit, 1984), 225–55; Laurie Kain Hart, "Culture, Civilization, and Demarcation at the Northwest Borders of Greece," *American Ethnologist* 26(1) (1997): 201; see also Basile Recatas, *L'Etat Actuel du Bilinguisme chez les Macedo-Roumains du Pinde et le Role de la Femme dans le Langage* (Paris: Libraire E. Droz, 1934), 14.

40. Evangelos Kofos, "Attempts at Mending the GreekBulgarian Ecclesiastical Schism (1875–1902)," *Balkan Studies* 25(2) (1984): 347–68.

41. FO 195/2182/286. No. 54. Salonica, 8 April 1904: Graves to O'Conor.

42. George Ditsias, *The Catastrophe of Krousovo: Atrocities by Bulgarians and Ottomans against the Hellenes* (Athens: S. Vlastos 1904), 109.

43. Dimitrios Livanios, "Conquering the Souls: Nationalism and Greek Guerrilla Warfare in Ottoman Macedonia, 1904–1908," *Byzantine and Modern Greek Studies* 23 (1999): 195221. For further discussion of Ditsias's account, and the cognitive shift it represents, see Keith Brown, *The Past in Question: Modern Macedonia and the Uncertainties of Nation* (Princeton: Princeton University Press, 2003), 92–102.

44. Gerasimos Augustinos, *Consciousness and History: Nationalist Critics of Greek Society 1897–1914* (New York: Columbia University Press, 1977), 61; Paul Stephenson, *The Legend of Basil the Bulgar-Slayer* (Cambridge: Cambridge University Press, 2003), 118–25.

45. Zaimis, *The Crimes of Bulgaria*, 40; Wallis, "The Devastation of Macedonia," 511.

46. Hart, "Culture, Civilization, and Demarcation," 201. In this argument, I focus on the cultural specificities of the Greek-Bulgarian interaction in the early twentieth century. An alternative explanatory model for the intensity of the violence of the Balkan Wars would be that developed by anthropologist Peter Loizos, writing on Cyprus, and sociologist Keith Doubt on the former Yugoslavia. In these cases, they argue, deadly violence was not an outcome of ancient hatred, but an index of the intimate connectedness between separable, but in fact coexistent, communities living in close

proximity and functionally intertwined. As noted above, in "Intercommunal Killing," Loizos terms the Greek and Turkish communities on Cyprus "culturally intimate," while Doubt notes the greater intensity of violence in precisely those parts of the former Yugoslavia which were a byword for multiculturalism and tolerance, such as Sarajevo. See Keith Doubt, *Sociology after Bosnia and Kosovo: Recovering Justice* (Lanham, Md.: Rowman and Littlefield, 2000). In each case, one group of actors seeks political capital by creating a (more or less) singular, well-defined constituency in what had been a context of trade-offs, bargains and compromises. To achieve this, "others" must be created, and in these particular contexts, they must be created out of people whose "selfness"—glimpsed in the experience of neighborliness—is at least as potentially open to development. In crude functionalist terms, then, the level of symbolic violence required to rearrange the categories of self and other involves "real" violence.

47. Larry Wolff, *Inventing Eastern Europe: the Map of Civilization on the Mind of the Enlightenment* (Stanford: Stanford University Press, 1994), 347.

48. Edson L. Clark, *The Races of European Turkey: Their History, Conditions and Prospects* (New York: Dodd, Mead, and Co., 1878), 446; Wolff, *Inventing Eastern Europe*, 346.

49. Omer Bartov, *The Eastern Front, 194145: German Troops and the Barbarisation of Warfare* (New York: St. Martin's Press, 1986), 95.

50. Augustinos, *Consciousness and History*, 20; Cassavetti, *Hellas*, 345, 311.

51. Michel Paillares, "Hellenism in Macedonia," in *Greece in Evolution: Studies Prepared under the Auspices of the French League for the Defense of the Rights of Hellenism*, ed. G. F. Abbott (New York: Wessels and Bissell, 1910), 152 (cited in Hart, "Culture, Civilization, and Demarcation"); Daniel Folkmar, *Dictionary of Races and Peoples* (Washington, D.C.: U.S. Congress, 1912), 27.

52. Folkmar, *Dictionary*, 26, 108; Cassavetti, *Hellas*, 311; see also William Sloane, *The Balkans: A Laboratory of History* (New York: The Abingdon Press, 1914), 72; Schurman, *The Balkan Wars*, 89.

53. Folkmar, *Dictionary*, 27.

54. Cited in Stephen Jay Gould, *The Mismeasure of Man* (New York: Norton, 1981), 119.

55. Kennan, ed., *The Other Balkan Wars*, 97.

56. Gustave Le Bon, *Psychology of the Great War: The First World War and Its Origins* (New Brunswick, N.J.: Transaction Publishers, 1999), 383–84.

57. James Creighton Miller, *"Benevolent Assimilation": The American Conquest of the Philippines, 1899–1903* (New Haven, Conn.: Yale University Press 1982), 188. For a discussion of terrorism, genocide, and what the author terms "institutional extremism" in Germany's colonial wars in the same period, see Isabel Hull, *Absolute Destruction: Military Culture and the Practices of War in Imperial Germany* (Ithaca, N.Y.: Cornell University Press, 2005).

58. Miller, *"Benevolent Assimilation,"* 207, 220.

59. John Horne and Alan Kramer, "German 'Atrocities' and Franco-German Opinion, 1914: The Evidence of German Soldiers' Diaries," *Journal of Modern History* 66(1) (1994): 12.

60. Le Bon, *Psychology of the Great War*, 391; see also Bartov, *Eastern Front*.

61. Mark J. Osiel, *Obeying Orders: Atrocity, Military Discipline, and the Law of War* (New Brunswick, N.J.: Transaction, 1999), 173; Daniel Pick, *War Machine: The Rationalization of Slaughter in the Modern Age* (New Haven, Conn.: Yale University Press, 1993), 91ff.

62. Daniel Goldhagen, *Hitler's Willing Executioners: Ordinary Germans and the Holocaust* (New York: Knopf, 1996); John Dower, *War Without Mercy: Race and Power in the Pacific War* (New York: Pantheon, 1986).

63. Zygmunt Bauman, *Modernity and the Holocaust* (Ithaca, N.Y.: Cornell University Press, 2001); Stanley Cohen, *States of Denial: Knowing About Atrocities and Suffering* (London: Polity Press, 2001); Osiel, *Obeying Orders*; Pick, *War Machine*.

64. Stanley Milgram, *Obedience to Authority: an Experimental View* (New York: Harper & Row, 1974), 13334.

65. Ibid., 9; see also Cohen, *States of Denial*, 96; Bartov, *Germany's War*, 183.

66. Christopher Browning, *Ordinary Men: Reserve Police Battalion 101 and the Final Solution in Poland* (New York: Aaron Asher, 1992). For an illuminating discussion of the debate between Goldhagen and Browning, as well as cultural biases in Milgram's approach, see Bartov, *Germany's War*, 139–91.

67. Fernand Van Langenhove, *The Growth of a Legend: A Study Based Upon the German Accounts of Francs-Tireurs and "Atrocities" in Belgium* (New York: Putnam's Press, 1916).

68. In the Belgian case there is also evidence that the *franc-tireur* was culturalized as "other," as German sources slip into allegations of Catholic fanaticism.

69. The Macedonian Revolutionary Organization had its own ambiguous relationship with the Bulgarian state, manifested by an internal, deadly schism between "autonomists" and pro-Bulgarian "centralists" or "*vrhovists.*" This is documented in Duncan Perry, *The Politics of Terror: The Macedonian Revolutionary Movements 1893–1903* (Durham, N.C.: Duke University Press, 1988).

70. Thanos Veremis, "The Selection and Education of Greek Officers From Independence to 1920," in *The East Central European Officer Corps, 1740–1920s: Social Origins, Selection, Education, and Training,* ed. Bela Király and Walter Scott Dillard (Boulder, Colo.: Social Science Monographs, 1988), 130. Hellenic Army General Staff, "The Hellenic Army," 159.

71. Wallis, "The Destruction of Macedonia," 521.

72. Iliya Iliyev and Momchil Yonov, "Evolution of the Bulgarian Armed Forces from the Eighteenth Century Until 1920," in *Essays on War and Society,* ed. Fischer-Galati and Király, 85–104; Ljudmil Petrov, "The Training of Bulgarian Officers 18781918," in *The East Central European Officer Corps,* ed. Király and Dillard, 107–124.

73. Iliyev and Yonov, "Evolution," 88.

74. Bartov, *Eastern Front,* 129.

75. Sloane, *The Balkans,* 226.

76. H. N. Brailsford, *The War of Steel and Gold* (London: G. Bell and Sons, Lt., 1914), 176–77.

77. Trotsky, *The Balkan Wars,* 148.

78. Milgram, *Obedience to Authority,* 146.

17

FAILED IDENTITY AND THE ASSYRIAN GENOCIDE

David Gaunt

The suffering of the Assyrian, Chaldean, and Syrian Christians in the Ottoman Empire during World War I is one of the least known genocides of modern times. If it is known at all it usually goes under the collective name of Assyrian genocide, which will be used here. A major reason for this obscurity is the failure of these religiously heterogeneous ethnic groups to agree on a common cultural and national identity. This resulted in a multiplicity of local experiences and selective memories. The story of the Assyrian genocide dissolves into a number of specific minor narratives framed by local contexts, most of which pale in comparison with the grand drama of the Armenian genocide, but were no less deadly for the populations involved. The declining Ottoman Empire found Oriental Christians that for centuries were split into antagonistic churches which had been locked into denigrating one another. Each cult had a strong exclusive in-group identity that militated against the very idea of a multilayered pan-Assyrian identity. Many outside observers considered these Christians curious, insignificant cultural relics, whereas the fate of the vigorous Armenian community loomed as a great concern in international diplomacy. One aspect of this invisibility is that the narratives of the Assyrian genocide build on testimonies of survivors whose perception was limited to local issues such as the struggle with nomadic tribes for agricultural land and the religious fanaticism of local Muslim sects. In the final analysis the Assyrians had no clear idea why they were being annihilated. In particular, they recognized only the local dimensions of their suffering and had no understanding of the overall policies and interests of the Young Turk government.

Two themes will be addressed in this chapter. The first concerns how the Assyrians got caught up in a state-orchestrated genocide that targeted Armenians. The second is about why the Assyrian genocide is still relatively unknown. Both are linked to the disputed nature of national identity and to the Assyrians' distant settlement in economically marginal borderlands. Some compensated for their impotence by seeking protection from Kurdish tribes, which of course only further complicated matters of cultural diversity and political loyalties.

Confessional and Political Heterogeneity

The historical origins of the Assyrian peoples are clouded. Historically they[1] lived in northern Mesopotamia or Kurdistan. They formed an unstable ethnic puzzle along the present-day frontiers of Iran, Iraq, Syria, and Turkey. All of them share a legacy from the ancient Assyrian Empire, but not all call themselves Assyrians. Basic divisions among them date to wars between the Roman Empire and Persia. An eastern group grew inside Persia and a western group evolved inside the Byzantine Empire. This ancient division nurtured permanent religious and linguistic sectarianism, which became expressed in mutual exclusivity and fierce theological conflicts.

A main feature of the Assyrian peoples is their early adherence to Christianity. A loose church organization spread from Antioch and imprinted its special version of Christian theology. After the Roman Empire accepted Christianity, a process of unification began. Key standpoints essential to the Antioch theology were deemed heretical. Rejecting the new Roman creed, the newly designated heretics simply created their own churches. They could only survive as isolated enclaves in the marginal tracts of northern Mesopotamia. Easterners, particularly those who belong to the Nestorian church, freely call themselves Assyrians.[2] The Chaldeans agree to the term Assyro-Chaldeans. But the large western group, led by the Syrian Orthodox Church, reject Assyrian as a meaningful identity and insist on being called Syrians or Syriacs.[3]

The theocratic Ottoman state conserved Assyrian religious differences by officially distinguishing the *Nasturiler* (Nestorians) from the *Keldaniler* (Chaldeans) and the *Süryaniler* (Syrian Orthodox). None of these churches had more than a few hundred thousand adherents by the early twentieth century.[4] For administrative reasons the non-Muslims were formed into separate *millets* (Turkish for nation) and were represented by the highest religious leaders, appointees of the sultan. The millet leader was also responsible for collecting the taxes from his community. Originally, the Ottomans recognized three non-Muslim millets: the Jewish, Greek Orthodox, and Armenian.[5] For centuries the Syrian Orthodox and Nestorian Assyrians were associated with the Armenian millet, while the Chaldeans as Catholics had no millet to belong to until much later.

In the course of the nineteenth century, the Sultan established new millets for the minor religions. Up to 1882 the Syrian Orthodox had been part of the large Armenian millet. When the Armenian Catholics received millet status, their millet spoke on behalf of the Chaldean and Syrian Catholics. Because of internal quarrels, all Assyrian churches were in desperately bad shape. All had serious problems with the legitimacy of the leaders, as appointment to high office was either hereditary or for sale. Further, in the shifting balance of power, the patriarchs proved increasingly unable to protect their own communities from lawlessness and violence. The Chaldean church was the largest Catholic organization among the Assyrians. But in 1873 the exodus of many of Mosul's wealthy families shook its foundations, splitting it in two.[6] On the eve of World War I a Chaldean priest published a study that showed a church in decline, particularly in the Anatolian provinces. Some parishes had no priest and the members would attend Armenian Catholic services.[7]

From about 1840, northern Mesopotamia emerged as an increasingly contested theater of ethnic and confessional civil war.[8] The ethnic balance of power shifted in favor of a few Kurdish tribes that were willing to be the instruments of the central government. The indigenous Christian minorities were on the losing end of local struggles over territory and social supremacy, as various Kurdish tribes and clans battled for local supremacy. Blocked by their mutual antagonism, the Christians could mount no unified opposition. Powerless alone, the Assyrians formed ties with Kurdish tribes and some even had Christian sections. Although this was a wise decision in the short run, it brought the Christians directly into the turmoil of Kurdish tribal warfare. Conditions grew particularly dangerous when the tribes split over resistance or submission to the Ottoman government's expanding control.

Reckoning the size of the Oriental Christian population is not a straightforward matter. However, a few sources can be combined to give a population on the eve of World War I. A delegation at the Paris peace conference published statistics tables for what they called the Assyro-Chaldean core areas. And the Armenian Patriarch supplied figures for non-Armenian Christians living in Armenian core areas. When the two sources are combined one gets a total of 608,000 divided about equally among Nestorians, Chaldeans, and Syrian Orthodox.[9] This is probably a maximum figure.

The Social and Economic Background to Massacres

Borderzones are sensitive militarized areas, and states make efforts to see that the populations are docile and loyal. The Assyrians and Syrians in the Ottoman Empire were not particularly docile, and they had grown even less loyal once the Young Turks came to power. Therefore, plans to deport them were just being implemented on the eve of World War I.

In northern Mesopotamia economic life revolved about the caravan trade, which was slow and costly. Avoiding the deserts to the south, caravans traversed the region because of its adequate supplies of water and food. Towns were situated at suitable distances and shops and crafts lived from provisioning the tradesmen. The farmers sold wool, tobacco, fruit, and nuts. However, the region declined economically during late Ottoman times. Caravan trade dwindled as the Suez Canal and the Trans-Caucasian railroad opened up quicker routes, which resulted in less transit through Mesopotamia. The price of wool, the most important local product, plummeted in the face of competition from Australia. Mardin saw the number of shops decline from 1,200 in 1875 to 700 in 1891.[10] In addition, Assyrians suffered from the depredations of Kurdish tribes and were steadily pushed off their land. Subsequently, new Christian villages grew up in the previously sparsely populated steppe along the desert's rim. But the new villages were very exposed to nomad attacks.

When Ottoman rule began seriously to falter the European powers intervened to protect the Christian minorities. By the Treaty of Berlin 1878 the Europeans assumed responsibility for supervising the progress of reforms toward social equality between Muslims and Armenians. From this date the Armenian Question became the object of international humanitarian concern. Many countries placed consuls in major cities to monitor the implementation of reforms. They often complained to the provincial government and demanded restitution and justice. Consular dispatches indicate that in certain localities the other Christians were treated just as harshly as the Armenians. The situation was particularly inflamed in Diyarbakir province, which formed a multiethnic transitional zone mixing Armenians, Kurds, Syrian Orthodox, Syrian Catholic, Chaldean,

Nestorians, and Arabs. The more numerous Kurds were increasingly influential at the local and provincial levels.

A French consul stationed in Diyarbakir warned that the "Armenian Question" concealed a universal Christian dimension.

> This state of affairs affects all Christians regardless of race, be they Armenian, Chaldean, Syrian or Greek. It is the result of a religious hatred that is all the more implacable in that it is based on the strength of some and the weakness of others. We might even say that the "Armenian issue" is foreign to this matter, for if the Armenians are indeed the worst treated, it is because they are the most numerous and because it is easy to portray the cruelty with which they are subjected as a form of repression necessary for public safety.[11]

In November 1895, deadly ethnic riots erupted in Diyarbakir with the torching of the bazaars. Mobs struck mainly against the large Armenian community with a thousand deaths and two thousand shops destroyed. But 167 non-Armenian Christians perished, 89 homes and 308 shops were plundered, some of them burned as well.[12] Observers listed massacres and destruction of 85 Syrian Orthodox villages around Diyarbakir. In two sub-districts the losses amounted to 84 Assyrians who were murdered, 10 women raped, 14 people taken captive, and 100 people forced to convert. In addition, 577 houses were burned.[13] These riots gave the appearance of being equally focused on damaging or destroying property as on outright killing and thus can be likened to the contemporary anti-Jewish pogroms in the Russian Empire.

Diplomats concluded that the government intended to substitute Muslims for the Christian peasants living in the borderlands. This large-scale transfer could occur only through government-sanctioned violence, for instance, using the newly created Hamidiye irregular cavalry as an instrument. Indeed, the main instigators of violence were often officers of the Hamidiye regiments, indicating the existence of a state policy (see chapter 9 for a detailed discussion of the Hamidiye violence). As such they were believed to have the Sultan's encouragement. They could organize campaigns against rural villages and never be taken to task. The French vice-consul in Diyarbakir expressed a common feeling among non-Muslims that the Hamidiye regiments were created in order to persecute the Christians. He wrote:

> By giving the Kurdish chieftains carte blanche to do whatever they please, to enrich themselves at the Christians' expense and to satisfy their men's whims under the pretext that that will prevent them from ever considering a revolt against Ottoman authority, the Sublime Porte has, for the last few years, been pursuing its goal of gradually annihilating the Christian element. But does my humble opinion not find ample proof in the very creation of the Hamidiye corps, a band of official highway robbers spreading terror throughout this vilayet [province] and many others, and in the impunity they enjoy for the crimes they commit every day?[14]

The suspected government involvement in the violence of the 1890s was a political novelty. Although there had been spontaneous riots before, the Christians as protected people had previously been safe from government-sanctioned harassment. Government passivity or collusion meant that the riots could continue for a long period and spread far and wide. However, because the massacres of 1895 took place in peacetime, the European powers managed to halt the process before it grew into a full-blown genocide. Still, 100,000 persons had been killed; 2,500 villages were reduced to rubble; 645 churches and monasteries were destroyed; under duress 559 parish communities had converted to Islam; 328 churches had been turned into mosques; and afterward 546,000 persons were left destitute.[15] Diplomats saw a common pattern in the massacres: they started at a predetermined hour, sparked by the blowing of a trumpet. Any Christians who approached the authorities for protection were arrested, and the known perpetrators were never brought to justice. All this seemed to indicate conspiracy among the powerful notables and the local authorities, as well as the blessing of the central government.

Contemporaries point to an intensification of religious violence in the borderland during the 20 years leading up to World War I. The intention was not just to kill, but even more to remove the economic livelihood of the non-Muslims. According to many accounts this violence was indiscriminate and survivors were left penniless. Ethnic rioters pillaged homes and all property that could not be carried away was willfully destroyed. The Syrian Orthodox Patriarch commented on the Hamidiye massacres: "The greater number of the people of our community became impoverished and in want after having been well-off [and] fell into lamentable condition. . . . Our hands have been emptied and there remains to us no power for carrying on desired work."[16] An American missionary explained "the plundered villagers have had but a tenth of their property restored to them; their burned and broken down houses are still in ruins; much of their grain has been either pastured while green, reaped when ripe by the Kurd, or carried from the threshing floor by the marauding Arab."[17]

Tribal attacks became everyday occurrences. "There have always been wars among *ashirets* [tribes], but ever since the events of 1895, they have become much more frequent in certain regions, such as around Mardin, Beshiri . . . and Jezire. In the space of two months, there have been ten of them."[18] A British missionary traveled through Hakkari just before World War I. Assyrian tribesmen told him that interethnic and interreligious violence was assuming insufferable proportions, because the government was supplying modern weapons to some of the Kurdish tribes. Among the tribesmen the situation had been

> by no means intolerable a generation ago . . . arms were approximately equal; and the Christians, though outnumbered, had strong positions to defend, and were of good fighting stock. . . . So, until Abdul Hamid's day, the parties were fairly matched on the whole; and generations of "cross-raiding" had evolved an understanding in the matter, capable of summary statement as "Take all you like, but do not damage what you leave; and do not touch the women." Thus livestock were fair lot, and so were carpets and other house-furniture, and arms of course. But the house must not be burnt, and standing crops and irrigating channels not touched, while a gentlemanly brigand would leave the corn-store alone. Women were never molested when a village of ashirets was raided, until a few years ago. And this was so thoroughly understood that it was not necessary even to guard them. . . . Of late things have changed for the worse in this respect. Women are not always respected now; and the free distribution of rifles among the Kurds has done away with all the old equality. This was done, when the late Sultan raised the "Hamidiye" battalions, partly for the defense of his throne, partly perhaps with the idea of keeping the Christians in subjection. Now when to odds in numbers you add the additional handicap implied in the difference between Mauser and flintlock, the position becomes impossible; and the balance has since inclined steadily against the Christian tribes.[19]

The causes of the intensified violence are complex and many are not connected with religious hatred, even though the victims emphasized that aspect in their testimonies. Political measures, motivated by the government's need to modernize administration and tax collection, exacerbated existing interreligious tension. Many of the reforms were interventions into the local balance of power between ethnic and religious groups. The ambition of the central government, which was notoriously weak in distant provinces, was to increase its direct control. This meant the intervention of troops in order to crush the autonomy of Kurdish tribal chiefs. The confrontation between troops and tribes was tantamount to civil war. The establishment of local Hamidiye regiments was one measure in the attempt to strengthen central control by buying the favor of a few tribes. These could act with impunity against their enemies. Throughout the borderlands there were Kurdish wars and the Assyrians had to choose to seek protection with oppositional or government-loyal groups. Some large Kurdish confederations even had Assyrian sections. Other measures that led to violence were reforms of tax collection and land ownership. Because of population increase there was great demand for farmland, and the Christians, as the original inhabitants, occupied the best arable land. The Ottoman reforms created provincial councils and these allowed the local elite to participate in politics and administration. From the late 1850s, tax collection was the responsibility of the local councils and they appointed some of their members as collectors. Taxes were high and led many famers to borrow money from the tax collectors at high interest, causing them to get in debt, which could only be resolved by giving the land to the creditors. Ambitious council members competed with each other in expropriating land. Even the Kurdish and Arab nomad tribes strove to gain land, but were inclined to use raw violence to get it. Assyrians who were under the protection of Kurdish tribes were sucked into the maelstrom of inter-tribal Kurdish warfare. The limited supply of good farmland was worsened by population growth, the in-migration of new tribes, the decline of the caravan trade, and the need to settle Muslim refugees from the Caucasus. All of this put the relatively better-off Christian farmers in danger.

After the Young Turk Revolution

The Young Turk Revolution of 1908 and the dethronement of Sultan Abdul Hamid looked at first sight like a golden opportunity for reconciliation of religious and ethnic conflicts. A general atmosphere of harmony evolved in the major cities and it was hoped that rural lawlessness would stop. Several choices lay open for the Assyrians. They could either go in wholeheartedly for the idea of a universal Ottoman citizenship with equality for all, or they could opt for "Assyrianism" and some form of autonomy. Both of these choices implied a break with exclusive sectarianism.

But there were also Assyrians who played down their ethnicity. By the early twentieth century no national political figures called themselves Assyrian. It is significant that when Davud Yusufani, a member of the Chaldean church in Mosul, was elected to the Ottoman National Assembly, he was designated as an Arab member.[20] Like most other Christians he was attracted to the liberal Party of Freedom and Understanding, which was the main opposition party to the radical nationalist Committee of Union and Progress.

The Young Turk revolution relaxed censorship, and some Assyrians began to publish journals. For the first time, a kind of Assyrian public opinion formed, however limited its scope. The prime issue was to overcome heterogeneity and reconcile enmity among the Assyrian churches. However, a concept of common ethnicity was completely lacking and the first efforts were no more than half-measures. Instead, there was an effort to place each sect separately within the umbrella of Ottoman citizenship. Sometimes the journals would reprint articles by national politicians who praised the virtues of Ottomanism. An often re-printed Turkish thinker was Riza Tevfik, a liberal who had broken with the CUP. His ideal is revealed in an appeal made at the outbreak of the Balkan wars, insisting:

> [It was] not a religious conflict. In this day and age, there can be no religious conflicts.... For now I wish only to ask of everyone, of every patriot, not to heed the words of hypocrites or look down on the Christians with whom we live, with whom we work side by side, who pay their taxes with us and who are soldiers; and do not forget that the Ottoman state and nation recognizes them, and our law protects their rights just as it protects ours.[21]

This statement appeals for a utopian multiethnic and multiconfessional society. At the same time, Riza admitted the reality that anti-Christian feelings were actually growing.

A few Syrian Orthodox intellectuals challenged the traditional sectarianism. Naum Faik Palak addressed an assembly of Assyrians gathered at Harput with the call, "if we desire progress, then we must unite."[22] What was new for the Assyrian context was that he began to toy with a concept of nation as an entity that was greater than simply a gathering of co-religionists. He used the term *Süryani* (Syriac) for all persons who in some way descended from the early Syrian Orthodox church. However, he avoided the term Assyrian and his vi-sion excluded the Nestorians and Chaldeans. When he felt the need to connect into a larger community he instead referred to Ottoman citizenship.

Faik's journal *Kevkeb Madenho* (*Star of the East*) was published in Diyarbakir until 1912, when he migrated to Paterson, New Jersey. His writings in Turkey reveal him as a clear-cut patriot praising the "glorious Ottoman constitution." In diaspora the term Assyrian was widely used. Once he arrived in America, Faik changed his self-identification and urged unity under the Assyrian umbrella. "These brothers are Nestorians, Chaldeans, Maronites, Catholics, Protestants.... I remind these groups [of] their pasts, their race, their blood and flesh, their tongue.... We must work to exalt the name of the Assyrians.... Our primary goal is to secure the rights of the Assyrians."[23]

Ashur Yusuf's paper *Mürşid-i Âsûriyûn* (*Guide of the Assyrians*) was published from 1909 up until his murder in the genocide of 1915. Yusuf was a teacher at Euphrates College, an overwhelmingly Armenian Protestant school, in the provincial capital Harput, where there existed an Assyrian enclave that spoke Armenian. One of his major issues was how to save the Assyrians from total assimilation. Politically Yusuf was a patriotic Ottomanist and encouraged Christian youths to do military service in the Balkan Wars.

Despite very high expectations for the new constitutional government, anti-Christian violence in the eastern provinces did not decrease. Instead its scale seemed to increase, and associates of the Young Turk party could break the law with impunity. In August 1908, the Kurdish emir of Berwari drove 11,000 Nestorian Assyrians from their homes in the Lizan valley. The British vice-consul in Van sent a communiqué on this subject. Someone at the embassy annotated the document with the optimistic hope "that under the Constitutional regime and with the disappearance of ruthless extermination of the Christian by the Mos-lem elements in the distant Asiatic provinces, the Nestorians like the Armenians, Syrians of Jezireh district etc. will not be exposed to such incidents which were most due to the incitement or connivance of Turkish officialdom."[24] However, the protests to the provincial government met with no response. Police sent to arrest the emir returned empty-handed. A few years later a tax collector killed an Assyrian village headman and a district governor stole thousands of sheep. The protests of the patriarch were met with the response that the accused were immune as "good constitutionalists."[25] Some believed conditions actually had gotten worse. One Assyrian remarked in 1911: "If this is Hurriet [freedom], give us back the other."[26]

Such frustration reflected a chronic problem of the Ottoman state: that the central government was forced to act in concert with powerful local notables and provincial officials were too weak to act without their approval.[27] As a consequence popular hate campaigns against the Christian minorities flourished as part of local political agitation. An attempt by the Young Turks to disband the disruptive Hamidiye irregulars led to revolt and they were soon reinstated under a new name, the Tribal Light Cavalry Regiments.

Anti-Christian Opinion

"Man-in-the-street" opinion held that because the Christians regularly appealed to foreign powers to ameliorate their conditions they had forfeited the traditional protection that Muslims were obliged to give them. In addition, after reforms established legal equality, they no longer observed the established cultural and social rules of deference to Muslims. Therefore, fanatics argued that, having broken the *dhimmi* (contract) of deference to the Muslims in return for tolerance, the Christians no longer needed to be protected. A feeling of insecurity emerged among the Assyrians and an even greater desire for outside protection. But the foreign interventions fed a vicious circle of repression. Calls for government action raised by foreign diplomats often fell on deaf ears. But the knowledge of such complaints unleashed renewed popular attacks. Conditions did not improve after the Young Turk revolution, but rather grew more desperate. A British missionary described the desperation of the Nestorian tribes as complaints only made the situation worse. He wrote:

> The attitude of the British Government makes it more and more difficult to afford even that [slight] amount of political help which was formerly possible. Mar Shimun has several times lately deprecated the reporting of acts of Kurdish oppression to the British Consuls, on the ground that their intervention will accomplish nothing beyond irritating the Turkish officials.[28]

The knee-jerk reaction among Muslims to the Young Turk revolution of 1908 was the feeling that "religion was being lost." Although based on a misunderstanding of the Young Turk position, it reinforced feelings of humiliation and nourished hate speech. The Sultan had been well known for his support of Islam, so the return to constitutional rule was interpreted as a reversal of that policy and a confirmation of religious equality. At first the Young Turks had received much support from non-Muslims. Voices from Diyarbakir complained: "We cannot tolerate the Caliph of Muslims becoming a toy in the hands of the CUP" and "Have the infidels become Muslims or the Muslims become infidels, such that they kiss each other and become equals?"[29]

A geographically limited but very bloody massacre occurred in Adana, capital of economically advanced Cilicia, during an attempted counter-coup by the Sultan's followers in April 1909. This massacre was seen as a turning point. An Armenian National Assembly delegate investigating the violence noted that the Adana riots marked a change from the previous anti-Christian policy, as for the first time Armenians were not the only targets.

> During the Abdul Hamid regime, the women and children were spared, and the Christians of other nationalities were not attacked, not even Armenian Catholics and Armenian Prot-

estants. But as at Adana, no distinctions were made among the Christians. The Syrian Orthodox and the Syrian Catholics who do not have any similarity with the language of the Armenians—because they speak Arabic—were killed: of the first, 400 victims, and of the second 65; the Chaldeans there were 200.[30]

This was actually not the first time Assyrians and Armenians were slaughtered together, but this statement reflects the lack of detailed information of earlier atrocities among National Assembly politicians.

The most common vulgarity used to designate non-Muslims was *gavur* or infidel. On several occasions official declarations were made to ban the word. For instance, on the Young Turk Revolution the Shaykh al-Islam preached that there was no justification in calling the Christians *gavur*. This position failed to penetrate the Anatolian provinces, however. There were many reports of local fanatics who fired up Muslims to eradicate all of the infidels. Diplomats noted a leaflet from a group calling itself the Committee for National Defense that urged each Muslim to kill three or four Christians. In Diyarbakir a pamphlet circulated deeming murder of infidels a religious duty.[31]

The Genocide

Memories of 1895 and 1909 were still fresh at the start of World War I. Some Christians considered the mass killings and ethnic cleansing as an unbroken spiral of escalating harassment culminating in 1915. Very early in the war, and particularly from New Year's Day 1915, the Christian population feared the outbreak of new massacres. Their leaders urged them to be calm, to ignore provocations and endure the various outrages. Meanwhile, among some Muslims a desire developed to carry out a more complete massacre than had been possible before.[32]

It was probably natural for the Assyrians to hope that they could survive relatively unharmed in a conflict the government described in purely Armenophobic terms. But in the local context of the northern Mesopotamian borderland the Christian population was a mix of Assyrians and Armenians. The Assyrians also possessed wealth and land so local politicians had no qualms about pretending that the Assyrians were Armenians in order to get government blessing to attack their settlements. Initially, there were serious attempts by appointed officials to shield the Assyrians from the deportations. However, after protests by local CUP politicians these officials were immediately replaced. Three district governors were killed on orders from the provincial governor of Diyarbakir. Authorities forced Kurdish chiefs who promised to rescue their Assyrian friends to change their minds. This difference reflects changes brought about by the rise of extreme nationalists to power and the local targeting of all Christians in eastern Anatolia. All were fingered as subversive elements and potential allies of the enemy—the Nestorians were perceived as the instrument of Russia, the Chaldeans and Syrian Catholics were perceived as close to France, and the Protestants were assumed to have contact with Britain.

Local conditions were markedly different, and the experience of each Assyrian community varied depending on whether it was hit by the combined forces of the national and local governments or solely by local forces. Because the central government focused on the Armenians, they undeniably had fewer chances than the Assyrians to survive the war. However, the Assyrians suffered rates of annihilation that were more than 50 percent, and in Diyarbakir the proportion rose to nearly two-thirds.[33]

The case of the Nestorian tribesmen of the Hakkari Mountains is that of a full ethnic cleansing enforced by the military. These Assyrians faced the direct wrath of the Young Turk government as well as the local Kurdish tribes. Thus their situation was analogous to that of the Armenians. Just before the Ottomans formally entered the war, Talât Pasha, the minister of the interior, saw them as a security risk and issued a decree for their deportation.[34] Their ongoing contacts with the Russians were no secret and since the Nestorians lived along the border with Iran it was deemed wise to deport them. They were to be sent to central Anatolia and dispersed so that they would never be more than 20 households in any village. This decree ignited a series of atrocities along the border strip. In self-defense the Assyrians tried to cash in on promises given by the Russians, but they only received a few surplus weapons and ammunition. In late May 1915 a window of opportunity appeared as a Turkish army was retreating from Iran through the Hakkari Mountains. The Assyrians joined Russian troops in a victorious battle. This military participation had dire consequences. Halil, a very influential general who was the uncle of the minister of war, headed the defeated army. He and his humiliated soldiers blamed both Armenians and Assyrians for their losses and began to punish civilian Ottoman Christians. The officers instigated horrible massacres of Christians of all faiths in the towns of Bashkala, Siirt, and Bitlis. The second consequence was the decision by the central government to send fresh troops to exterminate the Assyrian tribes. Talât ordered: "we should not let them return to their homelands."[35] Local Kurdish tribes reinforced the Turkish troops, and the Assyrians were outnumbered and outgunned. The Turkish campaign involved driving people out of their villages and up into the barren mountain peaks. The deserted villages, churches, fields, and orchards were destroyed. In September, after much loss of life, they poured over the Iranian border, seeking asylum behind Russian lines. At the most 35,000, clearly less than half the original population, made up the wave of refugees leaving Turkey.[36]

In comparison with the Nestorian tribes, the case of the Assyrians in Diyarbakir province was less clear-cut because it was basically a local initiative unconnected with national politics. The loss of life was staggering despite the absence of an order targeting the Assyrians. Provincial actions consisted of mass murder done very rapidly without the prior knowledge of the central government. A variety of local resources were mobilized: townsmen formed death squads, outlaws were pardoned, *jihad* rhetoric fired up nomad tribes. Instigated by local CUP politicians, the provincial administration of Diyarbakir organized attacks on Armenian and Assyrian villages starting in April 1915—ostensibly in search of rebels, weapons, and bombs. Arms searches were accompanied by mass arrests of the Christian leadership. By late May and early June, the urban Christian elite had been almost completely arrested. Many were tortured to get confessions. Their families were extorted to pay large sums of money for a release that never came. Prisoners were dehumanized and paraded in chains through the Muslim quarters and taken to places of execution. In Diyarbakir they were placed on rafts and then killed and thrown into the Tigris River.

The arrest and execution of urban Armenian males was near total, but that of the Assyrians was less complete. Catholic and Protestant Assyrians ran the greatest risk of being killed. Among the first group of notables who were arrested in Mardin were 230 Armenians and 255 Assyrians (113 Syrian Catholics, 30 Chaldeans, 27 Protestants, and 85 Syrian Orthodox). But suddenly all the Syrian Orthodox were released—some say the bishop paid a large bribe for their release; others say that the bishop signed a false accusation accusing the Armenians and other Assyrians of planning a revolt.[37] This was perhaps the most telling case of the lack of solidarity between the Assyrian sects. Something similar occurred in the town of Midyat when the Syrian Orthodox stood as bystanders when the Assyrian Protestants were killed in a mass execution.

There was some reaction on the part of the central government to news that all Christians, not just Armenians, were being annihilated. Several sources in Mardin write of the arrival of a decree sent by the Sultan ordering the release of all non-Armenian prisoners, said to have come in mid-June. Some prisoners were released temporarily from jail in several towns. However, massacres in the countryside continued and many of the released Assyrians were rearrested and executed later on. The German consul in Mosul urgently reported of an ongoing "general massacre" affecting all Christians.[38] Pressure from the German government prompted Talât to send a telegram to Diyarbakir to the effect that the "measures adopted against the Armenians are absolutely not to be extended to other Christians" because of the bad impression it made on world opinion.[39] By that time almost all rural villages had been eradicated.

Two villages were able to put up long-term resistance: Ayn Wardo near Midyat and Azakh near Jizre. They withstood first the efforts of amassed Kurdish tribes and then the siege by Ottoman troops. At Azakh the leader of the siege was a well-known CUP politician, Ömer Naci Bey, formerly the party's general inspector. In order to get government permission to deploy troops, the provincial government falsely claimed that the villagers were Armenians. After a month-long siege had failed, an armistice was arranged once it was acknowledged that the population of the village was Syrian and Chaldean. According to correspondence between the commander of the third army and the minister of war, the army would deal with the villagers later on. As the commander wrote to the war minister: "when to complete the destruction of the rebellion is a matter that is left to your discretion."[40] In Diyarbakir province and its neighboring region, 178 Assyrian towns and villages were cleansed and most were reduced to rubble. Later Muslim refugees from other parts of the empire were resettled in the villages, which authorities euphemistically termed "abandoned."

Thus there are several specific local contexts to the Assyrian genocide. The eastern Assyrians lived along the very border and had a history of contacts with Russia. This caught the attention of the central government and resulted in government-orchestrated and extremely violent ethnic cleansing. The local tribes aided the army, but did not take the initiative. The western context is quite different, as the Syrian Orthodox had no contacts with the enemy and lived far from the front line. The genocide was perpetrated for purely local reasons. There are indications that the government did not order the eradication of the Diyarbakir Syrians and Chaldeans. However, it acquiesced to the *fait accompli* and approved of the opportunity it presented to settle Muslim refugees. In certain situations the provincial authorities pretended that the Syrians and Assyrians were Armenians. The lack of a common Assyrian identity made it easy for the locals to conceal their real identity. In addition, since there was an existing conflict between confessions it was easy to apply divide-and-rule techniques. In several towns, Syrian Orthodox communities simply abandoned Assyrians who belonged to other faiths.

War Claims

Immediately after the Ottoman surrender in October 1918 it seemed as if the Assyrians might overcome their mutual antagonism and form a united political front. It was difficult to develop a common narrative, as easterners had been punished for participation in the war, while the westerners had merely defended themselves from aggressors. The tasks were calculating number of victims and raising the demand for independence at the Paris peace conference. The first estimates of population loss for all of the Assyrian churches totaled more than 250,000 deaths, with hundreds of destroyed villages. It was asserted that 175,000 of the Assyrian dead had been wrongly listed among the Armenian victims.[41]

A special challenge was to lift the suffering of the Assyrians out from under the shadow of the massive genocide that afflicted the Armenians. But this immediately revived sectarian antagonisms through clumsy comparisons. One Assyrian leader bitterly asserted: "No nation in modern history has suffered as much as our nation. We have endured our massacres silently. The horrors . . . infinitely surpass those of Armenia. Often at the expense of the Assyrian atrocities the Armenians have received the sympathy of the European nations. . . . A nation of many millions has been reduced to one twentieth of its original size."[42] This quote is symptomatic of how activists in their eagerness for recognition exaggerated their suffering and the degree to which they were ignored by international opinion. Exiles in the Caucasus echoed the same sentiment:

> We have suffered and suffered more than others, we should also be considered entitled to recognition and realization of our ideals. A nation that has fought and fought well; a nation that has given hundreds of thousands for the cause of the allies and its own freedom, it would be the very height of injustice not to receive the rights to which she is justly entitled. Every sacrifice has a reward, and the sacrifices of the Assyrians cannot be justly rewarded with anything short of their freedom.[43]

The sense of injustice can be felt in the complaint: "The Assyrian atrocities have erroneously been listed under the name of Armenia. The Assyrian gallantry on battlefield, amazing as it has been to the French, Russian and British officers who have witnessed it, has been attributed to the valor of the Armenians."[44] Although their tactics were somewhat misguided and inappropriate, the Assyrians, inspired by the spirit of self-determination declared by the victorious allies, began their national-political activity in the shadow of the Armenians whose terrible fate had been universally recognized.

The feeling of unfair neglect did have some basis. For instance, the voluminous report of Lord Bryce and Arnold Toynbee to the British Parliament included documents on the Assyrians, but this aspect of the events was fully obscured by the title, "The Treatment of the Armenians in the Ottoman Empire."[45] Some of the earliest systematic massacres perpetrated by the Ottoman army were on Assyrians living in northwestern Persia, and news about the atrocities committed there during the spring of 1915 were part of the background to the allied declaration that it would hold the Turkish government and its agents responsible for these crimes against "humanity and civilization." Humanitarian organizations aided both Armenians and Assyrians. When America began to organize relief its main instrument was the "American Committee for Armenian and Syrian Relief" which had a subsidiary named the "Assyrian Relief Fund."

Within days of the armistice, the governments of France, Great Britain, and the United States received proposals for an independent Assyria. These territorial claims covered areas in Ottoman and Persian territory.[46] One scheme staked out a region bordered on the west by the Euphrates River, in the north by the Murad Su River, and thereafter following a line south of Lake Van to Lake Urmia (which lies well inside Iran), east from Lake Urmia, and then following the Turkish–Persian border, extending in the south from the border to the Euphrates. The area designated included the important cities of Diyarbakir, Urfa, Mardin, Nisibin, Midyat, and Sairt in Turkey; Urmia and Salmas in Persia; Mosul, Kirkuk, Arbil, Suleimaniya, and Tikrit in Iraq; plus a chunk of northeastern Syria. Arguing for such a large territory, the delegates asserted that many of the Kurdish and Arabic groups living there originally had been Assyrians, thus arguing for a "racial" and "historical" bonding. They were to get none of this, and the Assyrian delegation at the Paris peace conference was barred from pleading its case. General works on the peace conference ignore the Assyrians.[47]

The reasons for the Assyrian diplomatic failure are extremely complex, but suffice it to say, they all converged on the same result: the Assyrians could not secure their independence or even a small autonomous province. The international situation was shaky. Much of what the Assyrians wanted had been given to the French in the Sykes-Picot Agreement of 1916. In addition, there was a fatal flaw to the claims—all included parts of northwestern Persia. But since Persia had officially been neutral throughout the war, all of the high-pitched demands for compensation and territory from that kingdom fell outside the mandate of the peace conference. Thus the Persian Assyrians, who were the most politically and intellectually advanced, had the bitter experience of being totally ignored by the only peace conference available.

Backbiting

A further complication to winning the world's attention was the deep disunity and divisiveness among the Assyrians themselves. Common features of the Assyrian churches were chronic problems with the legitimacy of their leadership, which expressed itself in quarrels, breakaways, and local loyalty to region, tribe, or clan. The fraternal divisiveness witnessed after the war was quite simply a continuation of the lack of unity in the years leading up to the war.

When World War I came to an end most survivors were in refugee camps. Very few of them remained in their original homes. All of the church leaders save one were safe outside Turkey. The sole exception was the Syrian Orthodox patriarch, who was bottled up in Mardin and without contact with the other churches. Believing that his community needed to plan for a future inside Turkey, the patriarch began to court the Turkish nationalists. He issued public statements in support of continued Ottoman dominance and sometimes denied that any damage had been done to his flock during the war. In a 1919 interview for an Istanbul newspaper he revealed that he had no complaint against the Turkish government and much preferred it to any alternative. Further, his church had been "almost wholly immune from massacre and deportation."[48] He also told a British intelligence officer that his community had been spared. The British officer agreed that "the Jacobites have suffered far less than the other Christian communities," but he had already gathered statistics showing tens of thousands of victims.[49] What lies behind the patriarch's statements cannot be lack of information, since he had received the report of an investigation showing the enormous damage to the rural parishioners.[50] What we see here is the first appearance of politically motivated silence about the Assyrian genocide.

The wartime suffering and the failure at the peace conference were followed by further disasters. The eastern Assyrians tried to return to the Hakkari area but were repulsed by Turkish troops and the few survivors were expelled. The Republic of Turkey in 1924 expelled a large number of Syrian Orthodox and seized their property. In exile the Assyrians began a process of selective amnesia. Memory of their tragedy in Turkey was silenced in the face of the tension of adjusting to the new social context of the Iraqi and Syrian mandate states. The Syrian Orthodox took advantage of their church's historic roots in the ancient Roman province of Syria, and thus voluntarily downplayed its Ottoman and Turkish experiences.[51] Here they waited 50 years before there was a commemoration of the expulsion from Turkey. The Nestorian refugees in Iraq soon had a more imminent tragedy to commemorate. Many had collaborated with the British mandate as hated mercenary soldiers, the so-called levies. When the mandate ceased in 1933, the Iraqis took revenge by massacring thousands as the British and the League of Nations stood by helplessly.[52] These massacres became the major catastrophe commemorated by the eastern Assyrians and a memorial "day of martyrs" is held on 7 August each year. Thus the commemoration became specific to a Nestorian event. Not until the 1980s was the silence broken when Assyrian groups began to commemorate the World War I genocide.

Conclusion

The religiously divided Assyrian peoples failed to attain political cooperation during the tragic events of the early twentieth century, and even today ideas of a common identity are controversial. Instead, the local communities were forced by increasing turmoil to ally with stronger ethnic groups, which only reinforced existing splits. During the wartime genocide the Assyrians were very exposed, especially as their Muslim neighbors were forced to abandon promises of help. The failure of the Assyrian churches to cooperate with each other has interfered with the presentation of a unified narrative of genocide. Other disasters, such as the expulsions of 1924 or the massacres of 1933 were instead adopted for the first memorials, which filtered out the memory of the earlier genocide that all Assyrians had suffered. Until recently it has sometimes been impossible to discuss the genocide issue within the official framework of the Syrian Orthodox Church.

Descriptions of the Assyrian genocide depend largely upon testimony from survivors and contemporaries. There is some documentation in the Turkish archives that specifically treats the Assyrians, but these deal with practical matters of deportations and army operations; none take up the political background. The testimonies have the advantage of emphasizing the details of violence and reveal the local contexts in which perpetrators, resistors, and rescuers acted. But they have the disadvantage of saying little about the underlying political reasons.

The Armenian genocide was motivated by a number of Young Turk ideological concerns: demographic engineering to create a homogeneous population as part of the effort to modernize the state, the drive to unite all Turkish-speaking peoples, and the total rejection of cultural autonomy for minorities. Turkish nationalist politicians portrayed Armenians as a threat to the very existence of the state. In contrast, the Assyrian peoples fell outside the formal political arena. Instead, their victimization was part of social problems played out in local contexts. The prime factor was the shortage of land, which intensified as the Ottoman Empire sought to settle nomadic tribes. From the late nineteenth century, powerful clans and tribes used the reforms instigated by the central government to appropriate land. Land could be taken from the Christian minority with little risk of sanction, even when property was stolen outright.

In the general history of genocide, the Armenian case emerges as one of the first examples of a political genocide inspired by nationalist ideology.[53] This meant that extermination involved much more than the appropriation of wealth and property. It was also conceived as a step toward building a unified nation out of a multicultural empire. Until there is more knowledge of the intentions of the Young Turk dictatorship, the many specific Assyrian massacres can best be categorized as variants of the "settler genocides" that characterized colonial land grabs in Africa, America, and Australia. These concerned above all the removal of the original inhabitants through a combination of killing and expulsion in order to redistribute their land to a completely new population.

NOTES

1. Here the term "Assyrian peoples" covers members of the Oriental Churches: the Nestorians, Chaldeans, Syrian Orthodoxy, and the Protestant and Catholic converts living in Anatolia, Kurdistan, and Mesopotamia. This excludes the Syrian and Assyrian churches in India and the Maronites of Lebanon.

2. See Surma D'Bait Mar Shimun, *Assyrian Church Customs and the Murder of Mar Shimun* (London: Faith Press, 1920).

3. Eugen Prym and Albert Socin, *Der Neu-Aramaeische Dialekt des Tur Abdin* (Göttingen: Vandenhoeck & Ruprecht, 1881), viii.

4. David Gaunt, *Massacres, Resistance, Protectors: Muslim–Christian Relations in Eastern Anatolia during World War I* (Piscataway, N.J.: Gorgias Press, 2006), 18–29.

5. Benjamin Braude and Bernard Lewis, eds., *Christians and Jews in the Ottoman Empire: The Functioning of a Plural Society* (New York: Holmes and Meier, 1982).

6. F. N. Heazell and Mrs. Margoliuth, eds., *Kurds and Christians* (London: Wells Gardner, 1913), 10–11; "Report by Consul-General Miles Respecting the Religious Dissensions Existing between the Chaldean and Syrian Communities at Mosul," 26 May 1880, in B. Destani, ed., *Assyrian Communities in the Levant and Iraq 1880–1938* (Cambridge: Archive Editions, 2007), 1–14.

7. Joseph Tfinkdji, "L'Eglise chaldéenne catholique autrefois et aujourd'hui," *Annuaire pontifical catholique* 17 (1914): 449–525.

8. Hirmis Aboona, *Assyrians, Kurds, and Ottomans: Intercommunal Relations on the Periphery of the Ottoman Empire* (Amherst, N.Y.: Cambria Press, 2008).

9. *La question assyro-chaldéenne devant la conférence de la paix* (brochure presented to the members of the peace conference, Paris, 1919; the copy used here is in the Hoover Library, Stanford University, Palo Alto, California). James Bryce and Arnold Toynbee, eds., *The Treatment of the Armenians in the Ottoman Empire, 1915–1916*, uncensored edition (Princeton: Gomidas Institute, 2000), 656.

10. Aydin, Suavi, Kudret Emiroğlu, Oktay Özel, and Süha Ünsal, *Mardin Aşiret-Cemaat-Devlet* (Istanbul: Tarih vakfi, 2000), 255.

11. French vice-consul in Diyarbakir report no. 2, dated 9 February 1895, cited in Sébastien de Courtois, *The Forgotten Genocide: Eastern Christians, the Last Arameans* (Piscataway, N.J.: Gorgias Press 2004), 101.

12. Gustave Meyrier, *Les Massacres de Diarbekir. Correspondance diplomatique du Vice-Consul de France 1894–1896* (Paris: L'Inventaire 2000), 134–35.

13. Manuscript in Alpheus N. Andrus papers, American Board of Commissioners of Foreign Missions, Houghton Library, Harvard University.

14. French vice-consul in Diyarbakir dispatch no. 2, dated 9 January 1901, cited in Courtois, *Forgotten Genocide*, 138.

15. Johannes Lepsius, *Armenien und Europa. Eine Anklageschrift* (Berlin-Westend: Faber 1897), 20–21.

16. Undated letter of Abdulmesih to Archbishop of Canterbury, cited in William Henry Taylor, *Antioch and Canterbury: The Syrian Orthodox Church and the Church of England 1874–1928* (Iscataway, N.J.: Gorgias Press, 2005), 80.

17. Cited in ibid., 77.

18. French vice-consul in Diyarbakir dispatch no. 6, dated 6 August 1903, cited in Courtois, *Forgotten Genocide*, 133.

19. W. A. Wigram and Edgar Wigram, *The Cradle of Mankind Life in Eastern Kurdistan* (London: Adam and Charles Black, 1914), 167–68.

20. For attribution as Arab: Aykut Kansu, *The Revolution of 1908 in Turkey* (Leiden: Brill, 1997), 292.

21. Reprinted in *Mürşid-i Âsûriyûn* 4(8) (1912), cited in Benjamin Trigona-Harany, "Naum Faik and Aşur Yusuf" (Master's Thesis, Boğaziçi University, 2008), 92–93.

22. Murat Fuat Çıkkı, *Naum Faik ve Süryani Rönesansı* (Istanbul: Belge, 2004), 133–36. For more on identity problems see Naures Atto, *Hostages in the Homeland, Orphans in the Diaspora: Identity Discourses among the Assyrian/Syriac Elites in the European Diaspora* (Leiden, Netherlands: Leiden University Press, 2011).

23. Ibid., 67.

24. Vice-consul to British Ambassador, 10 September 1908, FO 195/2284, cited in J. F. Coakley, *Church of the East and the Church of England: A History of the Archbishop of Canterbury's Assyrian Mission* (Oxford: Clarendon Press, 1992), 323.

25. Heazell and Margoliuth, *Kurds and Christians*, 205–207.

26. Ibid., 208.

27. Stephen Duguid, "The Politics of Unity: Hamidian Policy in Eastern Anatolia," *Middle Eastern Studies* 9 (1973): 139–55.

28. MacGillivray, Neesan, Barnard, Spearing, and Reed to Archbishop of Canterbury, 15 May 1913, cited in Coakley, *Church of the East*, 321.

29. Şevket Beysanoğlu, *Ziya Gökalp'in İlk Yazı Hayatı, 1894–1909* (Istanbul, 1956), 14–16.

30. Kévorkian, "La Cilicia," 167.

31. Swedish National Archives, Foreign Office 1902 dossier system, Embassy in Constantinople dispatch 106, 23 May 1915; for the pamphlet, see Ishaq Armale, *Al Quosara fi nakabat an-Nasara* (Beirut, Lebanon: El Sharfe, 1919), 150.

32. Jacques Rhétoré, *Les Chrétiens aux bêtes. Souvenirs de la guerre sainte proclamée par les Turcs contre les chrétiens en 1915* (Paris: Cerf, 2005), 314; Yves Ternon, *Mardin 1915. Anatomie pathologique d'une destruction,* Special Issue of *Revue d'histoire Arménienne Contemporaine* 4 (2002): 113.

33. Rhétoré, *Les Chrétiens aux bêtes,* 136; Gaunt, *Massacres, Resistance, Protectors,* 197–272.

34. BOA (Ottoman Archive Istanbul) DH. ŞFR 46/78, Talât to governor of Van, 26 October 1914.

35. BOA, DH. ŞFR 54/240, Talât to governors of Van and Mosul, 30 June 1915.

36. Gaunt, *Massacres, Resistance, Protectors,* 145–47.

37. Rhétoré, *Les Chrétiens aux bêtes,* 72–73.

38. Vice-consul in Mosul to German Embassy, 10 July 1915, in Johannes Lepsius, *Deutschland und Armenien 1914–1918* (Potsdam, Germany: Tempelverlag, 1919), 101–102.

39. BOA. DH. ŞFR 54/406, Talât to governor of Diyarbakir, 12 July 1915.

40. ATASE [Military History Archive Ankara], BDH. Kls. 17, dossier 81, file 58–1, Kamil to Enver, 28 November 1915.

41. *La question Assyro-Chaldéenne devant la conférence de la paix.*

42. Statement by the Assyrian National Associations of America, "The Assyrian Thanksgiving Day," *Izgedda; Persian American Courier,* 6 November 1918.

43. Letter to the editor from Fraydoon Atooraya, president of the National Assyrian Central Council in the Republic of Georgia, Tblisi, 22 March 1920, printed in the *Assyrian American Courier,* 26 May 1920.

44. "The Claim of the Assyrians," *Izgedda; Persian American Courier,* 13 November 1918.

45. Bryce and Toynbee, *Treatment of Armenians,* 135–222.

46. Joel E. Werda, President of the Assyrian National Association of America, "The Claim of the Assyrians," *Izgedda; Persian American Courier,* 6 November 1918, and 13 November 1918.

47. Article 62 of the Sèvres treaty limited its concern for the Assyro-Chaldeans to a call for safeguarding and protecting them within a projected independent Kurdistan.

48. Mary Caroline Holmes, *Between the Lines in Asia Minor* (New York: Fleming Revell, 1923).

49. *Diary of Major E. Noel on Special Duty* (Basra, 1919), entry for 22 April 1919.

50. He wrote in 1921 of hundreds of thousands of deaths and 166 church buildings sacked and destroyed (cited in Taylor, *Antioch and Canterbury,* 107).

51. Noriko Sato, "Selective Amnesia: Memory and History of the Urfalli Syrian Orthodox Christians," in *Identities: Global Studies in Culture and Power* 12: 315–33.

52. Annemasse (pseudonym), *The Assyrian Tragedy* (n.p., 1934). It is believed the author was a highly-placed Nestorian.

53. Ben Kiernan, *Blood and Soil: A World History of Genocide and Extermination from Sparta to Darfur* (New Haven, Conn.: Yale University Press, 2007).

18

FORMS OF VIOLENCE DURING THE RUSSIAN OCCUPATION OF OTTOMAN TERRITORY AND IN NORTHERN PERSIA (URMIA AND ASTRABAD)

OCTOBER 1914–DECEMBER 1917

PETER HOLQUIST

The area of the Caucasus and northern Anatolia was one of the areas of most intense and extended violence in the First World War. Factors both longstanding and contingent sparked this violence. But undoubtedly one key factor was that this was a borderland region, one of the shatterzones where empires crashed together like tectonic plates. In the early twentieth century the discipline of political geography developed models for these regions that are so particularly prone to instability and unrest. The Russian Empire was prominent as a foil in these theories. During the latter stages of the Great Game, Lord George Nathaniel Curzon thought up and even tried to implement a "buffer zone" between Russian and British interests in Persia and India. Of course, he would also pursue a related program in 1919 when he sought to impose the "Curzon Line" in Eastern Europe. In 1915, James Fairgrieve sketched out a model of a "crush zone" of small states existing between the German and Russian Empires.[1] In the aftermath of the Second World War and as the Cold War developed, other scholars elaborated this model. The Anglophone scholars who developed this concept of the "'shatter zone' in Europe" often employed quotation marks around the term, having adopted it from interwar German literature.[2] Not coincidentally, all these concepts emerged out of one or another iteration of the contest between the Atlantic West and Russia (be it the British Empire versus the Russian Empire in the nineteenth-century Great Game, or the United States versus the Soviet Union in the Cold War). In short, there is a history to the idea

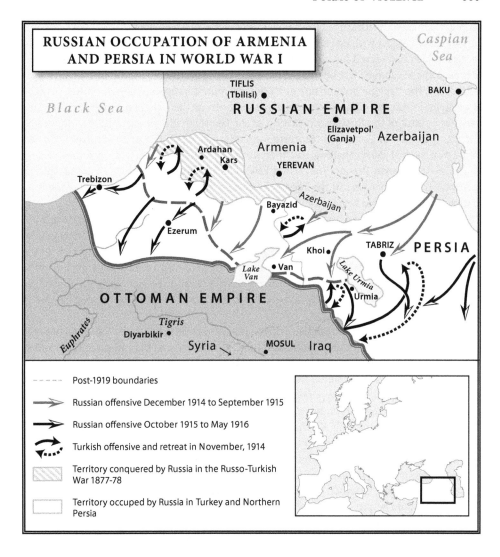

of "buffer zones," "crush zones," "shatter zones," and "shatter belts," the historicity of which determined which areas came to be identified as such "zones."[3] As critics of this literature have noted, it tends to reify historical conditions as near-permanent, quasi-geological features. One result is that such treatments tend to subordinate or overlook complex dynamics in favor of one-dimensional explanations—"the clash of civilizations," for instance. In this chapter I describe independent dynamics—military violence and the breakdown of order in revolution—that played out within a borderland region.

Regions sitting astride two empires indeed have specific features, as this literature has rightly noted. But we need not reify these concepts. In Alfred Rieber's felicitous formulation, such regions were shaped by "persistent factors" rather than "permanent conditions."[4] The Caucasus was one such "contact zone" between the Russian and Ottoman Empires. This "contact" emerged historically, rather than out of some "clash of civilizations." For both empires, greater contact with one another was itself the result of the disappearance of the "Wild Steppe" which had served for centuries as a buffer between them.[5] With the end of the Wild Steppe, a space subdued not by one power alone but collectively by the empires which surrounded it, the struggle became one of an overall contest between empires, particularly the Russian and Ottoman Empires. Russia came to confront the Ottoman Empire in the Caucasus as a result of the Russian annexation of the Georgian kingdom (in 1801) followed by the incorporation of Armenian territories—an advance which resulted more from Russian expansion against Persia than against the Ottomans. (The Treaty of Turkmenchai, ending the 1826–1828 Russo-Persian War, ceded Erivan and Nakhchivan provinces to the Russian Empire.) This advance against the Persian Empire set the stage for the escalation of the Russian–Ottoman duel that began from the mid-eighteenth century.

There is an extensive, and excellent, literature on the "Eastern Crisis" and struggle between the Russian and Ottoman Empires.[6] The struggle encompassed not only international relations, but also each empire's attempts to subdue its own borderlands—an ever-changing and morphing space. In this respect, the Russian Empire enjoyed a crucial advantage over the Ottoman Empire. Russia managed to incorporate new territories—less through "Russification" than through *étatist* centralization—to a greater extent than the Ottomans, particularly in the Caucasian borderlands.[7]

Thus the advance of the Russian army in late 1914 and 1915 into the Caucasus brought it into a region where it not only confronted the Ottoman Empire, but into a region in which *both* empires had a long history of seeking to subdue their own borderlands and had preexisting relations with ethnic populations on both sides of the border.[8] The extensive violence by both states' armies upon the population took its most extreme form in the massacre of the region's Armenian population, but it found expression in massacres and expulsions of the region's Muslim and especially Kurdish population as well. The conduct of the Russian Army was a major contributing factor to the spiral of violence here. Its impact was both direct, through its own conduct on the ground, and indirect, through its sanction of various irregular formations and its (ambivalent and tactical) endorsement of ethnic politics in this region (for discussion of the Ottoman part in events, see chapters 8, 9, 14, and 17).

Yet it would be a mistake to view the violence of the Russian military as flowing from a coherent policy, still less a specific ideology, be it a supposed overarching anti-Muslim bias or a cynical and programmatic desire to depopulate the region (particularly of Armenians) in order to pursue a policy of Russian colonization.[9] Various accounts have presented Russian policy as driven largely by the primacy of either Russian–Ottoman (or, often, Russian–Muslim) relations or, for scholars of Armenia, of Russian–Armenian relations.[10] Such interpretations read back nationalist agendas onto a polity that in many ways was pre-national or even a-national. Violence there was, but there were other, additional dynamics at play beyond nationalizing programs. The violence of the Russian military was in fact comprised of a set of overlapping forms and types of violence. The dynamic between these various forms of violence changed over time. Moreover, the various forms of violence were frequently at odds. What I wish to suggest is that an overarching, militarized violence, one which instrumentalized civilian populations but operated within certain bounds—and one which had analogues with Russian military conduct on other fronts—morphed over the course of 1917 into a more diffuse but much more destructive form of revolutionary violence. A major aspect of this revolutionary violence was the breakdown of military discipline and order, a discipline and order that had accounted for significant violence prior to 1917 but which had nevertheless operated with certain regularities. Yet this transformation was not specific to the occupied regions. Indeed, at least in the eyes of some Russian participants, the violence that washed over Russia in the period of 1917–1921 was at least in part in expiation for the violence Russians had meted out to populations in the occupied territories in 1914–1917.

Having indicated the structural and institutional factors for violence, I wish to highlight one additional aspect of this period: the efforts—both successful and unsuccessful—of individuals to place limits, often at great risks to themselves, on the spiral of violence against civilians. I turn first to the varieties of routinized military violence, and then to the nature of the violence that emerged after 1917 during the collapse of the Russian Army in the Russian Revolution.

Military Practices

The Russian military oversaw the administration of occupied territories. This form of rule extended equally to occupied areas of the Austro-Hungarian Empire and of the Ottoman Empire. With the opening of hostilities, the "Regulations on Field Administration of the Army in Wartime," hastily ratified in July 1914 as war approached, granted military authorities vast powers in the broad swaths of territory that were designated as front regions.[11] The "Regulations" now divided the Russian Empire itself into those areas under civilian rule and those areas which fell under military control. As a result, the military was largely a force unto itself, not only in the occupied regions but throughout the entire swath of territory the military had designated as the "front region." Indeed, one leading minister in the Russian government in August 1915 described the situation as one in which Russian territory had once again been divided into a *zemshchina* and an *oprichnina*—evoking the division that Ivan the Terrible had instituted in the Russian land in the sixteenth century between an area under normal administration (the *zemshchina*) and one under extraordinary rule by Ivan himself (the *oprichnina*). (The term *oprichnina* derives from a Russian word for "apart from, except.")[12]

When one discusses Russian policy in the occupied territories, then, one must first attempt to untangle what was generic Russian military conduct across the board from actions that were specific to occupied regions. Much of what is often described as specific or distinctive of Russian conduct in occupied Turkey can in fact be related to the general patterns of Russian military conduct, both in other occupied regions (Austrian Galicia in particular), and in Russia proper once military operations moved onto Russian territory. Russian policies in the occupied areas of Turkey must be situated against more overarching agendas and long-term trends, of both the Russian state in general and the Russian military in particular. For instance, the officials in charge of administering the occupied provinces of Turkey from mid-1915 until early 1917—Grand Duke Nikolai Nikolaevich and his aide, General Nikolai Ianushkevich—had earlier overseen the first Russian occupation of Galicia.[13]

It is tempting to view the actions of the Russian military as the result of a coherent policy or as guided by an overarching ideology. Yet two recent studies have argued (in the case of the German military in World War I) that military practices may have patterns yet still be the result of improvisation. John Horne and Alan Kramer, in analyzing German atrocities in occupied Belgium and northern France, point to the "cultural and political disposition that carried not just ordinary soldiers but the entire military command rapidly beyond its own legal code and even contemporary moral norms of acceptable violence against civilians." In their view, "brutality and inhumanity characterized the response to the 'franc-tireur war' because these reflected the prevailing doctrines of the German military on civilian involvement in warfare."[14] Isabel Hull has argued that military conduct in the German case was determined not simply by doctrine, but by an even more diffuse institutional culture embedded both in doctrine and in unarticulated presuppositions. When facing specific dilemmas in a wide variety of cases, the German military responded in nearly identical fashion, without guidance or central coordination. Indeed, Hull notes that the German military behaved in strikingly similar ways in colonial wars as it did during World War I in both Eastern *and* Western Europe. It did so, she argues, not because colonial methods were "brought home," but because the institutional culture of the German military—an unusually "strong" institution—transcended the particular arenas of its implementation. "When the military set about solving these problems, it came up with broadly the same techniques wherever it was."[15] The Russian military, subject to particular pressure from government ministries and especially the court, without a doubt, was an institution nowhere near as "strong" as its German counterpart.[16] Nevertheless, much of the Russian military's conduct in the occupied territories of Turkey derived from "standard operating procedure"—an operating procedure that was utilitarian and callous. The Russian military entirely subordinated the regions and their populations to its own military operations. On the other hand, these operations in occupied Turkey did not become supercharged with an overarching ideological program, such as the liberationist and overtly antisemitic occupation regime Grand Duke Nikolai Nikolaevich and Ianushkevich had pursued in Galicia in 1914–1915.[17]

The August 1914 Field Regulations granted the Russian military untrammeled control over occupied territory. At first, military authorities on the Caucasus Front simply directed civilian officials in provinces neighboring the occupied territories to oversee them.[18] Several months later, in September 1915, as the Russian advance made this earlier model untenable, the Russian army issued its first general guidelines for military officers serving as district captains.[19] These skeletal instructions—they directed military appointees to uphold peace and order—were superceded the following year by a more detailed "Temporary Guidelines for administering the regions of Turkey occupied by right of war."[20] At this time, over the summer of 1916, Foreign Minister Sazonov and the Viceroy for the Caucasus, Grand Duke Nikolai Nikolaevich (the former commander-in-chief, relieved in August 1915) exchanged notes regarding the aims and policies for Russian occupation of Armenia.[21] Sazonov noted that the occupation of Great Armenia and the decision to incorporate it had raised the question of the area's future organization. While it was still premature to determine the precise foundations for the conquered region, it was essential to determine guiding principles. "The greatest difficulty in our forthcoming task," noted Sazonov, "consists in posing and solving the Armenian question." He continued:

> Taken together, it somewhat extends beyond the boundaries of Russian State life. . . . As is well known, the two extremes between which the solution of the Armenian question has usually been posed by us are two currents. One is the desire of Armenian nationalists for full autonomy under the aegis of Russia, in the spirit of the reforms proposed by us in 1913, and the other—entirely contradictory to it—reduces the political significance of Armenians to nothing and seeks to put Muslims in their place. It seems to me that the solution of this question entirely in one or the other direction does not correspond to Russia's State interests, neither from the point of view of domestic nor of foreign policy. . . . It seems to me that the

best outcome for us in ordering the reconquered areas of Turkey would be to be led especially firmly by the principles of legality, justice, and an entirely nonpartisan relation to all the diverse elements of the region, not setting one against the other and not providing exclusive protection to any one particular nationality [*narodnost'*] at the expense of another.

Overall, the Grand Duke concurred with Sazonov's guidelines.[22] However, he noted that it was his "profound belief" that the Armenian question did not exist within the boundaries of the Russian Empire. In an offhand criticism of his predecessor as viceroy, Illarion Ivanovich Vorontsov-Dashkov, Grand Duke Nikolai noted that he did not favor any group in the Caucasus over any other. (The Grand Duke charged that Vorontsov-Dashkov had pursued a pro-Armenian orientation.) "The Armenian question as such," he expostulated, "exists only outside the borders of Russia." At another occasion, he proclaimed that "there is no more an Armenian question than there is a Yakut question," referring to an indigenous group found entirely within the bounds of the Russian Empire.[23] Insofar as the Armenian question did exist *outside* the borders of Russia, he concurred entirely with Sazonov's presentation: Armenians should be granted broad autonomy, but no special privileges vis-à-vis the Muslim population. These policies were formally expressed in the "Temporary Statute on the administration of the territories of Turkey, seized by right of war," issued in June 1916.

Such were the goals of Russian occupation policy in principle. These goals were attenuated by several factors. In my view, at least as important as the fitful embrace of ethnic mobilization (in regards to *both* Armenians and Kurds) was a template of military culture that instrumentalized the civilian population. The Russian military, rather than pursuing an overarching policy for the region, sought to come up with short-term solutions to immediate problems, solutions that privileged the military at the expense of the civilian population.[24] At some level the military had come to accept civilian losses as a military necessity. In early 1917 Nikolai Ianushkevich, the Grand Duke's chief of staff, declared bluntly that a ten percent mortality rate among civilians due to food shortages *in the Russian regions* of the Caucasus was "normal" and acceptable.[25] Ianushkevich here was not motivated by any specific colonial or anti-Muslim or anti-Armenian bias. He had operated by similar guidelines both in occupied Galicia (a Slavic region slated for incorporation into Russia proper) and in Russia proper.

The crucial role of this military dynamic is thrown into sharp relief by comparing Russian occupation policy in the occupied regions of Turkey and in Persia, which was formally neutral but in whose territory both the Russian and Turkish armies conducted military operations. The actual conduct of the Russian military was not terribly different in Persia. The military, in a rare fit of self-reflection, noted that its conduct in Persia was complicated by the fact that the "Regulations on Field Administration of the Army in Wartime" envisioned only two categories of the population: the population of the Russian Empire in those of its areas declared to be a war zone, and the population of enemy areas occupied by right of war. The population of Persia, of course, fell into neither category, but for over three years it was to find itself interacting with the Russian military. The Russian military's only solution was to try to appoint "people who knew the East and could apply the existing guidelines wisely."[26] Because of the dynamics of military necessity, however, such men did not act terribly differently than their compatriots in occupied Turkey. What was different in Persia was the presence of consular and diplomatic officials who were able to criticize both the military and the rationale it provided for its actions.[27] Indeed, throughout the war, but especially from late 1916 onward, consular officials in Persia criticized the military's myopia about its own operations, and its focus on military procedure to the exclusion of broader political considerations, in increasingly explicit terms. The Russian Army successfully prevented the appointment of diplomatic personnel to the occupied regions of Turkey.[28] It tried, but failed, to remove consular officials from the regions of Persia in which military operations were proceeding.[29] One reason we know so much about the (deplorable) conduct of the Russian military in Persia in 1917 is because consular officials were so excoriating in their reports on it. Russian conduct in the occupied regions of Turkey was no doubt equally bad. But without consular agents to criticize it and to report on it, we simply know much less about it.

REQUISITIONING

In the Caucasus, the Russian army was operating on a front designated to be of secondary importance and one that, due to the Armenian genocide and the flight of both the Kurd-ish and Armenian populations, faced a dire shortage of agricultural supplies.[30] In order to conduct military operations—the military's *raison d'être*—it had to acquire these goods. The quartermaster general was supposed to supply the army with goods or, failing that, purchase them from the local population. But the poor lines of communication and poor food sup-ply situation in Russia proper meant that the quartermaster could almost never supply the army's needs. As a result, military units took to requisitioning what they needed from the local population.

With the seizure of Erzerum in spring 1916, the Russian occupation administration set as its goal to do "all possible, on the one hand, to ease the burden of war on the units and, on the other, to secure their rear, securing the sympathy of the newly conquered region." But, reported the Foreign Ministry's appointee to the region,

> difficulties in bringing up the supplies of food and forage necessary for the units contributed greatly to the rise of marauding, and the unsystematic requisitions, which threatened a region already ravaged by war with total impoverishment. It also caused hostility and dissatisfaction among the population. Equally, the numerous military transports and passing cavalry units, without any plan or system, wastefully drove cattle over the sown fields . . . which threatened the units quartered in the Erzerum region with the prospect of being entirely without fodder.[31]

The local army command (the First Caucasus Army Corps) issued a directive establishing a minimal number of cattle that were to be left to the civilian population regardless of mili-tary needs. However, since the army quartermaster did not supply any of the units with the necessary cattle, army units were forced to supply themselves from the local population. In doing so, they "ignor[ed] the interests of the inhabitants as well as the orders issued for the Corps—and in fact it was not uncommon for units to fire on the [Russian-staffed] village police and to take the inhabitants' last head of cattle. As a result, the norms laid down by the corps for preserving the region's cattle were violated by roughly 50 percent."[32]

In a report to the new revolutionary authorities after the February Revolution of 1917 in Russia, the military governor-general for the occupied territories of Turkey described the prevailing state of affairs. The region had suffered both from the Turkish retreat and from the requisitions of the Russian army. These conditions produced a harvest shortage and the specter of hunger. The governor general, confronted with a region without its own resources, did his best to secure supplies for the population. Shortages in Russia itself along with trans-portation difficulties limited the aid, however. Russian civic organizations—the Union of

Towns, the Muslim Committee, the Armenian Committee—helped in providing aid. But the return of refugees further complicated the situation. "The army demands requisitions of cattle," reported the governor general, "but the population itself in many regions can survive only with such cattle. We need to establish certain norms, the transgression of which is possible only if we wish knowingly to condemn the local population to destruction. Of course, the demands of the army must be met, but the question of the civilian population's survival cannot be ignored."[33]

The governor general was charged with overseeing the region and caring for its population. Local military commanders had a narrower agenda: the functioning of their own units and the conduct of military operations. Their agenda therefore often conflicted with the desires of the governor-general to shield the civilian population from the excesses of requisitioning. Russian forces, in occupied Turkey as well as in northern Persia, increasingly faced a worsening supply situation. They responded by requisitioning even more rapaciously. The very process of this requisitioning allowed soldiers vast horizons for abuse. One Cossack officer recalled:

> In general the Kurds are a fine people, and we even came to like them. . . . And then with the start of war Russian forces came to this people in Turkey. We occupied their land, destroyed their buildings "for firewood," took all their grain to feed our own numerous head of horses, killed their sheep and cattle for our own provisioning, paying almost nothing for this. But mainly—in occupying this vast territory, we did not give them any kind of local administration. Any line commander of even the lowest rank who had stopped in a Kurdish settlement or having arrived for forage, could give himself free rein over the population. Any rank-and-file soldier, entering the dark stone dwelling of a Kurd, felt justified in doing whatever he wished: take the last *lavash,* dig into his rags "searching for weapons," he could take whatever he wanted, he could drive out the head of family from his hovel and right then and there to abuse his wife, sister, daughters.[34]

Such conduct grew out of an institutional dynamic, a dynamic that unfolded on other fronts and, later, within Russia proper.

REFUGEES

The military forcibly expelled tens of thousands of people, which I discuss below. But many people passed under the control of the Russian military of their own accord, as refugees.[35] The Russian military did not see its task to be caring for these people, particularly when the army believed that they interfered with the conduct of military operations—meaning, not least of all, the ability of the army to feed itself. Thus the Russian military often dispatched refugees from one region to another and sought to control their access to regions where the army was active. In doing so, its goals were usually limited and operational. In August 1916, for instance, General Iudenich, Commander of the Caucasus Army, banned any return of refugees to the occupied regions of Turkey. He was quite clear about his reason: their return "would complicate the already difficult food supply issue for these regions."[36] Later that year, in an interview with the newspaper *Novoe vremia,* the governor-general for the occupied regions of Turkey explained why he was barring the return of refugees to certain occupied regions:

> The question of the return of the Armenian population which had fled to Russia due to the Turkish atrocities depends, in the Governor-General's opinion, not only on completing the

administrative reorganization of the region, or guaranteeing the food supply, but also on the strategic situation at the front. The premature return of refugees often brings in its wake un-desirable panics and needless victims—both human and material—of which the population's rapid departure from Van recently can serve as an example. For this reason the state must treat this question very cautiously.[37]

Governor-General Peshkov was referring to the fact that the Russian army, in the face of the August 1916 Ottoman offensive, organized the evacuation of 50,000 refugees who had re-turned to Van, Bitlis, and Mush and distributed them further in the rear, to Basen and Igdyr. This relocation caused a new crisis, as the refugees now required food and medical supplies.[38] As this example shows, whenever a local field commander determined it necessary, he could order the "expulsion" of refugees from the region under his control to the rear.[39]

The Russian military, of course, was not a humanitarian organization. Just as it might seek to keep refugees out of harm's way—for its own interests, of course—it might just as soon exploit them to meet its operational needs. It channeled returning refugees to valleys and regions where there was a dire need for agricultural work. General Iudenich ordered that refugees be directed to certain regions closer to the front, so as to ease the delivery of these supplies to the army.[40] Should the food supply in a region prove insufficient for both the military and the refugees located there, the military's response was callous but predictable: the refugees would have to leave.[41]

The military had thus instrumentalized refugees and subordinated them to the needs of its own operations. Indeed, the military was most eager to avoid dealing with refugees at all. This outlook accounts in part for why the military was so eager to hand over care of the refugees to civilian organizations and especially to civilian welfare agencies such as the All-Russian Union of Towns, the Grand Duchess Tatiana Refugee Relief Committee, and the myriad Armenian and Muslim relief agencies. One of the great ironies of the Russian war effort is that the same state whose military expelled hundreds of thousands of civilians also provided vast sums to various charitable agencies that then cared for those same people.[42] In occupied Galicia, for instance, it was the All-Russian Union of Zemstvos and not the military that undertook the task of feeding not only the tens of thousands of refugees—many Jewish expellees—but also the nearly 200,000 civilians engaged in compulsory labor in the trenches and on roadwork.[43] Likewise on the Caucasus Front, the task of caring for refugees and for the remaining local civilian population fell largely to civilian relief organizations. There was of course a concerted effort to aid the Armenian refugees.[44] But after an initial decision in August 1915 to provide state credits only for aid to Christians in the occupied territories, the Russian government later approved credit also for the Muslim population there.[45] The Union of Zemstvos—operating largely with funds granted by the Russian government—distributed aid throughout the region without regard to religion. Armenian and Muslim relief agencies helped their own brethren.

I have discussed this humanitarian relief effort for two reasons. First, it demonstrates, I think, that the Russian military's policy of expulsion and management of refugees was meant primarily for operational reasons, rather than to eliminate certain populations. Expulsion was subordinate to military operations, not an end in itself. The Russian military had no ob-jections to the extension of humanitarian relief to these populations—indeed, it welcomed it. It did so not out of any high humanitarian ideals, but because its interests lay in displacing, for its own convenience, the population from the realm of military operations. The population was not a target *per se*. (My point of comparison here is obviously with Ottoman slaughter and expulsion of certain groups, Armenians and Greeks first and foremost, but also with the Russian army's conduct toward the Jews of Galicia.) My second reason for highlighting the central role of these civilian relief agencies is to underscore a change that was to occur in the course of 1917. As inefficient and wasteful as these agencies often were—they were often attacked on such grounds at the time—they played an absolutely crucial role in caring for the civilian population in the period 1915–1917. With the fraying of Russian public life in the course of 1917, and the eventual outlawing of the large relief organizations by the Bolsheviks, these agencies would cease to serve as a buffer between the Russian military and the local civilian population. This was one of the crucial and oft-overlooked reasons for the rapid deterioration in relations between civilians and the military as 1917 progressed.

POPULATION EXPULSIONS AND DEPORTATIONS

In addition to directing the flow of refugees, the Russian military also engaged in widespread expulsions of civilian populations. It has become increasingly clear that mass population expulsions were an intrinsic feature not just of the Second World War, but of the First World War as well. The mass population expulsions and deportations on the Caucasus Front the First World War have received attention, but others occurred on a widespread scale on the Western and Eastern fronts as well.[46] These expulsions were a military *practice,* one growing out of a disregard for civilian populations and a myopic focus on the conduct of military operations. (It is the same concern that underlay the development of concentration camps as a tool of military operations during the Spanish–American and Boer Wars.)[47] Deportations grew into something more than military practice when ideology came to inform the goals, and thus the means, of deportation. Clearly, what distinguished Ottoman policy in its expulsion of Armenians was not simply military necessity, but an ideological agenda. Similarly, the Russian treatment of the Jewish population in 1915 in occupied Galicia but also within Russia itself, culminating in the mass expulsion of perhaps one million people, occurred within an ideological envelope of antisemitism. Russian conduct upon the second occupation of Galicia, in 1916–1917, was strikingly different, in large part because the explicit antisemitic agenda of the 1914–1915 occupation was lacking.[48]

By and large, the Russian army on the Caucasus Front was driven by the generic institutional concerns of the military rather than any overarching ideological agenda. It did not seek, for instance, to expel the Armenian population or ban the return of Armenian refugees in order to colonize the region with Russians. Certain individuals and even ministries had such plans, to be sure. And the Russian army certainly entertained extravagant plans for resettling populations. General Peshkov, Governor General of the occupied regions, believed that separating the local population into its respective ethnic enclaves was the only way to ensure peace. He proposed "to deal with this difficulty by regrouping as far as possible the population, and getting the Armenians to settle east and the Kurds south of [Lake Van]." He continued:

> The regions of Trebizond and Erzerum are going to form two administrative areas separate from that of Van and Bitlis, which will form the third. Each of these three areas will be divided into four districts, and in the Van and Bitlis area as far as possible, the Moslems will be divided from the Christians and settled in particular districts. . . . As far as the Trebizond and Erzerum regions are concerned, only those Armenians who resided there before the war will be allowed to settle there. Those regions will be regarded as especially Moslem.[49]

Peshkov's plan, however, remained just that—a plan. Similarly, the progressive Ministry of Agriculture had grandiose plans for reordering the occupied provinces of Turkey as well as Astrabad province in Persia. The ministry, gripped by a technocratic planning mania, foresaw consolidating the landholdings of the local population and settling Russians on any remaining available land, rather than expelling the native population. The army command, however, blocked the Agriculture Ministry in no uncertain terms from pursuing its technocratic fantasies until the war was over.[50]

The first type of expulsions were those related to the conduct of military operations. The Russian army practiced population expulsion, clearing large swaths of the front of their native inhabitants, Armenian and Kurd alike. This was not, however, a policy specific to the Caucasus front, but was a generic feature of Russian military operations.[51] In the Erzerum region, for instance, the military commander resettled *all* inhabitants—10,000 people—from a seven-mile strip of the front line and moved them closer to the city of Erzerum, in the process thereby exacerbating the already dire food supply situation.[52] On a smaller scale, the military issued orders expelling the inhabitants of both Kurdish and Armenian villages from one half of the village into another in order to disinfect their dwellings. The rationale was not to help the civilian population so much as it was to prevent the spread of infectious diseases to the troops quartered in these regions.[53]

The subordination and instrumentalization of the civilian population to military needs also extended to drafting local people for compulsory labor. This side of the conduct of war by the Russian military has largely gone unstudied.[54] In occupied Galicia, for instance, the Russian military employed nearly 200,000 civilians drafted into compulsory labor for work on its trenches. The German Army acted similarly on both the Eastern and Western fronts. In the Caucasus, the Russian military as early as November 1914, one month into the war on that front, had drafted all male Kurds of the Bayazet valley for compulsory work on clearing the roads.[55] Upon its occupation of Erzerum, the Russian military drafted the entire population to dispose of unburied corpses (the concern again was the possibility of epidemic disease and the danger it posed to the military) and then assigned "almost the entire male population fit for work, from the age of 17 to 45, to compulsory labor of a military nature."[56] Armenians and Kurds alike were subject to compulsory labor. The head of the first district of the Erzerum region, Staff Captain Alekseev, detained 47 working-age Armenians for work details. (They were released—but only because the commissar of the Erzerum region determined that the men were farmers and their work in agriculture was more valuable.)[57] A short time later, the regional commanders were ordered to detain any males who had served in the Turkish army—or "generally any military-age Kurds or Turks"—and dispatch them to the construction and labor detachments. The apprehension of these individuals was to be done "gradually, as they are found, rather than by a mass search, with the goal that the army units will avoid any rash actions that might disturb the local population's economic life."[58] In many cases, then, the Russian military engaged in expulsion and detention out of what it perceived to be demands of "military necessity," demands that took absolute precedence over the region's civilian population. Such action, however, was not limited to the Caucasus Front, but was a generic feature of Russian military culture. The Russian military would resort to such measures within Russia itself as the army retreated. Both White and Red would draw upon such practices in the civil war that followed.[59]

If the first type of expulsion focused on the entire civilian population for reasons of "military necessity," the second type of expulsion focused on specific groups. The Russian

Army practiced more targeted expulsions of those populations it regarded as "unreliable." In Galicia and Russian Poland, this meant primarily the Jewish population. On the Caucasus Front, it meant first and foremost the Kurdish population. One must distinguish here between actual expulsions ordered at the operational level, and Russian troops' pillaging and marauding of the Kurdish population that derived from anti-Kurd sentiment among lower-level commanders and troops.

The Russian military, it must be emphasized, had a very ambivalent policy in regard to the Kurdish population. Court circles suspected that the Viceroy for the Caucasus, Vorontsov-Dashkov, harbored pro-Armenian sentiments. His program was one of Russian imperial greatness through management of ethnic difference—an old story. In fact, from 1912 he sought to enlist Kurdish leaders for the Russian cause.[60] In certain military and diplomatic circles, Russia's skillful use of the Kurds against the Ottoman Empire throughout the nineteenth century was a point of pride. These officials pointed in particular to the effective employment of Kurds by Mikhail Loris-Melikov, an Armenian serving the Russian Empire in the Caucasus from the 1860s through the Russo-Turkish War of 1877–1878.[61] Nevertheless, due in large part to court politics and bureaucratic infighting, Vorontsov-Dashkov was tarred as pro-Armenian. Significantly, his successor—Grand Duke Nikolai Nikolaevich—came to believe these rumors, and sought to "remedy" Vorontsov-Dashkov's "pro-Armenian" orientation.[62] His turn away from what he portrayed as "pro-Armenian" policies chronologically coincided with the Russian Army's advance into territories depopulated by the Ottoman slaughter of Armenians. The Grand Duke's shift away from what he believed were the previous "pro-Armenian" policies was most evident in his efforts to win over Kurdish tribal leaders and his order reforming Armenian volunteer formations into regular rifle regiments—resented by Armenian activists as an attempt to bring such units under greater Russian control. Armenian organizations excoriated him as pursuing heartless and unjust anti-Armenian policies.[63]

However, commanders at the corps level and below had the authority to expel individuals and entire groups of people they determined were "unreliable." Due to the irregular warfare practiced by those Kurds opposed to Russia, as well as to anti-Kurd sentiments among the Russian military, the military frequently resorted to expelling Kurdish communities *en masse*. Throughout the period 1915–1917, the Russian army expelled Kurds from entire districts.[64] This type of expulsion was distinct from, but overlapped with, marauding and pillaging by Russian units and Armenian volunteer formations against Kurdish communities.

First Intermezzo: The Case of Refugees and Deportees in Urmia, 1917

Here I want to present one case of how the Russian state—both military and diplomats—treated refugees and deportees. I turn the focus to northern Persia, both because it is unusually well-documented and because the presence of Russian consular agents there provides a critical perspective from outside the military on the military's activities.

By late 1916 several tens of thousands of refugees had gathered in northern Persia, especially around Urmia. Many were Assyrians and Armenians who had fled persecution and slaughter at the hand of Turkish forces, either in Turkey proper (in the region around Lake Van) or from Turkish forces and their Kurdish allies in Persia. They were cared for in part by the Russian Embassy and Russian relief organizations, but primarily by the various Christian missions in the town, especially the American Mission. Over the course of 1917 Russian diplomatic officials engaged in an extended correspondence with the Russian military over what should be done with these refugees, especially in light of the potential for intercommunal violence between the Christian and Muslim refugees. The Russian consul in Urmia, Vasilii Petrovich Nikitin, and the Russian mission's second official, Vladimir Fedorovich Minorskii, were sympathetic to the refugees' suffering but also urged the Russian military to pursue a more sensitive and conciliatory policy toward the local Kurdish population.[65] Due to the fact that this region was an arena of military operations, however, military authorities had to approve any movement of these refugees. In late April, for instance, the military authorities of the Caucasus Army, at the request of diplomatic officials, permitted a party of 500 refugees in Kazvin to return to their homes in Hamadan.[66]

In early April 1917 Minorskii telegraphed the Russian embassy in Tehran, informing it that he believed it "extremely desirable to take immediate measures to resettle the Urmia refugees in Turkey" because of the prospects of famine in Persia.[67] He returned to this issue in June 1917. He described how relations between the refugees and the local Muslim population had become increasingly tense as a result of political developments in both Russia and Persia. In Minorskii's view, "the refugee question in its present state cannot be solved by half-measures such as admonitions and attempts to reconcile the irreconcilable. We can only solve it by addressing its root problem—that is, by expelling [vyselenie] the refugees to regions that are entirely under Russian jurisdiction, whether that be in the regions of Turkey under our occupation or within the boundaries of Russia proper."[68] The Russian vice-consul in Urmia reported that the refugees had begun to plunder the local Muslim villages and requested that the Russian military take measures to prevent the pillaging by the refugees.[69] The Russian envoy in Tehran, Nikolai Sevastianovich Etter, endorsed this plan for a "transfer" [perevod] of the Urmia refugees, as did the Russian Foreign Ministry.[70] The Russian military authorities in Urmia had their own frustrations. The commander of the Seventh Caucasus Army Corps reported that over 18,000 refugees had massed in Urmia. A portion were living on lands abandoned by Kurdish tribes hostile to the Russians, while others survived on rations distributed by the Russian consulate. To the frustration of the commander, the refugees declined to work on military projects. They constituted, in his view, surplus mouths taxing the local food supply, a population that provided no useful labor. Moreover, they had started to pillage and rob the local Muslim population, so their presence, in his view, gave the erroneous impression that Russian authorities were siding with the local Christian population. General Vadbol'skii thus argued that

> from the point of view of military interests, the presence in the regions of Urmia of this [Christian refugee] population is harmful and undesirable, and thus it is necessary to resettle, if not all, then at least the tribes most irreconcilable and most disposed to pillaging (around 5000 people). There are no free agricultural lands in Azerbaidzhan; I propose that it would be more fitting to settle them in the region of Bayazet-Diadin-Bergi-kala—where they could practice peaceful labor if they so desired, and their bandit-like attributes could be directed against the Kurds. At the very least, they could serve as a kind of bulwark against the raids of these Kurds along our railroads on the line from Bayazet.[71]

The Russian mission in Tehran strongly endorsed General Vadbol'skii's proposal, noting that the Persian government had made similar requests. The commander of the Caucasus Army, however, forbade the expulsion of the 5,000 Assyrians from Turkey back into the occupied regions of Turkey.[72] It is important to note that Russian policy toward these refugees was driven not by a desire to pursue irredentist politics in support of the Christian population (a policy that the French and British governments would press insistently in early 1918), but rather by a concern for calm and order in the army's rear.

At the same time, over 12,000 Kurdish refugees who had been expelled by the Russian army from Mergever to Urmia petitioned Russian authorities for permission to return to their homes. Dying from famine and exposure, they wished to return home before winter.[73] Russian diplomatic officials supported the request. In their view, the refugees' return to Mergever was desirable because their continued presence in Urmia created "ever greater problems with food supply in Urmia, where they had been expelled." But Russian diplomatic officials now mobilized a new argument in favor of returning the refugees: banning their return "would be a violation of the laws of war, against which Russia had repeatedly protested in regard to Belgium, Armenia, and so on."[74] Invoking this precise rationale, the army command permitted the return of the Kurdish refugees to their homes.[75]

The situation of the Kurdish and Christian refugees in Urmia demonstrates, I believe, the Russian military's largely instrumental view of the civilian population. Rather than viewing the Christian refugee population as a potential basis of political support, the military and diplomats instead viewed them as source of disorder, unsettling the army's rear. Russian officials would embrace the ethnic mobilization and the arming of the Christian refugees—but only after the collapse of the Caucasus Army and at the strong urging of British and French military attachés.[76]

PUNITIVE EXPEDITIONS

A standard practice of European militaries, especially in "small war" operations, was to employ "punitive detachments." The Russians were no exception.[77] Given the nature of warfare on the Caucasus Front, particularly confronting Kurdish irregulars, the Russians routinely employed such punitive expeditions. The use of such detachments was predicated on the effect of terror. Given the shortage of troops, it was considered necessary to instill fear and obedience.[78] One must distinguish, however, between formally sanctioned punitive operations, directed specifically at those tribes which had attacked Russian forces, and the more indiscriminate and arbitrary operation of lower-level Russian units against entire populations they had come to believe were hostile. The limits of "sanctioned" punitive operations, and the transgressions of those limits, is the subject of the second intermezzo, at the conclusion of this section.

From the very first days of the war, Russian diplomatic and military leaders had sanctioned the use of "punitive expeditions" against Kurdish tribes operating against Russians.[79] However, officials insisted that such operations be limited only to those tribes that had actually acted against Russia. Concern that the operations would cause diplomatic complications, or extend beyond the actual perpetrators, led to the cancellation of some expeditions.[80] British observers noted that

> In the course of this war the Russian Government has been compelled in several districts to resort to punitive measures to protect for the future, posts which are garrisoned by necessarily small detachments from the treachery of the Kurds. . . . The Russian troops employed have been Cossacks, Armenian militia, frontier and other troops composed chiefly of Armenians and commanded by Armenian generals of the regular Russian Army, notably NAZIBEKOF, CHERNOZUBOF, and TEREMEN, whose compatriots have been massacred by the Kurds.[81]

Indeed, General Chernozubov, commanding Russian forces in Persian Azerbaidzhan, became particularly renowned for his reliance on punitive detachments against Kurdish tribes. His actions earned the condemnation and protests of Russian consular officials in Persia.[82] But Russian forces, forced to confront irregular units and without any hope for reinforcements, came to rely increasingly on such detachments. To the great dissatisfaction of Russian consular officials in Persia, Colonel Dumbadze gave a verbal order to the Second Border Regiment to "mercilessly exterminate the Kurds" and pursued a policy of counterproductive raiding, so much so that the British Government initiated its own investigation. Tellingly, the consular officials did not protest the use of punitive detachments, but demanded that they act only against those groups of the population "whose hostility to us has been definitively shown," and that women and children be allowed to leave any settlements before they were shelled. "Also," Minorskii added, "do not allow the soldiers to rape women and pillage everything in sight." Later he reported that Lieutenant Basevskii's unit had raped all the women in two Persian villages and Lieutenant Fedos'ev's unit had killed 28 men and 3 women in a raid on a Kurdish settlement.[83] (Again, we know about such conduct because Russian consular agents were much more likely to report on it than were Russian military officials.)

Second Intermezzo: General Depishich Cancels the Punitive Expedition of the Fifth Armenian Rifle Battalion against the Kurdish Tribes North of Van, 21–22 May 1917

To understand the boundaries of "legitimate" punitive operations and the dynamic of their transgression, it helps to examine a particular case. Here I will focus on the actions of the Fifth Armenian Rifle Battalion, dispatched by the Russian command on a punitive operation along the northern bank of Lake Van.[84] In order to combat the marauding of Kurdish bands along the Bayazid road, and "in order to make a fitting impression on the Kurdish tribes in the . . . region," General Depishich dispatched two punitive detachments to on the road to Bergi-Kala on 21 May 1917. As there were no other units available, the general dispatched the only force at hand, the Fifth Armenian Rifle Battalion, based in Van, and three companies of Black Sea Cossacks.

On the basis of reports from the Armenian battalion's commander as well as from the staff of an All-Russian Union of Towns feeding and medical station which had witnessed the event, the general was able to reconstruct the story. Two companies of the Armenian battalion had moved on Bergi-Kala. They heard rumors that the Kurds of that village planned to ambush them. When the Armenian soldiers moved into the village of Sor, along the way, they met no resistance and found that most of the population had fled. Upon trying to enter the local *bek*'s house, however, they were fired on, with four soldiers killed immediately. They then opened fire with shrapnel from their mountain cannon upon the settlement and soon took it. They suffered no more casualties. Most Kurds at that time had either been drafted by the military for work on the railroads or had entered the service of feeding station of the All-Russian Union of Zemstvos.

When the soldiers in Bergi-Kala heard of the exchange of fire in Sor, they took their rage out on the Kurdish inhabitants of Bergi-Kala. In the rampage that followed they beat all the Kurds they came across, killing over 40 people, all women, children, and old men. The crowd spared no one who fell into their hands and even chased those Kurds who had sought refuge in the canteen. One Russian nurse protected those Kurds seeking shelter by denouncing the Armenian soldiers as "bandits, who deserve no place in a Free Russia." She nearly paid for this statement with her life. Only after some time did the unit's officers manage to reestablish control. The officers placed the wounded Kurds in the unit's ambulance and set a guard over them.

Under these circumstances, General Depishich felt that a continuation of the "punitive expedition" would degenerate into the total extermination of the local Kurdish population and canceled it. He came to the belief that only individual bandits were marauding and that the mass of the population, if left alone, "might be useful, at least as workers on the railroad that was under construction." He traveled to Bergi-Kala on 25 May, where the Armenian battalion expressed its wish to meet with him. Through its spokesman, the regiment expressed its regret for the incident. The general lectured them "on a soldier's duty, on a soldier's obligations in relation to his foe and toward the civilian population, and on the shame for a soldier of the Russian Army to beat defenseless old men, women, children." The unit replied that it had been outraged that the canteen of the Union of Towns had been feeding Kurds but had barred Armenians. The situation, as the general pointed out, was quite different. The Union of Towns canteen had provided for the Kurds working on military projects; the canteen of the Armenian Relief Committee provided for Armenian refugees in the region. The Armenian delegates then concluded by expressing their desire to continue the punitive expedition. General Depishich replied that he had canceled any further punitive expeditions and ordered the Fifth Armenian Rifle Battalion back to its barracks in Van.

Undoubtedly, the general's decision to cancel the punitive expedition saved many lives. But with an ever-decreasing number of reliable troops, the command of the Caucasus Army had little choice but to rely on units such as the Fifth Armenian Rifle Battalion. Two months later, the chairman of the Van Soviet of Soldiers' Deputies informed the command of the Caucasus Army that the Fifth Armenian Rifle Battalion had "enlisted as an entire battalion as a battalion of death" (that is, as a shock battalion). No other unit of its size had done so.[85]

PILLAGING, LOOTING, RAPING. ANTI-KURD AND ANTI-MUSLIM SENTIMENTS AMONG LOWER-LEVEL OFFICERS AND THE RANK-AND-FILE IN THE RUSSIAN ARMY

By early 1917 Grand Duke Nikolai Nikolaevich, who was never terribly well-disposed toward the Armenians to begin with, had been swayed by Prince Shakhovskoi's arguments that the Caucasus Army should seek to some accommodation with the Kurds.[86] In fact, several of the Grand Duke's secret agents for conducting negotiations with the Kurdish tribes—Prince Shakhovskoi and College Assessor Gadzhemukov—were appointed, for purposes of conspiratorial cover, as district captains of areas of occupied Turkey.[87] Indeed, once the 1917 February Revolution occurred, Prince Gadzhemukov lobbied General Iudenich to pursue a more aggressive pro-Kurdish policy and to abandon any support for the Armenian cause. He concluded: "if one is to view [the Ottoman slaughter of the Armenians] not from a humanitarian, but from a political point of view, and as an already accomplished fact—one for which the Armenians bear the blame—one must say that there is this positive side: Turkey has left us an Armenia without Armenians."[88] Several works present Gadzhemukov's statement as revealing the Russian government's real intentions in Armenia.[89] In fact, rather than a statement of overall policy, his letter was a plea for the army to abandon what he believed were its pro-Armenian policies. "Armenia without Armenians" was Gadzhemukov's personal desire—not Russian policy.

The high military command's policies, however, were filtered through the conduct of individual army commanders. Most Russian commanders—entering a land that had just witnessed the systematic massacre of Armenians and with their own units under intermittent attack from Kurdish irregulars—came to hold abiding biases against the Kurds and Muslims in general. Cossack units in particular visited merciless retribution upon the local Muslim population.[90] When Cossack troops retook Ardahan, "a massacre and pogrom took place. The Cossacks looted the bazaar, burnt the Moslem quarter, and killed at sight all Turks they could see."[91] Armenian volunteer detachments, later reformed as rifle corps, similarly showed little mercy to Kurdish and Turkish communities.[92]

Thus the Russian occupation administration under the Grand Duke alienated Armenians because of its allegedly pro-Kurdish bias, while the conduct of individual army and corps commanders made the very Kurdish population the Grand Duke was seeking to win over hostile to Russian rule.[93] This criticism of the army's conduct from both sides has found reflection in the historiography, with Turkish accounts charging a systematic anti-Muslim bias and with Armenian accounts charging a callous disregard and indeed a pro-Kurdish orientation.

Certain Russian commanders early on began systematically persecuting the Muslim population. General Liakhov, for instance, retook Adjaria in early 1915 and advanced up the Chorokh. He "accused the Moslem natives of treachery, and sent his Cossacks from Batum with orders to kill every native at sight, and burn every village and every mosque. And very efficiently had they performed their task, for as we passed up the Chorokh valley to Artvin not a single habitable dwelling or a single living creature did we see."[94] There were intermittent attempts to impose order on such marauding.[95] But by and large they did not succeed. There were simply few institutional boundaries within the military to limit such conduct—especially in a situation where commanders faced an irregular foe, with insufficient forces, and believed that military necessity required firm action. The contrast with northern Persia is again striking: there, consular officials both criticized military officials and also sought to mediate between hostile segments of the population. The end result, however, was much the same by 1917. This was so not because there was no difference between the military and diplomatic officials, but because both had lost control of the situation by mid-1917. A different form of violence was emerging.

Revolutionary Violence

The military violence described above was callous and brutal. It subordinated civilian populations to the dictates of "military necessity" and often subjected populations suspected of disloyalty to expulsion and violence. But this was a goal-rational dynamic, albeit one with great violence and frequent excesses. The breakdown of military discipline and the political consensus on the purpose of legitimate force—the Revolution—produced a situation in which violence was much more ubiquitous but much more diffuse. If anything, it was worse, because it lacked the regularities of routine military violence. Rather than worrying about overall military necessity for the army or its operations, troops increasingly came to think about their own survival.

The Russian Revolution initially brought several positive developments to the dynamics of military violence. The military, overall as well in the occupied territories, now became politically accountable for its actions. (Thus General Chernozubov was relieved of his post and tried for his policies against the Kurds, while Prince Shakhovskoi was arrested for his pro-Kurdish policies.)[96] In both occupied Galicia and the areas of occupied Turkey, the shift to political accountability for military conduct was signified by the replacement of a "temporary military governor-general"—a military man appointed by the Commander in Chief—with a political commissar appointed by, and answerable to, the Provisional Government. The new political situation allowed increased reporting of military violations by a myriad of new organizations—such as regimental and army committees as well as local soviets and committees speaking on behalf of both Muslims and Armenians—and the possibility of actual judicial punishment of military officials for their misconduct. However, these positive developments were accompanied by the collapse of the state's ability to enforce its desires. As the year progressed, Armenians—as well as Kurds, Turks, Greeks, and Russians themselves—became increasingly subject to marauding, pillaging, looting, and rape by individual Russian military units.

The first problem to become evident was the total shortage of sufficient troops to uphold order.[97] In addition to the general shortage of troops, units increasingly refused assignment outside of their garrisons. This produced a situation in which the military officials appointed to administer the occupied districts, often very conscientious and decent men, lacked the necessary force to combat the marauding and pillaging of undisciplined units. The collapse of the food supply situation over 1917, which had already been dire on the Caucasus Front, only increased looting and pillaging by passing units.[98]

Third Intermezzo: The Vigorous but Vain Efforts of Ensign Kovalimov to Prevent a Rape and Massacre in Parsenik, Erzerum District

In mid-summer 1917 Ensign Kovalimov, the Russian officer in charge of the fourth district of the Terdzhano-Makhatun region, in Arlik, confronted a difficult task.[99] By statute, his office was supposed to have an aide, a clerk, and 30 soldiers to help him uphold order. Instead, he had a translator hired from the local population and three soldiers. On 16 July a Kurd came running to him and informed him that some unknown soldiers had driven off all the men in the village of Parsenik "for work on the roads." Soon afterward, women and children came to Kovalimov to report that soldiers of the machine-gun company of the Fourteenth Turkestan Regiment had begun to harass them. The ensign immediately sent off a note to the unit's commander, Lieutenant Polupanov, asking him to order his unit to conduct itself properly.[100] He received the following reply:

> I am astounded at your stupid report, which you saw fit to send to me. You direct me to issue an order and insult not only me personally, but my entire company for violence allegedly committed against women and children. I ask you to indicate what illegal actions my soldiers have taken. Are you certain things occurred in the form you say and that it was my people and not others? You did not investigate this but rush to insult us. I ask you to provide detailed facts of the aggressions committed by my troops or I will be forced to call you out for an apology before all my soldiers, which might end very sadly for you.[101]

Nevertheless, at the request of the village's women, all of whose menfolk were absent on compulsory labor, the district captain dispatched one of his three available soldiers to protect them. A group of 11 women and children awoke him at 1 AM and reported that the soldiers were raping all the women in the town. Another party arrived at 4 AM, declaring that they had just escaped the soldiers' clutches. At 5 AM Kovalimov headed off himself to the village of Parsenik. The soldier he had left to protect the women claimed that he had not reported the rapes because the soldiers had threatened him. The village inhabitants reported that the soldiers as well as Lieutenant Polupanov had all participated in the mass rape. Unable to identify the culprits himself, the district captain compiled a report, which he then submitted to the executive committee of the Mamakhatun region, so that it could take measures to protect the local population. All the women had left Parsenik and remained under his protection in Arlik. He also submitted a formal judicial report, including a list indicating the women who had reported being raped (there were 19 on the list, but others had fled and could not be interrogated), their age, and how many soldiers had violated them.

Judicial authorities took up the investigation. The acting commissar for the Provisional Government noted that it was "essential to prevent this repulsive assault of armed men on unarmed people who have been taken into the bosom as free citizens of our Great Republican Sovereign Russian Power, whose laws should be observed reverently by every citizen. The protector and defender of these laws ought to be each and every soldier of our Great Republic."[102] He requested that the local soviet of soldiers' deputies investigate the case. In late September 1917, the soviet replied. Because the Fourteenth Turkestan Rifle Regiment had moved to the front, it was impossible to pursue the investigation. The investigative materials were returned.[103]

Fourth Intermezzo: A Russian Formalist in a Persian Anabasis; or, Victor Shklovsky's Travails in Russian-occupied Persia

After having served as a commissar in occupied Galicia during Russia's failed 1917 summer offensive, the formalist literary critic Victor Shklovskii—now a soldier and a revolutionary—went as a commissar to Russian-occupied northern Persia in order to help with the withdrawal of Russian troops. He found a nightmare, a nightmare that he believed cast a long shadow over the Russian Revolution.[104]

The Russians came to Kurdistan, Shklovskii says, "already hating the Kurds—a hatred inherited from the Armenians and understandable in them. The formula 'The Kurd is the enemy' deprived the peaceful Kurds, and even their children, of the protection afforded by the laws of war."[105] But after the Revolution, recounted Shklovskii, "the relations between our units and the local population became worse. Before the revolution in Persia there was a regime for enslavement. Now they simply loot [the local population]." The entire valley of Meregev had been emptied of people, he reported; "It was Cossacks who did this." Villages were destroyed to their foundations. "I have seen Galicia [during the war], and I have seen Poland [during the war]—but that was all paradise compared to Kurdistan."[106] When one Kurdish tribe killed three soldiers who were foraging, the punitive detachment sent out in response slaughtered 200 Kurds "without regard to age or gender." On another punitive expedition, to Ushne, the soldiers were ordered to determine whether the enemy occupied the village. The troops found no enemy there. The Kurdish women sought to save themselves from rape by covering themselves with excrement. The soldiers wiped them off with rags and raped them one by one. Officers too participated.[107] It was common for generals to issue orders for their units to taken no prisoners and to kill everyone, "despite the fact that the units were not taking trenches, but hostile Kurdish villages."

Yet one could not explain the pillaging as simple hatred for the Kurds, because the soldiers pillaged not just Kurdistan, but all of Persia. In Shklovskii's view, this was the result not of the war, but of the revolution. "In all the hundreds of thousands of soldiers in our army, couldn't there have just possibly been something good, something worthwhile? There was. But the condition of our army—the total disillusionment, the deep despondency, the willingness to resort to sabotage if only to end the war—all this brought out the worst, not the best, side of men."[108]

And, thought Shklovskii, this could not but have an effect. Traveling back through the Caucasus, he passed through regions where Cossacks and Chechens were fighting. "By day, pillars of smoke; by night, pillars of fire encircled us. Russia was burning."[109] "Are we Russians not," asked Shklovskii, "reaping now what we sowed in Persia? In any case, in Persia the Russian Revolution was compromised and it will be difficult to restore it to its good name there. But who is there to restore it?" One did not have to be a literary critic to come to this same conclusion. Fedor Ivanovich Eliseev served throughout the war with a Cossack regiment on the Caucasus Front. He too came to believe that Russians would have to come to an accounting for their behavior in the occupied territories. "We only came to understand the psychological state of the Kurds," he recalled, "when the Red Army and Soviet power descended from the North to our Cossack lands and treated us Cossacks just as we had treated the Kurds."[110]

Conclusion

There is no doubt that the Russian Army engaged in extensive violence against civilian populations. It did so in occupied territories and it did so in Russian proper. It did so against Kurds as well as against Armenians—and Jews and, later, Russians too. My purpose here has been to try to untangle the various strands of violence—those strands that were sanctioned from those that were not, those that were, by their own lights, purposeful from those that were not. I have tried to show that this violence was not the product of some nationalizing project, or of an inevitable and timeless "clash of civilizations" in a "shatter zone of empires."

Some might say it makes no difference. But the actions of people like General Depishich, who canceled punitive operations that he recognized were about to degenerate into slaughter; of Ensign Kovalimov, who risked his life to try to protect the civilians under his charge; and of Victor Shklovskii, who repeatedly risked his life to protect civilians and prevent pillaging by Russian units in northern Persia—these all show that such men recognized and upheld the boundaries between legitimate force and naked violence. I am only trying to make sense of how such men distinguished between these two categories.

NOTES

This paper is part of a larger project examining how the Russians applied the "laws of war" to territories which they occupied "by right of war." I gratefully acknowledge the support of the National Council for Eurasian and East European Research for its support of this project.

KEY TO ARCHIVAL CITATIONS
AMAE: France, Archives du Ministère des Affairs étrangères/Guerre, 1914–1918/Turquie/vols. 887–94 (Paris: Service international de microfilms, 1981), 3 reels.

AVPRI: Arkhiv vneshnei politiki Rossiiskoi imperii (Moscow)
GARF: Gosudarstvennyi arkhiv Rossiiskoi Federatsii (Moscow)
HIA: Hoover Institution Archives, Stanford University
NAUK FO: National Archives of the United Kingdom, Foreign Office (London)
RGIA: Rossiiskii gosudarstvennyi istoricheskii arkhiv Rossiiskoi imperii (St. Petersburg)
RGVIA: Rossiiskii gosudarstvennyi voenno-istoricheskii arkhiv (Moscow)
SHAA: State Historical Archive of Armenia (Erevan)

1. James Fairgrieve, *Geography and World Power* (London: University of London Press, 1915), "crush zone of small states" at 329–31.

2. R. Hartshorne, "The Politico-Geographic Pattern of the World," *The Annals of the American Academy of Political and Social Science* 218 (Nov. 1941): 45–57, "shatter zone" (in quotes) at 52; Richard Hartshorne, "The United States and the 'Shatter Zone' in Europe," in *Compass of the World*, ed. H. Weigert and V. Stefannson (New York: MacMillan, 1944) 203–214; G. East, "The Concept and Political Status of the Shatter Zone," in *Geographical Essays on Eastern Europe*, ed. N. J. G. Pounds (Bloomington: Indiana University Press, 1961). In 1963 Saul Bernard Cohen developed his influential concept of a "shatter belt": *Geography and Politics in a World Divided* (New York: Random House, 1963).

3. See the incisive treatment of the parallel rise of "international relations" in the American academy in the post-1945 period: Martti Koskenniemi, *The Gentle Civilizer of Nations: The Rise and Fall of International Law, 1870–1960* (Cambridge: Cambridge University Press, 2002), ch. 6: "Out of Europe: Carl Schmitt, Hans Morgenthau, and the Turn to 'International Relations.'"

4. Alfred Rieber, "Persistent Factors in Russian Foreign Policy: An Interpretative Essay" in *Imperial Russian Foreign Policy*, ed. Hugh Ragsdale (Washington, D.C.: Wilson Center Press, 1993), 315–59.

5. Michael Khodarkovsky, *Russia's Steppe Frontier: The Making of a Colonial Empire* (Bloomington: Indiana University Press, 2002); Willard Sunderland, *Taming the Wild Field: Colonization and Empire on the Russian Steppe* (Ithaca, N.Y.: Cornell University Press, 2004); Brian L. Davies, *Warfare, State, and Society on the Black Sea Steppe* (New York: Routledge, 2007). For an analogous argument for a different region, see Peter Perdue, *China Marches West: The Qing Conquest of Central Eurasia* (Cambridge, Mass.: Harvard University Press, 2005).

6. E.g., M. S. Anderson, *The Eastern Question, 1774–1923: A Study in International Relations* (New York: St. Martin's Press, 1966).

7. On Russian incorporation of the Caucasus, see Austin Jersild, *Orientalism and Empire: North Caucasus Mountain Peoples and the Georgian Frontier, 1845–1917* (Montreal: McGill-Queen's University Press, 2002), and V. O. Bobrovnikov and I. L. Babich, *Severnyi Kavkaz v sostave Rossiiskoi imperii* (Moscow: NLO, 2007). For an analysis of center–periphery dynamic (and failure to resolve it in favor of the center) in the late Ottoman Empire, see M. Şükrü Hanioğlu, *A Brief History of the Ottoman Empire* (Princeton: Princeton University Press, 2008), esp. 3, 203–204. On the Ottoman state's difficulties in subduing the Kurdish territories bordering the Caucasus, see Martin van Bruinessen, *Agha, Shaikh, and State: The Social and Political Structures of Kurdistan* (London: Zed Books, 1992), and Janet Klein, *The Margins of Empire: Kurdish Militias in the Ottoman Tribal Zone* (Stanford: Stanford University Press, 2011).

8. In general, see Rieber, "Persistent Factors"; see also Peter Holquist, "The Politics and Practice of the Russian Occupation of Armenia, 1915–Feb. 1917," in *A Question of Genocide, 1915: Armenians and Turks at the End of the Ottoman Empire*, ed. Ronald Grigor Suny, Fatma Müge Göçek, and Norman M. Naimark (New York: Oxford University Press, 2011).

9. For various inflections of this argument, see: Richard Hovannisian, *Armenia on the Road to Independence* (Berkeley: University of California Press, 1967), 67; Manoug Somankian, *Empires in Conflict: Armenia and the Great Powers, 1895–1920* (London: I. B. Tauris, 1995), 106–119, esp. 111, 116; Alan Bodger, "Russia and the End of the Ottoman Empire" in *The Great Powers and the End of the Ottoman Empire* (London: George Allen and Unwin, 1984), 76–110, here at 99; Dzh. Kirakosian, *Zapadnaia Armeniia v gody pervoi mirovoi voiny* (Yerevan, Armenia: Izdatel'stvo Erivanskogo universiteta, 1971), 387–395; S. M. Akopian, *Zapadnaia Armeniia v planakh imperialisticheskikh derzhav* (Yerevan, Armenia: Izdatel'stvo Akademii Nauk Armianskoi SSSR, 1967); A. O. Arutiu-

nian, *Kavkazskii front, 1914–1917* (Yerevan, Armenia: Aiastan, 1971); A. Iu. Bakhturina, *Okrainy Rossiiskoi Imperii: Gosudarstvennoe upravlenie i natsional'naia politika v gody Pervoi mirovoi voiny* (Moscow: Rosspen, 2004); and esp. Justin McCarthy, *Death and Exile: The Ethnic Cleansing of Ottoman Muslims, 1821–1922* (Princeton, N.J.: Darwin Press, 1995), ch. 6: "Russian Imperialism."

10. This is beginning to change. See two excellent recent treatments: Halit Dündar Akarca, "The Russian Administration of the Occupied Ottoman Territories during the First World War, 1915–1917" (Master's Thesis, Bilkent University, 2002); Michael A. Reynolds, *Shattering Empires: The Clash and Collapse of the Ottoman and Russian Empires, 1908–1918* (New York: Cambridge University Press, 2011).

11. *Polozhenie o polevom upravlenii voisk v voennoe vremia* (Saint Petersburg: Voennaia tipografiia, 1914); Article 11 provides the framework for governing occupied territory. On the important unintended consequences of this document, see Daniel Graf, "Military Rule behind the Russian Front, 1914–1917: The Political Ramifications," *Jahrbücher für Geschichte Osteuropas* 22(3) (1974): 390–411.

12. *Prologue to Revolution: Notes of A. N. Iakhontov on the Secret Meeting of the Council of Ministers, 1915,* ed. Michael Cherniavsky (Englewood Cliffs, N.J.: Prentice Hall, 1967), 148 (Agriculture Minister Krivoshein in the meeting of 19 August 1915).

13. Peter Holquist, "The Role of Personality in the First (1914–1915) Russian Occupation of Galicia and Bukovina" in *Anti-Jewish Violence: Rethinking the Pogrom in European History,* ed. Jonathan Dekel-Chen (Bloomington: Indiana University Press, 2010), 52–73.

14. John Horne and Alan Kramer, *German Atrocities, 1914: A History of Denial* (New Haven, Conn.: Yale University Press, 2001), 167, 174.

15. Isabel Hull, *Absolute Destruction: Military Culture and the Practices of War in Wilhelmine Germany* (Ithaca, N.Y.: Cornell University Press, 2005), 228; see also 324. Most relevant to my argument here is Hull's ch. 10, "Civilians as Objects of Military Necessity." (Prof. Hull and I co-taught a course on World War I, and my thoughts are much indebted to our exchanges.)

16. William Fuller, *Civil Military Conflict in Imperial Russia, 1881–1914* (Princeton: Princeton University Press, 1985), 15–32; John Bushnell, "The Tsarist Officer Corps, 1881–1914: Customs, Duties, Inefficiency," *American Historical Review* 86(4) (Oct. 1981): 753–80.

17. Holquist, "Role of Personality."

18. Chancellery of the Viceroy to the Head of Field Headquarters, 8 February 1915; Field Commander Iudenich to Viceroy Vorontsov-Dashkov, 16 May 1915, (both in SHAA, f. 1262 [Kantseliariia namestnika na Kavkaze, 1846–1917], op. 3, d. 1563, ll. 3–4; *ibid,* d. 1597, l. 2).

19. *Instruktsiia nachal'nikam okrugov v oblastiakh Turtsii zaniatykh po pravu voiny,* 18 Sept. 1915 (HIA/Misc. Records/Russia—Armiia Kavkazskaia).

20. "Vremennoe polozhenie ob upravlenii oblastiami Turtsii, zaniatymi po pravu voiny" (5 June 1916), RGVIA, f. 2005 (Voenno-politicheskoe i grazhdanskoe upravlenie pri verkhovnom glavnokomanduiushchem), op. 1, d. 17, ll. 3 ob.-13 ob.

21. Sazonov to Grand Duke Nikolai Nikolaevich, 14/27 June 1916, RGVIA, f. 2005 (Voenno-politicheskoe i grazhdanskoe upravlenie pri verkhovnom glavnokomanduiushchem), op. 1, d. 17, ll. 1–2 ob.; reprinted in E. A. Adamov, *Razdel Aziatskoi Turtsii po sekretnym dokumentam b. ministerstva inostrannykh del* (Moscow: Litizdat, 1924), doc. 140.

22. Viceroy to the Caucasus Grand Duke Nikolai Nikolaevich to Sazonov, 3/16 July 1916 (AVPRI, f. 151, op. 482 [Politarkhiv], d. 3481, ll. 15–16 ob.; reproduced in Adamov, *Razdel aziatskoi Turtsii,* doc. 144). These overall guidelines were reconfirmed under Stürmer, Sazonov's replacement: Viceroy for the Caucasus to Chairman of the Council of Ministers Stürmer, 15/28 July 1916; Stürmer to the Viceroy, 19 July/1 August 1916 (AVPRI, f. 151, op. 482 [Politarkhive], d. 3481, ll. 21, 23; reproduced in Adamov, *Razdel Aziatskoi Turtsii,* docs. 148, 151).

23. Cited in Peter Gatrell, *A Whole Empire Walking: Refugees in Russia during World War I* (Bloomington: Indiana University Press, 1999), 152.

24. For an analysis of this outlook, see Hull, *Absolute Destruction,* ch. 10, esp. 233, 235.

25. A. Britnev, "Ot redaktsii," *Biulleteni glavnogo kavkazskogo komiteta Vserossiiskogo soiuza gorodov* no. 16 (20 Oct. 1917): 1–6, here at 1.

26. The staff of Russian forces in Persia to the Diplomatic Representative in the Caucasus Adamov, 31 December 1917 (HIA/N. N. Baratov Collection/Box 3/Folder 2: "Russian Expeditionary Force: Official Correspondence").

27. For what Minorskii believed was the proper policy for the Russian government in Persia, in contrast to how the military was conducting itself, see: secret telegram from Minorskii, the Russian Delegate in Tehran, to MID, 10 June 1917 (AVPRI, f. 133, op. 470 [Kantseliariia MID], 1917, d. 52, l. 407).

28. Secret telegram from Stolitsa, the Diplomatic Official for the Viceroy of the Caucasus, 25 May 1917, no. 617 (AVPRI, f. 151, op. 482 [Politakhiv], d. 4128, l. 4).

29. Secret telegram from Grand Duke Nikolai Nikolaevich to MID, 27 January 1917, no. 133 (AVPRI, f. 133, op. 470 [Kantseliariia MID], 1917, d. 142, l. 16).

30. For a military history of the Caucasus Front, see General E. V. Maslovskii, *Mirovaia voina na Kavkazskom fronte, 1914–1917 gg.: strategicheskii ocherk* (Paris: "Vozrozhdenie"-"La Renaissance," 1933); and W. E. D. Allen and Paul Muratoff, *Caucasian Battlefields: A History of the War on the Turco-Caucasian Border, 1828–1921* (Cambridge: Cambridge University Press, 1953). Both works emphasize the difficulties the Russian Army faced in obtaining supplies and forage.

31. Report of the head of the Erzerum Region, College Assessor Maksimov, to the Quartermaster-General of the Caucasus Army, 7 September 1916, no. 3051 (AVPRI, f. 151 [Politarkhiv], op. 482, d. 4128, ll. 18–24).

32. Ibid.

33. Report of the military Governor-General to the Special Caucasus Committee on the state of affairs in the occupied territories of Turkey (28 March 1917) (RGVIA, f. 13227 [*Upravlenie Generela-komissara Turetskoi Armenii i prochikh oblastei Turtsii, zaniatykh po pravu voiny*], op. 2, d. 149, ll. 1–20ob.)

34. F. I. Eliseev, *Kazaki na Kavkazskom fronte, 1914–1917: Zapiski polkovnika Kubanskogo kazach'ego voiska v trindadtsati broshiurakh-tetradiakh* (Moscow: Voennoe izdatel'stvo, 2001), 143–44, see also 131.

35. See the excellent treatment by Gatrell, *A Whole Empire Walking*. Gatrell devotes significant attention to the Caucasus Front.

36. Secret telegram from Petraiev, the Aide to the Second Political Department (Near East) to the General Consul in [illegible], 10/23 August 1916, no. 3644 (AVPRI, f. 151 [Politarkhiv], op. 482, d. 4128, l. 9).

37. Interview with General Peshkov in *Novoe Vremia*; excerpted in *Armianskii vestnik* no. 45 (4 December 1916): 9–10.

38. "Bezhentsy," *Armianskii vestnik* no. 32 (4 September 1916): 20–21.

39. General Liakhov to the Commander of the Caucasus Army, 8 April 1917 (RGVIA, f. 2168 [Shtab Kavkazskoi armii], op. 1, d. 288, l. 32).

40. General Iudenich to Glavnoupolnomochennyi po ustroistvu bezhentsev Kavkazskogo fronta, 17 Feb. 1917, no. 356 (RGVIA, f. 2168 [Shtab Kavkazskoi armii], op. 1, d. 288, l. 10); see also "Vozvrashchenie bezhentsev na rodinu," *Armianskii vestnik*, no. 31 (6 August 1917), 13 (originally reported in *Kavkazskoe slovo*).

41. E. Arutiunian, "General Kalitin v Armenii," *Armianskii vestnik*, nos. 35–36 (10 September 1917): 3–5, referring to an event in Erzindzhan in late 1916. Due to the lobbying of the local Armenian refugee committee, officials in Tblisi rescinded Kalitin's order to expel the refugees. The susceptibility of military officials to such political interventions stands in stark contrast to the German case. An analogous case is found in "Report of the head of the Erzerum Region, College Assessor Maksimov, to the Quartermaster-General of the Caucasus Army," op. cit., see n31.

42. See Gatrell, *A Whole Empire Walking*.

43. "Rech' E. A. Epapicha ob otdele pitatel'nykh punktov dlia okopnykh rabochikh," *Biulleten' komiteta Iugo-Zapadnogo fronta*, no. 5 (1 December 1915): 2–5; S. L. R., "Opyt ekonomicheskogo obsledovaniia naseleniia, postradavshego ot voennykh deistvii v raione tsentral'noi Galitsii," *Biulleten' komiteta Iugo-Zapadnogo fronta*, no. 18 (June 15, 1916): 28–33.

44. Gatrell, *A Whole Empire Walking*; see also Aide to the Viceroy for the Caucasus, Senator Peterson, to the Council of Ministers, 24 July 1915; Director of the Department of General Affairs to Peterson, 14 August 1915 (RGIA, f. 1276 [Sovet ministrov], op. 19 [*Kantseliariia Soveta ministrov po namestnichestvu na Kavkaze (1905–1917)*], d. 1146, ll. 2–4, 1), extending a 500,000 ruble line of credit for aiding Armenian refugees.

45. E.g., Grand Duke Nikolai Nikolaevich to the Council of Ministers, 16 February 1916; War Minister Polivanov to the Caucasian Viceroy's Delegate for the Council of Ministers, 19 February 1916 (RGIA, f. 1276 [Sovet ministrov], op. 19 [*Kantseliariia Soveta ministrov po namestnichestvu na Kavkaze (1905-1917)*], d. 1230, ll. 1, 4), authorizing aid to 33 Turkish villages "with a population of 5732 Muslim adults and 669 children"; "Ot upravleniia voennogo general-gubernatora oblastei Turtskii, zaniatykh po pravu voiny," *Kavkazskoe slovo,* 26 February 1917, no. 46: 3, establishing a civilian relief board for the occupied regions, with the charge to care for all inhabitants, regardless of religion. The official correspondent of *The Manchester Guardian* took part in a tour to distribute relief to the Muslim population of the Kars plateau and Lazistan: M. Philips Price, *War and Revolution in Asiatic Russia* (London: George, Allen & Unwin, 1918), chs. 6–7, esp. 184–85, 216–17.

46. For the Eastern Front: Gatrell, *A Whole Empire Walking;* Eric Lohr, "The Russian Army and the Jews: Mass Deportations, Hostages, and Violence during World War I," *Russian Review* 60(3) (July 2001): 404–19; Eric Lohr, *Nationalizing the Russian Empire: The Campaign against Enemy Aliens during World War I* (Cambridge: Harvard University Press). For the Western Front: Robert Armeson, *Total Warfare and Compulsory Labor: a Study of the Military-Industrial Complex in Germany during World War I* (The Hague: Martinus Nijhoff, 1964); Annette Becker, *Oubliés de la Grande Guerre. Humanitaire et culture de guerre 1914-1918. Populations occupées, déportés civils, prisonniers de guerre* (Paris: Noêsis, 1998); and Hull, *Absolute Destruction,* ch. 10.

47. S. B. Spies, *Methods of Barbarism: Roberts and Kitchener and Civilians in the Boer Republics, January 1900–May 1902* (Cape Town: Human and Rousseau, 1977); for Germany, see Hull, *Absolute Destruction,* ch. 3.

48. For the army's general treatment of the Jews, see Lohr, "Russian Army and the Jews"; for the specificity of the 1915 operations and the shift in policies in 1916, see Holquist, "Role of Personality."

49. [M. Philips Price], "Russia's Conquests in Armenia: Their New Governor," *Manchester Guardian,* 13 Sept. 1916, 6 (interview conducted 7 August 1916).

50. Peter Holquist, "'In accord with State Interests and the People's Wishes': The Technocratic Ideology of Imperial Russia's Resettlement Administration," *Slavic Review* 69(1) (Spring 2010): 151–79, here 170–71.

51. Lohr, *Nationalizing the Russian Empire,* 96–97, rightly treats these as general policies. He presents these policies, however, as the product of a broader nationalizing agenda, in this case the expulsion of Armenians in order to make way for Cossacks. Such measures were a *practice,* rather than a policy; they did not need any such rationalization. For similar conduct by the German Army on the Western Front, particularly in northern France, see Hull, *Absolute Destruction,* ch. 10.

52. Report of the Head of the Erzerum Region, College Assessor Maksimov, to the Quartermaster-General of the Caucasus Army, op. cit., n31. For the expulsion of the inhabitants—Armenian and Kurdish—of one entire district in the Erzerum region, see "Report of the Head of the Erzerum Region, College Assessor Maksimov, to the Aide of the Quartermaster-General of the Caucasus Army, 20 March 1917" (RGVIA, f. 2168 [Shtab Kavkazskoi armii], op. 1, d. 274, ll. 4–6).

53. Telegram correspondence between the Military Governor for the Regions of Turkey Occupied by Right of War and the head of the Erzerum district, 12 and 17 January 1917 (RGVIA, f. 13249 [Upravlenie nachal'nika Erzerumskogo okruga general-komissara Turetskoi Armenii], op. 3, d. 10, ll. 23, 45).

54. Joshua Sanborn has provided a promising start: see "Unsettling the Empire: Violent Migrations and Social Disaster in Russia during World War I," *Journal of Modern History* 77, no. 2 (June 2005): 290–324.

55. Eliseev, *Kazaki na Kavkazskom fronte,* 144.

56. Report of the Head of the Erzerum Region, College Assessor Maksimov, to the Quartermaster-General of the Caucasus Army, 7 Sept. 1916, op. cit., n31.

57. Head of the first district to the Commissar of the City of Erzerum, 8 May 1917, no. 896 (RGVIA, f. 13249 [Upravlenie nachal'nika Erzerumskogo okruga general-komissara Turetskoi Armenii], op. 2, d. 14, l. 112).

58. Circular from the Head of the Caucasus Army to the Heads of Army Corps, 26 August 1917 (RGVIA, f. 13249 [Upravlenie nachal'nika Erzerumskogo okruga general-komissara Turetskoi Armenii], op. 2, d. 10, l. 288).

59. See Peter Holquist, "Violent Russia, Deadly Marxism: Russia in the Epoch of Violence," *Kritika: Explorations in Russian and Eurasian History* 4(3) (Summer 2003): 627–52.

60. Reynolds, *Shattering Empires,* ch. 2. Reynolds' work is an important contribution to our understanding of the irrendentist programs fostered by both empires after 1908.

61. For Loris-Melikov's argument for the utility of the Turkish Kurds to Russian imperial policy, see his report as commander of the forces in the Terek Region (Chechnia), 15 November 1864 (RGIA, f. 866 [Graf Mikhail Tarielovich Loris-Melikov], op. 1, d. 35, ll. 1–8); V. F. Minorskii, in "Kurdy: Zametki i vpechatleniia," *Izvestiia Ministerstva inostrannykh del* 1915, no. 3: 189–231, argued for the strategic utility of a Russian pro-Kurdish policy and explicitly invoked Loris-Melikov's tactics.

62. Grand Duke Nikolai Nikolaevich to Sazonov, 3/16 July 1916 (AVPRI, f. 151, op. 482 [Politarkhiv], d. 3481, ll. 15–16 ob.; reproduced in Adamov, *Razdel aziatskoi Turtsii,* doc. 144).

63. For a general overview, see Reynolds, *Shattering Empires,* ch. 4. Specifically, see Report from Prince Shakhovskoi to the Headquarters of the Caucasus Army, 16 January 1916, no. 10 (AVPRI, f. 144, op. 489 [Persidskii stol "B"], d. 567, ll. 6–12); Prince Berdikhan and Prince Shakhovskoi to Lieutenant Chardigny (French military attaché to the Caucasus Front), translation from French, Tiflis, 29 September 1917 (AVPRI, f. 144, op. 489 [Persidskii stol "B"], d. 567, ll. 30–42, here at 36). The British were skeptical of Shakhovskoi's efforts: Colonel Marsh to the Department of Military Intelligence, 26 May 1916 (NAUK FO 371/1916/2778/no. 101880): Russia's Kurdish contacts "have proved to be unprofitable and even dangerous allies."

Samoukian (*Empires in Conflict,* 113) incorrectly identifies Prince B. N. Shakhovskoi as Dmitrii Ivanovich Shakhovskoi, who became the Minister for Social Welfare in the Provisional Government.

64. War Office to Commander-in-Chief, India, 4 October 1915 (NAUK FO 371/1916/2778/ no. 101879) (expulsion of "disloyal Kurds" between Bayazet and Diadin); from Prince Shakhovskoi to the Headquarters of the Caucasus Army, 9 January 1916, no. 7 (AVPRI, f. 144, op. 489 [Persidskii stol "B"], d. 567, ll. 2–5) (expulsion of Kurds from the the Giaverskii, Bashkalinskii, Saraiskii, and Koshurskii regions); "V Erzerume," *Armianskii vestnik,* no. 12–13 (24 April 1916): 37–38 (Kurds expelled from regions occupied by Russian Army); Chief of Staff to the Sixth Caucasus Army Corps to the Head of the Erzerum Region, 19 March 1917 no. 925 (RGVIA, f. 2168 [Shtab Kavkazskoi armii], op. 1, d. 274, l. 5).

65. On Nikitin, see Phillips Price, *War and Revolution,* 109–112. On Minorskii's attempts to negotiate with local Kurdish tribes, see his sympathetic 1915 article "Kurdy"; and secret telegram from Minorskii, the Russian Delegate in Tehran, to MID, 31 January 1917, no. 405; also 1 May 1917, no. 381; 10 June 1917, (AVPRI, f. 133, op. 470 [Kantseliariia MID], 1917, d. 52, ll. 179, 182, 407).

66. Telegraph exchange between the Chief Agent for settling refugees on the Caucasus Front and the Aide to the Quartermaster-General for the Caucasus Front, 8–28 April 1917 (RGVIA, f. 2168 [Shtab Kavkazskoi armii], op. 1, d. 288, ll. 40–42).

67. Minorskii to Russian Mission in Tehran, 3 April 1917 (AVPRI, f. 133, op. 470 [Kantseliariia MID], 1917, d. 52, l. 179. See also the treatment in M. S. Lazar'ev, *Kurdskii vopros, 1891–1917 gg.* (Moscow: Nauka, 1972), 348–53, esp. 353.

68. Minorskii to Russian Mission in Tehran, 3 June 1917 (GARF, f. R-4738 [Rossiiskaia missiia v Persii], op. 1, d. 222, l. 1).

69. Telegram from the "Vremennyi Genkvarkavfronta" to the Komkor in Urmiia, 15 July 1917 (RGVIA, f. 2168 [Shtab Kavkazskoi armii], op. 1, d. 288, l. 52).

70. Secret telegram from Etter, the Russian Envoy in Tehran, to MID, 28 June 1917, no. 608 (AVPRI, f. 133, op. 470 [Chancellery of the Foreign Minister], 1917, d. 52, l. 440); Girs to Etter, 22 July 1917 (AVPRI, f. 144, op. 489 [Persian Desk "B"], d. 31, l. 56).

71. General Vadbol'skii to the Commander in chief of the forces on the Caucasus Front, 8 August 1917, no. 398 (RGVIA, f. 2168 [Shtab Kavkazskoi armii], op. 1, d. 416, ll. 387–387ob.).

72. Telegraph exchange between the Headquarters for the Caucasus Army and diplomatic officials in Urmia, 29 September–10 October 1917 (RGVIA, f. 2168 [Shtab Kavkazskoi armii], op. 1, d. 416, ll. 382–385 ob.).

73. Diplomatic Official for the Caucasus Adamov to the Quartermaster for the Caucasus Army, 17 November 1917, forwarding refugees' petition; and telegrams from Commander of Caucasus Army to local military commanders (RGVIA, f. 2168 [Shtab Kavkazskoi armii], op. 1, d. 274, ll. 93–95).

74. Letter from Diplomatic Official for the Caucasus Adamov to the Quartermaster-General for the Caucasus Army, 17 November 1917, op. cit. n73.

75. Staff of the Caucasus Army to General Vadbol'skii, 25 November 1917, no. 4297, and replies of 2 December, 7 December 1917 (RGVIA, f. 2168 [Shtab Kavkazskoi armii], op. 1, d. 274, ll. 98–100).

76. Secret telegram from Etter, the Russian Envoy in Tehran, to Nikitin, the Vice-Consul in Urmiia, 10 December 1918 [*sic;* should read 1917], no. 1127 (GARF, f. R-4738 [Rossiiskaia missiia v Persii], op. 1, d. 216, ll. 282); Mr. Stevens to the Foreign Office, no. 10, Tiflis, 24 December 1917 (NAUK FO 371/3019/1917/243579); Letter from Nikitin, the Vice-Consul in Urmia, to the Russian Mission, 22 December 1917, no. 186, "secret" (GARF, f. R-4738 (Rossiiskaia missiia v Persii), op. 1, d. 216, ll. 81–82); Le Président du Conseil, Ministre de la Guerre, à Chef Mission Militaire Française, Paris, 13 January 1918, no. 745/BS3 (AMAE, Guerre 1914–1918, Turquie, vol. 894: Arméniens du Caucase (Oct. 1917–Jan. 1918), [reel 3], sheet 200); Russian Mission in Persia to the Official for Border Contacts in the Caucasus, Tehran, 23 March 1918, no. 1669 (GARF, f. R-4738 [Rossiiskaia missiia v Persii], op. 1, d. 216, ll. 24–24 ob.). Until fighting broke out in the city of Urmia in late February 1918, Russian officials *opposed* the arming of the Christian refugees in Urmia.

77. The classic work is C. E. Callwell, *Small Wars: A Tactical Textbook for Imperial Soldiers,* preface to new edition by Peter S. Walton (Novato, Calif.: Presidio Press, 1990; original, 1906). For the Russian military's use of "punitive detachments" both before and during World War I, see Peter Holquist "To Count, to Extract, To Exterminate: Population Statistics and Population Politics in Late Imperial and Soviet Russia" in *A State of Nations: Empire and Nation-Making in the Age of Lenin and Stalin,* ed. Terry Martin and Ron Suny (New York: Oxford University Press, 2001), 111–44.

78. See the analogous argument for the use of didactic and punitive violence by the German Army on the Western Front in Horne and Kramer, *German Atrocities* and Hull, *Absolute Destruction.*

79. E.g., Vorontsov-Dashkov to Sazonov, 19 October 1914 (reproduced in *Mezhdunarodnye otnosheniia v epokhu imperializma: Dokumenty iz arkhivov tsarskogo i vremennogo pravitel'stva, 1878–1917,* ed. M. N. Pokrovskii [Moscow: Gosizdat, 1935], series 3, vol. 6, pt. 1, doc. 400); Eliseev, *Kazaki na Kavkazskom fronte,* 132.

80. Secret telegrams from Stolitsa, the Official for Border Contacts under the Caucasian Viceroy to the Foreign Minister, and reply from Viceroy Vorontsov-Dashkov, 15–21 March 1915 (AVPRI, f. 133, op. 470 (1915) [Kantseliariia MID], d. 180, ll. 47–48, 50, 53).

81. Colonel Marsh to the Director of Military Intelligence, 24 May 1916 (FO 371/1916/2778/no. 101879); see also FO to Sir H. MacMahon (Cairo), 6 May 1916 (FO 371/1916/2768/file 938/no. 84129); Director of Military Intelligence to Colonel Marsh, 19 May 1916 (FO 371/1916/2768/file 938/no. 96903, 306).

82. Secret telegram from Etter, the Russian Envoy in Tehran, to MID, 20 Jan. 1917, no. 336, and from Russian Delegate in Tehran Minorskii to MID, 27 March 1917 (AVPRI, f. 133, op. 470 [Kantseliariia MID], 1917, d. 52, ll. 29, 175).

83. Secret telegram from Minorskii, the Russian Delegate in Tehran, to MID, 17 May 1917, no. 441 and from 21 May 1917, no. 462 (AVPRI, f. 133, op. 470 [Kantseliariia MID], 1917, d. 52, l. 326). The Mission in Persia reported to military authorities that one punitive expedition killed 52 men, six women, and two children: Russian Mission in Persia to the Commander of the Seventh Corps, 20 May 1917 (GARF, f. R-4738 [Rossiiskaia missiia v Persii], op. 1, d. 5, l. 223).

84. This account based on: Report of the Commander of the Fourth Caucasus Army Corps General Lieutenant Depishich to the Commander of the Caucasus Army, 4 June 1917 (RGVIA, f. 2168 [Headquarters of the Caucasus Army], op. 1, d. 15, ll. 7–9ob.); corroborated by telegram from the aide to the Commissar for Turkish Armenia, Tiflis, to the Chief of Staff of the Commander-in-Chief of the Army, Erzerum, 12 June 1917 (*ibid,* l. 11); and, Prince Berdikhan and Prince Shakhovskoi to Lieutenant Chardily [Chardigny], translation from French, Tiflis, 29 September 1917 (AVPRI, f. 144, op. 489 [Persidskii stol "B"], d. 567, ll. 30–42, here at l. 41).

85. Telegram from the Van Soviet of Soldiers' Deputies to the Commander of the Caucasus Army, 21 July 1917 (RGVIA, f. 2168 [Shtab Kavkazskoi armii], op. 1, d. 416, l. 93).

86. Secret Report of Prince Shakhovskoi to the Chief of Staff of the Caucasus Army, 31 January 1917, no. 14: Tiflis (AVPRI, f. 144, op. 489 [Persidskii stol "B", d. 567, ll. 13–28); the Grand Duke's marginal notations indicate his endorsement of Shakhovskoi's proposals.

87. Letter of appointment for Prince Gadzhemukov, 12 February 1917; General-Maior Tomilov to the General Commissar for the Occupied Provinces of Turkey, 9 August 1917 (RGVIA, f. 2168 [Shtab Kavkazskoi armii], op. 1, d. 274, ll. 32, 63).

88. Regional administrator for the Dersim region Gadzhemukov to the Commander of the Caucasus Army Iudenich, 14 March 1917 (RGVIA, f. 2168 [Shtab Kavkazskoi armii], op. 1, d. 274, ll. 1–3, here at 2 ob.).

89. Samoukian, *Empires in Conflict,* 111; Gatrell, *A Whole Empire Walking,* 152.

90. For a memoir of one Cossack participant, see Eliseev, *Kazaki na Kavkazskom,* esp. 104–107. See also the observations of an officer who served with the Ottomans, Rafael de Nogales, *Four Years Beneath the Crescent,* trans. Muna Lee (New York: Charles Scribner's Sons, 1926): "the Cossacks and the Armenian *comitadchis,* like our Kurd guerillas, killed without mercy all the enemy wounded and defenseless that fell into their hands."

91. Phillips Price, *War and Revolution,* 208

92. See, ibid., 140–41; also "Report from Prince Shakhovskoi to the Headquarters of the Caucasus Army," 9 January 1916, no. 7 (AVPRI, f. 144, op. 489 [Persidskii stol "B"], d. 567, ll. 2–5

93. Secret Report of Prince Shakhovskoi to the Chief of Staff of the Caucasus Army, 31 January 1917, no. 14: Tiflis (AVPRI, f. 144, op. 489 [Persidskii stol "B"], d. 567, ll. 13–28); Prince Berdikhan and Prince Shakhovskoi to Lieutenant Chardigny (French military attaché to the Caucasus Front), Tiflis, 29 September 1917, op. cit., n63.

94. Phillips Price, *War and Revolution,* 223–24.

95. The Grand Duke upheld the death penalty imposed on three soldiers accused of pillaging in the Persian city of Kangever: Petition from General Baratov for amnesty and reply of Grand Duke, 23 January 1916 (HIA/N. N. Baratov Collection/Box 3/Folder 3: Russian expeditionary force: Documents and correspondence).

96. "Otstavka Gen. Chernozubova," *Zakavkazskaia rech',* 24 March 1917, no. 69, 3; "Khronika: Delo kn. SHakhovskogo i Gen. Chernozubova," *Kavkazskoe slovo,* 9 June 1917, no. 126, 3. In June 1917 the Erzerum executive committee relieved the commander of the first district of the Erzerum region, Staff Captain Alekseev, for embezzlement during a mass search of a local village ("Khronika: Erzerumskii ispoln. komitet," *Kavkazskoe slovo,* 18 June 1917, no. 134, 3).

97. E.g., the repeated requests from the Erzerum regional commissar for military units to protect the roads and combat banditry and marauding, all declined by the high command, June–July 1917 (RGVIA, f. 2168 [Shtab Kavkazskoi armii], op. 1, d. 15, l. 15–17); or the complaints of the garrison commander in Kazvin that he lacked any reliable troops with which to combat the pillaging by his own units in the city: Commander of the First Caucasus Corps to the Head of the Kazvin City Garrison, 16 July 1917 (GARF, f. R-4738 [Rossiiskaia missiia v Persii], op. 1, d. 245, l. 11). Such cases are legion.

98. E.g., Russian Vice-Consul in Urmia to the Russian Mission in Tehran, 7 July 1917 (GARF, f. R-4738 [Rossiiskaia missiia v Persii], op. 1, d. 222, ll. 2–5); Minorskii to MID, 17 August 1917, no. 762 (GARF, f. R-4738 [Rossiiskaia missiia v Persii], op. 1, d. 5, l. 461).

99. This account is based on the ensign's reports to his superiors (RGVIA, f. 13235 [Upravlenie komissara Erzerumskoi oblasti] op. 1, d. 64).

100. Memo from the head of the fourth district to the commander of the machine gun company, 16 July 1917 (ibid., l. 21).

101. To the head of the fourth district (ibid., l. 22).

102. Ibid., l. 23.

103. Ibid., 14–15.

104. See Viktor Shklovksii, "Severnaia Persiia i nashi voiska," *Novaia zhizn',* 9 March 1918, no. 38, 3; his later memoirs, *Sentimental Journal: Memoirs, 1917–1922* (Ithaca, N.Y.: Cornell University Press, 1984; originally published in Russian: Berlin: Gelikon, 1923), also cover these events. All citations are from the 1918 article. Footnotes indicate where the event is described in the memoirs.

105. *Sentimental Journey,* 86; also 99.

106. An identical statement is found in ibid., 99.

107. Near-identical statement in ibid. 100–101.

108. Ibid., 113. In "Nashi voiska," Shklovskii writes: "Only a minority of the soldiers participated in pillaging, but the majority did not prevent it."

109. Ibid., 129. A less poetic, but similar description is found in "Nashi voiska."

110. Eliseev, *Kazaki na Kavkazskom fronte,* 144.

19

A "ZONE OF VIOLENCE"

THE ANTI-JEWISH POGROMS IN EASTERN GALICIA IN 1914–1915 AND 1941

ALEXANDER V. PRUSIN

"International boundaries [are] '. . . the razor's edge on which hang suspended the modern issues of war and peace, life and death to nations.'"

Lord Curzon

Although in the first half of the twentieth-century hardship was no novelty to Eastern Europe, the land-belt that in 1914 constituted the borderlands between the German, Austro-Hungarian, and Russian empires stands out as particularly volatile. During the two World Wars these regions became a huge front-zone that expanded and contracted in accordance with the fortunes of the opposing armies. Wartime ushered in a particularly tragic period for the Jewish communities of the borderlands. In 1914–1915 the Russian army initiated a brutal campaign of persecution and forcible relocation of more than half a million Jews to Russia proper; violent pogroms in Jewish settlements accompanied Russian offensives and retreats. The outbreak of the Soviet–German war in the summer of 1941 sparked another wave of pogroms that resulted in the deaths of thousands of Jews and heralded the beginning of the Holocaust in the German-occupied Soviet territories. In both cases considerable segments of the local population joined the invading forces in assaults on Jews, acting as unruly mobs or organized vigilante groups.

To be sure, Jews had been targets of religious, cultural, and economic prejudices that pervaded European societies for centuries and often erupted in violence, particularly in times of profound economic, social, or political crises.[1] However, from the assaults by the first Crusaders to the annihilation of entire Jewish communities during the Cossack wars in the seventeenth-century Polish-Lithuanian Commonwealth, anti-Jewish violence was more than just the scapegoating of an outcast minority for alleged social and economic ills. State and church policies, in the form of legal restrictions and limitations, created a propitious political and psychological environment in which the perpetrators acted under the assumption that their actions "punishing" Jews were sanctioned by the ruling elites.

Prejudices against Jews in the borderlands were heightened by state rivalries over these strategically sensitive areas. For centuries the political and territorial organization of the borderlands was shaped by their experiences as the areas of contact and conflict between different polities, cultures, and religions. With progression of time the administrative power-centers evolved into richer, more industrialized and urbanized settlements with fixed borders, whereas most of the borderlands remained largely agricultural and poor, culturally conservative, and characterized by frequent population migrations and blurred ethnic boundaries. Although in the early nineteenth century the Austrian, Prussian, and Russian empires consented to mutually acceptable border arrangements, the national and regional government agencies nurtured suspicions that the allegiances and identities of diverse ethnic groups living astride state and provincial borders were not necessarily, or at least not always, compatible with those envisioned by the state. Consequently, in search of the most efficient methods of control, the imperial authorities attempted to impose some form of political and administrative uniformity that would guarantee the diffusion or suppression of potential separatist and irredentist tendencies.[2]

Still, as long as the state's supremacy over all forms of social relations was unchallenged, it acted as the highest arbitrator, manipulating the conflicting claims of rival ethnic groups and maintaining relative stability in its domain. To be sure, until 1914 the German–Russian and the Austro-Hungarian–Russian borderlands were predominantly violence-free since the imperial authorities accorded their subjects a minimal modicum of stability and relative (by East European standards) political equilibrium. Hence, despite occasional eruptions such as the Polish uprisings of 1831 and 1863 and the 1905–1907 revolutionary turmoil in Russia's western provinces, the borderlands hardly resembled the "caldrons of conflict."[3]

The situation, however, changed dramatically in wartime. As the warring states mobilized their economic and human resources, suspicions of disloyalty among the diverse populations in the border-areas blurred the concept of external and internal enemies. Among the latter the state authorities considered most "corrosive" those who had acted as middlemen between different territorial and economic units, and outwardly pledged their loyalties to a cluster of values rather than to a single "national" culture. Consequently, Jews, who traditionally occupied the "gap" position between the upper and lower classes, found themselves at the receiving end of persecution and terror. On the other hand, when the state—"native" or foreign—initiated violent anti-Jewish policies, it engendered a specific cultural and psychological environment, encouraging similar reactions among the local population that had internalized violence as the means for social advancement, personal enrichment, or achievement of political goals. Similarly, in the 1920–1930s concerns over potentially seditious ethnic minorities dominated the policies of the "successor-states" that attempted to superimpose the national-state blueprint on the territories marked by linguistic, religious, and ethnic cleavages. Such policies contributed to profound fragmentation of the borderland societies that was reflected in their assorted affiliations and allegiances during World War II.

This chapter explores the dynamics and mechanisms of anti-Jewish violence in a "classic" borderland, Eastern Galicia, during the Russian occupation of the province in 1914–1915 and at the initial stage of German invasion in 1941. The chapter's main objective is not to seek the particular common patterns between the two cases—although some features replicated themselves across time—but to analyze the interplay of foreign occupation and internal conflicts in this second largest Jewish enclave in Europe before World War II. A part of the Austro-Hungarian Empire and a Polish province in the interwar period, Eastern Galicia stood out as a classic East European region, where asymmetrical socioeconomic development was tightly interwoven with ethno-religious and cultural differences. Although there was a profound discord among the province's three major ethnic groups—Ukrainians, Poles, and Jews—it remained dormant until wartime detonated the intercommunal hostilities. The ideologies of the invading armies—Russian nationalism versus the Nazi racism and anti-Bolshevism—were quite different in content, but both were predicated upon the elimination of Jews as the most "deviationist" group that did not fit into an envisioned new state order. Not only did the two invaders therefore both pursue brutal and systematic anti-Jewish policies, but they also encouraged and sanctioned "native" violence that acquired its own destructive logic. In other words, the state-driven violence was sustained and exacerbated by the active participation of Polish and Ukrainian "neighbors"[4] who strove to gain access to power and economic resources at the expense of Jews.

The first part of the chapter analyses the peculiarities of Eastern Galicia's socioeconomic and political history that heightened and intensified intercommunal enmities. The second and third parts examine the pogroms as the outcome of a murderous environment—a "zone of violence"—forged by the convergence of interests between the invading forces and native perpetrators. A special effort is made to analyze the ideological, socio-cultural, and psychological factors associated with the ritualization of anti-Jewish violence as a harbinger of a new political order.

The "Classic" Borderland

To a large extent the situation of Jews in Eastern Galicia reflected the particular character of the province, where a pyramidal socioeconomic and political structure was superimposed on a diversity of ethnicity, religion, and culture. The Ukrainians, who predominantly belonged to the Greek Catholic rite, constituted the demographic majority (2,711,400 persons or 65 percent of the population) and lived in the countryside, whereas the urban areas were dominated by the Roman Catholic Poles (879,400, 21 percent) and Jews (545,500, 13 percent); the representatives of the "imperial" nation, the Germans, constituted less than one percent of the total—just about 38,000 people in a region of over four million.[5]

Galicia's ethno-religious diversity in turn underscored its other conspicuous "borderland" feature—it was a highly stratified society, in which ethnicity and religion reflected each group's socioeconomic status and political influence. Since the Polish partitions of the late eighteenth century, the Austrian government had tolerated the primacy of the Polish landed nobility—a reliable "titular" group that possessed the legacy of a historic kingdom and preserved a well-developed culture that dominated regional politics, the justice system, education, and the economy in predictable ways. The Ukrainian peasantry occupied the bottom of the social hierarchy, facing limited prospects for upward mobility, while Jews acted as middlemen between the two groups and were prominent in trade, commerce, money-lending, and free professions. Although the overwhelming majority of Jews lived in poverty, on average they were still one grade above the Ukrainian and Polish peasants and laborers. Jews constituted about 50 percent all land renters and ten percent of estate stewards, and although the Jewish intelligentsia was inclined to German or Polish culture and education, most Jews lived in tight-knit communities, spoke Yiddish, and confined their relations with Poles and

Ukrainians entirely to economic transactions. Thus, despite the fact that Jews had lived in Galicia for centuries, for Poles and Ukrainians they remained "alien" on the account of their different religion, language, and culture.[6]

The era of modernization intensified socioeconomic and political rivalries in the province, for since the mid-nineteenth century the emancipation of peasants and the industrialization drive opened up Galician society to new political and cultural encounters and facilitated the nation-building process. Concerned about Polish irredentism—the uprising of 1847 in west Galicia was the case in point—the Austrian government encouraged the expansion of Ukrainian cooperatives, schools, libraries, and theaters. According to the classic formula suggested by Miroslav Hroch, modern nationalist movements in Eastern Europe began when native populists attempted to imbue their ethnic constituencies with a sense of common identity and destiny. To this effect, they began "recovering" lost symbols of national ethos such as language and folklore; political participation was envisioned as the second stage.[7] Starting in the 1860s the growth of the Ukrainian socioeconomic network was bolstered by more active participation in provincial and national politics. Ukrainian deputies entered the regional and imperial parliaments; the last decade of the century witnessed the formation of the first Ukrainian parties. In contrast to their kinsmen in Tsarist Ukraine, who suffered from abusive Russification policies, Galician Ukrainians largely appreciated their Habsburg rulers and considered Galicia their own "Piedmont"—the cradle of Ukrainian national culture.[8]

While these developments alarmed the Polish elite, the modernization of the provincial economy simultaneously propelled the "Jewish question" to the fore of provincial politics. Impoverished by the emancipation of peasants, many Polish nobles joined the growing Polish commercial and professional middle class, which engaged in fierce economic competition with the Jews. Accordingly, they embraced the ideological postulates of the Polish National Democratic Party (known casually as Endek or the Endeks, for the acronym ND) that promoted antisemitism as a symbolic realm embodying the socioeconomic and political resurgence of the Polish nation. Conflicts between Jewish traders and nascent Ukrainian cooperatives also grew in intensity. After the government introduced universal suffrage, socioeconomic rivalry spilled over to politics, reaching its peak during the municipal and provincial elections. In 1907 and 1911 Jewish voters cast their ballots in favor of Jewish and Ukrainian candidates. The Endeks responded with an escalation of antisemitic propaganda and organized a boycott of Jewish shops.[9]

* * *

If the Austrian government tried to maintain a relative economic and political equilibrium in Galicia, the post–World War I resurrection of independent Poland confirmed the dominant position of ethnic Poles in all spheres of public life, while relegating Ukrainians and Jews to second-class citizenship. In contrast to flexible Austrian policies, and despite its obligations as stipulated by the Minority Treaty of 1919, the Polish government was poised to build a "national" state, prioritizing the interests of the "core" ethnic constituency over the minority groups. Although the victorious Entente initially authorized Poland to administer Eastern Galicia until a national plebiscite, eager to establish a *cordon sanitaire* against Soviet Russia, they eventually consented to Galicia's annexation. Defeated in the Polish–Ukrainian War, the Ukrainians, however, did not give up their national aspirations, while anti-Jewish policies and the pogroms committed by Polish troops during the wars of independence in 1918–1920 made many Jews apprehensive about the new territorial arrangement. Accordingly, though state borders in the east were drawn, they remained in effect fluid frontier zones beset by political instability. The Ukrainians (as well as Belorussians and Lithuanians) boycotted national elections and the Ukrainian clandestine militant groups carried out anti-state propaganda, acts of sabotage, and assassinations of Polish officials. The government responded with brutal "pacifications"—the army and police descended upon Ukrainian villages, arresting thousands of individuals on flimsy pretexts. Police interrogations were accompanied by beatings and torture, while Polish courts imposed stiff prison terms upon hundreds of real and potential culprits. The "Polonization" campaign in the *Kresy* (the Polish term for the eastern provinces in Volhynia, Belorussia, and southern Lithuania) and in Galicia translated into a drastic reduction of Ukrainian schools; they dwindled dramatically from 1,050 in 1919 to 433 in 1922, and the remaining schools eventually became bilingual. The Ukrainian chair at the University of Lwów was closed and the attendance of Ukrainian students was restricted.[10]

The nationalization of Poland's socioeconomic sphere also profoundly affected the situation of Jews. Although in the early 1920s the Polish government initially introduced several liberal reforms, such as the abolition of the Russian imperial anti-Jewish restrictions, it increasingly adopted some of the Endeks' ideological viewpoints. The "de-Judaization" process began with the mass dismissal of Jewish civil employees. Out of 6,000 Galician-Jewish railroad and postal workers in 1914 only 670 retained their posts in 1923, and a similar situation prevailed in the police, legal professions, and education. These discriminatory practices forced more Jews to engage in the areas still open to them—trade, commerce, and artisanship—further aggravating competition with Poles and Ukrainians.[11] Low industrial productivity, a shortage of capital, and the predominance of the agricultural sector in Eastern Galicia were exacerbated by the Great Depression, which hit Poland especially hard. Economic difficulties and the rise of the Nazis in Germany contributed to the intensification of anti-Jewish policies and attitudes. From 1935 on the Polish government, dominated by right-wing senior officers and politicians, openly supported the economic boycott of Jewish businesses and imposed quota on Jewish applicants to the institutions of higher learning. With the encouragement of such official antisemitic attitudes, physical assaults on Jews in Poland became a frequent occurrence.[12]

Marked by political cooperation in the early the 1920s, Jewish–Ukrainian relations also worsened as a result of the deteriorating economic conditions and the radicalization of Ukrainian political circles. Created in 1929 the Organization of Ukrainian Nationalists (OUN) emulated the Italian fascist and Nazi ideology, adopting a political program that stipulated the "removal" of Jews and Poles from the "historical" Ukrainian lands. Radical and moderate Ukrainian political parties supported the boycott of Jewish businesses, and an anti-Jewish propaganda campaign by the Ukrainian press was accompanied by violence. Ukrainian vigilante groups blocked the entrances of Jewish shops and taverns, smashed windows, and attacked Jews on the streets. The right-wing agitators echoed the official Polish propaganda by portraying Jews as the vanguard of the Bolshevik movement.[13]

* * *

Despite the differences between the imperial and the Polish "national" political structure, in 1914 and in 1939 the situation in Eastern Galicia displayed similar socioeconomic and political patterns conducive to ethnic rivalries—intense competition for employment and limited access to education and politics for the majority of the population. In other words, due to the limits of modernization the Austro-Hungarian administration was *unable,* whereas the Polish government was *unwilling* to integrate the majority of population into collective decision-making processes. Conversely, engaged in fierce economic and political competition with each other, Poles, Ukrainians, and Jews tended to evaluate their relations through an emotional "double-bind process,"[14] perceiving a gain for one as a loss for the other two.

The Russian "Military" Pogroms in 1914–1915

Although by the mid-nineteenth century the imperial rule of each of the empires in the borderlands, Austro-Hungarian, German, and Russian, was fully consolidated, the imperial governments' concerns over these sensitive strategic regions were heightened in the era of nationalism. In the anticipation of armed conflict, the Russian and Austro-Hungarian governments were concerned that a national movement within or across the border could set in motion a dangerous chain reaction. As in such disputed borderlands as Alsace-Lorraine or Bosnia-Herzegovina, both sides invested Galicia with ideological and political significance. The Russian nationalist and liberal circles advocated the annexation of Eastern Galicia (along with Bukovina and Transcarpathia) as the long-lost "primordial Russian land" to be reunited under the scepter of the Tsar. Accordingly, they secretly supported and financed the Russophile factions in Austro-Hungary. In turn, the Austrian government used Galicia and Bukovina as the bases for the anti-Russian activities of Ukrainian and Polish political émigrés from Russia. As international tensions in prewar Europe gained momentum, St. Petersburg and Vienna repeatedly accused each other of harboring and abetting "subversive elements" across the border.[15]

After the outbreak of the war, in early August 1914, the first Russian units penetrated deep into Galicia. As the Austrian army and the civil administration began a hasty evacuation, the void of authority in several localities emboldened individuals and groups to engage in plundering abandoned houses, government offices, shops, and warehouses. Since many shops and businesses belonged to Jews, these first attacks were not necessarily antisemitic in character, but were rather driven by the opportunity to loot with no adverse consequences for the perpetrators. The Russian vanguard details, however, gave the random looting a more systematic character and anti-Jewish violence began increasingly to display both deliberate and reactive facets.

Ideology was a crucial element that informed the conduct of the Russian army. Since the second half of the nineteenth century the Russian military increasingly deployed comprehensive statistical data for the evaluation of the demographic and ethnographic makeup of the population of the Empire. As military statisticians determined that the imperial spatial core was "healthy and reliable," in contrast to the diverse and non-Christian populations on the imperial fringes, who were deemed "undesirable and unreliable," ethnicity and religion became the major criteria for loyalty to the state.[16] As the traditional imperial mode of peaceful conflict resolution was sidelined by wartime militant ideologies, such views were projected upon the territories marked for Russian occupation. Significantly, on the "black lists" of Russia's potential enemies none was vilified more than the Jews as the most resilient, wily, and dangerous. A number of Russian generals and senior officers, including the Supreme Commander Grand Duke Nicholas and his Chief of Staff, General Nicholas Yanushkevich, were vehement antisemites, and consequently the Russian Supreme Command—*Stavka*—

actively cultivated images of "traitorous" Jews. The Russian officer corps largely shared such attitudes. A Jewish doctor who spent a night with a group of Russian officers recalled that they were obsessed with the image of the "Jew"; it dominated all conversations. Officers, in turn, disseminated virulent antisemitic propaganda to the rank-and-file, who often were convinced that the war against the Central Powers was also a crusade against the Jews. As a result, upon arriving in towns and villages, Russian units conveyed to Poles and Ukrainians that they had come to free Galicia from the "Jewish yoke." In some instances the Russians incited the local population to anti-Jewish excesses or, after having looted Jewish stores and houses, distributed the booty to the villagers and townspeople.[17]

Crucially, the Russian military conceived its objectives in Eastern Galicia (as well as in Bukovina and Transcarpathia) as military and political. Having been invested by the Tsar with supreme powers in the front-zone, *Stavka* embarked upon dismantling the Austrian state system and integrating the occupied territories into the Russian imperial structure. Such measures entailed depriving Eastern Galicia of its specific "Austrian" features such as the "privileged" position of the Jews. By removing them from the provincial socioeconomic sphere the military conceived of "leveling" Galician Jews to put them on a par with their Russian co-religionists. Concomitantly, the pogroms were accompanied by a whole cluster of rituals that involved the degradation and humiliation of Jews, heralding the introduction of the new political order. Under the conniving eyes of the officers, the Cossacks and soldiers forced Jews to dance, ride on pigs—insulting the sensibilities of religious Jews—crawl, and run naked. Violence thus became a part of a socioeconomic and psychological campaign to relegate Jews to second-class status. Conversely, as soon as Poles and Ukrainians realized that their ethnic "credentials" could protect them from Russian depredations, they adorned their houses and apartments with icons and crosses.[18]

At the same time, knowing that the situation of Jews in Austro-Hungary was markedly more advantageous than in Russia, the Russian military anticipated that Galician Jews would constitute the backbone of resistance. Such "complimentary projections"[19]—the ascription of hostile intentions to the Jews—were bound to evolve into a self-fulfilling prophecy, especially when combined with the spy-mania that from the war's outset pervaded the Russian military and society. Russian wartime mentalities derived heavily from the military disaster in East Prussia, where in August 1914 the Germans surrounded and slaughtered two Russian armies. The ineptitude of the generals entailed an overwhelming atmosphere of fear of the "fifth columnists" lurking behind the frontlines. Suspicions of Jewish saboteurs were magnified by Austro-German propaganda that appealed to Russian Jews to rise against Tsarist oppression. Such instances as well as the preferential treatment initially accorded to Jews by the German and Austro-Hungarian troops gave the rumors of Jewish conspiracies wide credibility. The army facilitated these rumors by issuing reports of Jews spotting the enemy's fire from balloons, luring the Russian units into traps, or cutting telephone lines. The reports predominantly referred to the collective image of the "Jew/s" as an omnipresent subversive force rather than to specific cases.[20]

It should be noted that the Russian spy-mania was not a unique phenomenon and the fear of enemies lurking in shadows became a dominant psychological factor on all fronts of World War I. Thus, in Belgium the activities of the *franc-tireur* resisters generated mass German reprisals against civilians.[21] Similarly, on 2 September 1914 the Grand Duke ordered the "complete destruction" of localities in East Prussia where shooting at Russian troops took place. Reprisals involved executions of alleged spies and the destruction of houses from which shots were fired. Such actions seemingly did not contravene the provisions of the Hague Convention of 1899 that specified that combatants had to be clearly identified by uniforms and insignia. Since the guerrillas did not follow these rules and hid among the civilian population, the military logic was that the Convention did not apply to the culprits, or to the population that harbored them. In contrast to Belgium, however, there was no actual resistance in Galicia (although intense guerrilla warfare did occur in Bukovina, where the Austrians waged a successful hit-and-run campaign). Russian reprisals, therefore, were predicated merely upon the anticipated activities of the specific ethnic "out-groups."[22]

For soldiers and the Cossacks violence also became an expedient tool to make up for hardship and supply shortages, especially as communication lines were extended to the limit. In fact, letting troops go on a rampage as reward for capturing a locality has been a traditional practice of many armies since antiquity and is known as the "tax of violence."[23] Therefore, the Russian officers mostly tolerated the predatory habits of their subordinates who ran amok in Jewish residential areas. Time and again, the *modus operandi* of the pogromists was almost identical: a charge of some "treacherous act," such as allegations of shooting at the troops from Jewish houses or shops, would be followed in quick succession by plunder, rape, and massacre.

Since robbery was a ubiquitous element of the pogroms, greed could partially explain the participation of the local population in attacks. From the outset of hostilities, the news of the Russian invasion forced many Jews to flee Galicia. Their abandoned property attracted the throngs of looters, who were encouraged by the Cossacks and soldiers. Some individuals also guided the Russians to Jewish houses and shops, where they together robbed the residents and divided the booty. For example, on 3 September 1914 the Russian military personnel and the townspeople joined in a massive pogrom in Stanisławów. Although the assailants were mostly interested in plundering, in some instances they maimed or killed their victims and gang-raped women and girls. One of the most violent attacks took place in Lwów on 26–27 September, where local residents followed the Russians to the Jewish residential areas. Under the pretext of "searching" for concealed weapons, the soldiers looted apartments and murdered between 20 and 50 individuals; many more were wounded.[24]

On the other hand, it is possible that some local residents targeted Jews as the most "patented" Austrian patriots. When in the summer 1914 the Austrian military launched arrests, imprisonment, and executions of individuals accused of pro-Russian sentiments, some Jews displayed a conspicuously hostile attitude to the alleged traitors. In several instances, a mob comprised of Jews and Poles assaulted the columns of arrested "suspects." Some Jews also denounced the Ukrainians suspected of pro-Russian activities and the Austrian authorities carried out swift and merciless justice. The images of Jews brutalizing unfortunate victims (such images would be magnified tenfold in 1941) could have left an imprint in popular memory, invoking desire for revenge.[25]

*   *   *

In October 1914 after the establishment of the Russian administration and the front moving westward, "wild" violence was substituted by more systematic persecution consistent with the official anti-Jewish restrictions in Russia proper. The second cycle of pogroms began in the spring of 1915, when the Austro-German offensive in western Galicia shattered the Russian defenses. The Russian retreat soon turned into a rout and in June the Austrians recaptured Lwów. To deprive the enemy of human and material resources, the Russian High Command initiated a scorched-earth policy, which included the destruction of property along the front line and the forcible evacuation of the population. Conceived as a strategic device, the evacuation soon degenerated into widespread plunder, rape, and murder. Acting upon orders to "clean up" (*ochistit'*) the front-zone, the Cossacks and soldiers burned houses and crops, blew up bridges and mills, demolished railroads, and forced the population eastward. The same orders effectively institutionalized violence, for the Russian details now imbued with the official function of depriving the enemy of potential recruits and helpers hanged Jewish "spies," looted houses, and raped women. Assaults on Jews reached such magnitude that *Stavka* was compelled to issue an order that subjected commanders who incited violence to court martial. The uprooted Jewish communities were forced to endure long marches eastward while the guards mercilessly flogged anybody who tried to hand them a glass of water. Arriving to a point of destination, Jews were kept separated from other refugees. The Russian "Great Retreat" also opened the way for local residents to converge on abandoned Jewish houses and shops. Peasants in horse-driven carriages arrived at localities marked for Jewish expulsion and plundered houses and barns, while the Russian patrols, bands of deserters, and some villagers preyed upon the stragglers, robbing and murdering entire families.[26]

The "Jedwabne Syndrome" of 1941

In late June 1941 the German invasion of the Soviet Union sparked off a chain of violent anti-Jewish pogroms that in paradigmatic pattern swept through the borderlands. Eastern Galicia (alongside the *Kresy*) became a principal site for violence that claimed at least ten thousand lives. In contrast to the Russian pogroms in World War I, the "Jedwabne" violence displayed greater societal continuity reflecting a deep political and social fragmentation of the borderlands. By 1939 the Polish government's ethnic policies had effectively atomized Jews and Ukrainians, who either welcomed the Soviet invasion or remained indifferent to the collapse of Poland. Enticed by Soviet propaganda that called for the annihilation of the Polish *szlachta* (nobility), Ukrainian villagers were eager to settle old scores by murdering, robbing, or denouncing their Polish neighbors to Soviet authorities, and armed Ukrainian units ambushed small Polish detachments. In some localities Jewish houses and shops also came under attack.[27]

Aiming at dismantling the Polish state system, the Soviet administration altered the existing socioeconomic cleavages by initially favoring the "agricultural" Ukrainians at the expense of the "bourgeois" Poles and Jews, who were subjected to the state-nationalization campaign. The redistribution of land that had belonged to the Polish settlers and the Roman Catholic church, the expansion of hospitals and clinics, and the proliferation of Ukrainian-language schools, theaters, and libraries initially won large segments of the Ukrainian population to the Soviet cause. At the same time, the Soviet practice of promoting skilled or talented individuals, for whom higher education or elevation to a higher social rung had previously been inaccessible, attracted large numbers of Jewish and Ukrainian applicants. Antisemitism was officially outlawed and the hated student quota for Jews in colleges and universities was abolished. Such prospects reflected the positive and attractive features of the new regime, which, in the eyes of many Jews, offered a fair compensation for the years of discriminatory policies and humiliation in the Second Polish Republic.[28]

At the same time, the competition for employment fueled the traditional ethnic rivalries. In his report from July 1941 Stefan Rowecki, the commander of the main Polish underground force (the Union of Armed Struggle, later known as the Home Army or AK), noted that precisely because so many Jews had lost their livings to Soviet nationalization, many sought employment in the Soviet administration.[29] This visibility in the state apparatus on top of the preponderance of Jews in the white-collar professions imprinted images of the "Soviet-Jewish" regime in the collective psyche. Such attitudes were heightened by mass arrests and deportations that in 1939–1941 swept through the Soviet-annexed territories and affected all ethnic groups and social layers. From western Ukraine alone (Galicia, Volhynia, and northern Bukovina) the Soviets deported approximately 320,000 people, including 70,000 Jews. Denunciations, which were common, and various degrees of participation in the deportations added fuel to intercommunal animosities and portended a confrontation in the future.[30] However, despite the fact that many "class-acceptable" Poles and Ukrainians had collaborated with the Soviets, as the most discriminated-against minority in the interwar period Jews were singled out as the main beneficiaries of the Soviet regime. In the minds of nationalistically inclined societies antisemitism thus became inseparable from national patriotism and anti-communism. Consequently, in the summer of 1941 the jubilant Polish and Ukrainian crowds greeted the German troops as liberators from a regime tainted by "Jewish connection."[31]

Similarly to the situation in the early summer of 1914, the pogroms in Galicia in 1941 began with random robberies and looting that broke out during the Soviet evacuation. However, on the night of 27 June, as the Soviets were puling out from Galicia's capital, Lwów, large crowds descended upon the Jewish residential areas and a newly-organized Ukrainian militia began seizing Jewish men. Similar incidents transpired before and after the arrival of the first German units, which either joined in or "supervised" the assaults.[32]

Yet, in contrast to the Russian military pogroms, the anti-Jewish violence in the summer of 1941 was frequently "native-driven" even though it derived its momentum from the Nazi Operation Barbarossa. The Nazi culture and ideology of antisemitism are too well known to be rehearsed here. Suffice it to say that Hitler envisioned the war against the USSR as the war of annihilation against "Judeo-Bolshevism"—a view shared by the German military, the police, and the SS. The ideological crusaders—the *Einsatzgruppen*—had specific tasks of eliminating political opponents of the regime, having gained considerable experience in such operations during the war against Poland. On 17 June the chief of the Main Security Office, Reinhardt Heydrich, instructed his subordinates that "self-cleansing efforts" of the anti-communist groups in the East should be encouraged and "pointed in the right direction," without, however, leaving a trace of German involvement. Accordingly, upon entering Galicia, the German propaganda units concentrated upon inciting the population to avenge the wrongs done them by the "Judeo-Bolsheviks."[33]

Both OUN branches[34] were equally instrumental in promoting the "self-cleansing efforts" among the Ukrainians. Hoping to achieve its ultimate goal—the creation of an independent Ukraine—the OUN leadership was eager to take as much advantage of German policies as possible. Although initially its ideological platform stipulated the removal of Jews and Poles from the economy and public life, by the late 1930s it had embraced the Nazi racial postulates as fully corresponding with the creation of a homogeneous Ukraine. Such ideological affinity resulted in the vicious antisemitic propaganda that predicted a "final reckoning" with Jews in the future. At the beginning of the Soviet–German war, both OUN branches disseminated leaflets that called for the extermination of the "Bolsheviks and Jew-ish hirelings."[35]

The Nazi and OUN propaganda especially thrived on the discovery of mass graves left behind by the Soviets. During its hasty evacuation from the Polish eastern provinces, the Soviet secret police and the prison administration shot between 10,000 and 20,000 people held in Galicia's prisons.[36] In many localities corpses found in prisons were mutilated to an extreme degree—skulls opened, eyes put out, faces burned, and women's breasts cut off. Such gruesome sites certainly contributed to the overwhelming atmosphere of grief and desire for revenge against alleged culprits. Although there is no doubt that the Soviet secret police did torture its prisoners to extract confessions, there are indications that in some places the Germans and their native helpers also appropriately "prepared" the ground to arouse anti-Jewish violence. For example, after the Soviets pulled out from Lwów, the Ukrai-nian militia supervised by German officers deliberately disfigured and defiled corpses in the Łącki prison. In other localities Jewish corpses were removed from prisons before the crowds were let in.[37]

Although such "cosmetic" operations did not cause the pogroms, they facilitated pop-ular inclinations *to believe* that Jews were behind the massacres, since in a highly emotional atmosphere perceptions of reality are frequently distorted by "cognitive categories based on race and ethnicity [that] serve to simplify a highly complex world."[38] When the prisons were opened and many grieving individuals and families went inside to look for their relatives and friends, the sense of liberation from the hated Soviet regime and the horrors of the NKVD massacres glued the crowds together. Still, the assaults on Jews that followed dis-played a minimal degree of "organized-spontaneity," for while groups of vigilantes dragged Jews out of their apartments and escorted them to NKVD execution sites, others formed cordons through which Jews had to run the gauntlet or guarded Jewish exhumation details. Two other crucial ingredients of the pogroms were the timely arrival of peasants from the countryside, who partook in the plunder and the organization of the civil committees and the militia, which temporarily assumed power in small towns and villages. In some places the militia had prepared the proscription lists with the names and addresses of Jews and sus-pected communists. If initially only Jewish men were targeted, by early July the violence en-gulfed women and children, who were beaten and forced to exhume corpses or wash blood off the sidewalks.[39]

Although the NKVD massacres certainly contributed to the popular desire to pun-ish the culprits, the extreme brutality against defenseless men, women, and children tran-scended any notion of score-settling. This is especially revealing since the real perpetrators were long gone, and violence also erupted in localities where no NKVD killings had taken place. The surrogate victimization of Jews, therefore, calls into question the motivations of the perpetrators. From the German point of view, the annihilation of Jews was inseparable from the military and ideological preparations for the war against the Soviet Union, and the pogroms were integrated into the emerging pattern of the Holocaust. The units of the *Einsatzgruppe* C arrived to Lwów on the afternoon of 30 June, when the pogrom there had already begun. With the help of the Ukrainian militia, the German killing squads rounded up Jews and escorted them outside the city, where by 6 July they shot more than 6,000 people.[40]

The invasion of the Soviet Union simultaneously created a particular murderous en-vironment—aptly called the "Jedwabne state" by a prominent Polish historian after the infamous Jedwabne massacre of 1941[41]—whereby the Nazi crusade against "Judeo-Bolshevism" coalesced with the aspirations of the local nationalist groups that embraced anti-communism and antisemitism as the crucial building blocks of national independence. On 30 June an OUN-B group in Lwów announced the restoration of Ukrainian statehood. By this time, attacks on Jews had been in progress for some time, but they escalated within the next several days. Jews were forced to mop streets with toothbrushes and combs or wash sidewalks with their bare hands (one is prone to think of the considerable Nazi "experience" in such matters) and to exhume and wash corpses found in prisons. The militiamen and the crowds chanted anti-Jewish slogans, viciously beat their victims, and alongside the German soldiers amused themselves cutting off the beards of religious Jews. In Kolomeja the mob forced Jews to destroy Soviet monuments and shout anti-Soviet slogans, while in Stary Sambor Jews had to march through the town carrying pictures of Lenin and Stalin.[42] Therefore, anti-Jewish violence transpired under the specter of Ukrainian national statehood—whether the OUN intended it or not—giving it the appearance of a "native" initiative, precisely as the Germans had desired.

Similarly, the pogroms were internalized as a means to marginalize the Ukrainians' traditional socioeconomic rivals or to avenge alleged or real wrongs. In some localities the members of the Ukrainian intelligentsia acted as the main instigators, organizing civil committees and leading the assailants. Individuals who had suffered under the Soviet regime, or whose relatives were imprisoned or deported, also featured among the ringleaders. Although some apologetic studies have emphasized that central role of criminal and *Lumpen* (roughly, "rabble") elements in the violence,[43] the breakdown of the social order engendered a proclivity toward wanton destructiveness and cruelty among many ordinary people who partook in the pogroms. Indeed, a prominent American sociologist suggests that in times of crisis large segments of the population "become hysterical; mob-mindedness shows an upward trend. The perception of many phenomena becomes one-sided and distorted [leading to] erratic and chaotic associations, [and to] an uncritical acceptance of rumors and plots."[44]

Base instincts such as greed, jealousy, and personal animosities raged unabated, particularly because the conduct of the power-holders—either the Germans or the local civil committees and the militia—enabled the mobs to act with a modicum of confidence that the pogroms were sanctioned. Although Polish–Ukrainian animosities were further enflamed during the Soviet occupation in 1939–1941, in some localities such as Lwów and Borysław the culture of antisemitism and the opportunity for personal enrichment drew the members of the two groups together in the attacks on Jews. Importantly, participation in violence also served as a vehicle to redemption for previous political transgressions, for among the assailants there were former members of the Communist Union of Youth (*Komsomol*) and the Soviet militia. An OUN-M appeal, for example, specifically stressed that former Soviet employees who "retained national consciousness" could be readmitted as full-fledged members of the new Ukrainian community, if they turned against "Jews, Poles, *Moscovites* and communists."[45]

It should be noted that Jews were not the sole targets of violence. The Nazi killing units and the Ukrainian militia also targeted the Polish intelligentsia. On 3–4 July a special German unit murdered a number of leading Polish academics and intelligentsia in Lwów. Still, the non-Jewish victims were selected on an individual basis and as a rule their families were not murdered. In contrast, the Jewish community was targeted as a whole for the "crime" of being Jewish, regardless of whether they had any connection to the Soviet state.

Conclusion

Populated by different ethnic and religious groups, Eastern Galicia was a "classic borderland," an overlapping spatial and ethno-cultural domain that was easily infused with the territorial claims of the neighboring states. Having realized that efforts to create a homogeneous national identity were contradicted by the deeply rooted local cultural identities, the Austrian government tolerated the diversity of its realm even as, facing the confrontation with Russia, it was concerned over this strategically important area and the loyalty of its subjects. The Polish and Ukrainian national movements that came of age during the modernization period also claimed the rights to the province as "historically" their own and shared official concerns over the permeability of the state borders. Russia, on the other hand, invested Galicia with strategic and ideological significance as the "long-lost" land, thus threatening the territorial integrity of its neighbor.

Wartime turned the province into a veritable "zone of violence," where the invading armies attempted to restructure the national composition of Galicia by confining each ethnic group to clearly delimited space. Consequently, in 1914–1915 and in 1941 the traditional middlemen of the borderlands, Jews, were consistently singled out as the most "deviationist" elements that did not fit into the Russian national and the Nazi racial order. At the same time, the Russians and the Germans used situational determinants such as the objective socioeconomic and ethnic conditions in Galicia to foment and institutionalize existing intercommunal hostilities.

Although the Russian military pogroms partially mutated into a local heterogeneous form, the "live and let live" traditions of Austro-Hungarian imperial rule and the exclusionist rather than annihilationist policies of the Russian military mitigated its genocidal potential and contributed to the predominantly secondary role of local residents in violence. In contrast, by the late 1930s the ethnic minorities in the Second Polish Republic had grown alienated and bitter toward the regime. Shared traumatic experiences under the Soviet occupation only intensified mutual antagonisms that were set off by the Soviet–German war. The anti-Jewish violence in June–July 1941 was much more systematic and deadlier than the Russian pogroms precisely because of its dual character, at once organized by the state and enacted by significant segments of the population, who were cultivated and encouraged to participate in the genocide.

In both cases, however, it was the outbreak of war that created a climate in which violence was perceived as a tool to settle accounts, achieve power and economic benefits, or symbolize national resurgence. Accordingly, ethnic categories became major determinants in accessing the sources of power and economic resources, but also in determining one's safety, life, or death. The pogroms displayed the convergence of interests between the invaders and the local culprits, with the latter adjusting themselves to the conduct of the power-holders and benefitting from the socioeconomic marginalization of the ostracized minority or releasing negative emotions and frustrations associated with wartime. If for the Russian and German armies anti-Jewish violence heralded the dismantling of the old state systems—the Austro-Hungarian and the Soviet respectively—for the local perpetrators, who were removed from the epicenters of power, it was a way of integrating themselves into the new political order at the expense of Jews. Their conduct, therefore, derived from a whole range of motives, from the cumulative outcomes of Gentile–Jewish relations in the borderlands, radical political ideologies, and the human propensity to jealousy, greed, and violence.

NOTES

KEY TO ARCHIVAL CITATIONS
IPMS: Instytut Polski i Muzeum im. generała Sikorskiego (London, U.K.)
NARA: National Archives and Records Administration (Washington, D.C.)
TsDAVO: Tsentral'nyi derzhavnyi arkhiv vyshchykh orhaniv vlady i upravlinnia Ukrainy (Kiev, Ukraine)
TsDIAK: Tsentral'nyi derzhavnyi istorychnyi arkhiv Ukrainy u Kyevi (Kiev, Ukraine)
SPP: Studium Polski Podziemnej (London, U.K.)
USHMM: United States Holocaust Memorial Museum (Washington, D.C.)
dział = fond, sygnatura = file

(Referring to "Zone of Violence" in the chapter title) I paraphrased the term from Mark Levene, "Creating a Modern 'Zone of Genocide': The Impact of Nation- and State-Formation on Eastern Anatolia, 1878–1923," *Holocaust and Genocide Studies* 12(3) (1998): 393–433.

The epigraph is from Martin Pratt, "Foreword," in *Borderlands under Stress,* ed. Martin Pratt and Janet Ellison Brown (Cambridge, Mass.: Kluwer Law International, 2000), ix.

1. For example, John D. Klier, "The Pogrom Paradigm in Russian History," in *Pogroms: Anti-Jewish Violence in Modern Russian History,* ed. John D. Klier and Shlomo Lambroza (Cambridge: Cambridge University Press, 1992), 13–38.

2. Alfred J. Rieber, "Changing Concepts and Constructions of Frontiers: A Comparative Historical Approach," *Ab Imperio* 1 (2003): 23, 32–33.

3. Edward D. Wynot, *Caldron of Conflict: Eastern Europe, 1918–1945* (Wheeling, Ill.: Harlan Davidson, Inc., 1999), 3.

4. Jan T. Gross, *Neighbors: The Destruction of the Jewish Community in Jedwabne, Poland* (New York: Penguin Books, 2001).

5. Bohdan Wasiutyński, *Ludność żydowska w Polsce w wiekach XIX i XX* (Warsaw: wydawnic-two Kasy im. Mianowskiego, 1930), 90–91; B. Stopnevich, "Naselenie Galitsii," *Ukrainskaia zhizn'* 11–12 (1914): 48; S. E., "Galichina v tsyfrakh," *Ukrainskaia zhizn'* 3–4 (1915): 19.

6. Leila Everett, "The Rise of Jewish National Politics in Galicia, 1905–1907," in *Nationbuilding and the Politics of Nationalism: Essays on Austrian Galicia,* ed. Andrei S. Markovits and Frank S. Sysyn (Cambridge, Mass.: Harvard University Press, 1982), 156–57, 173–77.

7. Miroslav Hroch, *Social Preconditions of National Revival in Europe: A Comparative Analysis of the Social Composition of Patriotic Groups among the Smaller European Nations* (Cambridge: Cambridge University Press, 1985).

8. Paul Robert Magocsi, *The Roots of Ukrainian Nationalism: Galicia as Ukraine's Piedmont* (Toronto: University of Toronto Press, 2002), 73–82.

9. John-Paul Himka, "Ukrainian-Jewish Antagonism in the Galician Countryside During the Late Nineteenth Century," in *Ukrainian-Jewish Relations in Historical Perspective,* ed. Peter J. Potichnyj and Howard Aster (Edmonton: Canadian Institute of Ukrainian Studies, 1988), 121–39; Edward Dubanowicz, *Stanowisko ludności żydowskiej w Galicji wobec wyborów do parlamentu wiedeńskiego w r. 1907* (L'viv: Drukarnia "Polonia," 1970), 39–40.

10. O. H. Mykhailiuk, ed., *Istoriia Volyni z naidavnishykh chasiv do nashykh dniv* (L'viv: "Vyshcha shkola," 1988), 93; John-Paul Himka, "Western Ukraine in the Intewar Period," *Nationalities Papers* 20(2) (1994): 354; Grzegorz Mazur, "Problem pacyfikacji Małopolski Wschodniej w 1930," *Zeszyty Historyczne* 135 (2001): 3–39.

11. Szyja Bronstejn, *Ludność żydowska w Polsce w okresie międzywojennym: studium statystyczne* (Wrocław: Zakład Narodowy im. Ossolińskich, 1963), 71–73; Ignacy Schiper, *Dzieje handlu żydowskiego na ziemiach polskich* (Warsaw: nakładem Centrali Związku Kupców, 1937), 592–93.

12. Jerzy Tomaszewski, "Społeczność żydowska a Polacy w II Rzeczypospolitej," in *Polska-Polacy-Mniejszości Narodowe,* ed. Wojciech Wrzesiński (Wrocław: Zakład Narodowy imienia Ossolińskich, 1992), 117; Jolanta Żyndul, "Zajścia antyżydowskie w Polsce w latach 1935–1937—geografia i formy," *Biuletyn Żydowskiego Instytutu Historycznego* 159 (1991): 59, 61, 70.

13. Maksym Gon, *Iz kryvdoiu na samoti: ukrains'ko-yevreis'ki vzayemyny na zakhidnoukrains'kykh zemliakh u skladi Pol'shchi (1935–1939)* (Rivne, Ukraine: Volyns'ki oberehy, 2005), 77–79.

14. Jonathan Fletcher, *Violence and Civilization: An Introduction to the Work of Norbert Elias* (Cambridge: Polity Press, 1997), 57–58; Ralph H. Turner, "Collective Behavior," in *Handbook of Modern Sociology,* ed. Robert E. L. Faris (Chicago: Rand McNally & Company, 1964), 383.

15. Alexander Victor Prusin, *Nationalizing a Borderland: War, Ethnicity, and Anti-Jewish Violence in East Galicia, 1914–1920* (Tuscaloosa: The University of Alabama Press, 2005), 14.

16. Peter Holquist, "To Count, to Extract, and to Exterminate: Population Statistics and Population Politics in Late Imperial and Soviet Russia," in *A State of Nations: Empire and Nation-Making in the Age of Lenin and Stalin,* ed. Ronal Grigor Suny and Terry Martin (Oxford: Oxford University Press, 2001), 111–19.

17. Peter Holquist, "'The Raid of a 'Wild Horde': The Forms and Sources of Russian Military Violence during the First Occupation of Galicia, 1914–1915," unpublished manuscript, 29–31. I am grateful to Dr. Holquist for his generous permission to use this paper.

18. S. S. Ansky, *The Enemy at His Pleasure: A Journey Through the Jewish Pale of Settlement During World War I* (New York: Metropolitan Books, 2002), 272–73; Prusin, *Borderland,* 30.

19. Donald L. Horowitz, *The Deadly Ethnic Riot* (Berkeley.: University of California Press, 2001), 86–87.

20. Hoover Institution on War, Revolution, and Peace, "Zhurnal voennykh dieistvii," 3, 8, 10, 17.

21. John Horne and Alan Kramer, *German Atrocities, 1914: A History of Denial* (New Haven, Conn.: Yale University Press, 2001), 113–20.

22. T. Hunt Tooley, "World War I and the Emergence of Ethnic Cleansing in Europe," in *Ethnic Cleansing in Twentieth-Century Europe,* ed. Steven Béla Várdy and T. Hunt Tooley (New York: Columbia University Press, 2003), 77; John Klier, "Kazaki i pogromy. Chem otlichalis' 'voennye' pogromy?" in *Mirovoi krisis 1914–1920 godov i sud'ba vostochnoevropeiskogo yevreistva,* ed. O. V. Budnitskii et al. (Moscow: Rosspen, 2005), 47–70.

23. Mark Grimsley and Clifford J. Rogers, "Introduction," in *Civilians in the Path of War,* ed. Grimsely and Rogers (Lincoln, Nebr.: University of Nebraska Press, 2002), xv.

24. Tsentral'nyi derzhavnyi istorychnyi arkhiv Ukrainy u Kyevi (TsDIAK), 385/7/102, 51ob-52; Jacob Schall, *Żydostwo galicyjskie w czasie inwazji rosyjskiej w latach 1914–1916* (L'viv: nakładem Księgarni I. Madfesa, 1936), 6–7; Simon Spund, *Die Schreckenherrschaft der Russen in Stanislau: selbsterlebte Schilderungen* (Budweis, Czech Republic: Selbverlag, 1915), 6–8, 14–15, 19, 22, 24, 35.

25. Piotr Wróbel, "Barucha Milcha galicyjskie wspomnienia wojenne, 1914–1920," BŻIH 2/158 (1991), 91; *Voennye prestupleniia Gabsburgskoi monarkhii: Galitskaia Golgofa* (Trumbill, Conn.: Peter S. Hardy, 1964), 17–21.

26. TsDIAK, 363/1/86, 20, 22–26, 30, 46; 361/1/674, 61, 63–64; Ansky, *Enemy,* 155–56.

27. Lesław Jurewicz, "Niepotrzebny," *Zeszyty Historyczne* 15 (1969), 154; Alfred Jasiński, "Borysławska apokalipsa," *Karta* 4 (1991): 102–103.

28. *Instytut Polski i Muzeum im. generała Sikorskiego* (IPMS), dział "Ministerstwo Spraw Wewnętrznych," sygnatura A.9.III.2a/19, 5–7, 9–10, 70; Ryszard Torzecki, *Polacy i ukraińcy: sprawa ukraińska w czasie II wojny światowej na terenie II Rzeczy Pospolitej* (Warsaw: Wydawnictwo Naukowe PWN, 1993), 38–39.

29. Paweł Machcewicz and Krzysztof Persak, eds., *Wokół Jedwabnego,* (Warsaw: Instytut, 2002) 2: 133.

30. Grzegorz Mazur, "Polityka sowiecka na 'zachodniej Ukrainie' 1939–1941 (zarys problematyki)," *Zeszyty Historyczne* 130 (1999), 76, 81–82; I. F., Kuras et al., eds., *Politychna istoriia Ukrainy XX stolittia* (Kiev: vydavnytstvo "Geneza," 2003), vol. 3, 149.

31. Tadeusz Tomaszewski, *Lwów 1940–1944: Pejzaż psychologiczny* (Warsaw: UNI-DRUK, 1996), 62–63; Philipp-Christian Wachs, *Der Fall Theodor Oberländer (1905–1998): ein Lehrstück deutscher Geschichte* (Frankfurt: Campus Verlag GmbH, 2000), 78.

32. United States Holocaust Memorial Museum (USHMM), RG-15.069M, accession 1996.A.0228, "Teka Lwowska = Lwow files, 1898–1979," reel 1, 143; Samuel Lipa Tennenbaum, *Zloczow Memoir* (New York: Shengold Publishers, Inc., 1986), 167–68; 151, 175; Dieter Pohl, *Na-*

tionalsozialistische Judenverfolgung in Ostgalizien, 1941–1944: Organisation und Durchführung eines staatlichen Massenverbrechens (Munich: R. Oldenbourg Verlag, 1997), 54–67.

33. Peter Klein, ed., *Die Einsatzgruppen in der besetzten Sowjetunion, 1941/42: Die Tätigkeits- und Lageberichte des Chefs der Scicherheitspolizei und des SD* (Berlin: Edition Hentrich, 1997), 319.

34. In April 1940 the OUN split into two warring factions—OUN-M and OUN-B.

35. *Tsentral'nyi derzhavnyi arkhiv vyshchykh orhaniv vlady i upravlinnia Ukrainy* (TsDAVO), 3833/1/74, 24; 3833/1/70, 12, 15; Frank Golczewski, "Die Kollaboration in der Ukraine," in *Beiträge zur Geschichte des Nationalsozialismus,* vol. 19: *Kooperation und Verbrechen: Formen der "Kollaboration" im östlichen Europa 1939–1945,* ed. Christoph Dieckmann, Babette Quinkert, and Tatjana Tönsmeyer (Göttingen: Wallstein Verlag, 2003), 163.

36. Leon Weliczker Wells, *The Janowska Road* (New York: The Macmillan Company, 1963), 34–35; Tennenbaum, *Zloczow,* 174–75.

37. *Studium Polski Podziemnej* (SPP), B.II.715, Zygmunt Asłan, "Endlösung der Judenfrage in Lemberg," 23–25; Bogdan Musial, *"Kontrrevolutionäre Elemente sind zu erschiessen": Die Brutalisierung des deutsch-sowjetischen Krieges im Sommer 1941* (Berlin: Propyläen Verlag, 2000), 273; Jasiński, "Borysławska apokalipsa," 112.

38. Roger D. Petersen, *Understanding Ethnic Violence: Fear, Hatred, and Resentment in Twentieth-Century Eastern Europe* (Cambridge: Cambridge University Press, 2002), 46.

39. Musial, *Elemente,* 170; Jasiński, "Borysławska apokalipsa," 112–13; Andrzej Żbikowski, "Inny pogrom," *Karta* 6 (1991): 130–32; Andrzej Żbikowski, "Lokalne pogromy Żydów w czerwcu i lipcu 1941 roku na wschodnich rubieżach II Rzeczypospolitej," *Biuletyn Żydowskiego Instytutu Historycznego* 2–3 (1992): 14.

40. *National Archives and Records Administration* (NARA), RG-242, T175, reel 233, Ereignismeldung UdSSR, n. 14, 6 July 1941, n. 20, 12 July 1941, n. 24, 16 July 1941, n. 26, 18 July 1941.

41. Dariusz Stola, "A Monument of Words," *Yad Vashem Studies* 30 (2002): 46–47.

42. NARA, RG-242, T175, reel 233, Ereignissmeldung UdSSR n. 23, 15 July 1941; Zhanna Kovba, ed., *Shchodennyk L'vivs'koho getto: spohady rabyna Davyda Kahane* (Kiev: Dukh i Litera, 2003), 26–27, 29–30; Musial, *Elemente,* 166, 179, 258–60; Weliczker, *Janowska,* 37–43.

43. For example, Yevhen Nakonechnyi, *"Shoa" u L'vovi* (L'viv: Literaturna Ahentsiia "Piramida," 2006), 112–13.

44. Pitirim A. Sorokin, *Man and Society in Calamity: The Effects of War, Revolution, Famine, and Pestilence upon Human Mind, Behavior, Social Organization, and Cultural Life* (New York: E. Dutton, 1943), 44–45.

45. USHMM, "Teka Lwowska," sygn. 229/8, 163–64; sygn. 229/19, 153–54; TsDAVO, 3833/1/70, 9–15.

20

ETHNICITY AND THE REPORTING OF MASS MURDER

KRAKIVS'KI VISTI, THE NKVD MURDERS OF 1941, AND THE VINNYTSIA EXHUMATION

JOHN-PAUL HIMKA

Introduction

Violent discourse and discourse supportive of violence accompanied the conflicts that raged in the borderlands in the twentieth century. Here we look at an example of this that is particularly interesting because it involves the mass violence of two of the major competitors for the borderlands, Nazi Germany and the Soviet Union, in a discourse formulated in understanding with Germany by one of the autochthonous peoples of the region, the Ukrainians. It concerns crimes against humanity committed by the Soviet authorities as they were used in propaganda to justify the violence of the German occupiers and those who collaborated with them.

Specifically, this chapter looks at two incidents in which mass violence perpetrated by the Soviet political police, the NKVD, was exposed in the Ukrainian press under German occupation. The first incident is murders committed in the summer of 1941. After Germany and the Soviet Union put an end to the multinational Second Polish Republic in September 1939, the Ukrainian territories, Eastern Galicia and Volhynia, were incorporated into the Ukrainian Soviet Socialist Republic. The Soviets immediately undertook a massive deportation of the regions' Poles to Siberia, the first in a series of ethnic cleansings and genocides to unfold on the Polish–Ukrainian borderlands over the following eight years. Certain categories of Jews and a relatively small number of Ukrainians were also deported by the Soviets in 1939–41. The new Communist authorities Ukrainianized the region by subduing and deporting the Polish elite, but persecuted Ukrainian nationalists. When Germany attacked the Soviet Union on 22 June 1941, the prisons of Galicia and Volhynia happened to be full of Ukrainian nationalists, but also, in the larger cities, Jewish and Polish political prisoners. Because of the rapidity of the German advance into the new western borderlands of the USSR, the NKVD proved unable to evacuate these prisoners before the Germans would arrive. Not wishing to leave them as potential collaborators with the invaders, they killed them hastily. Thousands of corpses were found in prison basements after the Germans took the cities and towns of Western Ukraine.[1] The Nazis used these gruesome discoveries for propaganda and also to incite a series of murderous pogroms against the Jews by local inhabitants throughout the western borderlands.[2]

The second incident whose media coverage will be examined in this study is the Vinnytsia exhumation of 1943. In the aftermath of their defeat at Stalingrad, the Germans exhumed thousands of bodies from mass graves underneath a park and playground in Vinnytsia. An international team of forensic experts[3] as well as police investigators from Germany descended upon the exhumation site and determined that the victims had been shot in the back of the head by the NKVD in 1937–38, that is, during Stalin's Great Terror. The Nazis used the Vinnytsia exhumation for an international propaganda campaign similar to the one unleashed with respect to the exhumation of slain Polish officers at Katyn a few months before.[4]

I focus on how these incidents of mass violence committed by the Soviet state were reported, in particular on the issue of the ascription of ethnicity to both the victims and the perpetrators. It is a study of some of the uses that can be made of mass murder.

The newspaper that I have chosen to analyze is the Ukrainian-language daily *Krakivs'ki visti*. It was published in Kraków, which became a center of Ukrainian nationalist activity in 1939, after the Red Army marched into eastern Poland. Many Ukrainian nationalists left Eastern Galicia at that time and transferred their activities to the German zone. The German authorities allowed the establishment in Kraków of a Ukrainian Central Committee, with which *Krakivs'ki visti* was closely associated. The committee was headed by Professor Volodymyr Kubijovyč, a geographer who specialized in mapping ethnicity. Kubijovyč leaned toward the Mel'nyk rather than the Bandera faction of Ukrainian nationalists.(The two factions took their names from their leaders, Andrii Mel'nyk and Stepan Bandera. The Melnyk faction was stronger in emigration and in Bukovina, while the Bandera faction was stronger in Galicia and Volhynia. The leadership of the Mel'nyk faction was older than that of the Bandera faction.) Although carefully censored by the German press bureau, *Krakivs'ki visti* enjoyed more autonomy than any other legal Ukrainian-language publication under German occupation and also more autonomy than any of the legal Polish-language publications in the General Government. It was edited by a Ukrainian journalist, Mykhailo Khom"iak (Chomiak), and some of the most prominent Ukrainian intellectuals contributed to it. There is no direct evidence in the archives of *Krakivs'ki visti* that the German authorities intervened in the publication of any of the materials about the NKVD murders or Vinnytsia. The press run of *Krakivs'ki visti* was just over 10,000 in 1941 and just over 15,000 in 1943. It was circulated in the General Government, Germany, in most of German-occupied Europe, and in countries allied with Germany. It was not, however, allowed to be distributed in the Reichskommissariat Ukraine.[5] The paper can be described as the organ of established Ukrainian nationalists operating within the limits imposed by Nazi rule. It was not a local paper, as were most Ukrainian periodicals under Nazi occupation, since there were few Ukrainians living in Kraków; it was, rather, a paper that reflected a more generalized Ukrainian nationalist standpoint. The choice of *Krakivs'ki visti* as the object of analysis for this study was also motivated by the preservation of its editorial archive:[6] this is the most complete editorial archive of any of the papers of the General Government or of any of the Ukrainian-language papers of the German occupation.[7]

The Course of the Reporting

Krakivs'ski visti's first reports on the NKVD massacres were published on 6 July 1941, when three items appeared. One was an article, with the dateline 5 July, submitted by telephone from the paper's Berlin correspondent, Gennadii Kotorovych.[8] There was also an interview with Docent Dr. Hans Joachim Beyer, a Ukraine expert and SS *Obersturmbannführer,*[9] and an item translated from *Berliner Börsen Zeitung.*[10] Evidently, the topic was a sensitive one if the information came filtered first through German channels, rather than directly from Ukrainians in L'viv. The first publication on the murders that came from a Ukrainian source in L'viv was published in the 9 July issue, and it was based on a report already published in the first issue of the L'viv daily *Ukrains'ki shchodenni visti* (5 July 1941).[11] Throughout the reporting on the NKVD murders, materials taken from German papers, especially the Nazi party organ *Völkischer Beobachter,* appeared frequently. Original Ukrainian materials became more common after mid-July.

Articles on the subject appeared frequently in July and the first week of August, but then became old news. The last articles in this series were published on 21 and 24 August. The issues from 9 through 12 July 1941 published pictures of the corpses of NKVD victims and their mourners.

Although the local Vinnytsia paper, *Vinnyts'ki visti,* had been reporting on the exhumation of the mass graves since it commenced in late May 1943,[12] the first report to appear in *Krakivs'ki visti* was a small front-page article published on 23 June. It was taken from *Nova doba,* a weekly newspaper for Ukrainians in POW camps which was edited by *Krakivs'ki visti*'s Berlin correspondent, Kotorovych.[13] Although an editorial also appeared about the Vinnytsia mass graves on 27 June,[14] it was not until later that there was steady coverage of the issue. Kotorovych wrote to one of *Krakivs'ki visti*'s editors on 1 July: "The silence of the German press about Vinnytsia has its reasons. The press abroad has already mentioned the incident itself. For your information exclusively, I will tell you that this matter seems to be awaiting a complete investigation so that it can later become a topic for a large planned campaign à la Katyn."[15] The paper's Frankfurt correspondent, Anatol' Kurdydyk,[16] also wrote to one of the editors, Mariian Kozak, on the same subject on 10 July, at which time the press campaign about Vinnytsia had just taken off: "You surely know that they are writing a lot about Vinnytsia, and I will write you a separate article on it." He said that he had asked his superiors earlier about whether to write on Vinnytsia, and they had said "no," that after Katyn another such incident "will leave the impression of deliberate propaganda, sewn together with thick threads. But perhaps a different order came from 'ober.'"[17]

From 9 July until 10 August many articles about Vinnytsia appeared. A few also appeared in late August and in late September; the final article, on 29 September, reported the reburial of the last of the exhumed victims.

In the case of the NKVD murders, the editors of *Krakivs'ki visti* were able to obtain materials for publication directly from the sites of the massacres, since many of them were located in the General Government. Vinnytsia was located in the Reichskommissariat, however, which was mostly off limits to *Krakivs'ki visti*. *Krakivs'ki visti* did manage to maintain an unofficial exchange with the newspaper *Nova Ukraina,* which came out of Poltava in the Reichskommissariat, and published some material from it, but for the most part the articles on Vinnytsia were based on sources from Central and Western Europe. One article may have been written by a correspondent specifically sent from *Krakivs'ki visti* to Vinnytsia.[18] Another article claimed to be a review of the press of the Vinnytsia region,[19] but it is by no means certain that this review was based on materials actually in the possession of the editorial board of *Krakivs'ki visti*.

The Reporting of Atrocities

The first report of the NKVD murders stated that in L'viv thousands of corpses were found in the prisons and on the streets with marks of torture.[20] Dr. Beyer reported an initial tally: 4,000 were shot in L'viv, 600 in Ternopil', 300 in Iavoriv. There was, he said, evidence of torture.[21]

As the reporting developed, the description of the atrocities grew more elaborate. A report on 8 July translated from *Berliner Illustrierte Nachtausgabe* stated that so far 700 corpses had been recovered in L'viv, among them women, children, and elderly citizens. There were perhaps 2,000–3,000 victims in L'viv altogether. In the police presidium on Sapieha Street, 20 Ukrainians had been locked in a narrow cell. The "Bolshevik butchers" shot at them through the doors with machine guns and revolvers. They finished off some of the victims with knives and axes. In the investigative prison on Kazymyrivs'ka Street the Chekists threw the victims, dead or alive, into basement cells, then locked up the doors to the cells and walled them in. The retreating Bolsheviks set the prison on fire to hide their crimes, but the basement cells remained intact and were later opened.[22] According to an article translated from *Völkischer Beobachter,* "the animals in human form" ripped open the bellies of pregnant women and nailed the embryos to the wall.[23] The torture chamber in the secret police headquarters was covered with bloodstains up to the ceiling.[24] An unattributed report from Berlin said that first the victims in L'viv were crowded into cells and given little food or water. The ones who were buried according to this account were not shot, but instead their stomachs were cut open or their throats cut. Their bodies displayed marks of torture with sharp hooks. Some had their noses cut off, others their faces smashed in. Many victims were burned alive; perhaps they were thrown into boiling water. The skin was just hanging from some of the corpses. The torments were exacerbated by the so-called "red glove": the victims' arms and legs were placed into boiling water, then their skin was flayed from the joints to the fingers and toes.[25] Another report on L'viv said that women had their noses and breasts cut off, their wombs ripped open. Priests were found with crosses carved into their chests; some were crucified. Prisoners were shot in the basements and then hand grenades were thrown in. They were now counting 8,000 victims in L'viv.[26]

Similar atrocities were found elsewhere. A translation from *Berliner Illustrierte Nachtausgabe* stated that on the night of 24–25 June the Bolshevik-Jewish officials in Dubno shot 527 men and women and bestially stabbed infants.[27] A translated article from *Völkischer Beobachter* stated that 1,500 Ukrainians were killed by machine guns in Luts'k prison. The executioners started shooting them with machine guns, then threw hand grenades at them, then finished them off with pistols.[28] A correspondent from *Völkischer Beobachter* toured the citadel in Zolochiv. The ditch surrounding it was full of corpses. "Whatever could be cut off, the executioners cut off, whatever could be extracted or pulled out, they extracted it, pulled it out." One of the mourners pointed out his 15-year-old son among the victims. Perhaps over 400 persons were murdered there.[29] In Stryi the basements of the NKVD offices contained victims missing heads, arms, legs, and other parts of their bodies. A sewer there was found to be packed with corpses.[30] In Sambir over 50 children were shot. In the prison kitchens, kettles were discovered with boiled human arms and legs, and the prisoners had been fed some strange meat since March.[31] Fifteen-hundred Ukrainians were killed in Kremianets', including eight priests and a bishop. The Bolsheviks marched the bishop naked through the streets to the prison. There they set fire to his beard, cut off his heels, nose, and tongue, and plucked out his eyes.[32] In Shchyrets', a small town near L'viv, 27 Ukrainians were discovered buried in a stable. The bodies were without hands, legs, noses, ears.[33] About 700 were killed in the Dobromyl' region,[34] and 800 in Chortkiv.[35]

The first, terse report of the discovery in 1943 of a mass grave on the west side of Vinnytsia spoke of "about 10,000 corpses of killed Ukrainians."[36] The grave was located on what had once been NKVD property. The immediate impression was that the corpses originated from the period 1938–1941.[37] More precise information was published after the major press campaign started. A report at that time spoke of about 30 mass graves at Vinnytsia, in which "Ukrainians killed by the Bolsheviks in the years 1938, 1939, and later" were buried. Investigations showed that "the GPU and its Jewish *oprichniki* killed their victims with a shot to the back of the head and threw them with their hands behind their back into collective graves."[38] A special correspondent sent to Vinnytsia reported on the measures the perpetrators took to hide their activities: "With the innate refinement of Jews the NKVD was able to mask its crimes. The scene of the murders was surrounded by a high fence. Two dogs guarded the grounds. Anyone who looked inside was arrested and never heard of again. Documents on the victims said they were exiled to the farthest reaches of the Soviet Union without right of correspondence."[39]

The most sensational information came from an interview with Professor Niilo Pesonen[40] conducted by Bohdan Kentrzhyns'kyi,[41] identified by the newspaper as a representative of the Ukrainian Information Bureau in Helsinki. Professor Pesonen had been in Vinnytsia as one of the forensic experts working on the corpses. Many of the victims, he said, were buried alive and had swallowed earth.[42] The women were "completely naked, without underwear. . . . We can say with certainty that the chekists, before murdering these unfortunate women, threw macabre orgies with them."[43]

Propaganda Value for the Ukrainian Movement

The mass murders of the NKVD in 1941 and the Vinnytsia exhumation were major media events for the Ukrainian movement. Ukrainians as victims of Jewish Bolshevism were presented on newsreels and in the press across Nazi-dominated Europe. Never before had the Ukrainian nationalists enjoyed the kind of exposure that Joseph Goebbels could orchestrate for them. *Krakivs'ki visti* frequently highlighted what foreigners were writing and saying about the tragic events in Ukraine.

As we have already seen, many of the reports published in *Krakivs'ki visti* about the NKVD murders were in fact translations from the most important Berlin papers. One contributor wrote about the foreign press coverage of the murders:

> The fortunate thing in this great misfortune is that the frightful pogroms against the Ukrainians came to the attention of the entire world. The loss of tens of thousands of conscious, active

citizens is painful, their places won't be filled quickly by new people, the propaganda effect achieved in the context of the pogroms does not stand in any relation to the losses. But since they have already perished only because they were conscious Ukrainians and loved Ukraine above all else, then we should take care that their precious blood has not been wasted; we must use it for the benefit of the Fatherland. . . . We must make moral capital of it for our nation. . . . Now we have an opportunity, a sad opportunity, but nonetheless an opportunity which we cannot miss. For a long time the Jewish mafia in all its branches—from the Communist to the Masonic—has removed from the world press the word "Ukraine," or tried to debase it by any means. That is why now that our national name has appeared again on the front pages of the great periodicals, we cannot waste this interest, even though its background is so tragic.[44]

Frankfurt correspondent Anatol' Kurdydyk published a survey of the German press and its treatment of the murders. He was gratified that German papers linked L'viv with Ukraine (and not Poland or Russia). The Ukrainian name "L'viv," not "some foreign variant" (i.e., Lwów or L'vov) was being used in the press and newsreels. "Just two weeks ago I myself was afraid that no one thinks of us. But today? Everyone knows what Ukraine is and who the Ukrainians are, how they have written their page in blood in the history of our days."[45] The NKVD murders were reported in Swiss, Swedish, and American papers.[46] Vasyl' Grendzha-Dons'kyi,[47] a prominent Transcarpathian writer, published an account of the crimes as reported by the Slovak and Croatian press. His conclusion was: "Judeobolshevism must perish from the face of the earth so that not a trace of it is left."[48]

According to one editorial, the reporting of the NKVD murders broke the ban which the Jews had placed on coverage of Bolshevik crimes. In spite of the millions who had died in the Bolshevik hecatombs, the editorial stated, the world knew little about it.

It is obvious why. The international kingdom of Judah has always been in one yoke with the Muscovite tsardom of Satan. In this case the world press, which was mainly in Jewish hands, maintained silence about all the horrors, while gladly publicizing all sorts of so-called Bolshevik "achievements" and other lying inventions. Book publishing was also controlled by Jews. . . . And now the whole world witnesses [the horrors of the NKVD murders], and will believe, having seen it with their own eyes. We will not be surprised. For us this has been known for a long time. We are just convinced that over those long years nothing in the Bolsheviks has changed, that the Bolshevik sadists have brought their sadism to an even greater "art" and that Jewry continues to have the opportunity to enjoy the aroma of innocent blood and to abuse defenseless corpses.[49]

The international attention surrounding the Vinnytsia exhumation was even greater. On Vinnytsia *Krakivs'ki visti* was able to cite the German press, of course,[50] but also Belgian,[51] French,[52] Finnish,[53] Romanian,[54] Bulgarian, Danish,[55] and Serbian[56] sources. Kurdydyk surveyed the international press coverage: "And again, after a long silence, the names of Ukraine and Ukrainians, who have crawled bloody from the graves, fill the pages of European periodicals." "In Europe there are not many nations who could compete with them in the number of victims fallen in the battle against Bolshevism." He listed Portuguese, Spanish, Romanian, Italian, French, Bulgarian, Dutch, Swedish, and even Turkish periodicals that were printing stories about Vinnytsia. "And all emphasize that the only crime of these Ukrainians was their love for their native land and hatred for and aversion to the monstrous Bolshevik regime." The stories have printed photographs, so similar to those from L'viv in 1941.[57] Ievhen Onats'kyi[58] surveyed the Italian press. He omitted the details, because they were already widely known to

Ukrainian readers. "We just note that, as [Carlo Fettarappa] Sandri writes, at the entrance to the site of the exhumations the German authorities hung an appeal to the Ukrainian population, in which among other things we read: 'Ukrainians! Remember that your brothers who lie here were killed by cruel Stalin and his Jewish accomplices. . .'"[59] Bohdan Osadchuk,[60] another correspondent based in Berlin, reported the coverage by the German press in the Reich, a German-language newspaper in Bratislava, a Berlin correspondent of the Danish press, and a Croatian daily. Osadchuk's article ended with a quote from the Croatian paper:

> The mass graves in Vinnytsia, *Chrvacki Narod* states, are new proof of the politics of destruction that the Jews from the Kremlin have conducted among the Ukrainian people. The murdered Ukrainians again throw guilt on Stalin and his Jewish collaborators and summon the world to an implacable struggle against the Jewish-Bolshevik threat, which would like to bring upon Europe the same fate that the defenseless victims in Vinnytsia met.[61]

Krakivs'ki visti published an article translated from *Broen,* the Danish periodical for workers in Germany, which the editors said was "worthy of attention because of its approach to the issue and its warm attitude toward the Ukrainian people." The article referred to "an insane sadism that could only arise in the Jewish brain": building a park with swings and dance floors above mass graves. The chief of the NKVD in Vinnytsia was "Major Sokolins'kyi, a pure-blooded Jew." The head of the secret political division was also a Jew. Jews made up 60 percent of the personnel of the NKVD in Vinnytsia. They occupied all the top positions, including director of the prison, his deputy, the director of the "Special Division for Political Prisoners," and his deputy too.[62]

The sights at Vinnytsia were reported to have exercised a powerful effect on foreign visitors. On 22–23 July German arms workers from Berlin visited the exhumation site. Exposure to the horrors "strengthened the long-held conviction of the Berlin workers that Bolshevism is the mortal enemy of humanity." A Walloon who visited Vinnytsia was so moved by what he saw that he joined the Waffen-SS brigade Wallonia.[63]

Perhaps the most revealing moment is the interview that Kentrzhyns'kyi conducted with Professor Pesonen in Helsinki. It shows how easily the instrumentalization of tragic events can descend into kitsch. Kentrzhyns'kyi was interested in the impressions that his countrymen had made on the learned foreigner, and Pesonen offered all the right replies on cue. He stated that the Ukrainians he met in Vinnytsia "look very positive, are better dressed than he expected. They are distinguished by a more lively temperament than the Finns and other European peoples. . . ." He was especially impressed by an evening of Ukrainian folk songs and dances. He also praised "the excellent Ukrainian dishes" he was served in the hotel. The Ukrainians emphasized to him that Ukrainians differed from the Russians "just as Finns do" and wanted to live a free life like other European peoples. The interviewer asked him how he liked the Ukrainian landscape: he "liked it very much." The environs of Vinnytsia are "very attractive." "Everyone looks clean and well groomed." The men have beautiful voices. Vinnytsia has "a truly nice theater." "Your national costumes have great charm."[64]

Ethnicizing the Victims

Ukrainian nationalists wanted to use the victims of the NKVD as moral capital to gain support for their aims, particularly an independent Ukrainian state. As Bogdan Musial put it:

Then as now [referring to the 1990s war in Kosovo] the principle held that the greater the number of victims, the more convincing the martyrs-argument. In this context it is scarcely surprising that the Ukrainian nationalists frequently exaggerated the number of victims of the Soviet massacres. Even more conspicuous is the attempt to pass off all the victims of the Soviets as Ukrainians.[65]

As *Krakivs'ki visti* reported the NKVD murders, all the victims were Ukrainian.[66] What might have been meant as a singular exception came in a report about the executions in the Dobromyl' region: "Among those killed was also found a Bolshevik prosecutor." In this case, the nationality of the victim was passed over in silence.[67] Otherwise, the paper was monolithic in its presentation. A translation from *Berliner Illustrierte Nachtausgabe* stated that the victims "were no criminals, but loved their Ukrainian Fatherland and hated the Jewish-Bolshevik insanity."[68] In Luts'k, the paper reported, the Ukrainians, 1,500 in all, were singled out from a total of 4,000 prisoners and put to death.[69]

It is not possible to reconstruct the actual national composition of the victims, but the lists compiled by the NKVD itself leave no doubt as to the general picture. In L'viv, the nationality of the victims was mixed. The lists for L'viv have many characteristically Polish first names and fathers' names and some Jewish names as well.[70] Grzegorz Hryciuk estimates from the NKVD lists of victims that a minimum of 25 percent of the victims in L'viv prisons were Polish,[71] and Christof Mick writes that "up to two thirds" of the L'viv victims were Ukrainians.[72] In some localities outside L'viv the victims were also ethnically mixed, for example, in Drohobych,[73] and in others the overwhelming majority of the victims were Ukrainian, for example, in Ternopil'.[74] In sum, the evidence contradicts the paper's contention that the victims were all or with few exceptions Ukrainians.

The victims unearthed at Vinnytsia were also depicted as Ukrainians.[75] There were only two indications that a few victims of other nationalities ended up in the mass graves. One report singled out categories of victims on diverse, not necessarily ethnic grounds, e.g., "people with connections abroad." Another such category was "members of national minorities," but the example of a national minority cited was Galician Ukrainians.[76] Another report mentioned that an ethnic German, a driver at a collective farm, was killed for corresponding with his brother in Germany.[77] Otherwise, again, the presentation was monolithic.

And again, this was factually inaccurate. The German report stated that of the 679 identified victims, 490 were Ukrainian, 28 Polish, and 161 of unknown nationality.[78] The Polish victims were never mentioned in *Krakivs'ki visti*. Also, as Ihor Kamenetsky has observed, the category of unknown nationality "carries little credibility." The victims had been identified by relatives (in 468 cases) and/or on the basis of documents found on their persons (202 cases). "It would be unusual, indeed, if the relatives of the victims had not known their nationalities, or if the Soviet identification documents had not mentioned it either."[79] One of the editors of the local Vinnytsia paper, *Vinnyts'ki visti*, told the Harvard University Refugee Interview Project that there were Russians and Jews among the corpses as well as Ukrainians.[80] The translator for the Germans at Vinnytsia also recorded in his memoirs that a few corpses were exhumed that could be indirectly identified as Jewish, but the German police suppressed this fact.[81] Published NKVD documents also confirm that there were Jews among the victims.[82] (The ascription of homogeneous Ukrainian nationality to the victims can also be found in postwar émigré publications.)[83]

Krakivs'ki visti did not categorize the Vinnytsia victims by ethnicity alone. There was also some discussion of social class in order to demonstrate that the Bolshevik state was no friend of the common toiler. One of the seven categories of victim that one of the reports identified was farmers (*khliboroby*).[84] A certain Dr. H. Kurz from Berlin visited the mass graves himself and wrote: "In the graves at Vinnytsia there are no landowners, factory directors, high officials, only the poorest workers from factories and collective farms who had no political influence."[85]

Ethnicizing the Perpetrators

Irina Paperno has written a brilliant analysis of how the perpetrators of the Vinnytsia shootings have changed according to the political moment. During the exhumations themselves, the blame was placed on the Jewish NKVD. In 1959 the House Committee on Un-American Activities identified the perpetrator as an individual, Nikita Khrushchev, who was just then visiting the United States. In the postwar Ukrainian émigré press the perpetrator was "Moscow," a.k.a. the Russians. In independent Ukraine Vinnytsia has been presented as a crime of "Stalinism."[86]

So whom did *Krakivs'ki visti* identify as the perpetrators of the 1941 massacres and the Vinnytsia shootings?

One of the earliest statements on the NKVD murders was made by Professor Kubijovyč,[87] the head of the Ukrainian Central Committee and the person with the most influence on the *Krakivs'ki visti* milieu. He placed an editorial in the paper on 8 July under the title "Before the Majesty of Innocent Blood." He placed the blame for the murders squarely on the shoulders of "the eternal enemies of the Ukrainian people" (*vidvichni vorohy ukrains'koho narodu*) and called, as we shall see below, for stern retribution against them. But he was not explicit about whom he meant. "The eternal enemies of the Ukrainian people," he wrote, "did not let pass the opportunity to vent their rage and in a bestial manner spill the innocent blood of thousands of defenseless sons and daughters of the Ukrainian people. . . . In these bloody orgies a whole league [*tsila spilka*] of our eternal enemies took part."[88] Kubijovyč probably had in mind a broad set of others: the Russians, Jews, and Poles.[89]

The Poles were omitted from the ranks of perpetrators for the rest of the time the newspaper reported on the murders, but Kubijovyč was probably reacting to certain passages in the initial reports, found in the previous issue of the paper (of 6 July; there was no issue on 7 July). One of these, the one communicated by Kotorovych by telephone from Berlin, said that the massacred Ukrainians displayed "signs of terrible bestial abuses of NKVD sadists and the bestial Jewish-Polish mob."[90] In his interview, Beyer, said: "Also other elements [besides Jews] took part in this, in which connection it is particularly necessary to remember that a part of the Polish intelligentsia, under the leadership of former president Bartel,[91] was definitely favorably disposed to the Soviets."[92] The Poles soon disappeared as perpetrators, but the other "eternal enemies" remained.

Russians were blamed for both the NKVD murders of 1941 and the shootings at Vinnytsia. In connection with the NKVD murders, the Russians were always linked with the Jews. Thus in Mariian Kozak's interview with a former prisoner who survived the Luts'k massacre, reference is made to "Muscovite-Jewish executioners."[93] Another article ascribed the crimes to "Muscovy," which had now become "the kingdom of the Judeo-commune";[94] yet another blamed atheistic Muscovite Bolshevism as well as the Jews.[95] An eyewitness from

Sambir said the shooters in the prison were "a Jew from Sambir, two Muscovite Jews, two Georgians, two Muscovites (*moskali*), and even one of our own, a Cain from the village of Turchynovychi, Sambir county."[96] This, incidentally, was the only mention of a perpetrator of Ukrainian nationality (notably a West Ukrainian). According to the testimony of many Poles, West Ukrainians often functioned as perpetrators, collaborating with the Soviet authorities in deportation actions and outright plunder during the 1939–1941 period.[97] They are invisible in the *Krakivs'ki visti* reporting as well as in representative narratives of the postwar Ukrainian diaspora.[98] Moreover, there is some ethnic sleight of hand in the reporting regarding ethnic Ukrainian perpetrators from pre-1939 Soviet Ukraine, whom the West Ukrainians call *Skhidniaky* (Easterners). When they are victims, as in Vinnytsia, they are categorized as Ukrainians. When they are perpetrators, as they were in both Western Ukraine and Vinnytsia, they are categorized as Russians. The administration of Soviet Western Ukraine in 1939–1941 was largely made up of Communists recruited from pre-1939 Ukraine, where, as a result of the extensive violent purges and need to take in new members, almost two-thirds of the party was composed of ethnic Ukrainians.[99] Ukrainians were not a majority in the NKVD, but they were by no means absent from its ranks.

The most egregious example of the Muscovite/Jewish conflation came from the Berlin correspondent, Kotorovych, who said the victims were "massacred by Jewish-Muscovite beasts from the nihilist black regiment of the five-pointed star." He referred to a story in the *Berliner Börsen Zeitung*, which identified the perpetrators as "the Stalinist-Jewish commune," "the same Jewish-Bolshevik gang" that the chief plutocrats in London and Washington were allied with. Other German papers, he noted, also were also calling the world's attention to "the cruel-insane wildness of Muscovite-Jewish nonhumanity." Kotorovych himself seems to be the author of an allegation that Stalin was about to flee the country "to his 'democratized' friend Roosevelt, where in New York millions of dollars collected over many years await him in the safes of Jewish banks."[100]

Much of the reporting on Vinnytsia continued in the same vein: "The mass graves in Vinnytsia are a new, frightful proof of the system of methodical physical destruction to which Muscovite Bolshevism adheres. Jewish Bolsheviks and their lackeys introduced this policy of ruthless physical destruction in Ukraine from the first moment they came to power."[101] The review of the Vinnytsia regional press referred to the "Muscovite system of terror," but also wrote: "*Korostens'ki visti* charges Churchill and Roosevelt that they delivered all Europe and Ukraine to the mercy of the Bolsheviks through their alliance with world Jewry."[102] Another article identified Bolshevism as responsible for crimes at Vinnytsia, but Bolshevism was the work of "the deceitful and shameless Mongol-Muscovite spirit, impregnated with the heartless, cruel, adroit, and sharpened Jewish intellect."[103]

There were also two statements that singled out the Russians as responsible for the murders at Vinnytsia. One, by Mariian Kozak, who himself had earlier linked Muscovites and Jews, placed the emphasis on Russian imperialism. "The collective grave of Ukrainian victims of the mass Bolshevik terror near Vinnytsia characterizes the ways and means of red Moscow in respect to conquered nations and countries, that is, to those who have fallen victim to its expansionist foreign policy." Kozak proceeded to survey Russian imperialism in relation to Ukraine during the nineteenth and twentieth centuries. Bolshevism, he said, assumed the legacy of the old Russia, but added a messianic spirit and functioned without the restraints of Christian morality.[104] The other statement was submitted by Ivan Lysiak (later known as Ivan L. Rudnytsky).[105] Reflecting on the mass graves of Ukrainians murdered by the Bolsheviks, he concluded that Moscow was to blame. "The Russian nation is responsible for having sheltered, carried to the top, and given authority into the hands of a band of international murderers. Other nations will never forgive the Muscovites for that."[106]

But the dominant image of the perpetrator propagated by *Krakivs'ki visti* was the Jewish Bolshevik. I have already, in other contexts, cited some of the passages on this subject, and it is not necessary to cite all of them. I provide just a few more examples to confirm the flavor of the reporting.

An article translated from *Berliner Illustrierte Nachtausgabe* said of the NKVD murders: "We lay this all to the account of the Jewish potentates in the Kremlin, whose crimes against the whole world will find appropriate retribution."[107] Another translation from the same periodical cited a Ukrainian eyewitness saying that the shootings in L'viv on the night of 24–25 June were perpetrated by "Bolshevik-Jewish officials," including two Jewesses.[108]

After a lurid description of tortures suffered by the victims (the "red glove"), the unattributed article from Berlin continued: "No one earlier could imagine that there could be such monsters in human form as those Jews who executed their bloody duties as executioners. . . . This was done mainly by officials of the GPU, so called 'commissars' with a red stripe around their hat. These were Jews."[109]

The newspaper quoted extracts from Bishop Hryhorii (Ohiichuk)'s[110] anti-Semitic sermons at the funerals for the Vinnytsia victims:

> My dear sons! Arise from your graves and ask that bloodthirsty executioner, 'the father of all toilers'—Why did you drive us into your cursed collective-farm properties and acquire our good grain for the dinner table of your Jews? Because of our diligent work, which we performed for you and for your Jews? Or maybe because we took the milk away from the lips of our own children so that the children of your Jews could have butter? Why are you silent? You are silent, because you know, you executioner, that these victims were killed for the same reason as Christ was killed: because of the truth![111]

> They died like sheep that fell into the clutches of predators. They got into Stalin's hands, who used his 'excellent' constitution to torture millions of people to death. Millions of Soviet citizens were locked into the dungeons of the NKVD and even their hands were tied behind their backs so that the Jewish executioners could do what they wanted with them.[112]

The editors alerted readers that they considered Dr. H. Kurz's eyewitness testimony to be important. Kurz informed them that

> here, in the headquarters of the NKVD, were Jews, as in the local stations of all other localities. . . . Everywhere here in Vinnytsia we came upon the tracks of Jews, whether it was the boss of the NKVD or an investigative judge or a commissar of external service. In the face of the Vinnytsia victims we can understand the profound hatred of the Ukrainian people to the Jews and to Jewish Bolshevism. Let us hope that Europe learns from this truly horrible example.[113]

It should be noted that the reporting on the Vinnytsia exhumation (23 June–29 September 1943) overlapped in time with the publication in *Krakivs'ki visti* of a series of antisemitic articles specially commissioned by the German authorities (25 May–11 September 1943).[114] In this series Jewish collaboration with the Bolsheviks was a frequent theme. The same theme had also been evident in *Krakivs'ki visti*'s earlier reporting (17 April–6 June 1943) on the exhumation at Katyn of Poles killed by the Soviets.

The image of Jews as perpetrators was exaggerated. The Germans' translator at Vinnytsia, Mykhailo Seleshko, has left an account of how frustrated the German police commission was when it reconstructed the composition of the NKVD personnel in Vinnytsia and discovered that "among the supervisors and commissars of the NKVD there were fewer Jews than Muscovites."[115] (Similarly, in Latvia, where an identical propaganda campaign was being conducted, there was "only one person of indisputably Jewish origin" working in the NKVD in 1940–1941.)[116] Throughout the period 1937–1945, the percentage of Jews in the NKVD was declining, and the percentage of Ukrainians growing.[117]

Although not well grounded in fact, the anti-Jewish accusations of *Krakivs'ki visti* were accompanied by a violent rhetoric of retribution, usually formulated in an open-ended way. Professor Kubijovyč, in his editorial on "the eternal enemies" of the Ukrainian nation, heard the innocent blood of the victims issuing a call for

> RESOLUTE RUTHLESSNESS towards our eternal enemies, who more than once through our softheartedness stole into our confidence and became, indeed with our help, masters on our hospitable land. Of course, it is not a matter here of some sort of pagan cruelty, a base desire for vengeance, but only of firm justice dictated by the sacred right to defend the vital interests of our Native Nation. The innocent blood of our Victims imposes on us the irrevocable obligation to cleanse our Native Land of all enemy rabble and build a strong cordon against the enemy's onslaught.[118]

Another editorial, unsigned, wrote in connection with the prison murders: "We clench our teeth and our fists—from this pain is born in us still greater implacability and rancor: pay the executioners back. . . . We know what time has come. It's the trumpets of the cherubim, it's the last judgment. The moment has come when we must say: it is now or never."[119] With reference to the mass graves at Vinnytsia, *Krakivs'ki visti* cited *Vinnyts'ki visti:* "Only revenge, cruel, ruthless revenge can pay for the death of the martyrs of our nation."[120]

We can exclude the possibility that the inflammatory anti-Jewish materials published in *Krakivs'ki visti* in connection with the NKVD murders of 1941 served as an incitement for the pogroms that were perpetrated in Western Ukraine in late June and early July. Most of the pogroms occurred before *Krakivs'ki visti* began writing about the NKVD murders and blaming them on the Jews. Also, the pogroms all took place before it was even logistically possible to distribute the newspaper in the affected localities. It is clear, however, that the antisemitic propaganda of the paper contributed to create an atmosphere conducive to the mass murder of the Jews that was already underway. By the time the Vinnytsia articles appeared, most of the Jews of that city had been shot dead in large ditches in the open air. Most of the Jews of L'viv and Kraków were also dead, transported to killing centers in Bełżec and Auschwitz.

The pogroms were never directly mentioned in *Krakivs'ki visti,* but there are some passages that allude to them. An article about how L'viv had changed since the collapse of Soviet rule remarked that the Soviet bayonets and NKVD trucks had disappeared from the city.

> Now you meet on L'viv streets smiling, happy German soldiers, whom no one fears, to whom on the contrary the whole population gravitates. . . . In today's L'viv one more phenomenon strikes the eye: nowhere on the streets will you see Jews, with whom every corner of the city roiled until recently. 'The chosen people' have hidden in their mouse holes, afraid of the people's anger and retribution for the past two years of abuse.[121]

The pogroms usually began with having Jews retrieve the corpses of the victims. This activity is mentioned in a few accounts. After the German army entered Chortkiv, "the Jews began under guard to excavate the large courtyard and take corpses out of the earth."[122] An article translated from *Völkischer Beobachter* described the results of an NKVD massacre in an unnamed village. "The local people quickly brought the Jews, who are digging up the earth and finding the sadistically massacred corpses."[123] An article by the same correspondent to *Völkischer Beobachter* appeared in the next issue of *Krakivs'ki visti*. Again he mentioned an instance when the Jews were brought out for the exhumation. "As one might expect, the despair of the population was directed against the Jews who in their majority were employed as officials in Soviet offices and were precisely those who were instigating these crimes."[124]

Conclusions

From this investigation of how *Krakivs'ki visti* reported the NKVD murders and Vinnytsia exhumation, it is clear that the ascription of ethnicity, the right kind of ethnicity, to both perpetrators and victims was important for the newspaper.

The perpetrators were categorized as Jews, most emphatically, and secondarily as Russians. Although the perpetrators were also at times mentioned without ethnic modifiers, identified just as Bolsheviks or the NKVD,[125] this made little difference because so many articles ethnicized these state-associated categories, identifying Bolshevism and the NKVD with Jews and Russians.[126] For a brief moment, even Poles were identified as perpetrators. Only one Ukrainian, "a Cain," was mentioned in the role of perpetrator.

The victims, as has already been demonstrated, were presented by *Krakivs'ki visti* as almost homogeneously Ukrainian, but this was not the case, particularly with regard to the great massacres in L'viv in 1941. The writers and editors wanted to capitalize on the tragedies. They could then present the list of Ukrainian national aspirations written in the blood of martyrs. This was the discursive strategy adopted by some representatives of a borderlands people caught up in the immense violence of two large, expanding states. They denounced the violence of one of the states, accepted the violence of the other, and sought to use the violence and the rhetoric of violence to advance their own position and to injure those whom they perceived as their rivals or opponents.

The events of the war were to change forever the ethnic makeup of this Polish-Ukrainian borderland. In 1939, when World War II broke out, the Western Ukrainian territories were located in a multinational state, Poland. Neither Poles nor Ukrainians were, on the whole, happy with this mixture of ethnicities on the same territory. Polish politicians, especially on the nationalist right, imagined that they could, over the long term, assimilate the Ukrainian population to Polish nationality. Many of these politicians also imagined that they could make conditions for the Jews uncomfortable enough to induce them to emigrate. They pictured an ethnically homogeneous Polish national state instead of a polity riddled with national minorities. The Ukrainians imagined a state independent of Poland or any other state. Ukrainians associated with the Organization of Ukrainian Nationalists imagined this state as a "Ukraine for the Ukrainians," ethnically pure, with neither Poles nor Jews.

In 1939 the aspirations of both the Poles and the Ukrainians were shattered by the annexation of Western Ukraine to the Soviet Union. Although many Poles thought they could someday regain the annexed territories, they were, in fact, decisively excluded from them by the events of the war, deported by the Soviets and murdered by the Ukrainian nationalists.

Ukrainian nationalists recognized the danger that the Soviets posed to them and to their hopes. Many therefore fled to the German zone of occupation, where they plotted and propagandized for the nationalist cause. Those who remained at home in Galicia were murdered in the thousands by the Soviet state when Nazi Germany attacked.

The German invasion opened new possibilities to the Ukrainian nationalists to implement their program. The nationalists felt that if they worked closely with Germany, the state they wanted would find its place in Hitler's New Europe. Although this was not something that the radical Nazi leadership was willing to consider, the Ukrainians had no other options. They found common ground with the Germans on several issues. Both the Ukrainian nationalists and the Germans were interested in the destruction of the Soviet state and the displacement of the Russians further to the east. Moreover, the Ukrainians' ethnic cleansing project overlapped in part with the Germans' determination to destroy the Jews. From this violent context—of shattered borderlands and ethnic surgeries—the discourse which we have examined easily emerged.

NOTES

This article was first read as a paper at the Borderlands Workshop 2004: "Interethnic Coexistence and Violence in Europe's Eastern Borderlands: The Local Community and the State," Watson Institute for International Studies, Brown University, Providence RI, 15–16 May 2004. I am grateful to Omer Bartov for inviting me and to all the participants for their valuable comments. I would also like to thank Karyn Ball, Jeffrey Burds, Chrystia Chomiak, and Alan Rutkowski for their comments and suggestions. Thanks are also due to Taras Kurylo for research assistance.

1. On the NKVD murders see: Bogdan Musial, *"Konterrevolutionäre Elemente sind zu erschießen": Die Brutalisierung des deutsch-sowjetischen Krieges im Sommer 1941* (Berlin: Propyläen, 2000); there is also a Polish-language version: Bogdan Musiał, *Rozstrzelać elementy kontrrewolucyjne!: brutalizacja wojny niemiecko-sowieckiej latem 1941 roku* (Warsaw: Stowarzyszenie Kulturalne Fronda, 2001); see too the important critiques by Dieter Pohl in H-Soz-u-Kult, 30 April 2001, http://hsozkult.geschichte.hu-berlin.de/rezensio/buecher/2001/PoDi0401.htm (accessed 15 February 2012), and Per Anders Rudling, "Bogdan Musial and the Question of Jewish Responsibility for the Pogroms in L'viv in the Summer of 1941," *East European Jewish Affairs* 35(1) (June 2005): 69–89; Jan T. Gross, *Revolution from Abroad: The Soviet Conquest of Poland's Western Ukraine and Western Belorussia* (Princeton: Princeton University Press, 1988), 144–86; Alfred M. De Zayas, with the collaboration of Walter Rabus, *The Wehrmacht War Crimes Bureau, 1939–1945* (Lincoln: University of Nebraska Press, 1980), 214–27; Milena Rudnyts'ka, ed., *Zakhidnia Ukraina pid bol'shevykamy, IX.1939—VI.1941* (New York: n.p., 1958); Oleh Romaniv and Inna Fedushchak, *Zakhidnoukrains'ka trahediia 1941* (L'viv: Naukove tovarystvo im. Shevchenka, 2002); Krzysztof Popiński, Aleksandr Kokurin, and Aleksandr Gurjanow, *Drogi śmierci. Ewakuacja więzień sowieckich z Kresów Wschodnich II Rzeczypospolitej w czerwcu i lipcu 1941* (Warsaw: Karta, 1995); Iaroslav Lial'ka, et al., eds., *Litopys neskorenoi Ukrainy. Dokumenty, materialy, spohady*, vol. 1 (L'viv: Instytut ukrainoznavstva AN Ukrainy, 1993), 32–197.

2. On the pogroms in Western Ukraine, see: Dieter Pohl, *Nationalsozialistische Judenverfolgung in Ostgalizien 1941–1944: Organisation und Durchführung eines staatlichen Massenverbrechens* (Munich: R. Oldenbourg Verlag, 1997), 54–67; Andrzej Zbikowski, "Local Anti-Jewish Pogroms in the Occupied Territories of Eastern Poland, June–July 1941" in *The Holocaust in the Soviet Union: Studies and Sources on the Destruction of the Jews in the Nazi-Occupied Territories of the USSR, 1941–1945*, ed. Lucjan Dobroszycki and Jeffrey S. Gurock (Armonk, N.Y.: M. E. Sharpe, 1993), 173–79; Eliiakhu Iones, *Evrei L'vova v gody Vtoroi Mirovoi Voiny i Katastrofy evropeiskogo evreistva, 1939–1944* (Moscow: Rossiiskaia biblioteka Kholokosta, 1999), 93–99; Martin Gilbert, *Atlas of the*

Holocaust (London: Michael Joseph, 1982), 67. Some non-Jews who had collaborated with the Soviets were also targeted by the pogroms.

3. One member of the team, Dr. Gerhart Panning, had previously advised Nazi killing squads how best to execute their victims and also conducted medical experiments on Jewish POWs. Wendy Lower, *Nazi Empire-Building and the Holocaust in Ukraine* (Chapel Hill: The University of North Carolina Press in association with the United States Holocaust Memorial Museum, 2005), 79–83.

4. On Vinnytsia see the official report commissioned by the Ostministerium and published by the Nazi party: *Amtliches Material zum Massenmord von Winnica* (Berlin: Zentralverlag des NSDAP, Franz Eher, 1944). See also: Ihor Kamenetsky, ed., *The Tragedy of Vinnytsia: Materials on Stalin's Policy of Extermination in Ukraine during the Great Purge 1936–1938* (Toronto: Ukrainian Historical Association in cooperation with Bahriany Foundation Inc. and Ukrainian Research and Documentation Center, 1989). There is a superb analysis of the whole Vinnytsia incident and its place in collective memories: Irina Paperno, "Exhuming the Bodies of Soviet Terror," *Representations* 75 (Summer 2001): 89–118.

5. John-Paul Himka, "*Krakivs'ki visti*: An Overview," in *Cultures and Nations of Central and Eastern Europe: Essays in Honor of Roman Szporluk,* ed. Zvi Gitelman et al. (Cambridge, Mass.: Distributed by the Harvard University Press for the Ukrainian Research Institute, Harvard University, 2000), 251–61. Idem, "*Krakivski visti* and the Jews, 1943: A Contribution to the History of Ukrainian-Jewish Relations during the Second World War," *Journal of Ukrainian Studies* 21(1–2) (Summer–Winter 1996): 81–95.

6. Michael Chomiak Papers, Provincial Archives of Alberta, accession no. 85.191, items 24–68.

7. On the Polish-language press in the General Government, see: Lucjan Dobroszycki, *Reptile Journalism: The Official Polish-Language Press under the Nazis, 1939–1945,* trans. Barbara Harshav (New Haven: Yale University Press, 1994); Grzegorz Hryciuk, "*Gazeta Lwowska" 1941–1944,* Historia 89 (Wrocław: Wydawnictwo Uniwersytetu Wrocławskiego, 1992); Klaus-Peter Friedrich, "Die deutsche polnischsprachige Presse im Generalgouvernement (1939–1945): NS-Propaganda für die polnische Bevölkerung," *Publizistik* 46(2) (June 2001): 162–88; Klaus-Peter Friedrich, "Publizistische Kollaboration im sog. Generalgouvernement: Personengeschichtliche Aspekte der deutschen Okkupationsherrschaft in Polen (1939–1945)," *Zeitschrift für Ostmitteleuropa-Forschung* 48(1) (1999): 50–89. For a study of antisemitic iconography in another Ukrainian-language newspaper in the General Government, see: Henry Abramson, "'This is the Way It Was!' Textual and Iconographic Images of Jews in the Nazi-Sponsored Ukrainian Press of Distrikt Galizien," in *Why Didn't the Press Shout? American & International Journalism during the Holocaust,* ed. Robert Moses Shapiro (Jersey City, N.J.: Yeshiva University Press in association with KTAV Publishing House, Inc., 2003), 537–56; there is an expanded German version: Henry Abramson, "Nachrichten aus Lemberg: Lokale Elemente in der antisemitischen Ikonographie der NS-Propaganda in ukrainischer Sprache" in Irmtrud Wojak and Susanne Meinl, eds., *Grenzlose Vorurteile: Antisemitismus, Nationalismus und ethnische Konflikte in verschiedenen Kulturen* (Frankfurt: Campus Verlag, 2002), 249–68. On Jewish themes in the Eastern Galician press under the occupation, see Zhanna Kovba, "Periodychni vydannia Skhidnoi Halychyny (lypen' 1941–lypen' 1944) iak dzherelo doslidzhennia povedinky mistsevoho naselennia v umovakh fashysts'koho 'ostatochnoho vyrishennia ievreis'koho pytannia," in *Ievreis'ka istoriia ta kul'tura v Ukraini. Materialy konferentsii. Kyiv 2–5 veresnia 1996* (Kiev: Instytut iudaiky, 1997), 56–60. There is a collection of articles on the Ukrainian press during the Nazi occupation: *Naukovi zapysky,* Natsional'na akademiia nauk Ukrainy, Instytut politychnykh i etnonatsional'nykh doslidzhen' im. I. F. Kurasa, vol. 31 (Kiev, 2006). A study of antisemitism in a Russian-language newspaper under Nazi occupation: Robert Edwin Herzstein, "Anti-Jewish Propaganda in the Orel Region of Great Russia, 1942–1943: The German Army and Its Russian Collaborators," *Simon Wiesenthal Center Annual* no. 6, available at http://motlc.wiesenthal.com.

8. "Zhakhlyvi bol'shevyts'ki masakry u L'vovi," *Krakivs'ki visti* [hereafter KV], 6 July 1941. After the war Kotorovych edited a periodical (*Nedilia*) for Ukrainian displaced persons in Germany; it came out weekly in the camps in 1945–49 and then was published irregularly in Munich and Augsburg from 1950 until his death in 1956. I have only seen a few issues of *Nedilia*. One carries the story of a shady deal masterminded by a Jewish swindler in which several Ukrainians were also involved. It appears that this was written by Kotorovych himself. (R.) [Redaktor?] "Ukrains'ko-zhydivs'ka afera v SShA," *Nedilia* no. 14 (212) (September 1951): 4–5, 7.

9. "Podii na zakhidn'o-ukrains'kykh zemliakh (Interviu z dots. d-rom H.I. Baierom)," KV, 6 July 1941. In the editorial note Dr. Beyer is identified as "a coworker of the L'viv city commandant." For an account of Beyer's complicity in Nazi crimes, including atrocities against Jews and Poles in L'viv in the summer of 1941, see Karl Heinz Roth, "Heydrichs Professor: Historiographie des 'Volkstums' und der Massenvernichtungen: Der Fall Hans Joachim Beyer," in *Geschichtsschreibung als Legitimationswissenschaft 1918-1945*, ed. Peter Schöttler (Frankfurt am Main: Suhrkamp, 1997), 262–342.

10. "Bol'shevyts'kyi pohrom u L'vovi," KV 6 July 1941.

11. "Vistky zi L'vova," KV, 9 July 1941.

12. Amir Weiner, *Making Sense of War: The Second World War and the Fate of the Bolshevik Revolution* (Princeton: Princeton University Press, 2001), 67 n73.

13. "Masove vbyvstvo ukraintsiv bilia Vynnytsi," KV, 23 June 1943.

14. Mariian Kozak [mk], "Bez niiakykh oman," KV, 27 June 1943.

15. Michael Chomiak Papers, item 41.

16. In the "Lebenslauf" Anatol' Kurdydyk submitted to *Krakivs'ki visti* when applying to be their correspondent, he recommended himself as the author of many articles "about the NSDAP, Adolf Hitler, the Third Reich and its problems in the best tone." In 1937–38 he published "the anti-Communist and anti-Jewish weekly *Frontom*, which under Jewish pressure was banned by the Poles." In those years he also had relations with *Stürmer* and *Antikommintern* in Berlin. Michael Chomiak Papers, item 31. After the war Kurdydyk edited Ukrainian-language periodicals in Toronto and Winnipeg. See his obituary, "Anatol Kurdydyk, 95, Longtime Editor of Ukrainian Canadian Newspapers," *Ukrainian Weekly*, 15 July 2001; also R. L. Chomiak, in "Tribute to the Late Anatol Kurdydyk, 'a Mere Editor of the Ukrainian Press,'" *Ukrainian Weekly*, 2 September 2001.

17. Michael Chomiak Papers, item 41.

18. "Dal'shi podrobytsi zvirstva NKVD bilia Vynnytsi," KV, 11 July 1943.

19. "Oburennia i vidraza u vsikh ukraintsiv," KV, 11 July 1943.

20. Gennadii Kotorovych [KTV; the pseudonym derives from three consonants in his last name], "Zhakhlyvi bol'shevyts'ki masakry u L'vovi," KV, 6 July 1941.

21. "Podii na zakhidn'o-ukrains'kykh zemliakh (Interviu z dots. d-rom H.I. Baierom)," KV, 6 July 1941.

22. "Zhakhlyvyi pohrom ukraintsiv," KV, 8 July 1941.

23. Musial cogently argues that the crucifixions were staged and some of the mutilations were performed after the corpses were discovered, but before they were put on display for the public. He believes that Ukrainian nationalists tampered with the corpses in order to intensify the propaganda effect. Musial, "*Konterrevolutionäre Elemente sind zu erschießen*," 262–69. See also Hannes Heer, "Lemberg 1941: Die Instrumentalisierung der NKVD-Verbrechen für Judenmord," in *Kriegsverbrechen im 20. Jahrhundert*, ed. Wolfram Wette and Gerd R. Ueberschär (Darmstadt, Germany: Primus Verlag, 2001), 168–70. Further evidence is presented in Alexander V. Prusin, "The 'Zone of Violence': The Anti-Jewish Pogroms in East Galicia in 1914–1915 and 1941," paper presented at the final conference of the Borderlands Project, Marburg, 17–20 May 2007 (and see chapter 19). Alan Rutkowski has pointed out to me that the crucifixions may have been intended to evoke the image of Jews as Christ-killers.

24. "Kryvavi bol'shevyts'ki zvirstva u L'vovi," KV, 9 July 1941.

25. "Z bol'shevyts'koho pekla u L'vovi," KV, 9 July 1941.

26. "Vrazhinnia zi L'vova," KV, 18 July 1941. To date, using NKVD records and other information, 1,603 of the victims in L'viv have been identified by name. The NKVD reported 1,808 executions. Inna Fedushchak, a Memorial activist in Ukraine, used contemporary press reports to estimate the number of murders here at 4,000. Romaniv and Fedushchak, *Zakhidnoukrains'ka trahediia 1941*, 56, 109–41, 155–65, 346.

27. "Masakra u viaznytsi NKVD u Dubni," KV, 8 July 1941. This was reprinted in *Zlochyny komunistychnoi Moskvy v Ukraini v liti 1941 roku* (New York: Proloh, 1960), 30, 32, with references to Jews omitted, also with no mention that it originally came from a German periodical. Fedushchak accepts the estimate of 1,500 victims in Dubno that appeared in *Ukrains'ki shchodenni visti*, but notes that an NKVD document referred to 260 shot and 60 prisoners whom they should have shot but did not get to. Romaniv and Fedushchak, *Zakhidnoukrains'ka trahediia 1941*, 62–63, 380.

28. "Zhakhlyva masakra 1500 ukraintsiv u Luts′ku," KV, 9 July 1941. Fedushchak accepts the estimate of a German source that mentioned 2,754 victims. An NKVD document reported 2,000 executions. Romaniv and Fedushchak, *Zakhidnoukrains′ka trahediia 1941*, 61–63, 348.

29. "Strakhittia zolochivs′koi tsytadeli," KV, 17 July 1941. Feduschak estimates 749 victims; 485 have been identified by name. Romaniv and Fedushchak, *Zakhidnoukrains′ka trahediia 1941*, 63, 142–54.

30. "Zhakhlyvi dni v Stryiu," KV, 19 July 1941. Fedushchak accepts the NKVD figure of 1,101 victims. There are two very incomplete lists of victims with some overlapping names (one list has 29 names on it, the other 66). Romaniv and Fedushchak, *Zakhidnoukrains′ka trahediia 1941*, 59, 174–78. On Zolochiv, see also: Bernd Boll, "Złoczów. July 1941: The Wehrmacht and the Beginning of the Holocaust in Galicia: From a Criticism of Photographs to a Revision of the Past" in *Crimes of War: Guilt and Denial in the Twentieth Century*, ed. Omer Bartov, Atina Grossmann, and Mary Nolan (New York: The New Press, 2002), 61–99, 275–83.

31. "Ochevydets′ iz Sambora pro dni zhakhu," KV, 20 July 1941. Fedushchak accepts the figure of 1,200 victims from *Ukrains′ki shchodenni visti*. There is a list of 97 names. Romaniv and Fedushchak, *Zakhidnoukrains′ka trahediia 1941*, 59, 63, 179–82.

32. "1500 ukraintsiv zamorduvaly bol′shevyky u Kremiantsi," KV, 6 August 1941; reprinted in *Zlochyny komunistychnoi Moskvy*, 42, almost exactly. Using a Polish study from 1995, Feduschak cites 150 victims. Romaniv and Fedushchak, *Zakhidnoukrains′ka trahediia 1941*, 61.

33. L′vovianyn, "Zi L′vova i z kraiu. Masakra ukrains′kykh viazniv u Shchyrtsi," KV, 24 August 1941. Fedushchak accepts 30 victims from contemporary press reports; there is a list of 15 names. Romaniv and Fedushchak, *Zakhidnoukrains′ka trahediia 1941*, 58, 168.

34. "700 muchenykiv u Dobromyl′shchyni," KV, 23 July 1941. Based on contemporary press reports, Feduschak estimates 1,000 victims. Romaniv and Fedushchak, *Zakhidnoukrains′ka trahediia 1941*, 58–59, 63.

35. "Vistky z kraiu. Masakra viazniv u Chortkovi," 7 August 1941. Feduschak estimates 800 victims in Chortkiv based on contemporary press reports, but notes that another 954 were killed on a forced march to Uman. There are lists of 11 victims in Chortkiv prison and the 796 who died on the forced march. Romaniv and Fedushchak, *Zakhidnoukrains′ka trahediia 1941*, 61, 63, 209–30.

36. In the end, the official German report would state that 9,432 bodies were recovered from the graves at Vinnytsia; the report included a list of 679 victims who were identified by name. *Amtliches Material zum Massenmord von Winnica*, 21, 215–48.

37. "Masove vbyvstvo ukraintsiv bilia Vynnytsi," KV, 23 June 1943.

38. "30 masovykh hrobiv bilia Vynnytsi," KV, 9 July 1943.

39. "Dal′shi podrobytsi zvirstva NKVD bilia Vynnytsi," KV, 11 July 1943.

40. Niilo Pesonen was an anatomist who achieved fame as a physical anthropologist in the 1930s. In the postwar period he served as director-general of the National Medical Board in Finland.

41. During the war Kentrzhyns′kyi was the official representative of the Melnyk faction of the Organization of Ukrainian Nationalists (OUN-M) in Finland; during this time he wrote several popular histories of Ukraine in Swedish. After the war he headed the Ukrainian Information Bureau in Stockholm, lectured on history at Stockholm University, and served as a research associate of the Swedish Royal Academy.

42. From the German report:

> In two . . . cases, a dissection of the esophagus and a careful exposure of the throat revealed that a thick loam had forced its way down to the middle of the esophagus and into the piriform recesses. These findings indisputably point to the fact that a vital function—namely, the swallowing mechanism—had still been intact in the two victims. Accordingly, they had still been alive when they came into close contact with the mass of earth that was then forced down into the esophagus a certain distance by the intact swallowing function.

Amtliches Material zum Massenmord von Winnica, 45. The translation is taken from Kamenetsky, ed., *The Tragedy of Vinnytsia*, 117.

43. [Bohdan] Kent[rzhyns′kyi], "Fins′kyi uchenyi pro vynnyts′ki vbyvstva. Interv″iu z profesorom Niil′o Pesonenom," KV, 6 August 1943. There is a second-hand account of such an orgy in Ievhen Nakonechnyi, *"Shoa" u L′vovi*, 2nd ed. (L′viv: Piramida, 2006), 85.

44. B. Halit, "Ne rydai, a zdobuvai," KV, 29 July 1941.

45. Anatol' Kurdydyk, "Kryvava propahanda Ukrainy," KV, 23 July 1941.

46. "Zakord. zhurnalisty pro bol'shevyts'kyi teror u L'vovi," KV, 9 July 1941.

47. Grendzha-Donsky was interned in a concentration camp by the Hungarians for some months in 1939, but was released and moved to Bratislava where he worked for the Ukrainian-language program on Slovak radio. He joined the Czechoslovak Communist Party in 1945 and, except for a period in the 1950s, was well-treated by the Communist authorities until he died in 1974. Another antisemitic article by this author: V. Grendzha-Dons'kyi, "Na vlasnykh sylakh," KV, 28 August 1941.

48. V. Grendzha-Dons'kyi, "Slovats'ka ta khorvats'ka presa pro bol'shevyts'ki zvirstva nad ukraintsiamy," KV, 29 July 1941.

49. "Za zakliatoiu bramoiu," KV, 10 July 1941.

50. "Nimets'ka presa pro Vynnytsiu," KV, 10 July 1943.

51. "Bel'hiiets' pro Vynnytsiu," KV, 15 July 1943.

52. "Frantsuz'ki holosy pro Vynnytsiu," KV, 21 July 1943.

53. "Fins'kyi profesor pro vyslidy rozslidiv u Vynnytsi," KV, 21 July 1943.

54. "Reporter rumuns'koho radiia pro Vynnytsiu," KV, 21 July 1943. "Tserkovni dostoinyky Rumunii pro svoi vrazhennia z Vynnytsi," KV, 28 July 1943.

55. "Predstavnyky bolhars'koho i dans'koho uriadu u Vynnytsi," KV, 27 July 1943.

56. "Serby vidvidalay mistsia masovykh vbystv u Vynnytsi," KV, 19 September 1943.

57. A. Kurdydyk, "Vynnytsia i chuzhozemna presa," KV, 31 July 1943. Krakivs'ki visti did not print photographs from Vinnytsia.

58. A proponent of Italian fascism in the interwar period, Ievhen Onats'kyi had originally been critical of antisemitism and racism; by 1938 his views had changed (as evidenced by an antisemitic article he published in a Canadian Ukrainian-language newspaper). He lived in Rome between the wars and was the OUN representative there. The Germans imprisoned him for a year in 1943–44. In 1947 he moved to Buenos Aires and became the leading activist and writer of the Ukrainian community in Argentina. (I learned of Onats'kyi's involvement in the Canadian press and the change in his views on antisemitism from Orest T. Martynowych, "The Organization of Ukrainian Nationalists (OUN) and Ukrainian Canadians, 1929–1940," paper presented at the 35th National Convention of the American Association for the Advancement of Slavic Studies, Toronto, 20–23 November 2003.)

59. Ievhen Onats'kyi, "Vynnyts'ki strakhittia v italiis'kii presi," KV, 3 August 1943.

60. Osadchuk remained in Germany after the war and lives as a journalist. He has written frequently for Die Neue Zürcher Zeitung, Paris Kultura, and Suchasnist'. His relatively liberal attitudes and extraordinary gifts as a raconteur have made him a popular figure in both Polish and Ukrainian circles. An autobiography in the form of an interview mentions his connection with Krakivs'ki visti, but is not forthcoming about what he wrote there. Basil Kerski and Andrzej Stanisław Kowalczyk, eds., Ein ukrainischer Kosmopolit mit Berliner Adresse: Gespräche mit Bohdan Osadczuk (Alexander Korab) (Osnabrück, Germany: fibre, 2004), 30–32.

61. B[ohdan] O[sadchuk], "Kryvava propahanda Ukrainy. Vynnytsia v evropeis'kii presi," KV, 7 August 1943. Authorship established from Michael Chomiak Papers, item 32.

62. "Masovi bol'shevyts'ki vbyvstva v Ukraini," KV, 18 September 1943. Translated by K. The author of the original Danish article was Svend Aberg. The names of the periodical and the author were in Cyrillic characters, so my retransliteration into Latin characters may be incorrect.

63. P'ier Soné, "Val'onets' pro Vynnytsiu. Shcho ia pobachyv u Vynnytsi, novomu Katyni," KV, 10 August 1943. Translated from L'Effort Wallon, a weekly for Walloon workers published in Berlin.

64. [Bohdan] Kent[rzhyns'kyi], "Fins'kyi uchenyi pro vynnyts'ki vbyvstva. Interv''iu z profesorom Niil'o Pesonenom," KV, 6 August 1943.

65. Musial, "Konterrevolutionäre Elemente sind zu erschießen," 259–60.

66. "Bol'shevyts'kyi pohrom u L'vovi," KV, 6 July 1941. "Podii na zakhidn'o-ukrains'kykh zemliakh (Interviu z dots. d-rom H.I. Baierom)," KV, 6 July 1941. Volodymyr Kubiiovych, "Pered maiestatom nepovynnoi krovy," KV, 8 July 1941. "Zhakhlyvyi pohrom ukraintsiv," KV, 8 July 1941. "Kryvavi bol'shevyts'ki zvirstva u L'vovi," KV, 9 July 1941. "Vistky zi L'vova," KV, 9 July 1941. Gen-

nadii Kotorovych [KTV], "Svit klonyt' holovu pered trahediieiu Ukrainy," KV, 10 July 1941. Joseph Goebbels, "Zaslona opadaie," KV, 10 July 1941 (originally published in *Völkischer Beobachter,* no. 188, as the lead article). "1500 ukraintsiv zamorduvaly bol'shevyky u Kremiantsi," KV, 6 August 1941. "Vistky z kraiu. Masakra viazniv u Chortkovi," KV, 7 August 1941.

67. "Bol'shevyts'kyi pohrom u Dobromyl'shchyni," KV, 6 August 1941. There were Ukrainian prosecutors, of course; Mykhailo Seleshko learned of one in Vinnytsia. Mykhailo Seleshko, *Vinnytsia. Spomyny perekladacha komisii doslidiv zlochyniv NKVD v 1937-1938,* ed. Vasyl' Veryha (New York: Fundatsiia im. O. Ol'zhycha, 1991), 93.

68. "Masakra u viaznytsi NKVD u Dubni," KV, 8 July 1941.

69. "Zhakhlyva masakra 1500 ukraintsiv u Luts'ku," KV, 9 July 1941. The newspaper claimed the report was translated from war correspondent Kurt Hampe in *Völkischer Beobachter.*

70. Romaniv and Fedushchak, *Zakhidnoukrains'ka trahediia 1941,* 109-65.

71. Grzegorz Hryciuk, *Polacy we Lwowie 1939-1944. Zycie codzienne* (Warsaw: Książka i Wiedza, 2000), 188, 190.

72. Christof Mick, "Ethnische Gewalt und Pogrome in Lemberg 1914 und 1941," *Osteuropa* 53, no. 12 (December 2003): 1825.

73. Romaniv and Fedushchak, *Zakhidnoukrains'ka trahediia 1941,* 171-73.

74. Ibid., 193-208.

75. "Masove vbyvstvo ukraintsiv bilia Vynnytsi," KV, 23 June 1943. Mariian Kozak [mk], "Bez niiakykh oman," KV, 27 June 1943. "30 masovykh hrobiv bilia Vynnytsi," KV, 9 July 1943. "Dokumenty bol'shevyts'koi zhadoby nyshchennia," KV, 10 July 1943. "Vynnyts'ki mohyly," KV, 11 July 1943. "Oburennia i vidraza u vsikh ukraintsiv," KV, 11 July 1943. Ivan Lysiak [P. H.], "Nad vidkrytymy mohylamy u Vynnytsi," KV, 13 July 1943. "Dal'shi podrobytsi pro masovi mohyly u Vynnytsi," KV, 13 July 1943. D-r H.K[urz], "Na mistsi zlochynu," KV, 30 July 1943. A. Kurdydyk, "Vynnytsia i chuzhozemna presa," KV, 31 July 1943. Ievhen Onats'kyi, "Vynnyts'ki strakhittia v italiis'kii presi," KV, 3 August 1943.

76. "Vynnyts'ki zhertvy," KV, 16 July 1943.

77. "Vyna' vynnyts'kykh zhertv," KV, 17 July 1943.

78. *Amtliches Material zum Massenmord von Winnica,* 124.

79. Kamenetsky, ed., *The Tragedy of Vinnytsia,* 27.

80. Weiner, *Making Sense of War,* 67 n. 73.

81. Seleshko, *Vinnytsia,* 92.

82. Paperno, "Exhuming the Bodies of Soviet Terror," 105.

83. "The mass graves in the city of Vinnitsia, of these Ukrainian patriots shot by NKVD agents in 1937-38, uncovered during World War II, are witnesses to the terror exercised in Ukraine by Stalin's men." Isidore Nahayewsky, *History of Ukraine* (Philadelphia: "America" Publishing House of the "Providence" Association of Ukrainian Catholics in America, 1962), 232.

84. "Vynnyts'ki zhertvy," KV, 16 July 1943.

85. D-r H. K[urz]., "Na mistsi zlochynu," KV, 30 July 1943. The author wrote from Berlin. Author identified from the list of honoraria for *Krakivs'ki Visti,* Michael Chomiak Papers, item 32.

86. Paperno, "Exhuming the Bodies of Soviet Terror."

87. Kubijovyč eventually settled in Paris after the war. A geographer and prodigious scholar, he was in the leadership of the Shevchenko Scientific Society and was general editor of the Ukrainian encyclopedias published in Ukrainian and English in Europe and North America. He died in 1985.

88. Volodymyr Kubiiovych, "Pered maiestatom nepovynnoi krovy," KV, 8 July 1941.

89. The late Taras Zakydalsky, who read an earlier draft of this article, considered my interpretation to be "neither convincing nor fair" as well as "the most uncharitable interpretation." Letter of 24 January 2006. I base my interpretation upon the context of the reporting, but also upon Kubijovyč's political thinking in the summer of 1941. On 21 June 1941 he presented a memorial to Hans Frank requesting that a Ukrainian territory be established in the General Government and proposed "to purge the territory of the Polish and Jewish element by resettlement." Wasyl Veryha, comp., *The Correspondence of the Ukrainian Central Committe in Cracow and L'viv with the German Authorities 1939-1944,* 2 pts., Research Report No. 61 (Edmonton: Canadian Institute of Ukrainian Studies Press, 2000), 1: 242. On 29 August he wrote to Frank:

> Considering that all Jewish property originally belonged for the most part to the Ukrainian people and only through ruthless law-breaking on the part of the Jews and through their exploitation of members of the Ukrainian people did it pass into Jewish possession, we deem it a requirement of justice, in order to make restitution to the Ukrainian people for moral and material damages, that a very considerable portion of confiscated Jewish property be returned to the Ukrainian people. In particular, all Jewish land holdings should be given to Ukrainian peasants.

Ibid., 1: 342.

90. Gennadii Kotorovych [KTV], "Zhakhlyvi bol'shevyts'ki masakry u L'vovi," KV, 6 July 1941.

91. Kazimierz Bartel was a professor of mathematics at L'viv Polytechnic and was several times prime minister, but never president, of Poland. He was one of the 23 Polish professors arrested by the Germans on the night of 3 July 1941; he was executed on 26 July. For a first-hand admission of the involvement in this incident of the Banderist OUN, see Roman Volchuk, *Spomyny z peredvoiennoho L'vova ta voiennoho Vidnia* (Kiev: Krytyka, 2000), 89–90.

92. "Podii na zakhidn'o-ukrains'kykh zemliakh (Interviu z dots. d-rom H.I. Baierom)," KV, 6 July 1941.

93. Mariian Kozak [M. K.], "Peklo bol'shevyts'kykh viaznyts'. Ochevydets' pro kryvavu masakru ukraintsiv u Luts'ku," KV, 15 July 1941.

94. "Nema porivnan'," KV, 18 July 1941.

95. "Iak tryvoha, to do Boha," KV, 19 July 1941.

96. "Ochevydets' iz Sambora pro dni zhakhu," KV, 20 July 1941.

97. Jan Tomasz Gross and Irena Grudzińska-Gross, eds., *War through Children's Eyes: The Soviet Occupation of Poland and the Deportations, 1939–1941,* Hoover Press Publication 247 (Stanford: Hoover Institution Press, Stanford University, 1981), 115, 119, 131–32, 139, 141, 149–50, 169–70, 174, 180, 193–98, 201.

98. For example in Yury Boshyk, ed., *Ukraine during World War II: History and Its Aftermath: A Symposium* (Edmonton: Canadian Institute of Ukrainian Studies, 1986), or in the film *Between Hitler and Stalin: Ukraine in World War II—The Untold Story* directed by Slavko Nowytski and sponsored by the Ukrainian Canadian Research and Documentation Centre.

99. Sixty-three percent in May 1940. Bohdan Krawchenko, *Social Change and National Consciousness in Twentieth-Century Ukraine* (London: Macmillan in association with St Antony's College, Oxford, 1985), 150.

100. Gennadii Kotorovych [KTV], "Svit klonyt' holovu pered trahediieiu Ukrainy," KV, 10 July 1941.

101. "Vynnyts'ki mohyly," KV, 11 July 1943.

102. "Oburennia i vidraza u vsikh ukraintsiv," KV, 11 July 1943.

103. D. S., "Pidstava bol'shevyts'koho teroru," KV, 15 July 1943.

104. Mariian Kozak [mk], "Bez niiakykh oman," KV, 27 June 1943.

105. Ivan L. Rudnytsky was one of the founders of the Canadian Institute of Ukrainian Studies and professor of Ukrainian history at the University of Alberta from 1971 until his death in 1984. See the collection of his seminal articles: Ivan L. Rudnytsky, *Essays in Modern Ukrainian History,* ed. Peter L. Rudnytsky (Edmonton: Canadian Institute of Ukrainian Studies, University of Alberta, 1987). Rudnytsky was never attracted by the kind of nationalism represented by the OUN and in fact criticized it from a perspective that was a mix of classical liberalism and conservatism. At the time he submitted his article to *Krakiv'ki visti* he had just received his master's degree in Berlin.

106. Ivan Lysiak [P. H.], "Nad vidkrytymy mohylamy u Vynnytsi," KV, 13 July 1943. Authorship established on the basis of the Michael Chomiak Papers, items 32 (honorarium) and 41 (letter of Mariian Kozak to Ivan Lysiak, 14 July 1943).

107. "Zhakhlyvyi pohrom ukraintsiv," KV, 8 July 1941.

108. "Masakra u viaznytsi NKVD u Dubni," KV, 8 July 1941.

109. Bold type in the original. "Z bol'shevyts'koho pekla u L'vovi," KV, 9 July 1941.

110. Hryhorii was bishop of Vinnytsia for the Ukrainian Autocephalous Orthodox Church (UAOC). After the war he served as a bishop of the UAOC in Germany, but he split from the mainstream church in 1947 to support the conciliarist faction. In 1950 he moved to America as bishop of the Conciliarist UAOC.

111. "Masovi bol'shevyts'ki vbyvstva v Ukraini," KV, 18 September 1943. This was the article translated from the Danish periodical for workers in Germany.

112. "Pokhorony zhertv u Vynnytsi," KV, 16 July 1943. The full text of the sermon was printed separately: *Promova holovy Avtokefal'noi Pravoslavnoi Tserkvy Zhytomyrs'koi Heneral'noi Okruhy, Iepyskopa Hryhoriia proholoshena nad mohylamy zamordovanykh Ukraintsiv vid ruk NKVD mista Vinnytsi.* A copy can be found in United States Holocaust Memorial Museum RG-31.017M, reel 1, Derzhavnyi Arkhiv Rivnens'koi Oblasti, f. 30, op. 1, od. zb. 16, f. 16. For more antisemitic pronouncements from the hierarchy of the Ukrainian Autocephalous Orthodox Church, see Karel C. Berkhoff, *Harvest of Despair: Life and Death in Ukraine under Nazi Rule* (Cambridge, Mass.: The Belknap Press of Harvard University Press, 2003), 83–84, 250, 255.

113. D-r H.K[urz], "Na mistsi zlochynu," KV, 30 July 1943.

114. Himka, "*Krakivski visti* and the Jews."

115. Seleshko, *Vinnytsia,* 92.

116. Matthew Kott, "The Portrayal of Soviet Atrocities in the Nazi-controlled Latvian-language Press and the First Wave of Antisemitic Violence in Riga, July–August 1941," in *Collaboration and Resistance during the Holocaust: Belarus, Estonia, Latvia, Lithuania,* ed. David Gaunt, Paul A. Levine, and Laura Palosuo (Bern, Switzerland: Peter Lang, 2004), 137 n37.

117. N. V. Petrov and K. V. Skorkin, *Kto rukovodil NKVD 1934–1941. Spravochnik,* ed. N. G. Okhotin and A. B. Roginskii (Moscow: Obshchestvo "Memorial," 1999), 495. Weiner, *Making Sense of War,* 269 n101.

118. Volodymyr Kubiiovych, "Pered maiestatom nepovynnoi krovy," KV, 8 July 1941.

119. "Haslo dnia," KV, 9 July 1941.

120. "Oburennia i vidraza u vsikh ukraintsiv," KV, 11 July 1943.

121. "Vistky zi L'vova," KV, 12 July 1941.

122. "Vistky z kraiu. Masakra viazniv u Chortkovi," KV, 7 August 1941.

123. "Kryvavyi teror na ukrains'kykh zemliakh," KV, 10 July 1941.

124. "Chervonyi teror liutuie i nad ukrains'kymy selamy," KV, 11 July 1941.

125. "Kryvavi bol'shevyts'ki zvirstva u L'vovi," KV, 9 July 1941. "Zhakhlyva masakra 1500 ukraintsiv u Luts'ku," KV, 9 July 1941. "Bol'shevyky spalyly zhyvtsem 180 ukraintsiv. Zhorstokyi bol'shevyts'kyi teror u Stanyslavovi," KV, 15 July 1941. "Strakhittia zolochivs'koi tsytadeli," KV, 17 July 1941. "Zhertvy NKVD," KV, 27 July 1941, reprinted in *Zlochyny komunistychnoi Moskvy* 69, with minor omissions. "Masakra u tserkvi v Kamiantsi Pod.," KV, 27 July 1941. "Zhertvy NKVD v Drohobychi," KV, 3 August 1941, reprinted in *Zlochyny komunistychnoi Moskvy,* 30, as a slightly different text, with omissions and the wrong date. "1500 ukraintsiv zamorduvaly bol'shevyky u Kremiantsi," KV, 6 August 1941. "Bol'shevyts'ki strakhittia v Halychyni," KV, 21 August 1941. L'vovianyn, "Zi L'vova i z kraiu. Masakra ukrains'kykh viazniv u Shchyrtsi," KV, 24 August 1941. "Dokumenty bol'shevyts'koi zhadoby nyshchennia," KV, 10 July 1943. "Dal'shi podrobytsi pro masovi mohyly u Vynnytsi," KV, 13 July 1943. "Vynnyts'ki zhertvy," KV, 16 July 1943. A. Kurdydyk, "Vynnytsia i chuzhozemna presa," KV, 31 July 1943. "Nimets'ki robitnyky nad masovymy mohylamy u Vynnytsi," KV, 3 August 1943. [Bohdan] Kent[rzhyns'kyi], "F'nns'kyi uchenyi pro vynnyts'ki vbyvstva. Interv"iu z profesorom Niil'o Pesonenom," KV, 6 August 1943.

126. In addition to what has already been cited, see: "Zhydivstvo i bol'shevyky," KV, 11 July 1941. "Zhydivs'ka derzhava. Providni liudy bol'shevyzmu," KV, 15 July 1941. "Dynastiia Kaganovychiv. Rolia zhydiv u NKVD," KV, 15 July 1941.

21

COMMUNAL GENOCIDE

PERSONAL ACCOUNTS OF THE DESTRUCTION OF BUCZACZ, EASTERN GALICIA, 1941–1944

OMER BARTOV

I.

The borderlands of Eastern Europe were sites of interaction between a multiplicity of ethnic and religious groups. For city- and town-dwellers, as much as for villagers, living side-by-side with people who spoke a different language and worshipped God differently was part of their own way of life and that of their ancestors. For many, their difference in ethnicity and religion from their neighbors corresponded to different positions within the socioeconomic scale, and this differentiation between those with status and wealth and those living in poverty and subjugation created resentment and envy. As new national narratives began to supplement the old religious and social differentiation between groups, they also provided new retrospective meanings to the past and fueled a new urgency about mending the present in a manner that would conform to perceived historical rights and correct perceived historical injustices. In the fantasy each national movement shared, the future belonged to *them,* or to no one at all. The coexistence which had been the status quo of people's lives, with all its benefits and shortcomings, friction and cooperation, as well as its occasional outbursts of violence, came to be seen as unnatural, as a problem to be solved, often by radical social surgery. Cutting off unwanted, seemingly malignant and allegedly foreign elements would, it was said, enable the newly discovered and supposedly eternal national body to thrive.

It is, however, exceedingly difficult to understand and analyze how this transformation occurred on the ground and how it was perceived by its social protagonists. How was it that zones of coexistence were turned into communities of ethnic cleansing and genocide? To be sure, it was largely external forces, in the shape of occupying states or far-flung national movements, that determined the general course of events and provided the ideological impetus for population policies, mass displacement, and mass murder. But the way such policies and ideas were implemented on the ground had to do not only with the interaction between perpetrators and victims but also with the actions and interactions of the different local groups upon which these policies were enacted. A close look at what happened in small communities on Europe's eastern borderlands provides us with much insight into the social dynamics of interethnic communities at times of extreme violence. Yet such a view from below of borderland communities also necessitates making use of records of the past often eschewed by historians.

This chapter makes a case for the integration of personal accounts, or testimonies, into the historical reconstruction of the Holocaust as documents with equal validity to more official sources. By testimonies I mean all forms of evidence provided by individual protagonists in historical events. These include contemporary accounts and diaries, as well as postwar interviews, written, oral, audio- and video-taped testimonies, courtroom witness accounts, and memoirs. Such testimonies were given by people belonging to all three categories we have come to associate with the Holocaust and other genocides, namely, victims, perpetrators, and bystanders. But to a great extent, one benefit of using materials of this kind is that they largely, though not entirely, undermine this very categorization.

From the point of view of the historian, the single most important benefit of using testimonies is that they bring into history events that would otherwise remain completely unknown, since they are missing from more conventional documentation found in archives, which are mostly written by the perpetrators or organizers of genocide. Hence personal accounts can at times save events from oblivion. But they also provide a very different perspective on events that *are* known from conventional documentation. This other perspective has in turn two additional advantages. First, it may serve as a factual correction to official accounts; second, it provides the historian with a different vantage point and thereby helps to produce a richer and more complex—in a sense, a three-dimensional—reconstruction of the event as a whole. Finally, by virtue of being personal, or subjective, such testimonies provide insight into the lives and minds of the men, women, and children who experienced the events, and thus tell us much more than any official document about the mental landscape of the period, the psychology of the protagonists, and the views and perceptions of others.

Historians have traditionally been wary of using testimonies as historical evidence. Some have eschewed their use altogether, calling them subjective and therefore unreliable.[1] Others have preferred to use only testimonies very close to the event itself and largely avoided those given decades later.[2] Others still, most conventionally, use personal accounts only to illustrate the nature of a historical event whose reconstruction is based on seemingly more reliable documents culled from official archives.[3] This practice, to my mind, has greatly impoverished our understanding of the Holocaust, as it would that of any other historical event. There is no reason to believe that official contemporary documents written by Gestapo, SS, Wehrmacht, or German administrative officials are any more accurate or objective, or any less subjective and biased, than accounts by those they were trying to kill. Moreover, the use of testimonies only as confirmation of events already known through other documentation condemns to oblivion events only known through testimonies. Finally, the quest to understand the mentality and motivation of the perpetrators, which has already produced a small cottage industry, would benefit a great deal from knowing what their victims said about them and how *they* described their actions. And, of course, testimonies can tell us a great deal about the lives of those subjected to German occupation and the relations between the different ethnic groups that came under German rule.

As noted, some historians have argued that testimonies, if used at all, are more reliable the closer they are to the time of the event. Those given decades later are said to be suspect both because of the eroding effects of time on memory and because of the cumulative influence of other forms of representation and commemoration that mold the content and form of an individual's recollection. There is of course some truth to this argument. But anyone who has worked with large numbers of testimonies will know that there are two major qualifications to this assertion. First, that especially in the case of those who survived as young teenagers or even children—that is, those most likely to have still been alive six decades later—their experience in the Holocaust could often be recounted in full only after they reached greater maturity, thanks to the healing effects of time on their traumatized souls, and only long after rebuilding their lives and establishing new families. Second, that in some, though not all cases, testimonies given decades after the event do in fact have all the freshness and vividness of a first account that one may find in some early postwar testimonies. This makes particular sense in cases where the memory of an event was kept sealed inside the mind and never exposed to the light of day; without telling and retelling there is much less contamination by the "noise in the system" of external discourse and representation.

Many such "memory-boxes" were finally unlocked and opened up due to the advancing age of the witnesses and their desire to leave a record of events, whether simply to their own children and (especially) grandchildren, or more generally to posterity, at a cultural moment that many experienced as more attuned to listening (indeed, it has been designated by one scholar "the era of the witness").[4] Such testimonies are also strongly motivated by the urge to recall and inscribe in memory and history the names of the murdered that would otherwise sink into total oblivion with the passing of the witness, and at times also to record the names and actions of long-forgotten perpetrators, collaborators, and especially rescuers. Hence such testimonies contain much of the clarity and emotional impact of accounts given immediately in the wake of the events.

There has been, of course, a great deal of writing about testimonies as a form of memory, as a confrontation with trauma, a literary device, a means to gain insight into the psychology of survivors, or even as a therapeutic tool.[5] But what I am arguing for is that testimonies are also historical documents of invaluable importance that have been grossly underused by historians, especially in the case of the Holocaust, and despite the fact that this is an historical event that has produced a vast amount of such materials. Clearly, personal accounts do not tell a single story, and are full of contradictions, errors, misjudgments, and untruths—no less so than any other document. They should be treated with the same care and suspicion as any other piece of evidence pulled out of an archive, but also with the same respect, as yet another more or less important piece in the puzzle of the past. That they are concerned with traumatic events should not deter us from using them; quite to the contrary, the nature of those events must indicate to us that we would never be able to fathom them without making full use of the accounts of those who experienced them.

Integrating all these materials into a single text is clearly a difficult and complex undertaking. What one quickly realizes is that apart from such matters as chronology and geography—and not always even then—different protagonists saw and remembered the same event quite differently. Indeed, from the most elementary optical perspective, they did, since they were, so to speak, standing at different places, and because no two individuals can see the same event with precisely the same eyes. But beyond the optical perspective, such differences in view emanate from the fact that each person played a different role in the event. This, in turn, has also determined the manner in which they remembered it and in which they were willing or able to recall it in words or in writing.

There is, of course, nothing unique in this condition of historical documentation. Herodotus and Thucydides, whose different methods of treating their sources still guide us today, were already aware of this conundrum. The use of testimonies makes it more difficult to say what precisely happened at a given place and time; testimonies tell us more—perhaps more than we would like to know—about what happened, and they tell us that different people experienced and in some cases remembered and recorded the same events differently. We may decide to deliver a verdict on what actually happened on the basis of our documentation; or we may prefer to say that we are unable or unwilling to determine precisely what occurred and can simply report several versions or points of view.

Clearly, there are limitations to this kind of documentation. To my mind, testimonies can be most profitably used on two conditions. First, one must collect a critical mass of them, rather than relying on merely a few, if that is at all possible—although I would still argue that even a single testimony that "saves" an event from historical oblivion should and must be used. Second, such testimonies gain immensely from being focused on one locality and a relatively limited span of time and cast of characters. Within such a context, one can much more easily cross-check many testimonies that recount the same events from different perspectives, as well as integrate these individual perspectives into a historical reconstruction that uses all other available kinds of documentation. In the case of the Holocaust this would mean especially official reports by police, military, and civil administrations, as well as postwar trials and, finally, scholarly secondary literature.

One last issue cannot be avoided. The use of testimonies of trauma is a very difficult exercise for the historian. It is first of all difficult psychologically because these accounts almost invariably reveal aspects of human nature that one would rather not hear or know about. They are, in that sense, traumatizing. They may also undermine our trust in the historian's craft itself, since it is ultimately based on rationalist and Enlightenment values, on the alleged ability to divine the truth of the past and to identify humanity's progress and improvement. Testimonies also make it very difficult to retain the necessary detachment from the material; in other words, they may hamper the practice of the methods and undermine the philosophical assumptions that have come to be associated with good scholarly writing since the birth of the modern historical profession.

This is possibly the more profound reason for the reluctance of many historians to use testimonies. In other words, historians want to protect their own psychology from the damage they fear might be caused by, and to protect their profession from the undermining potential of, such testimonies. Yet these accounts are about an event that itself posed the greatest challenge to the values and methods on which the work of historians still bases itself today. These testimonies emanate from the very heart of that historical moment and site of darkness, and because they recount a historical event, they too are part of the historical record, perhaps the most crucial part of all.

Historians cannot escape the event and its implications for them as historians, as individual human beings, and as members of humankind, simply by leaving these accounts to gather dust in crumbling boxes. Historians need to face this challenge and cope with it as best they can. After all, these are accounts by individuals who were determined that what they experienced and saw and remembered would not be forgotten. Historians have largely betrayed these witnesses. By now the vast majority of them are dead. But their recorded accounts can and should still be used, not merely in order to respect those who left them behind, but in order to set the historical record straight.

In what follows, I will use testimonies by residents of the Eastern Galician town of Buczacz and by people who spent some time there during the German occupation, in order to explore some aspects of death and survival in an interethnic town at a time of genocide. In this region, the majority of the rural population was Ukrainian, while Poles and Jews constituted the majority of town and city dwellers. It belonged to Poland in the interwar period, was occupied by the Soviet Union in 1939–1941, and was ruled by the Germans in 1941–1944. My general argument here is that one of the central questions of historical research on the Holocaust in Eastern Europe—namely, the impact of local interethnic relations on the genocide of the Jews—must be analyzed through a close reading of testimonies by the protagonists in these events. I further suggest that this can be accomplished especially by examining a wide range of testimonies from a geographically limited locality.

I also make several more specific points based on these testimonies: first, that much of the gentile population in this region both collaborated in and profited from the genocide of the Jews. Second, I argue that most of the few Jews who survived the genocide in this area were helped by their gentile neighbors for a variety of reasons, which included both greed and altruism. Third, I suggest that the distinction between rescue and denunciation was often blurred and at times nonexistent, as was the distinction between perpetrators and victims; and that the category of bystander in these areas was largely meaningless, since everyone took part in the events, whether they suffered or profited from them. Fourth, I note that what we call the Holocaust and associate largely with mass-murder facilities and gas chambers was played out more intimately as communal massacres in vast parts of Eastern Europe, where the majority of Jews lived and were murdered. Finally, I point out that crucially important events—such as the otherwise sparsely documented chaotic and extraordinarily violent disintegration of the German occupation of this region in spring and summer 1944—have simply vanished from the historical record because such testimonies have not been used.

I begin with an examination of testimonies on collaboration, betrayal, and denunciation, and then proceed to analyze evidence of rescue and resistance. However, as will become clear, there is both a fair amount of overlap between these categories and a degree of inner contradiction depending on the nature, timing, and audience of eyewitness reports.

II.

Approximately half of those murdered in the Holocaust perished in ghettos and mass executions at or near their places of residence, in open-air, often public events. Of the 500,000 Jews living in Eastern Galicia in 1941, more than 90 percent of whom were murdered, half were deported to the extermination camp of Bełżec and half shot *in situ*. Even when the shootings were conducted in slightly more isolated forests or cemeteries, the brutal roundups, or *Aktionen*, which were accompanied by a great deal of gratuitous violence, took place in public view. Killing sites were frequently close enough for the shots to be heard by other residents. In most cases locally recruited auxiliary troops and policemen actively participated.

Such spectacles, rarely portrayed in any detail in official documentation or postwar historiography, are amply documented in contemporary diaries, postwar testimonies, courtroom witness accounts, and memoirs. These eyewitness reports shed new light on inter-ethnic coexistence and violence in Eastern Europe, and reveal both the peculiarities of the Holocaust and its affinity to other instances of modern genocide. Because the Holocaust in Eastern Europe was often experienced as a communal massacre, it left a deep and lasting imprint on all surviving inhabitants of these localities. In much of Central and Western Europe, the Jews were "simply" deported to the "East," and the few who returned rarely recounted their experiences or found willing listeners for many years thereafter. Conversely, the peoples of Eastern Europe, Jews and gentiles alike, were direct witnesses to and protagonists in a genocide that became an integral, routine, almost "normal" feature of daily life during the war, whether it targeted or spared or was exploited by them.[6]

It bears stressing what this "normality" of communal genocide literally meant. For in Eastern Europe large numbers of Jewish victims were slaughtered in front of family members, friends, and colleagues, in the cemeteries where their ancestors were buried, on the forested hills where they had strolled with lovers or picnicked with children, in the synagogues where they had prayed, in their own homes and farms and cellars.[7] Many postwar inhabitants of former Jewish property retained vivid recollections of the previous owners and the circumstances of their murder. This too is a characteristic of communal massacre, which is almost the exact inverse of the industrial killing in the extermination camps. Communal massacre devastates lives and warps psyches. It belies the very notion of passive bystanders: everyone becomes a protagonist, hunter and prey, resister and facilitator, loser and profiteer. Often, in the course of events, people come to play more than one role. And the resulting sorrow and shame, self-deception and denial, still infuse the way in which people remember, speak, and write about that past.

Nothing demonstrates these aspects of the Holocaust more clearly than testimonies. They expose its intimate, personally devastating effects as much as they reveal the opportunities it presented for greed and violence. Most important, testimonies repeatedly illustrate that even in the midst of the horror there was always a measure of choice, and that such choices could and did save lives and redeem souls. In these conditions, claims of indifference and passivity are meaningless: for what does it mean to remain indifferent to the murder of your classmates under your own windows, or to the sound of shots and screams from the nearby forest? What is the meaning of passivity when you move into a home vacated by your neighbors whom you have just heard being executed, when you eat with their silverware, when you tear out their floorboards to look for gold, when you sleep in their beds?

Interviewed 60 years after the Holocaust, some non-Jewish residents of Buczacz could still remember the events they witnessed during the war. They recalled seeing "how the Hitlerites committed crimes against the Jews . . . how those people dug their own graves . . . how they buried them alive . . . and how the ground was moving over the people who were still not dead."[8] The Germans, recalled another witness,[9] conducted regular roundups, after which "we could see . . . corpses of women, men and children lying on the road . . . infants . . . [thrown] from balconies onto the paved road . . . lying in the mud with smashed heads and spattered brains. . . . We could hear machine-gun fire" from the nearby killing site.[10] Yet such witnesses also describe relations between local Jews and non-Jews in positive terms. "Our people," says one, "Ukrainians and Poles alike—tried to help them however they could. They made dugouts in the ground, and the Jews hid there. Secretly people would bring food to those dugouts. . . . We pitied those people, for they were beaten, always scared for their lives and never knowing what would happen to them next."[11] Another reported that although "the local people were very careful about associating with the Jews . . . others did help, but very cautiously."[12]

Jewish witnesses interviewed at about the same distance of time provide a different perspective. Stories of local collaboration and denunciation, at times by the very people who had been hiding Jews, are a frequent feature of such accounts. Anne Resnik's family bunker was betrayed by the barber whose shop was over it, and much of her family was murdered. Her sister was shot shortly before the first liberation by "the same people that were pretending to hide" her.[13] Regina Gertner's sister was also denounced by a Polish neighbor and killed just before the end of the occupation.[14] Yitzhak Bauer and other witnesses reported that the Polish dogcatchers Nahajowski and Kowalski specialized in discovering Jews and handing them over to the Germans.[15]

The sense of betrayal runs deep many decades later. John Saunders, who had non-Jewish friends in school, remarked: "during the war you started to discover that they hate your guts . . . they didn't want to help us."[16] Robert Barton also had gentile friends. He assumed a Polish identity during the war. The Germans, he noted, "could not tell who the Jew is and who is a Polack . . . [but] the Polacks . . . used to say . . . you look like a Jew, you talk like a Jew, you walk like a Jew."[17] Jacob Heiss remembered local Ukrainians on horseback chasing and killing Jewish children.[18]

Similar observations can be found in a multitude of Jewish accounts written during the war, in its immediate aftermath, and throughout the following decades. Arie Klonicki wrote in his diary in 1943: "The hatred of the immediate surroundings . . . knows no boundaries. Millions of Jews have been slaughtered and it is not yet satiated!"[19] He and his wife were denounced and murdered shortly thereafter. Joachim Mincer wrote in his diary in 1943 that "executions in the prison yard" were carried out "mainly [by] Ukrainian policemen." "The main perpetrator," he wrote, "was an individual by the name of Bandrowski. He liked to shoot Jews on the street." Mincer was also killed soon thereafter.[20] Izio Wachtel recounted that in July 1941, after the Soviets retreated from his town of Czortków and "even before the Germans entered, the Ukrainians arrived at the town with . . . axes and scythes and other instruments and slaughtered and killed and robbed the Jews. With the arrival of the Germans the wild killing ceased and the murder by orders began."[21]

Stories of false rescue are especially striking in this context. Shulamit Aberdam recalled in 1998 that "a Polish woman . . . suggested . . . [to] hide me." Her mother refused. "After the war we heard that the Polish woman had taken another girl, and after getting all the money handed her over to the Germans." Aberdam's family was ejected time and again by rescuers who robbed them, down to their last belongings.[22] Fannie Kupitz, who survived as a girl by living with Ukrainians and often posing as one, commented in 1994: "They were good to me but they killed others."[23] As she told me in 2002, her German labor supervisor was fooled into thinking she was Ukrainian and wanted to send her to Germany to his wife.[24] The locals, on the other hand, could not easily be fooled, and the 13-year-old Fannie "just decided to go on my own. . . . I always was afraid; I only wished I would get a bullet in my back. . . . I . . . used to envy the people that were already dead, I used to envy when I saw a dog that is free and not afraid."[25] When she met a Ukrainian she knew in the forest, "he said to me, 'Oh, you are still alive?'" But his wife took her in for a while. Later her rescuers returned from church citing the priest's words: "Whoever has Jews, let them go, don't keep them!" Shortly afterward she was denounced and fled into the forest.

Girls, especially if they did not look Jewish, had a better chance of surviving than boys. But they were also targets of sexual abuse, rarely referred to directly in testimonies but often present in more subtle ways. One truck driver took Fannie into the forest. "He says to me, 'You probably had a husband.' And I was so afraid, I was pulling my hair, I was breaking my fingers, I was crying, I said, 'No, I don't have a husband and I am very young,' I said. 'Maybe you have a daughter and somebody would do this to your daughter and what would you do?'" He then left her in the forest and drove away.

Similarly, the 1945 testimony by the 13-year-old Rosa Brecher, who was hidden by Polish and Ukrainian women on a farm, reveals sheer terror from her main protector's brother-in-law, Hryń, a drunk and a collaborator: "Hryń came to the attic. . . . He hugged me and . . . [asked if] I was once before in German hands and faced death . . . and whether I was a communist. [He said] he would go to town to take part in the *Aktion*. At that moment I didn't want to live any longer . . ." On another occasion, "Hryń climbed up to the attic. . . . He was very drunk . . . and he asked who was my father and what organization [my parents] belonged to . . ." Then again, "At midnight . . . [Hryń] climbed up to the attic and grabbed me by the neck but I managed to scream and began to beg him to let me go. He said give me 1,000 . . . [or] I will denounce you." Rosa recounts that she made "a hole in the roof [of the attic] and . . . looked at the chickens [in the yard] and thought that soon I would be free."[26]

Much of the violence was about greed. Fannie observed how seven of her relatives were discovered by Ukrainian police: "They knew these people . . . they told them . . . 'We are not going to do nothing to you, just give us whatever you have, and we will let you go.' They gave them everything, [and] when they went out, everyone separately [got] a bullet in the head."[27] Some young Jews tried to prevent this kind of killing or denouncing for profit. Alicia Appleman-Jurman recounted in 1996 how her brother's small resistance group "burned the farmer's barn or beat the farmers up . . . as . . . retaliation, so that . . . people . . . who were hiding Jews should get a message that you can't just betray them [for money]." Eventually her brother too "was betrayed by a Polish boy who was . . . helping out" and was hanged in the local police station. Not long after, Alicia herself, who was just 12 years old, was arrested and registered by a Ukrainian police official, "my friend Olga's father . . . who," before the war, "said he loved me like a daughter." On the eve of the liberation her mother was shot right in front of her after they were denounced by their Polish building supervisor.[28]

Toward the end of the German occupation, the region slipped into total chaos, and the few surviving Jews were at the mercy of greedy peasants, antisemitic Ukrainian militias, Nazi murder squads, and local bandits of all descriptions. There is very little reliable official documentation on these last months and weeks of the war in Western Ukraine, but many vivid and terrifying testimonies. This is a history that can largely be told only on the basis of these accounts. It has some surprising twists and turns.

One striking account of these days was written in 1947 by the 17-year-old Eliasz Chalfen. This testimony implicates the Ukrainian police commander in Buczacz, Volodymyr Kaznovs'kyi, for taking an active part in the first mass execution there as early as 28 August 1941,[29] and goes on to describe many other roundups, in which "the Gestapo, with the help of the Ukrainian police, was trying to find hidden bunkers," and "our neighbors plundered [Jewish homes], taking everything they could," as well as collecting "valuables, gold teeth, etc.," from the thousands of victims of mass executions near the town. By the time of the chaos that preceded the German retreat, reports Chalfen, the "peasants . . . were murdering Jews, taking their belongings and leaving the naked victims in the fields. . . . The Ukrainian bandits . . . would go . . . to the houses that had been pointed out to them as hiding Jews . . . and immediately execute them. . . . Denouncing of Jews at that time," concludes Chalfen, "reached unprecedented levels, and the peasants themselves started murdering and chasing them out" for fear of Ukrainian nationalists.[30]

Ester Grintal testified in 1997 how as an 18-year-old at the time she tried to survive on a forced-labor farm: "The Ukrainian militia would pass through and . . . we would . . . hide in the toilet and count the shots knowing by that how many people were killed." As the Soviets came closer, "Cossacks and others who had collaborated with the Germans" appeared in the area. "They had never seen so many Jews, so they began murdering them. They did not have enough guns so they hanged people, or killed them with axes, etc. They came to our camp with some collaborators from the village. They locked [us] in an empty barn. . . . They began beating us. . . . They shot a line of people with one bullet . . . but the bullet didn't reach me. Again I was put in a line, and again the bullet didn't kill me. So they began killing people with knives. I was stabbed three times." Even the German military doctor who examined her a few days later said, "What did the Ukrainian swine do to you?"[31]

Yoel Katz, also 17 at the time, recalled in 1995 that when the inmates of his labor camp were struck by a typhus epidemic just before the liberation, the peasants called the police to kill them, surrounded the camp, and shouted: "All the children out, we are going to kill you!" Some were killed with axes; others put in a row and shot with a single bullet. The Ukrainians, he reports, "were very hard. . . . The Germans who came from the front protected us from the Ukrainians until the Russians came."[32]

Who would help and who would not was often entirely unpredictable. Joe Perl, who was 13 years old at the end of the occupation, testified in 1996 that he and his mother were hidden by a Ukrainian nationalist who was actually in charge of killing Jews and Poles.[33] Edzia Spielberg-Flitman, liberated at the age of 14, recalled in 1995 how her aunt and cousins were axed to death on the day the Red Army pulled out in July 1941 by a group of Ukrainians who included the children's female teacher. Conversely, her mother was saved from being murdered in a village by her female German friend. They were eventually hidden by a "poor farmer with a wife and four children." The peasant woman said to them: "It doesn't matter how long it takes, we will share our bread and potatoes with you." Yet the peasant who hid Edzia's relatives betrayed them and they were murdered by Ukrainian policemen.

What is curious about these last months and weeks of the occupation is that according to Jewish testimonies, the Jews often ended up being protected from Ukrainian militias and bandits by German army and administrative officers. Edzia, for instance, worked for a while as a washerwoman for a German army unit with a group of Ukrainian girls. When one of the girls denounced her as a Jew, the local German commander took Edzia, her 6-year-old brother, and her mother to safety: "And he left, and he then turned back with his horse one more time and he says, 'I hope you all live well.'" Edzia was "very happy to get away from the Ukrainians because they had pogroms after the war. . . . They were so brutal. I think they were worse than the Germans. . . . They left a big scar upon me. . . . I would say 80 percent [of my family] were killed by the Ukrainians who were our friends."[34]

The much older Mojżesz Szpigiel left a testimony of these events in 1948 at the age of 49. His is a relentless account of mayhem and brutality in the last months of the occupation. When the forced-labor farm where he and his family worked was liquidated in 1943, they hid in the forest, where "we were attacked by peasants. The Ukrainians began to catch people, torture them, take their money." Szpigiel's father and his two nephews were killed by a Ukrainian. Returning to the farm, they found that all inmates who fell ill from the rampant epidemics were killed by the Ukrainian police.

In January 1944 Ukrainian militiamen murdered most of the surviving 120 Jews in the farm, including Szpigiel's 14-year-old son. Szpigiel writes: "It is important to state that this killing was not a German action, that it was performed by Ukrainian policemen and bandits." Szpigiel and other survivors protested to the German administrator, but most of the few survivors were butchered with knives and pitchforks in yet another bandit attack just before the liberation. Szpigiel describes "the child orphans . . . stacked up in a pile . . . victims . . . lying with open guts. . . . Everybody," he remarks, "said they would rather die from a German bullet than from a bandit's knife." When the German administrator left, "The Jews earnestly cried." But the new commander, a young German army officer, said to them: "As long as I am here, nothing will happen to you." Indeed, when Ukrainian policemen attacked the last remaining Jews, reports Szpigiel, a German "major . . . went [there] with his aide and hit one policeman on the head with his revolver, threw them out and ordered them to leave immediately."[35]

The 15-year-old Izaak Szwarc reported on these same events shortly after the war. He recalled that at the labor camp, "the peasants . . . wanted roundups to take place so that they could rob the Jews. . . . The village head forbade the peasants to give us food. The peasants organized nightly guards around the camp so that the Jews could not escape. . . . The peasants supervised our work, they beat us, did not give us any water." When the camp was liquidated, "the peasants brought out hidden Jews. . . . In the forests Jews were attacked by bandits, and the peasants did not let us in." Under these conditions, the Jews "went to a village where the Germans were. We were safer there from the bandits. . . . We sensed that the peasants intended to remove us as witnesses to their crimes." On the eve of the liberation, as the Hungarian soldiers stationed in his village retreated, "the Vlasov-soldiers [former Soviet troops serving in the Wehrmacht] arrived. . . . They did not have any guns, only cold weapons. They murdered all the Jews they caught. . . . It was impossible to stay in the villages. The peasants organized roundups of Jews, killed them, discovered bunkers. Even those Jews who were hidden in bunkers at peasants' farms were killed by their hosts. The Jews began to gather in Tłusty. The [German commander] . . . promised that the Jews would not be harmed. 300 Jews gathered there . . . On 23 March the Soviets arrived."[36]

Rene Zuroff was only 7 years old when she was liberated. In 1995, she recalled roundups in which she and her 3-year-old sister would lie in the bunker and hear "the Germans . . . screaming, 'Juden, Juden raus, raus!' and . . . the Ukrainians and the Poles . . . calling 'żyd, żyd!'" and then the "bloodbath in your house, outside the door, in the street, bodies everywhere." Her last recollections of the Holocaust are the most terrifying. She remembers: "We were hiding in the forest and our shelter was a field of tobacco. . . . One night we heard terrible screaming and curses in Ukrainian and running, there was a whole massacre; the Ukrainian militia came at night hunting out the Jews from the woods. . . . [They] were chasing the Jews with dogs and we heard this rampage and started running for our lives . . . we were running blindly . . . and it was the scariest thing I can remember: we saw dismembered bodies, bodies without heads, and we saw death all around us; so that was my nightmare in the tobacco fields and forest."

Rene and her family were rescued by wretchedly poor Polish peasants; the Poles by then were also being massacred by Ukrainian nationalists. They hid in a hole in a "barn . . . full of rats and other vermin . . . and when the animals urinated the urine would spill into the hole." But "the old Polish woman was truly a saintly and wonderful human being who risked her life and that of her daughters. She gave us seven . . . pierogi . . . on Sunday, once a week we got food and very little in-between."

When she returned to Buczacz in July 1944, Rene was not given to compassion: "I was a little girl and we would go for our entertainment to the hangings . . . of collaborators . . . in the town square . . . we were totally happy to go to our daily hangings." She came to the United States in 1950, majored in foreign languages, married in 1962, and has two children, one of whom is a rabbi in Israel. She suffers from neuroses, hates the dark, doesn't like to be surrounded by people, and has to sit at the end of every table, "for a quick escape." She does not "have a great deal of . . . trust and confidence in people."[37]

III.

The testimonies cited above should demonstrate the importance of such eyewitnesses for reconstructing the typical experience of Jewish victims, especially survivors, in the small towns of Eastern Galicia, and by extension in much of the rest of Eastern Europe. These accounts also provide much insight into the psychological conditions that predominated during this period and thus help us understand both patterns of behavior at the time and the long-term effects of these events. In other words, these testimonies are crucial to any analysis of the mental makeup and resilience of those who endured the Holocaust and the effects of trauma on memory, recollection, and witnessing.[38]

Nonetheless, the picture sketched above remains incomplete without more substantial reference to rescue, resistance, and intra-communal conflict. Relatively rare in the record as a whole, rescue features prominently in testimonies, even as they recount numerous instances of betrayal and denunciation. If rescue was exceptional overall, it was a much more common experience for those survivors on whose testimonies we must rely. Indeed, the memories of most protagonists have remained ambivalent on precisely this score: they lay blame and assert humaneness, expose betrayal and recall altruism and sacrifice. Accounts by non-Jews often repress or marginalize Christian complicity and collaboration, while underscoring help and compassion, and in some cases blaming victims for their own fate. Jewish testimonies, quite apart from shifting uneasily between bitterness about the treachery of neighbors and gratitude for rescue by the righteous few, also flicker between repressing evidence of Jewish collaboration and corruption, and expressing profound rage and derision vis-à-vis those identified with the *Judenrat* and the Jewish police. Finally, compassion by Germans, perhaps precisely because of their local omnipotence, appears in such accounts as the strongest evidence for the possibility of choice and the potential for goodness even in the midst of genocide.

Choice constitutes the moral core of any discussion of mass murder; it also retains an underlying psychological dimension for those directly impacted by such events and for later generations.[39] Evidence of choice threatened to expose and shame those whose alibi for complicity was the alleged lack of an alternative. But instances of altruism, however few, provide flashes of light in what would have otherwise remained a period of utter darkness. Such glimmers of humanness, faint and far between though they might have been, should not be removed from the historical record. They should be recounted because they occurred; they should be remembered because they give us hope; and they should be contextualized because they serve to highlight the far more prevalent phenomena of glee and greed, complicity and collaboration, violence and cruelty. And there can be no more reliable evidence for gentile help, rescue, and sacrifice during the Holocaust than that derived from the testimonies of Jewish survivors.

Especially for children, survival depended on a combination of luck and the help of others, whether motivated by kindness or prospects of material gain. Safah Prüfer, a little girl from Buczacz interviewed soon after the liberation, recalled that her father "handed me and my little brother to a peasant we knew in our town." But following "a terrible *Aktion* . . . daddy built a hiding-place in the forest. . . . One day the Ukrainian police arrived and shot everybody, only I alone survived. From that day on I began to fight for my existence on my own. I wandered alone for seven months, unable to find any shelter; then finally the Red Army liberated us."[40]

It is inconceivable that such a small girl could have survived the long winter without some help from the locals, however grudging. Non-Jews often claimed that such help was offered quite willingly. A Polish resident of Buczacz related in 2003 that during the war a young woman came running to her with a baby, "crying and exhausted. . . . At my own risk I hid them in the attic of the cowshed. . . . I fed that little girl from my own breast . . . and I shared my own food with that woman." She stressed that this was not "the only case. I tried to help [the Jews] however I could, and my husband never objected."[41]

We do not know what eventually happened to that baby, though in all likelihood it did not survive. Conversely, Emil Skamene, raised as a Christian in Prague, was in fact born to the Kleiner family in Buczacz in 1941, "in a cellar of a Ukrainian peasant, who was hiding my parents." In desperation, Emil's father wrote his sister in Prague, begging her to rescue the baby. She in turn sent Rudolph Steiger, a German with "some function in the SS" who, for a fee, brought the 18-month-old baby "in a backpack . . . over two days . . . [on] the train" to Prague. Not long thereafter the peasant murdered Emil's parents as a means to get his hands on their valuables. Emil discovered his true identity only decades later; he subsequently also found out that both his adoptive parents were Jews. As he sees it, he owes his life to the fact that "it was very important for some people that I should survive." Even Steiger, who "originally did it for money," grew attached to the boy, becoming a regular guest at his birthday parties. His goodness paid off, since "as an SS official . . . [he] would have likely been killed by Czechs after the war," had it not been for "an affidavit from my parents." Steiger, concludes Emil, "lived . . . his life basically in exchange for this unbelievable act of heroism."[42]

Some older children adopted a false identity, a precarious choice in a society replete with stereotypes and prejudices. The 10-year-old Genia Weksler testified in 1946 that she spent the last months of the occupation in a Polish village with her mother and sister: "I grazed cattle. . . . In the house they often talked about Jews. 'Jews are cheaters.' . . . The children always played . . . 'manhunt' on Jews. . . . We lived as Poles until the liberation. I was often told that I have Jewish eyes, Jewish black hair. I answered that if 'You take a closer look it is possible that I'm completely Jewish.'"[43] Bronia Kahane, who was 10 when the Germans invaded in 1941, was initially hidden with her mother by a Ukrainian peasant who felt loyalty to her grandfather, even though his own son was a concentration camp guard. They were also saved from an execution by an Austrian SS-man thanks to her mother's excellent German and a $10 bill. But in spring 1944 she lost her entire family and began working as a farmhand. She lived in a house filled with Jewish goods looted by the owner's son, and was told by her employer: "You do everything like a Jew." When she returned to Buczacz after the liberation, Bronia "spoke only Ukrainian. . . . I forgot everything." She found the few surviving Jews terrified of being attacked: "I never went back to my house . . . because they said . . . 'They're going to kill you.'"[44]

Aliza Golobov, who was 14 when the Germans invaded, was also first saved by a German soldier, who hid her family during an *Aktion* in 1942. Although she was denounced several times, and similarly lost her entire family, Aliza was rescued by a number of Ukrainians and acquaintances of her father's in the town of Stanisławów. The lawyers Dr. Volchuk and Mr. Krochmichek, the latter's father, a priest, and a police inspector provided her with false papers and protected her until the liberation, receiving no compensation and at great risk to their own and their families' lives.[45] Hilda Weitz, who was also 14 in 1941, was sheltered by a Ukrainian family from Buczacz, despite the fact that "they were . . . very nationalistic" and that "two of the brothers were drafted to German army." She and her younger brother were later hidden by a blacksmith's family in a "very rough antisemitic town." The man, his wife, and their child eventually fled the village, "because they were afraid they will come to . . . look for Jews." Hilda and her brother were left alone: "I remember the light looked so beautiful, the sun, the nature, I said, 'Oh my God, life is so beautiful, but we will never see it anymore.' I thought this was our last day . . ."[46] Shortly thereafter the Soviets arrived.

In some cases love, passion, and loyalty also played a role. The 16-year-old Zofia Pollak jumped off a train headed to the Bełżec extermination camp near the town of Rawa Ruska, only to be arrested by the Polish policeman Smola, an ethnic German. He said to her: "You are so young . . . and so pretty, you shouldn't be killed." He took care of Zofia for six weeks. "He was really in love with me. . . . But he was a married man. And his wife and two children was on vacation." When his wife returned Smola sent Zofia back to her father and brother in Buczacz. She survived much of the remainder of the war thanks to the good will of a Polish work supervisor on the agricultural farm in which the father, a former estate manager, was employed. Almost murdered by Ukrainian partisans, they ended up in the barn of a poor peasant who had once been helped by Zofia's father. "He said: 'Whatever I have I will share with you . . .' He covered us with hay. It was very cold. . . . We were there in one position, we couldn't move and this is how we were liberated on 23 February 1944 in that place."[47]

In other cases, youngsters were saved thanks to split-second decisions by strangers. Eighteen-year-old Cyla Sznajder hid in the attic of the German administration's office during the liquidation of the Nagórzanka labor camp near Buczacz in 1942, and "thanks to the cleaner—a Pole, who found me by chance . . . I managed to get out . . . without being seen." During another liquidation action in January 1943 she hid with a friend in the backyard of a farm. The ethnic German peasant who discovered them there, "invited us into his hut . . . ordered his wife to prepare warm food . . . fed us . . . [and] found for us some old rags." Later she and a few others were supplied with food by another peasant woman. And, at the very end, Cyla and several other Jewish girls hid in the attic of a cloister: "The nuns comforted us that things would not last long, and brought us food."[48]

Rescuers were not made of the same cast, and we have contradictory reports about some of them. In 1946 the 21-year-old Shmuel Rosen testified that he, his two brothers, and their mother had hidden for nine months in a grave where they "built . . . a little apartment . . . with the help of the gravedigger," Mańko Świerszczak, in the Christian cemetery on the slope of the Fedor Hill overlooking the town of Buczacz.[49] In a 1960 testimony Shmuel described Świerszczak as "an illiterate but a very upright man" who, "in return for a fee," hid "40 Jews in the attic of the cemetery's chapel" during an *Aktion*, refusing to betray them even when the Ukrainian police "beat him up." The Rosens paid Świerszczak "1,000 złoty every

month for the supplies" in return for hiding them.[50] Shmuel's older brother Henry depicted
Świerszczak in 1997 as "a gorgeous man" and "a Christian. . . . He would say, 'If I will turn you
in, then my kids, my grandkids, and their grandchildren will have to pay for my sin.'"[51] But in
March 1944, a couple of months after the Rosens moved to "a shelter under the floor" of the
mortuary, "a group of German soldiers came into the [house and] the floor collapsed." The
brothers managed to escape, "but our poor mother . . . could not run with her sick legs. We
saw . . . how our mother was dragged out and shot."[52] Świerszczak later buried her.[53]

The three boys were subsequently hidden by an old Polish acquaintance, the peasant
Michał Dutkiewicz,[54] even as some of their relatives were denounced and murdered in the
same village.[55] It was thanks to them that Świerszczak's tale of heroism became known, and
in 1983 he and his Ukrainian wife Marynka were declared "righteous among the nations"
by Yad Vashem in Jerusalem.[56] Yet Yad Vashem's archives also contain an account written in
1947 by Moshe Wizinger, a friend of the Rosens, who had a very different recollection of the
undertaker. In June 1943 Wizinger also sought refuge in the cemetery, where he encountered
a "very frightened" Świerszczak, followed by his wife, who urged him to leave or to give
himself up to the Germans. Shortly thereafter he was captured by Ukrainian fighters, barely
managed to escape, and returned to the cemetery. This time Marynka "started to shout at me
to run . . . otherwise she herself would call the Germans." Remarkably, at this point Wizinger
was taken in by a local Polish resistance group, whose leader, Edek, decided to punish the
couple for refusing shelter to a Jew. After beating up Marynka while her husband was hiding
under the bed, Edek declared, according to Wizinger: "For what you did to him, I would have
killed you like dogs. And only your behavior before that . . . stops me from doing it. Fear of
the Germans cannot be an excuse for you . . . we will punish loyalty to German orders with
death. Remember this and tell the others."

By the standards of Edek's moral code, then, as reported by Wizinger, according to
which Polish honor required saving Jews, whether one liked them or not, Świerszczak did
not pass the test. But Edek's group was an uncommon local phenomenon—most nationalist
Polish and Ukrainian partisans were at best unfriendly to Jews—and he and most of his fighters were killed. The only record of his heroism is in Wizinger's unread account; consequently
he received no recognition by Yad Vashem and Świerszczak's status was never challenged.

This ambiguity of heroism was even more pronounced in the case of Jewish resisters.
At the end of his diary, Wizinger scans the handful of Jewish fighters still left on the eve of
the liberation and notes that they are "the last of a dying nation."[57] Inquiring who they were
and why there were so few of them tells us a great deal about the complexities of the historical
reality and the vicissitudes of memory.

An outstanding example is Yitzhak Bauer, 18 when the Germans invaded and 80 when
I interviewed him in 2003. Bauer recalled that "compared to other places the Christian population" of Buczacz "was relatively all right. . . . At least they did not harm us." Saved by a
Ukrainian friend during the first *Aktion*, Bauer ended up in a small Jewish resistance group
in the nearby forest. While he took action against denouncers, Bauer maintained a nuanced
view of Ukrainians, noting, for instance, that even the notorious chief of the local militia,
Volodymyr Kaznovs'kyi, refrained from action upon discovering that his own father, a priest,
was hiding Jews. Similarly, Bauer's Ukrainian friend Shenko, who provided the group with
food, later joined the police, explaining that "the alternative was to enlist for labor in Germany or join the SS-Division 'Galicia.'" Not long after, Shenko's house was burned down
as punishment for hiding Jews. Bauer also recalled an elderly Ukrainian family friend who

invited him and his brother to his home, gave them food, and parted from them saying "I wish that you manage to survive."[58]

From a deposition he submitted to a West German court in 1968 as evidence for the trial of former Nazi perpetrators in Buczacz, however, it turns out that before becoming a partisan, Bauer had served in the *Ordnungsdienst* (Jewish police, or OD). He was apparently not the only one who made the transition from collaboration to resistance. Bauer noted that he joined the OD in November 1941. The police, numbering some 30 men, "carried out the orders of the *Judenrat,* but during *Aktionen* . . . we were put at the disposition of . . . the Gestapo or the local gendarmerie." According to Bauer, on 27 November 1942, he "was assigned to participate in the cleanup of the Jewish hospital" which "was overflowing with . . . about 100 . . . sick people. . . . The sick who could not move were shot right there and then in their beds. The others were taken out to the railroad station . . . and transported to extermination in Bełżec." Bauer personally witnessed some of the shooting in the hospital, as well as during the *Aktion* of April 1943.[59]

There is no necessary contradiction between Bauer's two accounts; it may be simply a matter of relating different segments of his experiences appropriate to the circumstances in which they were presented. But it is also possible that Bauer could not assimilate the two parts of his story into one psychological and experiential whole: to the German court he asserted his role as an OD-man, in order established his ability to identify German perpetrators; to me he asserted his role as partisan, thus providing his survival with the more heroic aura befitting the Israeli context. Yet many of those who lived through that period would not share our understanding for the choices made by such men as Bauer or Shenko. Gershon Gross, a tough working-class 24-year-old in 1941, had only contempt for the *Judenrat* and OD: "What was their job? . . . No one wants to talk about it. . . . The Germans would say they need 500 people. The [Jewish] police went" to seize them. Gershon and his brothers refused to join the police. Of a *Judenrat* member who survived, Gershon noted dispassionately that he "had to hide, like Eichmann. If they found him they would kill him." Jewish collaborators, to his mind, were the worst, since they turned against their own. He had more sympathy for gentiles precisely because his expectations were lower. A Ukrainian policeman, a former classmate, let him go after the OD forced him to bury victims of a mass shooting. When Torah scrolls were "hanged . . . like you hang clothes" from the bridge over the Strypa River in Buczacz, "a Ukrainian priest hid one Torah in the church," retuning it to Gross after the liberation. And when one of his brothers was wounded in a partisan action, a poor Polish peasant sheltered and nursed him back to health. But Gross had no illusions. He knew that "Ukrainian police took" Hungarian and Czech Jewish refugees "to the Dniester River, tied them with wires and threw them alive into the Dniester." Closer to home, his own parents were denounced by a local Polish girl, taken out to their own yard, and shot.[60]

Moshe Wizinger was also harsher about Jewish collaborators than gentile neighbors. He similarly remembered the "harsh protest from the Ukrainian priests," who demanded from "the leader of the Ukrainian bands, Dankowicz . . . to stop desecrating Holy sites," and he noted the initiative of "the head of the Ukrainian Basilian Monastery . . . to carry the scrolls to the monastery where they would be safe." Wizinger distinguished between on the one hand "German soldiers led by Ukrainian dregs"—who in the early days of the occupation "forced their way into Jewish houses and raped young Jewish girls," as well as murdering former communists, including "Jews, Poles and even Ukrainians"—and on the other the Ukrainian community leaders who "were helpless" against "the leaders of the formerly secret Ukrainian bands . . . that were ruling now." He also stressed that those "Ukrainian bands" were soon thereafter "appointed as the police forces" which constituted the main local component of future mass killings. But it was about the Jewish leadership that Wizinger wrote most contemptuously, deriding the manner in which "the countless demands by the Germans or Ukrainians were fulfilled immediately" by the *Judenrat*. The OD, for its part, "robbed the Jews of furniture, bed linen and clothing," so that even "in those terrible times" Jewish officials "were able to lead a very good life and to amass large sums of money," while "Jews who were trying to hide their belongings were mercilessly beaten" by them. When Jews from neighboring smaller towns and villages were expelled to Buczacz, not only were they "attacked and robbed by the peasants," but once they arrived the Jewish police targeted them: "The OD are robbing, killing, worse than the Germans."

Some Jewish leaders did try to set a different moral standard. Thus when the Germans demanded 150 Jews for work in a forced labor camp, the head of the *Judenrat*, Dr. Engelberg, "announced that he would under no condition take part in selecting the people." But his assistants, Dr. "Seifer and Kramer Baruch . . . proposed to exchange those unable to work with healthy and young workers" and "supported their proposal with presents." As a result, "the names taken off the list belonged to those who could pay more," while Seifer and Kramer "made a great deal of money . . . and did not refuse to accept jewelry as well." There were some moments of heroism. Jankiel Ebenstein, "who during his few months of work at the *Judenrat* became hated by everyone," and "was called an agent of the Gestapo . . . was ordered to help . . . looking for hidden bunkers." He initially "tried to convince the Chief of the Gestapo that no Jews were hiding in" a certain house. But "when . . . they started pulling Jews out of there," he "grabbed a hatchet and tried to hit the Gestapo soldier," only to be immediately shot down. As Wizinger wrote, "that's how the man . . . died a heroes' death. That day he was forgiven everything."[61]

The effect of German rule on intra- and interethnic relations is noted in many testimonies. Zofia Pollak "had very close . . . gentile friends," but "after the Germans occupied our city they wouldn't even look at me because I was Jewish." As for the ghetto, "the *Judenrat* was very mean and the Jewish police was very mean. They thought that by being very obedient to the Germans, they will save their own lives. So the very nice people became very ugly." But, Pollack concluded, "at the end everybody was killed."[62] Shmuel Rosen recalled that "the 200 richest Jewish families found their way to the labor camp," considered the last safe site in Buczacz, by paying the *Judenrat* exorbitant sums.[63] Soon thereafter the labor camp was also liquidated. Yet Rosen did think that wealth and corruption made a difference in survival rate. Of the up to 1,000 Jews who came out of hiding following the first liberation of Buczacz in March 1944, "next to a handful of upright people, only dubious characters survived—denouncers, militiamen." To be sure, most of them were murdered when the Germans recaptured the town a few days later. Only a few managed to escape, and some became partisans. The Rosen brothers, for their part, joined the Red Army. By the second liberation in July 1944 fewer then 100 Jews were still alive in Buczacz.[64]

Survivors have often been reluctant to speak about internal Jewish corruption and complicity, invoking the phrase, "one does not speak ill of the dead." Yet this was a crucial component of life during the Holocaust and of its subsequent memory. Witnesses from Buczacz also observed that the Jewish leadership opposed and hindered the creation of armed resistance. In 2002 Shmuel Rosen recalled overhearing a conversation between *Judenrat* leaders and a man called Zuhler, who had "served in the Polish army before the war. . . . He said to them, 'We want to create partisan groups and to go to the forest . . . but we have no money for weapons.'. . . So they said, 'Sir . . . we will not agree to this.' And he left, and that was that."[65]

Rosen speculated that Jewish leaders "were scared," and that while some in the *Judenrat* wanted to organize resistance, others "were together with the Germans. Excuse me for saying that, to our regret, Dr. Seifer was one." By this Rosen meant that Seifer preferred collaboration to resistance, and his willingness to name the man must have also had to do with the fact that of all the *Judenrat* members, it was Seifer who survived: "They say he is in Australia." Zeev Anderman, another survivor, who was also present at the interview with Rosen, suggested: "Let's get off this subject, gentlemen, it is too painful. . . ." But Rosen insisted: "Look, they have to know this. . . . There were bad things in the *Judenrat* . . . they would seize a young man for work and they would exchange him [for another]. Who would [serve for the] exchange?" Now Anderman gave way: "One of the poor boys." And Rosen concluded: "Exactly, they would get the poor kids, [in exchange for] those of the rich. . . ." And Anderman added: "My uncle, they got him. . . ."[66]

These are fraught and agonizing issues. Ultimately, in conditions of communal genocide, no one remained entirely apart from the events. A passing remark by Shmuel Rosen revealed that, in fact, he too had worked in the *Judenrat,* if only in the position of a "helper" ("I made tea, coffee"). Zeev Anderman spoke with pride about his brother Janek's death in April 1943, when he pulled out a pistol and shot a Ukrainian policemen, only to be beaten, dragged to the town square, and burned alive.[67] Yet some sources suggest that Janek had a pistol because he was or had been an OD-man. Perhaps, just like Ebenstein, his heroic end made up for his past actions in the police.[68]

IV.

Personal accounts of genocide, by their very nature, do not allow for the creation of a single, uniform narrative of events. Rather, they offer a multitude of perspectives, some complementary, others contradictory, which, when put together, can provide an imperfect yet multidimensional picture of past reality. At times, this may be a contentious or opaque portrait, all the more so considering the extreme circumstances of World War II and the Holocaust. Yet listening closely to the witnesses allows us greater depth and nuance than can be derived from the tendentious obfuscation of official accounts. Individual, personal perspectives are all the more important in reconstructing events in the ethnically mixed borderlands of Eastern Europe.

Indeed, certain internal contradictions within individual accounts carry special significance for collective memory and historiography. Generalizing statements by witnesses on the conduct of entire ethnic groups tend to conform to conventional views, which are in part reflected in the overall course of events. Yet the same witnesses often cite specific cases of individual actions that belie the generalizations and, not least, were vital to the witnesses' own survival. Such instances of untypical but crucial behavior provide a corrective to widespread prejudices and undermine deterministic views of the past by introducing an element of choice.

The gap between conventional generalizations and unique individual experience makes for ambivalence. This reaction comes into particularly sharp relief in extreme situations such as genocide. Jewish accounts contain a large measure of mixed feelings about Christian neighbors, reflecting a general impression of universal betrayal mixed with individual experiences of rescue. Precisely because denunciation and murder were so pervasive, rare instances of mercy and altruism stand out all the more. And, of course, witness accounts disproportionately represent gentile rescue, since survival was so heavily dependent on such acts.

But testimonies also tell us that just as perpetrators occasionally showed pity or compassion, rescuers were hardly always altruistic, as motivations for action ranged from pure goodness to cynical exploitation. While a few men with blood on their hands occasionally chose to save someone, others masqueraded as rescuers only to rob and betray those they sheltered; while many upstanding citizens became complicit in plunder and murder, some wretchedly poor peasants shared their last crumbs with the desperate remnants of destroyed communities. Some sought a postwar alibi, others paid back moral debts: generalizing about motivation is futile. Habitual killers may have acted kindly only once; others might have been transformed by that first pang of conscience. Some began with good intentions and then turned to denunciation; others acted out of greed but became attached to those they rescued. Ambivalence was hardly restricted to survivors.

Observing the dynamics of communal genocide through a local perspective reveals that not a few of those who perpetrated violence at one point became its victims at another. Ukrainian nationalists collaborated with the Germans in killing Jews and massacred Poles; they were in turn targeted by the prewar Polish state, the Soviet authorities, and eventually also the Germans. Poles benefited from their prewar state's discriminatory anti-Jewish and anti-Ukrainian policies; in turn they were subjected to Soviet deportations and Ukrainian ethnic cleansing. Jewish community leaders and educated youths tried to save themselves by becoming complicit in the victimization of poorer and weaker fellow Jews, only to have their illusions of power and security dispelled as they too were murdered. Some saw this turning of tables as a kind of justice; but ultimately it merely resulted from the dynamics of unbound, unrestricted violence on a hitherto unimaginable scale.

And yet, many testimonies also contain a mélange of unspoken gratitude for the rescuers and inarticulate remorse for having failed to recognize and thank them for so long. The pervasive atmosphere of mayhem and violence, betrayal and abandonment, might have made such acts of mercy stand out all the more for a moment. After, they often receded into the background as survivors mourned the dead and tried to build a new life. But the testimonies uncover those buried stories. The multitudes of the drowned have left precious little behind; yet the few who were saved have given us a detailed record of these events—of which their rescuers constituted a vital component. This is of course an unbalanced historical record. But it has the benefit of enriching our understanding of the Holocaust and its aftermath. Ultimately, beyond saving their lives, acts of rescue also saved the souls of the survivors. After all, it is astonishing that men, women, and children who lived though that era had the inner resources to rebuild their lives, and yet many of them did just that. This is a testimony to their strength and resilience. But I would argue that what contributed no less to their determination to raise new families, and to their ability to instill in their children trust and humanity, was the memory of those who had selflessly saved them.

This memory remained deeply etched in the souls of the survivors. But it did not find public expression for decades, providing just enough sustenance to go on living but never completely resurfacing, perhaps because of the hardships of life after the catastrophe, or because allowing it to emerge would have brought back all the other horrors and betrayals and losses. When it did return, decades later, it came after lives had been lived, children and grandchildren had been born, and one could face the approaching inevitable end with more equanimity and sense of fulfillment. And with the memory of rescue came a recognition that those who had chosen to act then had done more than save lives but, unbeknownst to themselves perhaps, had rescued the very concept of a shared humanity—precisely that which the Nazis had set out to eradicate—by recognizing the human spark in those who were hunted down like animals.

What the witnesses I have cited here experienced hardly provides a single, one-sided lesson on human nature, or history, or even the events of the Holocaust. But these accounts, fraught and painful and contradictory as they are, constitute a crucial component of the past—in Buczacz, and by extension, in many other sites of communal genocide, most especially in the borderlands of Eastern Europe.[69] Ignoring them, setting them aside, using them merely to illustrate some point or thesis unrelated to their deeper meaning, not only constitutes abuse of these records of human experience, it also distorts and ultimately falsifies the historical record itself. No history should be written without listening to its protagonists, least of all the history of an event whose main goal was to silence these voices, and especially because the few who survived the disaster hoped more than anything else to transmit the memory of the events they experienced to posterity and thereby to save the multitudes of the dead from complete oblivion, statistical abstraction, and mass burial in the voluminous footnotes of scholarly publications.

Notes

1. For a forceful statement on the need for an objective and value-free use of documents, see David Engel, *Facing A Holocaust: The Polish Government-in-Exile and the Jews, 1943–1945* (Chapel Hill: University of North Carolina Press, 1993), 1–14; Engel has expressed strong reservations about the use of testimonies in several scholarly meetings.

2. For interesting comments on sources along these lines see Dieter Pohl, *Nationalsozialistische Judenverfolgung in Ostgalizien 1941–1944: Organisation und Durchführung eines staatlichen Massenverbrechens* (Munich: Oldenbourg, 1996), 17–21, who also writes: "Research of Jewish history under German occupation in East Galicia would have demanded knowledge of Yiddish and Hebrew, which I lack. This limitation is painful, but unavoidable"; ibid., 15. See also Thomas Sandkühler, *"Endlösung" in Galizien: Der Judenmord in Ostpolen und die Rettungsinitiativen von Berthold Beitz, 1941–1944* (Bonn: Dietz, 1996), 15–19. Skepticism over the use of diaries is expressed in Raul Hilberg, *Sources of Holocaust Research: An Analysis* (Chicago: Ivan R. Dee, 2001), 141–42, 155–59, 161–62. For a more sympathetic view that stresses the chronological proximity of accounts, see Saul Friedländer, *The Years of Extermination: Nazi Germany and the Jews, 1939–1945* (New York: HarperCollins, 2007, 2007), xxiv-xxvi.

3. This is ultimately the case even in Friedländer, *Years of Extermination*. A good example is Debórah Dwork and Robert Jan van Pelt, *The Holocaust: A History* (New York: Norton, 2002). A much more sophisticated discussion can be found in Alexandra Garbarini, *Numbered Days: Diaries and the Holocaust* (New Haven: Yale University Press, 2006), and Simone Gigliotti, *The Train Journey: Transit, Captivity, and Witnessing in the Holocaust* (New York: Berghahn Books, 2009).

4. Annette Wieviorka, *The Era of the Witness*, trans. Jared Stark (Ithaca, N.Y.: Cornell University Press, 2006).

5. A few examples: Lawrence L. Langer, *Holocaust Testimonies: The Ruins of Memory* (New Haven, Conn.: Yale University Press, 1991); Cathy Caruth, ed., *Trauma: Explorations in Memory* (Baltimore, Md.: Johns Hopkins University Press, 1995); Shoshana Felman and Dori Laub, *Testimony: Crises of Witnessing in Literature, Psychoanalysis, and History* (New York: Routledge, 1992);

Kenneth Jacobson, *Embattled Selves: An Investigation into the Nature of Identity Through Oral Histories of Holocaust Survival* (New York: Atlantic Monthly Press, 1994); Efraim Sicher, ed., *Breaking Crystal: Writing and Memory after Auschwitz* (Urbana: University of Illinois Press, 1998). An early exception is Terrence Des Pres, *The Survivor: An Anatomy of Life in the Death Camps* (New York: Oxford University Press, 1976).

6. Among the most harrowing texts on this "return," see Charlotte Delbo, *None of Us Will Return,* trans. John Githens (New York: Grove, 1968), and Primo Levi, *The Reawakening,* trans. Stuart Woolf (New York: Simon & Schuster, 1995).

7. For a detailed account of one such public massacre in an Eastern Galician town, known as "The bloody Sunday of Stanisławów" (now the city of Ivano-Frankivs'k in Western Ukraine), from various perspectives, see Pohl, *Judenverfolgung,* 144–47; Sandkühler, *Endlösung,* 150–52; Elisabeth Freundlich, *Die Ermordung einer Stadt namens Stanislau: NS-Vernichtungspolitik in Polen 1939–1945* (Vienna: Österreichischer Bundesverlag, 1986), 154–64; Avraham Liebesman, *With the Jews of Stanisławów in the Holocaust* (Tel Aviv: Hakibbutz Hameuchad, 1980, in Hebrew), 22–31.

8. Julija Mykhailivna Trembach, written on her behalf by her daughter, Roma Nestorivna Kryvenchuk, in 2003, collected by Mykola Kozak, translated from Ukrainian by Sofia Grachova.

9. Maria Mykhailivna Khvostenko (née Dovhanchuk), interview with Mykola Kozak, 2003, translated from Ukrainian by Sofia Grachova.

10. Ibid.

11. Trembach, 2003.

12. Tetiana Pavlyshyn, "The Holocaust in Buczacz," *Nova Doba* 48 (1 December 2000), collected by Mykola Kozak, translated by Sofia Grachova.

13. Anne H. Resnik (née Herzog), telephone interview with me, 11 September 2002.

14. Regina Gertner, telephone interview with me, 31 July 2002.

15. Yitzhak Bauer, interview with me, in Hebrew, Tel Aviv, November 2003.

16. John Saunders, telephone interview with me, 30 July 2002.

17. Robert Barton (Bertisz), telephone interview with me, 5 July 2002.

18. Jacob Heiss, telephone interview with me, 5 July 2003, and meeting in New York City, December 2002.

19. Arie Klonicki-Klonymus, *The Diary of Adam's Father* (Jerusalem: Hakibbutz Hameuchad, 1969, in Hebrew), 47.

20. Joachim Mincer, *Diary,* probably written in 1943, Yad Vashem, in Polish, translated by Eva Lutkiewicz.

21. Undated account by Yitzhak Shalev, formerly Izio Wachtel, sent to me by his son, Ziki Slav, on 25 February 2007.

22. Shulamit Aberdam (Freiberg), Shoah Foundation video, interviewed by Shlomit Saar in Haifa, Israel, 28 April 1998, in Hebrew.

23. Fannie Kupitz (Feldman), Shoah Foundation video, Forest Hills, 25 April 1994.

24. Salomon and Fania Kupitz, interview with me in New York City, 10 October 2002.

25. This and all subsequent citations of this witness are taken from Kupitz, Shoah Foundation video.

26. Rózia Brecher, "Recollections from the City of Buczacz," Yad Vashem Archives Division: 033, File: 765, E/32–3–, translation from Polish original with help from Joanna Michlic; Rosa Brecher, "Protocol, taken down in the refugee house, Bucharest, Calea Mosilor 128, on 20 May 1945," Jewish Historical Institute, Warsaw (hereafter ZIH) 301/4911, translation of German original.

27. Ibid.

28. Alicia Appleman-Jurman, Shoah Foundation video, interviewed by Catherine Renner, 29 January 1996, transcribed by Etan Newman, 8 November 2006.

29. See the extraordinary apologetic accounts of this man's career in: Yefrem Hasai, "Under Police Uniform there Beat the Heart of a Ukrainian Patriot," *Nova Doba,* no. 16 (8065), 23 April 2004; as well as Mykhailo Kheifetz, *Ukrayinski syluety* (Kharkiv, Ukraine: Folio, 2000), available at Kharkiv Group for Human Rights Protection: www.khpg.org—both translated by Sofia Grachova. And see records of Kaznovsk'kyi's 1957 trial in Ternopil', Branch State Archive of the Security Service of Ukraine (Haluzevyi derzhavnyi arkhiv Sluzhby bezpeky Ukraïny): HDA SBU, m. Ternopil',

spr. 30466, 26874, 14050-P, 736, 3713, 14340-P, 9859-P, 8540-P, 8973-P, 14320-P, multiple documents, in Russian and Ukrainian.

30. Eliasz Chalfen, Yad Vashem Testimony, M1/E 1559, translated from Polish by Eva Lutkiewicz.

31. Ester Grintal (Nachtigal), Shoah Foundation video, 21 September 1997, in Hebrew.

32. Yoel Katz, Shoah Foundation video, interviewed by Leah Shimoni, 11 December 1995, in Hebrew.

33. Joe (Yekhezkiel, Jechezkiel, Olszy) Perl, Shoah Foundation video, 14 October 1996, Los Angeles.

34. Edzia Spielberg-Flitman, Shoah Foundation video, 1995, transcribed by Joshua Tobias.

35. Mojżesz Szpigiel, USHMM, reel 37 301/3492, Łódź, 10 March 1948, translated from Polish by Evelyn Zegenhagen.

36. Izaak Szwarc, USHMM, RG-15.084 Acc.1997 A.0125, Reel 5, testimony 327, ZIH 301/327, translated from Polish by Evelyn Zegenhagen.

37. Rene Zuroff (Tabak), Shoah Foundation video, interviewed in Bellmore, New York, on 31 August 1995, by Charlotte Rettinger.

38. This has been discussed especially well by Lawrence L. Langer, *Holocaust Testimonies: The Ruins of Memory* (New Haven, Conn.: Yale University Press, 1991); Wieviorka, *The Era of the Witness.*

39. Rafael Moses, ed., *Persistent Shadows of the Holocaust: The Meaning to Those Not Directly Affected* (Madison, Conn.: International Universities Press, 1993); Dan Bar-On, *Legacy of Silence: Encounters with Children of the Third Reich* (Cambridge, Mass.: Harvard University Press, 1989); idem, *Fear and Hope: Three Generations of the Holocaust* (Cambridge, Mass.: Harvard University Press, 1995).

40. Safah Prüfer, USHMM, reel 49, from ZIH 301/4581, trans. Evelyn Zegenhagen, probably written in 1945–46.

41. Trembach, 2003.

42. Emil Skamene (Kleiner), Shoah Foundation videotaped testimony, 2002, transcribed by Rachel Hoffman.

43. Genia Weksler, USHMM, RG-15.084 Acc.1997 A.0125, Reel 19, Testimony 1865, ZIH 301/1865, sometime in 1946 in Wrocław, translated from Polish by Evelyn Zegenhagen.

44. Bronia Kahane, Shoah Foundation Video, interview with Karen Leeds in South Fallsburg, New York, in English, 8 August 1995, transcribed by Josh Tobias.

45. Aliza Golobov (Bernfeld), Division 0.3, Yad Vashem Testimonies, File # 10241, cassette # 033C/5361, recorded on 29 April 1997, in Hebrew.

46. Hilda Weitz, Shoah Foundation Videotape, Interview 47637, conducted in English by Sylvia Messeri, 4 November 1998, Fort Lee, transcribed by Rachel Hoffman.

47. Zofia Pollak (Zonka Berkowicz), Shoah Foundation video, Interview 05991, conducted in English by Louise Bobrow, 23 August 1995, transcribed by Rachel Hoffman.

48. Cyla Sznajder (Huss), Jewish Historical Institute, Warsaw (ZIH) 301/5699, Wrocław, 25 January 1960.

49. Samuel (Shmuel) Rosen, USHMM, translated from the Polish by Evelyn Zegenhagen, reel 20, testimony 1935, from ZIH 301/1935, given on 6 August 1946, in Kraków.

50. Samuel (Shmuel) Rosen, Yad Vashem, 03/2055, Tel Aviv, 20 December 1960, in file M-49/1935, translated from the Polish by Frank Grelka.

51. Henry Rosen, Holocaust Foundation, 10 November 1997, Chicago, interviewer Rosemarie Levin, transcribed by James T. Stever. A gist of Henry Rosen's story can also be found in Mordecai Paldiel, *The Path of the Righteous: Gentile Rescuers of Jews During the Holocaust* (Hoboken, N.J.: Ktav, 1993), 191–93, along with a photo of Świerszczak.

52. S. Rosen, Yad Vashem, 1960.

53. Omer Bartov interview with Shmuel (Samuel) Rosen and Zev Anderman, Tel Aviv, 12 March 2002, transcribed by Raz Bartov.

54. S. Rosen, Yad Vashem, 1960.

55. H. Rosen, Holocaust Foundation, 1997.

56. The Holocaust Martyrs' and Heroes' Remembrance Authority, *The Righteous Among the Nations Department, Righteous Among the Nations Honored by Yad Vashem,* 1 January 2010, available at the Yad Vashem website, www.yadvashem.org.

57. Wizinger, Moshe, Yad Vashem, 03/3799. The account was written in Cyprus in 1947. Wizinger was a radio technician from Buczacz. Polish text translated by Eva Lutkiewicz.

58. Bauer, 2003.

59. Bundesarchiv B 162/5182: "Aufklärung von NS-Verbrechen im Kreis Czortków / Distrikt Galizien, 1941–1944, Sammelverfahren gg. Brettschneider u.a.," deposition taken on 10 January 1968, 6212–14.

60. George (Gershon) Gross, Shoah Foundation video, 17 June 1996, in English.

61. Wizinger, Yad Vashem, 03/3799.

62. Zofia Pollak, Shoah Foundation video, interview 05991, 23 August 1995.

63. S. Rosen, Yad Vashem, 1960.

64. Ibid.

65. Members of the Zuhler family in Buczacz included Prof. Zuhler, who taught German at the *gymnasium* in 1939 and is said to have survived the war; Herzas Zuhler, who was a prominent prewar merchant; and Regina Zuhler, born in 1907, who testified at a German trial in 1965. Stanisław J. Kowalski, *Powiat Buczacki i jego zabytki* (Biały Dunajec-Ostróg, Poland: Ośrodek "Wołanie z Wołynia," 2005), 89; Adam Żarnowski, ed., *Kresy Wschodnie II Rzeczypospolitej: Buczacz* (Krakow: Wydanie Własne [privately published], 1992), 9; *Aufklärung von NS-Verbrechen im Kreis Czortków/Distrikt Galizien 1941–1944: Sammelverfahren gg. Brettschneider u.a.,* Bundersarchiv, B 162/5163, 492–93.

66. Bartov interview with Rosen and Anderman, 2002.

67. Yisrael Kohen, ed., *The Book of Buczacz* (Tel Aviv: Am Oved, 1956, in Hebrew), 246, 288.

68. Szwarc, ZIH 301/327. Another account mentions an Abraham Anderman who is said to have shot a policeman during an *Aktion* in July (more likely June) 1943: Zakhar Gerber, Shoah Foundation video interview, 28 November 1996, Akko, Israel, in Russian, translated by Jane Zolot-Gassko; similarly, Moshe Wizinger mentions a certain A. Anderman who shot and killed a Ukrainian policeman in June 1943 and then escaped: Wizinger, Yad Vashem, 03/3799; and Yitzhak Bauer's above-cited 1968 deposition speaks of "Max Andermann, a former member of the OD, [who] was killed in May 1944": Bundesarchiv B 162/5182. But Dr. Max Anderman, born in Buczacz in 1907, made a deposition in Israel to a German court in 1965. According to this document, he worked in the Jewish hospital until May 1942, after which he was in hiding until the liberation: Bundersarchiv B 162/5169, *Aufklärung von NS-Verbrechen im Kreis Czortków / Distrikt Galizien, 1941–1944, Sammelverfahren gg. Brettschneider u.a.,* deposition taken on 27 December 1965, 1977–1978.

69. For an effective use of oral histories in reconstructing interethnic violence in another part of the world, see Vazira Fazila-Yacoobali Zamindar, *The Long Partition and the Making of Modern South Asia: Refugees, Boundaries, Histories* (New York: Columbia University Press, 2007).

PART FIVE
Ritual, Symbolism, and Identity

22

Liquid Borderland, Inelastic Sea?

Mapping the Eastern Adriatic

Pamela Ballinger

Writing of the Mediterranean, Predrag Matvejević has argued, "Its boundaries are drawn in neither space nor time. There is in fact no way of drawing them: they are neither ethnic nor historical, state nor national; they are like a chalk circle that is constantly traced and erased, that the winds and waves, that obligations and inspirations expand or reduce."[1] This conceptualization of the Mediterranean owes much to Matvejević's personal experiences of (and on) the Adriatic, a body of water he deems a "sea of intimacy."[2] In attributing a fundamental indeterminacy to the Adriatic and the larger Mediterranean Sea of which it forms a part, Matvejević highlights a characteristic of most borderzones or borderlands: at different historical moments or in different contexts, they may figure as sites of coexistence or violent conflict, rigidity or fluidity, purity or hybridity. For the Mediterranean, for example, Bromberger has identified opposed "polyphonic" and "cacophonic" models, associated respectively with the metaphors of bridge and wall.[3]

These understandings of maritime border regions share much in common with representations of the largely terrestrial imperial shatterzones detailed in this volume, yet seas and watery spaces usually do not come to mind when discussing those East European borderlands that nurtured both coexistence and genocidal violence in the twentieth century. In this chapter, I argue that contests to define and possess terrestrial borderlands in the Adriatic region of southeastern Europe have not only extended into the watery realm but also that the sea itself has proven a key element in the construction of symbolic geographies that map some groups onto territories to which they are said to "belong" and which exclude others.

Seas: Spaces of Fluidity?

Matvejević's vision of the porous boundaries of the Mediterranean accords with a common view of seas as spaces of both literal and metaphorical fluidity, as media that confound efforts to draw rigid boundaries. Of late, watery metaphors have proven popular among theorists seeking to characterize the globalized post–Cold War order in terms that capture flux and mobility. Stefan Helmreich, for instance, deems water a "theory machine" for contemporary anthropology.[4] Zygmunt Bauman has gone so far as to define a new phase of modernity as "liquid," expressed in his belief that "'fluidity' or 'liquidity' [are] fitting metaphors when we wish to grasp the nature of the present, in many ways *novel*, phase in the history of modernity."[5]

Despite the vogue for using watery metaphors to capture the fluidity of the globalized world, along the contemporary Adriatic understandings of *actual* (rather than metaphorical) seawater suggest that sites of literal fluidity may not necessarily be sites of fluid or elastic understandings of territory. Since 1992, I have conducted field research in varied locales in the northeastern Adriatic, ranging from Trieste (Italy) to Piran (Slovenia) to Savudrija, Rovinj, and Lošinj (Croatia). I have investigated topics ranging from memories of the post-1945 exodus from the Istrian peninsula after it passed from Italian to Yugoslav control, to contemporary debates over privatization along the Croatian coast, to efforts to establish a marine protected area off the island of Lošinj. In all of these examples I have found that the sea figures prominently as a marker of identity and that inhabitants of the region often conceive of the sea not so much as a fluid space but as one delimited by boundaries, a vision embodied in cartographic representations of the Adriatic cut through by the rigid vectors of state borders.

It does not prove surprising, perhaps, that in the realm of state sovereignty, seaspace does not always carry with it associations of fluidity. The notion of the "high seas" as free dates only to the seventeenth century, for example, with its articulation by Dutch jurist Hugo de Groot (Grotius) in his 1609 work *Mare Liberum*. Grotius' advocacy of common access to the sea and its resources (*res communis*) did not entirely extinguish older ideas and practices of control of the seas (particularly of fisheries) by specific powers, an approach espoused by the Englishmen John Selden in his 1634 *Mare Clausum*.[6] By the twentieth century, international law began to recognize and expand national claims and rights to waters and their associated resources. The 1930 Hague Convention, for instance, provided legal recognition of a narrow band of waters, known as the territorial sea, over which states exercise national sovereignty.[7]

In the latter half of the twentieth century, the territorial sea concept was extended from 3 to 12 navigational miles. In addition, the United Nations Convention on the Law of the Sea codified the notion of Exclusive Economic Zones (EEZ) extending 200 miles out from coastal states, a concept with precedents in the Truman Declarations of 1945, the 1952 Santiago Declaration, and the more modest fisheries zones established by the 1964 European Fisheries Convention.[8] Seaspace, at least that adjacent to land masses, has thus increasingly become "contained" by lines and vectors on maps and charts, as well as signatures on international agreements. This political process followed a century of intense debate by cartographers and geographers about how to conceptualize seaspace, which by the twentieth century was predominantly modeled in terms of discrete and delineated ocean basins and seas.[9]

The Adriatic has long been defined by its position as a frontier space contested by competing empires and states, what sociologist Emilio Cocco calls a "maritime counterpart to the [Balkan] space poised between East and West."[10] Although by the twelfth century Venice effectively ruled the Adriatic as its sea (*mare clausum*), it also faced repeated challenges to its dominion. In practice, the Adriatic represented a shifting border between the Ottoman/ Muslim East and the Christian West.[11]

In subsequent centuries, the Adriatic would constitute a symbolic and political border between new competing powers. In the nineteenth century, for example, distinctions between peoples living along the coast and in the interior of the eastern Adriatic increasingly became mapped (figuratively and literally) onto exclusive ethno-national divisions even as the Habsburg Empire fostered a multiethnic, multiconfessional, and "cosmopolitan" maritime culture centered on Trieste/Trst and Rijeka/Fiume. The mapping of cultural difference among the peoples of the Eastern Adriatic and, more specifically, around the Gulf of Trieste reflects imperial projects of classification initiated by the Venetians and the Habsburgs and later reworked by ethnologists and cultural geographers in Italy, Yugoslavia, and beyond.

After 1945, the Adriatic became the borderland between the communist east and capitalist west. Yugoslav efforts to rigidify this marine border by controlling "incursions" on the part of fishermen from nearby Italy and by restricting maritime transportation to Italy proved particularly marked in the early years of the Cold War.[12] Between 1945 and 1954, the territory comprising the port city of Trieste and the adjacent Istrian peninsula was the object of competing Italian and Yugoslav claims, a contest within which unfolded the mass migration of between 200,000 and 250,000 individuals out of the area for a variety of reasons (political, ethno-national, religious, and economic).

Cocco argues that in the contemporary moment the Adriatic's role as a borderzone has gone from that of wall to bridge. He writes, "the Adriatic finds itself once again a frontier sea that, from the presumed immobility of the post World War II period (represented by the image of the "iron curtain") is now becoming a *space of mobility* favoring strategic contacts, the process of European integration, and transborder collaboration."[13] While this may be true of the larger Adriatic, interstate disputes like the two-decades-long squabble between Slovenia and Croatia over where to draw their maritime boundary or local resistance to a marine protected area off the island of Lošinj—examples I examine in the second half of the chapter—suggest that the notion of "a solid sea" (*un mare solido*) that Cocco locates in other historical moments persists. This solidity becomes evident in both the logic of certain state practices and in the imaginations of some local inhabitants.

Contemporary invocations of the Adriatic as simultaneously bordered and border sea remap durable symbolic boundaries of inclusion and exclusion. These boundaries both follow out of and express the thesis that the sea rightfully "belongs" to some cultures and peoples and not to others. In the territorial contests waged over the eastern Adriatic by Italy and Yugoslavia after World I and again after World War II, proponents of the Italian position (including folklorists) often posited a coastal/interior distinction as a key symbolic boundary between (putatively) distinct cultural-linguistic groups: Italians and Slavs. As a consequence of this politicized scheme of symbolic geography, Italian scholars tended to neglect the Slavic presence along the shores of the upper Adriatic. Ethnographers of the First Yugoslavia focused instead on key boundaries *within* the South Slav group, with relatively little attention paid to the Latinized/Italianized populations on the Dalmatian and Istrian coasts. The Yugoslav cultural geographer Jovan Cvijić (one of the founders of the Department of Ethnology in Belgrade), for example, included both Istria and Trieste as part of a Balkan cultural space.[14] These competing traditions continue to resonate in contemporary representations of cultural spheres around the Gulf of Trieste, drawing upon older imperial schemes of classification even as they refract new political exigencies.

In my anthropological work among individuals who self-identify as "Italian" and who migrated from the Istrian and Kvarner regions to Trieste and other parts of Italy after World War II, I have encountered frequent articulations of the coast–interior division as reflecting a split between Italian and Slavic cultural spheres. Many of my informants contended that as "Italians" left the Istrian peninsula *en masse* between 1945 and 1954, Slavic peoples came from the interior of Istria (or Yugoslavia more generally) and took up residence in a foreign and strange environment to which they did not belong by either custom or historical right. The incompatibility of these "inlanders" with coastal culture is said to become evident in intimate and familiar spheres such as cooking; advocates of the Italianist position point to practices such as cooking fish with vegetable oil rather than olive oil as evidence of the Slavs' inauthentic maritime and Mediterraneanist credentials. Despite the fact that Slavic-speaking peoples long inhabited areas along the coast near Trieste and in Istria, the powerful mapping of ethno-national identity onto place (coast/interior) underwrites persistent stereotypes that these peoples "belong" exclusively to certain environments and territories and vice versa.[15]

Istrian Italian exiles are not unique in questioning the authenticity of groups inhabiting the maritime environments of the contemporary Adriatic. Fishermen I interviewed in the Croatian town of Savudrija, which sits astride the maritime border contested between the independent states of Slovenia and Croatia, make similar arguments about the lack of a homegrown fishing tradition in Slovene Istria as a result of the post–World War II exodus, which largely emptied the coastal towns. The differentiation between Italians and Slavs on the coastal/interior axis thus parallels broader anthropogeographic distinctions historically employed to mark differences among South Slav peoples.

The following section sketches out a brief history of the symbolic geographies employed in competing national/ist visions along the eastern Adriatic. Elsewhere, I have examined the role of the museum and the census as key taxonomic instruments in boundary making in the northeastern Adriatic.[16] Here, I will focus on the map—both in its cartographic and ethnographic forms.

Maritime Cartographies, Social Geographies

The classificatory maps of coastal and interior peoples that became overlaid with ethno-national distinctions in the nineteenth and twentieth centuries refracted the larger symbolic geographies constructed by travelers to the areas that eventually became known as the Balkans and Eastern Europe. An extensive and rich body of scholarship has focused on the ways in which outsiders "invented" these regional designations and their attendant discursive configurations, with both Eastern Europe and the Balkans viewed as constituting a transitional zone poised between light and darkness, civilization and barbarism.[17] Yet Wendy Bracewell has recently reminded us that although "Much recent research has encouraged us to think of . . . the inhabitants of the east of Europe as the passive objects of western discursive construction—more mapped than mapping . . . the invention of Europe and of its constituent parts was hardly so one-sided."[18] Bracewell and her collaborators have focused on travel writing by East Europeans as a particularly significant site for such self-imagining or, more precisely, the dialectical relationship between external and internal ascriptions of identity and place. Here, I will instead focus on two particular forms of mapping—cartography and ethnography—that typically inform the kinds of travel accounts Bracewell analyzes and by which both insiders and outsiders have delimited the eastern Adriatic.

When judged by modern cartographic standards, Mediterranean *portolani* or sea charts (the oldest surviving example of which, the *Carte Pisane,* dates to the late 1200s) represent one of the most "accurate" mappings of medieval and early modern European space. A relatively large number of these *portolani* have survived, suggesting a long and fairly extensive tradition of such mapping for the Mediterranean Sea. These *portolan* charts appear to have served various functions, including the mapping of trade and navigational routes, the imagining of Mediterranean (and, successively, Atlantic) space by sovereigns and other elite consumers, and strategic military information vital to waging war.[19]

Although *portolani* focused on a specific region like the Adriatic were rare,[20] the popular genre of *isolarii* or illustrated "island books" usually featured maps focused on regional archipelagoes or coastal areas. Some scholars have viewed the *isolarii* as "early examples of regional island atlases" or "primitive tourist guides,"[21] combining as they did the ethnographic (information about customs) with the cartographic. The products of "Mediterranean people . . . all of [whom] had some sort of connection with the islands,"[22] the *isolarii* (and many *portolani*) reflected local knowledge. Venice became a center for the production of such *isolarii* and of cartographic works more generally,[23] reflecting the fact that in Venice cartography "was already playing an established role in the state bureaucracy for territorial management in the sixteenth century."[24]

In particular, the imperial struggle between Venice and the Ottomans for control of the Adriatic and beyond prompted the publication of many maps of the sea and islands.[25] It also encouraged efforts to map the military frontier between the Ottoman and Habsburg empires, although many of these maps were not published commercially owing to their secret military information.[26] The Ottoman navy of the sixteenth century, for example, used as a guide the "Book of the Sea" that Ottoman admiral and geographer Piri-Re'is put together drawing on *portolani* and *isolarii,* among other materials.[27] Both island books and *portolani* were therefore "linked with the European powers' vested interests in the eastern Mediterranean, and later with their colonial system in general."[28] In the case of the Venetians, who dominated the Adriatic for centuries, "the map became part of the process of government . . . the map's communicative efficacy made it into a tool for the furtherance of social strategies, a highly effective means for the promotion of political policies."[29] As this all too brief discussion suggests, the Mediterranean and its inner seas, including the Adriatic, have long histories as mapped and bounded spaces, or at least as sites that have invited intensive efforts at mapping and boundary making.

Portolani typically depicted features of the hinterland such as mountains schematically,[30] reflecting a valorization of the coast common throughout much of the Mediterranean region. In the eastern Adriatic, the coastal–interior divide frequently mapped onto distinctions between the urban (site of civilization and the urbane) and the rural (the place of backwardness). This axis of differentiation dates back at least as far as the Venetian period, though it has deeper roots in the patterns of settlement established during the Roman era. Eventually, this symbolic boundary between urban/rural and coastal/interior would merge with ethno-national (and class) distinctions. In turn, ethnographic elaborations of this symbolic geography would frequently (though not always) underwrite national and territorial claims.

Venetian imperial administrators primarily categorized difference among its subjects in and along the Adriatic in terms of civilization or its lack, rather than in terms of ethnic distinctions. The significant axis of differentiation distinguished the "civilized" peoples of the coast from the "rough" peoples of the interior (the Morlacchi of Dalmatia and Cicarija/Cicceria).[31] By the late imperial period, some Venetian observers began to reclassify these "Morlacchi" as Slavs more closely connected to a larger pan-Slavic world rather than an Adriatic sphere or culture.

The consolidation of these still unstable understandings of identity into more coherent ethno-national classifications took place during the Habsburg era thanks, in part, to more comprehensive projects of both cartographic mapping and ethnographic description.[32] Initially, these new maps reflected class (and, to some degree, regional) differentiations more than ethnic or national ones. Between the 1790s and 1830s, ethnic stereotypes in the Habsburg Empire served not so much to encode exclusive differences as to provide a guide for the construction of a civil society by illuminating which virtues (and, by extension, which peoples exhibiting them) should undergird the public sphere.[33] As the nineteenth century progressed, however, political identities increasingly became wed to exclusive ethno-national distinctions centered on religion and language (rather than rank in a society of orders), particularly in border areas and other mixed zones.[34]

A tradition of ethnographic study examining such ethnically mixed regions was already well established in the German-speaking lands in the eighteenth century. Eighteenth and nineteenth-century German observers of the Habsburg Adriatic perceived this region as belonging to the "South."[35] Writers often discussed the different languages of the region and placed the area's different groups into a hierarchy, which tended to treat the coastal "Italians" as more culturally advanced in contrast to the interior "Slavs," often deemed lazy and unkempt but also simple (in a state of nature). These representations of Slovenes and Croats converged with other negative stereotypes about Slavic peoples, often depicted by German-speaking scholars (particularly those in dialogue with the descriptive statistical school in Germany) as "naturmenschen: hardened, lazy, wild, sensual, poor, extravagant, and drunken."[36] These character differences ostensibly mirrored the physical landscapes these peoples inhabited, with the desolation of the (Slavic) karst contrasted to the fertility of the (Italian) coast. In his 1833 travel account, Carl Gottlob Kuettner phrased the contrast in these terms: "At length you arrive at the end of the Karst, and suddenly find yourself on the brink of a precipice which would make you shudder did you not anticipate the appearance of Hesperia's enchanting plains . . . what a contrast to the country we had just traversed."[37]

For authors like Kuettner, however, the primary differentiation still lay not between Italians and Slavs (both of them subject peoples of the empire) but between these groups and Germanic peoples, the latter becoming the sanctimonious upholders or "*Musterknaben* of progress and civilization."[38] Comparisons of Adriatic Slavs linked them with Slavic groups further afield, as well as with Tatars and other Caucasian peoples. Such comparisons inevitably praised Germans and made claims to territory on the basis of a civilizing mission, a logic shared by Italian nationalists and their cult of civilization or *civiltà*. As Cathie Carmichael puts it, "Looked at in this way, the Slavs were history's squatters."[39]

With its implicit focus on geography, Herder's work proved quite influential in the formulation of these ethnographic distinctions between peoples and their environments. "By discovering that 'Slavs' had a different kind of *Volksgeist* to their neighbours," writes Carmichael, "the question of what we might euphemistically call territorial incompatibility would eventually have to be raised, which was crucial in the multiethnic milieus of Central and Eastern Europe."[40] The discourse of territorial incompatibility would become particularly prominent in the upper Adriatic during the late Habsburg and Italian eras. Bracewell's caution about seeing the peoples of Central and Eastern Europe as "more mapped than mapping," however, should keep us attuned to the participation of those individuals self-identi-fying as Slavs in the discursive construction of Slavdom and its component parts. Bracewell reminds us, for example, that "Well before 1842, travellers had traced the coordinates of a Slav world in textual form, projecting a Slavic landscape of memory and of desire onto the physical space of Europe."[41]

Ethnographic projects like the Kronprinzenwerk (KPW)—24 volumes of ethnograph-ic descriptions published between 1886 and 1902 that mapped out the Habsburg Empire's array of peoples and cultures—took for granted the dimensions of this Slav world, further reifying notions of difference between the empire's Slavic, Germanic, and Italian peoples. Ironically, the KPW's promoters aimed "to undermine the idea of territorial exclusivity for individual ethnicities," thereby providing an alternative to the "land and peoples" model of ethnographic survey promoted by scholars like Wilhelm Heinrich Riehl.[42] The chapter devoted to the Littoral (Küstenland) comprising Trieste and Istria, for example, discussed physical traits together with "costume and custom." In the end, however, the KPW rein-forced stereotypical images of cultural difference that nationalists increasingly mapped onto demands for territory.

As Italian irredentists claiming Trieste and Istria became more strident during the late Habsburg period and then after World War I when these areas became part of the Italian state, many Italian folklorists sought to validate Italy's territorial claims by demonstrating Istria's Italian ethnic provenance. Triestine scholar Francesco Babudri, for instance, went as far as to claim the existence of a common regional language ("Veneto-giuliano"), despite a complete lack of evidence. Laura Oretti notes that Babudri's assertions sketch the "image of a monocultural area, rigidly determined and impermeable to foreign influence,"[43] an image that denied the reality of Istria's cultural and linguistic intermixture. Italian research derived from the anthropogeographic tradition noted the great "importance that the sea has in sta-bilizing/determining population," particularly its effects on climate, fishing, and navigation; one scholar even mapped out the population distribution in Istria in relation to its distance from the sea.[44] Contending that the majority of Istrians lived on or near the sea, Giannandrea Gravisi implicitly traded upon the association of the coast with Italian culture to claim Istria as belonging territorially to Italy.

From the other direction, cultural geographers and ethnologists like Jovan Cvijić, Dinko Tomašić, and Branimir Gušić powerfully shaped ethnological approaches in the First Yugoslavia by reworking older Habsburg anthropogeographic traditions. Key to the clas-sificatory systems of these scholars was an ethnographic division between peoples inhabit-ing distinctive environments, notably the Dinaric mountain area and the Pannonian Plain.[45] Trained in Vienna in the German tradition of anthropogeography and sociology, Cvijić gave great weight to environment as delimiting cultural characteristics of specific peoples.[46] For the area in and around Istria, he distinguished the karst not only as a particular type of environment but also as defining a mode of village settlement[47] that differed from a "Medi-terranean type" of town along the Adriatic coast. Central to the Dinaric type was a strong at-tachment to land and place of birth, suggesting a terrestrial orientation even for those Slavic peoples who lived along the Adriatic Sea.

Whereas Cvijić devoted little attention to the peoples of the Pannonian Plains, focus-ing instead on the Dinaric type he valorized, Yugoslav ethnographer Dinko Tomašić instead idealized the rural plains dwellers of Croatia in contrast to what he saw as the violent, emo-tionally unbalanced pastoralists of the Dinaric zone.[48] Later ethnologists of socialist Yugoslavia such as Milovan Gavazzi, who defined the anthropological research paradigm in and for Croatia into the 1980s, refashioned the coastal/interior terms somewhat but nonetheless kept the distinction in place. Gavazzi viewed the Adriatic coast as a place where the Mediterranean and Dinaric culture areas—distinguished primarily by modes of livelihood determined, in turn, by ecological conditions—intersected.[49] Though these distinctions central to Yugoslav ethnography refuted the Italian nationalist view of the littoral as belonging exclusively to an Italian culture complex, such ideas shared with those of the Italian nationalists an assumption that cultural values and psychological dispositions largely reflect the specific environments in which groups reside.

Similar arguments about territorial belonging (and incompatibility) featured prominently in the territorial struggle between Yugoslavia and Italy over the region after World War II and continue to figure in popular representations of ethnic and territorial identities today. Anthropologist Bojan Baskar, for example, has demonstrated how some of Cvijić's ideas implicitly inform the contemporary writings of Italians and Istrian Italians in Trieste with "an implicit but perfectly unambiguous extension of this menacing Dinaric habitat to [the] Karst immediately behind Trieste (which is inhabited by Slovenes) and indirectly to central Slovenia as well."[50]

Beyond Trieste and Istria, the coastal/interior distinction today often serves more to underscore differences between Slavic groups, rather than between "coastal" Italian and "karstic" Slavic peoples. In the 1990s, the coastal/interior distinction "was on occasions conflated with the distinction between the predominantly ethnic Croatian Littoral and the predominantly ethnic Serbian hinterland."[51] Drawing on the work of an older generation of Yugoslav ethnologists, for instance, some sociologists revived long-standing anthropogeographical distinctions to explain Yugoslavia's bloody breakup.[52] In analyzing the geographic elements of such ethnological work, Kaser highlights the pervasive link in both the scholarly and popular imaginations between "Balkan" peoples and specific places/environments. In the next section, I inquire into the afterlives of the various projects of mapping I have traced out here.

Redrawing the Map: The Inelasticity of Water

Scholars examining efforts to "make a society legible" (to borrow James Scott's phrasing) through the use of technical instruments such as censuses and maps designed to measure and consolidate clear-cut categorizations of identity usually focus on top-down directives. In the case of the cartographic traditions for the Adriatic already discussed, however, local knowledge and agency often proved quite significant. In today's world of increasingly standardized cartographic techniques and globalizing ethnographic perspectives, then, what role do maps play in the imaginations of locals in the eastern Adriatic? How does the symbolic geography of coast/hinterland continue to inform understandings of ethnic and national difference?

Since World War II and the large-scale migration of Italian populations out of Istria, the coastal/interior distinction has increasingly become an instrument for distinguishing between Slovenes and Croats in Istrian life. This is particularly true in the contemporary moment, in which Istria's maritime boundary between Slovenia and Croatia remains unresolved. (In November 2010 Slovenia and Croatia did, however, exchange diplomatic notes to ratify an agreement to finally submit the dispute to international arbitration and in January 2012 the two states agreed upon the members for an arbitral tribunal.) Together with a "fishermen's war" marked by occasional incursions and provocations by each side, the maritime dispute led to a war of maps and names, with at least some Croatian fishermen and one map privately published in Croatia proposing a name change for the bay in question from "Bay (or Gulf) of Piran" (referring to the town of Piran on the Slovene side of the gulf) to "Bay of Savudrija" (in reference to the settlement on the Croatian side of the bay).[53] I was surprised by the extent to which maps entered into everyday people's manner of conceptualizing the sea, although perhaps I should have expected this given the duration of a conflict at whose heart rest arguments about borders. Furthermore, maps proved crucial to how nonelite actors argued about who owns that sea. This relative "inelasticity of water" reflects the long history of state-making efforts in and around the Adriatic seaspace that I have already noted, as well as new contexts of post-socialist property privatization and European Union candidacy. Croatia completed accession negotiations in June 2011 and signed the accession treaty in December of that same year.

In referring to the "inelasticity of water," I adapt a concept developed by anthropologist Katherine Verdery in her study of land restitution in post-socialist Romania. As she began to study the restitution process, Verdery acknowledged, "I found my mental map of a fixed landscape . . . becoming destabilized. Parcels and whole fields seemed to stretch and shrink; a rigid surface was becoming pliable, more like a canvas. It was as if the earth heaved and sank, expanding and diminishing the area contained within a set of two-dimensional coordinates."[54] Detailing what she deemed the "elasticity of land," Verdery described property that "moves, stretches, evaporates."[55] Puzzled, she asked, "How can bits of the earth's surface migrate, expand, disappear, shrink, and otherwise behave as anything but firmly fixed in place?"[56] From another direction, as I began to examine debates about access to and ownership of the coast and the sea in Croatia I had to ask myself how that preeminent medium and site of fluidity—the sea—could behave as anything but shifting, mobile, and liquid? As with the politics of Romanian land restitution, contests over determining and restricting control of Adriatic seaspace reflect and refract the broader struggle of what Verdery deems "certain groups and persons to tie property down against others who would keep its edges flexible, uncertain, amorphous."[57]

Among those groups seeking to tie watery territory down along the Croatian coast are fishermen. In interviewing fishermen on both sides of the contested maritime border in Croatia and Slovenia, I was struck by the profound ways in which such fishermen have naturalized cartographic logics. Again and again, fishermen scribbled in my notebook or drew on napkins what they understood to be the demands of the Slovene and Croatian states regarding the delimitation of the border.

Although an administrative and republican land border existed within the Yugoslav federation prior to Slovene and Croatian independence in 1991, a strict maritime boundary did not.[58] As Kladnik and Pipan note,

> The border between the Yugoslav republics of Slovenia and Croatia was not precisely defined everywhere. The territory between the Blessed Odoric Canal (the southernmost channel of the Dragonja River) and the southern border of the cadastral district of Piran, which precisely follows the line between the alluvial plain of the Dragonja River and the corrosion plain slope of the Buje karst region, is an area that was covered by two record systems: it belonged to the Slovenian cadastral system on one hand and the Croatian administrative system on the other. Discussions over the border flared up considerably after both countries declared independence on 25 June 1991.[59]

In addition to the competing record systems that make for confusion, another issue at stake is whether the River Dragonja, often taken as the "traditional" border between Slovenia and Croatia in Istria, constitutes the "true" border, particularly since the Habsburgs had altered the waterway's course. In the case of the maritime border between Slovenia and Croatia, the vectors drawn on competing maps by fishermen and politicians only take away or add watery territory in the zero-sum game logic of sovereignty; the total space available does not appear to grow or shrink in the manner of the elastic property described by Verdery. Maps drawn for me by fishermen were produced spontaneously, rather than in response to any request. In their mappings, the fishermen replicated the proposals published in newspapers or challenged those of the opposing side. Marko (pseudonym), one of the fishermen I had first interviewed in 2002, reacted angrily several years later when I showed him a profession-ally produced map promoting Slovene maximalist claims and offering "historical evidence" in support of these arguments. Marko had already sent a letter of protest to the Slovene Ministry of Fisheries, finding it "scandalous" that such a map could be printed and sold in Slovenia. Yet a Croatian equivalent exists in the 2007 map "Topografska karta Umag," which prominently labels the contested waters the "Bay of Savudrija."[60]

The fishermen's internalized versions of these professional maps seem far from the kinds of mental mappings typically associated with fisherfolk, whether they be the mental images of rocky bottoms and fish spawning grounds recorded by Maine fisher-scholar Ted Ames (which often proved difficult to square with nautical maps)[61] or the "acoustemolo-gies"[62] and "soundings" by which Indonesian Mandars "call" fish.[63] One map jotted in my notebook and depicting marine life and currents in the Gulf of Trieste (represented as a sea without state boundaries) matched my expectations of what a fisher might draw. Ironically, given that fishers in a variety of cultures frequently use their local knowledge to contest the "scientific" paradigms of biologists and policy makers, this map was actually sketched by a marine biologist from Trieste, not a fisher. This is not to deny to the Slovene and Croatian fishers other kinds of local, place-based knowledge specific to their experiences of the sea but rather to emphasize the ways in which cartographic visions of *inelastic seaspace* and marine property have colonized at least a part of their imaginations. Yet mapping is never a mere re-flection of power relations (and the power/knowledge nexus) but also an active constitution of understandings of space, and thus the fishers should also be seen as active agents in this bordering process. As noted previously, fishermen created such maps in a context in which the border question had become extremely politicized. Some fishermen actively participated in the political mobilization around the border, as occurred on Croatian Independence Day in June 2002 when a fleet of fishing boats aimed to plant a Croatian flag on a floating marker in the middle of the bay. In the last two decades, incidents between Croatian fishermen and Slovene (marine) police or protests by Slovene nationalists at the land border Šecovlje on the Gulf of Piran regularly heated up during electoral campaigns in Croatia and Slovenia.

Was this just a watery version of the fighting over maps that characterized the Yugo-slav conflicts in the 1990s, a process in which—as geographer Jeremy Crampton wrote of Bosnia—the "map (or maps) are active solutions of the situation, rather than merely pas-sive outcomes"?[64] Do the fishermen merely internalize and replicate the logics of national-ism? Certainly, some local leaders in Croatian Istria believed so when they characterized the fishermen as "Balkan" and "politically immature."[65] Leaders voicing this negative judgment feared the opposition would harm cooperative relations with Slovenia and, thus, Croatia's prospects for EU membership.

Croatian fishermen with whom I spoke, however, rejected the suggestion that their defense of the maritime border represented a typical demonstration of "Balkan nationalism." Rather, they expressed the need to defend local interests in the face of demands posed by the EU accession process. In discussing the "disciplining" effects of EU candidacy and the clout wielded by their Slovene neighbors, fishermen also explicitly linked the debate over the border to the blight on the landscape created by privatization and construction of new summer homes and resorts, a process in which Slovene capital has proven critical. In another kind of mental map, then, the Croatian fishers connected a privatized terrestrial landscape with their imagining of sea and its borders. Slovenian fishermen instead expressed a fear of too narrowly contained a sea, what we might call a *mare claustrophobum.*

In other contexts, though, some Croatian fishers instead rejected altogether the logic of "lines in the water" when they feared that outsiders had imposed such maps. This is the case for the proposed marine protected area (MPA) off of the island of Lošinj. Responding in part to lobbying by the Lošinj-based NGO Blue World, which had long argued that the waters off of Lošinj constituted a critical dolphin habitat, in 2006 the Croatian government announced the establishment of a conservation area. The MPA declaration set out a three-year period of "preventive protection," during which time local stakeholders were to devise and agree upon a regulatory framework. A variety of local opposition forces—prominent among them local fishermen—succeeded in preventing the MPA's realization, however, and the preventive protection expired in 2009.

One common thread running through discourses of opposition on the island posited the "foreign" status of Blue World, with the MPA viewed as an imposition by outsiders seeking to maximize their own interests.[66] For some locals, the project appeared to be just another initiative in postsocialist "privatization" by outsiders, with the sea and its resources now the property to which access would be regulated and rendered private. Undeniably, the legislative decree establishing the MPA came from above with little consultation of local stakeholders; interestingly, the announcement of the MPA took even Blue World staff by surprise. The timing of the 2006 announcement, though, was anything but coincidental, intended as it was to send an explicit message to the European Union about the Croatian state's commitment to environmental protection. Fears and resentment about the MPA clearly drew on a larger reservoir of suspicion that Croatia aimed to sacrifice the interests and well-being of everyday citizens in order to enter the EU, a theme that echoes the fears of fishers on the Croatian side of the contested maritime border.

Although locals on Lošinj shared with fishermen in Savudrija fears about a privatized coast and sea from which they would be shut out, the plan for an MPA required that local stakeholders (including Blue World and the fishermen's council) work together to determine the rules governing the reserve. Researchers at Blue World made it clear that they were interested neither in formulating rules on their own nor in enforcing them. The regulatory recommendations that Blue World put forward to the Croatian government and to local entities reflected careful consideration of a host of factors, including pragmatic ones about what was politically possible. Some critics nonetheless complained about the arbitrary nature of the reserve's proposed boundaries, given the high mobility of dolphins.

The MPA's proposed borders, represented by straight lines on the map of the waters around Lošinj, rested on the cartographic logics that have governed the sea's partitioning for the last two centuries. Blue World scientists, however, had no illusions about the bordering processes at work in mapping the MPA. They openly acknowledged the mismatch of political and ecological maps; the proposed reserve boundary *was* arbitrary in ecological terms. The delimitation of the reserve coincided with Lošinj's administrative border with the neighboring islands of Pag and Rab, in strategic recognition that the MPA would be much easier to manage if lying within one *općina* (municipality) rather than cross-cutting several. Thus Blue World proponents of the MPA admitted the rigidity and inelasticity of the MPA border as one that did not match the fluidity of the resource (the local dolphin population) it aimed to protect. Despite Blue World insistence that the area would remain open to a variety of human uses, including fishing and tourism, many local critics feared other kinds of inelasticity that the reserve might bring, including restricted access and reduction of fishing.

Fishers on Lošinj and beyond fear a much tighter regime of fisheries regulation once Croatia comes under the aegis of the EU Common Fisheries Policy. The MPA, like the maritime border dispute, thus became a lightning rod for more diffused anxieties about the future not only of Lošinj but also of Croatia more generally—about sovereignty at its most macro and most micro levels. In these various contests, maps of the sea both reflected and furthered debates about where and how to redraw borders in a former imperial shatterzone.

Conclusions

As I have explored, bodies of water like the Adriatic have served as both fluid/elastic and rigid/inelastic borderlands in southeastern Europe depending on the historical moment and context. The symbolic geography that juxtaposes "maritime" or "coastal" cultures with those of the interior or karstic hinterland has played important roles in identity formation in a region in which anthropogeographic assumptions about peoples mapping onto specific environments and territories have been salient since at least the late eighteenth century. Despite this, the growing body of literature devoted to Europe's southern and eastern border zones has focused on terrestrial borders more than watery ones. This points to a larger "continental" bias in historical writing on the modern era.[67]

Faced with this continental bias and the historical baggage of a symbolic geography that has positioned Slavs as "squatters" along the Adriatic coastline, intellectuals from the area along the northeastern Adriatic have often turned their backs on the sea and embraced continental, terrestrial identities or, at the very least, have expressed ambivalence toward an Adriatic/Mediterranean identity. Indeed, the place of the sea in Croatian national identity has occasioned considerable scholarly debate.[68] Despite the importance of coastal tourism to the republic of Croatia in the socialist federation of Yugoslavia, for example, the so-called "Adriatic Orientation" often proved "inconsistent with the views and interests of the centre of power, far from the sea."[69] Likewise, studies of the coast occupied a marginal place within traditions of royalist and socialist Yugoslav ethnography, a lacuna that Croatian anthropologists have begun to challenge in recent years.

In this article, I have sought to demonstrate the scholarly purchase in attending to the maritime realms of Europe's eastern borderlands. The symbolic and political construction of the watery borderlands that I have discussed has much in common with that of terrestrial borderzones in the region. These symbolic geographies that have both informed and reflected political geographies have durable afterlives not just in the minds of scholars but also in the residents of these frontier regions, who may reproduce or challenge the cartographic and ethnographic maps that social actors in the region have themselves participated in mapping out historically. In the contemporary upper Adriatic, for instance, distinctions once used to ethnically demarcate "Italians" from "Slavs" and to make claims about the territories that "rightfully" belonged to each of these groups increasingly serve as markers of "Croatian" and "Slovene" identity in the struggle to define the maritime and terrestrial borders between the countries. Processes such as post-socialist privatization and the politics of European Union membership provide new contexts in which such symbolic geographies are reconfigured. In all this, the sea continues to play a prominent role. While the symbolic uses to which the sea and coast are put prove quite elastic, the borders being drawn down the maps of the sea become increasingly inelastic.

NOTES

The research for this article was made possible by fellowships from the National Council for Eurasian and East European Research, Wenner-Gren Foundation, and the Fletcher, Rusack, and Phocas Family Funds at Bowdoin College. I am grateful to the staffs at the Centro di Ricerche Storiche di Rovigno and Blue World for facilitating my research on the Adriatic.

1. Predrag Matvejević, *Mediterranean: A Cultural Landscape,* trans. Michael Henry Heim (Berkeley: University of California Press, 1999), 10.

2. Ibid., 14.

3. Christian Bromberger, "Bridge, Wall, Mirror: Coexistence and Confrontations in the Mediterranean World," *History and Anthropology* 18(3) (2007): 291–307.

4. Stefan Helmreich, "Nature/Culture/Seawater," American Anthropologist 114(1) (2011): 110.

5. Zygmunt Bauman, *Liquid Modernity* (Cambridge: Polity Press, 2000), 2.

6. James C. F. Wang, *Handbook on Ocean Politics and Law* (New York: Greenwood Press, 1992), 75.

7. Wang, *Handbook on Ocean Politics and Law,* 25.

8. Tatjana Rosen, "Exclusive Economic Zone (EEZ)," in *Encyclopedia of Earth,* ed. Cutler J. Cleveland (Washington, D.C., 2008), http://www.eoearth.org/article/Exclusive_economic_zone_ (EEZ) (accessed 20 March 2012).

9. Martin M. Lewis, "Dividing the Ocean Sea," *Geographical Review* 89(2) (1999): 207, 211.

10. Emilio Cocco, "I territori liquidi: Forme e confini di un immaginario adriatico," in *Immaginare l'Adriatico,* ed. Emilio Cocco and Everardo Minardi (Milan: FrancoAngeli, 2007), 19.

11. Wendy Catherine Bracewell, *The Uskoks of Senj: Piracy, Banditry, and Holy War in the Sixteenth-Century Adriatic* (Ithaca, N.Y.: Cornell University Press, 1992).

12. Pamela Ballinger, "La frantumazione dell'adriatico," in *Immaginare l'Adriatico,* ed. Emilio Cocco and Everardo Minardi (Milan, Italy: FrancoAngeli, 2007), 27–44.

13. Emilio Cocco, "I territori liquidi," 20.

14. Bojan Baskar, "Made in Trieste. Geopolitical Fears of an Istrianist Discourse on the Mediterranean," *Narodna umjetnost* 36(1) (1999): 122. See also Aleksandar Bosković, "Anthropology in Unlikely Places: Yugoslav Ethnology Between the Past and the Future" in *Other People's Anthropologies: Ethnographic Practice on the Margins,* ed. Aleksandar Bosković (New York: Berghahn Books, 2008), 158.

15. Historian Marta Verginella has deconstructed this pervasive association of Italians and Slavs with, respectively, the city and countryside. See Marta Verginella, "Rapporto città/campagna," *Qualestoria* 16(1) (1988): 5–25; M. Verginella, "Città e campagna nel tramonto asburgico: villaggio al confine tra Istria e Slovenia," *Rivista di storia contemporanea* 2 (1990): 183–218.

16. Pamela Ballinger, "Lines in the Water, Peoples on the Map: Maritime Museums and the Representation of Cultural Boundaries in the Upper Adriatic," *Narodna Umjetnost* 43(1) (2006): 15–39; Pamela Ballinger, "Opting for Identity: The Politics of International Refugee Relief in Venezia Giulia, 1948–1952," *Acta Histriae* 14(1) (2006): 115–36. Some of the material in this article contained in the section "Maritime Cartographies, Social Geographies" previously appeared in "Lines in the Water."

17. Larry Wolff, *Inventing Eastern Europe: The Map of Civilization on the Mind of the Enlightenment* (Stanford: Stanford University Press, 1994); Maria Todorova, *Imagining the Balkans* (Oxford: Oxford University Press, 1997).

18. Wendy Bracewell, "The Limits of Europe in East European Travel Writing" in *Under Eastern Eyes: A Comparative Introduction to East European Travel Writing on Europe,* ed. Wendy Bracewell and Alex Drake-Francis (Budapest: Central European University Press, 2008), 62–63.

19. James R. Akerman, "Finding Our Way," in *Maps: Finding Our Place in the World,* ed. James R. Akerman and Robert W. Karrow, Jr. (Chicago: University of Chicago Press, 2007), 52–54.

20. Corradino Astengo, "The Renaissance Chart Tradition in the Mediterranean" in *The History of Cartography: Cartography in the European Renaissance,* 2 pts., ed. David Woodward (Chicago: University of Chicago Press, 2007), pt. 1, 174, 178.

21. George Tolias, "*Isolarii,* Fifteenth to Seventeenth Century," in *The History of Cartography,* ed. Woodward, pt. 1, 263.

22. Tolias, "*Isolarii,* Fifteenth to Seventeenth Century," 280.

23. Tolias, "*Isolarii,* Fifteenth to Seventeenth Century," 268.

24. Emanuela Casti, "State, Cartography, and Territory in Renaissance Veneto and Lombardy," in *The History of Cartography,* ed. Woodward, pt. 1, 877.

25. Vasili Sphyroeras, Anna Avramea, and Spyros Asdrahas, *Maps and Map-Makers of the Aegean* (Athens: Olkos Limited, 1985), 28, 30.

26. Zsolt G. Török, "Renaissance Cartography in East-Central Europe, ca. 1450–1650," in *The History of Cartography,* ed.Woodward, pt. 2, 18.

27. Sphyroeras, Avramea, and Asdrahas, *Maps and Map-Makers of the Aegean,* 28.

28. Tolias, "*Isolarii,* Fifteenth to Seventeenth Century," 280.

29. Casti, "State, Cartography, and Territory in Renaissance Veneto and Lombardy," 908.

30. Sphyroeras, Avramea, and Asdrahas, *Maps and Map-Makers of the Aegean,* 25.

31. Larry Wolff, *Venice and the Slavs: The Discovery of Dalmatia in the Age of Enlightenment* (Stanford: Stanford University Press, 2001), 11.

32. Between 1763 and 1787, a comprehensive mapping project of the Monarchy was conducted. Irina Popova, "Representing National Territory: Cartography and Nationalism in Hungary, 1700–1848," in *Creating the Other: Ethnic Conflict and Nationalism in Habsburg Central Europe,* ed. Nancy M. Wingfield (New York: Berghahn Books, 2003), 17–38.

33. András Vári, "The Functions of Ethnic Stereotypes in Austria and Hungary in the Early Nineteenth Century," in *Creating the Other: Ethnic Conflict and Nationalism in Habsburg Central Europe,* ed. Nancy M. Wingfield (New York, New York: Berghahn Books, 2003), 39.

34. Pieter Judson, "Inventing Germans: Class, Nationality, and Colonial Fantasy at the Margins of the Hapsburg Monarchy," *Social Analysis* 33 (1993): 51.

35. Cathie Carmichael, "Ethnic Stereotypes in Early European Ethnographies: A Case Study of the Habsburg Adriatic c. 1770–1815," *Narodna umjetnost* 33(2) (1996): 201.

36. Vári, "The Functions of Ethnic Stereotypes," 5.

37. Cited in Carmichael, "Ethnic Stereotypes," 207.

38. Vári, "The Functions of Ethnic Stereotypes," 45.

39. Carmichael, "Ethnic Stereotypes," 203.

40. Carmichael, "Ethnic Stereotypes," 199.

41. Wendy Bracewell, "Travels through the Slav World" in *Under Eastern Eyes: A Comparative Introduction to East European Travel Writing on Europe,* ed. Wendy Bracewell and Alex Drake-Francis (Budapest: Central European University Press, 2008), 148.

42. Regina Bendix, "Ethnology, Cultural Reification, and the Dynamics of Difference in the *Kronprinzenwerk,*" in *Creating the Other,* ed. Wingfield, 154.

43. Laura Oretti, *A caminando che'l va: repertorio della narrativa di tradizione orale delle comunità italiane in Istria* (Trieste, Italy: Edizioni Italo Svevo, 2004), 29.

44. Giannandrea Gravisi, "Distribuzione della popolazione dell'Istria rispetto alla distanza dal mare: ricerche antropogeografiche," *Pagine Istriane* 1(7–8) (Sept.–Oct. 1903): 160.

45. Karl Kaser, "Peoples of the Mountains, Peoples of the Plains," in *Creating the Other,* ed. Wingfield, 219.

46. Cited in Svetozar Culibrk, "Cvijić's Sociological Research in Society in the Balkans," *The British Journal of Sociology* 22(4) (1971): 431.

47. Culibrik, "Cvijić's Sociological Research," 433.

48. Baskar, "Made in Trieste," 222.

49. Jasna Čapo Žmegač, "Ethnology, Mediterranean Studies, and Political Reticence in Croatia: From Mediterranean Constructs to Nation-Building," *Narodna umjetnost* 36(1) (1999): 38.

50. Baskar, "Made in Trieste," 130.

51. Čapo Žmegač, "Ethnology, Mediterranean Studies, and Political Reticence," 46.

52. Stjepan Meštrović, Slaven Letica, and Miroslav Goreta, *Habits of the Balkan Heart: Social Character and the Fall of Communism* (College Station: Texas A & M University Press, 1993).

53. Drago Kladnik and Primož Pipan, "Bay of Piran or Bay or Savudrija? An Example of Problematic Treatment of Geographic Names," *Acta geographica Slovenica* 48(1) (2008): 65.

54. Katherine Verdery, *What was Socialism and What Comes Next?* (Princeton: Princeton University Press, 1996), 138–139.

55. Ibid., 135.

56. Ibid., 139.

57. Ibid., 135.

58. Gerald H. Blake and Duško Topalović, *Maritime Briefing: The Maritime Boundaries of the Adriatic Sea,* ed. Clive Schofield and Mladen Klemenčić, vol. 1, no. 8 (Durham, U.K.: University of Durham, 1996), 19.

59. Kladnik and Pipan, "Bay of Piran or Bay or Savudrija?" 65.

60. Kladnik and Pipan, "Bay of Piran or Bay or Savudrija?" 72.

61. Ted Ames, "Putting Fishers' Knowledge to Work: The Promise and Pitfalls," *Fisheries Research Center* 11(1) (2003): 187.

62. Stefan Helmreich, *Alien Ocean* (Berkeley: University of California Press, 2008).

63. Charles Zerner, "Sounding the Makassar Strait: The Poetics and Politics of an Indonesian Marine Environment" in *Culture and the Question of Rights: Forests, Coasts, and Seas in Southeast Asia,* ed. Charles Zerner (Durham, N.C.: Duke University Press, 2003), 56–108.

64. Jeremy Crampton, "Bordering on Bosnia," *Geojournal* 39(4) (1996): 357.

65. For the comments of Ivan Jakovčić, President of the Istrian Region, go to *Il Piccolo,* 3 September 2002.

66. Branko Suljić, "Ne postoji Lošinjsko-cresko populacija dupina," *Novi List,* 14 January 2007.

67. John R. Gillis, *Islands of the Mind* (New York: Palgrave Macmillan, 2004), 85.

68. On this topic, see the special issue of *Narodna Umjetnost* 36(1) (1999).

69. Dunja Rihtman-Augustin, "A Croatian Controversy: Mediterranean-Danube-Balkans" *Narodna umjetnost* 36(1) (1999): 110.

23

NATIONAL MODERNISM IN POST-REVOLUTIONARY SOCIETY

THE UKRAINIAN RENAISSANCE AND JEWISH REVIVAL, 1917–1930

MYROSLAV SHKANDRIJ

In the early twentieth century two stateless peoples, Ukrainians and Jews, struggled to establish their cultural and political identities. Both were heavily concentrated in two mutually bordering empires—the Austro-Hungarian and Russian. Their increasing assertiveness during this time expressed itself in a growing number of publications, and a sharper focus in their literature and art on national self-representation and self-definition. One reflection of this assertiveness was the promotion of an identity that combined a modernist style with elements of the national tradition, a development that arguably reached its peak in Ukraine in the years immediately following the 1917 Revolution. Revolutionary Ukrainian society—first the Ukrainian National Republic (UNR) in the years 1917–1920 and then the Soviet Ukrainian state from 1923 onward—conducted a policy of Ukrainianization that created what is often referred to as "the cultural renaissance." Simultaneously the Jewish Kultur-Lige, which was headquartered in Kiev, pioneered a Jewish "cultural revival." The two movements were connected: both came out of the Ukrainian Revolution, and both embraced modernism (often in its most radical, avant-garde forms). The emergence of this "national modernism" was an important aspect of post-revolutionary life, and one that offers the possibility of re-conceptualizing cultural developments in the 1920s.

The collapse of the tsarist state provided Ukrainian and Jewish intellectuals with a hitherto unavailable opportunity to explore and develop the idea of their cultural uniqueness. At the same time, the rapid pace of revolutionary transformations demanded an immediate and radical reimagining of all identities, including the national-cultural. When Mykola Khvyl'ovy formed his organization VAPLITE (an acronym for "Free Academy of Proletarian Literature") and initiated the great Literary Discussion of 1925–1927, his aim was to accelerate the Ukrainianization process, which had been proclaimed by the Soviet Ukrainian government in 1923 and which, he felt, had stalled. But it was also to promote a new Ukrainian identity. How to achieve both these aims is the question that dominates his polemical pamphlets and fiction.[1] These writings represent one of the best expressions of the yearning for the new in the literature of the '20s, and inspired a vigorous debate over the future of Ukrainian culture. Khvyl'ovy argued that the culture had to be modern, European, and had to chart a course of its own, independent of Russia. This last, controversial call to escape Russian cultural hegemony has attracted most of the critical and scholarly attention, while the party's decision to close down the debate, VAPLITE's dissolution, and the writer's suicide in 1933 inevitably made him a martyr in the eyes of many commentators. By contrast, his attitude toward modernism's aesthetic of rupture and renewal and its promise of a new community has been understudied.

Khvyl'ovy produced daring, innovative work in the immediate post-revolutionary years, especially two collections of short stories *Syni etiudy* (*Blue Etudes,* 1923) and *Osin'* (*Autumn,* 1924). They already show evidence that the nation-building imperative, especially the articulation of a new national identity, was pulling him, as it was other writers (such as Pavlo Tychyna, the major poet of these years) toward historical allusions and narratives that could serve as allegories of the nation's fate. As a result, Khvyl'ovy, like most other "revolutionary" writers, found himself elaborating a modernist sensibility that both rejected traditionalism and continually invented ways of including and reconfiguring elements of the same national tradition. The ambivalent tone of these early stories emerges from the attempt to reconcile rejection of the past with historical references, to balance the rational with the intuitive, and to make the urban, as opposed to the rural, the stylistic matrix of a new culture.

World revolution was linked to the dream of modernity, access to the wider world, and to the triumph of justice. Many young people, such as Lev Kopelev, imagined that this world would have "no borders, no capitalists and no fascists at all," and that Moscow, Kharkiv, and Kiev "would become just as enormous, just as well built, as Berlin, Hamburg, New York," with skyscrapers, airplanes and dirigibles, streets full of automobiles and bicycles, workers and peasants in fine clothes, wearing hats and watches.[2] Kopelev's picture of the future was based on the assumption that modernity would be culturally Russian, perhaps uniformly so. These sentiments were echoed by others. Benedikt Livshits has described how he thought of David Burliuk and the early futurists: "[They] had destroyed poetical and painterly traditions and had founded a new aesthetics as stateless Martians, unconnected in any way with any nationality, much less with our planet."[3] Khvyl'ovy described the early post-revolutionary years differently: "Some kind of joyful alarm grips my heart. I see my descendants and see with what envy they look at me—a contemporary and eyewitness of my Eurasian renaissance. Just think, only a few years and such achievements. . . . What wonderful prospects appear in the future for this country, when these courageous innovators finally overcome the inertia of the centuries."[4] It was not material but cultural achievements that inspired him, and his focus was not on some abstract, borderless, geographical space, but on Ukraine ("this country") as the trailblazer of a new culture ("my Eurasian renaissance"). However, his excitement and fervor resemble Kopelev's. In his memoirs another Ukrainian writer of the '20s, Yurii Smolych, reflects this fervent faith in the arrival of the new: "This generation was called to liquidate the ruins of the war period and to create the first beginnings of the new way of life. And this took place at the break of two epochs—the destruction of the old worldly, reactionary norms and customs and the search for new customs and norms."[5]

What fascinates in this creative excitement is the combination of the revolutionary and national. A vehement rejection of the past was linked to the belief that the modern would be built on the release of long-suppressed, untapped national energies. The structure of Khvylovy's stories is built on this kind of "argument." His protagonists have often emerged from the whirlwind of revolutionary ideas and find themselves thrown into confusion by the horrors of the revolution. They are dissatisfied with revolutionary society, but find no inspiration in the prerevolutionary world, which they associate with symbolism and aestheticism, particularly the search for self-knowledge and retreat from the world. These protagonists suffer from arrested inner growth. Divorced from their surroundings, they focus obsessively on a beautiful illusion—the distant future in which the dreams of many past generations will become reality. However, the path to this future is blocked. The vision recedes year after year, and is eventually entirely blotted out by the corruptions of urban civilization. People from the countryside who have thrown in their lot with the revolution bring freshness, innocence, and idealism to the construction of revolutionary society, but soon succumb to the city's sterility and cynicism. Their vitality and excitement are extinguished. The loss of faith is caused in large part by the blocking of the national cultural movement, which authorities treat as something embarrassing or even evil. As a result, Ukrainian protagonists develop a feeling of self-hatred. The same message is carried in his polemical pamphlets, in which Khvyl'ovy challenged young people to create a cultural renaissance.

There is an underlying pull of mythic structures in the stories and pamphlets: illusions are destroyed by reality, heroism is disappointed by cowardice, and idealism is stifled by cynicism. Because of this, the stories can be given allegorical or symbolic readings, to which the pamphlets hold the interpretative key. The individual who is unable to tell his story openly can be seen as the nation that is not allowed to express itself, whose dream of cultural development has been dashed. In this way, the fictional works recount a familiar tale of national oppression and the need for emancipation, albeit in a fragmented and mysteriously allusive modernist style.

Nonetheless, the writer remained a caustic critic of conservative and populist views. He probed darkness at the heart of the village idyll, explored disturbing and anarchic forces in the human psyche, and exposed clichés such as romantic love. Like much of the literature and art of the early post-revolutionary period, Khvyl'ovy's writings show an aversion to populism and a refusal to embrace ethnographic traditions uncritically. Inspired by a vision of a blended social and national liberation, and by the prospect of introducing a new Ukrainian culture onto the world stage, his writings draw sustenance from the palingenetic myth (the idea of rebirth, regeneration, revival) that has been widely observed in twentieth-century modernism. The crucial concept is that of genesis. Both artists and writers sought to identify key elements out of which the culture had been formed. Thus the writers who contributed to the *Vaplite* journal and to the next journal formed by Khvyl'ovy, *Literaturnyi iarmarok* (December 1928–February 1930) searched for elements of the cultural code that represented the national experience and identity as it had evolved over the centuries. They examined archetypal forms, characters, canonical images and works, and then recoded these into a new format and a new identity. Abstraction and the investigation of fundamental concepts played an important role—whether in literature, painting, or theatre. The search for the "grammatical structure" of national identity became analogous to experimentation with pure color and form in painting, or with the search for basic patterns of sound and meaning in poetry, which were also typical of the avant-garde in the twenties. It was thought that, once discovered, these basic elements could by some mysterious alchemy be transformed into a new synthesis.

Others negotiated attitudes to the past in similarly ambiguous ways. The example of art is particularly instructive. Alexandra Exter's studio in Kiev in the years 1917–1920 was a good example of the modernist transformation of tradition. It blended cubo-futurism, constructivism, and folk-primitivism in innovative ways. Her interest in arts and crafts at this time led to collaboration with artists like Evheniia Prybyl's'ka and Nina Henke, who developed workshops in which local women mass-produced textiles and other products using patterns inspired both by folk motifs and by Suprematist art. These were shown in major exhibitions in Moscow and Paris to great acclaim. Exter's studio educated many important artists, including leading Jewish figures like Boris Aronson, Isaak Rabinovich, Nisson Shifrin, and Oleksandr (Aleksandr) Tyshler, and was visited by many figures from Moscow and Petrograd who found themselves in Kiev at the time, such as Illia Ehrenburg, Benedikt Livshits, Osip Mandelshtem, Viktor Shklovsky, and Natan Vengrov. Kazimir Malevich's Suprematist art can also be seen as a kind of recreation in an abstract and mystical key of the ancient and ethnographic; and Mykhailo Boichuk's monumentalist or neo-Byzantinist school also turned to national sources in its search for primitive, ethnographic, or folk features. This school came out of the thrilling "rediscovery" in prerevolutionary years of the icon as not only a popular but also a sophisticated form that could be linked to cubist and avant-garde experimentation. The artist turned to the icon and folk arts for national forms, and attempted to crystallize these traditional elements into a modern synthesis and a national style. Other artists, who were not part of the avant-garde, were also feeding this interest in the past. Hryhorii Narbut and Vasyl Krychevs'ky, for example, were famous for translating ornamental images into modern graphic art, particularly in book design: Narbut reworked baroque images and Krychevs'ky folk art patterns. Like the "national modernist" writers grouped around Khvyl'ovy, they were guided by a desire to give old, often very ancient forms a new expression.

These writers and artists felt no dichotomy between "ethnic loyalty" and participation in international modernism. Their interest in the traditional aimed at uncovering deeper generative principles. Figures like Alexander Archipenko, Kazimir Malevich, Alexandra Exter, and David Burliuk succeeded in bringing their discoveries to the international community. Like these artists, writers did not desire to remain strictly within the limits of their particular national tradition, but recognized the dialectical relationship between the national and international.

Abstracting, translating, or transforming tradition into modernist form became something of an obsession in Ukrainian culture in the following decades, and a major part of the continuing search for self-definition. In the forties, for example, Sviatoslav Hordyns'ky, an artist, poet, and critic who began exhibiting and writing in L'viv (then part of the Polish state) in the thirties before moving to the United States, contributed an article to *Ukrainske mystetstvo: Almanakh II* (*Ukrainian Art: Almanac II*) in which he argued for an abstract national art in terms very close to those used in the early twenties. He wrote that international modernism's interest in form had compelled twentieth-century Ukrainian artists to abandon historical styles and genre painting and forced them to study the compositional techniques and colors of their own popular traditions. The "strong, formalist features of the old Ukrainian art, its anti-naturalism" allowed them to create in an abstract manner that simultaneously echoed traditional forms.[6] He singled out Boichuk's school of the 1920s as an exemplary synthesis of traditionalism and formalism, and thought that the search for this synthesis continued to drive many contemporary artists.

A comparison with the key concepts of the Jewish revival is revealing. In the years 1918–1920 Kiev's Kultur-Lige championed the idea of a secular Yiddish culture that would be international and modern. Created on 9 January 1918, the organization had established 120 branches throughout Ukraine by the end of the year. Eponymous organizations were created in Petrograd, the Crimea, Minsk, Grodny, Vilnius, Bialystok, Chernowets (Romania; today's Chernivtsi in Ukraine), Moscow, Rostov-on-Don, and the far-eastern cities of Chita, Irkutsk, and Harbin. When at the end of 1920 the Kiev center came under Bolshevik control, some members left in order to reproduce the organization in Warsaw in 1921 and Berlin in 1922. A Kultur-Lige was created in Riga (Latvia) in 1922, New York and Chicago in 1926, Bucharest in 1931, and Mexico and Argentina in 1935. The Ukrainian organization was the largest and strongest in the years 1918–1920, and provided the model for developments elsewhere. Claims were made for its having "four evening folk universities, twelve grammar schools, twenty large libraries with reading rooms, seventy kindergartens and orphanages, forty evening programs, ten playing fields, three gymnasiums [high schools], twenty dramatic circles, choruses, and troupes."[7] The organization opened art studios, an art museum, a teachers' seminary, and a Jewish People's University. In 1918 its press accounted for over 40 percent of all titles in Yiddish produced in the lands of the former empire.[8] The literary section included leading modernists like Yehezkiel Dobrushin, Dovyd Bergelson, Der Nister (Pinkhas Kaganovich), Dovyd Gofshteyn, Leib Kvitko, and Nakhman Maizil, while its artistic section boasted many outstanding avant-gardists like Aronson, Tyshler, Rabinovich, Mark Epshtein, Solomon Nikritin, Abram Manevych, Isaak Rabichev, and Issachar-Ber Ryback. Other artists like El (Eliezer) Lissitzky, Sarra Shor, Joseph Chaikov, David Shterenberg, Polina Khentova, and Mark Sheikhel moved to Kiev to join the movement. Marc Chagall contributed illustrations to its publications. Kiev in fact became the center of an international Jewish avant-garde art. The book graphic art produced in these years is today universally admired precisely for the blending of modernism and national tradition that it was able to achieve. Two major art exhibitions were held in Kiev (in 1920 and 1922) and another in New York (in 1924).

Kultur-Lige's growth and the Jewish cultural revival took place against the background of the 1917–1920 Revolution. The revolutionary Ukrainian government (initially the Central Rada, later the Ukrainian National Republic or UNR) approved a multicultural policy, offering support in particular to the Jewish, Polish, and Russian minorities. They were granted cultural autonomy, representation at the ministerial level, and state funding for cultural development. The Rada was aware that the urban population was often less than one-third Ukrainian (with Russian, Jews, or Poles making up the majority) and sought an alliance with the Jewish population to bolster its support in crucial urban areas. The Ukrainian intelligentsia saw Jewish cultural development as an ally in the struggle to reverse the process of Russification that was tsarism's legacy.

The Kultur-Lige was formed in Kiev a day before the UNR's law on national-personal autonomy was proclaimed on 9 January 1918. The organization's statute was approved on 15 January. Its creation was supported by a coalition of Jewish socialist parties: the Bund, Fareinigte, Poale Zion, and Folkspartei (United Jewish Socialist Workers' Party). Since Moisei Zilberfarb, the Central Rada's Minister of Jewish Affairs, was in the Kultur-Lige's leadership, the organization was effectively an auxiliary organ of the Ministry. The Kultur-Lige continued to expand its activities under Hetmanate rule (from April to November 1918 Pavlo Skoropadky ruled as Hetman with German backing), when it "assumed the role of the organ of Jewish autonomy in Ukraine."[9] At this time it created the university, including a major library and a program of extramural education. The university began operating after a circular on national higher education allowing "teaching in the languages used in schools" was promulgated on 5 August by the Minister of Education and Art. When the UNR government returned to Kiev under the leadership of the Directory (November 1918–January 1919), lecturers from the Kultur-Lige's teacher-training school in Kiev formed the Department of Education in its Ministry of Jewish Affairs. The Kultur-Lige therefore embodied the concept of cultural autonomy under successive Ukrainian governments, receiving financial support from them, while at the same time also raising its own funds. In 1918 it employed around 260 people, and of the 21 individuals on its governing board three were ministers in the governments of the UNR. When the organization was brought under the control of the Communist Party in December 1920, the original leadership was squeezed out. By 1922 all branches throughout Ukraine had been subordinated to the Evsektsii (the Jewish Sections of the Commissariat of Education). Initially the Bolsheviks supported aspects of the Kultur-Lige's work, such as the university and theatres, but the Jewish sections of the Bolshevik Party argued that the Kultur-Lige was a class enemy and nationalist. More to the point, the Kultur-Lige presented a rival to the Jewish sections, which wanted exclusive control over organized Jewish cultural life.[10] The collapse of the UNR government was accompanied by the terrible wave of pogroms in 1919, in which troops ostensibly loyal to this government participated. These pogroms did much to destroy the Ukrainian–Jewish rapprochement, and encouraged some Jews to support the Bolsheviks.

In spite of its short existence, the Kultur-Lige achieved astonishing successes, including the development of a network of Jewish schools throughout Ukraine, a flowering of Yiddish literature, and the creation of an avant-garde art of international fame. Even after the Soviet takeover, many aspects of its work continued under other names. The music school was sponsored by a trade union organization; the major library in Kiev continued to function under other names; the art school was active until 1931; the Kultur-Lige's Jewish theatre began working in Kharkiv in 1924; and the publishing house continued using the organization's name until the end of the twenties.

It is hard to convey today how thrilling the vision of a cultural rebirth was to participants. In his memoirs Arthur Golomb, who lived in Kiev in the years 1917–1921 describes how in January of 1918, as the Bolsheviks began to sow disorder in Kiev and the Red Army commenced an artillery bombardment of the Ukrainian capital from the left bank of the Dnipro, he was running down the street to the Jewish student kitchen when he met Zelig Melamed, who called out: "It's ready!" He had in his pocket the statute of the Kultur-Lige. Both friends were so excited by the news that they stood up, entirely forgetting the danger and ignoring the flying bullets and the roar of the cannonade.[11]

The organization saw Yiddish, the language spoken by most Jews in Central and Eastern Europe, as the "natural" expression of Jewish life, and support for Yiddish as a turn to the creativity of the masses. It aimed at the creation of a new culture that would synthesize the universal and national, and that would unite the diaspora "from Moscow to New York and from London to Johannesburg," giving Yiddish-speaking Jews, who had no country of their own, a spiritual home wherever they found themselves.

The new culture was to be modern. For some this meant that it should be politically leftist and activist. Perets Markish, a leading figure in Kiev's Yiddish revival, who moved to Warsaw and then to Moscow in the thirties, was remarkably pro-Soviet, even after the regime repressed the Kultur-Lige. However, other members of the organization were not. When the Kiev organization was shut down, some of the main figures like I. I. Zinger, Moisei

Zilberfarb, Zelig Melamed, and Nakhmen Mayzel Maizil moved to Warsaw, hoping that this city would become the base of a Yiddish cultural flowering and that Jews in Poland would be granted the same cultural autonomy as they had received from the Ukrainian government.[12] Here, and wherever the members of the Kiev Kultur-Lige moved, they promoted their dream of a new but archetypically Jewish culture, a national sensibility that was modern (even avant-gardist), secular, progressive, and global.

The artistic section perhaps provided the clearest expression of national modernist theory and style. Several artists had been involved in the search for cultural roots in the prerevolutionary years. Natan Altman had in 1913 copied ancient tombstones on Jewish cemeteries in Shepetivka; Isakhar-Ber Rybak and El Lissitsky had in 1915 made drawings of the interiors of ancient synagogues in Right-Bank Ukraine; Solomon Yudovkin had taken over 1,500 photographs of *pinkas* (Jewish community books); Chaikov, Elman, and Kratko had studied Jewish embossed silver. The motivation in each case was the development of an art that drew on tradition in order to rework archetypal forms. In the Kultur-Lige period these same artists attempted to translate the traditional into an avant-garde idiom with the idea of abstract form as its purest expression. The approach was defended by Boris Aronson and Isakhar-Ber Rybak in an influential article published in 1919 in the Kiev journal *Oyfgang* (*Dawn*), which criticized the idea of an art focused on recognizably Jewish themes. Instead, the authors argued, the national could best be explored by examining formal qualities, such as the use of color and rhythm, and traditional ornamental patterns. The ensuing discussion on this subject evolved into an entire discourse in which Jewish journals in Berlin, Moscow, Lodz, and Vilnius participated.

Aronson developed this view in *Sovremennaia evreiskaia grafika* (*Contemporary Jewish Graphic Art,* 1924), which he published in Berlin. He elaborated the concept of a Jewish art based on specifically Jewish forms of ornamentation, compositional qualities, and archetypal imagery, all

Joseph Chaikov, cover for *Baginen* (Beginnings), no. 1 (Kiev, 1919). Located in Musée d'art et d'histoire du Judaisme, Paris.

Mark Epstein, "The Cellist" (also called "Cubist Composition"), 1920. Epstein was a product of the O. Murashko and the A. Exter studios in Kyiv. He was a leader of the Kultur-Lige's art section in Kyiv and illustrated many of its books. The National Museum of Art, Kyiv. From Hillel Kazovsky, ed., *Kultur-Lige: Artistic Avant-Garde of the 1920s and the 1930s* (Kyiv: Dukh i litera, 2007), p. 88.

of which, he felt, could already be found "in the distant sources of ethnography and in the first manuscript publications of sacred books."[13] A Jewish art, in his opinion, could be distilled from the entire range of objects that were used in rituals and daily life. However, the distillation could not be mere copying or stylization; it had to be a new individualization, as practiced by artists like Altman and Chagall, who had shown how popular elements could be transformed into unique and original combinations. By the time the book appeared, Aronson already felt that the search for a new national style had failed. Not only had the Kiev Kultur-Lige's great experiment been cut short, but a different artistic sensibility was ascendant—one that stressed dynamism, mechanics, and fragmentation, and seemed to deny the possibility of stable, recurring forms. However, he still claimed "one priceless achievement" for the earlier inspiration: "it enlivened a whole range of historical materials, blew the dust from the living face of grave stones, animated with warmth the relations between tradition and craft."[14] The traditional and ethnographic, he still maintained, could be reworked into a modernist idiom. In fact this combination was now in vogue, since primitivism had been widely embraced as one of modernism's programmatic features.

John Bowlt has emphasized the contradiction between loyalty to the community and commitment to the international art world, arguing that the attempt to create an international style in architecture and the plastic arts had to win out. According to him, these artists

... [sympathized] with the sincere attempts of their linguistic colleagues to accelerate the application of Esperanto. In the immediate context of Jewish art and the Russian avant-garde, this argument held a particular logic: few modern Jewish artists derived all their artistic inspiration from the patriarchal traditions of Jewish culture observed in the tortured environment of the shtetl, although, certainly, Chagall, Ryback, and Yudovkin did. In many cases, they attempted to interweave these traditions with the aesthetic systems of Cubism, Futurism, Suprematism, etc.[15]

This line of argumentation misses a crucial point: for many of these artists the road to an international style or abstraction passed through the national. After all, why should this route be any less acceptable than the exploration of "exotic" African or Polynesian art?

In the early Kultur-Lige years Aronson felt that Jewish folk traditions could be fused with contemporary art "to create a modern Jewish plastic art which seeks its own organic national form, color and rhythm."[16] This suggested a Jewish path to abstraction. Rybak and Aronson in the above-mentioned article of 1919 argued that even if the artist's work was successful internationally, it would still reveal the specific spiritual construction and emotions of the creator's milieu and the national element in its style, structure, and organization. However, at the same time, these leaders of Kultur-Lige believed that "traditional shtetl life was atrophied and a modern, secular, national culture should replace it. The role of art was to give aesthetic definition to new national and cultural longings."[17] Under the impact of Bolshevik pressure, the emphasis on national specificity was gradually removed. Abstraction came to mean not the refinement of a particular tradition, but the erasure of recognizable traditions and the embracing instead of a universalism that masked or denied national specificity.

The practical application of these theoretical premises can be seen in the work of many artists. Mark Epstein's cubist compositions, such as *The Cello-Player* (1920) and *Family Group* (1919–1920), or Joseph Chaikov's *The Seamstress* (1922), *Soyfer* (*The Scribe*, 1922), and *The Violin-Player* (1922) treat traditional themes in a Cubist manner. Rybak's decorative forms, such as his *Sketch for the Almanac Eygns* (Native, 1920) give a modern graphic interpretation of the forms he had copied from synagogue murals and carved tombstones. And the now famous book illustrations from 1917–1924 by El Lissitzky, Rybak, and Sarra Shor represent an avant-garde graphic art inspired by Jewish folk arts. These represented not a clash between the old and new, but a new aesthetic consciousness created by mingling tradition and modernism. There were, of course, works in which the tension between the old and new worlds was emphasized, as in Joseph Chaikov's image for the cover of the magazine *Baginen* (*Beginnings*, 1919). It depicts the artist with one eye open to the future and a second closed to the past, blind to the rural world he has left behind.[18]

The theorizing of the Ukrainian "renaissance" and the Jewish "revival" throw light on both movements. The literature and art of one finds analogous works in the other. This is to be expected, since there were often strong bonds between individuals in both groups, and both movements were inspired by the international avant-garde. Many artists had spent time abroad (especially in Paris, Munich, and Berlin) in prerevolutionary years. They had often come through the same art schools, in particular the Kiev Art School, Oleksandr Murashko's Art School, Alexandra Exter's studio, and Boichuk's studio of monumental art in the Ukrainian Academy of Arts (an institution that went through two name changes in the 1920s). They exhibited together in the earliest avant-garde exhibitions within the Russian empire (in Kiev, Moscow, and Petrograd) and continued to work together, both in the years 1917–1924, when the Kultur-Lige was most active, and later.

There were also numerous contacts between Ukrainian and Jewish writers at this time. Pavlo Tychyna and Leib Kvitko are a frequently cited example. Tychyna learned Yiddish and translated Kvitko's verse into Ukrainian, while Kvitko translated Tychyna into Yiddish. Tychyna's successful translation initiated translations into Russian and over 20 other languages. By the end of the thirties a hundred books by Kvitko had appeared in Yiddish, along with 30 translations each in Ukrainian and Russian. The author's works would disappear from bookstores and libraries when he was arrested and killed in 1952. Kvitko was also a member of VAPLITE, and, like Khvyl'ovy, made a spirited criticism of the Communist Party's control of literature in 1929. Yurii Smolych was a close friend of the Yiddish writer Der Nister (Pinkhus Kahanovych). Both came from Western Ukraine. During the 1905 pogrom, Smolych's family hid some Jewish families. In the twenties Smolych and Der Nister regularly attended and discussed Yiddish and Ukrainian theater performances. In his memoirs written in the sixties the Ukrainian writer looks back fondly on this time, although in order to please the censors his account alternatively veers between supporting non-Russian cultures and denouncing any attachment to them as "nationalistic." Even this carefully filtered version was criticized. One editor insisted that Smolych expunge his call for a revival of Jewish theater in Ukraine, reports of Der Nister's negative attitude toward the creation of the Birobidzhan Jewish autonomous region, and complaints about Soviet antisemitism.[19]

A third frequently cited friendship is that between the outstanding theatre director Les Kurbas and the famous actor Solomon Mikhoels. In 1933, Kurbas was dismissed from the innovative Berezil theatre in Kharkiv, which he had taken from success to success for over a decade. Mikhoels invited him to work in Moscow's GOSET (State Jewish Theater). Kurbas, who spoke Yiddish and had long maintained close contacts with Jewish theatres, enjoyed this collaboration, which produced *King Lear,* one of the great Shakespeare productions of the 1930s. Even though he was arrested on 26 December 1933 on his way to rehearsals, the production that premiered on 10 February 1935, with Mikhoels in a starring role, bore Kurbas's imprint.[20] Kurbas was shot in a labor camp in 1937, Mikhoels in 1952.

In his memoirs Smolych argues that in the twenties many Jews were "native speakers" of Ukrainian. They came from small Ukrainian towns and villages, and had only a faulty knowledge of Russian. The post-Stalin generation of Jews, according to Smolych, grew up without speaking Ukrainian and was prejudiced against the language. "Along the way," he writes, "we lost a good colleague in our cultural process."[21] In the twenties many Jews made major contributions to the development of Ukrainian literature, art, cinema, and scholarship. Olena Kurylo, a leading linguist, was an expert on Ukrainian dialects and folklore, and helped to codify the orthography in 1928–1929. Osyp Hermaize was a prominent historian and became one of the 45 accused in the great SVU (Union for the Liberation of Ukraine) show-trial of 1930, which was accompanied by the arrest of thousands of Ukrainian intellectuals. (The SVU, a supposed terrorist organization, was entirely dreamed up by the secret police.) Abram Leites, Samiilo Shchupak, Volodymyr Koriak, and Yarema Aizenshtok were leading critics. The first produced an important bibliography and anthology of critical materials that for many decades remained the best source on the writers of the twenties; the last prepared the complete edition of Shevchenko's diary, as well as numerous studies of Ukrainian writers and folklore. Accused of Ukrainian nationalism, he was forced to move to Leningrad.[22] Numerous writers of Jewish origin made names for themselves in Ukrainian literature in the twenties. The most prominent among them were Leonid Pervomaisky (Illia Hurevych), Sava Holovanivsky, Ivan (Izrail) Kulyk, Aron Kopshtein, and Raisa Troianker.

National modernism as a literary and artistic current was strongly in evidence in the twenties, but was most forcefully articulated by Khvyl'ovy on behalf of VAPLITE and by Aronson on behalf of Kultur-Lige. The Ukrainian and Jewish modernists associated with these groups saw the new literature and art as an expression of national identity, and attempted to theorize it accordingly. Their rhetoric and imagery were often aggressive. They left no doubt that the past was guilty: it bore responsibility for the catastrophic present. However, they simultaneously argued that, because the tsarist past had oppressed, denied, or marginalized national culture, its repressed energies and unexplored potential could be used to create new, popular and progressive artistic forms. Utopianism and faith in the future were a part of this modernism, but the local was the vehicle for reaching this future.

In the twentieth century's early decades the explosion of modernity simultaneously transformed millions of Ukrainians and Jews in analogous ways. In response to this development, both national revivals aimed at developing secular cultures that accepted European genres and modes of discourse, but simultaneously infused them with elements of their own tradition. A key to understanding the semiotics of this art lies in the cultural discourse out of which it grew.

Notes

1. For pamphlets, see Mykola Khvylovy, *The Cultural Renaissance in Ukraine* (Alberta: Canadian Institute of Ukrainian Studies, University of Alberta, 1986). A selection of his fiction has been translated in Mykola Khvylovy, *Stories from the Ukraine* (New York: Philosophical Library, 1960).

2. Lev Kopelev, *The Education of a True Believer* (New York: Harper and Row, 1980), 183–84.

3. Benedikt Livshits, *The One and a Half-Eyed Archer* (Newtonville, Mass.: Oriental Research Partners, 1977), 39.

4. Mykola Khvyl'ovy, "Une letter," *Nove mystetstvo* 26(10) (1926): 10.

5. Iurii Smolych, *Tvory u 8 t.,* vol. 8 (Kiev: Dnipro, 1986), 384.

6. Sviatoslav Hordyns'kyi, *Ukrainske mystetstvo: Almanakh II* (Munich: Spilka, 1947), 15.

7. *Der Fraytog,* 1 August 1919, 36, quoted in S. I. Wolitz, "The Jewish National Art Renaissance in Russia," in *Tradition and Revolution: The Jewish Renaissance in Russian Avant-Garde Art 1912-1928,* ed. Ruth Apter-Gabriel (Jerusalem: The Israel Museum, 1988), 35.

8. Apter-Gabriel has provided a bibliography, and those published in Ukraine are listed in M. O. Rybakov, *Pravda istorii: 'diial'nist 'ievrei'skoi kulturno-'prosvitnyts'koi orhanizatsii 'Kulturna liha' u Kyievi (1918-1925): Zbirnyk dokumentiv i materialiv,* 2nd ed. (Kiev, 2001), 163–64 and 176–87.

9. Hillel Kazovsky, ed., *Kultur-Lige: Artistic Avant-garde 1910-1920-kh rokiv* (Kiev: Dukh I litera, 2007), 27.

10. Zvi Y. Gitelman, *Jewish Nationality and Soviet Politics: The Jewish Sections of the CPSU, 1917-1930* (Princeton: Princeton University Press, 1972), 273–76.

11. Kazovsky, ed., *Kultur-Lige,* 24–25.

12. Meilekh Ravich, "Kratkaia istoriia dinamicheskoi gruppy trekh poetoc v Varshave, 1921–1925," in Grigorii Kazovskii, *O 'Khaliastre,'* 8, available at: http: //members.tripod.com/~barabash/zerkalo/19-20/Kazovsky.htm (accessed 31 August 2008).

13. B. Aronson, *Sovremennaia evreiskaia grafika* (Berlin: Petropolis, 1924), 24.

14. Ibid., 104.

15. J. Bowlt, "From the Pale of Settlement to the Reconstruction of the World?" in *Tradition and Revolution: The Jewish Renaissance in Russian Avant-Garde Art 1912-1928,* ed. Ruth Apter-Gabriel, (Jerusalem: The Israel Museum, 1988), 45.

16. *Kultur-Lige Zamlung* (gazette), November 1919, 38; quoted in S. I. Wolitz, "The Jewish National Art Renaissance in Russia" in *Tradition and Revolution: The Jewish Renaissance in Russian Avant-Garde Art 1912-1928,* ed. Ruth Apter-Gabriel (Jerusalem: The Israel Museum, 1988), 35.

17. Wolitz, "The Jewish National Art Renaissance in Russia," 36.

18. These works can be found in Kazovsky, *Kultur-Lige.* Epstein's *Cello-Player* and *Family Group* are reproduced on 88 and 89; Chaikov's *Seamstress, Soyfer,* and *Violin-Player* on 153–55; Rybak's *Sketch* on page 139; and the book illustrations by El Lissitsky, Rybak, and Sarra Shor on 111–23, 140–41, and 194–95, respectively; Chaikov's cover of *Baginen* is found on 52.

19. Tetiana Soloviova, "Memuaryst–Intelihent, humanist," *Prapor* 9 (1990): 175.

20. Irene Makaryk, *Shakespeare in the Undiscovered Bourn: Les Kurbas, Ukrainian Modernism, and Early Soviet Cultural Politics* (Toronto: University of Toronto Press, 2004), 191–95.

21. Iurii Smolych, "Zapysiv na skhyli viku," *Prapor* 9 (1990): 161.

22. Valerian Revuts'kyi, "Zustrich z Iaremoiu Aizenshtokom," *Diialohy* 9–10 (1985): 164–65.

24

Carpathian Rus'
INTERETHNIC COEXISTENCE
WITHOUT VIOLENCE

Paul Robert Magocsi

The phenomenon of borderlands together with the somewhat related concept of marginality are topics that in recent years have become quite popular as subjects of research among humanists and social scientists. At a recent scholarly conference in the United States I was asked to provide the opening remarks for an international project concerned with "exploring the origins and manifestations of ethnic (and related forms of religious and social) violence in the borderland regions of east-central, eastern, and southeastern Europe."[1] I felt obliged to begin with an apologetic explanation because, while the territory I was asked to speak about is certainly a borderland in the time frame under consideration—1848 to the present—it has been remarkably free of ethnic, religious, and social violence. Has there never been controversy in this borderland territory that was provoked by ethnic, religious, and social factors? Yes, there has been. But have these factors led to interethnic violence? The answer is no.

The territory in question is Carpathian Rus', which, as will become clear, is a land of multiple borders. Carpathian Rus' is not, however, located in an isolated peripheral region; rather, it is located in the center of the European continent as calculated by geographers interested in such questions during the second half of the nineteenth century.[2]

What, then, is Carpathian Rus' and where is it located specifically? Since it is not, and has never been, an independent state or even an administrative entity, one will be hard pressed to find Carpathian Rus' on maps of Europe. In that sense it is like many other European lands—Lapland, Kashubia, Euskal Herria/Basque Land, Occitanie, Ladinia, to name a few—a territorial entity that is defined by the ethnolinguistic characteristics of the majority of its inhabitants and not by political or administrative borders. Using the intellectual buzzwords of our day, Carpathian Rus' is a classic construct. Some skeptics would even say it is an "imagined community" or, at best, a construct or project still in the making.[3] What we

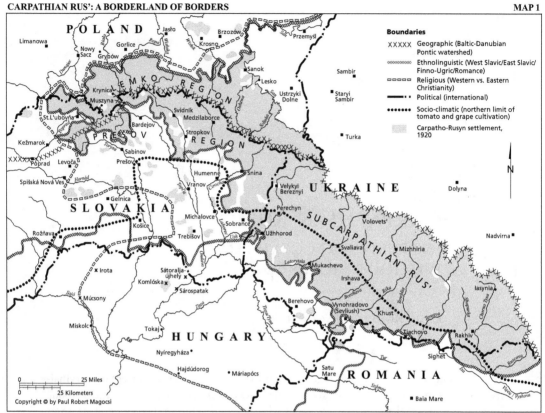

have in mind, however, is something quite concrete; namely, a geographically contiguous territory which at the outset of the twentieth century (when census data was still relatively reliable) included nearly 1,100 villages and some small towns in which at least 50 percent of the inhabitants were Carpatho-Rusyns.[4] Of the two component parts of the territory's name, *Carpathian* refers to the mountains which cover much of the land surface; *Rus'* refers to the ethnicity and traditional Eastern Christian religious orientation of the territory's majority East Slavic population whose historic ethnonym is *Rusnak* or *Rusyn.* That population will be referred to here as *Carpatho-Rusyn,* a term that reflects the group's geographic location and ethnic characteristics.

Carpathian Rus' is a borderland of borders (see map 1 above). Through or along its periphery cross geographic, political, religious, and ethnolinguistic boundaries. Geographically, the crest of the Carpathian mountains forms a watershed, so that the inhabitants on the northern slopes are drawn by natural as well as man-made facilities toward the Vistula-San basins of the Baltic Sea. The inhabitants on the southern slopes are, by contrast, geographically part of the Danubian Basin and plains of Hungary.

Politically, during the long nineteenth century (1770s–1918), Carpathian Rus' was within one state, the Habsburg Monarchy, although it was divided between that empire's Austrian and Hungarian "halves" by the crests of the Carpathians. Since 1918, its territory

CARPATHIAN RUS': POLITICAL CHANGE SINCE 1918   MAP 2

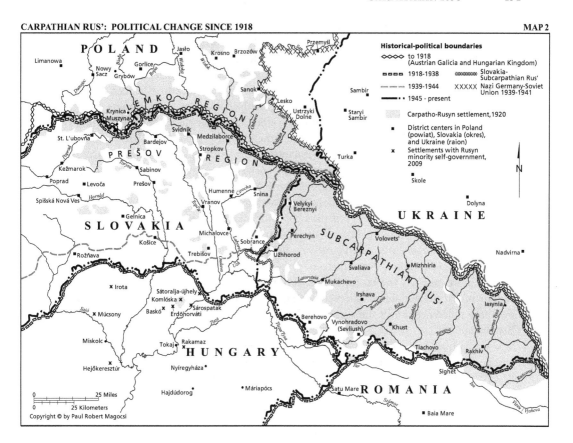

has been divided among several states: Poland, Czechoslovakia, Romania, the Soviet Union, Ukraine, and Slovakia, and for a short period Nazi Germany and Hungary (see map 2).

Carpathian Rus' is located along the great borderland divide between Eastern and Western Christianity, spheres which some scholars have described as *Slavia Orthodoxa* and *Slavia Romana.*[5] Most of the region's Rusnak/Rusyn inhabitants fall within the Eastern Christian sphere, although they are in turn divided more or less evenly between adherents of Greek Catholicism and Orthodoxy. Nor is the religious landscape limited to Greek Catholic and Orthodox Christians, since traditionally within and along the borders of Carpathian Rus' there have lived Roman Catholics, Protestants (Reformed Calvinists and a lesser number of Evangelical Lutherans), and a large concentration of Jews of varying orientations: Orthodox (Misnagdim), Reformed, but most importantly Hasidim.

Carpathian Rus' is also an ethnolinguistic borderland. All of Europe's major ethnolinguistic groups converge in Carpathian Rus', whose territory marks the farthest western extent of the East Slavic world and is bordered by speakers of three completely different language groups: West Slavic (Poles and Slovaks), Finno-Ugric (Magyars), and Romance (Romanians). The Germanic languages have also been a feature of the territory's culture, since until 1945 ethnic Germans (Spish and Carpathian Germans) and a large number of Yiddish-speaking Jews lived in towns and cities and also in the rural countryside of Carpathian Rus'.

Finally, there is another border that runs through Carpathian Rus' that to date has received no attention in scholarly or popular literature but is nonetheless of great significance. I refer to what might be called the socio-climatic border or, more prosaically, the tomato and grape line. It is through a good part of Carpathian Rus' that the northern limit for tomato and grape (wine) cultivation is found. Whereas tomato-based dishes are the norm in traditional cuisine south of the line, before the mid-twentieth century that vegetable was virtually unknown to the Rusyns and other groups living along the upper slopes of the Carpathians. The lack of grapes and wine cultivation north of the tomato-grape line has had a profound impact on the social psychology of the inhabitants of Carpathian Rus'. A warmer climate and café culture has promoted human interaction and social tolerance among Rusyns and others to the south. By contrast, those living farther north are apt to spend less time outdoors, and when they do interact in social situations the environment is frequently dominated by the use of hard alcohol that in excess provokes behavior marked by extremes of opinion, short tempers, and physical violence. Like all attempts at defining social or national "characteristics," the above assessment is based largely on impressionistic observation and, therefore, is liable to oversimplification.[6] Nevertheless, further empirical research should be carried out to define more precisely the exact location of tomato and grape cultivation, to describe the resultant interregional differentiation in food and drink, and more importantly, to determine how those differences affect the social psychology of the Rusyns and other inhabitants of Carpathian Rus'.

Carpathian Rus', therefore, certainly qualifies as a borderland par excellence. How, then, does it relate to the following themes: (1) the use of multiple constructs to define identity; (2) the development of ethnic and national identities; (3) the role of the state; and (4) the historic context of ethnic violence?

Multiple Constructs to Define Identity

Elsewhere, I developed a conceptual model for analyzing national movements among stateless peoples that contrasts the idea of a hierarchy of multiple identities with a framework of mutually exclusive identities.[7] The case study to which I applied this model concerned Ukrainians during the long nineteenth century, although I believe it can also be used to understand the evolution of most other stateless peoples in Europe.

I would argue that having multiple identities is the norm for most individuals in developed and developing societies. In other words, each individual has several potential identities from which to choose: a village, town, or city of residence; a region or state; a religious orientation; a language and/or ethnic group. Some of us also have strong loyalties and identity with the university we attended (there was a time when someone from Harvard was indeed different from a graduate from Yale or Princeton, not to mention a graduate from a state university), or with the clubs to which we belong, or with our sexual preference, especially if it is not heterosexual. Then there is identification with leisure activities, hobbies, and preferences, such as sports clubs, etc.

By way of illustration, may I be permitted a personal note. I can remember growing up in a part of New Jersey just opposite that state's largest suburb, New York City. Immersed in that environment, I had one primary identity. Whenever asked, I responded I was a Brooklyn Dodger fan—more precisely a vicarious Brooklyn Dodger.[8] This was a clear identity associated with certain personality traits that were demonstrably different from someone who identified with the rival New York Giants and the hated New York Yankees. Because my parents and grandparents were still alive, I had as yet no experience with personal loss, and my first such experience came in 1957, when the Dodgers left Brooklyn. In a sense, when I was 12 years old my "national" identity was taken away, not by some governmental decree or by planned ethnocide, but by greedy businessmen who saw that a bigger buck could be made by going to a foreign country—Los Angeles. The point is that it is perfectly normal for individuals to have more than one identity, and that the decision about which one to choose depends on the circumstances in which an answer to the question is needed. Put another way, situational identity is the handmaiden of multiple identities.

For self-proclaimed members of a nationalist intelligentsia, the very idea of multiple identities is an anathema. What in most circumstances might seem a normal phenomenon—such as a resident of pre–World War II Macedonia identifying as a Macedonian *and* Bulgarian (or Macedono-Bulgarian), or a resident of nineteenth-century Ukraine as a Little Russian (or Ukrainian) *and* Russian—is totally unacceptable to nationality-builders, who feel it their duty to make persons aware of their belonging only to a single nationality, in this case Macedonian *or* Bulgarian, Ukrainian *or* Russian. Hence, national identities should not be viewed as part of a hierarchy of multiple loyalties; rather, national identities, and by corollary language use, must be mutually exclusive.

Much of the history of Carpathian Rus' from 1848 to the present is a story of how the local nationalist intelligentsia has struggled—often in vain—against the natural tendency of the local Carpatho-Rusyn inhabitants to maintain more than one identity or, in some cases, no national identity at all. In the eyes of the nationalist intelligentsia, such persons are unenlightened, assimilationists, or, worse still, enemies of the nationalist cause.

The Development of National and Ethnic Identities

Questions regarding national and ethnic identity began to be raised in Carpathian Rus' during the 1830s and 1840s. The year 1848 was an important turning point for those discussions. During the next two decades Carpatho-Rusyns experienced their first national awakening.[9] Theirs was a classic national awakening—albeit on a small scale—of the central and eastern European variety. A small group of intellectuals, what we now call the nationalist intelligentsia, published the first books and newspapers in the native language; they founded organizations, village reading rooms, and schools in which the native culture and language were propagated; and they submitted petitions to the ruling Habsburg authorities calling for cultural and political autonomy based on territorial and/or corporate group rights.

To be sure, not all members of the intelligentsia—at the time they were mostly priests—favored the idea of promoting the local East Slavic Rus' culture. Many preferred instead association with the dominant nationality of the state, which before 1918 meant identifying as a Hungarian or, in the case of Carpathian Rus' territory north of the mountain crests, as a Pole.

As for those who believed in the desirability of association with the East Slavic and Eastern Christian world, the road to a clear national identity remained fraught with obstacles. Like many intellectual leaders stemming from stateless peoples, Carpatho-Rusyn national activists lacked pride and confidence in their own culture. Hence, it seemed easier to associate with an already existing East Slavic nationality and language. In essence, during the first national awakening in Carpathian Rus' (ca. 1848–1868), national activists proclaimed themselves to be of the Russian or Great Russian nationality; they tried to use the Russian literary language in their publications and for instruction in schools; and they tried to convince the local Rusyn inhabitants to adopt a Russian national identity. These early national awakeners, led by figures like Aleksander Dukhnovych and Adolf Dobrians'kyi, were partly successful in having a Russian national orientation accepted by the generation that was to follow them. By the 1890s, however, some younger intellectual activists (again mostly priests) argued that Russian was too far from the dialects spoken by the East Slavs of Carpathian Rus' and that instead the local vernacular should be standardized and used as the representative language of the region's inhabitants. It was never made clear, however, what that local language should be and what alternative, if any, should there be to the Russian national identity.

The problem of ethnic, national, and linguistic identity became more complex after World War I, when Carpathian Rus' was divided between Czechoslovakia and Poland. The Russian national orientation continued to be propagated by certain local activists, who were joined by postwar émigrés of Russian orientation from the former Habsburg province of Galicia (by then in Poland) and from the former Russian Empire (by then the Soviet Union). Among such émigrés were figures like "the grandmother" of the Russian Revolution, Ekaterina Breshko-Breshkovskaia, who considered Carpathian Rus' the last land where the spirit of Russia was preserved in pristine form.[10]

Also from Polish Galicia and the Dnieper Ukraine in the former Russian Empire came émigrés of Ukrainian orientation to Carpathian Rus'. They found a few supporters among local Carpatho-Rusyns and educated many more young people in the belief that the East Slavic inhabitants of Carpathian Rus' were ethnically Ukrainian, that is the same people as the Ukrainians of Eastern Galicia and the Dnieper Ukraine—and certainly not Russians.

It was not long before some local activists expressed dissatisfaction with the Russian/Ukrainian dichotomy and argued that the East Slavs of Carpathian Rus' were neither Russian nor Ukrainian, but rather a distinct nationality called Subcarpathian Rusyn, or Carpatho-Rusyn, or simply Rusyn. The result was that the entire period of what became known as the second national awakening, lasting from 1918 to 1939, was characterized by a fierce ideological rivalry between supporters of three national and linguistic orientations: the Russophile, the Ukrainophile, and the Rusynophile.[11]

As we have seen, the Russophile orientation was the oldest, having dominated the first national awakening and persisting through the second. It was the first orientation to disappear, however, so that during the third national awakening, which began in 1989 and continues to the present, there are only two orientations: the Rusynophile and the Ukrainophile.

The Role of the State

Carpathian Rus' has always been part of one or more state structures. Therefore, it should come as no surprise that the ruling authorities have always expressed an interest in the question of national identity among Carpatho-Rusyns.

During the last 70 years of Habsburg rule (1848–1918), the attitude of the state went through several phases. The first two decades of so-called Habsburg absolutism were marked by efforts of the central authorities to control and even suppress those nationalities with strong political ambitions, such as the Poles in Galicia and most particularly the Magyars in the Hungarian Kingdom. As a counterweight to the Poles and Magyars, the Habsburgs supported the efforts at national enlightenment among the East Slavs of Galicia and the Hungarian Kingdom, including Carpathian Rus'. In 1867, however, the Habsburg authorities reached an accommodation with the Magyars and Poles, who consequently regained their position as the dominant political and social factor in Hungary and Austrian Galicia. This political change had a particularly negative impact on Carpathian Rus' lands in Hungary, where until 1918 the local intelligentsia and school system became subject to a policy of Magyarization intended to eliminate all remnants of East Slavic culture.

The situation changed radically with the collapse of Austria-Hungary in late 1918 and the division of Carpathian Rus' territory between two new postwar states: Czechoslovakia and Poland. Czechoslovakia was especially favorable toward Carpatho-Rusyns who, alongside Czechs and Slovaks, became one of the founding peoples of the state. Rusyns living south of Carpathians voluntarily proclaimed their desire to join Czechoslovakia, and at the Paris Peace Conference that desire was confirmed with guarantees for "the fullest degree of self-government compatible with the Czecho-Slovak state."[12] A distinct administrative entity called Subcarpathian Rus' (Czech: Podkarpatská Rus) came into being in the far eastern end of Czechoslovakia. Although the Czechs never fulfilled their promise to grant autonomy, the province was nominally a Rusyn territory with its own governor and with Rusyn as the official language used in schools and alongside Czech in government administration.

With regard to the national identity of Rusyns and the closely related language question, the Czechoslovak authorities proclaimed neutrality. In practice, however, they supported the Ukrainophile, Russophile, and Rusynophile orientations at different times as warranted by political circumstances.[13] By the 1930s, when Czechoslovakia was in a desperate search for allies against revisionist Nazi Germany and Hungary, the territory of Subcarpathian Rus' took on special geo-strategic importance. It was the only direct territorial link to Czechoslovakia's fellow Little Entente allies, Romania and Yugoslavia. Therefore, the authorities in Prague gave greater support to the Rusynophile orientation, hoping to consolidate the formation of a distinct Carpatho-Rusyn nationality that would have no political interests beyond the borders of Czechoslovakia.[14]

Notwithstanding the change in government policy, the Russophile and Ukrainophile orientations did not disappear. On the contrary, the Ukrainian orientation continued to increase its grassroots support among various segments of the local Rusyn population, especially young people. So much was this the case that during the few months following the September 1938 Munich Pact, when the unitary structure of Czechoslovakia was transformed and Subcarpathian Rus' finally received its long awaited autonomy, the Ukrainian orientation soon dominated the region which it renamed Carpatho-Ukraine.

Carpathian Rus' territory within interwar Poland fared somewhat differently. The local Rusnaks, who by the outset of the twentieth century had adopted the name *Lemko* as an ethnonym, hoped at the close of World War I to unite politically with their Rusyn brethren south of the mountains in Czechoslovakia. It was in fact Lemko-Rusyn leaders who first formulated a clear territorial definition of Carpathian Rus' and submitted memoranda with maps to the Paris Peace Conference calling for its independence or autonomous status within a neighboring state.[15] The Lemko-Rusyn demand for union with Czechoslovakia was rejected, however, both by Rusyn leaders south of the Carpathians and by President Masaryk in Prague. Not wanting to be ruled by Poland, Lemko activists created an "independent" republic that lasted for about 16 months, until in March 1920 the area was brought under Polish control.[16]

Lemko opposition to Polish rule was quickly overcome—and without bloodshed. During the interwar years, the Russophile and Ukrainophile orientations were present in what became known as the Lemko Region of Carpathian Rus'. Ever fearful of the Ukrainian problem within its borders, the Polish government began openly to favor any national orientation among Lemko Rusyns as long as it was not Ukrainian.[17] Initially, it preferred those Lemko Rusyns who assimilated to Polish culture. For those who did not, the government permitted school programs in which Lemko-Rusyn vernacular was taught, and it welcomed the decision of the Vatican to create in 1934 a separate Lemko Greek Catholic church jurisdiction that was decidedly not Ukrainian in orientation.[18] The result of these efforts was the creation of a generation of individuals who believed they were part of a distinct Lemko nationality.

The relatively liberal environment of the interwar years came to an end with the onset of World War II. Subcarpathian Rus' was reannexed to Hungary, which banned the Ukrainian orientation, barely tolerated the Russian orientation, and openly supported the idea that the local East Slavs formed a distinct "Uhro-Rusyn" nationality loyal to the Hungarian state. North of the mountains the Ukrainian orientation was given a new lease on life by Nazi Germany, which incorporated the Lemko-inhabited part of Carpathian Rus' into the General Government of the Third Reich.[19]

The apex of state intervention in the nationality question was reached at the close of World War II. By 1945, former Czechoslovak Subcarpathian Rus' was annexed to the Soviet Union, while the other two parts of Carpathian Rus' remained within Poland (the Lemko Region) and Czechoslovakia (the so-called Prešov Region of northeastern Slovakia). The Soviet regime resolved the nationality question according to principles adopted by the Communist Party (Bolshevik) of Ukraine in December 1925. Regardless of what the inhabitants of Carpathian Rus' may have called themselves or believed themselves to be—Rusyns, Rusnaks, Carpatho-Russians, Uhro-Rusyns—they were formally designated as Ukrainians. The use of Rusyn as a nationality descriptor was simply banned. When, in 1948, Czechoslovakia became a Communist-ruled state, within a few years it adopted the Soviet model for Carpatho-Rusyns living in the northeastern corner of Slovakia. By 1951, the Rusyn population there was administratively declared to be Ukrainian. In the decades that followed, the Communist authorities of Czechoslovakia, in cooperation with those local activists who gave up a Russian national identity for a Ukrainian one, introduced a policy of Ukrainianization in schools and cultural life. Those Rusyns who were opposed to such a changes generally eschewed all further association with their East Slavic heritage and adopted a Slovak national identity and Slovak language.[20]

The nationality question among the Lemko Rusyns in Poland was resolved by state intervention in an even more drastic fashion. The Lemkos were simply deported en masse from their Carpathian homeland in two waves (1945–46 and 1947), thereby fulfilling the Stalinist precept—if there's no people there's no problem (net naroda—net problemy).

The role of the state had again a profound impact on the nationality question in Carpathian Rus' in the wake of the Revolution of 1989 and the implosion of the Soviet Union in 1991. As part of the effort to overcome the shortcomings of the Communist past, post-1989 Poland, along with Czechoslovakia and its successor states, the Czech Republic and Slovakia, made it legally possible for people once again to identify themselves as Rusyns in the sense of belonging to a distinct nationality. Consequently, Lemkos and Rusyns within Poland and Slovakia have been officially recognized in census reports since 1989 and are provided with state funds for education, publications, theaters, and other cultural events in the Rusyn language.

Independent Ukraine also styles itself a post-Soviet democratic republic and does not restrict privately sponsored cultural activity carried out by individuals and organizations in

Transcarpathia (former Subcarpathian Rus') who espouse the Rusyn national orientation. The government of Ukraine refuses, however, to recognize Carpatho-Rusyns as a distinct nationality and instead formally defines them as a "sub-ethnos" of the Ukrainian people.[21]

The Historical Context of Ethnic Violence

Carpathian Rus' has always been in an ethnically diverse region of Europe. To the northwest live Poles, to the northeast Ukrainians, to the southwest Slovaks, and to the southeast Romanians. Carpathian Rus' itself, that is the territory in which Rusnaks/Rusyns have traditionally formed the majority population, has also never been ethnically homogeneous. Living alongside Rusyns in villages, towns, and cities have been Magyars, Jews, Germans, Roma/Gypsies, Slovaks, Poles, Romanians, and since World War II Ukrainians and Russians. For illustrative purposes let us take one part of Carpathian Rus', the former Czechoslovak province of Subcarpathian Rus'. In 1930, its 725,000 inhabitants were comprised of Rusyns (63 percent), Magyars (15.4 percent), Jews (12.8 percent), Czechs and Slovaks (4.8 percent), Germans (1.9 percent), and others (1.9 percent).[22] There was no less religious diversity, with Greek Catholicism, Orthodoxy, Judaism, Reformed Calvinism, and Evangelical Lutheranism all serving one or more ethnic groups. Added to this mix are several Protestant and other Christian sects—Baptists, Seventh-Day Adventists, Jehovah's Witnesses—whose numbers have grown rapidly in the post-Communist era.

Such ethnic and religious diversity often led to rivalry and ideological conflict. I have already mentioned the rivalry among the pro-Russian, pro-Ukrainian, and pro-Rusyn oriented intelligentsia, not to mention the displeasure toward all these orientations on the part of those individuals who opted out of an East Slavic identity and favored assimilation with the Magyar, Slovak, or Polish nationalities. The twentieth century was also characterized by frictions between adherents of Greek Catholicism and Orthodoxy. Nearly one-third of the Carpatho-Rusyn population "converted" from Greek Catholicism to Orthodoxy in the decade after World War I. The resultant controversy between the two religious groups was less the result of liturgical or ideological differences than it was over church property. But perhaps the fiercest religious rivalries occurred among Jews, between the various Hasidic dynasties (the followers of rebbes Shapira, Rokeah, Weiss, and Teitelbaum being the most intolerant of each other) and between all the Hasidim, on the one hand, and the secular Zionists, on the other.[23]

The rhetoric spewed out by defenders of these various national and religious orientations was strong, even venomous. Nevertheless, while there may have occurred some scuffles at the individual level during public rallies on behalf of a specific national orientation or at protests on the steps of a church or a synagogue, there was never any organized violence and death that pitted one group against another.[24] True enough, pre–World War I Hungarian state officials and local gendarmes acted with disdain toward Carpatho-Rusyns, but there was never any violence between Rusyn and Magyar villagers or townspeople who lived alongside them or nearby. And Carpathian Rus' is perhaps unique in central and eastern Europe in that there has never been a pogrom of any kind perpetrated against Jews.

This is not to say that there was never any violence directed against ethnic or religious groups. There was, but in all cases it was inspired and carried out by the state. The worst fate has befallen that part of Carpathian Rus' inhabited by Lemko-Rusyns in what is present-day southeastern Poland. During the first months of World War I, the Habsburg government became suspicious of an estimated 2,000–5,000 Lemko-Rusyns who, because of their Russophile national orientation, were arrested for alleged treason and incarcerated for most of the war in concentration camps set up in the western part of the empire.[25] Many died there from disease and malnutrition. Three decades later, at the close of World War II, Lemko-Rusyns along with other East Slavs in postwar Poland were slated for resettlement as part of a "voluntary" population exchange with the Soviet Union. About 100,000 went eastward between late 1944 and 1946. Those who refused to go east (about 60,000) were forcibly driven from their homes in 1947 and scattered in villages and towns of western and northern Poland in territories (Silesia, Pomerania) that had belonged to prewar Germany.

There was also state-instigated violence against ethnic and religious groups in those parts of Carpathian Rus′ located on the southern slopes of the mountains. Perhaps the first instance occurred on the eve of World War I, when the Hungarian government tried to stop the early stages of the Orthodox movement by arresting some of its adherents and subjecting them to a trial in which religious conversion was equated with treason against the state. It was the Jews in Carpathian Rus′, however, who suffered the most at the hands of the state. In 1942, the German administration killed or sent to the Bełżec death camp all Jews living in the Lemko Region. Then, in the spring of 1944, Jews were deported *en masse* to the death camp of Auschwitz-Birkenau by the governments of Hungary (from Subcarpathian Rus′) and Slovakia (from the Prešov Region). As a result, no less than 80 percent of the Jews of Carpathian Rus′ perished.[26]

As World War II came to an end, it was the Magyars and Germans who became the object of state violence. In Subcarpathian Rus′, which was in the process of being annexed to the Soviet Union, all males of Magyar nationality between the ages of 18 and 50 were arrested and deported to forced labor camps in the Gulag. About 5,000 of the 30,000 deported Magyars died while in incarceration. In 1946, by which time Subcarpathian Rus′, renamed Transcarpathia, was formally part of the Soviet Union, all males of the German ethnicity were deported to eastern Ukraine or to the Gulag forced labor camps. Between 1949 and 1950, the Soviet Union and its Communist ally Czechoslovakia outlawed the Greek Catholic Church and arrested all its bishops and many priests who refused to embrace Orthodoxy as the only Eastern Christian religion recognized by the state.

Despite these numerous examples of state-inspired violence in the Carpathian Rus′ borderland, there has at the same time been a remarkable absence of interethnic violence. Why is this the case? Possible answers to that question can only be of a speculative nature. I would suggest two factors: socioeconomic status, and a common fear of the Other.

With regard to the socioeconomic factor, it should be noted that Carpathian Rus′ has traditionally been an economically marginal rural area in which most inhabitants have survived as subsistence-level peasant farmers, livestock herders, and forestry workers. Industry was virtually nonexistent until the second half of the twentieth century.   In   contrast   to many other parts of Europe, where ethnic groups are frequently differentiated according to their customary professions and socioeconomic status, in Carpathian Rus′ virtually all groups were engaged in agriculture and forest-related work. In other words, all the region's peoples were equally poor. For example, it was just as common to find Jewish peasant farmers and woodcutters as Jewish proprietors of small retail shops and taverns. The local ethnic Germans and Magyars—the "superior" nationalities in the Habsburg Monarchy—were also mostly peasant farmers and woodcutters in Carpathian Rus′.

Perhaps the only exception to this pattern occurred in Subcarpathian Rus′ during the interwar years of the twentieth century. At the same time the Czechoslovak government encouraged nearly 30,000 Czechs to settle in the region and to take up posts as government officials, teachers, physicians, businessmen, and other professionals. The Czechs clearly were an ethnic group associated with one socioeconomic stratum that was quantifiably different (and perceived as such) from all other ethnic groups in the region.

Ironically, the Soviet regime after World War II also contributed to socioeconomic disparity based on ethnic differences. To staff the new industrial plants it built in the region, the Soviets initially brought in managers, technical specialists, and workers from Ukraine and other parts of the Soviet Union. Almost all these newcomers settled in Transcarpathia's few cities. Some locals may have resented this intrusion, since at least in the first years of Soviet rule the newcomers seemed to get the most lucrative paying jobs and positions in the regional administration and professional spheres. In the end, however, the downturn and eventual collapse of the Soviet economy created a situation in which the economic and social status of the postwar "newcomers" from other parts of the Soviet Union turned out to be the same or worse than that of the locals, who were able to depend on family property in villages and socioeconomic opportunities provided by kinship networks. While it is certainly true that the lack of any correlation between socioeconomic status and ethnic origin may not have eliminated envy on an individual level, it did help to prevent the basis for envy and hatred on a group level.

At first glance fear of the Other might be considered as a factor which contributes to interethnic violence. The question, however, is what specifically was the Other that produced fear? There were and still are many ethnic and religious Others in Carpathian Rus'. Those Others have never been unfamiliar, since ethnic interaction continually occurs in the workplace, village tavern and store, town market, and through the exchange of mutually symbiotic labor services (Christians cooked and cleaned for Jews on their Sabbaths; Jews operated stores and provided other services on Sundays). The comfort level on the part of the numerically dominant Carpatho-Rusyns toward other peoples in their midst was also enhanced by their ongoing inclination toward maintaining multiple identities.[27]

Rather, the Other that all groups feared equally was the state. For people at the lower end of the socioeconomic scale—and this accounts for a significant portion of all ethnic groups in Carpathian Rus'—the state has always been a threat to the individual, whether in its role of collecting taxes or drafting young male family members into the army. As such, the state was to be avoided as much as possible. In that regard, the Magyar peasant was as fearful and probably as mistreated as the Rusyn peasant by the Hungarian gendarme. In other words, there was no "correct" ethnic identity that in and of itself could save one from the wrath of the state. Since, in general, most inhabitants of Carpathian Rus', regardless of ethnic or religious background, were resentful and fearful of the state, it was difficult if not impossible for the authorities to mobilize one group against another in its periodic campaigns of group-directed violence.

Conclusion

By way of conclusion it might be useful to assess the value of studying Carpathian Rus' in the context of borderlands. If, as many historians and social scientists have argued, east-central, eastern, and southeastern Europe is composed of borderlands characterized by ethnic, religious, or social violence, then is it possible that Carpathian Rus' is unique? I am skeptical about arguing for the uniqueness of any phenomenon, especially in the presence of scholars who are always likely to come up with counterexamples. If not unique, then we might agree that Carpathian Rus' is somewhat exceptional. To understand any norm, one needs to account for and explain the exceptions. If violence is considered the norm in ethnic relations, then Carpathian Rus' may be an example against which other case studies may be compared and contrasted.

Notes

1. The conference took place in May 2005 as part of the international research project: "Borderlands: Ethnicity, Identity, and Violence in the Shatter-Zone of Empires since 1848," sponsored by the Watson Institute for International Studies at Brown University in Providence, Rhode Island.

2. The exact geographic center is near the village of Dilove (formerly Trebushany), in the far southeastern corner of Carpathian Rus', present-day Ukraine's region of Transcarpathia. There, in 1875, the Hungarian government set up a monument, and a century later, in 1975, the Soviet government erected a new monument; both are still standing.

3. Benedict Anderson's now well-known concept of imagined communities and its relationship to the post-1989 revival of Rusyns is discussed with provocative irony and insight by British and German specialists on central Europe: Timothy Garton Ash, "Long Live Ruthenia!," *The New York Review of Books,* 22 April 1999, reprinted in his *History of the Present: Essays, Sketches and Dispatches from Europe in the 1990s* (London: Penguin Press, 1999), 376–82; and Stefan Troebst, "Russinen, Lemken, Huzulen und andere: zwischen regionaler Identitätssuche und EU-Ost-Erweiterung," *Frankfurter Allgemeine Zeitung,* 16 January 2001, 9, reprinted in his *Kulturstudien Ostmitteleuropas: Aufsätze und Essays* (Frankfurt am Main: Peter Lang, 2006), 361–66.

4. All 1,100 settlements (with their various names) are listed in Paul Robert Magocsi, *Our People: Carpatho-Rusyns and Their Descendants in North America,* 4th rev. ed. (Wauconda, Ill.: Bolchazy-Carducci Publishers, 2005), 110–206, and mapped in Paul Robert Magocsi, *Carpatho-Rusyn Settlements at the Outset of the 20th Century with Additional Data from 1881 and 1806,* 3rd rev. ed. (New York: Carpatho-Rusyn Research Center, 2011).

5. These concepts were developed by the Italian Slavist, Riccardo Picchio, "Guidelines for a Comparative Study of the Language Question among the Slavs," in Riccardo Picchio and Harvey Goldblatt, eds., *Aspects of the Slavic Language Question,* vol. 1 (New Haven, Conn.: Yale Concilium on International and Area Studies, 1984), 1–42.

6. An early attempt at describing the differences in cuisine and the sociopsychological characteristics of Carpatho-Rusyns is found in Sándor Bonkáló, *A Rutének (Ruszinok)* (Budapest: Franklin-Társulat, 1940), 70–101; English translation in Alexander Bonkáló, *The Rusyns* (New York: Columbia University Press/East European Monographs, 1990), 57–84.

7. The conceptual framework was first laid out in Paul Robert Magocsi, "The Ukrainian National Revival: A New Analytical Framework," *Canadian Review of Studies in Nationalism,* 16(1–2) (Charlottetown, Canada: E. I., 1989), 45–62, and fleshed out in greater detail in chapters 29 to 35 of idem, *History of Ukraine: The Land and its Peoples,* 2nd rev. ed. (Toronto: University of Toronto Press, 2010), 374–488.

8. Lest this example be perceived as idiosyncratic, it should be noted that there is an extensive literature on the Brooklyn Dodger phenomenon in twentieth-century American culture. Many consider the classic work on this topic to be Roger Kahn, *The Boys of Summer* (New York: Harper and Row, 1972), but to my mind the best of all is the elegantly written autobiographical essay by the devoted female follower of the Dodger cult—a native of Brooklyn and distinguished American political scientist—Doris Kearns Goodwin, *Wait Till Next Year: A Memoir* (New York: Simon and Schuster, 1997). Others that capture very well the psychology of "Dodgerness" are: Peter Golenbock, *Bums: An Oral History of the Brooklyn Dodgers* (New York: G. Putnam, 1984); Harvey Frommer, *New York City Baseball: The Last Golden Age, 1947–1957* (New York: Atheneum, 1985); and Bob McGee, *The Greatest Ballpark Ever: Ebbets Fields and the Story of the Brooklyn Dodgers* (New Brunswick, N.J.: Rutgers University Press, 2005).

9. For details on this first national awakening, see Ivan Žeguc, *Die nationalpolitischen Bestrebungen der Karpato-Ruthenen 1848–1914* (Wiesbaden, Germany: Otto Harrassowitz, 1965); and Paul Robert Magocsi, *The Shaping of National Identity: Subcarpathian Rus', 1848–1948* (Cambridge, Mass.: Harvard University Press, 1978), esp. 42–75.

10. This attitude was best summed up in the words of another Russian émigré: "I remember with fascination how a few years before the [First] World War I learned that Russians live in Carpathians! . . . From that moment I felt inside of me an urgent desire to get to . . . Subcarpathian Rus', to learn more about this land, to see its people in their everyday life, and to hear a Russian song sung in the Carpatho-Russian land." Konstantin Bel'govskii, "Krai Russkii—krai neviedomyi: vpechatlieniia iz Podkarpatskoi Rusi," *Staroe i novoe* no. 3 (Tallinn, Estonia, 1932), 177.

11. For details on these controversies, see Magocsi, *Shaping*, 105–187.

12. *Traité entre les Principales Puissances Alliées et Associées et la Tchécoslovaquie* (Paris, 1919), 26–27.

13. For details on the evolution of Czechoslovak policy, see Magocsi, *Shaping*, 191–233.

14. The experience of Czechoslovak rule was to a degree successful in creating a sense of Carpatho-Rusyn distinctiveness. Part of this process was related to the group's ethnonym. The term *Rusyn* had also been used by the East Slavs of Galicia and Bukovina until at least 1918; thereafter, most Galician and Bukovinian East Slavs adopted instead the ethnonym *Ukrainian,* arguing since then that it is the modern equivalent of the older name *Rusyn.* The Rusynophiles of Carpathian Rus', both during the Czechoslovak period and subsequently under Hungarian rule, used the term *Rusyn* (or *Carpatho-Rusyn, Subcarpathian Rusyn,* and *Uhro-Rusyn*) in the sense of a distinct fourth East Slavic nationality. Carpatho-Rusyn national specificity was also helped by the appearance of several synthetic surveys propagating the view that Carpatho-Rusyns had a distinct historical, literary, and artistic tradition. Among works in this genre were: Yrynei M. Kondratovych, *Ystoriia Podkarpatskoî Rusy dlia naroda* (Uzhhorod, Russia: Tovarystvo "Prosvîta," 1924; 3rd ed., 1930); Evgenii Nedziel'skii, *Ocherk karpatorusskoi literatury* (Uzhhorod: Podkarpatorusskii narodnoprosvietitel'nyi soiuz, 1932); [Stepan Dobosh], *Ystoriia podkarpatorus'koi lyteraturŷ* (Uzhhorod, Russia: Regentskii komissariat, 1942); and A. Yzvoryn [Evgenii Nedziel'skii], "Suchasnî rus'kî khudozhnyky," *Zoria/Hajnal* 2(3–4) (Uzhhorod, Russia, 1942): 387–418, and vol. 3(1–4) (1943): 258–287.

15. Anthony Beskid and Dimitry Sobin, *The Origin of the Lems, Slavs of Danubian Provenance: Memorandum to the Peace Conference Concerning Their National Claims* (Prešov, Slovakia: National Council of Carpatho-Russians in Prešov, 1919).

16. For details on the little-known Lemko Republic, see Bogdan Horbal, *Działność polityczna Łemków na Łemkowszczyźnie, 1918–1921* (Wrocław, Poland: Wyd. Arboretum, 1997); and Paul Robert Magocsi, "The Lemko Rusyn Republic, 1918–1920 and Political Thought in Western Rus'-Ukraine," in idem, *Of the Making of Nationalities There is No End,* vol. 1 (New York: Columbia University Press/East European Monographs, 1999), 303–315.

17. For details on Polish policy toward the Lemko Region during the interwar years, see Jarosław Moklak, *Łemkowszczyzna w drugiej rzeczypospolitej: zagadnienia polityczne i wyznaniowe* (Krakow: Towarzystwo Wyd. "Historia Iagellonica," 1997).

18. The new jurisdiction was known as the Lemko Apostolic Administration. It was called into being because of the Vatican's concern with the large-scale defections of Lemkos to Orthodoxy. The "return to Orthodoxy" was in part a reaction by Lemko Rusyns against the Ukrainian national orientation of the Greek Catholic Eparchy of Przemyśl, of which the Lemko Region had been a part. The Vatican hoped that, having their own ecclesiastical jurisdiction headed by Rusynophile (and Russophile) prelates, Lemkos would feel they were still part of a Rus' and not Ukrainian church structure.

19. The Nazis allowed the formation of a Ukrainian Central Committee in Cracow, which organized Ukrainian-language schools in the Lemko Region staffed largely by refugee Ukrainian nationalists fleeing from Eastern Galicia after that territory had come under Soviet rule in September 1939.

20. For details on these developments, see Pavel Mačů, "National Assimilation: The Case of the Rusyn-Ukrainians of Czehoslovakia," in Magocsi, *Of the Making of Nationalities There is No End,* vol. 1, 242–289.

21. The official Ukrainian position was formulated in a *Report Submitted by the Ukraine to the Council of Europe Pursuant to Article 25, Paragraph 1 of the Framework Convention for the Protection of National Minorities,* 2 November 1999, in particular the Appendix, "Ethnic Groups of the Nationalities of Ukraine," 137–140.

22. *Statistický lexicon obcí v Zemi podkarpatoruské* (Prague: Orbis, 1937), xv.

23. On the various conflicts among Jews of the region, see Yeshayahu A. Jelinek, *The Carpathian Diaspora: The Jews of Subcarpathian Rus' and Mukachevo, 1848–1948* (New York: Columbia University Press/East European Monographs, 2007), esp. 113–224.

24. The one exception of "ethnically" motivated violence occurred among Carpatho-Rusyns themselves when, in 1930, a local student of Ukrainian national orientation at the Teacher's College in Uzhhorod, Fedir Tatsynets', attempted to shoot the Greek Catholic priest and respected patriarch of the Russophile orientation, Evmenii Sabov. The assassination attempt failed and the student was apprehended. Tatsynets' had been persuaded to carry out the deed by one of his teachers at the Uzhhorod Teachers' College, Stefaniia Novakivs'ka, a radical Galician-Ukrainian nationalist, who was head of the recently-founded Subcarpathian branch of the underground Ukrainian Military Organization based in neighboring Polish-ruled Galicia. Both Tatsynets' and Novakivs'ka were arrested and sentenced to several years in prison. Although local Ukrainophile leaders disavowed the act, it did suggest the extremes to which Ukrainian émigrés from Galicia might go in order to achieve their goals. On the "Tatsynets' Affair," see Mykola M. Vegesh, ed., *Vony boronyly Karpats'ku Ukraïnu* (Uzhhorod, Russia: Vyd. "Karpaty," 2002), 522–27.

25. The most infamous of the camps was at Thalerhof, a village in Austrian Styria now replaced by a runway of the airport in Graz.

26. For details, see Jelinek, *The Carpathian Diaspora,* 227–321.

27. To be sure, local Carpatho-Rusyns were not enamored of the treatment they received from Soviet "Russian" officials and bureaucrats in the first years after 1945 annexation, or by the condescending attitude of Galician Ukrainians who considered—and still consider—Transcarpathia their land as much as they do Galicia or any other part of Ukraine. Nevertheless, Carpatho-Rusyns who studied the Russian and Ukrainian languages and cultures, and who may have identified themselves in the past or present as Russians or Ukrainians, find it instinctively difficult to dislike fellow Transcarpathians from those ethnic groups.

25

TREMORS IN THE SHATTERZONE OF EMPIRES
EASTERN GALICIA IN SUMMER 1941

KAI STRUVE

During the first days and weeks after the German attack on the Soviet Union on 22 June 1941 a wave of violence against Jews swept those territories that had been occupied by the Soviet Union since September 1939 or summer 1940 and now were invaded by the German armed forces and its Romanian and Hungarian allies. The violence consisted mostly of mass executions by the German Security Police's infamous *Einsatzgruppen* and pogrom-like excesses by the local Christian population. Often both forms of violence were closely connected.[1]

The anti-Jewish violence in the region sprung from both external and internal sources. Both sources of violence characterized the region a borderland in the sense of a contested space where competing claims of states, nations, religions, and ideologies clashed with one another. Thus, the violent events of summer 1941 epitomize greater conflicts that arose from the relations of the powers in the region and from the fundamental political and socioeconomic changes of the nineteenth and early twentieth centuries. Local anti-Jewish violence was one expression of larger structural tensions that characterized the region.

This chapter will focus on Eastern Galicia. It does not aspire to a comprehensive presentation of all anti-Jewish violence or all pogroms, but is intended as an analysis of certain motifs and contexts and, therefore, refers to specific cases as exemplary.[2] As a starting point, we look at the central violent event in the region, i.e., in Lwów (L'viv). It was central not so much because of the scale of violence in Eastern Galicia's capital—although it was probably the place that saw the most victims of mass executions during the first weeks of the war in June and July—but more so because the aspirations, perceptions, expectations, and strategies of the different collective actors here became more clearly visible than in other places.[3]

Lwów

During the weeks before the German invasion a new wave of deportation and arrests had started in the territories that the Soviet Union had occupied since 1939 and 1940. In Eastern Galicia and Volhynia the arrests focused on people who were suspected of Ukrainian nationalism and of having links to the Ukrainian nationalist underground.[4] Many more were arrested after the German attack. Just one or two days after the German attack the Soviet People's Commissar for Internal Affairs, Lavrentii Beriia, seems to have given the order to execute all inmates of the prisons in Western Ukraine who had been imprisoned for "counter-revolutionary crimes as well as persons who caused damage on a large scale."[5] The advance of the German armies in Western Ukraine—the Seventeenth Army, the First Tank Group, and the Sixth Army—after 22 June was comparatively slow because of the strong Soviet forces that were concentrated here. This gave the NKVD more time to complete this order than in other parts of the border regions. The number of murdered prison inmates in Lwów alone was more than 3,000.[6] Altogether, probably 20,000-24,000 prison inmates were murdered in the territories of eastern Poland, two-thirds to three-quarters of them in Eastern Galicia.[7] In contrast to earlier periods of the Soviet occupation of the region, the majority of prison inmates at the time of the German invasion were Ukrainian. Nevertheless, there were also many Poles and Jews among them.

The first units of the German army entered Lwów in the early morning of 30 June, without fighting except for some short exchanges of gunfire with departing Soviet units. Among them was the Ukrainian battalion with the codename *Nachtigall* (Nightingale) as part of the I. Battalion of the special command regiment Brandenburg 800. This unit had to occupy and secure important objects within the city. Among them were the prisons.[8] Nachtigall had been staffed in cooperation with the radical Ukrainian nationalists of the OUN's (*Orhanizatsiia Ukraïns'kykh Natsionalistiv*) self-styled "revolutionary" faction under the leadership of Stepan Bandera (usually referred to as OUN-B).[9] It soon became evident that there were some German soldiers among the dead in the NKVD remand prison at Łąckiego Street.[10] Many corpses showed signs of torture and some apparently were also mutilated.[11] The information about the mass killings of prison inmates spread rapidly through the city (see also chapter 20).

The prisons were in the center of a pogrom that unfolded between 30 June and the afternoon of 2 July. Jews were forcibly brought to the prisons in large numbers by members of a Ukrainian militia (often identified by yellow and light blue badges) supported by civilians. They caught Jews on the streets or took them from apartments, beat and otherwise mistreated them, and droved them to the prisons, were the mistreatment continued. Before the entrances of the three major prisons in the city a crowd had assembled to beat the Jews being forced inside. Many were killed in the streets. Inside the prisons, Jews were forced to recover the corpses from cells, cellars, and from mass graves in a prison yard. They had to lay them in lines in order to allow for their identification and to prepare their burials.[12] However, many more Jews were brought to the prisons than were needed for the work. Only a portion of the corpses in the prisons were retrieved and laid out because in the hot summer climate many had reached such a stage of decomposition that not only identification but even retrieval was difficult or impossible.[13]

Mistreatment and murder of Jews continued in the prison yards. Here, mostly members of the militia and civilians, but also German soldiers and policemen, participated in the violence. The Nachtigall unit that first occupied the prisons on the morning of 30 June seems to have been replaced during the afternoon by German Feldgendarmerie, though Bataillon 800 seemed to have remained in command of the prisons.[14] The violence in the prisons ended on the evening of 1 July. This suggests an approval of the violence on the part of the commanding officers of the German armed forces, who for a certain period clearly allowed it to continue. In fact, from 30 June onward large numbers of German troops and police forces visited the prisons because they were curious to see the Bolshevik atrocities. Some commanders even asked their troops to see for themselves the crimes of the "Jewish-communist gang" or led them personally into the prisons.[15]

By forcing Jews to go to the prisons, to confront the murdered inmates, to pull out the corpses from the cells or from mass graves and clean them, and to pull the corpse carts from the prisons to the cemeteries (instead of using horses),[16] as well as by mocking, humiliating, and beating them, the people of Lwów used violence as a ritual to put the guilt for the Soviet crimes on the Jews and punish them.[17] The actual perpetrators from the ranks of the NKVD had left Lwów already in the days before. But Jews in general were considered to be supporters and beneficiaries of the Soviet rule during the previous 21 months; even more damningly, they were seen as informers to the NKVD and creators and carriers of communism and Bolshevism in general. Eliyahu Yones relates how a Ukrainian-speaking man in German uniform, who he believes was a member of Nachtigall, spoke to him and other Jews who were pulling out corpses from the cellar of the Brygidki prison, pointing to the bodies: "Look, what you have done."[18]

The Germans shared this view of the Jews. Yones reports that a German officer who visited the scene of the Soviet crimes together with some soldiers turned to the Jews and stated: "The whole world is bleeding because of you! Numerous soldiers are dying because the Jewry has wanted the war."[19] Mostly, German soldiers only watched (and took pictures of) the pogrom violence. But some soldiers also participated in the excesses, beat and shot at Jews who retrieved the bodies.[20]

Jews were also mocked, forced to humiliating work, robbed, beaten, and killed in many other parts of the city. They were forced to crawl on hands and knees toward the prisons; they had to sing Russian songs while being marched there; they were made to clean broken glass from the streets with their bare hands.[21] Near the Zamarstynów prison, Jews, primarily Jewesses, were stripped of their clothes and beaten.[22] Mistreatments of a sexual character occurred also at other places in the city.[23]

Amidst the pogrom, on the evening of 30 June Stepan Bandera's deputy, Iaroslav Stets′ko, as a leader of the OUN-B, declared the "Renewal of the Ukrainian State" at a meeting of Ukrainians in the building of the Prosvita society at the market square where he also read an order from Bandera that appointed himself as the head of a provisional Ukrainian government. Stets′ko had just that day come to Lwów together with other leading OUN-B members.[24] Among their first activities was the organization of the local militia, based on existing underground structures.[25] A bill that announced the declaration of a Ukrainian state also called for an armed fight for it. It was signed by Ivan Klymiv in his capacity as OUN leader of the Ukrainian territories, and it declared: "People! Know! Moscow, Poland, the Hungarians and the Jewry—these are your enemies. Destroy them."[26] A second leaflet, signed by Klymiv in his second capacity as "Chief Commander of the Ukrainian Revolutionary Army," declared: "I am introducing mass (ethnic and national) responsibility for crimes against the Ukrainian state and the Ukrainian army."[27]

The humiliations, mistreatments, and killings can be understood as rituals that estab-lished or reestablished, after the period of Soviet rule, the "right" and "just" order by pun-ishing the Jews for an alleged transgression of accepted borders in relation to the Christian population, because they were seen as having been treated better than Christians by the Soviets, as well as being supporters and informers of the Soviets and the NKVD. The humili-ation and violence not only punished them for transgressions, but also referred them back to the restricted social space that they had allegedly transgressed in the period of Soviet rule. The national triumph of liberation from Soviet suppression and the high expectations for the realization of the great aim of the Ukrainian national endeavor—excitement heightened even more by the ordeal of the Soviet mass murder of many Ukrainians in the prisons—be-came expressed in a "carnival of violence" that mocked and reversed the previous order and celebrated the new national one.[28]

However, neither did the Ukrainian nationalists' high expectations for the future come true nor did the violence against Jews end with the initial celebration of the victory over the Soviet enemy. There was some support for the Ukrainian national aims from the Wehrmacht, especially from its intelligence unit, called the *Abwehr,* and from the designated Minister for the Occupied Eastern Territories, Alfred Rosenberg (although he distrusted the OUN). But they represented only a minority opinion within the German power structure. During a meeting of high-ranking German officials on 16 July 1941 Hitler announced his decision that there would be no semi-independent states on the former Soviet territory, but the whole ter-ritory would remain under direct German rule. Eastern Galicia was attached to the General Government and the rest of the occupied Ukrainian territories under civil administration became part of the Reichskommissariat Ukraine. This started a brutal policy of exploitation, suppression, and mass murder.[29]

But in the end of June and the beginning of July, it was still an open question what the future German policy on the occupied Ukrainian territories would look like. Nevertheless, the Einsatzgruppen of the German Security Police from the beginning had clear instructions to avoid entering into any obligations toward the national movements in the newly occupied territories.[30] The bold step of Bandera and his followers led to a clear alienation between them and the Germans and to efforts by the Security Police to reduce their influence. On 5 July Bandera was arrested in Krakow and transported to Berlin, and on 9 July the same happened to Stets'ko and some other members of his government in Lwów.[31] However, in the first days after 30 June the Security Police tried to avoid an open confrontation with the OUN-B because they did not want to lose the support of the Ukrainian militia in Lwów and other localities for their own "security" and "reprisal" operations.[32]

On 2 July the violence on the streets of Lwów mostly stopped, but it was now replaced by organized arrests and mass executions by parts of Einsatzgruppe C. An advance unit of Einsatzkommando 4b had arrived in Lwów during the afternoon of 30 June; the bulk of the Einsatzgruppe joined them the next day.[33] On 29 June, the day before they began arriving, Reinhard Heydrich had sent his well-known order to the commanders of the Einsatzgruppen "not to constrain any self-cleaning attempts of anti-communist and anti-Jewish circles in the newly occupied territories. On the contrary, they should be initiated, but without any traces, intensified, if necessary, and channeled into the right direction."[34]

It seems likely that the Security Police encouraged the Ukrainian militia to intensify the violence against Jews. This may have occurred as early as the inception of violence in the afternoon of 30 June, or begun 1 July after the commander of Einsatzgruppe C, SS-Brigadeführer Otto Rasch, and his staff arrived in the early morning. During that day the pogrom violence reached its greatest intensity.

Beginning possibly on 3 July, certainly on 4 July, the Ukrainian militia and members of Einsatzkommandos 5 and 6 started to arrest people who were suspected as communist supporters, but mostly Jews, and to assemble them on a sports field near the former NKVD headquarters in Pelczyńska Street that had been taken over by the Einsatzgruppe. Here 2,500-3,000 people were assembled.[35] Most of them were executed on 5 July in forests near Lwów.[36] The executions were declared to be a reprisal for the murder of the prison inmates in Lwów by the Soviets.[37]

After the occupation of Lwów the Soviet atrocities became a prominent subject in German propaganda. When the first information about the piles of corpses in the Lwów prisons had reached the command of the Seventeenth Army it had asked to send journalists from national and international media to Lwów in order to use the scenes for propaganda purposes.[38] On 6 July Joseph Goebbels, the Reich's Propaganda Minister, noted in his diary about the impact of film material from Lwów: "The Führer wants us to start the big anti-bolshevist campaign now."[39] The German newsreel *Deutsche Wochenschau* presented material about the Soviet massacres through the whole of July and interpreted them as an example of the normal procedures of "Jewish-Bolshevik" rule.[40]

However, mass executions of alleged "communists" and of Jews as "reprisal" for Soviet atrocities had already begun before the murdered inmates of the prisons in Lwów were found. They also took place at about the same time in other localities. The Einsatzkommando 6 had already shot 132 people, nearly all of them were Jews, on the evening of 30 June in Dobromil as reprisal for a Soviet massacre of prison inmates. Its commander, Erhard Kröger, received an order for this execution from the chief of the Einsatzgruppe C, Otto Rasch, and the Higher SS- and Police Leader Friedrich Jeckeln, who both were present in Dobromil.[41] Jeckeln is known as a radical antisemite and as one of those high-ranking SS officers whose activities strongly contributed to the escalation of the murder of the Jewish population during the following months. He was the chief organizer of the large massacres in Kamenets' Podil's'kyi in mid-August and at Babyn Yar near Kyïv at the end of September 1941.[42]

The Chief of Sonderkommando 4a, Standartenführer Paul Blobel, was a similar character. During the first days of the war he initiated large massacres. Between 28 and 30 of June, according to *The Einsatzgruppen Reports,* his unit shot a total of 317 people in Sokal: on 28 June 17 "Communist functionaries, agents and snipers"; on 29 June "117 active Communists and agents of the NKVD"; and on 30 June "183 Jewish Communists." Both in Dobromil and in Sokal the executed had been identified and arrested with the help of a local Ukrainian militia.[43] In the next city that Blobel's Sonderkommando reached, Łuck in Volhynia, a much larger number of people was shot. This execution was legitimized as a "reprisal" for the Soviet massacre of prison inmates. In Łuck, about 2,800 prison inmates had been killed. After Lwów, that was the largest Soviet massacre in the region.[44] The Sonderkommando reported that Ukrainian survivors of the massacre told them "the Jews again played a decisive part in the arrests and shooting." The Sonderkommando shot "300 Jews and 20 looters" who were considered to be responsible for arson and large-scale looting in the city on 30 June. Only on 2 July were the corpses of 10 murdered German POW found in the city. "As a reprisal," as the report of the Einsatzgruppen says, "for the murder of the German soldiers and the Ukrainians 1160 Jews were shot with support from a platoon of the Order Police and a platoon of the Infantry."[45]

"... Bolsheviks and Jews ..."

The view that Jews not only had been the main supporters and beneficiaries of Soviet rule in 1939-1941, but that Jews basically represented the core of Bolshevism and of the Soviet regime in general was prevalent within the higher ranks of the Nazi regime, including its police forces and many officers of the German armed forces. This view constituted a decisive factor in the development of the German course of action against the Jews during the first weeks of the war and paved the way for the policy of all-out murder that was adopted during August and September 1941. In the German view the Jews gained a fundamentally greater importance for the war against the Soviet Union than for previous wars. Despite all the excessive anti-Jewish violence that had also occurred during the campaign against Poland in 1939, during that war the Polish elites and not the Jews had been the focus of German "actions of pacification." Klaus-Michael Mallman has grasped this difference well:

> The war [with the Soviet Union] was about the destruction of the racially defined main enemy, the "Jewish Bolshevism." The claimed identity [of Jewish race and Bolshevism] made possible a permanent reinterpretation and conversion of both sides. For that reason, the significance of the Jewish population had changed from the beginning. They were no longer a group, held in contempt, but they were now considered to be the carriers and creators, the biological substance of the Soviet system. Only through the fact that the two central images of enemies—the Jews and communism—mutually penetrated and reinforced was a dynamic development kindled that led to genocide.[46]

Already from the beginning of the war Jews were regarded as actual or at least potential carriers of resistance and the liquidation of Jews was seen as a measure to increase security.[47]

The instructions that the commanders of the Einsatzgruppen and its subunits, the so-called Einsatzkommandos and Sonderkommandos, received before the start of the war apparently did not clearly reflect the fact that among their main tasks would be the killing of Jews, let alone the extermination of the whole Jewish population, but remained largely within the framework that was set through agreements between the Security Police and the Wehrmacht.[48] This included the execution of Soviet state and party officials and "radical elements" within the population, but not a general liquidation of the Jewish population.[49] It was probably not till August 1941 that the Einsatzgruppen received orders that aimed at the total extermination of the Jewish population.[50] Nevertheless, there was a clear understanding from the beginning of the war that the enemies to be executed were "Bolsheviks and Jews," as Heydrich said so explicitly in his letter to the chiefs of the Einsatzgruppen from 1 July: "It is obvious that the cleansing activities have to extend first of all to the Bolsheviks and Jews."[51]

Before the war there was already a widespread expectation among German officials that spontaneous violent reckonings with the "Jewish-Bolshevik oppressors" would start after areas were liberated from Soviet rule. Apparently, they approved of them.[52] This was especially true for the Security Police, because these reckonings were expected to work in the same direction as the main task of the Einsatzgruppen, i.e. to liquidate communist supporters.

In his letter of 29 June Heydrich refers to a meeting with the commanders of the Einsatzgruppen and their high-ranking officers on 17 June in Berlin where, as Heydrich implies, the question of pogroms had been discussed.[53] However, it seems that the task of actually instigating the pogroms had not been stressed strongly enough or the instructions had not been sufficiently clear, for he later clarified this task in a separate letter.[54]

If the instigation of pogroms appeared as a priority task of the Einsatzgruppen only during the first week after the German attack, then that would suggest a negative answer to the disputed question of whether there had been a clear prior agreement between the Germans and the OUN about the instigation of pogroms.

There was, however, detailed planning on the side of the OUN-B, finalized in an extensive document with the title "Fighting and Activity During the War," dated May 1941, about how to proceed when the German-Soviet war began, which its authors expected to see in the near future. The organization's initial aim for the beginning of the war was to start uprisings in the Soviet-occupied territories, to liberate as many territories as possible and to start with the organization of local administrations and local militias as soon as the Soviets left in order to support the claim to a Ukrainian state and demonstrate the Ukrainians' ability to establish it.[55]

Attacks by Ukrainian underground forces on the Soviet army and police occurred in many places. Usually the Ukrainians themselves were not able to drive out the Soviets, but often they took over localities when the Soviets had left and before the Germans arrived.[56] Here members and supporters of the OUN-B played a central role.

Among the central tasks that the OUN-B guidelines assigned to the newly created administrations and militias was "to cleanse the territory from enemy forces."[57] This included Soviet forces, but the OUN-B also considered "Muscovites, Poles, and Jews as enemy minorities on Ukrainian territory."[58] The guidelines declared: "[. . .] at a time of chaos and confusion liquidation of undesirable Polish, Muscovite, and Jewish activists is permitted, especially supporters of Bolshevik-Muscovite imperialism."[59]

However, a resolution of an OUN-B Congress in Krakow in April 1941 had warned against pogroms because "the anti-Jewish sentiment of the Ukrainian masses could be used by the Muscovite-Bolshevik government in order to distract the masses' attention from the real producer of evil," i.e. "Moscow." But at the same time the resolution stated: "The Jews in the USSR are the most devoted pillars of the governing Bolshevik regime and the avant-garde of the Muscovite imperialism in Ukraine. . . . The Organization of Ukrainian Nationalists fights the Jews as pillars of the Muscovite-Bolshevik regime and, at the same time, explains to the masses of the people: Moscow—that is the main enemy."[60] This statement sometimes is referred to as proof that the OUN was not involved in the pogroms of summer 1941.[61] However, together with the instructions for the initial phase of the war this statement seems rather to sketch the background of OUN perceptions and strategies that paved the way for the involvement of local militias and OUN supporters in anti-Jewish violence. It shows the strong influence of the perception of Jews as supporters and collaborators of "Muscovite-Bolshevik" rule in the OUN. And the "clean[sing] of the territory from the enemy" is precisely the goal which which most of the militias would have motivated their acts of violence against Jews.

It is clearly documented that Lithuanian nationalists had a strategy of using the German-Soviet war to drive out the Jews. Leaflets of the Front of Lithuanian Activists (LAF) from spring 1941 called on Lithuanians "to drive out the Jews along with the Red Russians" when the German-Soviet war started. It argued that the Jews had lost the right to live on Lithuanian soil "because of their repeated betrayals of the Lithuanian nation to its oppressors."[62] Other leaflets expressed explicit threats of violence and murder and called upon the Jews to leave the country in order to avoid "unnecessary victims."[63]

There are no documents from the OUN that would show a comparably explicit strategy. However, there are statements from the OUN's leading personnel expressing approval of the "German methods" for dealing with the Jews.[64] Antisemitic paranoia may, in fact, have been of lesser influence within the leading circles of the OUN than, for example, in an organization like the LAF. Clearly, it was less important than within the German leadership. For the OUN, Russia—"Muscovy" in their terminology—remained the most important enemy; the Jews were considered to be its supporters, but not its core. Nevertheless, the OUN's nationalist radicalism and the readiness to use highly violent means to achieve their national aims paved the way for anti-Jewish violence and for consent to the German killing operations.[65] The actual events clearly indicate that the OUN's rank-and-file members embarked on anti-Jewish violence on a large scale, and when they did so, they were far from ignoring the political program or the instructions of the leadership; on the contrary, they found encouragement in them.

The role and attitude of the third major organized actor besides the German Security Police and the Ukrainian nationalists, the Wehrmacht, is less clear. Did it support or disapprove of the pogrom strategy of the Einsatzgruppen? In Lwów the Wehrmacht did not interfere to end the violence, at least not for about 24-48 hours.

In addition, at many other places the pogroms took place in the immediate presence of Wehrmacht units that did not intervene. For example, in Borysław and Drohobycz south of Lwów, which were occupied by the German armed forces at about the same time, it was only after two or three days that the Wehrmacht stopped the violent pogroms that began in close connection to the discovery of murdered prison inmates. German soldiers were present during the pogroms, and, at least in Borysław, some of them actively participated.[66] Jewish survivors report about rumors that the Germans had a policy of allowing locals one or two days to settle accounts with Jews and communists.[67] However, it does not seem that explicit orders had been issued telling commanders to allow for pogroms. The attitude of the army units in localities where they apparently tolerated pogroms was mostly directed by the view of Jews as supporters of Soviet rule and as bearing responsibility for the Soviet atrocities. Thus, the violent outbreaks were basically considered to be a just and healthy phenomenon in a phase of transition from Soviet to German rule.

Nevertheless, the High Command of the Seventeenth Army and its commander, General Carl-Heinrich von Stülpnagel, in all likelihood knew about the pogrom strategy of the Einsatzgruppen and seem to have approved of it. Heydrich mentioned in his "Einsatzbefehl Nr. 2" of 1 July 1941 that it was based on a suggestion of Army High Command 17, headed by von Stülpnagel; the document said that Poles in the newly occupied territories could be expected "on the basis of their experiences, to be anti-Communist and also anti-Jewish." Therefore, Poles "need not to be included in the cleansing action [i.e., be executed], especially as they are of great importance as elements to initiate pogroms and for obtaining information."[68] In fact, the suggestion by von Stülpnagel that is referred to is not known. While it is sometimes interpreted as a call for pogroms, it may rather have been intended to prevent the Einsatzgruppen from undertaking large-scale executions among the Polish elite as they had after the German occupation of Polish territories in 1939.[69] Nevertheless, whatever the original content of "the suggestion" to Heydrich had been, it shows that the command of the Seventeenth Army were aware of the Einsatzgruppen's pogrom strategy. The timing of the suggestion may even indicate that it was in reaction to Heydrich's letter to the chiefs of the Einsatzgruppen of 29 June. In contrast to the executions among the Polish elites, von

Stülpnagel did not try to prevent the Einsatzgruppe from inciting pogroms. It is known also from other documents that von Stülpnagel shared the view of Jews as pillars of Bolshevism.[70] Heydrich sent copies of his letter of 1 July to the commanders of the Einsatzgruppen, to the High Command of the German Army (*Oberkommando des Heeres*), and to the three Army Group Commands.[71]

Pogroms

Besides Lwów, the pogroms with the largest number of victims were those in Złoczów and Tarnopol. The murder of several hundred Jews in Zborów belongs in the same context. The high number of victims in these cities resulted from a killing rampage by the Waffen-SS division "Wiking," more specifically its regiment "Westland" and some supply units. Wiking was part of the combat troops and not of the police force and therefore had no assigned task in the police's "security" and "cleansing" operations.[72] It would be inappropriate to use the term "pogrom"—understood as an excessive, public, and to a certain degree spontaneous event with respect to participants and forms of violence—for the executions of the Einsatzgruppen. But the term does fit well in the cases of violence perpetrated by division Wiking in Złoczów, Zborów, Tarnopol, and perhaps also other places.

On the morning of 2 July the commander of the Westland regiment, Standartenführer Hilmar Wäckerle, was killed by a sniper, very likely a Soviet soldier, near the town of Słowita east of Lwów. This seems to have triggered the rampage. The unit had only crossed the border on 30 June and had not participated in major combat operations so far. The Wiking division had been newly created in November 1940, and among its men were a large number of volunteers from the Netherlands, Belgium, and the Scandinavian countries.[73] Those from the Netherlands and Belgium were in the Westland regiment. The death of their commander seems to have triggered large-scale revenge against the Jewish population.[74] On the morning of 3 July the Chief of the General Staff of the Seventeenth Army complained that since the day before the SS Wiking had been blocking the traffic on the road from Lwów to Złoczów: "In the meantime, individual members of the division go hunting Jews."[75] According to a postwar testimony during the Nuremberg trials, an order had been read to the soldiers that stated that a Jew had shot Wäckerle and that henceforth they were allowed to shoot at Jews without warning.[76]

Złoczów had already been occupied on 1 July by the 9th Tank Division. Several hundred murdered inmates had been found in the town's prison.[77] A Ukrainian committee that formed that day in the city blamed the Jews for the murders and, according to Marco Carynnyk's finding, turned to the German authorities for permission to take revenge. On 2 July the Ukrainian militia posted announcements on the walls of the city stating that all Jews had to appear on the next morning at 8:00 AM in the marketplace and threatening those who did not appear with death. But already on that day the mistreatment, beating, robbery, and killing of Jews had begun. The Jews who assembled in the marketplace on the morning of 3 July were driven to the castle where the NKVD prison had been. Jews who tried to hide were taken out of their houses, heavily beaten, and also driven to the castle. They were beaten again at the entrances of the castle and then forced to take the corpses out of the mass graves, wash them, and put them in lines beside the castle. In all these acts of violence SS men and Ukrainians alike took part. Many Jews were beaten to death while working at the castle. But the greatest number were probably shot down by the SS with machine guns on the evening of 3 July and on 4 July. Women and children were freed on the evening of 3 July after an officer of the 295th Infantry Division intervened on behalf of the town's German military commander. In the afternoon of 4 July the killings were finally stopped by the commander of the 295th Infantry Division. This commander, Otto Korfes, had been urged to intervene by his First Staff Officer Helmuth Groscurth, who displayed more moral sensibility and responsibility than most of the Wehrmacht officers.[78]

Parts of SS Wiking were apparently also responsible for another major massacre during the first days of July that occurred in the town of Zborów. About Zborów the Einsatzgruppen report of 11 July stated: ". . . 600 Jews liquidated by the Waffen-SS as a retaliation measure for Soviet atrocities."[79] However, in Zborów itself only one murdered Ukrainian prisoner had been found buried in the yard of the local police station. According to reports of Jewish survivors 850 men were shot on the second day after the Germans occupied the town.[80]

On 2 July, Tarnopol was captured by the Ninth Tank Division. On 3 July several hundred murdered inmates were found in the NKVD prison, among them ten German soldiers.[81] Some attacks on Jews or their property occurred on the same day, but a major pogrom and executions started only on 4 July and continued for the next two or three days. Here again, both Ukrainians and men from SS Wiking played a major role. Jews were brought in large numbers to the prison, as well as other places in the city, and beaten to death or shot by the German forces. The excessive character of the pogrom violence is also shown by the fact that here soldiers, probably from SS Wiking, raped Jewish women.[82]

It is not very clear what role the Sonderkommando 4b had during this pogrom. The unit probably arrived in Tarnopol on 4 July.[83] The operational reports of the Einsatzgruppen listed among Sonderkommando 4b's achievements for Tarnopol 127 executions as well as "liquidation of 600 Jews in the course of the persecutions of Jews as inspired by the Einsatzkommando."[84] Apparently, neither the SS Wiking men nor local Ukrainian forces needed much inspiration to attack Jews. On the contrary, the Ukrainian city administration seems to have deliberately tried to instigate the Germans to "reprisals" against Jews by stressing the role of Jews in the Soviet atrocities and especially the murder of German soldiers.[85]

In other places public displays of violence were closely connected with the "cleansing operations" of the German Security Police. They were usually accomplished with the help of local administrations and militias who were needed to identify the "communists" and often also to assemble them. In various places the Jewish population, or a part of it, and usually also some non-Jewish alleged communists, were gathered on the market place, where beatings and mistreatment occurred that sometimes resulted in murder. Later a larger or smaller number from among them would be taken out of town and executed by a German Police unit.[86]

In contrast to the army in German-occupied territories, where the police forces actively supported and instigated pogroms and the Wehrmacht in many places at least tolerated them, the Hungarian troops who occupied the southeastern part of Galicia from the beginning of July usually prevented pogroms, at least if they threatened to result in killings. This applies mostly only to the larger cities in the area[87]; in smaller localities and in rural areas the Hungarians apparently did not exert very close control. Here, according to testimonies of Jewish survivors, several major acts of violence occurred that sometimes took on an exterminatory character. So, for example, in the town of Ottynia violence increased from day to day until on 6 and 7 July 138 Jews were killed in the town and neighboring villages. The following day Hungarian troops from Delatyn arrived who stopped the violence. They had been called in by local Poles who feared to become the next victims.[88]

Probably one of the worst acts took place in the region of Niezwisko near Obertyn. During one night in the first half of July "hooligan groups" of "Ukrainian fascists," as one witness for these events, Markus Willbach, calls them, under the leadership of the local doctor Anatol' Jurevych and the local Greek-Catholic priest Gavdunyk, brought together the Jews—men, women, and children—from Niezwisko and surrounding villages at the banks of the nearby Dniester river, tied their hands with barbed wire, and threw them into the river from a ferry at the village of Łuka.[89] Willbach relates that the "hooligans" from Niezwisko during the following days also tried to convince the Ukrainians of Obertyn and other towns and villages in the region to do or to allow them do the same with the Jews from these localities. But the determined opposition of local Ukrainian priests and other respected persons prevented similar murderous acts.[90]

Jabłonica at the Czeremosz river in the mountainous Hutsul region south of Kosów was another place where an act of murder occurred that may have been intended to exterminate the local Jews. According to testimonies 74 people died there. As in Niezwisko the local priest may have had a major role in initiating the killing. According to one testimony the Jews were handcuffed with barbed wire and then thrown from a cliff into the canyon of the Czeremosz river, where they drowned. According to another one their bodies were thrown into the river after they had been killed. The pogromists wanted to continue their murderous work on the following day in the nearby village of Hriniawa, but the local Ukrainian peasants did not allow it. Nevertheless, villagers of Hriniawa later drove out the Jews and took their property.[91] Looting, robbery, and other actions around property were typically connected with pogroms in many places. They may have had a special significance in rural areas because there villagers could not only rob goods and valuables, but also actually acquire the houses and land of killed or expelled Jews.

In Jabłonica and its environs the fact that the area had been briefly occupied by Romanian troops probably contributed to the violence. The large-scale pogrom violence in neighboring Northern Bukovina, in which the Romanian army was strongly involved, apparently encouraged violence on the Galician side of the border even in those regions where no Romanian troops appeared.[92]

A number of killings also occurred in another part of the region neighboring with Northern Bukovina, around the cities of Borszczów and Tłuste, though in these cities itself anti-Jewish violence remained limited. In Borszczów the head of the local Ukrainian administration, Mykhailo Motyl', apparently worked successfully to limit the violence, while in Tłuste the Greek-Catholic priest Izvols'kyi and other local Ukrainian dignitaries did not allow it.[93] One of the major pogroms in that region took place in the village of Ułaszkowce on 7 July, shortly after the Soviet retreat. Here the pogrom began during a parish fair after an inciting sermon by the local priest. The events here are said to have instigated the violence in other villages.[94] However, another report relates that pogroms with many murders started in villages around Czortków with the occupation of that city by German troops on 6 July, and this was probably an encouragement for violence in Ułaszkowce, which was located south of Czortków in the Hungarian zone.[95]

Another mass murder, this one in the village of Laszkowice in the same region but north of Czortków and therefore in the German-occupied area, is related by Izak Orensztein. According to his testimony 60 Jewish families fell victim to this massacre of which he was an eye-witness: "Ukrainians armed with sickles, axes and knifes threw themselves on to the Jews and killed them all."[96]

A relatively large number of highly violent pogroms seem to have taken place in the region south of Drohobycz and Borysław. Probably during the third week of July 1941 the Jewish Committee of Drohobycz compiled a list of incidents of murder in localities in that region that it sent to the local German Feldkommandantur.[97] For the town of Schodnica it mentioned 240 killed. A large number of killings there is also confirmed in other sources.[98] In addition, the Committee's list reported that in the villages of Majdan and Lastówki all Jews had been killed and that 50 people had been murdered in Rybnik. The Jewish youth of that village had been burned alive in a barn. In Nowy Kropiwnik and Stary Kropiwnik 40 had been killed. In the village of Bystrzyca the family of Leiser Koppel, about 30 people, had been slain, and the villagers of Dereżyce had driven all the Jews out of their locality.[99]

It is difficult to assess how widespread such incidents in Eastern Galicia were at this time. Those mentioned here clearly are not the only ones. But the information on villages usually is very scarce and insufficient to reconstruct events in a more detailed way.

Conclusion

The spreading phenomenon of anti-Jewish violence in summer 1941 was a symptom of the fact that the region was a contested space between empires, ideologies, nations, and religions. The different conflicts focused during this short period in a specific way on the Jews. Jews were humiliated, robbed, beaten, and killed both by locals and by the German invaders because they were identified with Bolshevism and Soviet rule. This antisemitic stereotype of Jews as communists was not isolated from other antisemitic prejudices. The view that Jews had supported the Soviet occupation of the area, had participated in and benefited from the suppression and persecution of other national groups was a perception that was widespread among the local population as well as the local nationalist political activists and that was also shared by the Germans. In fact, the executions of the Einsatzgruppen and other German police units during the first weeks of the war usually were declared to be liquidations of communist functionaries or supporters or to be reprisals for the Soviet mass murder of prison inmates. In both categories the vast majority of the executed were male Jews between 15 and 60, considered to be the most dangerous group. Usually, they were taken from the better-educated strata that were seen as especially pro-communist. On the German side this perception of Jews was an important element that fueled and justified a further escalation of the murderous policy against Jews.

The discovery of the murdered prison inmates produced anger and hate that increased the pogrom violence, but it was not its only background, and there seems to be no doubt that there would still have been violence against Jews from local militias or civilians if prison inmates had not been murdered. The same applies for actions of the Einsatzgruppen against Jews. The large executions declared as "reprisals" in Lwów and Łuck might not have happened, but there was a firm belief among the Germans that the Jews were the "core" of Bolshevism and of Soviet rule, so mass executions as a means of liquidating "communists" were a task assigned to the Einsatzgruppen before there was any knowledge about the Soviet atrocities. Bogdan Musial argues that the Soviet atrocities contributed significantly to the radicalization of the German persecution of the Jews and the brutalization of German warfare.[100] However, it seems to be quite clear that the radicalization was hardly a consequence of Soviet crimes, but rather of the identification of "Bolshevists" and "Jews." That is the reason why the war against the Soviet Union also became a war of annihilation against the Jews.

Another highly controversial issue is what caused the rise of hostility toward Jews in the period of Soviet occupation 1939-1941. Was it truly the result of a pro-Soviet attitude among the Jews or more of antisemitic stereotypes among the gentile population? Findings for some parts of "Western Belarus" seem to suggest that Jews, at least after the initial months of the Soviet occupation, did not really have a disproportionate share in most segments of the Soviet administration.[101] Jewish religious, political, economic, and cultural life was suppressed or forcefully transformed according to Soviet ideology, and not to a lesser degree than that of the other communities in the area. The widespread perception among the Christian population of broad Jewish collaboration and "treason" seems to have been, as the rituals of punishment analyzed above suggest, rather the result of the fact that the Soviet regime actually brought equality to Jews as individuals, albeit under the condition of a general lack of individual rights that characterized the Soviet citizen. Before the Soviet occupation Jews, though officially equal citizens, had faced many discriminatory practices. Under the Soviets, many of these practices were abolished, antisemitism became a punishable crime, and positions in public service became open to Jews that earlier had been denied to them. Many Jews, especially from the younger generation, took opportunities that arose when the Soviets removed the former, mostly Polish elites whom they mistrusted. So even a percentage of Jews in state offices proportional to their percentage in the general population meant a considerable shift, and could appear to the Christian population as an undue improvement of the social position of the Jews. The pogroms were rituals that were intended to reverse this unacceptable change, show the Jews their subordinate social position, and punish them for the transgression of its limits during the time of Soviet rule.

NOTES

Research for this article has been supported by a Raul Hilberg Fellowship at the Center for Advanced Holocaust Studies, United States Holocaust Memorial Museum, and a research grant of Deutsche Forschungsgemeinschaft.

1. New insights into the complex events of summer 1941 in this region have resulted from the controversial discussion of Jan T. Gross's study on the pogrom in the town of Jedwabne on 10 July 1941, that, however, focused on the mostly Polish region of Łomża and Białystok: Jan T. Gross, *Neighbors: The Destruction of the Jewish Community in Jedwabne, Poland* (Princeton: Princeton University Press, 2001); see Paweł Machcewicz, Krzysztof Persak, eds., *Wokół Jewabnego, t. 1: Studia, t. 2: Dokumenty,* (Warsaw: IPN, 2002); and Andrzej Żbikowski, *U genezy Jedwabnego. Żydzi na kresach północno-wschodnich II Rzeczypospolitej, wrzesień 1939–lipiec 1941* (Warsaw: Żydowski Instytut Historyczny, 2006). A revised version of the latter book's chapter on summer 1941 has been published in English as Andrzej Żbikowski, "Pogroms in Northeastern Poland—Spontaneous Reactions and German Instigations" in *Shared History—Divided Memory: Jews and Others in Soviet-Occupied Poland, 1939–1941,* ed. Elazar Barkan, Elizabeth A. Cole, and Kai Struve (Leipzig: Leipziger Universitätsverlag 2008), 315–54.

2. The most comprehensive, though not complete overview on pogrom violence in Eastern Galicia that we have so far can be found in Andrzej Żbikowski's early attempt to present an overview of pogroms in Eastern Poland, Andrzej Żbikowski, "Lokalne pogromy Żydów w czerwcu i lipcu 1941 roku na wschodnich rubieżach II Rzeczypospolitej," *Biuletyn Żydowskiego Instytutu Historycznego*

1992, nos. 2–3 (162–63): 3–18, esp. 12–18. The state of research for Eastern Galicia and Volhynia is discussed by Dieter Pohl in "Anti-Jewish Pogroms in Western Ukraine: A Research Agenda" in *Shared History—Divided Memory*, ed. Barkan, Cole, and Struve, 305–313. In a recent article Wendy Lower compared Western Ukraine with other regions and discussed various models of explanation for the violence: "Pogroms, Mob Violence, and Genocide in Western Ukraine, Summer 1941: Varied Histories, Explanations, and Comparisons," *Journal of Genocide Research* 13 (2011): 217–46. See also A. Kruglov, "Pogromy v vostochnoi Galitsii letom 1941 g.: organizatory, uchastniki, masshtaby i posledstvija," in *Vojna na unichtozhenie: Nasitskaia politika genotsida na territorii Vostochnoi Evropy: Materialy mezhdunarodnoi nauchnoi konferencii*, ed. Aleksandr. R. Diukov (Moscow: Fond "Istoricheskaia pamiat," 2010); and Vladimir Melamed, "Organized and Unsolicited Collaboration in the Holocaust: The Multifaceted Ukrainian Context," *East European Jewish Affairs* 37 (2007): 217–48. This article refers primarily to the pogroms in Lwów and Borysław.

3. The violent events in Lwów have been discussed in the research literature more or less extensively for a long time, but have only recently been studied more thoroughly, John-Paul Himka, "The Lviv Pogrom of 1941: The Germans, Ukrainian Nationalists, and the Carnival Crowd," *Canadian Slavonic Papers/Revue canadienne des slavistes* 53 (2011): 209–43. But neither Himka nor other researchers who discussed the pogrom and German mass executions in early July are certain about the number of victims. The Operational Situational Report No. 24 of the Chief of the Security Police and the SD on the activities of the Einsatzgruppen from 16 July 1941 reports for Einsatzgruppe C, apparently with respect to Lwów: "Approximately 7,000 Jews were rounded up and shot by the Security Police in retaliation for the inhuman atrocities," cited in Yitzhad Arad, Shmuel Krakowski, and Shmuel Spector, eds., *The Einsatzgruppen Reports: Selection from the Dispatches of the Nazi Death Squads' Campaign Against the Jews in Occupied Territories of the Soviet Union July 1941–January 1943* (New York: Holocaust Library, 1989), 31. However, Dieter Pohl believes that this number includes both the victims of pogroms and of the mass executions by Einsatzgruppe C, which occurred mostly on 5 July, with perhaps 2,500–3,000 executed. Dieter Pohl, *Nationalsozialistische Judenverfolgung in Ostgalizien 1941–1944. Organisation und Durchführung eines staatlichen Massenverbrechens* (Munich: Oldenbourg, 1996), 69. Jakub Gerstenfeld-Maltiel reports in his memoirs that the Jewish burial society established (according to information of the later Lwów Judenrat) that about 2,000 Jews were killed in the first days of German occupation of Lwów. Jakub Gerstenfeld-Maltiel, *My Private War: One Man's Struggle to Survive the Soviets and the Nazis* (London: Valentine Mitchell, 1993), 54. John-Paul Himka believes that the Judenrat might have underestimated the number of victims and that the German Security Police might have exaggerated it (Himka, "The Lviv Pogrom," 221).

4. On the wave of arrests and deportations (with further literature), see Grzegorz Hryciuk, "Victims 1939–1941: The Soviet Repressions in Eastern Poland" in *Shared History—Divided Memory*, ed. Barkan, Cole, and Struve, 173–200, here 191–94.

5. Quoted in Ivan Bilas, *Represyvno-karal'na systema v Ukraïni 1917–1953*, vol. 1 (Kiev: Lybid 1994, 128f.); see also Marco Carynnyk, "The Palace on the Ikva—Dubne, September 18th, 1939 and June 24th, 1941" in *Shared History—Divided Memory*, ed. Barkan, Cole, and Struve, 263–301, here 280f.

6. Grzegorz Hryciuk estimates the number of murdered prison inmates in Lwów at 3,100–3,500. Grzegorz Hryciuk, *Polacy we Lwowie 1939–1944. Życie codzienne* (Warsaw: Książka i Wiedza, 2000), 186–91. Oleh Romaniv and Inna Fedushchak estimate the number at 4,000 in *Zakhidnoukraïns'ka trahediia 1941, L'viv*, (New York: Naukove Tovarystvo im. Shevchenka, 2002), 56.

7. Krzysztof Popiński, "Ewakuacja więzień kresowych w czerwcu 1941r. na podstawie dokumentacji 'Memoriału' i Archiwum Wschodniego," in *Zbrodnicza ewakuacja więzień i aresztów NKWD na Kresach Wschodnich II Rzeczypospolitej w czerwcu-lipcu 1941 roku* (Warsaw: Głowna Komisja Badania Zbrodni Przeciwko Narodowi Polskiemu-Instytut Pamięci Narodowej, 1997), 73–77; idem, "Zbrodnie sowieckie na kresach wschodnich II Rzeczypospolitej czerwiec-lipiec 1941 r.," http://www.electronicmuseum.ca/Poland-WW2/soviet_atrocities/soviet_atrocities_annex_I.html (accessed 23 January 2009). Bogdan Musial believes that it could have been up to 30,000: *"Konterrevolutionäre Elemente sind zu erschießen." Die Brutalisierung des deutsch-sowjetischen Krieges im Sommer 1941* (Berlin: Propyläen, 2001), 138. Romaniv and Fedushchak have collected evidence on

the killing of about 22,000 prisoners in Eastern Galicia and Volhynia and they consider their data incomplete: *Zakhidnoukraïns'ka trahedija*, 63, see also the information on the prisons on 55–63.

8. Batallion 800, Kommandeur, Schlussmeldung über Einnahme Lemberg und vollzogene Objektsicherung, Bundesarchiv-Militärarchiv (henceforth: BA-MA) Wf-03/34170.

9. On the OUN see also below. On Nachtigall and "Roland" see I. K. Patryliak, *Viis'kova diial'nist' OUN (B) u 1940–1942 rokakh* (Kiev: Instytut istoriï Ukraïny NAN Ukraïny, 2004), 253–321; Andrii Bolianovs'kyi, *Ukraïns'ki viis'kovi formuvannia v zbroinykh sylakh Nimechchyny (1939–1945)* (L'viv: L'vivs'kyi Nacional'nyi Universytet im. Ivana Franka, 2003), 40–86.

10. Three other murdered German soldiers were later found in the Soviet military hospital, "Schlussbericht über die in der Zeit vom 1.–10. Juli 1941 in Lemberg getroffenen Feststellungen, betreffend russische Greueltaten," 16 July 1941, Oberkommando der Wehrmacht, Wehrmacht-Untersuchungstelle für Verletzungen des Völkerrechts, BA-MA RW 2/148, 375f.; see also Alfred M. de Zayas, *Die Wehrmachtsuntersuchungsstelle. Deutsche Ermittlungen über alliierte Völkerrechtsverletzungen im Zweiten Weltkrieg* (Berlin: Ullstein, 1987), 336–38 (published in English as *The Wehrmacht War Crimes Bureau, 1939–1945,* trans. Kai Struve [Lincoln: University of Nebraska Press, 1989]).

11. Hryciuk, *Polacy we Lwowie*, 190f.; Musial, *"Konterrevolutionäre Elemente,"* 262–69.

12. Himka: "The Lviv Pogrom," 210–21. For the Zamarstynów prison see also Ivan Khymka [John-Paul Himka], "Dostovirnist' svidchennia: Relatsiia Ruzi Vagner pro L'vivs'kyi pohrom vlitku 1941," *Holokost i suchasnist'* 2 (4) 2008: 43–79; and the account of Zygmunt Tune, Wałbrzych, 12 March 1947, Archiwum Żydowskiego Instytutu Historycznego we Warszawie (henceforth: AŻIH) 301/2242, 1f. For the Brygidki prison see Eliyahu Yones, *Die Straße nach Lemberg. Zwangsarbeit und Widerstand in Ostgalizien 1941–1944* (Frankfurt am Main: Fischer, 1999), 21–24.

13. Because of the decomposition most of the corpses in the cellars of the Brygidky and Zamarstynów prisons were not retrieved, but the doors were bricked and only reopened in the beginning of 1942. De Zayas, *Die Wehrmachtsuntersuchungsstelle*, 338.

14. Philipp Christian Wachs, *Der Fall Theodor Oberländer (1905-1998). Ein Lehrstück deutscher Geschichte* (Frankfurt: Campus, 2000), 82; Hannes Heer, "Einübung in den Holocaust: Lemberg Juni/Juli 1941," *Zeitschrift für Geschichtswissenschaft* 49 (2001): 409–427, here 419. In a letter to the German city command (Stadtkommandant) from 2 July 1941 the commander of Bataillon 800, Major Heinz, stated that his unit was still occupying three prisons in the city, Derzhavnyi arkhiv L'vivs'koï oblasti (DALO) R-31/1/1, 11.

15. See, for example, for the Third Battalion of the First Mountain Division, Hermann Frank Meyer, *Blutiges Edelweiß. Die 1. Gebirgs-Division im Zweiten Weltkrieg* (Berlin: Links, 2008), 62. Brigadeführer Rasch, the head of Einsatzgruppe C, probably also gave a speech before a group of his men in the prison yards at Łąckiego Street; see interrogation of Rudolf Hohenschildt, 12 December 1961, Bundesarchiv (henceforth: BArch) B 162/1570, 270.

16. The pulling of carts is not reported for Lwów, but for Sambor, see Musial, *"Konterrevolutionäre Elemente,"* 179.

17. Similar rituals took place also at other localities where murdered prison inmates had been found. On Drohobycz and Borysław see below.

18. BArch B 162/27345, 55.

19. Ibid., 56.

20. See Heer, "Einübung in den Holocaust," 423.

21. See Jan Rogowski, "Lwów pod znakiem swastyki. Pamiętnik z lat 1941–1942," BOss. 16711/II, 188f.; Musial, *"Konterrevolutionäre Elemente,"* 175–78; Tadeusz Zaderecki, "Gdy swastyka Lwowem władała . . . (Wycinek z dziejów okupacji hitlerowskiej)," Yad Vashem Archives (henceforth: YVA) O-6/367, 9–12 (published in Hebrew as "Bi-meshol tselav haqeres bi-Lvov: Churban haqehilla ha-yehudit be-enei mechabber polani," Jerusalem 1982).

22. Photos from these scenes have been published many times. Perhaps among the first publications was Gerhard Schönberner, *Der gelbe Stern. Die Judenverfolgung in Europa 1933–1945* (Frankfurt am Main: Fischer, 1991 [1st ed. 1960]), 132f.; see now also Khymka, "Dostovirnist' svidchennia," 53–60.

23. Zaderecki, Gdy swastyka, 11f.; Himka: "The Lviv Pogrom," 213f.

24. See Frank Grelka, *Die ukrainische Nationalbewegung unter deutscher Besatzungsherrschaft 1918 und 1941/42* (Wiesbaden: Harassowitz, 2005), 251–70; see also the comprehensive collection of documents about these events in Orest Dziuban, ed., *Ukraïns'ke derzhavotvorennia: akt 30 chervnia. Zbirnyk dokumentiv i materialiv, L'viv* (Kiev: Piramida, 2001). Stets'ko's view can be found in Iaroslav Stets'ko, *30 chervnia 1941. Proholoshennia vidnovlennia derzhavnosti Ukraïny* (Toronto: Liga Vyzvolennia Ukraïny, 1967).

25. The Einsatzgruppen Report of 2 July said: "Some elements of the Bandera-group under the direction of Stechko [!] and Ravlik [!] have organized a militia force and a municipal office [. . .]," *The Einsatzgruppen Reports*, 3f. Ivan Ravlyk ("Ravlik" was a misspelling) belonged to the group of OUN members that came to Lwów together with Stets'ko. He is considered to be one of the organizers of the militia. At the end of 1941 he was arrested by the Gestapo in Lwów and died in 1942 in prison after long torture. On the organization of the militia on 30 June, see also Khymka, "Dostovirnist' svidchennia," 64 n27.

26. Dziuban, ed., *Ukraïns'ke derzhavotvorennia,* 126–29, here 129. However, in the original printings this line in contrast to many others was not produced in bold type or larger letters, see the copies in Central'nyi derzhavnyi arkhiv vyshchykh orhaniv vlady ta upravlinnia Ukraïny 3833/1/63, 9a, 10, 12.

27. Ibid., 131. The Hungarians had attracted the Ukrainian nationalists' hatred because they had destroyed the Ukrainian state-building attempt in Carpatho-Ukraine by occupying that region in March 1939.

28. Siegfried Gasparaitis interpreted the parallel event of the pogrom in the Lithuanian capital Kaunas after 23 June 1941, which also took place simultaneously with the formation of a new Lithuanian government, as a "performance of a national resuscitation" after the suffering under the Soviet occupation. Siegfried Gasparaitis, "'Verrätern wird nur dann vergeben, wenn sie wirklich beweisen können, dass sie mindestens einen Juden liquidiert haben.' Die 'Front Litauischer Aktivisten' (LAF) und die antisowjetischen Aufstände 1941," *Zeitschrift für Geschichtswissenschaft* 49 (2001): 886-904, here 901. For an interpretation of the pogroms of summer 1941 in Lithuania and eastern Poland as a "punishment" of the Jews for Soviet rule see also Roger D. Petersen, *Understanding Ethnic Violence: Fear, Hatred, and Resentment in Twentieth-Century Eastern Europe* (Cambridge: Cambridge University Press, 2002), 95–136; and Kai Struve, "Rites of Violence? The Pogroms of Summer 1941," *Polin: Studies in Polish Jewry* 24 (2011): 257–74. On this aspect of the violence see also Himka: "The Lviv Pogrom," 235-38, who, however, tends to restrict this aspect of the violence maybe too strongly to the "crowd" in contrast to the Ukrainian militia.

29. See, on the German occupation of the Ukrainian territories, Karel Berkhoff, *Harvest of Despair: Life and Death in Ukraine under Nazi Rule* (Cambridge, Mass.: Belknap Press, 2004); on the example of the Zhytomyr region, Wendy Lower, *Nazi Empire-Building and the Holocaust in Ukraine* (Chapel Hill: The University of North Carolina Press, 2005).

30. See Heydrich's first written order to the commanders of the Einsatzgruppen from 29 June where he also asked them to initiate pogroms, Peter Klein, ed., *Die Einsatzgruppen in der besetzten Sowjetunion 1941/42. Die Tätigkeits- und Lageberichte des Chefs der Sicherheitspolizei und des SD* (Berlin: Edition Hentrich, 1997), 319.

31. Grelka, *Die ukrainische Nationalbewegung,* 259–61.

32. The Operational Situation Report USSR No. 10 of 2 July said about the situation in Lwów: "The Einsatzgruppe has created a Ukrainian political city administration as a counter-balance against the Bandera group" (my own translation from Ereignismeldung UdSSR Nr. 10 des Chefs der Sicherheitspolizei und des SD, 2 July 1941, BArch 58/214, 53; in a somewhat awkward translation also in *The Einsatzgruppen Reports,* 3).

33. *The Einsatzgruppen Reports,* 3, and Operational Report no. 9, 1 July 1941, 46.

34. Klein ed., *Die Einsatzgruppen,* 319.

35. Affidavit of Erwin Schultz, 26 May 1947, NO-3644, in *Trials of War Criminals Before the Nuremberg Military Tribunals Under Control Council Law* No. 10, Vol. 4 (Washington, D.C.: U.S. Government Printing Office, 1949-1953), 135f.; Leon Weliczker Wells, *The Janowska Road,* (Washington, D.C.: United States Holocaust Memorial Museum 1999), 45-54.

36. According to the Operational Situation Report No. 11 from 3 July 1941 Einsatzkommando 6 already on 2 July reported the execution of 133 Jews, *The Einsatzgruppen Reports,* 5. How-

ever, this may have referred to an execution in Dobromil on 30 June. The activity report of the Intelligence officer (Ic) in the staff of the Seventeenth Army stated under 5 July: "Einsatzkommando 6 (Standartenführer Dr. Kroeger) in Lwów, NKVD headquarter, reports: more than 400 Jews have been shot as reprisal for murdered Ukrainians. 200 more will follow," BA-MA, RH 20-17/769. See also the diary of Felix Landau, a member of an Einsatzgruppen unit sent from Krakow, in Ernst Klee et al.: *"Schöne Zeiten." Judenmord aus der Sicht der Täter und Gaffer,* 4th ed., (Frankfurt am Main: Fischer, 1989), 89f. Landau reports that his unit had been summoned already in the morning of 3 July for an execution of 500 Jews, but later he says that the execution did not take place.

37. See Affidavit by Erwin Schultz, 137; many testimonies about the executions can be found also in the judicial investigations against members of Einsatzkommandos 5 and 6; see, for example, BArch B 162/1570–1573, 5224, 5226, 5227, 5343, 5344, 20190, 20200.

38. The journalists reached Lwów in the evening of 2 July; see AOK 17, Tätigkeitsberichte Ic/AO, Beilage Nr. 1 zum KTB Nr. 1, 15.1.-12.12.41, BA-MA 20-17/768, entries for 1 and 2 July 1941; see also Heer, "Einübung in den Holocaust," 417.

39. Joseph Goebbels, *Tagebücher,* vol. 4, ed. Ralf Georg Reuth (Munich: Piper, 1992), 1622.

40. On how the German propaganda used the massacres see also Bianka Pietrow-Ennker, "Die Sowjetunion in der Propaganda des Dritten Reiches: Das Beispiel der Wochenschau," *Militärgeschichtliche Mitteilungen* 2 (1989): 79-120, here 94–96; Musial, *"Konterrevolutionäre Elemente,"* 200-209; Bernd Boll, "Zloczow, Juli 1941: Die Wehrmacht und der Beginn des Holocaust in Galizien," *Zeitschrift für Geschichtswissenschaft* 50 (2002): 899-917, here 916 (published in English as: "Złoczów, July 1941: The Wehrmacht and the Beginning of the Holocaust in Galicia; From a Criticism of Photographs to a Revision of the Past" in *Crimes of War: Guilt and Denial in the Twentieth Century,* ed. O. Bartov, A. Grossman, and M. Nolan [New York: New Press, 2002], 61-99).

41. *The Einsatzgruppen Reports,* 31. See the "Judgment of Landgericht Tübingen," 31 July 1969, against Erhard Kröger and Andreas von Koskull, in *Justiz und NS-Verbrechen. Sammlung deutscher Strafurteile wegen nationalsozialistischer Tötungsverbrechen,* vol. 32 (Amsterdam: Amsterdam University Press, 2004), 704–734, here 714-16.

42. On Jeckeln see Richard Breitman, "Friedrich Jeckeln—Spezialist für die 'Endlösung' im Osten" in *Die SS—Elite unter dem Totenkopf. 30 Lebensläufe,* ed. Ronald Smelser et al. (Paderborn, Germany: Schöningh, 2000), 267-75.

43. *The Einsatzgruppen Reports,* 31. See also the ruling of Landgericht Darmstadt against Kuno Callsen et al., 29 November 1941, in *Justiz und NS-Verbrechen* 31, 7–275, here 56.

44. This number is mentioned in the Einsatzgruppen report no. 24, 16 July 1941, *The Einsatzgruppen Reports,* 32. Romaniv and Fedushchak mention 2,754 murdered prison inmates in *Zakhidnoukraïns'ka trahediia,* 61f.

45. Ereignismeldung UdSSR Nr. 11, 16 July 1941, 192. The translation in *The Einsatzgruppen Reports* 32 wrongly ascribes the execution to Ukrainians.

46. Klaus-Michael Mallmann, "Die Türöffner der 'Endlösung'. Zur Genesis des Genozids" in *Die Gestapo im Zweiten Weltkrieg. 'Heimatfront' und besetztes Europa,* ed. by Gerhard Paul and Klaus-Michael Mallmann (Darmstadt, Germany: Wissenschaftliche Buchgesellschaft, 2000), 437–63, here 443f. About the war with Poland in 1939, see Alexander B. Rossino, *Hitler Strikes Poland: Blitzkrieg, Ideology, and Atrocity* (Lawrence: University Press of Kansas, 2003); and Jochen Böhler, *Auftakt zum Vernichtungskrieg. Die Wehrmacht in Polen 1939* (Frankfurt am Main: Fischer, 2006).

47. See also Jürgen Matthäus, "Controlled Escalation: Himmler's Men in the Summer of 1941 and the Holocaust in the Occupied Soviet Territories," *Holocaust and Genocide Studies* 21(2) (2007): 218–42.

48. Jürgen Förster, "Das Unternehmen, Barbarossa' als Eroberungs- und Vernichtungskrieg" in *Das Deutsche Reich und der Zweite Weltkrieg, Bd. 4: Der Angriff auf die Sowjetunion* (Stuttgart: DVA, 1983), 413–47.

49. Such a definition of the tasks of the Einsatzgruppen is reflected in a letter that Heydrich sent to the Higher SS and Police Leader in the East on 2 July 1941; see Klein, ed., *Die Einsatzgruppen,* 320.

50. The question of which orders the Einsatzgruppen received before 22 June 1941 and if and when a "general killing order" had been issued has been the subject of a long controversy; the most

extensive discussion is found in Ralf Ogorreck, *Die Einsatzgruppen und die "Genesis der Endlösung"* (Berlin: Metropol, 1996).

51. Klein, ed.: *Die Einsatzgruppen,* 320f. The text of this order is included also in the Einsatzgruppen report of 2 July, see *The Einsatzgruppen Reports,* 2f.

52. During a multidepartmental meeting on planning for propaganda on 29 May 1941, Georg Leibbrandt, a future high-ranking official of the Ministry for the Occupied Eastern Territories, presented "political guidelines for propaganda" that stated: ". . . it is probably advisable to leave to the population itself to settle its accounts with the Jewish-Bolshevik oppressors initially, and then after gathering more detailed knowledge to deal with the remaining oppressors," quoted in Karlis Kangeris, "Die nationalsozialistischen Pläne und Propagandamaßnahmen im Generalbezirk Lettland 1941-1942" in *Collaboration and Resistance During the Holocaust: Belarus, Estonia, Latvia, Lithuania, Bern et. al.,* ed. David Gaunt, Paul A. Levine, Laura Palosuo (Bern: Peter Lang, 2004), 161-86, here 169.

53. Klein, *The Einsatzgruppen,* 319.

54. Alexander Rossino assumes that Heydrich's order of 29 June 1941 originated from a meeting of Heinrich Himmler with several high-ranking SS and Police leaders held on 28 June in eastern Prussia where Himmler seem to have criticized the fact that there had not been pogroms in the neighboring region of Białystok as there had been in Lithuania. In fact, the course of events in Kaunas, where a large pogrom apparently had intensified under the influence of the Chief of Einsatzgruppe A Franz Walter Stahlecker, may have been instructive for Heydrich's letter, see Alexander B. Rossino, "Polish 'Neighbours' and German Invaders: Anti-Jewish Violence in the Białystok District during the Opening Weeks of Operation Barbarossa," *Polin* 16 (2003): 431-51, here 443.

55. "Borot'ba i diial'nist' OUN pid chas viiny" in *OUN v 1941 rotsi,* ed. O. Veselova et al (Kiev: Instytut istorii Ukraïny NAN Ukraïny, 2006), vol. 1, 58-176; also in Patryliak, *Viis'kova diial'nist',* 426-596. On the intentions and activities of the OUN-B in the summer of 1941 see also Grzegorz Rossoliński-Liebe: "The 'Ukrainian National Revolution of 1941': Discourse and Practice of a Fascist Movement," *Kritika: Explorations in Russian and Eurasian History* 12 (2011): 83-114.

56. On the OUN-B's planning for the initial phase of the war and for military activities behind the Soviet army, see Patryliak, *Viis'kova diial'nist',* 96-207. Patryliak tends to stress the significance of the military activities of the OUN.

57. Veselova et al., eds., *OUN v 1941 roci,* vol. 1, 69.

58. Ibid., 103f.

59. Ibid., 93. On the OUN's attitude toward Jews see Marco Carynnyk, "Foes of Our Rebirth: Ukrainian Nationalist Discussions about Jews, 1929-1947," *Nationalities Papers* 39 (2011): 315-52; on spring and summer 1941, ibid., 328-32; see also Karel C. Berkhoff and Marco Carynnyk, "The Organization of Ukrainian Nationalists and Its Attitude toward Germans and Jews: Iaroslav Stets'ko's 1941 Zhyttiepys," *Harvard Ukrainian Studies* 23(3-4) (1999): 149-84, here 153.

60. Veselova et al., eds., *OUN v 1941 rotsi,* vol. 1, 43.

61. See, for example, Volodymyr V'iatrovyč, "Stavlennia OUN do ievreïv. Formuvannia pozycii na tli katastrofy, L'viv: Vydavnyctvo," Mss. (2006), 54-60; and the critical review by Taras Kurylo and Ivan Khymka [John-Paul Himka], "Iak OUN stavylasia do ievreïv? Rozdumy nad knyzhkoiu Volodymyra V'iatrovyča," *Ukraïna moderna* 13(2) (2008): 252-65.

62. Michael MacQueen, "The Context of Mass Destruction: Agents and Prerequisites of the Holocaust in Lithuania," *Holocaust and Genocide Studies* 12(1) (1998): 27-48, here 34; see also idem, "Massenvernichtung im Kontext: Täter und Voraussetzungen des Holocaust in Litauen," in *Judenmord in Litauen. Studien und Dokumente,* ed. by Wolfgang Benz and Marion Neiss (Berlin: Metropol, 1999), 15-34, here 23.

63. MacQueen, "The Context of Mass Destruction," 29-32.

64. Berkhoff and Carynnyk, "The Organization of Ukrainian Nationalists," 152 and passim. See also Stepan Lenkavs'kyi in a discussion of the Council of Seniors of policies of the future Ukrainian state in mid-July 1941 in Lwów: "With regard to the Jews we will adopt all methods that will contribute to their destruction," in *Ukraïns'ke derzhavotvorennia,* ed. Dziuban, 190.

65. The conviction deeply rooted in the OUN that violence was legitimate, necessary, and the only way of achieving the national aims included also the expectation that the members of the OUN should be prepared to sacrifice their own lives for the national cause. This is expressed in the often

repeated phrase "Prevail in the battle for the Ukrainian state or die!" But the readiness to sacrifice one's own life included also a readiness to take ruthlessly that of the perceived enemy among not only other national groups but also among fellow Ukrainians who were considered to be "traitors."

66. Gina Wieser, 31 May 1945, AŻIH 301/176, 1.

67. See for Borysław, for example, Ana Antler, 12 September 1945; for Drohobycz Zofia Cukier, 1 June 1946; both in AŻIH 301/2569, 1. A Polish witness reports that a German "general" allowed for the violence (which he, however, interprets as directed only against "communists") describing the scenes of the pogrom in great detail. Alfred Jasiński, "Borysławska apokalipsa," *Karta* no. 4 (1991): 98–114, here 112. Another source from Borysław reports that the allowance was given by the Gestapo, but the pogrom was ended by the Ortskommandantur of the Wehrmacht, see Salomon Rosenberg, 29 November 1947, AŻIH 301/3119.

68. Klein ed., *Die Einsatzgruppen,* 320f. Heydrich's order was also included in the Operational Situation Report no. 10 of 2 July 1941, see *The Einsatzgruppen Reports,* 2.

69. In fact, a special Einsatzkommando, usually referred to as Einsatzkommando z.b.V. (for special tasks), executed on 4 July and later dates 25 Polish professors from universities in Lwów along with some of their family members, altogether 45 persons; see Dieter Schenk, *Der Lemberger Professorenmord und der Holocaust in Ostgalizien* (Bonn: Dietz, 2007).

70. Christian Streit, "Angehörige des militärischen Widerstandes und der Genozid an den Juden im Südabschnitt der Ostfront" in *NS-Verbrechen und der militärische Widerstand gegen Hitler,* ed. Gerd R. Ueberschär (Darmstadt: Primus, 2000), 90–103, esp. 93f. For an apologia for Stülpnagel, who belonged to the military opposition and was sentenced to death and hanged after the failed coup of 20 July 1944, see Barbara Koehn, *Carl-Heinrich von Stülpnagel. Offizier und Widerstands-kämpfer: eine Verteidigung* (Berlin: Duncker & Humblot, 2008).

71. See BA-MA WF-03/9121, Bl. 106f.; see also Pohl, *Die Herrschaft der Wehrmacht,* 156f.

72. As for Lwów, it is difficult to establish a clear and certain number of victims for these cities. The numbers in German sources are usually only estimates based on limited information. The numbers that are mentioned in reports of Jewish survivors in most cases reflect estimates and rumors that existed among Jews in the different localities. Because of the traumatic character of the event they may have become exaggerated, but sometimes they also may be fragmentary or remembered inexactly. In any case, for Złoczów Jewish survivors mention 2,000–3,000 victims or more, while a report of the Einsatzgruppe mentions 300–500 Jews who had been arrested and shot by the militia "by order of the Wehrmacht" (see *The Einsatzgruppen Reports,* 33). In fact, most of the shootings had been carried out by units of Division Wiking. This number clearly seems to be too low; see for a discussion of the numbers Boll, "Zloczow," 909. For Tarnopol, Jewish survivors mostly mention 5,000 victims or more. However, Salomon Hirschberg mentions a number of about 4,000 and gives a concrete source for his estimate: the Ukrainian public health authority in the city had established this number according to data received from the victims' families (Salomon Hirschberg, 20 July 1948, AŻIH 301/3774). If these numbers for Złoczów and Tarnopol are true then the number of victims of pogrom violence here would be probably larger than in Lwów. However, here the share of them slain and shot by members of the German armed forces was much larger than in Lwów. *The Einsatzgruppen Reports* contain various information on Tarnopol that sums up the number of victims of pogrom violence and executions at no fewer than 900, but maybe several hundred more, see *The Einsatzgruppen Reports,* 12, 19, 32f., 39.

73. There seems to be no critical research on this unit. See instead the presentation of their history from the veterans' point of view in Peter Straßner, *Europäische Freiwillige. Die Geschichte der 5. SS-Panzerdivision Wiking* (Osnabrück, Germany: Munin, 1977); and the popular Rupert Butler, *SS-Wiking: The History of the Fifth SS Division 1941–45* (Staplehurst, U.K.: Spellmount, 2002).

74. See for this background of the bloody trail that SS Wiking left behind in Eastern Galicia Marco Carynnyk, "Zolochiv movchyt'," *Krytyka* 2005 no. 10 (96): 14–17, here 14. The battle log of the 2nd Battalion of Westland says for 2 July 1941: "At 11.00 the battalion receives the message that SS-Standartenführer Wäckerle had been shot by snipers. Burial takes place in manor Slowida [!]. 5th company guard of honour. At 14.00 7th company is put on to the village in retaliation where the snipers had hidden," Kriegstagebuch II./SS Rgt. "Westland," 1.4.1941-25.5.1942. The battle log was originally preserved in BA-MA RS 3-5/7, but in February 2009 the file had disappeared. A copy of some pages, including that cited above, can be found in BA-MA N 756/144a (collection Vopersal).

A bound photocopy of the whole battle log, presumably produced by veterans of the regiment, was acquired by the author as a second-hand book at the end of February 2009. In Słowita 36 Jews were shot after long ordeals, see Carynnyk, "Zolochiv movchyt'," 14f.

75. BA-MA, RH 20-17/46, quoted in Heer, "Einübung in den Holocaust," 424.

76. Carynnyk, "Zolochiv movchyt'," 14. The sniper had not been caught, but it is very likely that it was a Soviet soldier. The Soviet tactic of having sharpshooters target officers caught the Germans by surprise and resulted in relatively high numbers of casualties among officers in the beginning of the war. Sometimes the snipers also hid and let German troops pass before they opened fire on a target that they considered worthy and then disappeared. Also, many dispersed Soviet soldiers or small Red Army units had remained behind the German front lines and occasionally attacked German units.

77. The sources mention between 649 and 752 victims; Carynnyk, "Zolochiv movchyt'"; see also Boll, "Zloczow," 904.

78. Boll, "Zloczow," 903–908. On Groscurth see Helmuth Groscurth, *Tagebücher eines Abwehroffiziers: 1938–1940. Mit weiteren Dokumenten zur Militäropposition gegen Hitler* (Stuttgart: DVA, 1970). Groscurth was part of the military opposition against the Nazi regime and also intervened unsuccessfully against the murder of 90 Jewish children by Sonderkommando 4a at Bielaia Tserkov on 20 August 1941, see ibid., 534–42.

79. *The Einsatzgruppen Reports,* 19.

80. Maria Cukier, 27 June 1947, AŻIH 301/2520; see also Sonia Zeiger, no date, AŻIH 301, 1643. See also the entry on Zborów in Pinkas Hakehillot, *Entsiklopedyah shel ha-yishuvim ha-Yehudiyim le-min hivasdam ve-'ad le-ahar Sho'at Milhemet ha-'olam ha-sheniyah: Polin,* vol. 2, ed. Danuta Dabrowska, Abraham Wein, and Aharon Weiss (Jerusalem: Yad Vashem, 1980), 202–205. It mentions more than 1,000 victims. One memoir describes how Jews before they were murdered were led in a kind of procession through the city being mistreated and mocked. According to this memoir one local Jewish notable had been nailed to a board in a kind of imitation of Christian symbolism; see Solomon Berger, *The Jewish Commonwealth of Zborow* (New York: Regsol, 1967), 84f. Several memoirs with more details are found in Eliyahu Zilberman, ed., *Sefer Zikaron Leqehilat Zborov* (Haifa, Israel: Irgun Yots'e Zborov veha-sevivah be-Yiśra'el, [1971]).

81. *The Einsatzgruppen Reports,* 39f. According to Soviet sources 574 prison inmates had been executed in Tarnopol; witnesses mention 1,000 and more victims; see Musial, *"Konterrevolutionäre Elemente,"* 128; Romaniv and Fedushchak, *Zakhidnoukraïns'ka trahediia,* 63.

82. Anna Terkel and Sara Frydman mention that the perpetrators had the sign of skull and crossbones on their uniforms; see Anna Terkel, n.d., AŻIH 301/367, and Sara Frydman, 12 May 1948, AŻIH 301/3551. This applied to SS units as well as the personnel of the tank divisions. The SS had it on its caps, the tank troops on their collar tabs.

83. The Einsatzgruppen report of 5 July mentions Tarnopol as position of Sonderkommando 4b, *The Einsatzgruppen Reports,* 8; see also BArch B 162/18184.

84. *The Einsatzgruppen Reports,* 19; see also 39. Among the 127 executions that *The Einsatzgruppen Reports* mentions were probably about 100 members of the leading circles of the Jews in Tarnopol who had been identified under the pretext of preparing a list of possible members of a Judenrat in Tarnopol and were executed on 7 July; see Salomon Hirschberg, 20 July 1948, AŻIH 301/3774, 4f.; Klara Katz, 26 November 1946, AŻIH 301/2165.

85. See the documents on Tarnopol presented in Musial, *"Konterrevolutionäre Elemente,"* 236–41.

86. See, for example, about Rudki Leib Tell, 1945, AŻIH 301/527, 1; about Sokal Moses Brüh, 28 April 1945, AŻIH 301/4971; Maria Ostermann, 16 November 1945, AŻIH 301/1167. In Busk, on the second day after the Germans had entered the town the Gestapo rounded up the Jewish men and also some women in the market place and kept them there, beating and threatening them, until the evening, when they were released. After some days about 30 people, listed by the Ukrainians, were arrested as communist supporters and killed by the Gestapo in a nearby forest. Maria Steinberg, 1945, AŻIH 301/477, 1; see also Izrael Hecht, AŻIH 301/1704. In Jaworów, the Ukrainian militia compiled a list of Jews who allegedly collaborated with the Soviets. Twelve were arrested and about five days after the Germans had occupied the city on 25 June they were executed in a nearby forest by Gestapo. Izrael (Ignacy) Manber, 12 July 1946, AŻIH 301/1912, 5. Sometimes these "cleansing

operations" occurred rather late. In Sasów, for example, such a selection of "communists" from the assembled Jews took place perhaps only at the end of July, after Jews had already been mistreated and killed by Germans and Ukrainians as public spectacles in the first half of July. See Herman Weigler, 26 June 1948, AŻIH 301/3701. In Brody Jews had been forced to do humiliating work and had been mistreated immediately after the Germans occupied the city; several days later, probably on 11 July, the Jewish intelligentsia was assembled, brought out of the city, and shot by the Gestapo—Kalman Harnik, n.d., AŻIH 301/1777.

87. Pohl, *Nationalsozialistische Judenverfolgung*, 65f.; see also, for example, on Mielnica, Mechel Kassirer, 4 August 1947, AŻIH 301/2540, 1; on Kołomyja, Anna Moritz, 20 June 1946, AŻIH 301/2579. Another memoir from Kołomyja ascribes the prevention of large-scale killings during a pogrom to the Ukrainian mayor: Szaje and Róża Feder, 27 January 1946, AŻIH 301/1398. On Horodenka see Tomasz Miedziński, interviewed by Anka Grupińska, December 2003-February 2004, http://www.centropa.org/index.php?nID=30&x=PXVuZGVGVmaW51ZDsgc2VhcmNoVHlwZT1CaW9EZXRhaWw7IHNlYXJjaFZhbHVlPTIyODsgc2VhcmNoU2tpcD0w (accessed February 2009).

88. Tzvi Schnitzer, "Hedim Migey Tsalmavet. Hoshana Rabba—'Ha'aqtsya Harishona,'" in D. Noy, M. Schutzman, eds., *Sefer zikaron le-kehilat Kolomey ve ha-sevivah* (Tel Aviv: Irgun yots'e Kolomyah veha-sevivah ba-'arets uba-tefutsot, 1972), 325–31.

89. See the memoirs of Markus Willbach, AŻIH 302/105, 22–24; excerpts have been published as Markus Willbach, "Skupiska żydowskie w Obertynie podczas II wojny światowej," *Biuletyn Żydowskiego Instytutu Historycznego* 1960, no. 35: 106-128; see also T. Lipiński (Teofil Jetel), 20 March 1961, AŻIH 301/5775; Szaje and Róża Feder, 27 January 1946, AŻIH 301/1398, 4; Izak Plat and Sabina Charasz, AŻIH 301/1434, 3; Tomasz Miedziński, interviewed by Anka Grupińska, December 2003–February 2004, http://www.centropa.org/index.php?nID=30&x=PXVuZGVGVmaW51ZDsgc2VhcmNoVHlwZT1CaW9EZXRhaWw7IHNlYXJjaFZhbHVlPTIyODsgc2VhcmNoU2tpcD0w (accessed February 2009). There are some discrepancies among the witnesses' accounts about the date of the murder. Willbach and Miedziński date it on the first days of July, while T. Lipiński in his quite detailed account gives 13 July.

90. Willbach, AŻIH 302/102, 24f.

91. See the anonymous memoir "Das Schicksal des Grenzstreifens Jablonitza bis Snyatyn in den Kriegsjahren 1941 bis 1944," Yad Vashem Archives, O-33/172, 1f.; Schoszne Gertner (J. Gärtner), n.d., AŻIH 301/134, 3 (an English translation of an excerpt from Gertner's Hebrew-language memoirs is available on www.yadvashem.org); Dawid Likwornik, October 1946, AŻIH 301/2153, 1; Szaje and Róża Feder, AŻIH 301/1398, 4; Schnitzer, "Hedim Migey Tsalmavet," 330f. According to Schnitzer's report many Jews were killed in the neighboring villages also.

92. On the pogroms in neighboring Northern Bukovina and the role of the Romanian armed forces see the excellent study by Vladimir Solonari: "Patterns auf Violence: The Local Population and the Mass Murder of Jews in Bessarabia and Northern Bukovina, July–August 1941," *Kritika: Explorations in Russian and Eurasian History* 8 (2007): 749-87.

93. On Borszczów see Bernard Kremer, 31 July 1948, AŻIH 301/3770, 1; on Tłuste, Maria Königsberg (Kenigsberg), 17 January 1948, AŻIH 301/3281, and 15 March 1948, AŻIH 301/3491, 1.

94. Hilary Kenigsberg, 28 March 1948, AŻIH 301/3337. In Ułaszkowce perhaps 68 people were killed; see the entry on that town in Pinkas Hakehillot, *Polin*, vol. 2, 54f. Another testimony estimates the number of victims in the villages in that region at 1,500, see Jehuda and Eliasz Albin, 2 May 1945, AŻIH 301/4976.

95. Fischel Winter, AŻIH 301/835, 2.

96. Izak Orensztein, 22 May 1947, AŻIH 301/2440, 1. See also Tzvi Fenster, "Megillat Hasho'ah," in M. A. Tenenblatt, ed., *Sefer ozieran ve-ha-seviva* (Jerusalem: Hotsa'at Entsiklopedyah shel galuyot, [1959]), 289-364, here 290f. Fenster mentions 68 victims for Laszkowice.

97. The document has no date, but bears the remark "Z.d.A. (Juden)" [To the files (Jews)] with initials and the date of 22 July 1941; see "Zusammenstellung der Vorfälle, betreffend die jüdische Bevölkerung in der Umgebung von Drohobycz," DALO R-1928/1/4, 10–12 (a copy is in U.S. Holocaust Memorial Museum Archives—henceforth: USHMMA—Acc. 1995.A.1086, reel 31).

98. On Schnodnica see various reports by Fay Walker, *My Memories, 1939–1945*, USHMMA RG-02.050, part 2, 2–3; the somewhat dramatized memoirs, Fay Walker and Leo Rosen, with Caren S. Neile, *Hidden: A Sister and Brother in Nazi Poland* (Madison: University of Wisconsin

Press, 2002); and under the name Fela Walka or Walke, given in a letter from 4 October 1947 to H. Ajchenbaumowa, AŻIH 301/2931, 2. See also Jakob Steinberg, testimony 6 May 1945, AŻIH 301/4920, 1.

99. On 7 July a subunit of the Einsatzkommando z.b.V. arrived in Drohobycz and probably participated the same day in an execution in the village of Pohorodce. Pohl, *Nationalsozialistische Judenverfolgung,* 70. Because the exact dates of the killings in the other villages and more details about them have not been established, it cannot be excluded that this Einsatzkommando inspired at least some of them. Also other German Police units came through this region shortly after the German troops.

100. Musial, *"Konterrevolutionäre Elemente,"* esp. 284–95.

101. See on the controversies on 1939–1941 Kai Struve, "Geschichte und Gedächtnis—Polen und Juden unter sowjetischer Herrschaft 1939–1941," *Jahrbuch des Simon-Dubnow-Instituts* 7 (2008): 495–530.

26

Caught in Between
BORDER REGIONS IN MODERN EUROPE

Philipp Ther

Introduction

The metaphorical term "lands in between" alludes to the fact that many border regions in modern Europe, and in particular in Central Europe, were shaped by a distinct mixture of cultures and languages. Precisely because of this mixture many borderlands stood under the competition of two or more national movements and nation states. This was already an issue in the age of empires that preceded World War I. When an order of nation states was established in 1918–1920, this competition often turned into a bitter struggle over disputed regions. While these disputes have been a very important topic of historiography, a discourse often tailored to legitimize the competing claims of various nationalisms and nation states, the issue of human identification with regions has for a long time been relatively neglected.[1]

In this chapter the term regionalism is used to explore the political and social dimensions of regional identification. In certain periods regional movements achieved a high degree of political mobilization and developed their own ideologies. However, the European nation states perceived regional movements as competitors and fought against political projects that stressed the autonomy of border regions. On the one hand, this was an issue of the administrative power of the centers over the periphery, in particular over disputed borderlands. On the other hand, it was a struggle over ideological domination. The centers aspired to define the national codes, i.e. the ways in which the various nations defined themselves. There was little toleration for regional identifications that stressed the particularity of regions and their blends of cultures and languages. A "compulsory unambiguity" (*Zwang zur Eindeutigkeit*) was not only directed against regional movements and regionalisms, but imposed on society at a very basic level.

As the second part of this chapter shows through the example of Upper Silesia, the population of the borderland in the age of nationalism had to find various strategies to cope with the compulsion to be unambiguous. The first ideal type (in the Weberian sense) was to join one of the competing national movements, the second one to resist and to establish regional movements, the third one to retreat into the private sphere and to keep a distance from political activities in general, including the competing nationalisms. Quite often, the population of border regions would show conformity with the ruling ideology in public, especially when confronted with National Socialist and Stalinist regimes, while preserving a strong identification with the region in the private sphere or the neighborhood.

But the preservation of regional identification and the perseverance of a peculiar mix of cultures and languages should not be romanticized as a case of multiculturalism. The population of the borderlands was often "caught in between," and was discriminated against, persecuted, or even deported. This will again be shown specifically in the case of Upper Silesia (in Polish the specification "Upper" is unusual, the region is mostly called Śląsk/Silesia, in contrast to Dolny Śląsk, and its center is Wrocław/Breslau), which forms the empirical core of this article. The evidence for other European border regions is gathered from a project about "Regional Movements and Regionalism" which was carried out in 2001–2003 at the Center for Comparative History of Europe in Berlin.[2]

Problems of Historiography

As Ron Suny once pointedly stated, the institutionalization of history is more closely linked with the project of the nation than that of any other science.[3] Although historiography has largely freed itself from misuse by various nationalisms, the nation and the nation state have remained the most important units of analysis or at least points of reference for historians until the end of the twentieth century. Ernest Gellner once found a wonderful metaphor for this still prevailing *nation state perspective,* which for him resembles a modernist painting.[4] Thereby, the historical map of Europe is shaped by homogeneously painted areas of various sizes and colors, sometimes bizarrely shaped, but always clearly outlined. These colored territories demarcate the European nations which were able to form their own states over the course of their history. Shading or transitional areas between the individual colors, or nations, is certainly not provided; nor is any grading of color tone, although some national categories that persist in the language, such as German or Polish, meant something quite different 200 years ago than they do today.

This state-national or modernistic view does not do justice to the borderlands. For example, in Upper Silesia, an intermediary space between today's Czech Republic, Poland, and Germany, it was not possible to clearly define the nationality of inhabitants until well into the twentieth century. The same is true of Alsace, where the population was torn between France and Germany until the 1940s. One could also point to the example of the former Polish East (the so-called *Kresy*), to the southern Balkans, in particular to greater Macedonia, and to numerous other regions in Europe. In these "lands in between," national standard languages were only spoken to a limited extent. The population communicated mainly in mixed local and regional dialects. Social distinctions and purposes determined the usage of language, rather than national standards. This was not only true for rural areas and small towns, but often also larger cities. One should add that in Central and Eastern Europe, such multilingual borderlands are not just narrow marginal areas, but in fact cover large parts of the entire large region. Although these cultural and social nuances defined people's everyday life—and in the twentieth century, even influenced international politics and the domestic policy of the states concerned—they become almost imperceptible when the history of Europe is packed into a cabinet consisting entirely of national compartments. It is a mistake to perceive European history as the sum of its national histories.[5] One should also look at regional specifics or characteristics, which are of course not exhausted with the cases of the borderlands presented in this article.

Even the term "borderlands" has potential drawbacks, because of prominence of the word "border," which in today's perspective automatically connotes the boundaries of nation states. The "lands in between" dealt with in this article do not necessarily end *at* state borders, but often transcend them and encompass areas of both sides. If a less metaphorical and more analytical term is preferred, one can label "the lands in between" as *intermediary spaces*. This term has a geographical dimension, in the sense of a location between (inter) national centers and spaces. There is also a political dimension, which will be shown below in the section on "regionalism." Finally, there is an important cultural dimension. All of the regions mentioned in the last paragraph are areas of linguistic, cultural, and ethnic transition in which various influences meet and frequently mingle.

A vivid example can again be provided by Upper Silesia, where Czech, Austrian, Prussian, German, and Polish rule not only shaped the region's history but also its language. Up to the present, the regional dialect has been shaped by elements taken from various national languages. In the early 1990s the sociologist Danuta Berlińska, one of the most prominent specialists on the region, noted a sentence spoken by a teenager: "Jechoech na kole, trzaszech sie ze stromem i sie skrzywia linksztanga."[6] The content of this sentence is quite simple: the teenager rode on a bicycle, hit a tree, and as a result of this his handlebar broke. Linguistically speaking, the sentence is much more complicated and hardly understandable for an outsider coming to the region. If one looks at this sentence from the viewpoint of standardized national languages, the Silesian boy rode a Czech bicycle with an old Polish verb and archaic Polish grammar into a Czech tree and then the German handlebars broke.[7] This example is of more than anecdotal significance.

In recent years linguists and literature scholars have proven that "continuous dialects" such as Silesian were not only an everyday means of communication but also served to differentiate between the familiar and the foreign, i.e. were points of identification.[8] The linguist Hans-Christian Trepte has demonstrated this as well for the Polish–Belarusian border area.[9] In view of the close linguistic relationship of the various Slavic languages, the existence of transitional dialects is not surprising. It displays similarities with the situation in Teschen Silesia, for example, where areas of Czech and Polish linguistic influence intersected and where until recently people communicated mainly in a regional dialect.[10] Yet even in places where quite different linguistic families had an influence, such as in the Slavo-Germanic border area, mixed dialects and modern Creole languages developed which assumed elements of the standard languages of both neighboring countries. If one approaches the history of Upper Silesia, Alsace, the eastern Polish borderlands, or Macedonia only with the conventional nation state categories, these linguistic phenomena are easily lost, along with their political significance.

But if there was any awareness of consistent dialects and other regional traditions or cases of syncretism in the "short" twentieth century (1918–1989/91), they were generally regarded as backward and inferior. Population groups which opposed clear national classification or cultural monopolization were considered to be premodern. In an ideological move aptly criticized by Celia Applegate, modernization was frequently equated with nation-alization[11] so that, except for purposes of legitimization, the study of regions such as Upper Silesia, Polesie, Moravia, Transylvania or the Vojvodina was largely neglected.

It is characteristic of many intermediary spaces that their cultures serve as a point of departure for political projects and movements. Also for this reason, intermediary spaces cannot be regarded as a peripheral phenomenon of European history, where one studies only bizarre dialects. Precisely their location at the (changing) borders specified a certain central-ity, for major traffic arteries and channels of communication ran through them.[12] This is true of the late nineteenth century as well as of the situation today. From a European perspective Strasbourg or Katowice are more centrally located than Paris or Warsaw. In her program-matic essay on "A Europe of Regions," Celia Applegate describes the extent to which regions have shaped the economic and political development of the individual European nations and states. This can also be said of most of the intermediary spaces treated here. Their border location often gave rise to their symbolic significance for the respective national movements and nation states.

The study of nationalism is, for reasons inherent to the subject, an end in itself. In spite of the disputes between constructivists, ethnosymbolists, and other schools of study,[13] the telos of nationalism studies, and frequently the finale of scientific narratives, is the fully developed modern nation and the nation state.[14] This focus on the "success" of nationalism entails a hermeneutic problem. This is particularly true of nationalism studies in the Federal Republic of Germany, which has always started from the premise that the German nation project possessed a strong assimilating power and that the population was nationalized by the turn of the century.[15] Christian Geulen recently transposed this theory to the modern self and maintained that "all other differences and identities have been made to disappear by the national."[16]

Recent research, chiefly prompted by Michael G. Müller, has expressed criticism of this teleology. In their recently published book on regional and national identities in Eu-rope, Müller and his two coeditors come to the conclusion that, "It is no longer possible to maintain the tacit assumptions long made that the impact of national propaganda increases with its intensity and that the advance of the nation-building process means that thinking in national categories takes primacy over regional and local loyalties."[17] One possibility for solv-ing the hermeneutic problem of the study of nationalism is to analyze potentially competing identification options on the political, social, and cultural levels. On closer examination, it emerges that religion, political convictions, social standing, a dynasty, or a monarchist state were often more important to people than national beliefs or identities. The problem with this kind of relativization, however, is that it defies measurement and does not take into ac-count the fact that nation and religion, for example, often effectively complemented each other.

One possible way of avoiding this dilemma is to first examine nationalism from the perimeters of its range of influence and to look at identification alternatives which at least partly offered competition. In many intermediary spaces, regional identification options could not be combined with the ideologies of national movements and nation states. For this reason, it seems appropriate to take a closer look at regional identities, movements, and pro-grams. The initial question is, then, to what extent regional identities in the various "interme-diary spaces" competed with national identities starting from the middle of the nineteenth century, followed by to what extent regional movements were able to mobilize the masses, and which political programs arose from this mobilization.[18]

The Concept of Regionalism

In the context of the theoretical state of nationalism studies today, regions are constructs which should not be assumed as units, as this leads to incorrect assumptions regarding territorial continuity and internal homogeneity.[19] Following Rogers Brubaker's approach to nationalism,[20] the emphasis should be placed on examining European regions as a cultural practice. Therefore, one needs to look at a region not as a territory with fixed boundaries, but as an object of discourses. One particularly informative empirical example is the above-mentioned region of Upper Silesia, which will be looked at more closely below. The question is, why this and other regions at times played an important role in political, social, and cultural discourses or were even considered as alternative projects to already existent state nations and nation states. Taking this approach, regional movements are viewed as modern mass movements which support the autonomy of the region in question in relation to greater units such as empires or nation states. The term regionalism describes the programs and ideologies on which the construction of a given region is based. It also contains a dimension of social history, for without knowledge of the social extent of regionalism, its development as an ideology cannot be understood.

In principle, transitional forms of identification can also exist between regionalism and nationalism. The difference between the two phenomena is that regionalism does not strive for sovereignty or independence of the area it lays claim to. While people's belonging to a nation state is defined by clearly identifiable criteria such as citizenship, the right to vote, military service, etc., regions do not have such sources of legitimization and institutions of power at their disposal. The *feeling* of belonging to a region is determined more by identification elements involving mainly "soft" cultural criteria, such as dialects, customs, traditions, personal relationships, and specific historical experiences and "memories". People evidently have a close affinity to areas of a manageable size, while nations are more often based on a cognitive "invention" or "imagination."[21] These dissimilarities also make it clear that regionalism and nationalism should not be regarded only as competing concepts and social movements. Even in the age of nationalism, multiple identities were widespread, with beliefs about belonging to a region and in belonging to a nation often complementing and augmenting each other. Thus the question is: Why in certain circumstances does a situation of competing identifications arise?

The Case of Upper Silesia

It would go beyond the scope of this chapter to describe the already mentioned region of Upper Silesia in great detail.[22] Nevertheless, a brief, concise outline of the history of the region in the "age of nationalism" can convey an idea of why regions and particularly the "intermediary spaces" treated here could form a component in a new kind of transnational history of Europe.

In modern German history, a general congruence of regional and national identifications has been shown in various studies. Celia Applegate and Alon Confino have provided persuasive evidence of this in central areas of Germany with an exclusively German-speaking population.[23] In Silesia, and particularly in the mainly Catholic, Slavic-dialect-speaking region of Upper Silesia, however, different circumstances prevailed. Even when it was part of the German Empire, national identities spread relatively slowly in Upper Silesia. The reasons for this lay in the religious and social specifics of the activity of the German national movement in the eastern territories of Prussia, including Upper Silesia, and in the antagonistic, counterproductive attempts at nation-building in the German Empire and the ideological narrowing of German nationalism.

The revolution of 1848 was a boost for the activities of the German national movement in the area. The Polish national movement took the same moment to hit on the Upper Silesians, who to a large extent still spoke an ancient Polish dialect, especially in rural areas. Both movements were confronted with obstacles in the shape of the social and religious specifics of Upper Silesia. The German national movement was mainly supported by Protestants and members of the Prussian administration and met with little response from the mixed population of these mainly Catholic and rural areas. The distance between them was increased by the struggle between the Prussian state and the church in the *Kulturkampf* and the narrowing definition of who and what was to be perceived as German. These splits were not fully overcome until the First World War.[24] Furthermore, a social gulf formed between the elites and the German middle class, often "imported" from the interior of imperial Germany, on the one hand, and what they disparagingly called the *Schlonsaks,* the Slavic-speaking workers and rural proletariat, on the other. The relationship between the two sides was markedly asymmetrical. For this reason, the Krakow sociologist Maria Szmeja even describes the Prussian-German rule of Upper Silesia as an example of "internal colonialism."[25]

Polish nationalism also came up against considerable obstacles despite the fact that many Poles immigrated to Upper Silesia's industrial district. The Polish national movement, unlike the German, was not backed up by an own state, so it had organizational deficits. And since Upper Silesia had not been part of Poland since the fourteenth century, there was there no common remembrance of the Polish state that had existed until 1795. Furthermore, the numerous cultural differences between the Poles and the Polish-speaking Upper Silesians which had developed over the centuries of Austrian, Prussian, and German rule all played a part. Many Poles could barely understand the Upper Silesian dialect, or considered it a strange mixture with German. For this reason, identification with the more immediate homeland among the Polish-speaking population, particularly in rural areas, continued to dominate and usually prevailed over any secondary German or Polish national consciousness.[26] This identification with Silesia did not, however, manifest itself in a strong political movement and the Upper Silesians did not produce a secular political elite in the German Empire.

Poland was refounded after the First World War and claimed a large part of Upper Silesia on the basis of ethnic principles. The German Empire, however, insisted on keeping the largest industrial district in East Central Europe. The conflict between both states caused deep ruptures in the region. Violence broke out, and the two sides fought each other in armed combat in the three Silesian uprisings (1919–1921). It is undisputed that Upper Silesians took part in these conflicts, but more decisive was the intervention and mobilization from abroad. The paramilitary units which fought on both sides brought in Germans and Poles who had little or no connection to the region but basically continued the war in the name of the "national interest." The major cause of the violence, then, was the choice not to demobilize troops who had fought in World War I, not a nationalist mobilization of the population in Upper Silesia.

The vast majority of the political elites in Upper Silesia, for their part, called for unity in the region and tried to mediate in the dispute between Germany and Poland. After World War I, a strong regional movement emerged, the *Bund der Oberschlesier* (Alliance of Upper Silesians), which demanded autonomy and at times even Upper Silesia's independence. In 1919 the regional movement had around 300,000 adherents, i.e. a seventh of the population. Publications of the Bund der Oberschlesier even tried to invent an Upper Silesian nation. They spoke about a "multilingual unitary nation" (*multilinguales Einheitsvolk*) and a blend of slavo-germanic blood (*slavo-germanische Blutmischung*),[27] i.e. ancestry. The regional activists mixed ethnic elements with arguments of multiculturalism in order to construct a regional community or even nation. But how could this invention have attracted a population which was already familiar with German and Polish nationalism?

The regional movement failed eventually due to its inability to maintain neutrality in the conflict between Poland and Germany. Furthermore, neither Germany, Poland, Czechoslovakia, nor the Allies wanted another free state like Danzig/Gdańsk. In March 1921, the inhabitants of Upper Silesia were called on to align themselves with either Germany or Poland in a plebiscite. Around 700,000 people voted to stay with Germany while 480,000 voted for union with Poland. The areas with a majority in favor of Germany were mainly urban and left of the Oder River; those in favor of Poland were right of the Oder and small-town or rural.[28] It would, however, be wrong to interpret this voting behavior as an expression of a deeply rooted national identity (in the hardly translatable terms of the time: *Volkstum, Deutschtum,* or *Polskość;* or very roughly "local culture," "Germanness," and "Polishness") or to equate the number of votes for each side with the number of resident Germans or Poles. At local elections in November 1919, Polish candidates still had gained over 60 percent of the votes—this roughly corresponded with the proportion of the population that was Polish-speaking or bilingual. Economic considerations and loyalty to the Prussian-German state evidently carried more weight in the plebiscite than "objective" criteria of national belonging such as language.

The division of Upper Silesia left large minorities on either side of the new border. A total of 226,000 people who had voted for Germany remained in eastern Upper Silesia while 195,000 people who had voted for Poland became residents of Opole Silesia. Under the Geneva Convention on Upper Silesia of 1922, the people in the areas where the vote was held were entitled to adopt the nationality of the respective neighboring country and emigrate to Germany or Poland. By 1925, about 100,000 people on both sides had taken advantage of this right of "option." The plebiscite and the Geneva Convention show that not only the nation states, but also the international community in the League of Nations wanted to enhance the homogeneity of the nation states. There was no "option" to remain Polish *and* German, or to declare an allegiance to Silesia.

During the Weimar Republic, in Opole Silesia, the western part of Upper Silesia that remained German, many members of the mixed population adopted Germany's language and culture for pragmatic reasons. Not only was this a prerequisite for social advancement, but even school children distanced themselves from their regional roots and Slavic mother-tongue in order to avoid teasing and isolation from the German majority. This "pragmatic assimilation" manifested itself in censuses in the drop in numbers of people who declared themselves bilingual or Polish-speaking and in elections in the decrease in votes for Polish candidates. This tendency to assimilate was, however, disrupted by a seizure of power National Socialist's, who gained only 30 percent of the votes in Upper Silesia in 1932. When the National Socialists began to take steps against the Catholic church, dissolved the Catholic

Center Party in 1934, and finally also persecuted priests, the mixed population was driven into the arms of Polish minority organizations.[29] Nazi church policy provoked a similar reaction to that which the *Kulturkampf* had elicited two generations earlier: resistance to anything henceforth defined as German and the linking of the struggle for linguistic and cultural freedom with defense of the church. The head of the regional government in Breslau recognized this problem and dispatched a report in 1935 to the Prussian and Reich Minister for the Interior, Wilhelm Frick, stating that "the unrestrained attacks which were customary in the past and went way beyond the fight against political Catholicism, have to stop. In any case, the state and the movement must not identify with them."[30] Racial prejudice against the Upper Silesians proved to be just as counterproductive.

In the eyes of many National Socialists, the only options were to be either German or Polish. The idea of a "floating national character" (*schwebendes Volkstum*), as it was pejoratively called, was only accepted as a temporary phenomenon. In general, the popular image of Upper Silesia's mixed population transformed in the interwar years from that of a nationally and otherwise underdeveloped community to that of a group of freeloaders. Indeed, the National Socialists noted with pleasure how they were able to entice Upper Silesians to their functions with free tickets to cultural events and complimentary cake at women's meetings[31] but in other reports bemoaned the fact that this was a nationally unreliable and corruptible ethnic group.

In 1935, the National Socialists proceeded with the Germanization of personal and place names and extended their pursuit of the population into the private realm, suspecting that, underneath the cloak of outward conformity, anti-German or even pro-Polish identities continued to exist. As the official reports from Upper Silesia, edited by Przemysław Hauser and Mathias Niendorf, show, the authorities were not entirely wrong in this assumption. One sign of the endurance of cultural traits was the popularity of Polish church services. In 1938, 30 percent of services were still held in Polish according to the nationalist Association of the German East (*Bund Deutscher Osten*, BDO). The BDO estimated the total number of people in the "Polish minority" at about 400,000, or about 550,000 with the "Germanized section" included.[32] Nevertheless, very few people openly professed their Polishness, as that would have lead to persecution and possibly even internment in a concentration camp. As is well known, Silesian Jews experienced an even more terrible fate, regardless of their nationality. Many Upper Silesians who outwardly conformed or even spoke German at home preserved close family, religious, and cultural ties with Polish Upper Silesia. Paradoxically, the nationalist propaganda against the "*Diktat* of Versailles" and the revisionism in regard to the border established in 1921 helped to preserve a mental mapping that encompassed the entire region of Upper Silesia.

Parts of the Silesian society activated an Upper Silesian or Polish identification, whether out of sympathy for Poland or an aversion to National Socialism, or for pragmatic reasons. The further tightening of the policy on nationality and the ban on Polish-language church services in the run-up to the Second World War increased the old tendency among Upper Silesia's mixed population toward self-isolationism.[33] Not until Germany achieved its first war victories and troops on the home front had been mobilized was it possible to win over a section of the population. Following Germany's defeats on the eastern front, however, personal and public attitudes toward Germany changed. Despite the Nazi terror, a willingness to show symbols of a Polish or Upper Silesian identification in the private sphere and in the limited public of neighborhoods increased.

In Polish eastern Upper Silesia, which requires special consideration in the interwar period, national and regional identification changed even more than in the German part of Upper Silesia. The number of inhabitants who considered themselves definitely German had dropped, mainly due to emigration, from about a third to a seventh of the total population between 1921 and 1931.[35] But many Polish-speaking or bilingual Upper Silesians turned toward German political parties in order to express their dissatisfaction with economic and political developments in Poland. In local elections in 1926, German parties gained 42 percent of the votes, and 18.4 percent in the Polish parliamentary elections in Upper Silesia in 1930, i.e. far more than the proportion of the corresponding population. These results were, however, less an expression of "unbroken Germanness," as was thought in the Weimar Republic, and more a sign of the vitality of the identification with Upper Silesia. Many Silesians voted for German parties in protest against the undermining of the autonomy of Silesia as a Polish province (*Województwo*). Arkadiusz Bożek, who became vice president of the province of Upper Silesia in 1945, summarized the general feeling of disappointment with the Polish administration in the interwar period thus: "Only the men in charge have changed. The Berliners went and the Warsaw-Krakovians came."[36] This quote indicates the gap between the regional society and those who came from outside.

At the end of the twenties, as the situation in Poland began to temporarily stabilize, German parties enjoyed much less electoral success, and participation in German-national rallies also decreased rapidly. Even the opponents of the Polish state evidently grew accustomed to its existence.[37] Furthermore, in Upper Silesia, social and economic considerations gave rise to a willingness to adapt oneself to the majority nation. This pragmatism could, however, swing in the opposite direction at any time. For example, parents often signed their children up for wealthier German schools because they tended to provide more plentiful school meals than their state-run Polish competitors.[38] But this pragmatic attitude was not tolerated by the Polish state, which thought in dialectic national terms and was afraid of a strengthening of the *German* minority. The Polish administration wanted to compel parents of mixed origin to send their children to Polish schools. Eventually the conflict about these children was decided by the League of Nations. It decided that the nationality of children, and therefore their choice of school, had to be decided by the state bureaucracy according to objective indicators (primarily the language spoken by the parents), and not by the parents. One can conclude that it was not only radical nationalists and "nationalizing nation states" (Brubaker) who though in terms of a binary nationalism, but also the international community of states. Moreover, nationality was not perceived as subjective and changeable, but as objective. The regional society was indeed caught in between.

A person's sense of being German, Polish, or Silesian often depended on their individual social and professional standing. Some cases are known, for example, of the wives of Polish policemen in eastern (Polish) Upper Silesia who belonged to the German People's Association.[39] These cases were recorded because the Supreme Commander of the Polish Police in the district of Silesia was angered at the lack of national feeling among officials and suspected that state secrets were being betrayed. In Opole Silesia, the authorities also reported on behavior which could not be reconciled with their view of a proper national standing. There was no understanding at all for several members of the local Hitler Youth who had joined Polish sports clubs.[40] As the reports show, Upper Silesians sometimes switched languages and cultures within the space of one evening. This is illustrated by an incident reported by the chief of police in Gleiwitz/Gliwice in 1929, when a local celebration organized by the Polish choral society presented a guest choir which sang in Polish first before performing German military songs.[41]

Nevertheless, one should be wary of romanticizing this multicultural mélange. If a person failed to opt for a particular nationality, they faced life with a bad reputation and sanctions. Even after 1945, the "struggle for national character" (*Volkstumskampf*)—which today would be described as a conflict over identities—was fought out primarily at the expense of the regional society.

After the Second World War, attempts to nationalize the region continued—although in different circumstances and without an equivalent procedure to the mass murder of the Jews. Poland had been granted all of Upper Silesia in 1945 through the Potsdam treaty. Its main goal was to Polonize (or "re-Polonize," as the propaganda formulated it) the region once and for all. For reaching this goal the postwar Polish state deployed the entire toolkit of violent, totalitarian nationality policy. The "enemy" language was forbidden, the regional culture eliminated by all possible means, books destroyed, and personal as well as place names changed. The aim of this policy was to "de-Germanize," as the apt title of a book by Bernard Linek translates,[42] i.e. to eliminate all traces of the German era. This also entailed the expulsion of inhabitants who could be clearly identified as German. In comparison to Lower Silesia, where almost all citizens of the German Empire were compelled to leave their homelands, the stance toward the Germans in Upper Silesia was liberal. In the areas where the plebiscite was held in 1921, a declaration of loyalty to the Polish state and the Polish nation was generally enough to earn one's "verification" or "rehabilitation" as a Pole and so avoid expulsion. The authorities upheld the argument that a large part of the population of Upper Silesia was actually Polish; this also formed the basis for territorial claims to the former territories of the German East. About 850,000 "Autochthones" were therefore permitted to stay, making up the majority of the population after the war in the later provinces of Katowice and Opole.

Yet this majority section of the population was regarded with deep mistrust and often disapproval by the Polish government, the immigrant population from central Poland, and expellees from eastern Poland,[43] who equated the indigenous Upper Silesians with Germans—the most negative categorization possible in view of the recent experience of National Socialist occupation. This bipolar national discourse or a "compulsory unambiguity" had existed since World War I: one had to be either German or Polish and nothing in between. The suspicion persisted that the *Ślązacy* (the Silesians) were secret Germans. In fact, after the war, many Upper Silesians could speak German better than Polish, which they pronounced with a strong accent anyway, as a result of Nazi-era pressures. Even the term "Autochthon" has a derogatory connotation, as the immigrants who used it regarded themselves as Polish missionaries leading the formerly German citizens of Polish extraction back to the path of rightful nationality and drumming Polishness into them, by force if necessary. Furthermore, deep social conflicts arose after the Second World War, particularly over property in Upper Silesia. Locals and immigrants fought over farms, apartments, everyday necessities, and soon also over positions in the state and the party.

These conflicts and the frequent discrimination and persecution of native inhabitants led to the latter's complete rejection of Poland as a nation and a state. For the deeply Catholic population, the rejection of communism was also connected with their religious affiliation. By contrast, the German era in Upper Silesia was often idealized, especially as the "economic miracle" was beginning to take effect in the Federal Republic of Germany. In 1950, Arkadiusz Bożek recorded bitterly that, "the Germans are laughing up their sleeves—what we could not achieve in seven hundred years, because the Silesians persistently defended their faith and their language, they accomplished in seven years: the complete eradication of Polishness in these lands, down to the very last root."[44] This statement contained the nationalist myth of timeless Polishness; nevertheless, it was right about the disaffection with Poland and Poles.

The change in orientation toward Germany was, however, also motivated by the fact that the identification with the region of Upper Silesia was suppressed in the People's Republic of Poland, being regarded as a remnant of the interwar period and a possible Trojan Horse of the Germans. Open declarations of Germanness were the most effective method for gaining permission to leave the country and so escape Communism. Moreover, the Upper Silesians were discriminated against as Germans.

Until 1989, the situation in Upper Silesia remained by and large stable. The People's Republic of Poland proceeded with oppression—the ban on the German language, for example, remained in force to the last—and Upper Silesians reacted to this with inner emigration or actual emigration to Germany. Thus the old-established Upper Silesian population became the minority, estimated at 250,000–300,000 of a total population of around one million in the province of Opole in 1989. Those who felt drawn to German culture or simply saw no future in communist Poland left the country.

When the communist regimes collapsed, the troubled history of the interwar period threatened to repeat itself. The minority, which as a result of the Polish nationality policy indeed had become a *German* minority, demanded their official authorization, and individual demands for the borders to be redrawn were also made. The situation quickly eased with the conclusion of the 2+4 Treaty in 1990, in which Germany relinquished all territorial claims in favor of reunification, and the German–Polish treaty of 1990–1991, which finally confirmed the Oder-Neiße border and enforced the official recognition of the minority in Poland.

For this reason, among others, Poland tolerated the *de facto* revisionist citizenship policy of the Federal Republic of Germany. In Upper Silesia, all Polish citizens who could provide evidence of their German ancestry could apply for German citizenship. Well over 200,000 German passports were issued as a consequence of this policy up to the mid-1990s. They secured the holders' free access to the job market in Germany and the EU. The Germanness of the minority in Upper Silesia was once again officially confirmed.

Freedom to travel and reunification, however, rapidly brought about a change in the popular image of the Federal Republic of Germany in Upper Silesia. The former spiritual homeland became simply a neighboring state that could be reached within a few hours. Nearly all Upper Silesians took advantage of their newly established right to travel to visit the country, especially those who held German passports and therefore also work permits. The reality of Germany, however, was often surprising, and did not always correspond with images conjured up by television, brochures of expellee associations, and letters from relatives who had emigrated there before. Especially at work Upper Silesians were not greeted as compatriots but rejected as Poles, particularly in the new federal states (i.e. the former German Democratic Republic). Those with a good command of German still spoke a dialect which sounded foreign to people west of the Oder and Neiße. In addition to this, job-seekers from Silesia were hardly regarded as lost sons of the fatherland but frequently as competition. Because of this renewed experience of national differences after the 1989 revolution, many members of the mixed population turned away from Germany and German nationality.

As Danuta Berlińska, a sociologist from Opole, has shown, some years after the 1989 revolution more than two thirds of the minority population considered themselves exclusively or primarily Silesian, while only about one tenth defined themselves as German.[45] Less is known about changes in the identities of the majority population, which migrated or were forced to migrate to Silesia in the postwar period. Most of them clearly and sometimes exclusively identify with Poland as a nation and as a state. The changes in Poland since 1989 contributed to a generally stronger perception of the regional or local homeland as a point of reference. In the province of Opole, the minority possessed a concrete territory in which they could realize their political ideas. Since the 1989 revolution, the "socio-cultural society of Germans in Poland" has produced numerous mayors, chief administrative officers, some members of the Sejm, and a few senators in the second chamber of the Polish parliament. In the 2003 census, however, 173,000 people unexpectedly declared themselves "Silesian."[46] Among these were many former members of the German minority that had sharply decreased in numbers to become the second largest minority in Poland. With this result, the minority demonstrated that their regional allegiance was stronger than a national Polish or German one.

After the census was taken, the leadership of the regional movement tried to gain recognition as national minority. This was first denied by the Polish government and courts, then also by the highest European court in Strassbourg. The refusal in Poland was based on fears that a new separatist movement might arise. Indeed, the widespread discontent in Upper Silesia with the social and economic situation of the region might feed some discontent. But the reaction against the Silesian movement was driven rather by historical memories than by rational calculations or public opinion polling. In Strassbourg, the underlying issue was that if the Silesians were to gain recognition, then other groups might organize themselves as national minorities. That would be in contrast to the still dominant vision that the European states are homogeneous nation states. None of these states would today repeat the coercive nationality policy of the interwar and postwar period. But it still seems to be difficult to accept diversity and to overcome the utopia of homogeneous nation states if divergent groups come into existence.

Summary

By looking at the case of Upper Silesia, one can show the endurance of regions as objects of identification, which is surprising precisely because of the wide range of references they host. The Upper Silesia which the Silesian or German minority refers to today has little in common with the Prussian region of Upper Silesia of the early twentieth century. The size of the area, its social and demographic structures, and its state affiliation changed several times, quite dramatically, between 1900 and 2000. And yet today a significant number of people identify themselves primarily with the substratum called Upper Silesia. National identities, by contrast, appear volatile and context-dependent. Such processes can be shown to have taken place not only in Upper Silesia but also in other intermediary spaces such as Alsace. With these intermediary spaces and their inhabitants frequently crushed between national millstones, the European idea presented itself as a possible solution. It is no coincidence that some prominent figures of the European movement or a European historiography, such as with Robert Schuman and Lucien Febvre, originated from such intermediary spaces.

Although the regionalism in Upper Silesia has so far failed to achieve its aims to the extent other regional movements have—with any comprehensive autonomy still lacking—it proves the limits of concepts of nationality and nation states. The relationship between nationalism and regionalism is fundamentally defined by the attractiveness and inclusive ability of the concept in question. That means, however, that nation and region should not be understood as firmly established quantities but as relational options employed in political discourses and practices. Collective identification models such as the nation or the region are transitory. The history of Europe is, then, in this respect an open book. It remains to be seen whether it will continue to be a matter of a Europe of fatherlands or whether a Europe of regions will gain in significance. This is even more true for the enlarged European Union and hence, academic disciplines studying not past but present-day changes, making it just one more reason to take the study of regions as a way of approaching European history. The Schengen Treaty and its expansion to the East in 2007 have removed all border controls from the Bug in eastern Poland to Portugal in the West. This means that the European borderlands have ceased to be located at state borders. Of course, Schengen has not removed linguistic, social, and political borders. But it remains to be seen how this reconfiguration will influence the intermediary spaces in Europe.

Looking back at their history again, one can distinguish three major periods. The late age of empires between 1848 and 1918 was undoubtedly an age of nationalism. People's identification with regions did not diminish, however, but was spread in various borderlands as a result of a generally rising tide of politicization of the population. The national movements hit their limits in the horizontal and vertical mobilization of societies. Because of their mostly bourgeois character and other factors such as religious and linguistic differences, the national movements had problems mobilizing the urban and the rural under-classes. This is especially true for borderlands such as Upper Silesia or Alsace. World War I was a catalyst of nationalism, but especially in countries which had lost the war, regional movements also gained power. However, they were always hampered by the lack of a secular elite. So even when nation states were weakened, such as Germany in 1918–1919, the regional movements could not achieve autonomy, let alone secession or independence.

The second period lasted from 1918 until 1939, in which the old and new nation states demanded an unambiguous identification from their citizens. This created conflicts with national minorities, and in particular with and within disputed borderlands. As a reaction, the nation states intensified their nationalizing policies. Regional movements became suspicious of helping enemy states across the borders or guessed that minorities could be Trojan Horses within the body of an organically understood nation. Various nation states such as France in Alsace, both Germany and Poland in Upper Silesia, Romania in Transylvania, Italy in South Tirol, or the states which had carved up Macedonia, developed repressive policies. Instead of accepting at least a minimum of regional specifics, any demands for autonomy were interpreted as a danger for the nation state. The repressions ranged from discrimination to persecution and deportations of elites. This created deep conflicts which should not be interpreted in the framework of minority politics only, but also as conflicts between centers and marginalized borderlands.

The suppression of regionalism was mostly counterproductive. For a demonstration of this we can look not only to Upper Silesia, but also to Alsace. Christiane Kohser-Spohn has shown how the French policy against the regional movement in the 1920s turned sour an Alsatian society which had welcomed French troops in 1918. Similar conclusions can be made about other nation states and their nationality policy in disputed borderlands.[47] Although discontent was widespread, none of the regional movements were able to reach their ideal goals or even reduce the degree of suppression by nation states. This was mostly due to their weakness in term of organization and political ideology, and their late start compared to national movements. Moreover, the nation states could offer careers which were of course pursued by inhabitants of the borderlands. The regional movements were caught in between the nation states. Looking for support beyond the border was not a viable solution anymore after 1945 because the regional movements in Alsace, the Silesians in Poland, and the Schleswiger in Denmark were tainted by collaboration with the National Socialists.

After World War II, our third period, Europe was structured into nation states that were more homogenized than ever before. The borderlands lost all opportunity to raise a political voice, let alone to form a regional movement again. Only in the late 1960s did new dynamics emerge. In Western Europe this was mostly due to the activities of the student movement. The regionalistic component of 1968 has, however, not received much attention by historians. In Alsace, Bretagne, and parts of southern France regional initiatives gathered and established institutions. Similar developments can be observed in Wales and Scotland, in parts of Italy, and in Spain after the death of Franco. This "new" regionalism was partially inspired by the political Left, and it utilized the vocabulary of the anticolonial struggle.[48] In France, the activists also spoke about a "renaissance" of the region, revealing the relevance of invented traditions. Altogether this regionalism was very different from the interwar period, when there still was a strong influence from clerics and right-wing parties, and is ripe for attention as a distinct era.

In the late 1960s, identification directed against hegemonic nation states also increased in Central and Eastern Europe, but developed a different dynamic. Officially the autonomist Slovak, Croat, Macedonian, and other elites asked for more regional autonomy, but the political discourses soon focused on national interest and rights. The regimes in both countries responded with federalization (1969 in Czechoslovakia, 1974 in Yugoslavia), but this did not have the same results as in France or Britain, where regions also gained power in the 1970s and '80s. In Eastern Europe, the devolution of political power strengthened national discourses and national movements. Similar conclusions could be made about post-Franco Spain, where the regional movements called themselves national movements. But only a minority of Catalans or Galicians called for independence from their regions. Hence, one can label these movements as predominantly regionalist according to the definition here provided. In the Basque Country and in Northern Ireland, events took a different course because violence was introduced.[49]

In Western Europe the postwar regionalism was also strengthened by the European Community/Union. This seems to be paradoxical on first view because originally the concept of the EC had been a "Europe of fatherlands." But the European Union organized its various programs for agriculture and in particular for infrastructure in such a way that the entities who could apply for funds were not entire nation states, but rather the less developed parts of them. Inequality was defined on a regional not on a national basis. This motivated regional interest groups to become politically active in order to get funding from Brussels. One can explain this development through a comparison with the UN. While it is necessary on a global level to make political claims as a nation because only nation states can become members of the United *Nations,* in Europe certain benefits, especially the structural funds, are distributed at a regional level. Moreover, the states which already had a federal structure, such as Germany and Spain, pressed for a general federalization of the EC and its single member-states. This culminated in the establishment of the "Committee of the Regions" (CoR) in the Maastricht Treaty, which is more well-known for having laid the groundwork for the common currency, the Euro. It is disputed how much power the CoR really has. Since the enlargement of the EU in 2004, this consultative body has rarely produced any headlines or public discourses. But this institutionalization might be more relevant in the future. It is an open question how the "Europe of nations" will develop into a "Europe of regions."

Independently of this process, regions and in particular borderlands are an important object of study for historians. They make it possible to overcome the dominant national paradigm, they reveal the contingency in nation building and nation state formation, and they demonstrate that no territorial and group identification, be it on a national, regional, or local level, is set and stable. Last but not least, the "lands in between" demonstrate that the much-debated subject of transnational history can be studied beneath and not only beyond the nation.

NOTES

1. The term "identification" is preferred in this article because it indicates an active process which can be gradual, fluid, or multiple. For the debate about the term "identity" see Rogers Brubaker and Frederick Cooper, "Beyond Identity," *Theory and Society* 29 (2000): 1–47. See also the genealogical treatise in Lutz Niethammer, *Kollektive Identität. Heimliche Quellen einer unheimlichen Konjuktur* (Reinbek, Germany: Rowohlt Taschenbuch, 2000).

2. This project is documented in a publication by Philipp Ther and Holm Sundhaussen, eds., *Regionale Bewegungen und Regionalismen in europäischen Zwischenräumen seit der Mitte des 19. Jahrhunderts* (Marburg: Herder-Institut, 2003).

3. See: Ronald Grigor Suny, "History and the Making of Nations," in *Cultures and Nations of Central and Eastern Europe: Essays in Honor of Roman Szporluk*, ed. Zvy Gitelman (Cambridge: Harvard University Press, 2000), 569–89. Note that due to limitations of space, this chapter quotes only a few important works as an introduction to the topic.

4. On the comparison with modern painting see: Ernest Gellner, *Nations and Nationalism* (Ithaca, N.Y.: Cornell, 1983), 139 ff. Rogers Brubaker used this in his essay "Myths and Misconceptions in the Study of Nationalism" in *The State of the Nation: Ernest Gellner and the Theory of Nationalism*, ed. John A. Hall (Cambridge: Cambridge University Press, 1998), 272–306, here 294 ff.

5. See Mary Fulbrook, "Introduction: States, Nations, and the Development of Europe" in *National Histories and European History*, ed. Mary Fulbrook (Boulder, Colo.: Westview Press, 1993), 1–20.

6. On the change of identities among the Silesian population see Danuta Berlińska, *Mniejszość niemiecka na Śląsku Opolskim w poszukiwaniu tożsamości* (Opole, Poland: Instytut Śląski, 1999).

7. In standard Polish the sentence would read "Jechałem na rowerze, zderzyłem się z drzewem i skrzywiła się kierownica."

8. On the social function of such "consistent dialects," explored through the example of Teschen Silesia, cf. Kevin Hannan, *Borders of Language and Identity in Teschen Silesia* (New York: Peter Lang 1996).

9. Cf. Hans-Christian Trepte, "'Die Hiesigen' (Tuejsi/Tutejšyja)—Regionales Bewußtsein im polnisch-weissrussischem Grenzraum" in *Regionale Bewegungen und Regionalismen in europäischen Zwischenräumen seit der Mitte des 19. Jahrhunderts*, ed. Philipp Ther and Holm Sundhaussen (Marburg: Herder-Institut, 2003), 145–60.

10. Cf. Kevin Hannan, *Borders of Language and Identity in Teschen Silesia* (New York: Peter Lang, 1996).

11. Cf. Celia Applegate, "A Europe of Regions: Reflections on the Historiography of Sub-National Places in Modern Times," *American Historical Review* 104 (Oct. 1999): 1157–82.

12. Center–periphery models are therefore hardly suited to analyzing the cases examined here. On the problematic nature of such models, see also Applegate, "A Europe of Regions," 1167.

13. Among the main proponents of the debate were and are Ernest Gellner, *Nations and Nationalism* (Oxford: Blackwell, 1983); Benedict Anderson, *Imagined Communities: Reflections on the Origin and Spread of Nationalism* (London: Verso, 1983); Antony D. Smith, *Nations and Nationalism in a Global Era* (Cambridge: Blackwell, 1995). Miroslav Hroch came up with a convincing compromise on this contentious issue in which he accepts that the nation is to be regarded as a project which is basically formed by previously existing economic, political, and linguistic areas of communication: Hroch, "Real and Constructed: the Nature of the Nation" in *The State of the Nation: Ernest Gellner and the Theory of Nationalism,* ed. John A. Hall (Cambridge: Cambridge University Press, 1998), 91–106.

14. See as prototypical examples Eugen Weber, *Peasants into Frenchmen: The Modernization of Rural France, 1870–1914* (Stanford: Stanford University Press, 1976);

Alexej Miller, "Russko-ukrainskije otnošenija v 19 i načale 20 veka. Rusifikacija i pričiny jejo neudači," *Ruskij istoričeskij žurnal,* 1 (1998): 131–48.

15. This mainstream point of view on postwar West German history writing is expounded in Hans-Ulrich Wehler, *Deutsche Gesellschaftsgeschichte, Dritter Band. Von der "Deutschen Doppelrevolution" bis zum Beginn des Ersten Weltkrieges* (Munich: Beck, 1995), 962. More recent publications have modified or revised the assumption that minorities were largely assimilated: see Hans Henning Hahn and Peter Kunze, eds., *Nationale Minderheiten und staatliche Minderheitenpolitik in Deutschland im 19. Jahrhundert* (Berlin: Akademie Verlag, 1999). On Upper Silesia in particular, see Philipp Ther, "Die Grenzen des Nationalismus: Der Wandel von Identitäten in Oberschlesien von der Mitte des 19. Jahrhunderts bis 1939," in Ulrike v. Hirschhausen and Jörn Leonhard, eds., *Nationalismen in Europa: West und Osteuropa im Vergleich* (Göttingen: Wallstein, 2001), 322–46.

16. Cf. Christian Geulen, "Die Metamorphose der Identität. Zur 'Langlebigkeit' des Nationalismus" in *Identitäten, Erinnerung, Geschichte, Identität* 3, ed. Aleida Assmann and Heidrun Friese (Frankfurt am Main: Suhrkamp, 1998), 346–73, here 359.

17. Heinz-Gerhard Haupt, Michael Müller, and Stuart Woolf, eds., *Regional and National Identities in Europe in the XIXth and XXth Centuries* (The Hague: Kluwer, 1996), 4, 14. Michael G. Müller and Rolf Petri, eds., *Zur Konstruktion nationaler Identität in sprachlich gemischten Grenzregionen* (Marburg: Herder-Institut, 2002).

18. A recently published volume on the incorporation of borders into the concept of the nation formulates a similar question, albeit indirectly: Michael G. Müller and Rolf Petri, eds., *Zur Konstruktion nationaler Identität in sprachlich gemischten Grenzregionen* (Marburg: Herder-Institut, 2002). The introduction to this volume contains a comprehensive bibliography on this subject.

19. On the problematic nature of the tendency to regard regions and towns as given or essential see, for example, Jaques Revel, "La Région" in *Les Lieux de Mémoire,* vol. 3: *La France,* part 1: *Conflicts et partages,* ed. Pierre Nora (Paris: Gallimard, 1992), 851–83, here 854. A convincing definition can be found in Wolfgang Schmale, *Historische Komparatistik und Kulturtransfer. Europageschichtliche Perspektiven für die Landesgeschichte* (Bochum, Germany: D. Winkler, 1998), 54. Neither this article nor the comparative volume on regionalism published in 2003 (cited in note 2) intend to contribute to the establishment of regional identities.

20. See the introduction of Rogers Brubaker, *Nationalism Reframed: Nationhood and the National Question in the New Europe* (Cambridge: Cambridge University Press, 1996).

21. On the potential of these terms (in German, "invention" is often simply translated as "*Erfindung*" although it can also mean "*Entdeckung*") see: Eric Hobsbawm and Terence Ranger, eds., *The Invention of Tradition* (Cambridge: Cambridge University Press, 1983); Anderson, *Imagined Communities.*

22. A detailed account of the relationship between regional and national identities in Upper Silesia can be found in Kai Struve and Philipp Ther, eds., *Nationen und ihre Grenzen. Identitätenwandel in Oberschlesien in der Neuzeit* (Marburg: Herder-Institut, 2002). Most of the relevant literature published up to 2001 is listed in the introduction to this book.

23. Alon Confino, *The Nation as a Local Metaphor: Württemberg, Imperial Germany, and National Memory, 1871–1918* (Chapel Hill: University of North Carolina Press, 1997); Celia Applegate, *A Nation of Provincials: The German Idea of Heimat* (Berkeley: University of California Press, 1990). For an attempt at a theoretical classification of the relationship between region and nation in Germany see: Siegfried Weichlein "Das Spannungsfeld von nationaler und regionaler Identität" in

Politische Kultur in Ostmittel- und Südosteuropa, ed. Werner Bramke in cooperation with Thomas Adam (Leipzig: Leipziger Universitätsverlag, 1999), 241–52. On the regional basis and orientation of the German national movement: Dieter Langewiesche, "Föderativer Nationalismus als Erbe der deutschen Reichsnation: Über Föderalismus und Zentralismus in der deutschen Nationalgeschichte" in *Föderative Nation. Deutschlandkonzepte von der Reformation bis zum Ersten Weltkrieg,* ed. Dieter Langewiesche and Georg Schmidt (Munich: Oldenbourg, 2000).

24. On the struggle between state and church in Upper Silesia see Joachim Bahlcke, "Die Geschichte der schlesischen Territorien von den Anfängen bis zum Ausbruch des Zweiten Weltkrieges" in *Schlesien und die Schlesier,* ed. Joachim Bahlcke (Munich: Langen Müller, 1996), 14–154, here 103–104.

25. Cf. Maria Szmeja, *Niemcy? Polacy? Ślązacy! Rodzimi mieszkańcy Opolszczyzny w świetle analiz socjologicznych* (Krakow: Universitas, 2000), 65–74.

26. For a complete panorama of the various national and subnational population groups in Upper Silesia and their identification designs see: Tomasz Kamusella, *Schlonsko: Horní Slezsko, Oberschlesien, Górny Śląsk* (Elbląg: Elbląska Oficyna Wydawnicza, 2001), 30–40.

27. Quoted from materials of the Bund der Oberschlesier in Andrea Schmidt-Rösler, "Autonomie- und Separatismusbestrebungen in Oberschlesien 1918–1922," *Zeitschrift für Ostmitteleuropaforschung* (1999): 1–49, here 11.

28. It has become difficult to navigate the sheer amount of literature on the plebiscite, which cannot be listed here due to lack of space. On Upper Silesia after World War I: Kai Struve, ed., *Oberschlesien nach dem Ersten Weltkrieg. Studien zu einem nationalen Konflikt und seiner Erinnerung* (Marburg: Herder-Institut, 2003).

29. Wojciech Wrzesiński, *Polski Ruch Narodowy w Niemczech 1922–1939,* (Poznań, Poland: Poznańskie, 1970), 222–32. At the national census of 1933, about 100,000 people stated that Polish was their mother tongue and 266,375 declared Polish and German to be their native languages.

30. "9.12.1935: Der Oberpräsident in Breslau an den Reichs- und Preußischen Minister des Innern. Lagebericht," in *Deutsche und Polen zwischen den Kriegen,* Institut fur Zeitgeschichte (Sauer, Germany, 1997), 877–81, here 878. Cf. a report of March 1935 with similar content by the president of the local government in Opolskie in ibid., 857–62, here 862.

31. Cf. various reports in *Deutsche und Polen zwischen den Kriegen,* 872, 881, 895.

32. Quoted in Józef Kokot, "Wojenne i powojenne losy byłej ludności niemieckiej Śląska," *Ekonomia* 1 (1965): 5–51, here 13–15.

33. Cf. Wrzesiński, *Polski Ruch Narodowy w Niemczech,* 374–80. Cf. on the National Socialist policy on nationalism during World War II: Piotr Madajczyk, *Przyłączenie Śląska Opolskiego do Polski 1945–1948* (Warsaw: Instytut Studiów Politycznych PAN, 1996), 45, 121.

34. Cf. Popiołek, 131–137; 238 ff.

35. For an estimate of the German proportion of the population see Kazimierz Śmigiel, ed., *Die statistische Erhebung über die deutschen Katholiken in den Bistümern Polens 1928 und 1936* (Marburg: Herder-Institut, 1992), 220; Maria Wanatowicz, "Niemcy wobec problemu integracji Górnego Śląska z Rzeczpospolitą (1922–1939)" in *Niemcy wobec konfliktu narodowościowego na Górnym Śląsku po I wojnie światowej,* ed. Andrzej Szefer, ed., 141–56, here 154; Franciszek Serafin, "Wpływ Drugiej Rzeczypospolitej na przemiany demograficzne i społeczne w województwie Śląskim w latach 1922–1939," in *Rola i miejsce Górnego Śląska w Drugiej Rzeczypospolitej,* ed. Maria Wanda Wanatowicz (Katowice, Poland: Katowice: Muzeum Śląskie, 1995) 163–82, here 169 ff.

36. Quoted in Maria Wanatowicz, *Ludność napływowa na Górnym Śląsku w latach 1922–1939* (Katowice: Uniwersytet Śląski, 1982), 345. Cf. on the national attitudes of the population particularly in eastern Upper Silesia: Przemysław Hauser, "Zur Frage der nationalen Identität der oberschlesischen Bevölkerung in der Zeit zwischen den beiden Weltkriegen" in *Grenzen und Grenzräume in der deutschen und polnischen Geschichte. Scheidelinie oder Begegnungsraum?* ed. Georg Stöber and Robert Maier (Hanover: Hahn, 2000), 205–216.

37. Cf. Marian Marek Drożdowski, "Górny Śląsk czasów Drugiej Rzeczypospolitej. Rzeczywistość, stereotypy, mity" in *Rola i miejsce Górnego Śląska,* ed. Wanatowicz, 65–83, here 75 ff.

38. Cf. Tomasz Falęcki, *Niemieckie szkolnictwo mniejszościowe na Górnym Śląsku w latach 1922-1939* (Katowice: Instytut Śląski, 1970), 67.

39. *Deutsche und Polen zwischen den Kriegen,* 983.

40. Ibid. 949.

41. Ibid, 933

42. Cf. B. Linek, *"Odniemczanie" województwa śląskiego w latach 1945-1950 (w świetle materiałów wojewódzkich)* (Opole, Poland: Instytut Śląski, 1997).

43. This immigrant population deserves special attention already for the mere fact that in the course of postwar history, it came to be a large majority in historical Upper Silesia and the present-day provinces of Opole and Katowice. Since the third postwar generation has already been born, it would seem anachronistic to call them "settlers," and the Silesian society "indigenous population," as they were labeled in the 1990s. But within the framework of this article I cannot deal in detail with the (former) "settlers" (*osiedlency*) who came to Silesia after 1945.

44. A similar conclusion was drawn by sociologist Kazimierz Żygulski already in communist times. See his uncensored manuscript his *Przyczyny wyjazdu ludności rodzimej z woj. opolskiego na Zachód,* (Archive of the Silesian Institute in Opole, Opole Instytut Đlski A 1454), 24. The grounds for Bożeks disappointment lay in the fact that he, as one of the proponents of Polishness among the Upper Silesians, strongly overestimated their actual link to the Polish nation. The same thing applies to Żygulski, whose essay was suppressed by the censors.

45. Cf. Danuta Berlińska, "Identität und nationale Identifikation der Schlesier nach 1989," in Struve and Ther, *Nationen und ihre Grenzen,* 275–308.

46. Cf. Aleksandra Klich, "Czy Đlązacy są narodowością," *Gazeta Wyborcza,* 1 July 2003.

47. On Alsace see the work by the Swiss historian Karl-Heinz Rothenberger, *Die elsaß-lothringische Heimat- und Autonomiebewegung zwischen den beiden Weltkriegen* (Bern: Peter Lang, 1976); also, Alfred Wahl and Jean-Claude Richez, *L'Alsace entre France et Allemagne 1850–1950* (Paris: Hachette, 1994).

48. Traces of anticolonial terms can also be found in academic literature, which invented the term of "internal colonialism." See for example Michael Hechter, *Internal Colonialism: The Celtic Fringe in British National Development 1536–1966* (Berkeley: University of California Press, 1977); Jochen Blaschke, *Volk, Nation, interner Kolonialismus. Konzepte zur politischen Soziologie der westeuropäischen Regionalbewegungen* (Berlin: BIVS, 1984).

49. See about these conflicts the comparative research by the sociologist Peter Waldmann, who published widely in German and Spanish. See in German Peter Waldmann, "Gewaltsamer Separatismus. Westeuropäische Nationalitätenkonflikte in vergleichender Perspektive," in *National-ismus—Nationalitäten—Supranationalität,* ed. H. A. Winkler and H. Kaelble, eds. (Stuttgart: Klett-Cotta, 1993), 82–107; see in Spanish Peter Waldmann, *Radicalismo Étnico. Análisis comparado de las causas y efectos en conflictos etnicos violentos* (Madrid: AKAL, 1997).

CONTRIBUTORS

Taner Akçam is Professor of History and holder of the Kaloosdian/Mugar Chair in Modern Armenian History and Armenian Genocide Studies at Clark University. Among many other books, he has published *A Shameful Act: The Armenian Genocide and the Question of Turkish Responsibility*, which has been translated into seven languages, including Farsi and Armenian. His latest book is *The Young Turks' Crime Against Humanity: The Armenian Genocide and Ethnic Cleansing in the Ottoman Empire*.

Tomas Balkelis is an ERC Research Fellow working at University College Dublin. He is the author of *The Making of Modern Lithuania* and was recently published in the journals *Past and Present* and *Contemporary European History*. He has a particular interest in the history of Eastern Europe (especially the Baltic states, Russia, and Poland). His research fields include nationalism, paramilitarism, forced migrations, population displacement, and military violence.

Pamela Ballinger is the Fred Cuny Professor of International Human Rights at the University of Michigan. She is the author of *History in Exile: Memory and Identity at the Borders of the Balkans*. Her research interests include refugees, forced migration, Italy, and the Balkans.

Omer Bartov is the John P. Birkelund Distinguished Professor of European History at Brown University. He received his D.Phil. from Oxford in 1983, was a research fellow at Harvard, Princeton, and the Berlin American Academy, and has received NEH and Guggenheim fellowships. He is a member of the American Academy of Arts and Sciences. His books include *The Eastern Front, 1941–45; Hitler's Army; Murder in Our Midst; Mirrors of Destruction: War, Genocide, and Modern Indentity; Germany's War and the Holocaust; The "Jew" in Cinema* (IUP, 2005); *Erased: Vanishing Traces of Jewish Galicia in Present-Day Ukraine*; and *The Voice of Your Brother's Blood: Buczacz, Biography of a Town* (forthcoming).

Keith Brown is Professor of International Studies (Research) at the Watson Institute for International Studies at Brown University. As well as extensive research on ethnonationalism and the role of national history in the Balkans, with a particular focus on Macedonia, his more recent work explores the cultural dimensions of modern warfare, especially in contexts of occupation, insurgency, and peacekeeping. He is the author of *The Past in Question: Modern Macedonia and the Uncertainties of Nation* and the forthcoming *Loyal Unto Death: Trust, Terror, and Solidarity in Revolutionary Macedonia*.

Gary B. Cohen is Professor of Modern Central European History and chair of the History Department at the University of Minnesota, Twin Cities. He directed the Minnesota Center for Austrian Studies, 2001–2010. His publications include *The Politics of Ethnic Survival: Germans in Prague, 1861–1914; Education and Middle-Class Society in Imperial Austria,*

1848–1918, and numerous articles and chapters in the *Journal of Modern History, Central European History, The Austrian History Yearbook, Český Časopis historický, Jewish History,* and various collections. Among numerous other volumes, he has co-edited *Embodiments of Power: Building Baroque Cities in Europe,* with Franz A. J. Szabo; and *Diversity and Dissent: Negotiating Religious Difference in Central Europe, 1500–1800,* with Howard P. Louthan and Franz A. J. Szabo.

Patrice M. Dabrowski received her Ph.D. in 1999 from Harvard University. She is the author of *Commemorations and the Shaping of Modern Poland* (IUP, 2004). Her most recent articles (several of them prize-winning) have appeared in *Austrian History Yearbook; East Central Europe, L'Europe du Centre-Est: Eine wissenschaftliche Zeitschrift;* and *Slavic Review,* and she has authored chapters in a number of edited volumes, including *Capital Cities in the Aftermath of Empires: Planning in Central and Southeastern Europe.* Dabrowski's current book-length projects include a second monograph, tentatively entitled *"Discovering" the Carpathians: Episodes in Imagining and Reshaping Alpine Borderland Regions,* and a popular thousand-year history of Poland. She has taught at Harvard, Brown, and the University of Massachusetts, Amherst, and since 2009 has served as Director of the Harvard Ukrainian Summer Institute.

Dan Diner is Professor of History at The Hebrew University, Jerusalem and Director of the Simon Dubnow Institute for Jewish History and Culture at Leipzig University. He is a member of the Saxonian Academy of the Sciences. Diner is author of numerous articles and books on the history of the twentieth century, the history of the Middle East, and German history, especially the history of National Socialism and the Holocaust. His publications include *Lost in the Sacred: Why the Muslim World Stood Still; Cataclysms: A History of the Twentieth Century from Europe's Edge;* and *Beyond the Conceivable: Studies on Germany, Nazism, and the Holocaust.*

David Gaunt is Professor of History at Södertörn University, Stockholm. Among his most recent publications are *Massacres, Resistance, Protectors: Muslim–Christian Relations in Eastern Anatolia during World War I; Anti-Jewish Violence: Rethinking the Pogrom in East European History* (co-editor, IUP, 2010); and chapters on the Baltic countries in *The Routledge History of the Holocaust,* edited by Jonathan Friedman, and the Assyrian genocide in *A Question of Genocide,* edited by Fatma Müge Göcek, Ronald G. Suny, and Norman Naimark).

Eyal Ginio is Senior Lecturer for Turkish Studies and the chair of the Department of Islamic and Middle Eastern Studies in the Hebrew University of Jerusalem. His research and publications have focused on the social history of the Ottoman Empire with a particular emphasis on eighteenth-century Salonica. He is currently preparing a manuscript on the sociocultural history of Ottoman society during the Balkan Wars.

Elke Hartmann is a research fellow at the History Department at the Freie-Universität Berlin. In 2010 she co-founded "Houshamadyan," a project to reconstruct Ottoman Armenian town and village life. Her book *Die Reichweite des Staates. Wehrpflicht und moderne Staatlichkeit in der Spätzeit des Osmanischen Reiches* is forthcoming. She is currently working on a monograph on the self-narratives of Armenian revolutionaries in the Ottoman Empire.

John-Paul Himka is Professor of East European History at the University of Alberta. His area of specialty is Ukrainian history. At present he is researching and writing about Ukrainian nationalist participation in the Holocaust. Together with Joanna Michlic he is co-editor of *Bringing the Dark Past to Light: The Reception of the Holocaust in Postcommunist Europe,* forthcoming.

Peter Holquist is Associate Professor of History at the University of Pennsylvania. He is the author of *Making War, Forging Revolution: Russia's Continuum of Crisis, 1914–1921* and founder and editor of the journal *Kritika: Explorations in Russian and Eurasian History.* He is currently completing a project on the role of Imperial Russia in developing and applying the laws of war in the nineteenth and early twentieth centuries.

Yaroslav Hrytsak is Director of the Institute for Historical Research at L'viv University and Professor of Modern Ukrainian History at the Ukrainian Catholic University. His interests include the modern history of Central and Eastern Europe. Among many other publications, he has written *Essays in Ukrainian History: The Making of the Modern Ukrainian Nation,* and *"A Prophet in His Fatherland": Ivan Franko and His Community.*

Pieter M. Judson is Isaac H. Clothier Professor of History and International Relations at Swarthmore College and editor of the *Austrian History Yearbook.* His book *Guardians of the Nation: Activists on the Language Frontiers of Imperial Austria* was awarded the Karl von Vogelsang State Prize by the Austrian government, and the Jelavich prize of the Association of Slavic, East European, and Eurasian Studies. *Exclusive Revolutionaries: Liberal Politics, Social Experience and National Identity in the Austrian Empire 1848–1914* won prizes from the American Historical Association and the Austrian Cultural Forum. He has held fellowships from Guggenheim, Fulbright, NEH, and the American Academy in Berlin.

Paul Robert Magocsi is holder of the John Yaremko Chair of Ukrainian Studies at the University of Toronto and a Fellow of the Royal Society of Canada. He has authored many studies on central Europe and Ukraine. Among his over 30 books are *The Shaping of a National Identity: Subcarpathian Rus', 1848–1948; A History of Ukraine and Its Peoples,* 2nd rev. ed.; and *Historical Atlas of Central Europe,* 2nd rev. ed.

Robert Nemes is Associate Professor of History at Colgate University. He is the author of *The Once and Future Budapest,* a monograph on nationalism and urbanism in nineteenth-century Hungary. His current book project, entitled *Another Hungary,* examines the intersection of politics, religion, and violence in provincial Hungary from the late 1700s through the First World War.

Alexander V. Prusin received his Ph.D. from the University of Toronto and teaches history at the New Mexico Institute of Mining and Technology in Socorro, New Mexico. He is the author of two books: *Nationalizing a Borderland: War, Ethnicity, and Anti-Jewish Violence in East Galicia, 1914–1920,* and *The "Lands Between": Conflict in the East European Borderlands, 1870–1992,* as well as a number of articles.

Frithjof Benjamin Schenk is Professor of Russian and East European History at University of Basel, Switzerland. He graduated from the Freie-Universität Berlin, where he wrote his dissertation on the history of the image of Alexander Nevsky in Russian and Soviet cultural memory (published in German and in Russian translation). His second book, *Russia's Ride Towards Modernity: Mobility and Social Space in the Railway Age,* is forthcoming.

Myroslav Shkandrij is Professor in the Department of German and Slavic Studies at the University of Manitoba. He has curated exhibitions and edited books on the avant-garde art of the 1920s, and published several studies of modern Ukrainian literature, including *Russia* *and Ukraine: Literature and the Discourse of Empire,* and *Jews in Ukrainian Literature: Representation and Identity.*

Kai Struve is a research fellow at the Institute of History at Martin Luther University in Halle, Germany. He received his Ph.D. in 2002 at the Freie-Universität Berlin and held positions at the Herder Institute, Marburg, and the Simon Dubnow Institute of Jewish History and Culture at Leipzig University. Among his publications are *Bauern und Nation in Galizien. Über Zugehörigkeit und soziale Emanzipation im 19. Jahrhundert;* "Rites of Violence? The Pogroms of Summer 1941," in the journal *Polin;* and "Geschichte und Gedächtnis—Ostpolen unter sowjetischer Besatzung 1939–41," in the Yearbook of the Simon Dubnow Institute. He co-edited with Elazar Barkan and Elizabeth A. Cole *Shared History—Divided Memory: Jews and Others in Soviet-Occupied Poland, 1939–1941.*

Philipp Ther is Professor of Central European History at the University of Vienna. He has published several books about nationalism and borderlands, among them *Redrawing Nations: Ethnic Cleansing in East-Central Europe 1944–1948,* co-edited with Ana Siljak; *Regionale Bewegungen und Regionalismen in europäischen Zwischenräumen seit der Mitte des 19. Jahrhunderts,* co-edited with Holm Sundhaussen; and a new monograph on ethnic cleansing in modern Europe, *Die dunkle Seite der Nationalstaaten: "Ethnische Säuberungen" im modernen Europa.*

Gregor Thum is Assistant Professor of German and East Central European History at the University of Pittsburgh. He is the author of *Uprooted: How Breslau Became Wrocław During the Century of Expulsions,* and the editor of *Traumland Osten: Deutsche Bilder vom östlichen Europa.* He is currently working on a book titled *Mastering the East: The German Frontier from 1800 to the Present.*

Theodore R. Weeks is Professor of History at Southern Illinois University, where he teaches European and world history. He is the author of *From Assimilation to Antisemitism: the "Jewish Question" in Poland, 1850–1914,* and *Across the Revolutionary Divide: Russia 1861–1945.* His present research project is tentatively entitled *Vilna-Wilno-Vilnius: History of a Multicultural City, 1795–2000.*

Eric D. Weitz is Dean of Humanities and the Arts and Professor of History at City College, City University of New York. Trained in modern German and European history, in recent years his work has extended to the history and politics of international human rights and crimes against humanity. His major publications include *Weimar Germany: Promise and Tragedy; A Century of Genocide: Utopias of Race and Nation;* and *Creating German Communism, 1890–1990.* He is currently writing *A World Divided: Nations and Human Rights from the Age of Revolution to the Present.*

Larry Wolff is Professor of History at New York University, and director of the NYU Center for European and Mediterranean Studies. His newest book is *The Idea of Galicia: History and Fantasy in Habsburg Political Culture.* He is also the author of *Venice and the Slavs: The Discovery of Dalmatia in the Age of Enlightenment; Inventing Eastern Europe: The Map of Civilization on the Mind of the Enlightenment; The Vatican and Poland in the Age of the Partitions: Diplomatic and Cultural Encounters at the Warsaw Nunciature;* and *Postcards from the End of the World: Child Abuse in Freud's Vienna.* He has received Fulbright, American Council of Learned Societies, and Guggenheim fellowships, and is a member of the American Academy of Arts and Sciences.

INDEX

CPSIA information can be obtained
at www.ICGtesting.com
Printed in the USA
LVHW022351200723
752921LV00006B/359